REFORMING ART IN RENAISSANCE VENICE

The spiritual turmoil of the sixteenth century had a profound impact on religious life throughout Italy. Art and architecture were directly implicated in the seismic historical events of the age, as the Catholic Church countered Protestant iconoclasm through the embrace of sacred images as decreed by the Council of Trent in 1563. In this volume, Marie-Louise Lillywhite considers the impact of religious reform on the devotional art and architecture of sixteenth-century Venice. Interrogating early modern censorship, artistic liberty, notions of decorum tied to depictions of the body, and the role of sacred images in the shaping of local identity, she shows how Venice, a crossroads city exposed to a rich gamut of religious and artistic currents, serves as a fascinating case study through which to explore these themes. Her study reconstructs the conditions that enabled artistic invention to prevail and how artists became interpreters of spiritual values.

Marie-Louise Lillywhite is the senior tutor of the Middlebury College Centre for Medieval and Renaissance Studies in Oxford, as well as a research associate at Keble College and a member of the History Faculty at the University of Oxford.

REFORMING ART IN RENAISSANCE VENICE

MARIE-LOUISE LILLYWHITE
University of Oxford

CAMBRIDGE
UNIVERSITY PRESS

CAMBRIDGE
UNIVERSITY PRESS

Shaftesbury Road, Cambridge CB2 8EA, United Kingdom

One Liberty Plaza, 20th Floor, New York, NY 10006, USA

477 Williamstown Road, Port Melbourne, VIC 3207, Australia

314–321, 3rd Floor, Plot 3, Splendor Forum, Jasola District Centre, New Delhi – 110025, India

103 Penang Road, #05–06/07, Visioncrest Commercial, Singapore 238467

Cambridge University Press is part of Cambridge University Press & Assessment, a department of the University of Cambridge.

We share the University's mission to contribute to society through the pursuit of education, learning and research at the highest international levels of excellence.

www.cambridge.org
Information on this title: www.cambridge.org/9781009557498

DOI: 10.1017/9781009557474

When citing this work, please include a reference to the DOI 10.1017/9781009557474

First published 2025

Printed in the United Kingdom by CPI Group Ltd, Croydon CR0 4YY 2025

A catalogue record for this publication is available from the British Library

A Cataloging-in-Publication data record for this book is available from the Library of Congress

ISBN 978-1-009-55749-8 Hardback

Publication of this book has been supported by a grant from the Gladys Krieble Delmas Foundation, for which the publisher and author are most grateful.

CONTENTS

ACKNOWLEDGEMENTS

The idea for this book first occurred to me many years ago during a term spent in Venice as part of my BA in History of Art at the University of Warwick. On the advice of my wise professors, I set myself the task of visiting all the churches of the city that were open to the public. Not only did I get to see lots of wonderful art, but I decided I wanted to learn more about why so many of these remarkable sites underwent significant architectural and artistic renovations towards the end of the sixteenth century and the beginning of the seventeenth, a fact briefly referred to in the guides to the churches available at each site. Since then I have been fortunate enough to spend many years living in Venice in order to answer this question, as well as in Rome and Florence. Writing this book has brought me into contact with some of the most beautiful places and artworks in Italy and has led to many meaningful friendships and collaborations, some related to art history, many with no relation to it whatsoever!

The writing of any academic book inevitably accrues a series of debts of gratitude, of a financial, collegiate, and personal nature. Proceeding in this order, without the financial assistance that I received during my academic career this book would never have been possible. Attending university in the United Kingdom just before the dawn of the huge hike in fees, I was the beneficiary of a system that covered my academic costs, ensuring that my student loan was relatively low. I am thankful to the Arts and Humanities Research Council, which completely funded my MA and PhD; to the Gladys Krieble Delmas Foundation, which awarded me grants for research in Venice as well as a scholars' publication subvention for this monograph; to the Kunsthistorisches in Florence where I held a postdoctoral award; and, in more recent years, to employers that have provided necessary research funds to cover the costs of illustrations. Too many institutions (particularly British ones) charge astronomical prices for permission to use images in their collections for academic projects, presenting yet another economic barrier to publication in the discipline. Happily, many smaller European collections and churches generously shared image reproductions. I am particularly indebted to the photographer Francesco Turio Böhm, whose beautiful photographs can be found in this book.

During the miserable circumstances brought about by the COVID-19 pandemic, the Bodleian libraries operated a wonderful service, making huge volumes of material available online and offering a scan and deliver service to users unable to consult materials in person. I am very grateful to those anonymous librarians who emailed me articles and book chapters with such diligence. Without them the completion of this monograph would have been seriously delayed. In Venice I wish to thank the charming staff of the Biblioteca Correr, Fondazione Cini, Archivio del Patriarcato, and the Archivio di Stato. Towards the tail end of the pandemic, when I was in the final stages of pregnancy, a few of the librarians at the Marciana very considerately carried heavy books to and from my desk and tended to my every research need. Their assistance has not been forgotten. Back in Oxford, Keble College provided a stimulating environment in which to complete this book, and I gained much from conversations with academics in other disciplines, particularly those belonging to the history and English literature faculties. As senior tutor of the Middlebury College Centre for Medieval and Renaissance Studies in Oxford, I learnt a tremendous amount from a series of splendid colleagues, some of whom read multiple chapters and provided much sage advice, and others who assisted with equally important administrative or moral support. My thanks to all of them: Bernard Gowers, Octavia Cox, Paul Monod, Joanna Perks, Guy Perry, Kenisha Morgan, and Fiona Kilby. Teaching the seminar course 'Art and Censorship 1500–1650' to some very bright students on the programme helped to crystallise the ideas presented in this study, as did the years spent teaching in Venice and Rome where we had the great privilege of examining some of the images featured here in situ.

Many art historians shared their specialist knowledge with me or offered valuable bibliographic suggestions. Their names are included at relevant points in the notes. I am especially grateful to those individuals who generously read or commented upon my work: Tom Nichols, the late Thomas Worthen, Julian Gardner, and Gianmario Guidarelli. I also enjoyed stimulating conversations with both the co-founders and various members of the Venetian Art History group: Peter Humfrey, Giulia Zanon, Giorgio Tagliaferro, and Penelope Gardner-Chloros, in particular. Finally, the enthusiasm and charisma of my doctoral supervisor, Louise Bourdua, deserves a special mention. I recall leaving every supervision session with Louise imbued with a newfound energy and interest in my topic. In the years after completing my doctorate she was equally supportive, thanks to her boundless positivity and wise counsel.

Perhaps my biggest academic debt with relation to this book is to the three friends and scholars of history and history of art who read the entire manuscript: Celeste McNamara, Maria Aresin, and Michael Tymkiw. The suggestions of this trinity were astute and stimulating, and I am deeply appreciative of their help. The comments of the two anonymous peer reviewers have undoubtedly resulted in a better book. Any remaining errors are of course my own. Beyond academia, I offer heartfelt thanks to all my family and friends, particularly to Anjum Khan, who proved to be a stalwart companion at London exhibitions; my siblings, who valiantly helped with childcare in the final stages of submitting the revised document; and my parents, who have always been most encouraging of my interest in the history of art.

From driving me around the Veneto to visit remote abbeys, to photographing archival material or helping me to find the perfect translation for a word in Venetian dialect, my husband Sebastiano's intellectual companionship and unselfish assistance has been constant. This book is dedicated to him and to our son Xavier, who was born just a few days after this book was first submitted for peer review and whose boundless good humour and joie de vivre has proved to be a delight ever since.

INTRODUCTION

This study is about how the spiritual turmoil of the sixteenth century impacted devotional art and architecture in Venice and the ways in which the artistic climate changed over the course of the century. In the aftermath of the Reformations that transformed western Christendom from 1517 onwards, and the closure of the Council of Trent (1545–63), which aimed to reform the Catholic Church and clarify contested aspects of dogma, the sacred image was an element in this agenda for change. In some ways images lay at the heart of the Reformations, both Protestant and Catholic, especially if we consider that Martin Luther's ire was in part provoked by the indulgence used to fund the construction of the pope's new basilica of Saint Peter's in Rome.[1] The destruction and defacement of visual representations of the divine, taking place with various degrees of intensity in Protestant areas of Europe, had brought the question of their necessity to the fore, stimulating the official response of the Church on the matter, decreed at the final session of the Tridentine Council in 1563. With the exception of the Byzantine image controversies of the eighth and ninth centuries, this was a period when the sacred image in Europe had never before been invested with such urgent and polemical importance. If it is true that 'no Westerner can ever hope to know him – or herself, or the world he or she lives in, without first understanding this crucial turning point in history', then the same applies for better comprehending what happened to the arts in this period given their consequence for the seismic debates of the age.[2] Rather than interpreting the visual achievements (or failures) of artists in

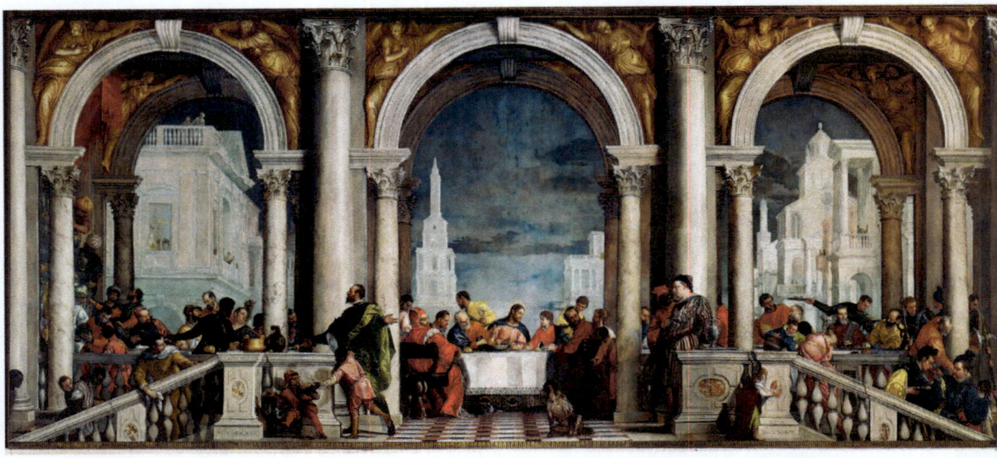

1 Veronese, *The Feast in the House of Levi,* 1573, oil on canvas, Gallerie dell'Accademia, Venice (Photo: Cameraphoto)

Venice as the inevitable outcome of the brief conciliar statements on images, this book explores the extent to which they set the agenda for sacred art in the city and the role they played in articulating the key beliefs of the epoch.

Discussions of the climate for artmaking in the late sixteenth century habitually commence with one of the most infamous episodes of early modern censorship that exists and that happened in Venice: the case of Paolo Veronese's (1528–88) *Last Supper*, painted for the refectory of the Dominican convent of Santi Giovanni e Paolo, now in the Gallerie dell'Accademia, Venice (Fig. 1). Questioned by the Inquisition about the curious iconography of the painting, Veronese subsequently added inscriptions to the canvas, transforming it into the *Feast in the House of Levi* (Luke 5:27–32). For a long time Veronese's experience was interpreted as evidence of the sombre creative atmosphere at the end of the century, as well as the tendency of artists in the city to refuse to comply with the contemporary requirements for devotional art. This reading conveniently dovetailed with a now outdated, although still potent, historical analysis that has focused above all on the Serenissima's resistance to various aspects of Tridentine reform in the late sixteenth and early seventeenth century, rather than its obedience: most obviously with the excommunication of the city during the Papal Interdict of 1606, but also with the polemical 1618 critique of the Council of Trent written by the Venetian Servite friar Paolo Sarpi (1552–1623).[3] Scholars have presented more holistic views of Veronese's career as a religious artist for years now, yet narratives that focus solely on resistance are still pervasive and popular.[4] This is predominantly in literature for non-specialist audiences (where it is arguably most important that misleading generalisations should be corrected), but it also lingers on in some scholarly approaches too. The simplistic portrayal of Venice as a quasi-secular state that stood up to the papacy and was far removed from the exigencies of the Counter-Reformation has proved too attractive to resist. The artistic equivalent to this has tended to be the example of Veronese before the Holy Office. Owing to the fact that the painter made minimal changes to the image, rather than to dramatically transform the composition, this has even been interpreted in the British press as evidence that he somehow 'outsmarted' this key instrument of religious repression in a triumph of artistic liberty over censorship.[5] Yet this highly unusual event became common knowledge only in the nineteenth century when the original account was found in the Venetian State Archives. Before that it had never even been so much as referred to, either by the artist's biographers or by any other document in existence.[6] The impression that this interrogation subsequently created was at odds with the predominant reception of Venetian devotional art at the time, which influenced artists as stylistically diverse as El Greco (1541–1614) and Federico Barocci (1533–1612), and was avidly collected by the Catholic Emperors Charles V (1500–58) and his son Philip II of Spain (1527–98). One of the aims of this book is therefore to consider Venice's place in the history of art as it was perceived and received in the early modern period and not as it was subsequently altered by the Veronese paradigm.

My central argument is twofold. First, to a greater extent than the Church, it was artists who forged the way for the visual developments of the age, their creations offering intense ocular experiences that validated a particular set of spiritual ideas. This imbues artists with an agency that is all too often denied in analyses of artistic production post-Trent that tend to emphasise top-down enforcement to the point of disregarding creative autonomy. As we shall see, change was not achieved solely through repression or censorship. In fact, the Venetian Church was more likely to insist that more devotional artworks should be commissioned than they were to order their removal or destruction. The result of this was not always of the highest quality artistically speaking, but it did ensure quantity, which was what they wanted, as well as employment opportunities for the jobbing artist. Taken alone, the Tridentine decrees of 1563 left room for artistic creativity and a degree of interpretation, and they were not severe enough to present an insurmountable barrier to innovation, something lost on those who over-sensationalise their rigidity. The analysis here presented will demonstrate how unusual cases like Veronese's were, and it argues against the reductive tendency, eloquently noted by Gauvin Bailey, to pit the Church and artists against each other 'in a romantic (and post-Enlightenment) battle between artistic freedom and ecclesiastical dogma'.[7] This does not mean glossing over the occasions when this happened, but it does involve considering the more numerous examples of parties negotiating mutually beneficial solutions together, as well as understanding what artists and patrons were trying to achieve in this period. When this is done, the implications for how we approach late sixteenth- and early seventeenth-century art are evident. Artists neither are reduced to the role of obedient propagandists of religion, nor are they understood as engaged in a constant struggle for their creative liberty. Narratives of visual reform emerge that seek not to replace ones of artistic control and coercion but to complement and nuance them. Devotional images are appreciated on their own terms, in accordance with what was considered ideal or praiseworthy when they were made, rather than for how they correspond to what we might value as ideal today. In doing this, I hope that this book offers correctives to some lingering assumptions in the history of early modern Italian art, as well as drawing attention to methods that might equally be applied to other places.

Second, although there were instances when Venice rigorously resisted the more centralising instruments of reform emanating from the papacy in Rome, those that presented a direct threat to the relative independence of her Church, one arena in which the city *was* able to flaunt its orthodoxy was through the visual arts. In his 1605 *Relatione della Republica Venetiana*, the onetime assistant to both Carlo and Federico Borromeo and former Jesuit, Giovanni Botero (1544–1617), understood the marvellous ornamentation of the churches of Venice as being convincing evidence of the city's religion, at a time of heightened tensions between the Serenissima and the Holy See. Botero praised the material aspects of devotion in the city at length, waxing lyrical about the quantity and beauty of the churches that featured delicate sculptures, graceful paintings, precious marbles, and majestic mosaics. Botero contended that the beauty of these sites elevated the soul of the spectator to contemplation of the divine, his impression being that no expense had been spared in their decoration.[8] For individuals like Botero, as well as other contemporary visitors, persuasive evidence of Venice's commitment to religion was the city itself, with its sumptuous sacred edifices and their magnificent embellishment.[9] We also know that successive Venetian ambassadors fulminated against the iconoclasm in war-torn France, suggesting that this was perceived as one of the more senseless aspects of the Reformations.[10] It should be remembered that in the years that followed Luther's definite break with the Catholic Church, one's approach to visual representations of the divine was even interpreted as reliable proof of true spiritual loyalties. The case against a wealthy German merchant, one 'Zuanne Sfogger', who was investigated by the Inquisition in 1571 after various allegations of his heterodoxy came to their attention, including his apparent hatred of representations of the saints, appears to have been dropped after witnesses attested to the quantity of devotional images in his homes in Venice and Mestre and his commitment to 'good works'.[11] Conversely, in seventeenth-century England, Archbishop William Laud's (1573–1645) involvement in the addition of a Baroque portico to the church of Saint Mary the Virgin in Oxford, complete with Solomonic columns and an effigy of the Madonna and Child (completed 1637), was interpreted as compelling evidence of his popish sympathies during his trial for treason. The 'very scandalous statue' was disfigured in 1642 when Parliamentarian troops shot at it, and Laud was beheaded a few years later.[12]

MINDSET

This leads to the question of the prevailing mentality relating to images in Venice in the period this study examines, which was in many ways different to today's attitudes. The majority of the paintings, sculptures, and buildings that will be encountered in this text were devotional ones, invested with symbolic meanings and uses, and valued for reasons beyond their aesthetic qualities.[13] This is not to infer that the issues traversed here are no longer relevant even if the context is completely different. As David Freedberg demonstrated many years ago, discomfort surrounding the potency of visual representations has existed throughout history and will continue to do so.[14] In the time I have been studying this material, we have seen attacks on Nimrud and Palmyra by Daesh in 2015, conversations about the removal of statues tied to racist histories in the wake of the 2020 Black Lives Matter protests, vigorous objections to the vast expenditure on the renovations to Notre Dame in the aftermath of the fire of 2019 (ones that neatly echoed statements expressed centuries earlier in various degrees of intensity by Luther, Zwingli, and Calvin),[15] and the censorship of artists due to their political opinions.[16] Most recently, there has even been a polemic in France relating to complaints made by students and their parents after schoolchildren were shown a Renaissance painting that featured female nudity, demonstrating that many of the themes explored in the book continue to cause tension.[17]

Yet the most significant difference between then and now is that because the modern category of art inhabits a predominantly secular sphere, often seen as something of a frivolity to be indulged in once other exigencies have been satisfied, it can be challenging to appreciate a mindset that perceived the material culture of devotion in the form of beautiful paintings, luxurious vestments, swathes of candles, and costly churches as not just important but essential. This was an approach that to a greater or lesser extent was at odds with the opinions of Protestant reformers – whose outlook might have more in common with the majority of the public today – but it was what motivated the laity to pool their funds in the late fifteenth century to erect the church of the Madonna dei Miracoli, or what caused the Venetian State to cover the costs for the votive constructions of Andrea Palladio's (1508–80) basilica of the Redentore and Baldassare Longhena's Santa Maria della Salute after outbreaks of pestilence in 1575–77 and 1630–31, respectively. Such acts were viewed as ones of charity and sometimes thanksgiving, that gave honour to God, served the community, and reflected well on the laity, clergy, and Venice itself.

Indeed, in 1592 the confraternity of the Blessed Sacrament in the church of San Giacomo dall'Orio justified their considerable expenditure on the decoration not just of their chapel but on the church as a whole since 'in this way it will be pleasing to Christ'.[18] Even much later, during the instability of Napoleonic and Austrian rule, the laity at San Polo banded together to renovate their beloved church, an act of generosity that is all the more poignant considering the dissolution of the parish in 1810, but one that points to the survival of a resilient communal mentality.[19]

For the majority of the early modern Catholics that we will encounter in this book, devotional images were a necessity because they served a practical purpose, not only as the 'bibles of the illiterate' (as Gregory the Great's famous dictum observed) but as a focus for intercessory prayer, and because they functioned as material access points to the spiritual realm.[20] Yet in the sixteenth century there was a growing consensus that some of the excesses of Renaissance devotional art needed to be reined in, particularly with relation to nudity and the intrusion of profane elements in sacred scenes. This happened at the same time as artists in some parts of Italy were challenging the guild system and forming academies, investing them with greater independence and creative liberty, and announcing the conception of the 'artist' as we later came to know it. These ostensibly conflicting aims were the focus of a study by Marcia Hall, who pointed out that the year 1563 was both the foundation date of the first artistic academy in Florence and the year of the Council of Trent's decrees concerning images.[21] Even if the establishment of the Accademia di Pittura e Scultura in Venice would have to wait until 1754, in 1566 a number of Venetian painters, architects, and sculptors (including Palladio, Jacopo Tintoretto, and Titian) petitioned to join the Florentine academy.[22] We also know that even before this date patrons in Venice deferred to the expertise of painters regarding subject matter, an example of this being the freedom given to Giovanni Antonio da Pordenone (c. 1483–1539) in 1538 by the board of the Scuola Grande della Carità, pointing to a recognition of the inventive talents and professional status of artists.[23] On other occasions the command of the patron was to be upheld, even if the artist disagreed. Tasked with completing an altarpiece of the baptism of Christ for a church on the Venetian mainland in what is now Veronella, Melchiorre Galluzzi wrote to his patron from Venice to argue that even if he had been requested to show Christ standing, he had it on the good authority of not just other artists in the city (including Alessandro Vittoria, 1525–1608), but even the city's patriarch, that it would be 'more devout' to show Christ kneeling. This was in keeping with current artistic practice in the city, and it is perhaps to be expected that if the patriarch really had been sought out for advice, then he would have endorsed this local variant, since Patriarch Giovanni Trevisan (1503–90, r. 1559–90) was a passionate defender of Venetian devotional customs and traditions. Galluzzi's pleading evidently failed to have the desired effect, since the resulting image shows Christ in the pose corresponding to the original brief.[24] Yet the tension between the two big events explored in Hall's study can be exaggerated. Unless numerous more examples come to light, cases of artists being punished for falling foul of the Church's new regulations are still unusual in Italy, and to a greater or lesser extent, artists had always had to work within climates of compromised artistic liberty and concede to the stated desires of those paying for their works. Galluzzi's letter also demonstrates that artists were invested in finding the most beautiful and spiritually uplifting ways in which to depict the sacred episodes and that they were willing to try to negotiate with their patrons in order to achieve these aims.

CHAPTER OVERVIEW

This book is divided into two parts, consisting of four lengthier chapters in the first half, and three shorter thematic studies in the second. Part I traces the varied ways in which the religious climate in Italy during the Cinquecento impacted artistic production, and how this climate transformed itself over the course of the century, drawing conclusions on the extent to which the arts were controlled and censored by the Church post-Trent. Part II of the book concentrates on the more generative relationship between art and the spiritual reform of the age. It concentrates on three key visual phenomena that can be convincingly tied to this: images of the body of Christ, the miraculous feats and martyrdom of the saints, and representations of the heavens and of purgatory. Often these iconographies had their roots in older visual practices and local traditions even when they were dynamically reinvented; on other occasions they necessitated novel solutions. These vignettes encompass works by a number of the canonical artists and architects associated with Venetian artistic traditions, as well as their lesser studied protégés and colleagues.

Arranged broadly chronologically and commencing with examples from the 1520s, Chapter 1 explores how the relative fluidity of belief that was tolerated prior to the 1540s in Italy was manifested visually, with the majority of the examples cited having been created either on the Venetian mainland or in overseas outposts of the Serenissima. The chapter analyses artists who may have been interested in heterodox ideas, but it also highlights the complexities of tying iconographies that may have been dictated by the patron to the innermost spiritual beliefs of their creators. The Serenissima's status as a significant locus for innovative visual experiments in the early sixteenth century is explored, on the one hand, as well as its infamy as one of the principal gateways through which Protestant ideas entered Italy, on the other. This duality is examined through visual examples that were often ahead of their time, boldly anticipating elements that were later to be actively encouraged after the Council of Trent, as well as cases of artists who may have embraced ideas that would later be deemed unacceptable, underlining how these seemingly paradoxical impulses could co-exist in this period, and the conclusions that one might reasonably draw from this.

Chapter 2 is about the boundaries of visual decorum both before and after the Council of Trent. The shifting parameters of what was deemed appropriate for public display in devotional sites can only partially explain why certain images came to be censored, particularly with relation to nudity. To my mind it seems more the case that certain artistic creations tested the boundaries of acceptability as never before. Complaints about nudity in devotional images had a long pre-history, but it was the infamous nakedness of the saints in Michelangelo's (1475–1564) 1541 *Last Judgment* – and their subsequent censorship – that brought the question of the limits of artistic license to the forefront (Fig. 22). Thus, the vicissitudes of the fresco were just as important for defining standards of visual decorum as the Tridentine decrees on images, if not more so, since there is clearer evidence that Venetian artists were familiar with the polemics that the fresco ignited. In this chapter, I look at the reception of the work in Venice, from where some early invectives against the painting emanated. Representations of total nakedness in Venetian ecclesiastical settings were rarer than in other centres like Florence or Rome, something that is rarely commented on. Even an artist as profoundly influenced by Michelangelo as Tintoretto (c. 1518–94) shrouded the groins of the saints in his own paintings of the same, and similar themes, as the Sistine Chapel fresco. Thus, in late sixteenth-century Venice censorship of devotional images was rarely resorted to. Since the Council of Trent had warned against 'lascivious' works and those that displayed a 'beauty exciting to lust' (rather than the unclothed body per se), these terms left room for a degree of interpretation, allowing for local peculiarities that furnish us with a richer portrayal of how artistic practices at this time varied from one place to another.

Chapter 3 is about artistic censorship in Venice. Although my concern is predominantly with the institutional variety, it should be understood that a censorious climate can equally be established without direct recourse to it, especially when it relates to the boundaries of acceptable speech or behaviour. Artists such as the Tuscan Leone Leoni (1509–90) and, later, Caravaggio (1571–1610) were engaged in terribly violent crimes and continued to enjoy a stream of patronage, in Leoni's case even being highly favoured by Emperor Charles V, but publicly voicing 'heretical' statements would have certainly been a provocation too far, demonstrated by those artists and craftsmen who suffered the wrath of the Inquisition not for their creations but for their heterodox beliefs. In this chapter, I explore the instruments of enforcement and methods of communication available for controlling the arts in Venice and the extent of their efficacy. This includes the Tridentine decrees and those of local synods, the records of the Inquisition, and published treatises on devotional images and architecture. As will be shown, the supposed marshalling of art in the service of religion towards the end of the sixteenth century has traditionally been portrayed as having a negative impact on quality, initiating a bleak new climate of artistic control at odds with the relative freedom synonymous with how the Renaissance has been historically interpreted. Theoretically, the late sixteenth century heralded a new era of censorship, and the activities of the Inquisition and the Indexes of Prohibited Books were very real instruments of repression in the Venetian Republic, even if in the latter case their efficacy was debatable. But if images were the 'bibles of the illiterate', to what extent were they censored in the same manner as books were in the late sixteenth century, and for what reasons?[25] How common was a case like Veronese's questioning by the Inquisition? What precisely were the new restrictions placed on artists, and how were they communicated to them and then enforced? This chapter highlights the perils of taking documents like local synodal decrees or instructions contained in any of the many treatises on the topic of 'appropriate' devotional art at face value, since written prohibitions were sometimes ignored even by their ecclesiastical authors, and image censorship proved to be far more haphazard than programmatic.

Chapter 4 focuses on the visitation records of Patriarch Lorenzo Priuli (1537–1600, r. 1590–1600), who carried out exhaustive inspections of Venice's parish churches in the 1590s. Priuli was a major figure in the history of late sixteenth-century Venice but has been the subject of very few studies, with the exception of recent publications examining his involvement in the renovations to the cathedral of San Pietro di Castello and Michael Matile's partial use of his visitation records for his project on lateral paintings in the churches of Venice.[26] A Venetian noble with an extensive background in dedicated service to the state, including distinguished ambassadorial posts in Spain (1572–76), in France (1579–82), and to the Holy See (1583–86), at the time of his election to the patriarchate Priuli was a layman.[27] Upon ascending to the office he embarked on an ambitious and wide-ranging programme of Tridentine reform, efforts that culminated in him being elevated to the cardinalate in 1596. Priuli's rigorously compiled visitation records include lengthy advice on the new standards for the organisation and embellishment of the sacred space; these documents provide fascinating insights into his prerogatives as both a censor and an ecclesiastic tasked with ensuring that standards of architectural and visual decorum were being maintained in the churches of his diocese. The evidence demonstrates that the patriarch was far more likely to insist that more artworks should be commissioned than he was to order their removal or destruction for reasons of propriety, something that was resorted to only on extremely rare occasions. Priuli was deeply committed to ushering in Counter-Reformation reforms to Venice, being something of an austere 'Tridentine hard-liner',[28] yet during the visitation he proved to be far more tolerant of pictorial practices that his own synodal instructions condemned, once again illustrating the difference between the ideals of official instruction and the reality of reform efforts. Nevertheless, Priuli's obsession with visually exalting the eucharist by insisting upon the construction of ever more lavish tabernacles and chapels led to radical transformations throughout the city's parishes. Rather than reform imposed purely from above, however, this most often depended on the cooperation of the eucharistic confraternities, or the 'Scuole del Santissimo Sacramento', whose membership was drawn from a broad spectrum of Venetian society. Changes were often initially advised by the visitations and then swiftly actioned by these increasingly popular and wealthy confraternities, who often went beyond the directives suggested.[29] Here this is conceptualised as a kind of inverted iconoclasm, one that was indirectly destructive, but that conversely provided a boost to artistic production since it required the creation of new chapels, architectural fittings, and paintings à la mode.

Leading on from Patriarch Priuli's vigorous promotion of the cult of the eucharist, Chapter 5 explores depictions of the body of Christ, covering a rich terrain of painted and illustrated images to ever more lavishly embellished tabernacles, designed both to contain the consecrated communion wafers and to signal the site of its mystical presence in the church interior. Here we will see how iconographies that had been explored prior to the Reformations by earlier generations of artists in Venice were revisited afresh by the leading local painters of the day. The visual evidence speaks for itself in demonstrating the space for artistic invention and experimentation that prevailed at the time, and the power invested in the figure of the artist as an interpreter of spiritual values. The topic of Chapter 6 is the relatively sudden proliferation of images of the virtuous deeds and dramatic martyrdom of the saints in altarpieces in Venice, exploring first the apparent visual solidarity with the dispossessed in many of these works and the soteriological emphasis on acts of charity. The consistent inclusion of recipients of charity in paintings was in contrast to the more stigmatising aspects of poor laws enacted by the Venetian State, reminding the viewer of Christ's affinity for the outcast and possibly even acting as sites of resistance to the more brutal attitudes towards poverty that developed in the wake of the Reformations.[30] In the same period, images of the martyrdoms of the saints began to insist upon their mental fortitude, showing them not in the throes of earthly agony, but as exemplars of self-control, consciously ignoring their earthly torments and setting their sights firmly on the heavens. In these altarpieces the supernatural realm at the height of the painting is almost never acknowledged by any of the bystanders to the event; the cruelty of the pagan torturers renders them unable to visualise the vision of paradise perceived by the saint and witnessed by the spectator, who is thus invited to participate in its magnificence.[31]

Leading on from this, Chapter 7 examines images of the greatest artistic challenge of all: the depiction of the beauty of heaven, a beauty that was unknowable and supposedly greater than anything one's earthbound experience could prepare them for, and thus had to be imagined and brought to life by dint of the artist's brush. In these paintings a series of artistic devices are deployed to insist that the supernatural exists, the heavens are real, and so too are the visions and ecstasies of the saints. Mystics had agreed that any experience with the transcendent was indescribable and unrepresentable, but this proved to be no barrier in trying to do so.[32] Following on from the innovations of Raphael (1483–1520), then, Titian (c. 1490–1576), Lorenzo Lotto (c. 1480–1556/7), and Veronese authored some of the most spectacular visions of paradise of the century, paintings that pulse with vibrancy and life. In the hands of such gifted artists, the mastery of oil paint in the city and the example of the shimmering mosaics of the Marcian basilica combined to activate an artistic tradition that in some ways heralded the dawn of the Baroque. We see this too with representations of purgatory, with which the book concludes. Palma il Giovane (c. 1550–1628) painted an important cycle of paintings on the theme for the ceiling of the Scuola di San Fantin (now the Ateneo Veneto), images that sought to persuade the viewer of practices of almsgiving, papal indulgences, and the offering of masses as an efficacious method of freeing suffering souls from the antechamber of heaven. Perhaps the earliest cycle of its kind, one that Emile Mâle's important iconographic compendium of art after the Council of Trent overlooked completely in favour of Federico Zuccaro's (c. 1542–1609) near contemporaneous frescoes for the chapel of the Angels at the mother church of the Jesuit Order in Rome, the San Fantin cycle expressed one of the fundamental beliefs of the early modern Catholic world: that the realm of the dead could be transformed by the actions of the living.[33]

Although the visual themes explored in Part II generally correspond to the dogmas reasserted at the Council of Trent and then promoted in its aftermath, I have attempted to be scrupulous in identifying their pre-history. For example, there is a wealth of evidence from the Priuli visitation that encouraging devotion to the eucharist was a fundamental aspect of his programme for reform. Yet eucharistic imagery already had an important pre-history in Venice, so should not be understood solely as a consequence of later historical changes.[34] What can be asserted is that in this particular case a lively local visual tradition coincided with the broader aims of the post-Tridentine Church. It is also true that in areas of Europe that remained Catholic, those rituals and beliefs that had been directly critiqued and rejected by the Protestant Reformations tended to be newly elevated. This can be seen even in those places where the reformed movements had far less of a direct impact, including the Iberian Peninsula and Southern Italy.[35] This climate of 'hypersacralisation' is usually associated with the flourishing of the Baroque in Rome, but it can be seen early on in Venice. Rather than associate this with a considered 'counter-attack', it would be more accurate to interpret these visual outcomes as the product of a culture newly reinvested in the emotive power of the devotional image, as the fruit of a period of spiritual change, rather than as a blunt reflection of the Tridentine decrees. In Part I of this book the lack of a broadly implemented strategy for reforming the sacred image by the Catholic Church is demonstrated. In Part II it is shown how this approach left space for the possibility of innovation and experimentation, since stylistically artists responded to the requirement for an emotive devotional art in diverse ways. Art may have changed in terms of content, with particular themes and iconographies enjoying a newfound popularity, but there was no fixed consensus about what the perfect devotional image looked like in terms of its style. Centuries later this was confirmed at the Second Vatican Council (1962–65), when it was asserted that the Church 'has not adopted any particular style of art as her very own; she has admitted styles from every period according to the natural talents and circumstances of peoples, and the needs of the various rites'.[36]

Thus, one cause did not always lead to one stylistic effect, and the spiritual events of the Cinquecento impacted artists in very different ways, particularly in Venice where they were exposed to a range of religious and artistic currents.[37] This is why a local approach matters, because the extent to which the visual arts were regulated differed from one place to another.[38] For example, although he later called for an 'Index' of forbidden images, Cardinal Gabriele Paleotti (1522–97) had written in his earlier treatise of 1582 on sacred and profane images that his recommendations were relevant only to his own diocese, since he had no intention of 'playing the censor of usages' that might have differed from those found in Bologna.[39] It is equally true that ecclesiastical visitors often had their own personal priorities and irritants. In Verona, for example, at seventeen churches the coadjutor Agostino Valier (1531–1606) ordered the removal of images showing the blood of Christ flowing from the wounds of his resurrected body and filling a chalice.[40] In Rome, Pope Clement VIII (r. 1592–1605) ordered changes even to fully dressed figures, whose poses he considered indecorous.[41] Neither of these tendencies can be traced in Priuli's visits, and even when orders like these were made, it cannot be taken for granted that they were acted on. Just as sensitivity to time and place is crucial for the histories of sixteenth-century religion, so too are regional art histories in allowing us to reach a more nuanced and ultimately more accurate portrayal of how visual representations developed in this epoch. This is particularly the case in Venice, where the geographical location of the city, its singular environment, and the relatively independent nature of its Church and its links to the East are local peculiarities that complicate the idea of a centralised and enforceable 'Counter-Reformation'. This follows the reality of Tridentine reform more broadly: with the exception of the Papal States perhaps, nowhere in sixteenth-century Europe was it accepted that a good Catholic was a thoroughly Tridentine Catholic.

WHY VENICE?

Before proceeding, it is worth providing a deeper rationale of the reasons why Venice presents such an interesting subject for the themes this book examines. First, as noted by Hall, if one compares the artistic achievements of Venetian artists in the latter half of the sixteenth century with the artifice of late *maniera* in central Italy, often (unfairly) perceived as a nadir in the history of art, one can see that the sensuous appeal of light and colour synonymous with the city's visual heritage was well placed to fulfil the requirements of legibility and emotive potential that the Church and the laity expected.[42] Second, whereas Pope Sixtus V (r. 1585–90) considered pulling down the pagan statues in Rome during his papacy towards the end of the Cinquecento (in imitation of Gregory the Great's actions centuries earlier), Venice was believed to be without an antique past. The myth of the city as uniquely blessed and divinely favoured provided it with excellent religious credentials in an age when this was of renewed importance.[43] Transcendent beauty had always been a prerogative of the Venetians, from the glimmering mosaics of the Basilica of San Marco to the jewellery-box loveliness of the church of the Miracoli, meaning that the city's inhabitants were enthusiastic protagonists in the redecoration and embellishment of the environment in a period when this was actively encouraged. Third, the Venetian art critic Marco Boschini (1613–c. 1700) might have written in 1660 that a 'painting without a nude is like a meal without bread', but the sensual nudes for which Venetian sixteenth-century artists were renowned were mostly consigned to paintings of a profane subject matter, and the majority of the city's artists and patrons appear to have shown little enthusiasm for 'scandalous' religious paintings, particularly when these were on public display in a ritual context.[44] Raffaello Borghini (c. 1537–88), the Florentine whose 1584 *Il Riposo* had a moralising tone, and which criticised the painters Agnolo Bronzino (1503–72) and Jacopo Pontormo (1494–1556/7) for the 'lascivious' aspects of their art in no uncertain terms, even if their technical skills were praised, had kind things to say about Venetian artists, and the text never critiqued them for the lapses of decorum that his Tuscan compatriots were believed to have indulged in.[45] At least from a contemporary viewpoint, then, the artists he praised could even be said to have been more 'modern' and forward thinking in their shrewd grasp of what was now required from the sacred image than their colleagues working elsewhere.

This can also be appreciated by thinking about the ways in which the visual solutions adopted by Venetian artists in their religious paintings were harnessed by painters as stylistically diverse as El Greco or Peter Paul Rubens (1577–1640), both of whom were notably interested in the affective power of art, and made journeys to Venice towards the beginning of their careers: El Greco in the late 1560s and Rubens in the first years of the 1600s.[46] El Greco owned his own copy of the Tridentine decrees, and the deeply pious Rubens was at the helm of Counter-Reformation painting in Hapsburg Antwerp. His *Deposition* for the guild of the Arquebusiers at Antwerp Cathedral demonstrates the extent to which he looked to artists like Veronese for their compositional and painterly innovations.[47] The left-hand panel of this triptych depicts the Virgin Mary greeting her cousin Elizabeth, an apparent meditation on Veronese's altarpiece of the *Visitation* once displayed in the church of the convent of San Giacomo on the island of Murano.[48] Rubens adopted the same unusual visual solution of the raised bridge upon which the two women meet, while denoting the hierarchy of the figures and the significance of the episode slightly differently, in keeping with the eucharistic themes of the Antwerp triptych (Figs. 2 and 3).[49] Rubens emphasises the Virgin Mary as the mother of Christ: in his painting a visibly pregnant Mary points to her womb, as does Elizabeth. Mary is here garbed in red, meaning not only is the sacrificial fate of her son emphasised (who is shown being taken down from the cross in the main panel of the triptych), but her relationship to the disciple John is too, depicted dressed in garments of the same hue. Just as Rubens demonstrated an obvious enthusiasm for Venetian religious painting, drawing upon the innovations of recent artists in his own *arte sacra*, some years earlier Philip II of Spain had requested the services of either Tintoretto or Veronese for the decoration of the Escorial outside Madrid. Since neither of his first choices was inclined to leave Venice, the Hapsburg King had to make do with the central Italian painter Federico Zuccaro, who arrived in 1585. Despite Zuccaro's status as something of a reformer of devotional art, his *Adoration of the Shepherds* failed to impress the emperor, who concluded that the blame did not lie with the artist, but with those 'who sent him this way'.[50]

The artists that Borghini complimented, including Jacopo Bassano, Titian, Veronese, Tintoretto, and Palma il Giovane, are amongst the most renowned and famous in the history of Venetian art. Their achievements have hardly been undervalued, yet they have not necessarily been adequately appreciated in terms of how their output corresponded to the objectives of devotional art and architecture in modern scholarship until relatively recently. Surveys of Venetian art and architecture rarely mention these themes, or if they do it is limited to the example of Veronese and the Inquisition, or as part of a discussion of either Palladio's ecclesiastical architecture or Tintoretto's paintings for the Scuole del Santissimo Sacramento.[51] Landmark monographs such as Mâle's, which first appeared in 1932, left Venice almost completely out of the picture (apart from a brief mention of Tintoretto's paintings at the Ducal Palace), since his emphasis was predominantly on the Seicento and Baroque artists of the Roman and Spanish schools, where it was thought that the impact of the century's religious transformation could be most clearly traced.[52] Broadly speaking, the visual trends perceptively observed by Mâle

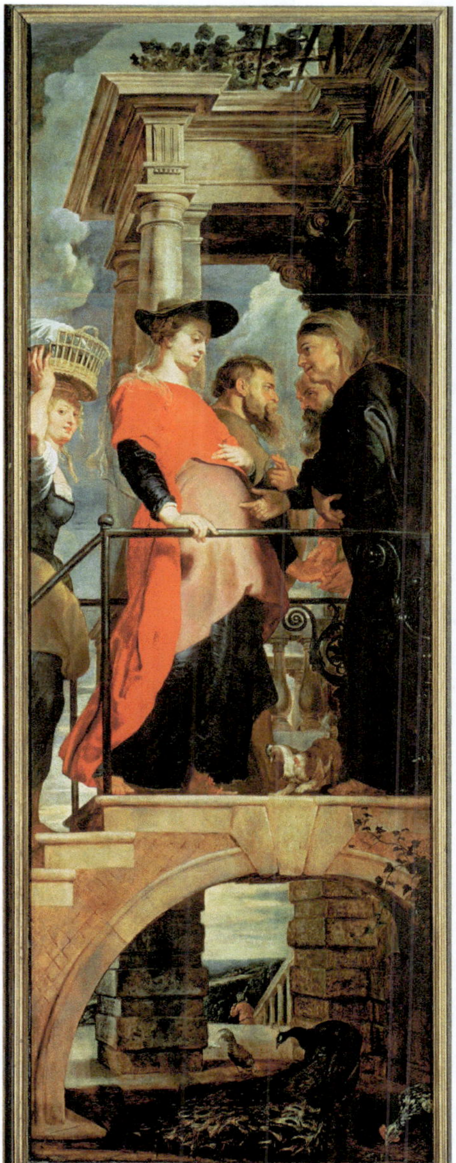

2 Rubens, *The Visitation*, 1611–14, oil on panel, Cathedral of Our Lady, Antwerp (Photo: Erich Lessing/Art Resource New York)

are confirmed by my own study. Yet due to Mâle's tendency to concentrate on papal Rome he often ignored precedents for his findings, too readily assuming that the images he discussed were a straightforward visual response to the Protestant Reformations.[53] Because the achievements of late sixteenth-century Venetian artists were so marked, this also caused a problem for scholars who tended to link Catholic reform to artistic decline. For example, influential art historians such as Sydney Freedberg praised the 'libertarian and energetic' painting of

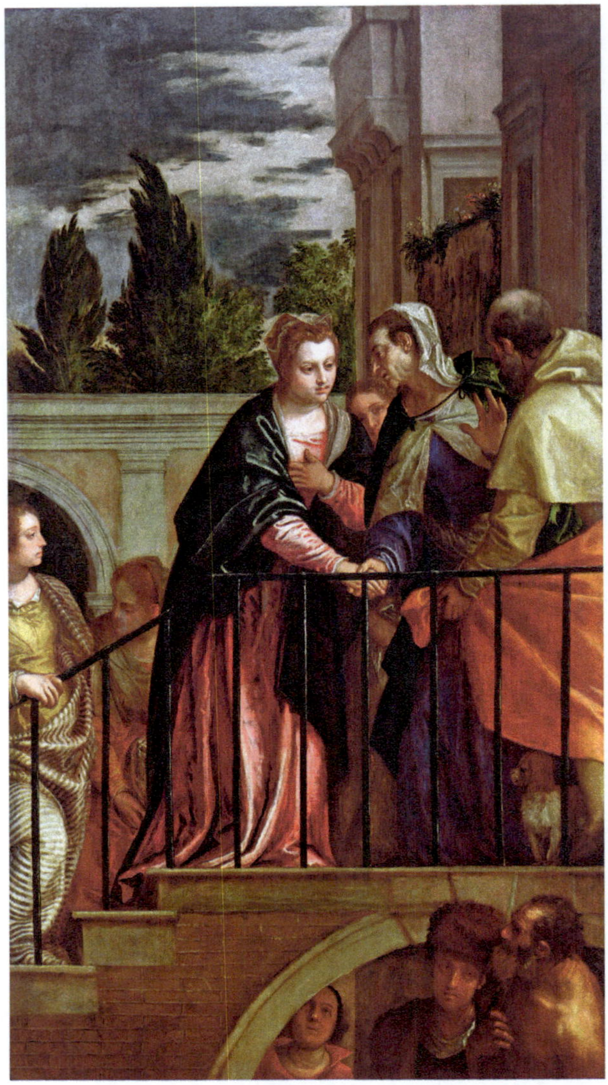

3 Veronese, *The Visitation*, c. 1585, oil on canvas, Barber Institute, Birmingham (Photo: Barber Institute of Fine Arts/The Henry Barber Trust, the Barber Institute of Fine Arts, University of Birmingham/Bridgeman Images)

mid-sixteenth-century Venice, in contrast to the perceived lack of achievement in Rome and central Italy, attributing this in part to very different spiritual and religious values.[54]

In a similar vein to Freedberg, in 2002 Augusto Gentili contended that 'one after the other, the great Venetian artists of the sixteenth century came close to, or actually manifested outright dissent when faced with the crucial test of religious painting during the period of post-Trent 'normalization'.[55] Gentili's assertions are similar to those of other Italian scholars that came of age in 1968, such as Sergio Marinelli or Giandomenico Romanelli in more recent publications, whose approaches will also be discussed in Chapter 1. Since it is evidently very difficult not only to show how artists visually manifested dissenting beliefs in early modern Venice and why patrons would have wanted such works, but also to demonstrate that they even held them in the first place, these interpretations are often reached through obscure and complex iconographic readings.[56] It sometimes appears that the more revered and famous the artist is considered to be, the more likely it is that sooner or later they will be associated with heterodoxy, since this parallels a characterisation of the genius creator as an outsider at odds with the will of the establishment.[57]

One idea proposed by Gentili that has been widely disseminated in numerous publications and is pertinent to the question of the relationship between art and the spiritual crises of the century is 'figurative Nicodemism'. This theory can be summed up as follows: like the Pharisee Nicodemus in the Gospel of John who secretly followed Christ and prepared his corpse for burial, Nicodemites were individuals who concealed their reformist beliefs. Gentili supposes that Titian must have been a Nicodemite towards the end of his life, the evidence being that he was close friends with Pietro Aretino (1492–1556), who had expressed evangelical ideas in his writings, and that Titian apparently appears in the guise of the saint in the 1559 *Entombment,* now in the Museo del Prado, this identification thus revealing his true spiritual allegiances.[58] This situation is complicated by the fact that the visual evidence is evidently ambivalent. In the Prado painting Titian's self-portrait is reserved for the figure by Christ's head, identified by Gentili as Nicodemus.[59] The figure at the other end of the tomb who gently supports Christ's legs is thus Joseph of Arimathea, even though he is depicted in far plainer clothing, unusual considering both established iconographic tradition and his status as a rich man. In a later version of the same episode by Titian and his workshop of 1572 in the Prado, Joseph of Arimathea is evidently the figure at Christ's head, not at his feet.[60] Michelangelo famously depicted himself as Nicodemus in the sculpted *Deposition* of 1547–55, but in the Prado *Entombment* it appears to me that Titian equates himself not with Nicodemus but with Joseph, the wealthy Israelite. In sum, images offer powerful evidence, but we have to be careful not to bend this evidence to ideas that are at best thought-provoking theories that should justly be considered, but do not have to be grandiosely insisted upon as the sole correct interpretation of the painting.[61] By its very nature, the theory of figurative Nicodemism is impossible to prove or disprove: Nicodemites had to hide their true sympathies so we cannot know for sure if Titian even held these beliefs, and if he did, the visual evidence had to be deliberately obfuscated, which means it becomes feasible to take into consideration hidden meanings that must have been completely lost on spectators or patrons of these paintings, in this case the Catholic King of Spain, Philip II.

Whereas an iconographic reading of an image can be at the least suggestive, arguably the least convincing kind of evidence used to promote an artist as nonconformist is entirely circumstantial, merely tying them to a location where Lutheran conventicles were known to flourish. An example of this would be W. R. Rearick's theory that Jacopo Bassano harboured Protestant sympathies because he worked in Enego for a few months, a town known for harbouring religious dissidents. As Bernard Aikema pointed out in his refutation of Rearick's theory, a number of Bassano's altarpieces were explicitly anti-heretical, as indeed were those of Titian.[62] This is not to deny that there were examples of artists active in Venice who may have adhered to creeds that would be condemned by the Church. Lorenzo Lotto, for example, is someone for whom convincing visual and documentary evidence exists to suggest this, analysed in Chapter 1. But against many of the less persuasive assertions concerning the religiosity of painters described is the reality that they worked extensively and repeatedly for patrons that included the new religious orders of the Catholic Reformation, eucharistic confraternities, and Catholic kings and emperors. All of the oeuvres of these artists included highly orthodox masterpieces. The fact that the Bassano workshop was commissioned to complete an altarpiece for one of the crucibles of devotional art in Rome, the Gesù, or that Veronese, despite his experience with the Inquisition, was paradigmatic of a great devotional artist for later painters, tells us something about how their achievements were appreciated in their own times, a reception very much at odds with the modern scholarly constructions that have been described.

AGENDAS AND APPROACHES

Venice

The well-known hubs of artistic reform in Italy are naturally Rome, followed by Milan, Florence, and Bologna, all of which have been the subject of important studies. There now also exists a sizeable bibliography for Northern Italy, Venice in particular, although the themes that this book examines have mostly been approached through the oeuvres of individual artists: such as Aikema's analysis of Jacopo Bassano's 'moralising' paintings, Stefania Mason's catalogue raisonné of Palma il Giovane, Una d'Elia's and Christopher Nygren's monographs on Titian's religious works, as well as Roland Krischel's and Tom Nichols's studies on Tintoretto, even if with the exception of Nygren, the most recent of these date to almost twenty years ago.[63] This book's themes have also been explored through the studies of heterodoxy described, the more successful of these including the work of Massimo Firpo and Fabrizio Biferali on the artist Battista Franco (c. 1510–61) and the more general volume on *Images and Heresy in Sixteenth-Century Italy*, which focuses its attention on the volatile climate of the 1540s and 1550s.[64]

This corpus of literature has been complemented by illuminating studies of patronage in Venice, particularly those of Peter Humfrey (co-ordinated altarpiece programmes), Tracy Cooper (Palladio), and Aikema and Dulcia Meijers (charitable institutions tied to Catholic Reform), as well as through iconographic analyses and explorations of the social conditions of Venetian artists in the same years this monograph focuses on: primarily Maurice Cope's investigation of chapels of the Blessed Sacrament, Michel Hochmann's work on painters and patrons in Venice from 1540 to 1628, Matile's study of lateral canvases in Venetian churches, and Martin Seidel's analysis of Venetian painting at the time of the Counter-Reformation, which examined paintings by Titian, Tintoretto, Veronese, and Palma in light of treatises on the subject of devotional art.[65] Finally, special mention should go to the detailed and sensitive reconstructions regarding the patronage of the eucharistic confraternities in Venetian parishes by the late Thomas Worthen.[66] Each of Worthen's studies was the fruit of years of direct observation and painstaking research in the city's archives and libraries, resulting in a small but influential body of scholarship. As a whole, these and other scholars have done much to present balanced analyses of the multifaceted ways in which artistic production in Venice was shaped by the historical context of religious change, although they differ in the extent to which they suggest the city was an important site for these developments.[67] One of the outcomes of these studies, which often pivoted around careful archival research and persuasive visual analysis, was that their findings were brought to the attention of a wider public through recent blockbuster exhibitions on Veronese and Tintoretto in particular, both of which presented sensitive characterisations of their status as religious artists.[68] Despite this, it is still fair to say that Venetian artists are mostly examined tangentially with regard to the question of the visual arts and reform during the late Renaissance; and they were mostly absent from the two excellent edited volumes on this topic that were published in the last few years.[69]

Art and Religion

For much of the last century the impact of the Catholic response to the Reformation on the arts was seen as a negative one, closely tied to the later flourishing of the Baroque in Rome and the machinations of the Jesuit Order, who were regarded with great suspicion.[70] Bailey noted that 'nothing in the history of Italian painting may be as detested as the religious painting of the last four decades of the 1500s'.[71] Although his focus was on images produced for the Society of Jesus in Rome, it is true that the latter decades of the Cinquecento were not considered worthy of extensive study until relatively recently, primarily because they were not believed to be ones of great artistic achievement, but rather of decline. To give a few examples: in a series of lectures given from 1894 to 1902 Alois Reigl argued that the period was one of profound artistic crisis; for Nikolaus Pevsner writing in 1925 Trent suppressed the Renaissance 'spirit'; and for Anthony Blunt in his hugely influential *Artistic Theory in Italy*, first published in 1940, the art of the late sixteenth century faltered due its intrinsic links to a religion of repression and intolerance.[72]

The analysis of many of these scholars was predicated upon an understanding of the art in this time as a method of indoctrination or propaganda, something that had clear ramifications for the extent to which it was even considered a suitable topic for art historical investigation.[73] This is not to say that there was no truth to some of their observations. Confronted with some of the more lugubrious and repetitive seventeenth-century depictions of purgatory it is not difficult to appreciate why they might fail to appeal to a modern audience. Nor would it be correct to say that contemporary images or architecture never aimed for a level of indoctrination: one could argue that this is inherent in the very justification of devotional images as the 'bibles of the illiterate', and in the early modern period the use of visual tools as a method of evangelisation on the global missions was of great importance.[74] But not only does such a judgement run the risk of reductivism, it presupposes that the will of the institution (in this case the Church) is fundamentally at odds with the desires of the individual (in this case the artist). Rather than a process of negotiation, the former is seen as enforcing their agenda on the latter, meaning that the end product – whether that be a painting or a sculpture or a building – is dismissed since the dynamic is understood as binary, with the ironic result that the creator is denied any agency and thus is of little interest to the art historian.[75] Furthermore, since images reflect not just the religious persuasions of the patron and artist, but also that of the laity, this interpretation denies agency to them also, bypassing a consideration of the ways in which the people could play a role in constructing devotional identity.[76]

Blunt was famously employed as a Soviet spy in his youth, so it was unlikely that he was ever going to have much sympathy for the devotional *aims* of images in this period, even if he did have a keen interest in the Sicilian and Neapolitan Baroque.[77] To be fair to Blunt, he later expressed discomfort not only with his earlier political sympathies but with aspects of his influential analysis, the preface to the second edition describing the book as the result of 'the rashness of youth'.[78] The analysis presented in *Artistic Theory in Italy* drew upon a narrative of Counter-Reform that tended to claim the humanism of the Renaissance as the natural precursor to both Protestantism and secularism, arguing that the movement 'opposed all the achievements of Renaissance Humanism', aiming to 'undo all that the Renaissance had achieved, and get back to a feudal and medieval state of affairs'.[79] Indeed, for much earlier seminal figures like Jacob Burckhardt (1818–97), the period after the Council of Trent signalled the death knell of the Renaissance and 'annihilated the higher spiritual life of the people', something that had long-lasting consequences for how the climate for artistic production in this period was perceived. It was seen mainly as anti-artistic (in that it insisted on didacticism) and emotionally manipulative (in that it appealed to the senses, in contrast to the cerebral nature of much Renaissance art).[80] As noted by Rachel Miller, particularly with regard to images commissioned by the Jesuit Order, opinions such as those of Blunt and his ilk can also be found in popular art history surveys written in the 1970s and 1980s (with reprints perpetuating these ideas well into the twenty-first century), the most pertinent example of this being Sydney Freedberg's bestselling *Painting in Italy, 1500–1600*, which remains one of the standard English-language surveys of Italian art for this period.[81]

Challenging the biases of this scholarship, which often ran along confessional lines, from the mid 1980s onwards advances were made to present a more holistic view of artistic production in early modern Italy, meaning that there is now a large and ever-expanding scholarship on the subject.[82] Often hailing from North American institutions of higher education, scholars examined the effects of the contemporary religious controversies on the visual arts in new ways, by thinking about the apparent paradox of how a climate of religious intolerance and limited creative freedom could also be one of artistic and architectural innovation (Hall), by considering the nature of reform movements prior to the Council of Trent and their links to artistic practice (Alexander Nagel), or by examining the place of the sensuous in the Counter-Reformation Church (Hall and Cooper).[83] Bailey's extensive work on the arts of the Jesuit Order, in terms of both their global missions and their decorative programmes in Rome and Florence, has dismantled many of the myths concerning the society's patronage of art and architecture.[84] Rome might have been the traditional epicentre for studies on changes to the visual arts in Italy during this period, but in recent years these studies have been complemented by a host of monographs on patrons, painters, sculptors, and architects from a range of larger centres and smaller peripheries, as well as English-language translations of the treatises that will be explored in Chapter 3.[85] This diversification in terms of geography and approach has been complemented by new ways of examining miracle-working images, and has even encompassed imaginative studies of one the most lampooned of all Catholic devotions: the holy house of Loreto.[86] As a whole, these studies can be said to have punctured the Burckhardtian view of the Renaissance (a process that has been ongoing since the 1950s), contributing to a more inclusive and complex portrayal of a broad range of images and devotional practices in early modern Italy, whilst also underlining the importance of local contexts and histories in achieving this.[87]

TERMINOLOGY

Reform and Reformation

As with all terminology, 'reform' comes with its own set of limitations but is used throughout this text, together with the label 'sacred art' (*arte sacra*), because these are the words that are most frequently encountered in the contemporary texts and documents here examined. The two main shortcomings of this term are worth stating. First, reform brings to mind a uniform process of improvement and standardisation that could be applied to any significant shift in religious practice or, for my purposes, any change in artistic style or content. This is why it tends to be overused and is often deployed by art historians for any innovation that is apparently without precedent, even when the broader apparatus to suggest that a formal process of 'reform' took place is missing. Second, reform denotes a pre-existing level of corruption, or institutional failure, that through a process of purification is improved. This has clear implications for how the changes in art and architecture in this period are understood, since these transformations were not always positive. As shall be shown, in the hands of talented artists and architects these reforms were often innovative, requiring new architectural and artistic responses, but they could also be deeply traditional and at times repetitive. The ramifications are also evident in the singular use of the word 'Reformation' to describe the period of European history that saw western Christendom fragmented and transformed after Luther's break with the Roman Church. As pointed out by Carlos Eire, '*the* Reformation' suggests that this was the definitive step in the correct direction towards a purified Christian faith, one cleansed of the superstitions, idolatry, and 'popishness' of the Catholics.[88] In late sixteenth-century Italy, however, reform had different connotations, and it was associated with the institutional Roman Church and with conciliar legislation.[89]

Stylistic Labels

Interwoven with the trends described in the previous section is the question of which stylistic label (if any) should be used to refer to artistic production in the years between the movements known as Mannerism and Baroque.[90] Although labels can be useful for categorising and classifying artistic movements, they are flexible; their parameters shift and change, usually with all sorts of qualifications; and there are always exceptions to the rule. To some extent, labels reflect the norms and preferences of the period in which one writes, and I neither take them too seriously nor reject them outright. I unapologetically refer to Renaissance art in the title of this book, knowing full well that, on the one hand, the chronology and very nature of this phenomenon is extensively debated, but also, on the other, that a number of the artists and architects who will be examined are generally grouped under the 'late Renaissance' in art historical surveys of Venice intended for students and the interested public, who are often less familiar with terms like 'early modern' that are more extensively employed by scholars. Moreover, given the lack of one single stylistic movement immediately after the Council of Trent, attempts to establish the terms of an aesthetic that can be closely associated with it tend to founder, although thought-provoking stylistic studies do exist.[91] Musing upon Rubens's sensuous *Holy Family with Saint Anne*, the historian John O'Malley was right to ask himself, 'Would this painting have been any different had there been no "Counter-Reformation"?,' and I have endeavoured to do the same.[92] I reject the label 'Counter-Reformation art' that is sometimes used, since this is usually employed as a pejorative one, bringing to mind the picture of a mediocre artist slavishly following the dictates of the clergy as they conjure up straightforward explications of dogma, bereft of any sense of innovation or nuance. It also harkens back to an understanding of the 'age of the Counter-Reformation' as signalling a decisive break with Renaissance ideals, a viewpoint that the historian William Hudon (amongst numerous others) has argued presents a major stumbling block to understanding early modern Italian religiosity and, by extension, its effects on art.[93] As noted by Bailey, the quantity of labels that have been applied to late sixteenth-century painting, from 'anti-maniera' to 'Counter-maniera' to 'mannered Mannerism', are only of limited use, particularly when you try to apply them to Venice, where the stylistic individuality of the city's artists often has little in common with these categorisations.

Periodisation

Just as stylistic labels are almost always invented after the period they refer to and were rarely employed contemporaneously, the terminology used to apply to this period of history is similarly contested, and some scholars have argued that it would be better to do away with it completely.[94] Anyone trying to get to grips with the wealth of conflicting literature devoted solely to what name to give to this period of history cannot help but sympathise with them. Thus, Simon Ditchfield's oft-repeated comment concerning Tridentine Catholicism that 'it is high time we stopped arguing what label to use when describing it – i.e. what it *was* and, instead, ask ourselves what it *did*' is a cogent one, and undoubtedly more fruitful in terms of the future direction of research.[95] The various nomenclatures given to the reform of the Catholic Church in the Cinquecento – 'Counter-Reformation', 'Catholic Reformation', 'Early Modern Catholicism', and 'post-Tridentine' – all have their own distinct advantages, disadvantages, and inherent bias, and they seem to go in and out of vogue. Not one of them was used during the early sixteenth or late seventeenth century, and this is why I use the simple term 'reform' – for the reasons just outlined – as well as referring to 'Reformations' in the plural, in order to reference diverse movements that come under the umbrella of both Protestantism and Catholicism, and the ways in which they were intertwined.[96]

Yet I do also make reference to the 'Counter-Reformation' and the 'Catholic Reformation' throughout this book in order to highlight different impulses. Numerous excellent literature reviews exist on the use of these terms, and I do not intend to exhaustively repeat these historiographies in detail.[97] As a term, 'Counter-Reformation' was first employed in 1776 by the Lutheran lawyer and historian Johann Stephan Pütter in his introduction to his edition of the Augsburg Confession and later in 1843 by Leopold von Ranke in his German History in the Reformation, which ended with his portentous declaration: 'After the era of the Reformation came the era of the Counter-Reformation.'[98] More recently, Firpo argued that Counter-Reform was not just a battle against external enemies of the Church, but was 'above all an internal battle for the control of conscience, social discipline and repression of dissent', with those instruments of enforcement and censorship such as the Inquisition or the Index of Prohibited Books becoming emblematic of it.[99] The second term, 'Catholic Reformation', tends to be employed to underline the more generative results of reform, such as the new religious orders or innovative charitable activities. This also has its pitfalls, and its most dogmatic adherents suggest that Catholic reform efforts had nothing to do with Protestantism, an interpretation that stresses continuity to such an extent that it can appear that little changed and that avoids the fact that without the Reformation it is unlikely (although not completely implausible) that the Council of Trent would ever have been called.[100] Like 'Counter-Reformation', 'Catholic Reformation' has a Teutonic origin, coined by Wilhelm Maurenbrecher in 1880 in his *History of the Catholic Reformation*.[101] Catholic Reform can be defined as diverse religious movements that existed both before and after the Council of Trent and that were in harmony or in tension with its objectives. Catholic Reform underlines the historical continuity of the reform process and the flowering of devotions that in the light of the later Reformation could be assumed to respond directly to it. In this book I use both nomenclatures interchangeably to show the different outcomes of a desire both to repress dissent and to encourage spiritual regeneration. Finally, since even the most accepted terms are now extensively debated by scholars, to round off my justifications regarding terminology, I have no objection to referring to the 'Church', in the sense of the institution of the Catholic Church, which is how it was referred to in the documents and literature produced in Italy during the years that this book covers. Although I distinguish between local variants of the Venetian Church where necessary, when referring to something like the decrees of the Council of Trent, for example, I understand these texts as the official promulgations of the 'Church', even if aspects of them might have been subsequently resisted.

To conclude, although the question of the image was given a new urgency due to the negation of its role in various parts of Europe, even before the Reformation critiques of the appearance and use of sacred images were routinely voiced by clerics. The immediate impetus for the reassertion of the

Church's stance on images was the reality of Protestant iconoclasm abroad, but the growing consensus regarding image reform in Italy was also the result of homegrown sentiments, and we will see how it was stimulated by the spectacular fallout over Michelangelo's *Last Judgement* for the Sistine Chapel. At Trent, the question of images was low on the list of priorities, and it was rushed through in the last session under pressure from the Cardinal of Lorraine, Charles de Guise (1524–74), who was concerned about outbreaks of iconoclasm in France.[102] The council prelates might have noted the emotional power of the image, but they did not stipulate how such power was to be achieved, what such an image might look like, and whether it depended upon iconography, style, the religious convictions of the artist, or the pious inclinations of the viewer. Perhaps they understood that the effectiveness of an image depends on a myriad of factors that are beyond the control of the artist and the Church, and that these general guidelines provided sufficient information to ensure the production of decorous images, as well as including the standard (although arguably ineffectual) reminder to the laity that in terms of response, images were not to be worshipped, but rather venerated. In short, their demands were hardly onerous. That they were not found to be difficult to interpret is evidenced by the fact that of the thousands of requests that the Congregazione del concilio received relating to problems with implementing the Tridentine decrees, not one was related to the veneration of images.[103]

Nevertheless, as the sixteenth century wore on it was increasingly felt by a number of the writers who are examined in Chapter 2 that artists could not be trusted to be left completely to their own devices, and that they should be guided by more detailed norms that could assist them in creating 'appropriate' sacred art and architecture. The aims of one of them, Cardinal Paleotti, were rejected as over the top by figures in the very orbit of the Inquisition itself, with one opponent arguing that 'surely the Catholic Church does not need to be taught, after fifteen hundred years, how to paint sacred images?', something that artists doubtless agreed with.[104] In other places controls could be much more rigid. In Seville, for example, there was an official artistic censor appointed by the Inquisition: the painter Francisco Pacheco (1564–1644), who was the father-in-law of Diego Velázquez. Carmen Fracchia uses the existence of said censor and the fact that El Greco's *Martyrdom of St Maurice* for King Philip II was replaced with another version by the artist Romulo Cincinato (d. 1597) to argue that 'total semiotic control' was placed on the production of visual representations in Spain after the last session of the Council of Trent.[105] Yet complicating the mixed reaction that more than one of El Greco's sacred images were greeted with is the fact that said Pacheco stated that his Cretan contemporary had succeeded in producing the most appropriate and decorous images of St Francis of all.[106]

Finally, the significance and background relating to the 1563 decree on images will be analysed in Chapter 2, but it should be noted that while the Tridentine declarations are often understood predominantly in terms of challenging artistic freedom, they were also favourable to the inherent need and power of the image, by arguing that 'great profit is derived from all sacred images'. The decrees reissued the Church's historic justification regarding visual representations of the divine first established at the Second Council of Nicaea (787): that images were useful for their educative potential, and that despite the inherent risks of idolatry, honour was due not to the image but to the prototype that it represented.[107] At Trent, this was intended foremost as a firm rebuttal of Protestant iconoclasm, but although it is often repeated that the council said little that was new on the image issue, this is not quite true, since it was also stipulated that they should avoid indecency and be appropriate to their setting. In addition to their communicative usefulness, it is worth emphasising that the decrees powerfully endorsed images as capable of encouraging the faithful to 'adore and love God, and to cultivate piety', imbuing the images with a portent far beyond their function as a mere didactic tool and providing a renewed impetus to make sacred spaces ever more honorific and splendid. As pointed out by Maarten Delbeke in his study of art theory in Bernini's Rome, mere imitation was no longer the ultimate justification of artistic practice for figures like Cardinal Sforza Pallavicino (1607–67). Their insistence on the capacity of art to provide access to God was an assumption from which emerged 'a powerful and striking plea for formal experiments and artistic innovation'.[108] Crucially, how this was to be done was never spelled out in great detail by the brief Tridentine decrees, and ultimately it was left up to artists and patrons to work out how best to achieve this. The novel and visually arresting solutions forged by both of these groups, and the ways in which the visual arts were variously exploited, controlled, and promoted in this turbulent period of Venice's history is the subject of the next chapters.

NOTES

1 Thesis fifty of Luther's ninety-five statements read: 'Christians are to be taught that if the pope knew the exactions of the indulgence preachers, he would rather that the basilica of St Peter were burned to ashes than built up with the skin, flesh and bones of the sheep.' Carlos M. N. Eire, *Reformations: The Early Modern World, 1450–1650* (New Haven, CT: Yale University Press, 2016), 151.

2 Eire, *Reformations*, viii.

3 For recent research that has partially dismantled this interpretation, see Chapter 3. This interpretation was promoted above all by Gaetano Cozzi, *Il doge Nicolò Contarini: ricerche sul patriziato veneziano agli inizi del Seicento* (Venice: Istituto per la collaborazione culturale, 1958); Gaetano Cozzi, *Paolo Sarpi tra Venezia e l'Europa* (Turin: Einuadi, 1978); William J. Bouwsma, *Venice and the Defense of Republican Liberty: Renaissance Values in the Age of the Counter Reformation*, 2nd ed. (Berkeley: University of California Press, 1984). An analysis of these approaches and

how subsequent historians challenged them is provided by James S. Grubb, 'When Myths Lose Power: Four Decades of Venetian Historiography', *Journal of Modern History* 58, no. 1 (1986): 43–94. For a more recent discussion, see Alfredo Viggiano, 'Politics and Constitution', in *A Companion to Venetian History, 1400–1797*, ed. Eric Dursteler (Leiden: Brill, 2013), 47–84.

4 For a few examples of the former, see Madlyn Kahr, 'The Meaning of Veronese's Paintings in the Church of San Sebastiano in Venice', *Journal of the Warburg and Courtauld Institutes* 33 (1970): 235–47; Bernard Aikema, 'Pictor religiosus', in *Paolo Veronese: L'illusione della realtà*, ed. Bernard Aikema and Paola Marini, Exhibition Catalogue, Palazzo della Gran Guardia, Verona, 5 July–5 October 2014 (Milan: Electa, 2014), 241–54; Richard Cocke, *Paolo Veronese: Piety and Display in an Age of Religious Reform* (Aldershot: Ashgate, 2001).

5 To name just two recent articles that demonstrate this tendency: Jonathan Jones, 'A Jester at the Last Supper? How Veronese Became His Era's Ai Weiwei', *Guardian*, 19 March 2014; Martin Gayford, 'How Veronese Outwitted the Inquisition', *Telegraph*, 3 April 2014. Jones stated that 'Venice was a "libertine" city of free thought and free love and Veronese was its perfect artist.'

6 The interrogation was discovered by Armand Baschet, 'Paul Véronèse appelé au Tribunal du Saint Office à Venise (1573)', *Gazette des Beaux-Arts* 23 (1867): 378–82.

7 Gauvin A. Bailey, *Between Renaissance and Baroque: Jesuit Art in Rome, 1565–1610* (Toronto: University of Toronto Press, 2003), 15. Similar opinions are expressed in Pamela M. Jones, *Federico Borromeo and the Ambrosiana: Art Patronage and Reform in Seventeenth-Century Milan* (Cambridge: Cambridge University Press, 1993), 7.

8 Giovanni Botero, *Relatione della Republica Venetiana* (Venice: Giorgio Varisco, 1605), 105–6. For Botero, see Luigi Firpo, 'Giovanni Botero', in *Dizionario Biografico degli Italiani*, vol. 13 (Rome: Treccani, 1971), 352–62. The *Relatione* was subject to censorship by the heads of the Council of Ten, who approved an imprimatur for the first edition in 1603 on condition that it was subject to the 'removal of the many things canceled out by the ... [ducal] secretary'. The precise nature of the edits is unknown, but the resulting account presented the Serenissima in an unsurprisingly positive light when it finally appeared in 1605. Paul F. Grendler, *The Roman Inquisition and the Venetian Press, 1540–1605* (Princeton, NJ: Princeton University Press, 1977), 157. Edits may not have involved this passage, since similar sentiments were expressed earlier in Giovanni Botero *Delle cause della grandezza delle citta libri 3* (Rome: Giovanni Martinelli, 1588), 8–9.

9 The French ambassador Canaye de Fresnes commented on the improvements in the city's devotional life in 1602 compared to thirty years earlier, stating that 'everything that can be desired for the consolation of the soul abounds here as much as in any city of Christendom'. Bouwsma, *Venice and the Defense of Republican Liberty*, 268.

10 For examples, see Eugenio Albèri, *Le relazioni degli ambasciatori veneti al senato durante il secolo decimosesto*, vol. 4, series 1 (Florence: Società editrice fiorentina, 1860), 135, 161, 192, 244, 288.

11 Sfogger has been identified as a member of the great Fugger banking dynasty by John Jeffries Martin, *Venice's Hidden Enemies: Italian Heretics in a Renaissance City* (Berkeley: University of California Press, 1993), 190–91. The investigation included a reconnaissance to Zuanne's palace in Mestre and the inspection of his home in Venice by the local priest, who pretended to be interested in borrowing tapestries to honour the Blessed Sacrament. Recounted by Richard Mackenney, *Venice as the Polity of Mercy: Guilds, Confraternities, and the Social Order, c. 1250–c. 1650* (Toronto: University of Toronto Press, 2018), 265–69.

12 Geoffrey Tyack, *Oxford: An Architectural Guide* (Oxford: Oxford University Press, 1998), 112. Tyack argued that nothing 'in Oxford, or indeed in England, represents more vividly the High Churchmanship and ultramontane artistic sympathies of the Laudian era'.

13 A cogent discussion of the differences is provided by Geraldine A. Johnson, *Renaissance Art: A Very Short Introduction* (Oxford: Oxford University Press, 2005), 3.

14 David Freedberg, *The Power of Images: Studies in the History and Theory of Response*, 2nd ed. (Chicago: University of Chicago Press, 1991).

15 A few examples: Joe Roberts, 'Anger at Fundraiser for Notre Dame Instead of Homeless Parisians', *Metro*, 16 April 2019; Aditya Chakrabortty, 'The Billionaires' Donations Will

Turn Notre Dame into a Monument to Hypocrisy', *Guardian*, 18 April 2019; Colleen Ford, 'Humanity Chose Notre Dame over Starving Children', *Easterner*, 2 May 2019. Chakrabortty pointed out that 'not least among this litany of ironies is that it takes a Catholic cathedral to remind us that we have barely advanced an inch from the medieval buying of indulgences'.

16 I am quoted in Xochitl Gonzalez, 'That's Not Censorship. Artists Are Free to Say What They Want, and Free to Face the Consequences', *Atlantic*, 15 December 2023.

17 The painting in question was Giuseppe Cesari's *Diana and Actaeon* of 1603. See Gareth Harris, 'Renaissance Nude Painting Row at French School Sparks Teacher Walkout', *Art Newspaper*, 13 December 2023.

18 Marie-Louise Lillywhite, 'The Decoration of the Church of San Giacomo dall'Orio in Venice, 1567–1606: Palma Il Giovane, Giovanni Maria da Ponte and the Counter-Reformation', *Artibus et Historiae* 40, no. 79 (2019): 118.

19 See Nora Gietz, 'The Parish of San Polo and Its Patrimony after the Fall of the Venetian Republic (1797–1814)', in *La chiesa e la parrocchia di San Polo: Spazio religioso e spazio pubblico*, ed. Gabriele Matino and Dorit Raines (Rome: Viella, 2020), 325–39.

20 Prior to Gregory, Saint Basil had pronounced that 'artists do as much for religion with their pictures as orators do with their eloquence'. Howard Hibbard, 'Ut picturae sermones: The First Painted Decorations of the Gesù', in *Baroque Art: The Jesuit Contribution*, ed. Rudolf Wittkower and Irma B. Jaffe (New York: Fordham University Press, 1972), 29. Gregory's statement was contained in his letter of 599 to the iconoclastic Bishop Serenus of Marseilles. See Lawrence G. Duggan, 'Was Art Really the "Book of the Illiterate"?', *Word & Image* 5, no. 3 (1989): 227–51. As noted by Koerner, this shifted the emphasis away from cult to pedagogy. See Joseph Leo Koerner, *The Reformation of the Image* (London: Reaktion Books, 2004), 137. For the history of the Western Church's attitudes to religious art, see the opening chapter of Sixten Ringbom, *Icon to Narrative: The Rise of the Dramatic Close-Up in Fifteenth-Century Devotional Painting* (Åbo: Åbo Akademi, 1965). See also chapter 14 on iconoclasm in Freedberg, *The Power of Images*, 378–428.

21 Marcia B. Hall, *The Sacred Image in the Age of Art: Titian, Tintoretto, Barocci, El Greco, Caravaggio* (New Haven, CT: Yale University Press, 2011). See also Gauvin A. Bailey, Review of 'The Sacred Image in the Age of Art: Titian, Tintoretto, Barocci, El Greco, Caravaggio' by Marcia B. Hall, *Renaissance Quarterly* 65, no. 3 (2012): 885–86. Here Bailey warns against perceiving the establishment of the Florentine Accademia as a 'secular counterpart to Trent', noting that it had more in common with a confraternity, and 'placed issues of faith to the fore'.

22 Only in 1682 did the Senate first allow for the foundation of a new guild called the Collegio dei Pittori (not Academy) that disassociated painters from the gilders, card-makers, miniature painters, and others who were part of the venerable Arte dei Depentori. David Rosand, 'The Crisis of the Venetian Renaissance Tradition', *L'arte* 11–12 (1970): 29–34.

23 Frederick Ilchman, 'Tintoretto as a Painter of Religious Narrative', in *Tintoretto*, ed. Miguel Falomir, English ed., Exhibition Catalogue, Museo Nacional del Prado, Madrid, 30 January–13 May 2007 (Madrid: Museo Nacional del Prado, 2007), 87. Described in a document of 6 March 1539 after the painter's death. David Rosand, *Painting in Cinquecento Venice: Titian, Veronese, Tintoretto* (New Haven, CT: Yale University Press, 1982), 141–42, 234–35, doc. 20.

24 Giulia Zavatta, 'Documenti inediti per Alessandro Vittoria e il pittore Melchiorre Galluzzi da Cologna Veneta', *Verona Illustrata* 29 (2016): 36, doc. 3. For an English translation, see David Ekserdjian, *The Italian Renaissance Altarpiece: Between Icon and Narrative* (New Haven, CT: Yale University Press, 2021), 397–99.

25 The lack of a policy for censoring the arts in a similar manner to forbidden books was examined by Michael Douglas-Scott, 'Prohibition of Text and License of Image: Painters and the Vernacular Bible in Counter-Reformation Venice', in *Il Rinascimento italiano di fronte alla Riforma: letteratura e arte*, ed. Chrysa Damianaki, Paolo Procaccioli, and Angelo

Romano, Proceedings of the International Conference, Warburg Institute, London, 30–31 January 2004 (Rome: Vecchiarelli Editore, 2005), 231–51.

26 Areli Marina, 'From the Myth to the Margins: The Patriarch's Piazza at San Pietro Di Castello in Venice', *Renaissance Quarterly* 64, no. 2 (2011): 353–429; Gianmario Guidarelli, 'Venice's Cathedral of San Pietro di Castello 1451–1630', in *Architecture, Art and Identity in Venice and its Territories, 1450–1750: Essays in Honour of Deborah Howard*, ed. Nebahat Avcioglu and Emma Jones (Farnham: Ashgate, 2013), 185–99; Gianmario Guidarelli, *I patriarchi di Venezia e l'architettura: la cattedrale di San Pietro di Castello nel Rinascimento*, Saggi IUAV (Padua: Il Poligrafo, 2015); Gianmario Guidarelli, Michel Hochmann, and Fabio Tonizzi, eds., *La chiesa di San Pietro di Castello e la nascita del patriarcato di Venezia* (Venice: Marcianum Press, 2018); Michael Matile, *'Quadri laterali' im sakralen Kontext: Studien und Materialen zur Historienmalerei in venezianischen Kirchen und Kapellen des Cinquecento* (Munich: Scaneg, 1997); Michael Matile, '"Quadri laterali" ovvero conseguenze di una collocazione ingrata: sui dipinti di storie sacre nell'opera di Jacopo Tintoretto', *Venezia Cinquecento* 6, no. 12 (1997): 151–206.

27 Priuli has never been subject to a full-length biography. Overviews are provided by Giuseppe Cappelletti, *Storia della Chiesa di Venezia dalla sua fondazione sino ai nostri giorni*, vol. 1 (Venice: Tipografia Armena di S. Lazzaro, 1849), 486–94; Antonio Niero, *I patriarchi di Venezia: da Lorenzo Giustiniani ai nostri giorni* (Venice: Studium cattolico veneziano, 1961), 99–106; Giuseppe Trebbi, 'Lorenzo Priuli', in *Dizionario Biografico degli Italiani*, vol. 85 (Rome: Treccani, 2016), 435–38.

28 Jutta Gisela Sperling, *Convents and the Body Politic in Late Renaissance Venice* (Chicago: University of Chicago Press, 1999), 154.

29 Sometimes transformations were made without ever having been ordered by the ecclesiastical authorities, as Hall demonstrated with the examples of the renovations made to Santa Croce and Santa Maria Novella at the initiative of Duke Cosimo de' Medici. Marcia B. Hall, *Renovation and Counter-Reformation: Vasari and Duke Cosimo in Sta Maria Novella and Sta Croce, 1565–1577* (Oxford: Clarendon Press, 1979); Marcia B. Hall, 'Introduction', in *The Sensuous in the Counter-Reformation Church*, ed. Marcia B. Hall and Tracy E. Cooper (Cambridge: Cambridge University Press, 2013), 3–4. More recently, see also Joanne Allen, *Transforming the Church Interior in Renaissance Florence: Screens and Choir Spaces, from the Middle Ages to Tridentine Reform* (Cambridge: Cambridge University Press, 2022).

30 Musing on new iconographies, Camille argued that they 'do not merely describe or reflect a new situation but are products of social processes and often instruments for social action'. Michael Camille, *The Gothic Idol: Ideology and Image-Making in Medieval Art* (Cambridge: Cambridge University Press, 1989), 9.

31 See number five of the theses of Victor I. Stoichita, *Visionary Experience in the Golden Age of Spanish Art* (London: Reaktion Books, 1997), 198.

32 Pointed out by Stoichita, *Visionary Experience*, 7.

33 Emile Mâle, *L'art religieux de la fin du XVIe siècle, du XVIIe siècle et du XVIIIe siècle: étude sur l'iconographie après le Concile de Trente, Italie-France- Espagne-Flandres*, 2nd ed., rev. and corr. (Paris: Armand Colin, 1951), 60–61.

34 That images of the dead Christ 'reached full maturity in the course of the sixteenth century' was argued by Catherine R. Puglisi and William L. Barcham, *Art and Faith in the Venetian World: Venerating Christ as the Man of Sorrows* (Turnhout: Harvey Miller, Brepols, 2019), 289.

35 Eire, *Reformations*, 754.

36 Chapter 7 of the constitution on the sacred liturgy (4 December 1963). See www.vatican.va/archive/hist_councils/ii_vatican_council/documents/vat-ii_const_19631204_sacrosanctum-concilium_en.html (accessed 16 July 2023).

37 This problem was described by Freedberg, who observed that 'almost everything art historians claim about the relations between stylistic change and post-Tridentine attitudes can be qualified, modified or supplemented'. David Freedberg, 'Painting and the Counter

Reformation in the Age of Rubens', in *The Age of Rubens*, ed. Peter C. Sutton, Exhibition Catalogue, Museum of Fine Arts, Boston, 22 September 1993–2 January 1994, Toledo Museum of Art, 2 February–24 April 1994 (Boston: Ludion Press, 1993), 141.

38 The difference between what the Council of Trent decreed and how these decrees were then implemented was pointed out by Giuseppe Alberigo, 'De Concile de Trente au tridentisme', *Irénikon* 54 (1981): 192–210.

39 Gabriele Paleotti, *Discourse on Sacred and Profane Images*, trans. William McCuaig, introduction by Paolo Prodi (Los Angeles: Getty Research Institute; Brighton: Roundhouse Distributor, 2012), 50.

40 Ottavia Niccoli, *Vedere con gli occhi del cuore: Alle origini del potere delle immagini* (Rome: Laterza, 2011), 142.

41 Opher Mansour, 'Censure and Censorship in Rome, c. 1600: The Visitation of Clement VIII and the Visual Arts', in *The Sensuous in the Counter-Reformation Church*, ed. Marcia B. Hall and Tracy E. Cooper (Cambridge: Cambridge University Press, 2013), 136–60.

42 Hall, *The Sacred Image in the Age of Art.*

43 The implications of the city's pervasive myth were not lost on Botero, who dutifully pointed out in his *Relatione* that, 'of all the great cities of Italy, rather of Europe, and of the universe, only this one was born Christian and Catholic'. Botero, *Relatione della Republica Venetiana*, 102.

44 A point made also by Humfrey, see Chapter 2, note 13. Boschini's quip was noted by Taryn Marie Zarillo, 'Artistic Patrimony and Cultural Politics in Early Seicento Venice' (doctoral thesis, University of Columbia, 2016), 173. Marco Boschini, *La carta del navegar pitoresco. Edizione critica con la 'Breve instruzione' premessa alle 'Ricche minere della pittura veneziana'*, ed. Anna Pallucchini (Venice: Istituto per la collaborazione culturale, 1966), 380.

45 Raffaello Borghini, *Il Riposo* (Florence: Giorgio Marescotti, 1584). His accounts of Venetian artists are contained in book three of this text. Borghini's biography of Tintoretto was the longest that he wrote for any living artist, apart from the Florentine Alessandro Allori. See Raffaello Borghini, *Raffaello Borghini's Il Riposo*, ed. and trans. H. Lloyd Ellis Jr. (Toronto: University of Toronto Press, 2007), 34–35.

46 For El Greco in Venice, see Lionello Puppi, 'Il soggiorno italiano del Greco', *Studies in the History of Art* 13, no. El Greco: Italy and Spain (1984): 133–51; Peter Humfrey, *Painting in Renaissance Venice* (New Haven, CT: Yale University Press, 1995), 226–29; Andrew R. Casper, *Art and the Religious Image in El Greco's Italy* (University Park: Pennsylvania State University Press, 2014), 2–6. El Greco was documented in Crete on 26 December 1566 and he is thought to have travelled to Venice at some point the following year. The only record of his presence in the city is a letter referencing drawings that he was to send to the Cretan cartographer Giorgio Sideris on 18 August 1568. Rubens was in Italy from 1600 to 1608, leaving only once on a diplomatic trip to Madrid from 1603 to 1604. Rubens left no written record of his time in Venice, but his nephew asserted that it was his first port of call, whilst Bellori stated that he went to Mantua and Rome first, and then to Venice, where he concentrated 'his study entirely on Titian and Paolo Veronese'. See Giovanni Pietro Bellori, *The Lives of the Modern Painters, Sculptors and Architects; a New Translation and Critical Edition*, ed. Alice Sedgwick Wohl, Hellmut Wohl, and Tomaso Montanari (Cambridge: Cambridge University Press, 2005), 194; Levy Robert Lind, 'The Latin Life of Peter Paul Rubens by His Nephew: A Translation', *Art Quarterly* 9 (1946): 38.

47 Javier Docampo and José Riello Velasco, *La Biblioteca del Greco*, Exhibition Catalogue, Museo Nacional del Prado, Madrid, 1 April–29 June 2014 (Madrid: Museo Nacional del Prado, 2014), 214–15, cat. 39.

48 Peter Humfrey, 'Made in Venice', *Apollo* 178, no. 612 (2013): 76–82.

49 See the entry of Paul Huvenne in *From Quinten Metsijs to Peter Paul Rubens: Masterpieces from the Royal Museum Reunited in the Cathedral*, Exhibition Catalogue, Cathedral of Our

Lady, Antwerp, 5 June–15 November 2009 (Antwerp: De Kathedraal VZW & Bai, 2009), 160–68.

50 For the decoration of the Escorial, see, in particular, Jonathan Brown, *Painting in Spain, 1500–1700* (New Haven, CT: Yale University Press, 1998), 57–60; Marcus B. Burke, 'Spanish Painters in the Forefront of the Tridentine Reform', in *Art and Reform in the Late Renaissance: After Trent*, ed. Jesse Locker (London: Routledge, 2018), 54–55.

51 Two notable exceptions to this are Humfrey, *Painting in Renaissance Venice*; Tom Nichols, *Renaissance Art in Venice: From Tradition to Individualism* (London: Laurence King, 2016).

52 Emile Mâle, *L'art religieux après le Concile de Trente: étude sur l'iconographie de la fin du 16e siècle, du 17e, du 18e siècle en Italie, en France, en Espagne et en Flandre* (Paris: Armand Colin, 1932). Years later, Scavizzi identified three key centres of artistic reform in late sixteenth-century Italy: Rome, Florence, and Bologna, arguing that 'nothing comparable to the new naturalism we have just observed in Rome and Florence occurred in Venice or in other Italian cities, in the Flandres, in Spain or in Prague'. Giuseppe Scavizzi, *The Controversy on Images from Calvin to Baronius* (New York: Peter Lang, 1994), 255.

53 Noted also by Maurice E. Cope, *The Venetian Chapel of the Sacrament in the Sixteenth Century* (New York: Garland, 1979), 264. An example is Mâle's discussion of Blessed Sacrament chapels, which he referred to as a creation of the papacy, rather than a phenomenon that emerged in Northern Italy much earlier. Mâle, *L'art religieux de la fin du XVIe siècle, du XVIIe siècle et du XVIIIe siècle*, 82–83.

54 Sydney J Freedberg, *Painting in Italy: 1500–1600*, 3rd ed. (New Haven, CT: Yale University Press, 1993), 503; Anthony Blunt, *Artistic Theory in Italy, 1450–1600*, 8th ed. (Oxford: Oxford University Press, 1985), 116–17. Blunt stated that 'compared with other parts of Italy, Venice was little affected by the Tridentine phase of the Counter-Reformation' since 'the Jesuits were never firmly established there'. Quite the contrary is true for the late sixteenth century at least; see Marie-Louise Lillywhite, 'The Decoration of the Jesuit Church of the Madonna dell'Umiltà in Venice, 1560–1606', *Artibus et Historiae* 39, no. 77 (2018): 161–200.

55 Augusto Gentili et al., *Paintings in Venice* (Boston: Bulfinch Press, 2002), 314.

56 See Xavier F. Salomon, 'Review of "La Cena in casa di Levi di Paolo Veronese. Il processo riaperto" by Maria Elena Massimi', *Burlington Magazine* 154, no. 1313 (2012): 581–83. Salomon points out that 'this type of approach to the reading of paintings and related wild iconology has been unfortunately only too common in recent years among art historians trained in Venice. For the present reviewer this convoluted iconological construction is altogether unconvincing'. Gentili provided a polemic defence of his ex-student's book in Augusto Gentili, 'Invenzione di linguaggio, ragioni di significato', in *Paolo Veronese: Giornate di Studio*, ed. Bernard Aikema, Paola Marini, and Thomas Dalla Costa (Venice: Linea d'acqua, 2016), 91–99.

57 See also Brian G. H. Ditcham, review of 'Immagini ed eresie nell'Italia del Cinquecento', by Massimo Firpo and Fabrizio Biferali, *Sixteenth Century Journal* 48, no. 3 (2017): 807. Ditcham notes that 'there seems to be a sense that the greater the artists, the more likely they were to create their own images – Michelangelo is given full credit for the "Last Judgement", Battista Franco's abortive scheme for Urbino supposedly came from the duke's advisors – a view which deserves some unpacking'.

58 See, in particular, Augusto Gentili, 'Tiziano e la religione', *Studies in the History of Art* 45, no. 25: Titian 500 (1993): 146–65; Augusto Gentili, 'La pittura religiosa dell'ultimo Tiziano', *Studi Tizianeschi* 1 (2003): 9–18; Augusto Gentili, 'Il prudente dissenso di Tiziano: dipingere di religione negli anni del disciplinamento', in *L'ultimo Tiziano e la sensualità della pittura*, ed. Sylvia Ferino-Pagden, Exhibition Catalogue, Kunsthistorisches Museum, Vienna, 18 October 2007–6 January 2008, Gallerie dell'Accademia, Venice, 20 January–20 April 2008 (Venice: Marsilio, 2008), 239–45.

59 Gentili, 'Tiziano e la religione', 150.

60 Agreed upon by Gentili, 'Tiziano e la religione', 150–51. Even though this also appears to be a possible portrait of Titian, Gentili rejects this evidence and attributes the painting largely to the workshop.

61 A similar conclusion is drawn by Puglisi and Barcham in *Art and Faith in the Venetian World: Venerating Christ as the Man of Sorrows*, 258. As the authors note after musing on a series of examples of the dead Christ, 'it would be imprudent to classify specific paintings as promoting nonconformist as opposed to orthodox doctrine, when many nuanced positions could fall somewhere between'.

62 Bernard Aikema, *Jacopo Bassano and His Public: Moralizing Pictures in an Age of Reform, ca. 1535–1600*, trans. Andrew P. McCormick (Princeton, NJ: Princeton University Press, 1996), 67.

63 Stefania Mason Rinaldi, *Palma il Giovane: L'Opera Completa* (Milan: Alfieri, 1984); Roland Krischel, *Tintoretto* (Reinbeck bei Hamburg: Rowohlt, 1994); Aikema, *Jacopo Bassano and His Public*; Una Roman D'Elia, *The Poetics of Titian's Religious Paintings* (Cambridge: Cambridge University Press, 2005); Tom Nichols, *Tintoretto: Tradition and Identity*, 2nd revised ed. (London: Reaktion, 2015); Christopher T. Nygren, *Titian's Icons: Tradition, Charisma and Devotion in Renaissance Italy* (University Park: Pennsylvania State University Press, 2020). This list highlights a few key publications; it is not an exhaustive list.

64 Massimo Firpo and Fabrizio Biferali, *Battista Franco 'pittore viniziano' nella cultura artistica e nella vita religiosa del Cinquecento* (Pisa: Edizioni della Normale, 2007); Massimo Firpo and Fabrizio Biferali, *Immagini ed eresie nell'Italia del Cinquecento* (Bari: GLF editori Laterza, 2016).

65 Cope, *The Venetian Chapel of the Sacrament in the Sixteenth Century*; Bernard Aikema and Dulcia Meijers, 'L'immagine della "Carità Veneziana"', in *Nel regno dei poveri: arte e storia dei grandi ospedali veneziani in età moderna, 1474–1797* (Venice: Arsenale Editrice, 1989), 71–98; Peter Humfrey, 'Co-ordinated Altarpieces in Renaissance Venice: The Progress of an Ideal', in *The Altarpiece in the Renaissance*, ed. Martin Kemp (Cambridge: Cambridge University Press, 1990), 190–211; Michel Hochmann, *Peintres et commanditaires à Venise (1540–1628)*, Collection de l'École française de Rome, 155 (Rome: Ecole française de Rome, 1992); Martin Seidel, *Venezianische Malerei zur Zeit der Gegenreformation: kirchliche Programmschriften und künstlerische Bildkonzepte bei Tizian, Tintoretto, Veronese und Palma il Giovane* (Lit Verlag: Münster, 1996); Tracy Cooper, *Palladio's Venice: Architecture and Society in a Renaissance Republic* (New Haven, CT: Yale University Press, 2005).

66 Thomas Worthen, 'Tintoretto's Paintings for the Banco del Sacramento in S. Margherita', *Art Bulletin* 78, no. 4 (1996): 707–32; Thomas Worthen, 'Soazoni, or The Venetian Reformation of San Nicolò dei Mendicoli', in *Celebrazione e autocritica. La Serenissima e la ricerca dell'identità veneziana nel tardo Cinquecento*, ed. Benjamin Paul (Rome: Viella; Venice: Centro tedesco di studi veneziani, 2014), 253–83; Thomas Worthen, 'The Altar and the "banco" of the Scuola del Sacramento in San Giacomo dall'Orio', in *La chiesa di San Giacomo dall'Orio: Una trama millenaria di arte e fede*, ed. Massimo Bisson, Isabella Cecchini, and Deborah Howard (Rome: Viella, 2018), 187–204.

67 For example, Mason suggested that they were, pointing particularly to the embellishment of the chapels of the Blessed Sacrament, whereas Humfrey was undecided, noting that more needed to be known about parallel progress in different artistic centres. Stefania Mason, 'Images of Christ for Venetian Piety and Devotions in the Light of the Council of Trent', in *New Perspectives on the Man of Sorrows*, ed. Catherine R. Puglisi and William L. Barcham, Studies in Iconography: Themes and Variations (Kalamazoo: Medieval Institute Publications, Western Michigan University, 2013), 295–322; Humfrey, 'Co-ordinated Altarpieces in Renaissance Venice', 211.

68 Xavier F. Salomon, *Veronese*, Exhibition Catalogue, National Gallery, London, 19 March–15 June 2014 (London: National Gallery Company, 2014); Bernard Aikema and Paola Marini, eds., *Paolo Veronese: L'illusione della realtà*, Exhibition Catalogue, Palazzo della Gran Guardia, Verona, 5 July–5 October 2014 (Milan: Electa, 2014); Robert Echols and Frederick Ilchman, *Tintoretto: Artist of Renaissance Venice*, Exhibition Catalogue, Palazzo Ducale, Venice, 7 September 2018–6 January 2019, National Gallery of Art, Washington, 24 March–7 July 2019 (New Haven, CT: Yale University Press, 2018).

69 Marcia B. Hall and Tracy E. Cooper, eds., *The Sensuous in the Counter-Reformation Church* (Cambridge: Cambridge University Press, 2013); Jesse Locker, ed., *Art and Reform in the Late Renaissance: After Trent* (London: Routledge, 2018).

70 See the introductions to Bailey, *Between Renaissance and Baroque*; Evonne Levy, *Propaganda and the Jesuit Baroque* (Berkeley: University of California Press, 2004).

71 Bailey, *Between Renaissance and Baroque*, 3.

72 Nikolaus Pevsner, 'Gegenreformation und Manierismus', *Repertorium für Kunstwissenschaft* 46 (1925): 243–62; Blunt, *Artistic Theory in Italy*, 134–35; Locker, *Art and Reform in the Late Renaissance*, 6.

73 For the changed implications of the term 'propaganda' in the post-war period compared to the early modern, see, above all, Levy, *Propaganda and the Jesuit Baroque*. For example, Rudolf Wittkower eagerly linked Jesuits to propaganda in his *Art and Architecture in Italy, 1600 to 1750* of 1958 and he incorrectly attributed the founding of the Collegio di Propaganda Fide to the Society of Jesus rather than Pope Gregory XV in *Baroque Art: The Jesuit Contribution* of 1972. See the analysis of Gauvin A. Bailey, '"Le style jésuite n'existe pas": Jesuit Corporate Culture and the Visual Arts', in *The Jesuits: Cultures, Sciences, and the Arts, 1540–1773*, ed. John W. O'Malley, Gauvin A. Bailey, and Steven J. Harris (Toronto: University of Toronto Press, 1999), 42.

74 The bibliography is ample. For a survey, see Gauvin A. Bailey, *Art on the Jesuit Missions in Asia and Latin America, 1542–1773* (Toronto: University of Toronto Press, 1999).

75 In his study of early Jesuit art in Rome, Marciari made a similar plea 'for painters of the era as *painters*, rather than seeing them firstly as agents of reformist churchmen and patrons'. John Marciari, 'Girolamo Muziano, Scipione Pulzone, and the First Generation of Jesuit Art', *Journal of Jesuit Studies* 6, no. 2 (2019): 199.

76 With reference to the Baroque, Argan pointed out that 'in the majority of Baroque religious figurations, we find expressed not the religiosity of the artist, but a reflection of the religion of the devoted'. Giulio Carlo Argan, 'La rettorica e l'arte barocca', *Lettere Italiane* 6, no. 3 (1954): 262.

77 Anthony Blunt, *Sicilian Baroque* (London: Weidenfeld & Nicolson, 1968); Anthony Blunt, *Neapolitan Baroque and Rococo Architecture* (London: Zwemmer, 1975).

78 Analysed by Maarten Delbeke, *The Art of Religion: Sforza Pallavicino and Art Theory in Bernini's Rome* (London: Routledge, 2016), 1.

79 Blunt, *Artistic Theory in Italy*, 104–5.

80 Jacob Burckhardt, *The Civilization of the Renaissance in Italy*, trans. S. G. C. Middlemore (New York: Harper & Brothers, 1958), vol. 1: 210. Burckhardt's stance was matched in many late nineteenth-century Italian academic circles, like that of Francesco de Sanctis, and later in the first half of the twentieth century with Benedetto Croce. O'Malley points out that for them the Counter-Reformation came to symbolise 'opposition to the freedom of the human spirit'. John W. O'Malley, 'A Historiographical Frame for the Paintings: Recent Interpretations of Early Modern Catholicism', in *Saints & Sinners: Caravaggio & the Baroque Image*, ed. Franco Mormando (Chicago: University of Chicago Press, 1999), 20.

81 Rachel Miller, 'Patron Saint of a World in Crisis: Early Modern Representations of St. Francis Xavier in Europe and Asia' (doctoral thesis, University of Pittsburgh, 2016), 32.

82 For the increasingly sympathetic approaches of North American scholars, in particular, see O'Malley, 'A Historiographical Frame for the Paintings', 20.

83 Hall, *The Sacred Image in the Age of Art*; Alexander Nagel, *Michelangelo and the Reform of Art* (Cambridge: Cambridge University Press, 2000); Alexander Nagel, *The Controversy of Renaissance Art* (Chicago: University of Chicago Press, 2011); Hall and Cooper, eds., *The Sensuous in the Counter-Reformation Church*.

84 Of his many publications, see, in particular, Bailey, *Art on the Jesuit Missions in Asia and Latin America, 1542–1773*; Bailey, *Between Renaissance and Baroque*.

85 Referred to throughout the text. By comparison Southern Italy has been notably ignored in English-language scholarship on art in the decades after the Council of Trent. For studies that

focus on Naples, see, in particular, Sebastian Schütze, 'The Politics of Counter-Reformation Iconography and a Quest for the Spanishness of Neapolitan Art', in *Spain in Italy: Politics, Society, and Religion, 1500–1700*, ed. Thomas James Dandelet and John A. Marino (Leiden: Brill, 2007), 555–68; Helen Hills, *The Matter of Miracles: Neapolitan Baroque Architecture and Sanctity* (Manchester: Manchester University Press, 2016); Helen Hills and Melissa Caleresu, eds., *New Approaches to Naples 1500–1800: The Power of Place* (Farnham: Ashgate, 2013). De Maio produced a study of painting and the Counter-Reformation in Naples: Romeo De Maio, *Pittura e controriforma a Napoli* (Rome: Laterza, 1983).

86 Two of the more recent examples: Jane Garnett and Gervase Rosser, *Spectacular Miracles: Transforming Images in Italy from the Renaissance to the Present* (London: Reaktion Books, 2013); Megan Holmes, *The Miraculous Image in Renaissance Florence* (New Haven, CT: Yale University Press, 2013). For Loreto, see Karin Vélez, *The Miraculous Flying House of Loreto: Spreading Catholicism in the Early Modern World* (Princeton, NJ: Princeton University Press, 2018). Important older studies on miraculous images, or so-called cult images, include Gerhard Wolf, *Salus Populi Romani: die Geschichte römischer Kultbilder im Mittelalter* (Weinheim: VCH, 1990); Freedberg, *The Power of Images*, chap. 7; Hans Belting, *Likeness and Presence: A History of the Image before the Era of Art*, trans. Edmund Jephcott (Chicago: University of Chicago Press, 1994).

87 As Black puts it, historians have 'increasingly seen the Buckhardian Renaissance as a great deal more enthusiastically religious, less 'individualistic', less pagan'. Christopher F. Black, 'The Development of Confraternity Studies over the Past Thirty Years', in *The Politics of Ritual Kinship: Confraternities and Social Order in Early Modern Italy*, ed. Nicholas Terpstra (Cambridge: Cambridge University Press, 2000), 16.

88 Eire, *Reformations: The Early Modern World*, ix.

89 Jones, *Federico Borromeo and the Ambrosiana*, 3.

90 For two useful reviews on the question of artistic labels, see the introductions of Marcia B. Hall, *After Raphael: Painting in Central Italy in the Sixteenth Century* (Cambridge: Cambridge University Press, 1999); Bailey, *Between Renaissance and Baroque*.

91 As Freedberg puts it, the examples of failure are legion. Freedberg, 'Painting and the Counter Reformation in the Age of Rubens', 136, 144, note 43. For one of the more sensitive stylistic studies, see Federico Zeri, *Pittura e Controriforma: l'arte senza tempo di Scipione da Gaeta* (Turin: Einaudi, 1957). See also Francis Haskell's entertaining review of 'Painting and the Counter-Reformation', by Federico Zeri, *The Burlington Magazine* 100, no. 668 (1958): 396–99.

92 John W. O'Malley, *Trent and All That: Renaming Catholicism in the Early Modern Era* (Cambridge, MA: Harvard University Press, 2000), 4.

93 William V. Hudon, 'Religion and Society in Early Modern Italy: Old Questions, New Insights', *American Historical Review* 101, no. 3 (1996): 783–804. See also Nicholas Terpstra, 'Renaissance Religions: Afterwards?', in *Renaissance Religions: Modes and Meanings in History*, ed. Peter Howard, Nicholas Terpstra, and Riccardo Saccenti (Turnhout: Brepols, 2021), 365–73.

94 See Hudon, 'Religion and Society in Early Modern Italy'.

95 Simon Ditchfield, 'Of Dancing Cardinals and Mestizo Madonnas: Reconfiguring the History of Roman Catholicism in the Early Modern Period', *Journal of Early Modern History* 8 (2004): 408.

96 For 'Reformations', see Eire, *Reformations: The Early Modern World*, xi.

97 Particularly useful is O'Malley, *Trent and All That*. See also Hubert Jedin, 'Catholic Reformation or Counter Reformation?', in *The Counter Reformation: The Essential Readings*, ed. David Luebke (Oxford: Blackwell, 1999), 21–45; Simon Ditchfield, 'Tridentine Catholicism', in *The Ashgate Research Companion to the Counter-Reformation*, ed. Alexandra Bamji, Geert H. Janssen, and Mary Laven (Surrey: Ashgate, 2013), 15–31.

98 See O'Malley, *Trent and All That*, 19–20. The term was first used to refer to art by Charles Dejob, *De l'influence du Concile de Trente sur la littérature et les beaux-arts chez les peuples catholiques: Essai d'introduction à l'histoire littéraire du siècle de Louis XIV* (Paris: Thorin, 1884).

99 Massimo Firpo, *Inquisizione romana e Controriforma: Studi sul cardinal Giovanni Morone (1509–80) ed il suo processo d'eresia*, 2nd enlarged ed. (Brescia: Morcelliana, 2005), 47. The implications of Firpo's argument are discussed by Simon Ditchfield, 'In Sarpi's Shadow: Coping with Trent the Italian Way', in *Studi in memoria di Cesare Mozzarelli* (Milan: Vita e Pensiero, 2008), 604.

100 See Adriano Prosperi, 'Seminario sulle visite pastorali del vescovo G. M. Giberti (1525–42)', *Richerche di storia sociale e religiosa* 39 (1991): 172. Prosperi mentions the scholarship of both Jedin and Delio Cantimori, noting that the latter advised avoiding the term 'Reformation' unless it was explicitly mentioned by documents.

101 O'Malley, *Trent and All That*, 25.

102 John W. O'Malley, 'Trent, Sacred Images, and Catholics' Senses of the Sensuous', in *The Sensuous in the Counter-Reformation Church*, ed. Marcia B. Hall and Tracy E. Cooper (Cambridge: Cambridge University Press, 2013), 28–48.

103 Noted by Garnett and Rosser, *Spectacular Miracles* 274, note 95. The congregation was founded in 1564, offering answers to bishops across Europe. See Celeste McNamara, *The Bishop's Burden: Reforming the Catholic Church in Early Modern Italy* (Washington, DC: Catholic University of America Press, 2020), 6.

104 Paolo Prodi, *Ricerca sulla teorica delle arti figurative nella Riforma Cattolica* (Bologna: Nuova Alfa, 1984), 112. See also Paleotti, *Discourse on Sacred and Profane Images*, 25–26.

105 Carmen Fracchia, *Black but Human: Slavery and Visual Arts in Hapsburg Spain, 1480–1700* (Oxford: Oxford University Press, 2019), 5, 58.

106 Bonaventura Bassegoda i Hugas, ed., *Arte de la pintura: Francisco Pacheco, 1564–1644* (Madrid: Ediciones Cátedra, 1990), 698.

107 Scriptural accuracy is not specifically exhorted by the Tridentine decree, but artists were reminded that 'no images, [suggestive] of false doctrine, and furnishing occasion of dangerous error to the uneducated, be set up'. Rev. James Waterworth, ed., *Canons and Decrees of the Council of Trent* (London: Dolman, 1848), 235. For the image decrees of Nicaea, see Norman P. Tanner, *Decrees of the Ecumenical Councils* (Washington, DC: Georgetown University Press, 1990), vol. 2: 137–56.

108 Delbeke, *The Art of Religion*, 206.

PART I

CHAPTER ONE

THE APPEAL OF THE SUBVERSIVE

Art and Heresy (1520–1544)

Imprisoned in the Castel Sant'Angelo on the orders of Pope Paul IV in 1557, who suspected him of heresy, Cardinal Giovanni Morone (1509–80) provided an eloquent description of the religious climate in Italy during the early 1500s: 'many years ago religious matters in Italy progressed with scant controls, since the office of the Holy Inquisition had not yet been instituted and it was not yet well founded or powerful. But in every corner ecclesiastical dogma was spoken of and everyone acted as if they were a theologian... it was almost allowed and tolerated that everyone could do and say as they pleased'.[1]

Morone eventually cleared his name, and his diplomacy brought the Council of Trent to a successful conclusion in 1563. But his experience with the Inquisition demonstrates how fluidity of opinion concerning doctrine and religious practice was far less likely to be tolerated by the Church in the latter half of the Cinquecento than it had been in the earlier decades of the century. The precise date of when this shift took place is contested, but sometime around the late 1530s and the early 1540s the religious climate changed, and since religion affected every facet of life in early modern Italy, this also had ramifications for artistic production. The narrative favoured by some art historians has been that a period of invention and experimentation under the broad-minded aegis of the so-called Catholic reformers known as the *spirituali* moved towards one of decline and obedience as the century wore on, and the severe *intransigenti* gained the upper hand, with the Church increasingly encroaching upon the licence of the artist as part of its efforts to enforce orthodoxy and stamp out heresy.[2] As Hudon put it, the simplistic division of early modern churchmen into 'warring camps of *spirituali* versus *intransigenti* always sounded like the good guys against the bad guys'.[3] The example most often cited as evidence of this depressing transformation to the artistic climate is the expurgation of the nudity in Michelangelo's *Last Judgment*, beginning with the alterations of Daniele da Volterra in 1564, shortly after the conclusion of the Council of Trent. This is the only episode of Renaissance artistic censorship more notorious than Veronese's questioning by the Inquisition. Anyone who has been taught survey courses on late sixteenth-century art will be familiar with this account, and it remains a standard one for many undergraduate students first encountering the social conditions of late Renaissance Italian artists.

Artists who may or may not have held heterodox sympathies in early sixteenth-century Italy are given great attention by art historians. This is in part because of the reasons underlined in the introduction, but it is also because the topic of heresy is an exciting one – dealing as it does with those individuals who stood removed from the religion of their community and as such can be considered rebels or outsiders. It has also proved to be an area of enquiry that is far out of proportion with the numbers or influence of heretics in early modern Italian society, as Silvana Seidel Menchi observed.[4] More often than not, the visual evidence used to support an interpretation of an artist as heretical is slight (as we might expect it to be), something illustrated by a case like the painter Riccardo del Perucolo (c. 1520–68), who was born in the province of Treviso on the Venetian mainland. He was burnt to death on the orders of the Inquisition in 1568; it was not the unfortunate Perucolo's artworks but his personal beliefs that were deemed to be heretical. Despite efforts to the contrary, almost nothing can be learnt from whether or not Perucolo's faith was expressed in his oeuvre because the work that is most convincingly attributed to him is a mere fragment of a monochrome frieze in the Palazzo Sarcinelli of Conegliano, part of a decorative programme at the palace that in any case involved other masters.[5] Notwithstanding these glaring lacunae in our knowledge, his plight has been the subject of two monographs, a number of articles, and even appears in the title of a recent exhibition catalogue, meaning that more has been written about Perucolo since the 1990s than other far more significant artists active in the same years.[6]

This chapter probes what examples of artists like Perucolo, who held religious sympathies that would ultimately be outlawed by the Church, reveal about the extent to which these heterodox sentiments could ever be manifested visually. If they were, was this the result of their own religious convictions or those of their patrons? This examination of the level of creative freedom that artists enjoyed in the first half of the century helps to contextualise and frame the exploration of censorship in the subsequent chapters, complicating the simplistic interpretation of events described above. Yet it also raises a larger problem, which is a tendency to indiscriminately interpret any devotional image with reference to Reformation polemics, especially those produced in the first half of the century, long before the debates on the decorum of images erupted in the aftermath of the unveiling of Michelangelo's *Last Judgment* and the decrees on images established at Trent. Although the first half of the Cinquecento was one of great artistic experimentation, as we shall see, it was only in the latter half of the century that the necessity of reforming art became a distinct and widespread concern.[7] Nevertheless, even peasants living in remote areas of Friuli were aware of 'Lutherans', and there is little doubt that the artists examined in this book could have remained ignorant of the iconoclasm that was taking place with various degrees of intensity in neighbouring countries and beyond.[8] But if Venice and its land territories were one of the principal routes through which information on Protestantism was diffused into Italy, why are there not more examples of artists expressing interest in these ideas visually? What was the fate of images that were inspired by controversial theologies? Since the new creeds emanating from Northern Europe were mostly hostile to sacred images, in this chapter I argue that it is of little surprise that they won relatively few adherents from amongst those who made their living by producing images. This is intended to infer neither that artists were all paragons of Catholic orthodoxy nor that they could not have been interested in Protestant ideas. What it does do is emphasise the various reasons, of which the market for devotional art was surely one of the most significant, which explain why artists in Italy were mostly disinclined to heterodoxy.

CHRIST IN METAMORPHOSIS

In the case of one Venetian-born painter, the question of whether he should be cast as a crypto-Protestant or a devout Catholic has divided scholarly opinion to such an extent that his religion has at times threatened to overshadow his creations.[9] This is of course Lorenzo Lotto, whose peripatetic career brought him into close contact with groups that held very different views on the Reformations: from devout Catholics to close friends and family who would later be denounced for heresy.[10] In a sense Lotto is paradigmatic of the very paradoxes that the early 1500s present, and this is something that can be eloquently illustrated by his authorship of arguably the most explicitly anti-heretical cycle of paintings to be found anywhere in this period in Italy: the frescoes for the Suardi Chapel in Trescore Balneario, province of Bergamo (at this point part of the Venetian Empire).[11]

This small oratory was frescoed by Lotto between 1523 and 1524 (Fig. 4). In 1502 it had been dedicated to Saints Barbara and Brigid of Ireland, who were invoked against bad weather and for protection against lightning and sudden death, powers of particular relevance given the agrarian location of the Suardi chapel.[12] The patrons of the cycle were Battista Suardi and his cousin Maffeo Suardi, with the inscription at the centre of the left wall recording also the participation of Orsolina Suardi, wife of Battista, and his sister Paolina.[13] Members of the Suardi clans are depicted at various points in the chapel as pious observers and protagonists in the sacred events that unfold. On the same wall as the inscription, the massive figure of Christ dominates the space, his arms shown outstretched as his fingers transform themselves from flesh into vines (Fig. 5). A visual allegory of the parable of Christ the True Vine (John 15:1–12), these vines encoil themselves to create medallions that enclose the pairs of saints shown arranged horizontally across the length of the wall above. The saints are the 'fruit' that the life-giving vine bears, the vine that turns from flesh into grapes, symbolic of the eucharistic transformation from wine to blood believed to take place during the celebration of the mass. Behind the Christ-vine, the narrative of Saint Barbara's trials takes place. Her gory flaying presents a visual manifestation of Tertullian's maxim that the blood of martyrs is the seed of the Church, symbolised by the retinue of saints arranged above her, some of whom endured similar trials. At each extremity of the vine's branches, the Church Doctors Jerome and Ambrose purge the branches of those who attempt to alight them on ladders, their malevolent intent to destroy the vine made clear by the machetes that they brandish (Fig. 6). Inscriptions identify the invaders as early Christian heretics, including Helvidius, Vigilantius, Jovinian, and Arianus, whose writings on the perpetual virginity of the Madonna, clerical celibacy, the nature of grace, and the power of saintly intercession had been refuted by Jerome and Ambrose centuries earlier.[14] These were all issues of renewed concern in light of the Protestant Reformations, and the message here is self-evident: the actions of the Church Doctors who cast down the heretics present a visual manifestation of Christ's words 'if any one abide not in me, he shall be cast forth as a branch and shall wither' (John 15:6).

The themes of the Suardi chapel were dictated by patrons' concerns about the immediate geographical realities of the Cavallina valley and the diffusion of heresy in the vicinity, particularly the denigration of the eucharist.[15] However local these preoccupations might have been, the second of them also points to the universal preoccupations of the Church in the early sixteenth century, thus demonstrating the significance of the rural context as the site of one of the earliest artistic responses in Northern Italy to the events of the Reformation.[16] Trescore was not so far from the Swiss cantons where Ulrich Zwingli's uncompromising Protestantism had begun to make Luther seem like a

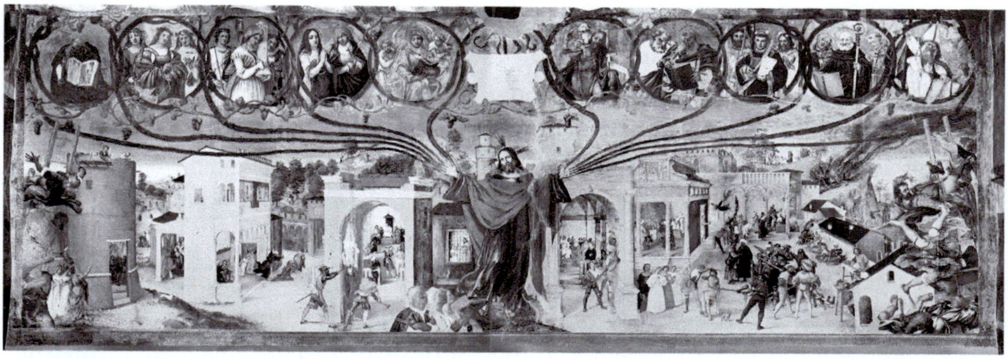

4. Lorenzo Lotto, *Christ the Vine and The Miracles of Saint Barbara*, 1523–24, fresco, Suardi Chapel, Trescore (Photo: Erich Lessing/Art Resource New York)

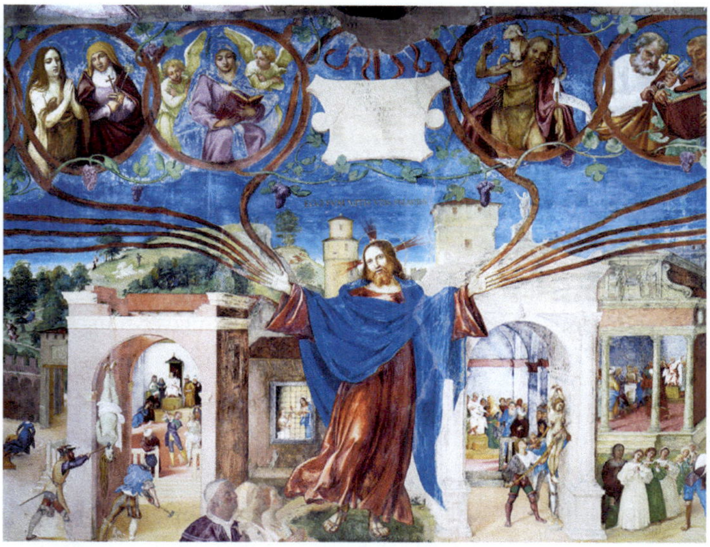

5. Detail of *Christ the Vine*, Suardi Chapel (Photo: DeA Picture Library/Art Resource, New York)

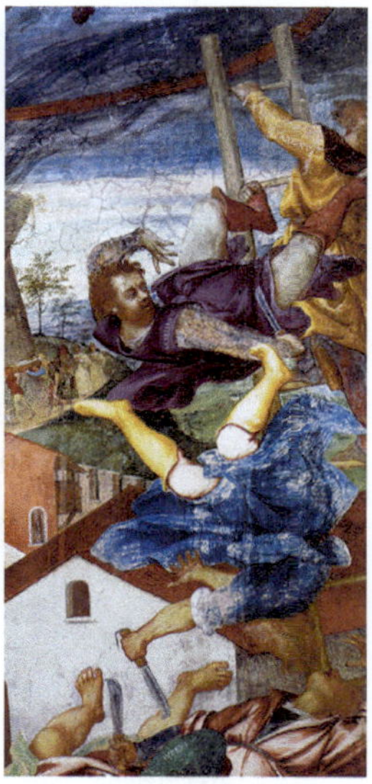

6. Detail of the *Fall of the Heretics*, Suardi Chapel (Photo: DeA Picture Library/Art Resource, New York)

moderate by comparison, and the oratory was located on a road where German mercenaries were known to have passed. Anxieties concerning religious dissent would have troubled the Suardis, since Giovanni Battista in particular was a pious Catholic: one of the presidents of the powerful Misericordia Maggiore of Bergamo in 1493 and 1502, and one of the founders of the Scuola del Santissimo Corpo di Cristo at the church of San Michele al Pozzo Bianco in 1511, a devotion reflected in the eucharistic emphasis of the chapel's decoration.[17] The dire predictions that a natural catastrophe would strike in 1524 after the destructive floods of one year earlier mean that the commission has been understood as a kind of atoning 'good work', one that underlined the orthodoxy of the Suardi family by repudiating what they believed was heresy in a period when natural disasters were commonly attributed to the sins of a wayward humanity.[18]

The sources for Lotto's almost surrealist conception of Christ have been given limited attention, his magnificent artistic inventiveness seemingly defying attempts to trace its origins and subsequent impact.[19] The relationship of the imagery of Christ the Vine to issues of Church unity can be illustrated with reference both to visual precedents that Lotto might have known and to subsequent Catholic propaganda. The vine that forms the individual frames at Trescore has its roots in the ancient iconography of the genealogical Tree of Jesse, and the idea of bloodlines is also present in Lotto's fresco, where Christ's mother and his cousin John the Baptist appear directly above him.[20]

Icons from Crete had begun to explicitly link the New Testament parable to the vine shoot in the first half of the fifteenth century, as demonstrated by some important portable versions by Angelos Akotantos (Fig. 7).[21] Even though Crete was part of the Venetian Empire at this point, Lotto may not have known about these specific examples, but even so the similarity to his Trescore fresco is intriguing. The appearance and popularity of this typology has been convincingly linked to debates surrounding the union of the Eastern and Western churches at the 1438 Council of Ferrara, and the emphasis on lineage and unity was one equally present at Trescore. A similarly persuasive visual equivalent to Lotto's fresco is a gilded-silver communion chalice made in Venice in the sixteenth century and now held in the monastery of the island of Patmos. It shows the enthroned Christ the Vine embossed around the base, the gesture of the raised hands and outstretched fingers from which a vine burst forth to form individual frames for each of the disciples bearing a clear resemblance to the metamorphosising body at Trescore. The presence of this iconography on a chalice used for communion wine points to the increasingly eucharistic conception of the parable at the point it was made (Fig. 8).[22] Representations of the Tree of Jesse were also a clear stimulus upon Lotto, something further demonstrated by his later use of medallions to recount the mysteries of the rosary in his 1539 altarpiece for the Dominicans at Cingoli. Another interesting precedent is an altarpiece by the Venetian painter Luca Antonio Busati (finished by Girolamo Tessari between 1518 and 1519) for the chapel of Saint Sebastian in the Santo of Padua (Fig. 9).[23] Christ was believed to have been crucified on wood derived from the Tree of Life described in Genesis, and here he is shown nailed to a tree rather than a crucifix. From the twelve branches leaves sprout and encircle the portraits of the Old Testament prophets, accompanied by Saints Bonaventure,

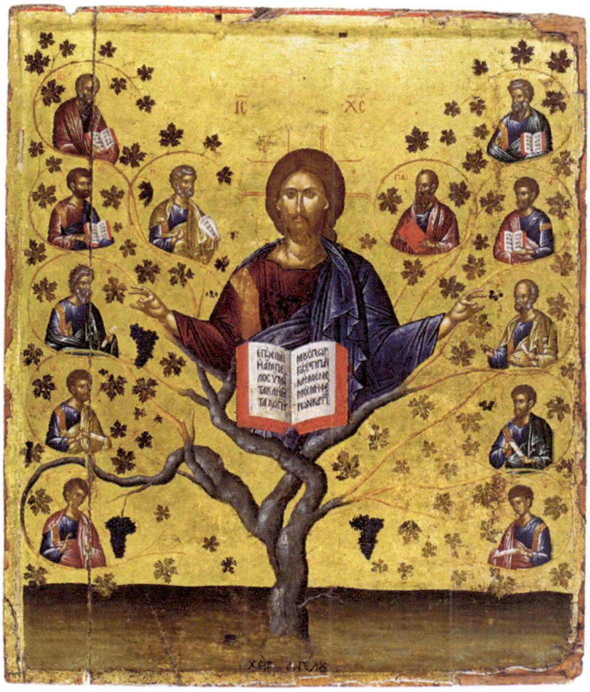

7. Angelos Akotantos, *Christ the Vine*, first half of 1400s, Malles, Hierapetra, Crete (Photo: Holy Metropolis of Ierapytni and Sitia)

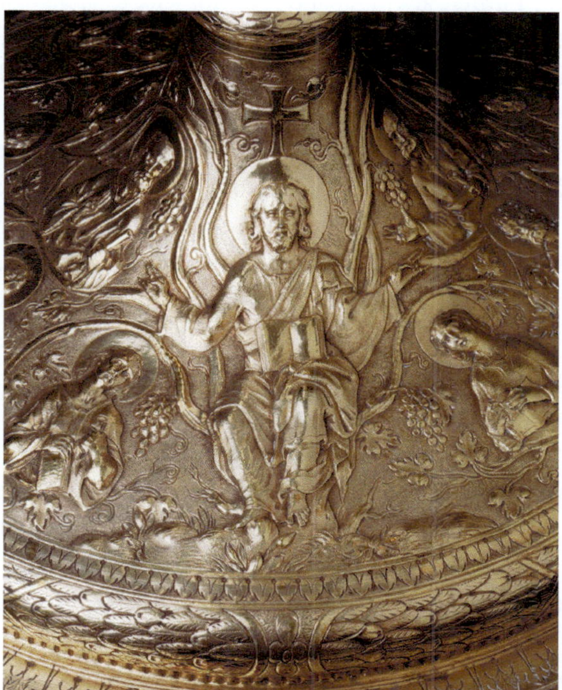

8. *Communion Chalice*, sixteenth century, Monastery of St John the Theologian, Patmos (Photo: Monastery of St John the Theologian, Patmos)

Sebastian, Gregory the Great, and Ursula below. The eucharistic relevance of the iconography of the blood that nourishes is heightened by the presence of the pelican above, a trickle of blood streaming down from her breast to feed her offspring. Enrico Pozzolo has pointed to the influence of Franciscan spirituality on the iconography, to the writings of Bonaventure on the *Lignum crucis* and his interpretation from the passage of Apocalypse 22:2: 'on both sides of the river, was the tree of life, bearing twelve fruits, yielding its fruit every month, and the leaves of the tree were for the healing of the nations'. Pozzolo mentioned the possible relationship between the background of Lotto's Edinburgh *Madonna and Child with Saints* (c. 1504–5) to the later altarpiece – which depicts the preparation of wood chopped down from a tree by two woodsmen and may have had a Franciscan patron – but Lotto could also have been aware of the Santo altarpiece when he created his later fresco cycle in Bergamo, his image of the Christ-vine thus drawing upon both antecedents from outposts of the Venetian Empire and artistic centres of the terraferma.[24]

The imagery of Doctors of the Church as bulwarks against heresy at Trescore was one later deployed by a Catholic broadside of c. 1570 (Fig. 10).[25] Here, the complete set of the four Latin doctors are represented as the metaphorical towers of the Church, defending it from a band of iconoclastic Protestant reformers. Aided and abetted by a band of devilish creatures, Calvin, Luther, Zwingli, and their ilk seek to attack and destroy, but despite the size and number of this mob, their efforts are in vain. The chain wrapped around the tower of Saint Gregory the Great has already broken, and the imminent victory of the Church is hammered home by the ominous title of the print. In making this comparison, I am not suggesting that the author of this image had direct knowledge of Lotto's cycle. What is clear is that the similarities between the routing of the ancient adversaries of the Church Doctors at Trescore and their contemporary enemies in the later broadside indicate the polemical intent of the iconography at the Suardi chapel. The messages that the Trescore frescoes communicated were ones that clearly related to the specific devotions and fears of the Suardis as patrons, so it cannot be assumed that Lotto sympathised with their meaning in his role as the artist. A level of scepticism regarding the extent to which his religious leanings were expressed in his orthodox works should be equally applied to examples used to support an interpretation of him as a Protestant: namely, the portraits of Martin Luther and his wife Katharina von Bora of 1540, and his attributed authorship of the frontispiece for the Vernacular Bible of Antonio Brucioli, first published by Luc'Antonio Giunta in Venice in 1532, which was placed on the 1559 Index of Prohibited Books.[26] One possible clue about Lotto's stance at Trescore is provided by a figure above the entrance to the chapel

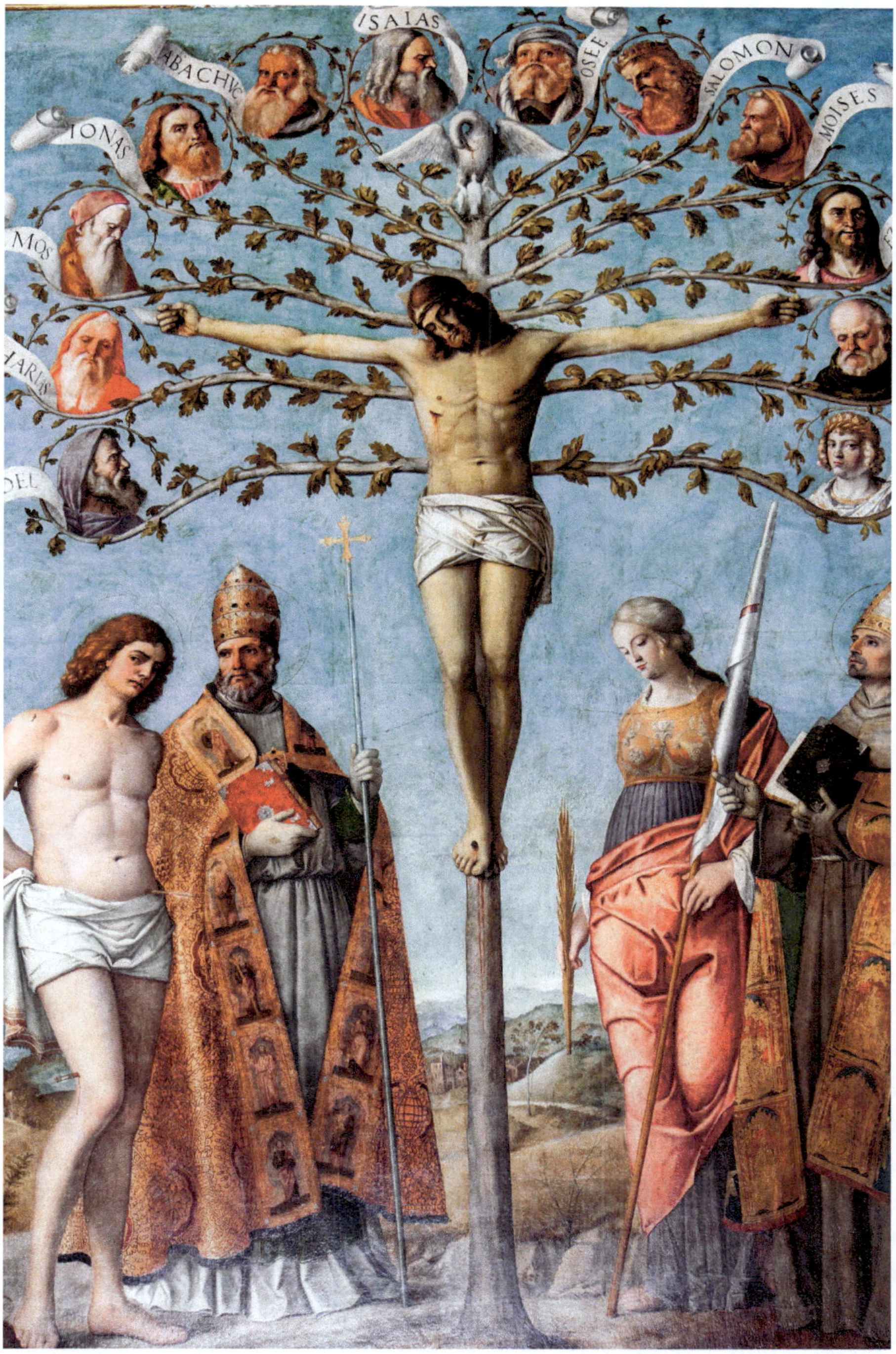

9. Luca Antonio Busati (finished by Girolamo Tessari), *Crucified Christ with the Prophets and Saints Sebastian, Gregory the Great, Ursula and Bonaventure*, 1510–19, Basilica di Sant'Antonio, Padua (Photo: Alamy Stock)

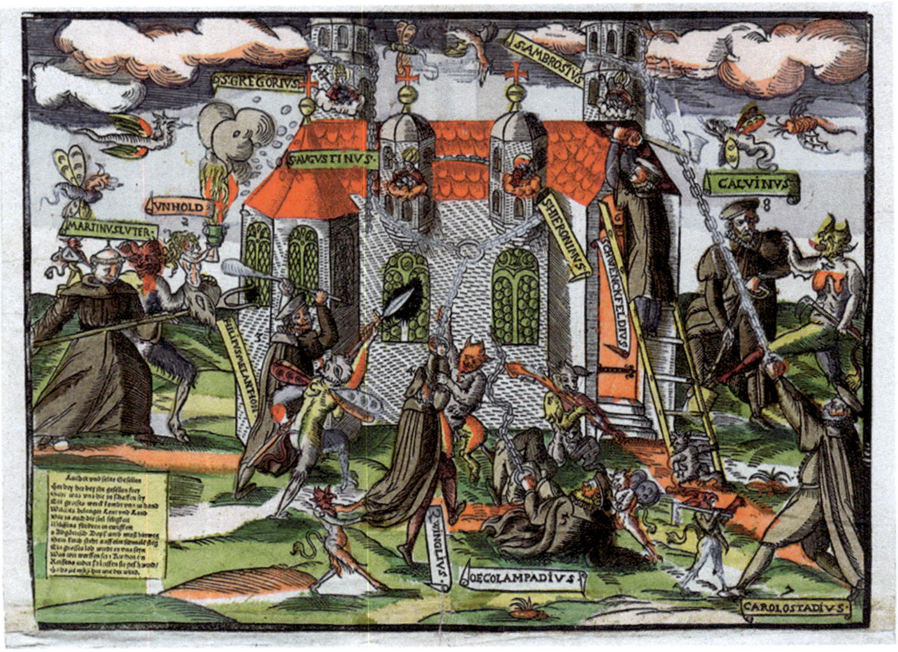

10. *Mirror of the militant, true, steadfast, age-old Catholic Church of God, against which many tyrants, heathens, Jews and heretics revolt, tear down, burn and break by storm*, c. 1570, Bridwell Library Special Collections, Perkins School of Theology, Southern Methodist University (Photo: Bridwell Library Special Collections, SMU)

shown as a bird catcher, armed with a trap and an owl. This has been identified as a self-portrait of Lotto, and Stephen Campbell has recently linked the image both to the writings of the Venetian Catholic reformer Cardinal Gasparo Contarini (1483–1542), who characterised heretics and the superstitious as bird catchers, as well as to the poetry of Giovanni Battista Suardi himself.[27] Considering also that the *Hexameron* of Saint Ambrose compared false believers to owls, the inclusion of catcher and owl is suggestive.[28] Yet as with so many aspects of Lotto's oeuvre, and as pointed out by Campbell, the artist's relationship to the ideas expressed here remains decidedly ambiguous. Whether this is or is not a self-portrait is an open question, and if the literary allusion linking bird catchers to heresy was well-known, then presumably his identification as one of them was not common knowledge.

Observing the Trescore frescoes, it is clear why interpretations of Lorenzo Lotto have been so divided. The painter of the early anti-heretical content of the Suardi chapel must be reconciled with the same figure who was paid to produce an image of the Church's 'heretic' par excellence: Martin Luther, whose effigy had been burnt in Rome already in 1519.[29] The commission was detailed in Lotto's own account book at a point when the subversive implications of this action must have been evident. They were made for the artist's nephew Mario D'Armano, to give to a friend. Mario was investigated by the Inquisition in 1559 (after the artist's death in 1556/57), along with other members of his family, as was the Venetian jeweler Bartolomeo Carpan, possibly the subject of Lotto's *Portrait of a Goldsmith* of c. 1525–35 and a close personal friend of the artist.[30] Later in the century, clerics like Gabriele Paleotti and Johannes Molanus (1533–85) agreed that such portraits should be prohibited, and their destruction was advised. This was the only category for which they promoted iconoclasm, and destruction was possibly the ultimate fate of D'Armano's paintings.[31] That Lotto painted these portraits could be evidence of nothing more than his pragmatism and a desire to fulfill the wishes of the person who requested and paid for them. Yet he spent extended periods of time in the homes and company of these individuals, so it is reasonable to suggest that he may well have had sympathy for the more unorthodox strands of Italian evangelism. In the end, though, the visual traces that link Lotto to heterodoxy are slight, and he died as the 'Painter of the Holy House', having taken the partial vows of a perpetual oblate of the Marian sanctuary of the Santa Casa di Loreto in the Marche. Even if Lotto did adhere to contentious theological ideas at points during his life, this was never apparent from the overwhelming majority of his artistic output, and nor was it so unusual for this period, as the quote from Cardinal Morone at the beginning of this chapter demonstrated.[32]

PETER AND PAUL

Just a few years after Lotto's frescoes were completed, Bishop Gian Matteo Giberti (1495–1543) initiated an ambitious project in 1527 for the renovation of the presbytery of Verona's cathedral Santa Maria Matricolare (Fig. 11).[33] Although this proved to be an early site of significance for architectural and visual reform in Northern Italy, the mixed reactions to Giberti's trailblazing efforts demonstrate that in the early sixteenth century there was often a thin line between the actions of a reformer and those of a heretic.[34] Not only were the transformations that the bishop championed met with resistance from the laity when he tried to enact them, but he was even accused of iconoclasm by his enemies, and at the end of his life he passionately described to the Council of Ten in Venice his frustration at the complaints the cathedral renovations had caused, and his anger at the accusation that he had overspent on them.[35] Giberti might have been at the vanguard of modernising the cathedral of his diocese, but some of his efforts were misunderstood in his lifetime, and found broad acceptance only after his death, when they were imitated by that exemplar of a Counter Reformer: Saint Carlo Borromeo (1538–84).[36] Giberti's architectonic and decorative changes to the Veronese cathedral

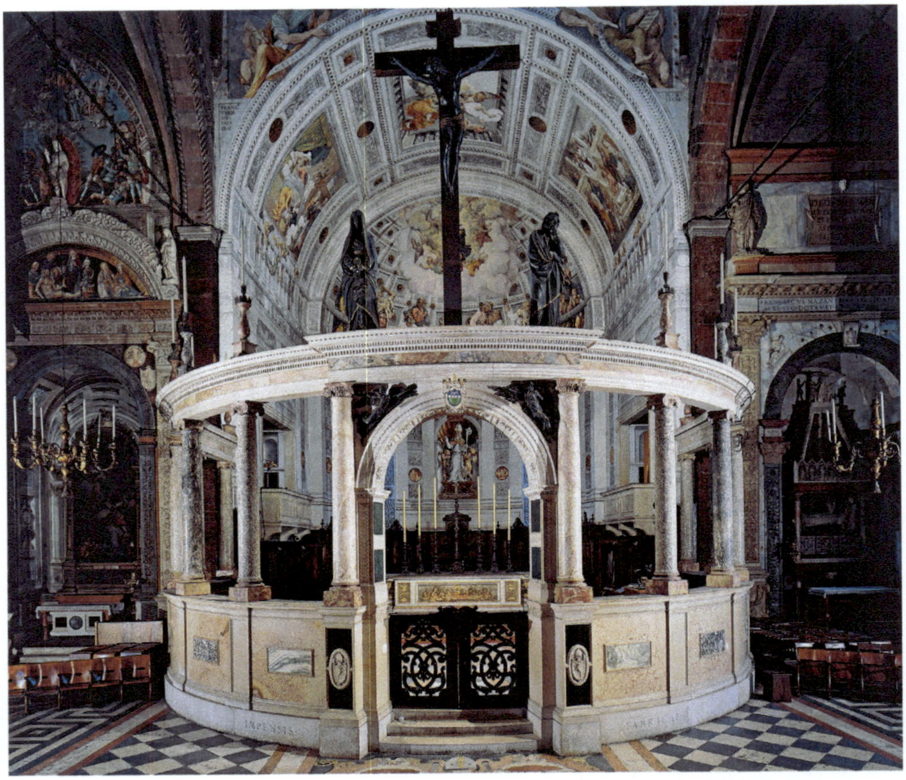

11. *Presbytery of Verona Cathedral* (Photo: A. dagli Orti/NPL – DeA Picture Library/Bridgeman Images)

inspired Borromeo's own later project for the presbytery at the cathedral of Milan designed by the architect Pellegrino Tibaldi (1527–96) in 1577, as well as the advice set out in the archbishops' influential treatise on ecclesiastical architecture and furnishings of the same year. The lost high altar tabernacle supported by angels designed by the architect Michele Sanmicheli (1484–1559) for Giberti in Verona was a typology subsequently used not just at the Milanese cathedral under Borromeo, but by Pope Sixtus V for his chapel in Santa Maria Maggiore in Rome (begun in 1585).[37] Borromeo's publications, in particular the *Acta ecclesiae mediolanensis* of 1582, which brought together the texts of his diocesan synods, provincial councils, and pastoral letters, had a sustained impact on Catholicism not just in Italy, but globally. In turn, this points to the significance of the territories of the Venetian Republic for enacting early visual and pastoral reforms that would go on to be imitated by leading churchmen from the late sixteenth century onwards.[38]

Giberti's outfitting of the presbytery of Verona cathedral encompassed a number of different elements in a variety of mediums, including the magnificent lost marble tabernacle, a pulpit, two new tombs for Bishop Lodovico Canossa of Bayeaux and Pope Lucius III (r. 1181–85), and frescoes of the assumption of the Virgin Mary and the city's patron saint Zeno, which were designed by Giulio Romano (c. 1499–1546) and executed by Francesco Torbido (c. 1482–1561).[39] The project also included an unusual semi-circular *tornacoro* by Sanmicheli that ranged around the high altar, a sort of vast protective balustrade. On the surface, Giberti's changes to the duomo appear to present a paradigm of orthodoxy, with their focus on the Virgin Mary, the city's patron saint, and the eucharist.[40] The bishop understood the construction of decorous ecclesiastical buildings as potentially relevant to reform efforts, something suggested by a later catechism of 1540 where one of the anonymous interlocutors has been identified as the voice of Giberti. Here the reasons given for such expenditures were that contrary attitudes in Germany had led not only to no new building projects, but to them 'destroy[ing] every single thing'.[41] Giberti was doubtless well versed on this topic: as a friend of Johann Eck (1486–1543), one of Luther's most formidable adversaries, he would have been familiar with his *De non tollendis Christi & sanctorum imaginibus* (1522), which set out a spirited defence of the Catholic position on sacred images.[42]

Notwithstanding this, in 1542 the cleric Filiberto Veronese, who had previously accompanied Giberti on visitations, issued a slanderous tract that indirectly accused the bishop of iconoclasm, arguing that some heretical bishops removed beautiful and devout images of Christ, the Madonna, and the saints under the pretext of 'wanting to accommodate, or give proportion to a site'.[43] On occasion, the populace had been angered by Giberti's attempts to remove images that he considered to be unconvincing in their claims of miraculous powers, as well as those that were damaged or incongruous, demonstrating their deep attachment to local cults and images.[44] A degree of scepticism regarding new miracles or unusual representations was later recommended by the Council of Trent, but in the decades that preceded the council, Giberti's actions might well have appeared to be verging on the iconoclastic. Since the average layperson may not have known much about the specifics of the Tridentine decrees, the reaction of the laity might not have been so different decades later had a cleric followed the same course of action. In addition to his attempts to remove some images, Giberti was one of the earliest promoters of displaying the tabernacle on the high altar, a practice that eventually displaced the traditional high altarpiece.[45] His changes at Verona cathedral pronounced the site where the eucharist was held, in the form of the consecrated host, as the most holy and significant of the ecclesiastical space. Although this is a change that became extremely popular, as we shall see in Chapter 4, it often led to radical and sometimes destructive architectural interventions.[46] Traditionally of equal importance was the exaltation of the saints, and although the city's patron saint, Zeno, was present in the fresco decoration, his representation was limited to only one scene. At least in the 1530s, Giberti appears to have shown a slight reluctance to over-emphasise the cult of the saints, and he emphatically stated that devotion to them should represent devotion to God himself, a position that would become anathema later in the century.[47] As an adversary of Giberti, Filiberto's comments regarding iconoclasm were incendiary, but the collision between orthodoxy and heresy was something that many of the early sixteenth-century reformers grappled with, and the innovative Giberti was no exception to this.

In 1546 Giberti appeared on the Capuchin Bernardino Ochino's list of those who believed in salvation (or justification) by faith alone, a theological position that was promoted by Luther, and later by other reformers like Zwingli and John Calvin.[48] Giberti was dead at this point, and Ochino had become one of the most infamous apostates of the period when he fled to Calvinist Geneva in 1542.[49] The previous year at the Colloquy of Ratisbon, Contarini and Philipp Melanchthon had managed to achieve a compromise formula on justification. But this was rejected both by Luther and the pope, marking the failed culmination of attempts to find common ground between Protestants and Catholics. A year later the Roman Inquisition was established. From this point onwards, the ideas on the nature of salvation that Giberti supposedly supported would prove to be increasingly controversial, and ultimately untenable for the Catholic Church after the Council of Trent's 1547 decrees on justification that confirmed the equal efficacy of charitable works. Yet in the years before the 1540s, this was not an unusual belief amongst Catholic reformers, and it did not necessarily signify collusion with Protestant doctrine. Giberti's contemporary Contarini, for example, decided that he was justified by faith in Christ's sacrifice already in 1511, prior to the Reformations having even begun.[50]

A fresco cycle commissioned by Giberti and completed by Torbido, which appeared not in the cathedral of a major artistic centre, but in the abbey of Rosazzo in Friuli, has been alluded to by scholars as possibly reflecting Giberti's views on justification by faith alone (Fig. 12).[51] Giberti was Commendatory Abbot of the site from 1527 until his death, and he proved to be a committed guardian of the abbey, ordering extensive restorations and embellishments. In 1535 the frescoes for the presbytery of the church were completed, including the pair at the height of the entrance to the high altar that depict Saints Peter and Paul on either side of the coat of arms of Pope Clement VII (who had died in 1534). The dedication of the abbey to Peter informs the Petrine subject matter of the fresco cycle, and in this particular scene the two saints are

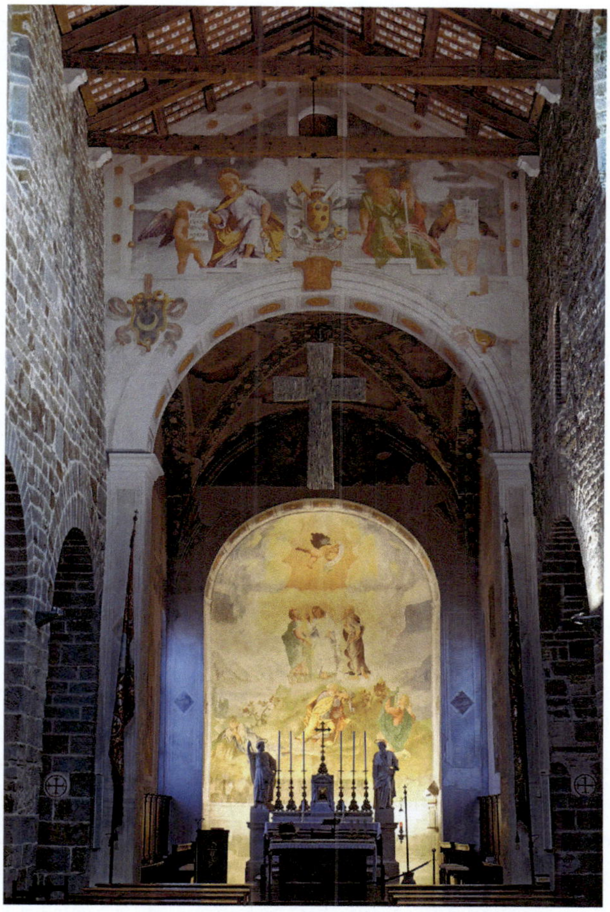

12. Francesco Torbido, *Saints Peter and Paul and the Transfiguration*, 1535, frescoes, Abbey of Rosazzo, Friuli (Photo: Sebastiano Giannesini)

shown accompanied by Latin inscriptions held aloft by cherubs. Peter's refers to faith: 'Love is the foundation of faith' (*Fidei fundamentum amor*) and Paul's to grace: 'My grace is sufficient for you' (*Sufficit tibi gratia mea*). Luther's views on justification had been inspired by the Pauline epistles, and so it has thus been argued that the inscription from 2 Corinthians 12:9 expounds sensibilities relating to the idea of *sola fide*, presenting Giberti's allegiance to these ideas in his capacity as patron.[52] Yet if love is understood as charity, then the Petrine inscription gives equal weight to the role of this virtue in salvation. Moreover, the centrality given to the pope's coat of arms demonstrates a defence of the Bishop of Rome's supremacy and his relationship to Saint Peter, neutralising any potentially problematic message.[53] The subject matter of the rest of the cycle is similarly orthodox: the main scene behind the high altar depicts the *Transfiguration*, the figure of the sleeping Peter prominently depicted directly below Christ, and on either side of the presbytery walls are scenes of the *Calling of Saint Peter and Andrew* (left wall) and the *Miraculous Draught of*

Fishes (right wall), emphasising the Apostolic succession. On the ceiling above are the symbols of the Evangelists, and at the centre of the inner arch the Virgin is shown holding the Christ-child. As outlined in the introduction to this chapter, in the absence of convincing visual and documentary evidence there is a risk that any image – or, in this case, element in a larger whole – can take on a polemical aspect when it is viewed in light of the Reformation, or when its chronology means that it was produced subsequent to it. This tendency can be appreciated not only with the example of Rosazzo, but also with reference to the aforementioned frontispiece of the Brucioli Bible attributed to Lotto, where the presence of Saint Paul as an impassioned preacher in one of the episodes excited one scholar so much that the image was declared to 'undoubtedly reveal a spirituality quite close to that of the Protestants',[54] a judgment that overstates the significance of choosing one saint over another (i.e., Paul instead of Peter), and elides the fact that the design was reused by the publisher for the 1538 edition of the Santi Marmocino translation, a rebuttal by the Dominicans of Brucioli's earlier text, demonstrating that its iconography was in no way considered outwardly suspect.[55]

Giberti was a devoted and innovative reformer, but he was also controversial for some of his practices, and even had to defend himself against accusations of espionage and heresy at the end of his life.[56] This was not so unusual for the period, and it anticipated the experiences of those who tried to enforce Tridentine reforms in the wake of the council and who often met with resistance, the most extreme case of this being the two assassination attempts on the life of Carlo Borromeo in Milan, one by the canons of La Scala and another by a member of the Humiliati Order. In the second quarter of the sixteenth century, contact with currents that would unequivocally be condemned in the latter half of it was almost inevitable for someone of Giberti's status in Northern Italy. Evidence of this is provided by the closely interlinked networks in which such individuals operated. For example, a member of Giberti's household, the Friulian cleric Ludovico Mantovano da Serravalle, was prosecuted in 1539 (likely at Giberti's insistence) for his opposition to the cult of saints and various sacraments.[57] Mantovano was a friend of Marcantonio Flaminio, who was in turn secretary to Giberti, but left Verona to join the circle of Juan de Valdés in Naples (c. 1490–1541), whose theological works were placed on the very first Index published in Venice in 1549.[58] Other contemporaries of the Veronese bishop such as Cardinal Contarini were similarly criticised for their opinions on justification by faith alone (as were numerous other prominent ecclesiastics), and, like Giberti, Contarini had been a friend of Ochino prior to his dramatic departure from Italy.[59] Finally, even the staunchest defender of orthodoxy such as the Bishop of Pula, Altobello Averoldi – best known to art historians as the patron of Titian's polyptych for Santi Nazaro e Celso of c. 1528–30 – mixed in these circles. Averoldi's funeral oration was delivered in San Marco on 4 November 1531 by none other than Pier Paolo Vergerio, the Bishop of Capodistria who famously fled to the Grisons in 1549.[60]

A GREAT MOUNTAIN OF BODIES, 'SOMETHING DIRTY TO BEHOLD'

Venice was exposed to a rich gamut of religious currents in the years spanning from the early 1520s to the 1540s. This was not only because of its printing industry, its large population, and the presence of diverse nationalities in the city (one only has to think of the *fondaco* for the German community at Rialto) but also because of its vicinity to northern countries and the vast extent of its land and sea empire.[61] As we have seen, figures like Giberti moved in milieus that included individuals who later became notorious for their dissenting creeds: in 1539, for example, Ochino delivered a series of lectures promoting the doctrine of *sola fide* in Venice, his presence there having been encouraged by the Venetian cardinal Pietro Bembo (1470–1547). For these reasons Giberti, Contarini, and their associated networks have been described as *spirituali*, to denote their adherence to some of the aims and beliefs of a loosely interconnected group of contemporary reformers.[62] As the name suggests, the *spirituali* focused on interior spirituality and an individual relationship with God. They believed in justification by faith alone and defended the authority of the pope, although they had initially hoped for conciliation with the Protestants. Like the seemingly insatiable interest amongst scholars for nomenclature described in the introduction, categorisations like *spirituali* or evangelism are extensively debated and contested. In part this is because the mingling of diverse opinions and theological positions in these years defies precise groupings, but also because these terms place more orthodox individuals like Giberti or Contarini in the same category as Ochino, Juan de Valdés, or Peter Martyr Vermigli (1499–1562), the latter of whom fled to Protestant Strasbourg in the same year as Ochino left.[63] Reservations about oversimplifications aside, some *spirituali* did indeed refer to themselves as such, including Giberti himself.[64] Camilla Russell's point that the group were distinct enough to warrant this categorisation is a valid one, keeping in mind her important qualification about the obvious complexities relating to the beliefs and transformations that the group underwent over the years.[65]

One of the most famous texts associated with the *spirituali* was Benedetto da Mantova's *Beneficio di Cristo*, printed anonymously in Venice during the 1540s in at least three editions.[66] Influenced by the preachings of Ochino, the theology of Valdés in Naples, and Calvin's *Institutes* of 1536, the publication was placed on the Venetian Index in 1549, although it had already been criticised by Ambrogio Catarino (1484–1553), a fierce opponent of Luther, in 1544.[67] Vergerio, by this point in religious exile, attested to the immense success of the book, claiming that 40,000 copies of it had been sold in six years alone. If this many copies of the *Beneficio di Cristo* had really been bought, then we would expect more of them to have found their way into Protestant territories and thus escaped censorship.[68] But even if Vergerio greatly exaggerated the *fortuna* of the book, it was still a popular text, as evidenced by its various editions. Figures like Morone described how initially they believed the book to be 'very spiritual', and since they had been taught that 'heretical books were contrary to all the sacraments', it had not occurred to them that the text, 'which spoke so highly of the Blessed Sacrament, could have had something evil hidden within it'.[69] The *Beneficio di Cristo* exhorted its readers to concentrate on Christ's sacrifice on the cross, to receive the 'benefit' of his death through their trust in him, proposing that we are saved by our faith alone. Theoretically, then, any image of the Crucifixion could reflect this idea, but scholars have gone to great lengths to tie the theology of the *spirituali* and that of their most notorious publication to specific paintings. Despite its popularity in Venice, the *Beneficio di Cristo* does not appear to have had any clear impact on the output of artists in the city, which does not mean to suggest that none of them sympathised with or even adhered to its doctrines. Rather, as we shall see, this demonstrates how difficult it is to identify or convincingly prove if contested theological ideas were made visually manifest. Nonetheless, the *Beneficio di Cristo* has been repeatedly linked to the lost frescoes of a Tuscan artist, Pontormo, for the church of San Lorenzo in Florence. A brief diversion to that city in order to consider whether the frescoes did indeed correspond to the theology of the *Beneficio* will allow us to appreciate why unusual iconographies were rarely greeted with a positive reception in Italy, ensuring that few of them were ever produced in the first place.

Pontormo's frescoes in the choir of San Lorenzo were destroyed in 1738 when a new cupola was installed in the church, and so they are known to us primarily through extant drawings by him and by those after him (Figs. 13 and 14).[70] Combined with the textual descriptions, these visual traces have allowed scholars to reconstruct the subject matter of the San Lorenzo cycle as covering the story of the salvation of humanity from the flood to the Last Judgment. Begun in 1545 and finished after Pontormo's death in 1557 by his pupil Agnolo Bronzino, the frescoes were revealed to the public of Florence in 1558. It was not until 1950 that the cycle was first tied to the ideas dear to the *spirituali* in an article by Charles de Tolnay.[71] After the careful reconstruction of the cycle by Janet Cox-Rearick in 1964,[72] subsequent scholars linked the iconography closely to specific texts: Raffaella Corti proposed the *Beneficio di*

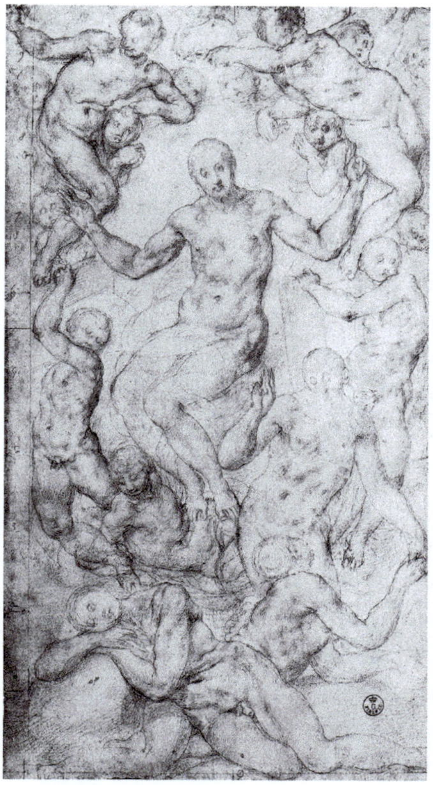

13. Pontormo, *Christ in Glory and the Creation of Eve*, c. 1550, Gabinetto dei Disegni e delle Stampe, Uffizi, Florence (Photo: Finsiel/Alinari/Art Resource, New York)

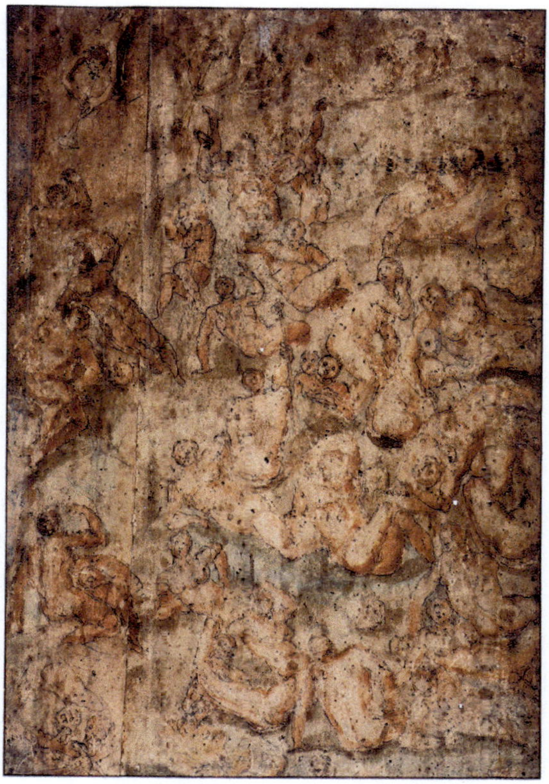

14. Anonymous, copy after Pontormo's *Resurrection of the Dead*, late sixteenth/early seventeenth century, Victoria & Albert Museum, London (Photo: Victoria & Albert Museum, London)

Cristo as a source, whilst first Salvatore Caponetto and then Massimo Firpo argued that they reflected the popular catechism of Valdés, published posthumously in the same year that works on the cycle began.[73] Even if Pontormo was influenced by these writings, the lack of consensus about precisely what theological point he was trying to make at San Lorenzo is demonstrated by the different ideas amongst scholars about which theologies he was representing in more recent times.[74] But it was also something that equally mystified his contemporaries, who greeted his innovations with a lukewarm reception.

We can appreciate this first with reference to Vasari's thoughts on the San Lorenzo frescoes. Vasari was particularly bemused by Pontormo's image of *Christ in Glory*, where God the Father is shown creating Adam and Eve as his Son sits in judgment above him. Disrupting the traditional hierarchy of God the Father and Son, Vasari commented, 'I have never been able to understand the significance of this scene, although I know that Jacopo had wit enough for himself and associated with learned and lettered persons.' Vasari had a tendency to demur to the expertise of the 'learned' when confronted with any potentially heretical images, the reasons for which will be explored presently. Not only did he find this image strange, but he thought the cycle as a whole was an outright failure. Worse, he wrote that whilst Pontormo had envisaged the works as the summit of his professional career, he not only failed to surpass 'all the painters in the world of art' (his original aim apparently), but he couldn't even manage to equal his past achievements![75] Similar opinions were expressed in more forceful terms by Borghini in *Il Riposo*, a text well-known for its prudery. Borghini found the dizzying quantity of nudes and genitalia in the cycle to be predictably off-putting, and pronounced the *Last Judgment* that featured a mountain of 'ugly bodies' to be 'something dirty to behold'.[76] Confronted with the artist's rendition of the *Deluge* consisting of a mass of corpses, Pontormo's imaginative tendencies elicited despair, the interlocutor Vecchietti concluding: 'see how many errors painters make by inconsiderately explaining in their paintings their own opinions'.[77]

A few years after the destruction of Pontormo's frescoes in the eighteenth century, the Jesuit Giuseppe Richa agreed with Borghini's earlier critique of 1584, noting that the frescoes had garnered little praise and that their loss was 'nothing to cry about'.[78] In Vasari's biography of Pontormo, he wrote that the artist had taken inspiration from Michelangelo for the cycle, whose *Last Judgment* for the Sistine Chapel had met a similarly divisive reception, as we shall see in the next chapter. By the time Vasari, and to a greater extent Borghini, surveyed the frescoes, there was less tolerance for overt nudity, partly because the debacle over Michelangelo's frescoes had brought the question of artistic decorum to the fore. Even more sympathetic commentators like Francesco Bocchi writing in 1591 about the San Lorenzo cycle could not fail to conclude that Pontormo would have done a much better job if he had just adhered more closely to scripture.[79] The unusual iconography of the cycle was thought to be bizarre and nonsensical and the wealth of nudes obscene. If anything, the negative reception of the frescoes would have reminded artists to avoid the 'lascivious' and 'unusual' imagery that the Council of Trent warned against in 1563, just a few years after they were unveiled. But even if the images were inspired by heterodox theologies, as many scholars have insisted, this was not necessarily deduced by viewers. Treatises like Borghini's limited themselves to enumerating the 'errors' committed by thoughtless artists, a practice with far lesser consequences that an outright condemnation of subversive intent. This paternalistic attitude arguably protected artists from the consequences of such accusations. Since they were not theologians, they could not be expected to get things right all the time, hence why they should be mindful of iconographic traditions. When in doubt they could consult the Bible or a member of the clergy. Later on, if they were especially punctilious, they could even have read one of the treatises on the subject analysed in the next chapter to ensure that they were not inadvertently representing doctrinal or iconographic 'errors' in their devotional artworks.

Borghini's text does, however, underline the impact of German prints on Pontormo, the only time that this is mentioned in *Il Riposo* with reference to an artist. We are told that Pontormo first became enraptured by some of Albrecht Dürer's (1471–1528) prints, leading him to imitate a 'German manner', abandoning his own style, which had been 'full of sweetness and grace'.[80] Dürer of course had a great influence on countless Italian artists, but Borghini's comments might have had a deeper significance pertaining to Pontormo's religious allegiances.[81] The frescoes were commissioned by Duke Cosimo de' Medici (1519–74) via his *maggiordomo* Pier Francesco Riccio, the prior of San Lorenzo. The anonymous author of a letter owned by Riccio and sent from Venice in 1544 boasted that 'I find in my possession all the writings of Melanchthon in five volumes, a beautiful work' and offered to send them on.[82] The diffusion of Valdensian thought at the court of Cosimo in this period is well documented, and Pontormo may have come into contact with these ideas through Riccio.[83] Yet even if the iconography had been influenced by the theology of these reform movements, it is still not clear why Cosimo would have wanted frescoes that expressed ideas that were already becoming problematic in the late 1540s.

To suggest that Riccio's later ownership of the *Beneficio di Cristo* in 1557, the year of Pontormo's death, closely informed the iconographic programme of the San Lorenzo cycle is tenuous at best.[84] The major new reconstruction of the project by Elizabeth Pilliod, far from demonstrating that Pontormo's works referenced heretical ideas, has instead come to the opposite conclusion: that this was in fact one of the most fundamentally orthodox commissions of the period.[85] This may be taking the alternative line of argument a touch too far. If the cycle was so orthodox, then it was certainly not greeted as such by any of the subsequent commentators who were offended by both the nudes and the odd iconography. Whilst the close connection with the *Beneficio di Cristo* is convincingly refuted by Pilliod, the letters that belonged to Riccio do demonstrate an interest in heterodox creeds.[86] It is also telling that Vasari, who enjoyed a close relationship to Cosimo de' Medici, criticised a project that the Grand Duke had paid for.[87] Combined with the evidence presented by Firpo, Vasari's response allows us to speculate that the frescoes may have been partly inspired by controversial theologies, and that his reason for feigning confusion concerning their intent was to protect both the powerful patron of the works and himself. This is because Vasari may well have been interested in similar ideas diffused in Italy at the time, something that is hinted at by his 1546 preparatory drawing of *The Last Supper*, completed contemporaneously to Pontormo's works at San Lorenzo.[88] This drawing has two inscriptions, neither of which appears in the painting completed for the nuns of the

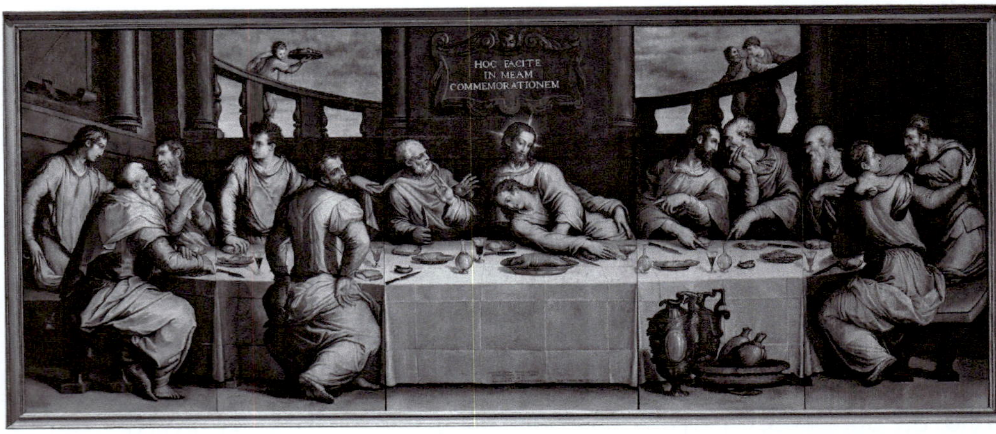

15. Giorgio Vasari, *The Last Supper*, 1546–47, oil on panel, Museo dell'Opera di Santa Croce, Florence (Photo: Ghigo C. Roli/Art Resource, New York)

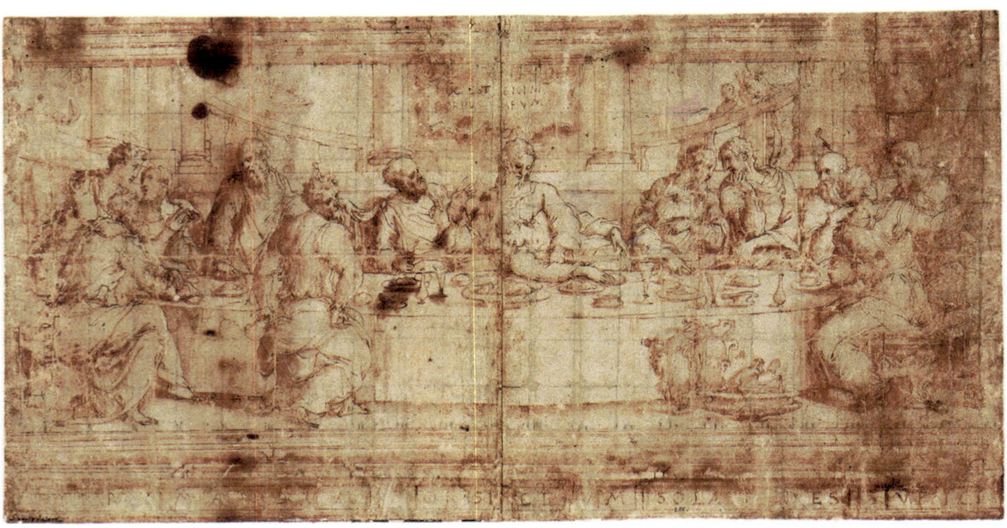

16. Giorgio Vasari, drawing of *The Last Supper*, 1546, Staatliche Graphische Sammlung, Munich (Photo: Staatliche Graphische Sammlung München)

Murate in Florence (Figs. 15 and 16). The first of these, 'For this in my body' (HOC EST ENIM/CORPVS MEVM), underlines the sacramental significance of the episode through the inclusion of Christ's words spoken at his final supper.[89] The second, which translates as 'Faith only is sufficient to fortify a sincere heart' [(AD) (FI)RMANDVM COR SI(N)CERVM SOLA F(I)DES SVFFICI(T)], suggests a potentially heretical undercurrent relating to *sola fide*, something noticed by Kate Lowe and underlined by Alessandro Nova.[90] Richard Harprath was the first to note that the inscription repeats the words of the *Pange lingue*, attributed to a paragon of orthodoxy – Thomas Aquinas – and that this hymn was traditionally sung at vespers on the most Catholic of feast days, Corpus Christi.[91] Yet despite the Aquinian source, these words could well have been interpreted in a Protestant light during the increasingly tense religious climate of the 1540s, and to avoid this, either Vasari or the sisters of the Murate, or someone else entirely, advised that it should be omitted from the final painting. As Nova points out, notwithstanding his many other many qualities, Vasari 'was never an intellectual'. The drawing reflects his experimentation with ideas that he would have heard his friends discussing, perhaps without fully realising their implications.[92]

Vasari's account of the San Lorenzo frescoes placed the blame for their appearance not with the patron who paid for them, but squarely with the artist who had produced them. Vasari may also have been envious of Pontormo, since they were in competition for Medici patronage, but it is telling that he emphasised Pontormo's decision to work away in secret, keeping his progress shielded carefully from view for eleven years, suggesting that Cosimo had been completely in the dark about their actual appearance.[93] Pilliod has taken issue with this, pointing out that Pontormo's diary records two visits by the Duke and Duchess Eleonora to San Lorenzo, suggesting the contrary.[94] Perhaps Vasari was unaware of these visits, but it seems more likely that he deliberately suppressed the information. Less than a decade after Pontormo's death, and in the year after the conclusion of the Council of Trent, Duke Cosimo instigated of his own accord an orthodox programme of architectural interventions at the two mendicant churches of Santa Maria Novella and Santa Croce in Florence.[95] Since Vasari was in charge of these works, it is plausible that he deliberately downplayed any involvement his patron had had in Pontormo's problematic cycle due to the connection with Riccio's heretodox leanings in the 1540s.[96] In this context, the Santa Croce and Santa Maria Novella projects can even be seen as a way for Cosimo to atone for the earlier failure of Pontormo at San Lorenzo.

Whatever Vasari's motives may have been, Pontormo's frescoes were evidently considered neither grave enough nor offensive enough to warrant their destruction (in the sixteenth century at least). But even if they had been, the elite nature of this commission would have almost certainly ruled out this option. For example, when iconoclasm hit Nuremberg in 1519, Veit Stoss's *Angelic Salutation* for the Saint Lorenzkirche was decommissioned and covered, but it was never destroyed since it had recently been paid for by the city official Anton Tucher. Given Cosimo's status, it was unlikely that too many people in Florence would have had the nerve to denounce artworks that he had paid for as heterodox; Borghini's snub, for example, was made at a safe distance of some years subsequent to his death.[97] Local evidence of these tendencies is also provided by the events related to Francesco Botticini's *Assumption* (c. 1475/76), a painting that Vasari tells us was the subject of gossip since both its artist and patron were believed to have committed 'the grievous sin of heresy' in

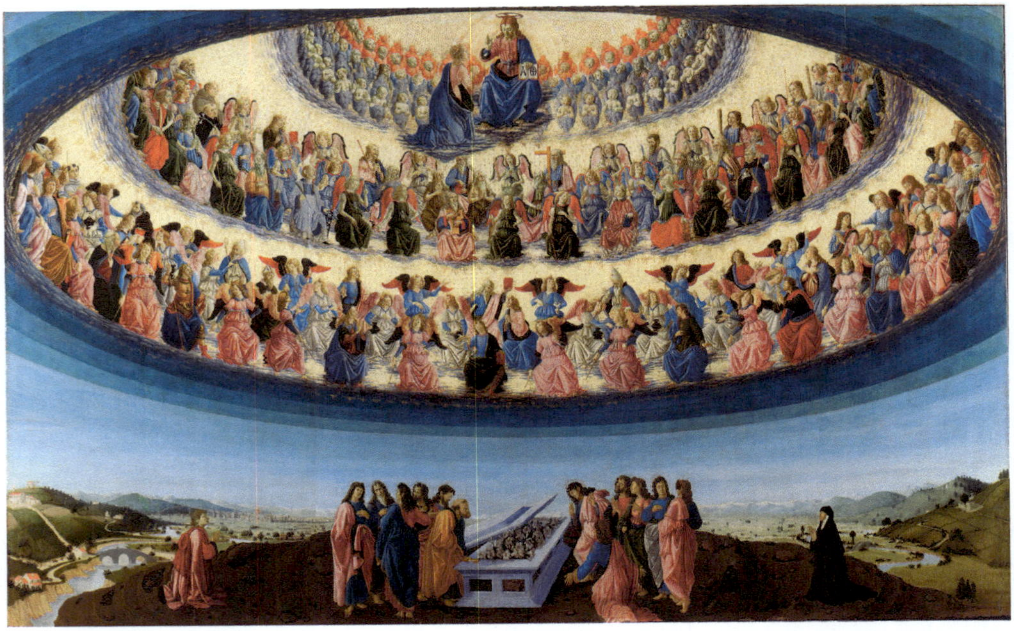

17. Francesco Botticini, *Assumption of the Virgin*, c. 1475–76, tempera on wood, National Gallery, London (Photo: National Gallery, London)

producing it (Fig. 17).[98] The patron of the work, Matteo Palmieri, was author of the 1465 *Citta di vità*, a text that was denounced as heretical. In essence, it adapted the third-century views of Origen to describe the souls of incarnate humanity as being derived from angels, thus suggesting that souls transmigrated, and so were not entirely individual.[99] Bagemihl argued that Botticini's painting reflected the last canto of the *Citta di vità* by presenting the Virgin received into heaven surrounded by nine tiers of angels, although he pointed out that although unusual, this arrangement was hardly unorthodox. Bagemihl also maintained that Palmieri's ideas on the nature of the soul were expressed through the stars that marked the chest of each saint and angel in Botticini's painting. Closer examination of the work shows that in fact the saints and angels mingle in seven of the nine tiers, and the stars are not deployed consistently, appearing on the chests of some figures and not on others. Even if they had been, Bagemihl conceded that only a viewer primed in the ideas of the *Citta di vità* could ever have recognised this.[100] Even if the painting was inspired by Palmieri's Dantesque text, its patronage by Palmieri likely gave credence to the rumours that the painting reflected his heretical ideas to a greater extent than the iconographic specifics, and at some point the faces of the donor portraits of Matteo and his wife Niccolosa were scratched out as a kind of *damnatio memoriae*. As with Stoss's *Angelic Salutation*, the solution appears to have been not to destroy or remove the image from the now demolished church of San Pier Maggiore, where it was originally placed on the end wall of the south transept and where its donor was interred. Instead, it was covered up, something that seems to have only caused gossip about its supposedly heretical iconography to grow.[101] True to form, Vasari made it clear that although he valued the painting for its beauty, he was not a theologian, so whether the accusations against artist and patron were true or false, 'I cannot be expected to judge.'[102]

A FALLEN POPE

On the whole the production of sacred images for public display made the expression of contested ideas in visual form both improbable and undesirable, particularly in the latter half of the sixteenth century. For example, there are no known cases of individual religious prints being banned in sixteenth-century Venice, and neither is there any recorded censorship of devotional woodcut prints in books.[103] Pontormo's lost works at San Lorenzo might have tested the boundaries of what was considered acceptable, but their theological message was presumably vague enough that the intended meaning would have been evident only to those directly involved in the commission. Images deemed doctrinally deficient or misleading rarely posed a great problem in the Cinquecento, something that partially supports Charles Hope's view that altarpieces in particular were most often focused on figures that could be invoked and venerated rather than about complex ideas or dogmas. Although I am not in complete agreement with Hope's assertions (see Chapter 5), he does provide one compelling reason for why there are not more images that reflect the ideas on justification that were popular amongst elite Italian reformers.[104]

In his recent analysis of Poussin's *Sacrament of Marriage* T. J. Clark summed up the problem of how the religious scepticism of an artist might be reflected visually: 'Doubters in the seventeenth century learned to cover their tracks. Only a fool would have risked actually staging such doubts in paintings having to do with the central mysteries of faith.'[105] The same applies equally for the preceding century, and this is what makes the job of the art historian difficult: if doubters covered their tracks visually, and we have only scant information regarding their religious sympathies, it is tempting to sensationalise the image as having a covert heretical message, perhaps one only evident to those who deliberately set out to find it. What is more, images reflect not just the beliefs of the artist, but those of the patron, and in some cases also of the laity more generally. Artists painted for profit, and some worked for both Protestant and Catholic patrons, adapting their style to the religious inclinations of their clients. Lucas Cranach (1472–1553) the Elder is a good example of this.

Although his loyalties were firmly with the Lutherans (Cranach and Luther were godparents to each other's children), he had to earn a living, and so he continued working for Catholic patrons, producing affective images of the Virgin and the saints, at the same time as he was engaged on the Protestant woodcuts and reformed altarpieces for which he is best known.[106]

The cases that have been discussed so far are of images and individuals that can be tied to Italian evangelism and to the ideas of the *spirituali*. But what about images that express a Protestant viewpoint, or a demonstrably anti-Catholic one? This question is worth asking since Venice was relatively tolerant of heterodox thought in the early years of the Reformations, and together with other Italian 'hotbeds of heresy' such as Parma, Lucca, and Modena, numerous sources attest to the presence of nonconformist groups in the city during the sixteenth century, ranging from Anabaptists to Lutherans.[107] Protestantism also spread to the terraferma, particularly Vicenza, where the Calvinist congregations associated with the nobleman Alessandro Trissino (c. 1523–c. 1609) initially flourished. Already in 1547 the podesta, Lorenzo Venier, wrote that 'we see the city badly infected by these new opinions against the honour of God, against the faith and Christian religion'.[108] It was from a town on the Venetian mainland that one artist who swapped Italy for the court of King Henry VIII in England hailed: his name was Girolamo da Treviso (1498–1544) and works attributed to him both before and after his emigration appear to show that he went from painting standard images of sacred themes to possibly producing the grisaille *Protestant Allegory* of c. 1542–44 whilst in the employ of the Tudor court (Fig. 18).[109]

Girolamo left his homeland in 1538, at a point in the English Reformation that Diarmaid MacCulloch has pronounced as being 'characterised by its hatred of images'.[110] Vasari suggests Girolamo emigrated for purely economic reasons, his role there having been as a military engineer, rather than as a painter.[111] Few Italian painters journeyed to England after Henry's split from Rome in 1532, so Girolamo must have mostly abandoned his artistic aspirations when he decided to take up gainful employment as an engineer, a switch that proved to be lucrative.[112] Earning a living was what had caused Girolamo to move frequently around Italy prior to his departure in search of work, just as it was the reason that Holbein swapped Basel for England in 1526; and it was the primary motivating factor behind the emigration of Italian artists and architects to the court of King François I in the same period. This is not to disregard the possibility that escaping religious persecution may have been of paramount importance, but to point out that the tendency to assume that this was the overarching cause for such journeys – as Sergio Marinelli did when he surmised that the Italian 'exiles' (as he called them) were 'undoubtedly heretics' – is too often predicated upon supposition, particularly if we consider that in this case the French king was a Catholic.[113]

That Girolamo still dabbled in his original line of work after emigrating is attested to by the *Protestant Allegory*, and although his authorship has not been universally accepted, the visual evidence is nevertheless intriguing. Girolamo was an expert in grisaille, attested to by his 1525–26 cycle of paintings for the Saraceni Chapel in San Petronio of Bologna, and there are clear similarities between his work here and the Hampton Court palace allegory (Fig. 19).[114] A polemically anti-papal image, the *Protestant Allegory* reflects Henry's political stance in this period of his reign. It depicts the pope, the metaphorical rock upon which the Roman Church was believed to be founded, vanquished by the authors of the Gospels who are poised to stone to death the figures below. The Evangelists are shown engaged in violence, suggesting that the image could be read as a veiled justification for Henry's methods of enforcement in his realms. In the *Protestant Allegory* the true word of Christ is triumphantly reclaimed as the foundation-stone of belief, as the pope falls to ground, accompanied by the material accoutrement of the Church and the personifications of avarice and hypocrisy. In the distance there is a city, probably the heavenly Jerusalem, and above it a candle burns. This light of truth contrasts to the second candle in the foreground, its flame about to be extinguished as it topples to the ground, suggestive of the false doctrine of Rome.[115]

The *Protestant Allegory* depends upon the iconography of the kinds of Catholic images that Girolamo da Treviso was well versed in. The composition draws clear inspiration from images of the stoning of Saint Stephen, in particular, the altarpiece for the cathedral of Genoa of 1519–21 by Giulio Romano, under whom the artist had worked at the Palazzo Te.[116] Given both the irascible temperament of Henry VIII and the fact that Girolamo da Treviso was directly dependent on his patronage and reliant on his judgment as a foreign worker, whether or not the *Protestant Allegory* reflects the artist's own sympathies can only be speculated on in the absence of further documentary evidence regarding his authorship. Composers such as Thomas Tallis (c. 1505–85) and William Byrd (c. 1540–1623) worked successfully at the Tudor court, even being jointly granted a monopoly on printing music in England under Queen Elizabeth, whilst privately continuing an allegiance to Catholicism and covertly creating compositions for Catholic patrons.[117] On the other hand, producing an image that offered an outright denunciation of the Church of Rome would have been considered a serious heretical act in Girolamo's home country. In seventeenth-century Japan the devotion of those suspected to have converted to Christianity was tested by forcing them to

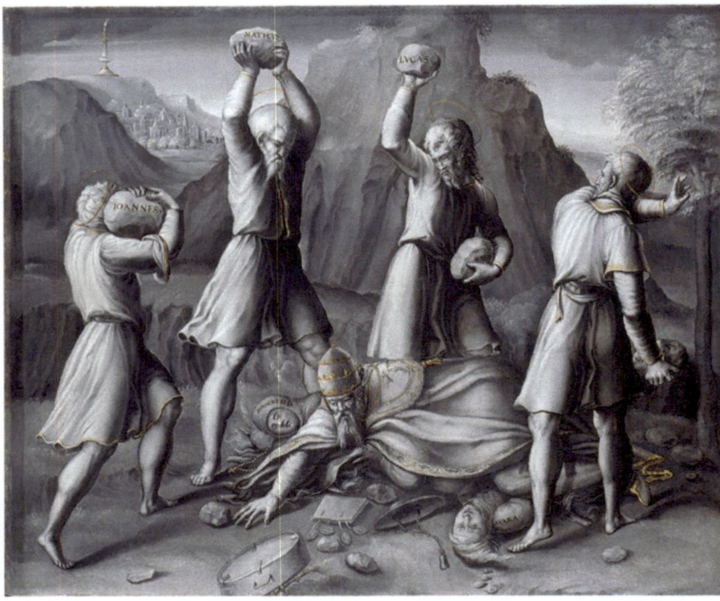

18. Attributed to Girolamo da Treviso, *Protestant Allegory*, c. 1542–44, oil on panel, Hampton Court Palace (Royal Collection Trust/His Majesty King Charles III/Bridgeman Images)

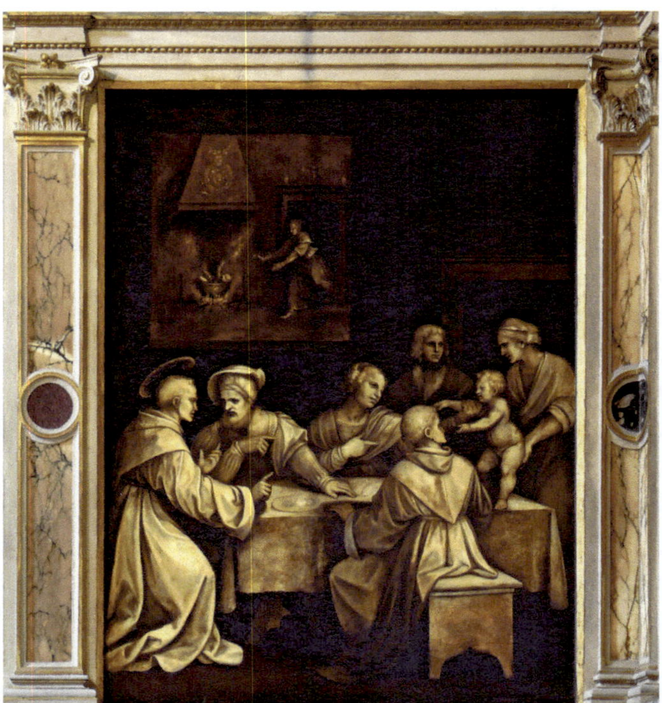

19. Girolamo da Treviso, detail of the *Miracle of the Baby in the Cauldron*, 1525–26, oil on wall, Saraceni Chapel, San Petronio, Bologna (Photo: Photographic Archive of the Basilica of San Petronio)

trample on an image of Christ or the Virgin Mary (*fumi-e*), the most faithful refusing to desecrate the images. Creating an image like the *Protestant Allegory* was akin to this, but without knowing the precise circumstances of the commission it is difficult to be sure of the extent to which the painting reflects the artist's religious sympathies or those of his patron. What the example of Girolamo's *Protestant Allegory* seems to really highlight is that in the overwhelming majority of cases, early modern devotional artworks reflect the predominant religion in the place where they were produced. This is intended not to diminish artists' agency but to challenge a tendency to all too swiftly link the individual circumstances of either patron or artist to the appearance of the creations that they were responsible for. An example of this relating to Venice is Manfredo Tafuri and Antonio Foscari's analysis of the decoration of the Barbaro chapel at San Francesco della Vigna.[118] The altarpiece of the *Baptism of Christ* by Battista Franco of c. 1552–54 was interpreted as demonstrating an anti-heretical agenda relating to the impact of Daniele Barbaro's trip to Protestant England upon him and his growing preoccupations about the diffusion of Anabaptism in Venice. The apparent emphasis on what was interpreted as a scene of purgatory in the bottom section of the altarpiece was thus read as placing a particular emphasis on a devotion rejected by Protestantism, yet as shown by Anne Lauder and Deborah Howard, a detailed investigation of the sources revealed that the altarpiece had not been commissioned by the Barbaro family but was funded by the confraternity dedicated to the name of Jesus that had rights to the altar space.[119]

In this chapter I have explored examples that include frescoes with a decidedly anti-heretical outlook authored by an artist who also painted portraits of infamous heretics (in the view of the Church), the presbytery renovations of a reforming bishop whose agenda often met with resistance, a cycle of paintings that may or may not have been influenced by the theology of the *spirituali*, and a polemically anti-papal grisaille attributed to an Italian artist working as an engineer in Protestant England. Yet these cases mostly add up to exceptions, and examples of images that promote ideas contrary to the established religion are few and far between.[120] The primary reason for this would appear to be self-censorship: market demands regulated an artist's output, meaning there was little reason for heretical images to exist, let alone to be displayed publicly. Even if artists might have harbored subversive sympathies, it is unlikely that their clients would have wanted works that expressed problematic ideas or disputed dogmas that could land them in trouble. This is of course the obvious answer to the question, one pointed out by Marilyn Perry and Philip Fehl some years ago.[121] While undoubtedly a valid assertion, to conclude I would like to build upon a further point that these scholars made as an aside, which was that, generally speaking, the Reformation rejected the very necessity of sacred images, a fact that to my mind ensured that it probably held limited appeal for artists by rendering unnecessary the bread and butter of their output (devotional images for display in churches). Although there was a variety of attitudes towards sacred images within Reformation movements, ranging from Luther's relative tolerance to Zwingli's unrelenting condemnation, by the end of the sixteenth century most of Protestant Europe had stopped commissioning new religious art, even if other genres began to flourish.[122]

This viewpoint is supported by some contemporary reactions to iconoclasm in the North, such as Karel van Mander's account of the Dutch painter Pieter Aertsen's (1507/8–75) rage at suffering the ignominy of having twenty-five of his altarpieces in various towns of the Low Countries destroyed by the 'vicious hands of raving, insane iconoclasts – a tragic loss to art'.[123] Van Mander wrote that Aertsen was 'often in an incensed state of mind, because the works which he once hoped to leave to the world were destroyed in this tragic way; and many times he had such bitter arguments with the enemies of art that he almost brought himself into danger'.[124] Even artists like Dürer, who supported Luther, spoke out against iconoclasm and the threat that images were supposed to present in his 1525 *Art of Measurement*. The impact of these policies on the livelihood of artists was already notable in the mid 1520s, when Erasmus of Rotterdam wrote to Thomas More in England that 'here the arts are freezing', and as such Holbein (1497/98–1543) was emigrating 'in order to scrape together a little money'.[125] Heterodox ideas were reasonably widespread in Venetian territories, but that artists seem not to have been particularly interested in them is not just an impression gained from the absence of artworks that clearly manifest subversive imagery, but is one backed up by evidence provided by the documents of the Inquisition in Venice. Records demonstrate that only twelve artists were accused of heresy between 1547 and 1586, compared with thirty jewellers and twenty-four apothecaries.[126] In light of such data, provocative discussions of the impact of the Counter-Reformation on artists in the lands of the Venetian terraferma published as recently as 2014 need to be re-evaluated, and the statement made at the beginning of this chapter that early modern Venetian artists were more inclined to orthodoxy rather than heterodoxy needs to be taken seriously when assessing the extent to which their artistic freedom was compromised in the later sixteenth century.

NOTES

1 Morone's account was part of his defence at having read the *Beneficio di Cristo*. Translated from Massimo Firpo and Dario Marcatto, *Il processo inquisitoriale del Cardinal Giovanni Morone: edizione critica*, vol. 2, part 1 (Rome: Istituto storico italiano per l'età moderna e contemporanea, 1984), 465. See also Firpo, *Inquisizione romana e Controriforma: Studi sul cardinal Giovanni Morone (1509–80) ed il suo processo d'eresia*, 395.

2 See Chapter 2, notes 96 and 98. Recently, historians have illustrated the importance of a nuanced approach for even the most seemingly dogmatic of the Catholic 'intransigents'.

See Giorgio Caravale, *Beyond the Inquisition: Ambrogio Catarino Politi and the Origins of the Counter-Reformation*, trans. Don Weinstein (Notre Dame, IN: University of Notre Dame Press, 2017).

3 Hudon, 'Religion and Society in Early Modern Italy', 794.

4 Silvana Seidel Menchi, 'The Age of Reformation and Counter-Reformation in Italian Historiography, 1939–2009', *Archiv für Reformationsgeschichte* 100, no. 1 (2009): 193.

5 See the catalogue entry in Giandomenico Romanelli and Giorgio Fossaluzza, eds., 'Un Cinquecento inquieto: da Cima da Conegliano al rogo di Riccardo Perucolo', Exhibition Catalogue, Palazzo Sarcinelli, Conegliano, 1 March–8 June 2014 (Venice: Marsilio, 2014), 190–93.

6 See, for example, Lionello Puppi, *Un trono di fuoco: arte e martirio di un pittore eretico del Cinquecento* (Rome: Donzelli, 1995); Achille Olivieri, 'Dipingere ed immaginar: arte ed eresia nel Cinquecento: Riccardo Perucolo', *Odeo Olimpico* 22 (1995–96): 99–109; Romanelli and Fossaluzza, 'Un Cinquecento inquieto. Da Cima da Conegliano al rogo di Riccardo Perucolo'; Giandomenico Romanelli, *Il pittore prigioniero* (Venice: Marsilio, 2014). A new edition of Puppi's text appeared in 2015. Similar to Perucolo, the Veronese painter Ventura Caliari was also given the capital sentence in 1584. See Gino Benzoni, *Venezia nell'età della Controriforma* (Milan: Mursia, 1973), 7. A second painter from Verona, Girolamo Vaienti, was accused of heresy in 1559. See Giulio Sancassani, 'Il pittore Girolamo Vaienti da Vicenza in carcere a Verona per eresia nel 1559', *Atti e memorie dell'Accademia di Agricoltura, Scienze e Lettere di Verona* 26, no. 6 (1976): 191–95. Massimo de Massimi, a miniature painter in Padua, was denounced for making heretical statements, but this had nothing to do with his artistic production. See Philipp Fehl and Marilyn Perry, 'Painting and the Inquisition at Venice: Three Forgotten Files', in *Interpretazioni veneziane: studi di storia dell'arte in honore di Michelangelo Muraro*, ed. David Rosand (Venice: Arsenale Editrice, 1984), 376, note 6. In Venice, an itinerant pedlar of the name Battista Amai, who created small dolls and sold his wares around the Rialto, was arrested by the Inquisition in 1572 for heretical beliefs. See Martin, *Venice's Hidden Enemies*, 158, 210–11; Rosa M. Salzberg, 'The Margins in the Centre: Working Around Rialto in Sixteenth-Century Venice', in *The Place of the Social Margins*, ed. Andrew Spicer and Jane L. Stevens Crawshaw (London: Routledge, 2016), 139.

7 Recently discussed by Marsha Libina, *Sebastiano del Piombo and the Sacred Image: Mediating the Divine in the Age of Reform* (Turnhout: Brepols, 2022), 20.

8 Indeed, in 1573, the Inquisition reminded Veronese of the polemical use of images in Germany and 'other places infected with heresy' during his interrogation. For Friuli, see Carlo Ginzburg, *The Night Battles: Witchcraft & Agrarian Cults in the Sixteenth & Seventeenth Centuries*, trans. John Tedeschi and Anne Tedeschi (London: Routledge & Kegan Paul, 1983).

9 See Massimo Firpo, *Artisti, gioiellieri, eretici: il mondo di Lorenzo Lotto tra Riforma e Controriforma* (Rome: Laterza, 2004). The introduction to Firpo's monograph provides a useful and entertaining literature review on scholarly approaches to the question of Lotto's orthodoxy, as does Massimo Firpo, 'Storia religiosa e storia dell'arte. I casi di Jacopo Pontormo e Lorenzo Lotto', in *Storia per parole e per immagini*, ed. Ugo Rozzo and Mino Gabriele (Udine: Forum, 2006), 213–34. It should be noted that Firpo criticises attempts to portray Lotto as a straightforward Protestant. The same author has also interpreted the oeuvres of other painters including Pontormo and Battista Franco primarily in terms of dissent. Massimo Firpo, *Gli affreschi di Pontormo a San Lorenzo: eresia, politica e cultura nella Firenze di Cosimo I* (Turin: Einaudi, 1997); Firpo and Biferali, *Battista Franco 'pittore viniziano' nella cultura artistica e nella vita religiosa del Cinquecento*; Firpo and Biferali, *Immagini ed eresie nell'Italia del Cinquecento*.

10 See Renzo Fontana, '"Solo, senza fidel governo et molto inquieto de la mente": Testimonianze archivistiche su alcuni amici di Lotto processati per eresia', in *Lorenzo Lotto. Atti del convegno internazionale di studi per il V centenario della nascita, Asolo, 18–21*

September, 1980, ed. Pietro Zampetti and Vittorio Sgarbi (Treviso: Comitato per la celebrazioni lottesche, 1981), 279–97; Firpo, *Artisti, gioiellieri, eretici*; Firpo, 'Storia religiosa e storia dell'arte. I casi di Jacopo Pontormo e Lorenzo Lotto'.

11 For the Suardi cycle, see, in particular, Francesca Cortesi Bosco, *Gli affreschi dell'Oratorio Suardi: Lorenzo Lotto nella crisi della Riforma* (Bergamo: Bollis, 1980); Francesca Cortesi Bosco, 'Riforma, religiosità, arte, alchimia negli affreschi di Lorenzo Lotto dell'Oratorio Suardi di Trescore', *Notizie da Palazzo Albani* 9 (1980): 28–38; Francesca Cortesi Bosco, 'Il problema della posizione religiosa di Lorenzo Lotto', *Notizie da Palazzo Albani* 13, no. 1 (1984): 81–89. More recently, see Stephen J. Campbell, *The Endless Periphery: Toward a Geopolitics of Art in Lorenzo Lotto's Italy* (Chicago: University of Chicago Press, 2019), 181–93. Even though the orthodox nature of the fresco cycle is obvious (it should be stressed that it depicts heretics being brusquely vanquished by the Doctors of the Church), Maria Calì argued vigorously against the analysis of the cycle presented by Cortesi Bosco, and instead interpreted the frescoes somewhat unconvincingly with reference to the *Deharmonia mundi* of Francesco Zorzi (which was still unpublished in 1524). See Maria Calì, 'La "religione" di Lorenzo Lotto', in *Lorenzo Lotto: atti del convengo internazionale di studi per il V centenario della nascita, Asolo, 18–21 September, 1980*, ed. Pietro Zampetti and Vittorio Sgarbi (Treviso: Comitato per la celebrazioni lottesche, 1981), 243–77.

12 The oratory was dedicated to Brigid and Barbara, but the choice of the Irish Brigid is to the best of my knowledge a very unusual one for this period and location. Cortesi Bosco, *Gli affreschi dell'Oratorio Suardi*, 12.

13 The inscription is now damaged but was transcribed in the past. Cortesi Bosco, *Gli affreschi dell'Oratorio Suardi*, 13.

14 On the right side of the fresco a further figure is unnamed, and two others represent 'pagans' and 'Jews'. Cortesi Bosco, *Gli affreschi dell'Oratorio Suardi*, 70–73; Peter Humfrey, *Lorenzo Lotto* (New Haven, CT: Yale University Press, 1997), 77–78.

15 See, in particular, the analysis of Campbell, *The Endless Periphery*, 186–90.

16 Pope Leo X's bull of 1520, *Exurge domini*, which denounced Luther and likened him to a wild boar destroying the vineyard of the Lord, was directly connected to the iconography of the Suardi chapel by Cortesi Bosco, 'Il problema della posizione religiosa di Lorenzo Lotto'. For arguments against this clear-cut connection, see Adriano Prosperi, ed., 'The Religious Crisis in Early Sixteenth-Century Italy', in *Lorenzo Lotto: Rediscovered Master of the Renaissance*, Exhibition Catalogue, National Gallery of Art, Washington, 2 November 1997–1 March 1998, Accademia Carrara di Belle Arti, Bergamo, 2 April–28 June 1998, Galeries nationales du Grand Palais, Paris, 12 October 1998–11 January 1999 (Washington, DC: National Gallery of Art, 1997), 21–26.

17 Cortesi Bosco, *Gli affreschi dell'Oratorio Suardi*, 8.

18 The hypothesis put forward by Cortesi Bosco, *Gli affreschi dell'Oratorio Suardi*, 3–6. The location of the chapel is discussed in further detail by Carlo Pirovano, 'Ego vitis vos palmites', in *Lotto: gli affreschi di Trescore*, ed. Carlo Pirovano (Milan: Electa, 1997), 35–36.

19 Most recently, the influence and deliberate subversion of Raphael's *Transfiguration* of 1519 by Lotto for the figure of Christ was noted by Campbell, *The Endless Periphery*, 185–86. The impact of Guadenzio Ferrari on the Suardi Chapel was explored by Cortesi Bosco, *Gli affreschi dell'Oratorio Suardi*, 46–53.

20 For the development of the iconography, see Gertrud Schiller, *Iconography of Christian Art* (London: Lund Humphries, 1971), vol. 1, 15–21. Note that at Nicaea II, Jeremiah 12:10 was referenced when the Council declared 'they had the effrontery to criticise the beauty pleasing to God established in the holy monuments ... They were those of whom God calls out by prophecy, '*Many pastors have destroyed my vine, they have defiled my portion.*' Tanner, *Decrees of the Ecumenical Councils*, vol. 1: 133.

21 See Myrtalē Acheimastou-Potamianou et al., *Byzantine and Post-Byzantine Art* (Athens: Ministry of Culture, 1986), 101–4, cat. 101; Apostolos G. Mantas, 'The Iconographic Subject "Christ the Vine" in Byzantine and Post-byzantine Art', *Δελτίον Χριστιανικής*

Αρχαιολογικής Εταιρείας 24 (2003): 348. For two late seventeenth-century icons of Christ the Vine and the Tree of Jesse in the collection of the Greek Institute in Venice, see Manolēs Chatzēdakēs, *Icônes de Saint-Georges des Grecs et de la collection de l'Institut*, Bibliothèque de l'Institut hellénique d'études byzantines et post-byzantines de Venise, no. 1 (Venice: Neri Pozza, 1962), 148–49, cats. 128, 129.

22 Athanasios D. Kominēs, *Patmos: Treasures of the Monastery* (Athens: Ekdotikē Athēnōn, 1988), 225–26; Mantas, 'The Iconographic Subject "Christ the Vine" in Byzantine and Post-Byzantine Art', 354–55.

23 Mentioned in Claudio Bellinati et al., *La Basilica del Santo: Storia e Arte* (Padua: De Luca, Messaggero di S. Antonio, 1994), 292; Enrico Maria Dal Pozzolo, 'Alcune precisazioni intorno al "Lignum Crucis" di Luca Antonio Busati e all'iconografia della passione in ambito francescano', *Il Santo* 30 (1990): 107–14; Enrico Maria Dal Pozzolo, 'Anatomia di un S. Girolamo (e una postilla)', *Il Santo* 32 (1992): 63–82.

24 Dal Pozzolo, 'Alcune precisazioni intorno al "Lignum Crucis" di Luca Antonio Busati e all'iconografia della passione in ambito francescano', 112.

25 Recently published in Eire, *Reformations: The Early Modern World*, 745.

26 Lotto's authorship is disputed, but supporters of the hypothesis underline the similarities between this design and that of the intarsias for Bergamo cathedral of 1531. See Giovanni Romano, 'La Bibbia di Lotto', *Paragone* 27, nos. 317–19 (1976): 82–91; Humfrey, *Lorenzo Lotto*, 114. Gentili argues that Lotto may have contributed a drawing for the frontispiece to his friend Brucioli, but that there is not enough evidence to show that he executed it personally. Augusto Gentili, 'Lorenzo Lotto, la questione della religione e l'indipendenza intellettuale', *Bergomum* 113 (2019): 51, note 11.

27 Campbell, *The Endless Periphery*, 192–93.

28 Cortesi Bosco, *Gli affreschi dell'Oratorio Suardi*, 124–28.

29 At the Diet of Worms in 1521 Luther's portrait was also burnt. Robert W. Scribner, *Popular Culture and Popular Movements in Reformation Germany* (London: Hambledon Press, 1987), 326.

30 Humfrey, *Lorenzo Lotto*, 140–41, 177; Firpo, 'Storia religiosa e storia dell'arte. I casi di Jacopo Pontormo e Lorenzo Lotto', 221.

31 See Chapter 3, note 97.

32 Lotto's personality is sensitively analysed by Humfrey, *Lorenzo Lotto*, 145–49.

33 For the project, see Alessandro Serafini, 'Gian Matteo Giberti e il Duomo di Verona: Il programma, il contesto', *Venezia Cinquecento* 6, no. 11 (1996): 75–161; Alessandro Serafini, 'Gian Matteo Giberti e il Duomo di Verona. 2: Gli affreschi di Francesco Torbido', *Venezia Cinquecento* 8, no. 15 (1998): 21–142; Paul Davies and David Hemsoll, *Michele Sanmicheli* (Milan: Electa, 2004), 101–14; Nagel, *The Controversy of Renaissance Art*, chap. 6.

34 For Giberti, see Adriano Prosperi, *Tra evangelismo e controriforma: G. M. Giberti, 1495–1543* (Roma: Edizioni di storia e letteratura, 1969). For his visitations, see Don Antonio Fasani, *Riforma pretridentina della diocesi di Verona: Visite pastorali del vescovo G.M. Giberti 1525–1542*, 3 vols. (Vicenza: Istituto per le ricerche di storia sociale e di storia religiosa, 1989).

35 Giberti was accused of political intrigue with the French by the Venetian State and in 1542 he had to justify himself to the Council of Ten. It was during this *Giustificazione* that he defended himself from the critiques of over-expenditure. See Giovanni Battista Pighi, *G. M. Giberti, Vescovo di Verona* (Verona: Marchiori, 1900), 182; Nagel, *The Controversy of Renaissance Art*, 254.

36 Borromeo was so impressed by Giberti's achievements that he chose as his vicar general Nicolò Ormaneto, a former protégé of Giberti and future bishop of Padua. See Paolo Preto, 'Un aspetto della riforma cattolica nel Veneto: l'episcopato padovano di Niccolò Ormaneto', *Studi veneziani* 11 (1969): 325–63. For some important reflections on the relationship between Giberti and Borromeo, see Adriano Prosperi, 'Note in margine a un opuscolo di Gian Matteo Giberti', *Critica Storica* 4 (1965): 373–74.

37 Davies and Hemsoll, *Michele Sanmicheli*, 113–14.

38 See Simon Ditchfield, 'Carlo Borromeo in the Construction of Roman Catholicism as a World Religion', *Studia Borromaica* 25 (2011): 3–23 Ditchfield, 'Tridentine Catholicism', 21. As Ditchfield puts it in the 2011 publication, 'if the decrees and canons of the Council of Trent might be considered the "theory" of Tridentine Catholicism, then the AEM should perhaps be viewed as a practical "how to" manual for the conscientious prelate'. Ditchfield's comments in light of Borromeo's impact on church architecture have recently been discussed by Allen, *Transforming the Church Interior*, 295–96.

39 Giberti was a friend and collaborator of Canossa. After his death he convinced Pope Paul III to approve a modification to Canossa's will in order to divert 500 ducats to the building of the presbytery in Verona. An inscription in the paving notes that Bartolomeo and Galeazzo Canossa, nephews of Lodovico, also helped finance the project. Sanmicheli may have become involved in the commission due to his connections to the Canossa family as designer of their palace in Verona. The nature of the patronage is clarified by Davies and Hemsoll, *Michele Sanmicheli*, 106–7.

40 A broader analysis of the bishop's pastoral activities also evinces this, since alongside his proclivity for the eucharist, Giberti was notably dedicated to the Virgin Mary. During a pastoral visit of 1530 he ordered the construction of a new oratory for the miracle-working image of the Madonna della Corona that supposedly appeared on Monte Baldo in 1522. See Serafini, 'Gian Matteo Giberti e il Duomo di Verona', 54. In Verona cathedral he supported the cult of the Madonna del Popolo; and in his 1542 *Constitutiones* – which provided a practical guide for the administration and reform of a diocese based on his own tried and tested methods – Giberti advised that upon leaving a church one should stop to sing either an *Alma*, a *Salve* or a *Regina coeli*. Gian Matteo Giberti, *Constitutiones* (Verona: Antonio Putelleto, 1542), 9r–v, 31r.

41 See *Alcune Interogationi delle cose della fede & del stato overo vivere de Christiani* (Verona: Antonio da Portesco, 1540), chap. 32. Thanks to the Biblioteca Civica of Verona for kindly digitising a copy of this for me. Discussed by Serafini, 'Gian Matteo Giberti e il Duomo di Verona', 122. Serafini argues that through this text Giberti was inadvertently providing a justification for his own expenses in the choir of Verona cathedral.

42 Eck's hugely popular 1525 anti-Lutheran *Enchiridion* mentioned Giberti in the afterword, who had encouraged Eck in his literary endeavours. For the correspondence, see Prosperi, *Tra evangelismo e controriforma*, 126–27.

43 Francesco Filiberto, *Ragionare pio, e catholico della veneratione debita a Santi, composto da Pier Francesco Philiberto Veronese*, Biblioteca Civica di Verona, Cinq. D. 1247. 10 (Venice, 1542). Quoted in Serafini, 'Gian Matteo Giberti e il Duomo di Verona', 120–21. For Filiberto, see Prosperi, 'Seminario sulle visite pastorali del vescovo G. M. Giberti (1525–42)', 176. A letter from Contarini to Cardinal Ercole Gonzaga of 1539 references a priest who had become an enemy of Giberti over the question of ecclesiastical benefices. If this letter indeed refers to Filiberto, then it could provide the real motive for the falling out. See Edmondo Solmi, 'Lettere inedite di Gasparo Contarini nel carteggio del cardinale Ercole Gonzaga', *Nuovo Archivio Veneto* 7, no. 14 (1904): 257.

44 See Gabriele de Rosa's introduction for Fasani, *Visite pastorali del vescovo G. M. Giberti*, XV–XXXI.

45 Davies and Hemsoll, *Michele Sanmicheli*, 112. For some examples of tabernacles being placed on high altars that predate this, see Nagel, *The Controversy of Renaissance Art*, 206. At San Marco in Venice the Pala d'Oro remained on the high altar, but in 1518 the sacrament altar behind it was commissioned from Lorenzo Bregno by the Procuratori di San Marco de Supra. The Sienese architect and theorist Francesco di Giorgio Martini wrote about a church space focused around the tabernacle on the high altar already in the fifteenth century. See Allen, *Transforming the Church Interior*, 289.

46 This is also demonstrated by Giberti's *Constitutiones*. See the following sections in particular, all of which are concerned with the eucharist: Giberti, *Constitutiones*, 11r–v, 23v, 25r–v, 30r–33v. In addition, the *Breve ricordo* of 1530 intended for the instruction of the diocesan

clergy noted that the host should be kept in a clean and secure place under lock and key and that a lamp should be left burning there during the night. See Prosperi, 'Note in margine a un opuscolo di Gian Matteo Giberti', 398.

47 Giberti's comments appear in the *Breve Ricordo* of 1530. See Prosperi, 'Note in margine a un opuscolo di Gian Matteo Giberti', 395; Prosperi, *Tra evangelismo e controriforma*, 270–71.

48 Nagel, *The Controversy of Renaissance Art*, 240.

49 Prior to his flight the pair had been close friends, although Giberti had encouraged Ochino to give himself up the tribunal in Rome. Fragnito argued that Giberti deliberately sought to buy Ochino time to complete his flight so as not to betray him. It may also be the case that Giberti feared that he would implicate their friends and contacts. Gigliola Fragnito, 'Gli "spirituali" e la fuga di Bernardino Ochino', *Rivista storica italiana* 84 (1972): 783.

50 Elisabeth G. Gleason, *Gasparo Contarini: Venice, Rome, and Reform* (Berkeley: University of California Press, 1993), 14–18.

51 The possibility was first raised by Serafini, 'Gian Matteo Giberti e il Duomo di Verona', 127. It was referred to in stronger terms by Nagel, *The Controversy of Renaissance Art*, 240.

52 Nagel, *The Controversy of Renaissance Art*, 240. Nagel does point out that Giberti never opposed papal authority or questioned the legitimacy of the sacraments.

53 These ideas are close to those of Contarini, who emphasised the importance of faith and God's freely given grace, yet never questioned the validity of the sacraments and defended papal supremacy in his *De potestate pontifices, quod divinitus sit tradita* of the early 1530s. See Gleason, *Gasparo Contarini*, 107–10; Oliver Logan, 'Grace and Justification: Some Italian Views of the Sixteenth and Early Seventeenth Centuries', *Journal of Ecclesiastical History* 20, no. 1 (1969): 67–78.

54 Fontana, '"Solo, senza fidel governo et molto inquieto de la mente": Testimonianze archivistiche su alcuni amici di Lotto processati per eresia', 287.

55 Pointed out by Douglas-Scott, 'Prohibition of Text and License of Image: Painters and the Vernacular Bible in Counter-Reformation Venice', 239.

56 Giberti was also criticised for practices such as laymen preaching and frequent communion. Prosperi thus argued that efforts to frame Giberti as the 'ideal bishop' ignore the resistance he encountered in his own lifetime. See Prosperi, 'Note in margine a un opuscolo di Gian Matteo Giberti'.

57 Mantovano declared that 'the number of saints in Friuli makes me despair'. Adriano Prosperi, 'Un processo per eresia a Verona verso la metà del Cinquecento', *Quaderni Storici* 15 (1970): 779–80. As noted by Prosperi, in Luigi Lippomano's *Confirmatione e stabilimento di tutti i dogmi catholici* (Venice, 1554) arguments regarding the saints analogous to those of Mantovano were voiced by heretics in the text.

58 Nagel, *The Controversy of Renaissance Art*, 197; Grendler, *The Roman Inquisition and the Venetian Press*, 86; Massimo Firpo, *Juan de Valdés and the Italian Reformation*, trans. Richard Bates (Burlington: Ashgate, 2015), 150.

59 The Capuchin friar wrote that it was Contarini who indirectly warned him against travelling to Rome where he would have faced charges of heresy. Fragnito, 'Gli "spirituali" e la fuga di Bernardino Ochino', 782–83.

60 Anne Jacobson Schutte, *Pier Paolo Vergerio: The Making of an Italian Reformer* (Geneva: Droz, 1977), 44.

61 Venice reached its highest population before the 1575–77 plague. Estimates are of a populace of 120,000 in 1500 and 190,000 prior to 1575. Frederic Chapin Lane, *Venice: A Maritime Republic* (Baltimore: Johns Hopkins University Press, 1973), 19.

62 The literature on the *spirituali* and evangelism is extensive. A classic study is provided by Paolo Simoncelli, *Evangelismo italiano del Cinquecento: questione religiosa e nicodemismo politico* (Rome: Istituto storico italiano per l'età moderna e contemporanea, 1979). Particularly useful for a cogent literature review is Camilla Russell, 'Religious Reforming Currents in Sixteenth-Century Italy: The Spirituali and the Tridentine Debates over Church Reform', *Journal of Religious History* 38, no. 4 (December 2014): 457–75. The complexities of religious

life in the early sixteenth century were explored by Eva-Maria Jung, 'On the Nature of Evangelism in Sixteenth-Century Italy', *Journal of the History of Ideas* 14, no. 4 (1953): 511–27. A number of her assumptions were criticised by other historians, such as Elisabeth G. Gleason, 'On the Nature of Sixteenth-Century Italian Evangelism: Scholarship, 1953–1978', *Sixteenth Century Journal* 9, no. 3 (1978): 3–26. Cantimori specified three distinct phases of Italian heretical history; see Delio Cantimori, *Prospettive di storia ereticale italiana del Cinquecento* (Bari: Laterza, 1960). These were evangelism from c. 1513 to 1541/42, the crisis of evangelism from 1541/42 to c. 1560, and 'the second generation: their hopes and defeat' from c. 1560 to c. 1580. While noting the importance of Cantimori's studies, Schutte argued that the 'crisis' of Italian heretics in 1541/42 was simplistic. See Anne Jacobson Schutte, 'Periodization of Sixteenth-Century Italian Religious History: The Post-Cantimori Paradigm Shift', *Journal of Modern History* 61, no. 2 (1989): 269–84.

63 The very existence of Italian evangelism has been questioned by scholars such as Susanna P. Rambaldi, 'Ancora sull'evangelismo italiano: Categoria o invenzione storiografica?', *Società e storia*, no. 18 (1982): 935–67. The most vocal critic of the terms *spirituali* and *intransigenti* is Hudon, 'Religion and Society in Early Modern Italy'.

64 Letter of 28 August 1542 from Giberti to Cardinal Ercole Gonzaga. Fragnito, 'Gli "spirituali" e la fuga di Bernardino Ochino', 777.

65 Russell, 'Religious Reforming Currents in Sixteenth-Century Italy', 460, note 12.

66 Pier Paolo Vergerio's oration to Doge Francesco Donà of November 1545 noted that for almost three or four years the title had been on sale in Venice. See Benedetto Da Mantova, *Il Beneficio di Cristo: con le versioni del secolo XVI. Documenti e testimonianze*, ed. Salvatore Caponetto (Florence: Sansoni; Chicago: Newberry Library, 1972), 438–39. For the editions, see Grendler, *The Roman Inquisition and the Venetian Press*, 81–82. See also Carlo Ginzburg and Adriano Prosperi, 'Le due redazioni del "Beneficio di Cristo"', in *Eresia e riforma nell'Italia del cinquecento*, Biblioteca del Corpus Reformatorum Italicorum, Miscellanea I (Florence: Sansoni; Chicago: Newberry Library, 1974), 135–204; Carlo Ginzburg and Adriano Prosperi, *Giochi di pazienza: un seminario sul Beneficio di Cristo* (Turin: Einuadi, 1975); Philip McNair, 'Benedetto da Mantova, Marcantonio Flaminio, and the "Beneficio di Cristo": A Developing Twentieth-Century Debate Reviewed', *Modern Language Review* 82, no. 3 (1987): 614–24.

67 Ambrogio Catarino Politi, *Compendio d'errori, e inganni Luterani, contenuti in un Libretto, Senza nome de l'Autore, intitolato, Trattato utilissimo del benefitio di Christo crucifisso* (Rome, 1544). For Catarino, see, in particular, Caravale, *Beyond the Inquisition*; Da Mantova, *Il Beneficio di Cristo*, 347–422. For the Index, see Grendler, *The Roman Inquisition and the Venetian Press*, 86.

68 A figure of 10,000 copies is more realistic, as estimated by Grendler, *The Roman Inquisition and the Venetian Press*, 82, note 58.

69 Firpo and Marcatto, *Il processo inquisitoriale del Cardinal Giovanni Morone: edizione critica*, 2, part 1:465.

70 Elena Ciletti, 'On the Destruction of Pontormo's Frescoes at S. Lorenzo and the Possibility that Parts Remain', *Burlington Magazine* 121, no. 921 (1979): 764–70.

71 Charles De Tolnay, 'Les fresques de Pontormo dans le choeur de San Lorenzo à Florence: essai de reconstitution', *La Critica d'arte* 9 (1950): 49.

72 Janet Cox-Rearick, *The Drawings of Pontormo* (Cambridge, MA: Harvard University Press, 1964), vol. 1: 318–27.

73 Raffaella Corti, 'Pontormo a San Lorenzo: un episodio figurativo dello "spiritualismo" italiano', *Richerche di storia dell'arte* 6 (1977): 5–36; Salvatore Caponetto, *La Riforma protestante nell'Italia del Cinquecento* (Turin: Claudiana, 1992), 110–14; Firpo, *Gli affreschi di Pontormo a San Lorenzo*, 93.

74 A warning against tying the frescoes too closely to a single written text is provided by both Carlo Falciani, 'Il Pontormo a San Lorenzo fra echi valdesiani e riflessi conciliari', in *Il Concilio di Trento e le arti 1563–2013: atti del convegno, Bologna, 10 dicembre 2013*, ed. Marinella

Pigozzi (Bologna: Bononia University Press, 2015), 54, and Jessica A. Maratsos, *Pontormo and the Art of Devotion in Renaissance Italy* (Cambridge: Cambridge University Press, 2021), 125.

75 Giorgio Vasari, *Lives of the Painters, Sculptors and Architects*, ed. David Ekserdjian, trans. Gaston du C. De Vere (New York: Alfred A. Knopf, 1996), vol. 2: 369–70.

76 Borghini, *Il Riposo*, 82.

77 Borghini, *Il Riposo*, 81.

78 Giuseppe Richa, *Notizie istoriche delle chiese fiorentine, divise ne' suoi quartieri*, vol. 5, part 1 (Florence: Pietro Gaetano Viviani, 1757), 29. Negative appraisals of the frescoes had continued until the point of their destruction. See Ciletti, 'On the Destruction of Pontormo's Frescoes at S. Lorenzo and the Possibility That Parts Remain'.

79 Francesco Bocchi, *Le bellezze della città di Firenze* (1591), ed. Giovanni Cinelli (Florence: Giovanni Gugliantini, 1677), 516.

80 Borghini, *Il Riposo*, 482–83.

81 That Borghini's criticisms of the cycle might have alluded to its potentially pro-Lutheran elements was suggested by David Franklin, *Painting in Renaissance Florence, 1500–1550* (New Haven, CT: Yale University Press, 2001), 205.

82 First cited by Caponetto in Da Mantova, *Il Beneficio di Cristo*, 502–3. See also Firpo, *Gli affreschi di Pontormo a San Lorenzo*, 163.

83 See Firpo, *Gli affreschi di Pontormo a San Lorenzo*.

84 The problems with the dating were raised by Carlo Falciani, *Pontormo: disegni degli Uffizi* (Florence: Leo Olschki, 1996), 164.

85 Elizabeth Pilliod, *Pontormo at San Lorenzo: Art, History, Ritual. The Making and Meaning of a Lost Renaissance Masterpiece* (London: Harvey Miller, 2022), 12.

86 Pilliod writes that 'it cannot be ascertained if Riccio's acquisition of the *Beneficio* in 1557 reflected his thinking in the 1540s'. Pilliod, *Pontormo at San Lorenzo*, 104. On page 106 Pilliod agrees that Vasari's critique of the cycle may reflect the changed religious climate in Florence by the mid 1560s.

87 Noted also by Anton Boschloo, *The Limits of Artistic Freedom: Criticism of Art in Italy from 1500–1800* (Leiden: Primavers Pers, 2008), 80.

88 Vasari frequented followers of the Spanish theologian Juan de Valdés and he was familiar with the *spirituali*. See Alessandro Nova, 'L'Ultima Cena di Giorgio Vasari per il convento delle Murate: contesto, committenza e un episodio della crisi religiosa del Cinquecento', in *Dall'alluvione alla rinascita: il restauro dell'Ultima Cena di Giorgio Vasari. Santa Croce cinquant'anni dopo (1966–2016)*, Problemi di conservazione e restauro. 47, ed. Roberto Bellucci, Marco Ciatti, and Cecila Frosinini (Florence: Edifir edizioni, 2016), 30.

89 Nova, 'L'Ultima Cena di Giorgio Vasari', 30. The final inscription on the painting records Christ's exhortation at the Last Supper: HOC FACITE IN MEAM COMMEMORATIONEM (do this in memory of me).

90 Nova, 'L'Ultima Cena di Giorgio Vasari', 28–30; Kate Lowe, *Nuns' Chronicles and Convent Culture in Renaissance and Counter-Reformation Italy* (Cambridge: Cambridge University Press, 2003), 359–61.

91 Richard Harprath, *Italienische Zeichnungen des 16. Jahrhunderts aus eigenem Besitz*, Exhibition Catalogue, Staatliche Graphische Sammlung, Munich, 1 July–28 August 1977 (Munich: Kastner & Callwey, 1977), 159–60, cat. 111.

92 Nova, 'L'Ultima Cena di Giorgio Vasari', 31.

93 Vasari, *Lives of the Painters, Sculptors and Architects*, vol. 2: 368–69.

94 Elizabeth Pilliod, *Pontormo, Bronzino, Allori: A Genealogy of Florentine Art* (New Haven, CT: Yale University Press, 2001), 20.

95 Cosimo's policies towards the Church were already beginning to change in the late 1540s but decisively shifted after the election of the Medici Pope Pius IV in 1559. See Hall, *Renovation and Counter-Reformation*; Ludovica Sebregondi, 'Churches, Convents, Monasteries and Confraternities in Counter-Reformation Florence', in *The Cinquecento in Florence: 'Modern*

Manner' and Counter-Reformation, ed. Carlo Falciani and Antonio Natali, Exhibition Catalogue, Palazzo Strozzi, Florence, 21 September 2017–21 January 2018 (Florence: Mandragora, 2017), 107–17. See also chapter 8 of Allen, *Transforming the Church Interior.*

96 That Vasari criticised the cycle in order to distance himself from any suggestion of heterodoxy is noted by Philippe Costamagna, *Pontormo* (Milan: Electa, 1994), 93. Costamagna, unlike myself, believes that the San Lorenzo cycle illustrated the themes of the *Beneficio di Cristo*.

97 Pilliod argues that if the fresco had really been informed by heterodox ideas then they would have been destroyed sooner, rather than 200 years after the event. However, as we shall see in the next chapter it was highly unusual that existing devotional images were destroyed due to concerns relating to iconoclasm. Nevertheless, she rightly points out that they must have met the minimum requirements for survival. Pilliod, *Pontormo at San Lorenzo*, 106.

98 Vasari attributed the painting to Botticelli. He was the first to connect its patron directly to the iconography of the image, stating that the work was 'all from the design given to him by Matteo, who was a learned and able man'. Vasari, *Lives of the Painters, Sculptors and Architects*, vol. 1: 537.

99 Rolf Bagemihl, 'Francesco Botticini's Palmieri Altar-piece', *Burlington Magazine* 138, no. 1118 (1996): 311; Blunt, *Artistic Theory in Italy*, 109. Blunt stated that the authorities had ordered Botticini's painting to be covered between 1485 and 1500. Blunt cites Margaret Rooke's study, which stated that the painting was covered with a black veil and the chapel placed under an Interdict until c. 1745. See Matteo Palmieri, *Libro del poema chiamato Citta di vita composto da Matteo Palmieri Florentino*, ed. Margaret Rooke (Northampton, MA: Smith College, 1927), viii.

100 Bagemihl, 'Francesco Botticini's Palmieri Altar-piece', 311; Jennifer Sliwka, *Visions of Paradise: Botticini's Palmieri Altarpiece* (London: National Gallery Company, 2015), 98; Martin Kemp, *Visions of Heaven: Dante and the Art of Divine Light* (London: Lund Humphries, 2021), 190–95. Slikwa (p. 52) stresses that 'nothing in the altarpiece can be specifically identified as unorthodox'. Kemp believes the hierarchical interspersing of angels and mortals in the heavens closely reflects Palmieri's ideas of incarnated intelligences striving for salvation and notes that the patron must have been closely involved with the commission.

101 In 1657 Stefano Rosselli observed that the painting had been covered by a curtain 'for a long time', adding that this was 'out of envy or ignorance'. See Bagemihl, 'Francesco Botticini's Palmieri Altar-piece', 311. Bagemihl believes the veiling of the painting was a 'subsidiary legend', and that it was probably only covered by a curtain to limit its exposure to feast days. Roselli's claim was embellished by Richa, who wrote that the image was believed to depict a false hierarchy of semi-human angels (reflecting the contested theology of Palmieri's text) and as a result it had been covered up and the chapel placed under Interdict. The church of San Pier was demolished in the 1780s. Giuseppe Richa, *Notizie istoriche delle chiese fiorentine, divise ne' suoi quartieri*, vol. 1 (Florence: Pietro Gaetano Viviani, 1754), 161.

102 Vasari, *Lives of the Painters, Sculptors and Architects*, vol. 1: 537.

103 Douglas-Scott, 'Prohibition of Text and License of Image: Painters and the Vernacular Bible in Counter-Reformation Venice', 240. Scott points out that it is possible that there was some pre-publication censorship, since publishers had to include woodcut illustrations in their applications to the Senate for printing privileges.

104 Charles Hope, 'Altarpieces and the Requirements of Patrons', in *Christianity and the Renaissance: Image and Religious Imagination in the Quattrocento*, ed. Timothy Verdon and John Henderson (Syracuse, NY: Syracuse University Press, 1990), 536.

105 T. J. Clark, *Heaven on Earth: Painting and the Life to Come* (London: Thames and Hudson, 2018), 165.

106 Andreas Tacke, *Der katholische Cranach* (Mainz: Von Zabern, 1992); Andreas Tacke, 'With Cranach's Help: Counter-Reformation Art before the Council of Trent', in *Cranach*, ed.

Bodo Brinkmann, Exhibition Catalogue, Städel Museum, Frankfurt Am Main, 23 November 2007–17 February 2008, Royal Academy of Arts, London, 8 March–8 June 2008 (London: Thames & Hudson, 2007), 81–89.

107 This is demonstrated by the activities of the Inquisition in Venice. From 1547 to 1582 more than 717 individuals accused of Lutheranism were tried among its first 1,200 cases, plus 30 Anabaptists, 68 cases of 'general heresy', 20 of eating meat in Lent, and almost 90 of reading or possessing prohibited books. In the table of sentences issued from 1580 to 1582 by the Venetian Inquisition, 59 Protestants were charged with heresy, compared with just 15 in the Duchy of Milan and one in the Kingdom of Naples. See John Tedeschi and William Monter, 'Toward a Statistical Profile of the Italian Inquisitions', in *The Inquisition in Early Modern Europe: Studies on Sources and Methods*, ed. John Tedeschi and Gustav Henningsen (DeKalb: Northern Illinois University Press, 1986), 133, 139. As a complement to the data, see also Andrea del Col, 'Problemi per la catalogazione e repertoriazione unificata degli atti processuali dell'Inquisizione romana', *Critica Storica* 25, no. 1 (1988): 155–64.

108 Achille Olivieri, *Riforma ed eresia a Vicenza nel Cinquecento* (Rome: Herder, 1992), 8. As religion became increasingly regulated, one by one the Vicentine group took flight or were imprisoned, with Trissino fleeing for Chiavenna in 1563.

109 The painting was first mentioned in an inventory of the king's collection of 1547 and so it must have been produced at some point between 1542, the date of an earlier inventory that does not mention the painting, and the artist's death in 1544. See Philip Pouncey, 'Girolamo da Treviso in the Service of Henry VIII', *Burlington Magazine* 95 no. 603 (1953): 208, 210–11; Paolo Ervas, *Girolamo da Treviso* (Saonara: Il Prato, 2014); Pietro Caiazza, *Un candeliere valdese nel 1540? 'La Lapidazione del Papa' di Girolamo da Treviso il Giovane* (Salerno: Scala, 2017).

110 Diarmaid MacCulloch, *The Later Reformation in England, 1547–1603*, 2nd ed. (Basingstoke: Palgrave Macmillan, 2001), 57. For Girolamo's career in England, see Vasari, *Lives of the Painters, Sculptors and Architects*, vol. 1: 888–89; Alessandro Serafini, 'Girolamo da Treviso, il Giovane', in *Dizionario Biografico degli Italiani*, vol. 56 (Rome: Treccani, 2001), 594–95.

111 Vasari, *Lives of the Painters, Sculptors and Architects*, vol. 1: 888–89.

112 A letter of 1542 from Pietro Aretino congratulated Girolamo on his success, although his luck ran out when he was caught in cannon crossfire at the battle of Boulonge just two years later and was mortally wounded. Vasari reports that King Henry was so pleased with his work that he gave him 400 crowns per year. Vasari wrote that the catalyst for the move to England was Girolamo's annoyance at having lost out on an important commission in Bologna. Serafini hypothesised that he might have come to English attention through his *Presentation of the Virgin with Saint Thomas Becket* for the English students at San Salvador in Venice. See Vasari, *Lives of the Painters, Sculptors and Architects*, vol. 1: 888–89; Serafini, 'Girolamo da Treviso, il Giovane', 594.

113 'Many of the Italian "exiles" in French territories, such as the architect Sebastiano Serlio, were in fact undoubtedly heretics.' Sergio Marinelli, 'Adesioni e resistenze al Concilio di Trento nel territorio della Repubblica di Venezia', in *Il Concilio di Trento e le arti 1563–2013: Atti del convegno, Bologna, 10 dicembre 2013*, ed. Marinella Pigozzi (Bologna: Bononia University Press, 2015), 74. See also Luca Molà, *The Silk Industry of Renaissance Venice* (Baltimore: Johns Hopkins University Press, 2000), 50. Molà notes that Inquisition depositions show the emigration of silk weavers was prompted more by job opportunities than by religious faith.

114 For the Bologna grisailles, see Diana Bullen Presciutti, 'Miracles in Monochrome: Grisaille in Visual Hagiography', *Art History* 42, no. 5 (2019): 862–91.

115 Caiazza argued that the lit candle is symbolic of the Valdensian church. Yet he admits that this symbolism was used only much later by the Valdensians on the frontispiece of Valerio Grosso's 1640 *Lucerna Sacra*. Caiazza, *Un candeliere valdese nel 1540?*, 5, 17.

116 Observe the close resemblance between the figure of Mark, who clenches a stone above his head, ready to smash it down upon the pope below, and one of Stephen's tormentors in

the Genoese painting. The connection was first noted by Fabrizio Biferali in 2017: www.casadevelazquez.org/es/la-casa/novedad/tre-lapidazioni-a-confronto-raffaello-giulio-romano-e-girolamo-da-treviso (accessed 21 July 2023).

117 Andrew Cichy, 'English Catholic Music after the Reformation to 1750', in *Oxford Bibliographies*, 2014.

118 Manfredo Tafuri and Antonio Foscari, *L'armonia e i conflitti: la chiesa di San Francesco della Vigna nella Venezia del '500* (Turin: Einaudi, 1983), 131–32.

119 Deborah Howard and Anne Varick Lauder, 'New Light on Battista Franco in Venice: Part I; The Barbaro Chapel in S. Francesco Della Vigna and the Scuola del Nome di Gesù', *Burlington Magazine* 148, no. 1244 (2006): 747–53. More recently, see Firpo and Biferali, *Battista Franco 'pittore viniziano' nella cultura artistica e nella vita religiosa del Cinquecento*, 209–29.

120 The same point could also be made about contemporary documentary evidence such as wills, which are more likely to support a view of artists as orthodox rather than heterodox, since they are based upon formulas that correspond to dominant social mores and religious norms.

121 Fehl and Perry, 'Painting and the Inquisition at Venice: Three Forgotten Files', 375.

122 Bryan Mangrum and Giuseppe Scavizzi, *A Reformation Debate* (Toronto: CRRS Publications, 1991), 4. This situation began to change in the seventeenth century, when Lutheranism became an increasingly visually magnificent faith in areas such as Saxony; see Bridget Heal, *A Magnificent Faith: Art and Identity in Lutheran Germany* (Oxford: Oxford University Press, 2017).

123 Carel van Mander, *Dutch and Flemish Painters: Translation from the Schilderboeck*, ed. Constant van de Wall (New York: McFarlane, 1936), 205.

124 Mander, *Dutch and Flemish Painters*, 206. Freedberg pointed out that even for successful and wealthy artists this was not a happy time in the Netherlands, questioning who would have wanted to paint a picture when there was the risk that it would be decimated in the next round of iconoclasm. It is important to note that Freedberg does not see the impact of iconoclasm in the Netherlands as completely negative, noting the stimulus it had on other kinds of image-making. He also discusses committed Protestant artists like Frans Pourbus and Philips Galle. David Freedberg, 'Art after Iconoclasm', in *Art after Iconoclasm: Painting in the Netherlands between 1566 and 1585*, ed. Koenraad Jonckheere and Ruben Suykerbuyk (Turnhout: Brepols, 2012), 22.

125 Dürer wrote that 'they [all eager students of Art] will not be misled by those now amongst us who, in our own day, revile the Art of Painting and say that it is the servant to Idolatry. For a Christian would no more be led to superstition by a picture or effigy than an honest man to commit murder because he carries a weapon by his side. He must indeed be an unthinking man who would worship picture, wood or stone. A picture therefore brings more good than harm, when it is honourably, artistically and well made'. William Martin Conway, ed., *The Writings of Albrecht Dürer*, trans. William Martin Conway (New York: Philosophical Library, 1958), 212. For Erasmus' letter of introduction, see Hugh Honour and John Fleming, *The Visual Arts: A History*, 7th ed. (Upper Saddle River, NJ: Pearson Education, 2010), 463.

126 Martin, *Venice's Hidden Enemies*, 245.

CHAPTER TWO

NAKEDNESS AND THE LASCIVIOUS

The Boundaries of Decorum before and after the Council of Trent

That presumptuous painter, who has represented Saint Mark as he knew or could, in the judgment of everyone has made a great mistake. He hasn't represented an evangelist, but a man dressed up in a military fashion, not to say a monster of a man; I don't know what mercenary or barbarian he has represented. He is only missing a sword at his side and a quiver on his shoulder, and then he will be ready to slaughter and slit the throats of the masses, rather than calm them with his preaching of the divine word of Christ. On his head we do not see the venerable white hair of which the sacred scriptures speak, instead he is shown bald with a haughty expression. Under his nostrils he is abundantly hairy, with thick stubble and a head of unkempt hair that falls to his shoulders. It is truly frightening.[1]

On 12 July 1501 the deacon of the chapter of the cathedral of Udine, Giacomo di Marano, wrote to the Patriarch of Aquileia, Domenico Grimani (1461–1523, r. 1498–1517), to express his unhappiness with a recently completed altarpiece by the artist Giovanni Martini da Udine (c. 1470/75–1535) (Fig. 20). Marano's indignant reaction to the depiction of Saint Mark had shades of the Inquisition's later critique of Veronese's *Last Supper*, and we can well imagine him being similarly incensed if he had been presented with the iconographic novelties of Veronese's painting. In contrast to the instruments of enforcement that were available later in the century, Giacomo lacked the means to be able to do much about the altarpiece that he so despised, and it is still on display in the site for which it was intended. Although he appealed to his superior, the complaint was likely to have been in vain, considering the prominence of its patron: Antonio Loredan, who had been Lieutenant of Friuli until March of that year, and whose likeness may have been reflected in the

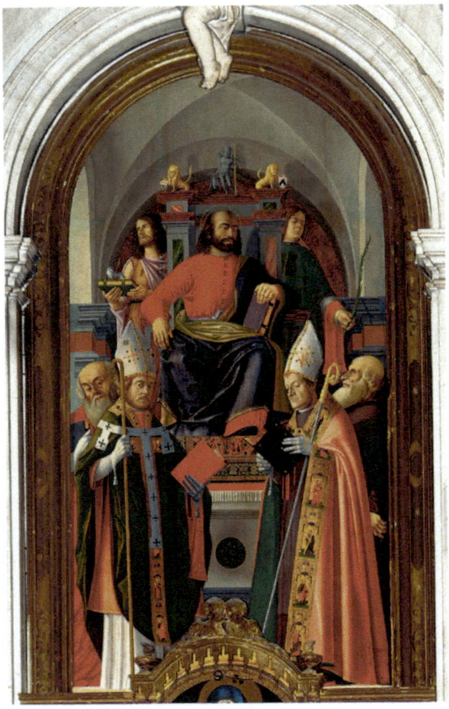

20. Giovanni Martini, *Saint Mark Enthroned with Saints,* 1500, Cathedral of Udine (Photo: Cameraphoto Arte, Venice/Art Resource, New York)

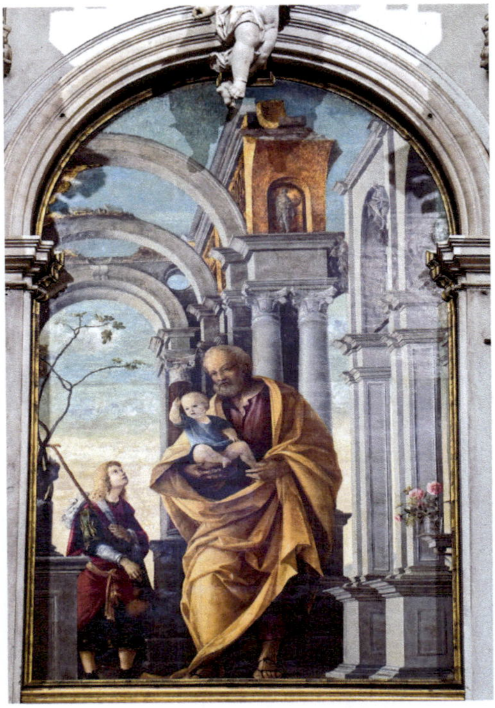

21. Pellegrino da San Daniele, *Saint Joseph,* 1500, Cathedral of Udine (Photo: Cattedrale di S. Maria Annunziata, Parrocchia S. Maria Annunziata, Udine/ Reproduced with permission of the Arcidiocesi di Udine, ufficio Arte Sacra e Beni culturali)

figure of the Evangelist Mark.[2] In contrast to his harsh judgment of Giovanni Martini's efforts, in the same letter the deacon expressed his satisfaction with a second altarpiece, which had also been commissioned by the Lieutenant and was painted by Pellegrino da San Daniele (c. 1467–1547) in 1500. Still displayed in the chapel next to Martini's work, here we see the aged Saint Joseph tenderly holding the Christ-child (Fig. 21). Due to the sweetness of the scene and the sympathetic representation of Joseph as the protector of the babe, it is perhaps unsurprising that the deacon praised it. It might have been similarly well received if it had been produced a century later, when the Counter-Reformation was in full swing. What this episode illustrates, then, is that although some of the mechanisms for controlling the arts did change in the Cinquecento, the expectation that images of the saints should respect iconographic norms did not.

In the previous chapter it was shown that devotional images with a subversive or potentially heretical message were small in number, as were those perceived to be theologically inaccurate. Yet unusual or strange iconographies of the saints or the biblical episodes presented more of a problem. In the opinion of the deacon, the artist had overstepped the mark in deciding to paint the saint with a bald head and stubble because he was no longer identifiable as the Evangelist. These artistic liberties, combined with the saint's stern expression, were thought capable of striking terror rather than reverence into the hearts of those who viewed the offending altarpiece. We know that some devotional images were indeed capable of inciting such a dramatic reaction from their spectators: in 1518 a sketch of the projected *Spedalingo Altarpiece* by Rosso Fiorentino (1494–1540) apparently caused the horrified patron (Lorenzo Buonafede) to flee from his house upon sight of it, since 'the Saints appeared to him like devils'.[3] Rejected for its intended site at the church of the Ognissanti in Florence, Buonafede's reaction might have been unusual, but then the blackened eyes of the Christ-child and the skeletal figure of Saint Jerome in Rosso's work made it a particularly unusual painting, his representation of the holy personages radically departing from the visual precedents that Buonafede would have been accustomed to.

In flouting these norms, both Giovanni Martini and Rosso Fiorentino pushed the boundaries of what was accepted as decent, dignified, and appropriate: in short, what was deemed decorous. Understanding notions of decorum helps to explain the mindset behind the censorship of some sacred images in the early modern period, so that we can better comprehend the significance given to the location and contexts in which artworks were viewed by different audiences.[4] In 1444 the humanist Lorenzo Valla provided a straightforward definition of decorum as 'what men and common opinion consider to be virtuous, beautiful, and fitting' in his lexicographical book, the *Elegantiae*.[5] This common opinion could function to regulate the appearance of images, but by the mid-sixteenth century some artworks were being greeted with a decidedly mixed reception due to the perception that they were taking impermissible and potentially offensive iconographic liberties that were anything but virtuous. It would thus appear that standards of decorum had not altered at the same speed as artistic experimentation. Still, whilst decorum has been seen in modern times as potentially repressive and something enforced upon artists, to a certain extent this group also set the very limits for what was acceptable and what was not, and in the overwhelming majority of instances their efforts were accepted and even encouraged by their patrons. In the first part of this chapter, I will thus explore how ideas about the boundaries of decorum most often coalesced around specific kinds of nakedness in devotional images that were on public display. This was an area where a consensus of opinion emerged that some artists were demonstrating a lack of sensitivity both to the nature of their subject matter and to their audiences: aspects that on occasion were considered of even greater importance than adherence to scripture. Because these grumbles increased as the Cinquecento wore on, this is usually interpreted as evidence of the new prudishness of the Counter-

Reformation, which showed little tolerance for nudity, even on the occasions where it made an important theological point.[6] The readiness of ecclesiastics to police the appearance of devotional images is associated above all with the veiling of the genitalia in Michelangelo's *Last Judgment*. Since the alterations to the fresco began in the year after the conclusion of the Council of Trent in December 1563, the event is often framed as an ideological decision on behalf of the Catholic Church that heralded the beginnings of a dark new era of artistic censorship and decline.[7]

It is not my intention to deny that a shift towards greater clerical oversight of images existed. Indeed, there are well-known examples of rejected or censored works that, to some extent, bolster this narrative. Yet until relatively recently there has been a preference amongst scholars to pay far greater attention to what was censored and repressed than to ever consider the nature of what was tolerated and why, as if these were mutually exclusive phenomena.[8] By giving attention also to the latter, a more accurate (although arguably less sensational) portrayal emerges of the ways in which the limits of artistic liberty were negotiated by different groups, one that presents a serious challenge to the tendency to pit Renaissance artistic freedom against iron-fisted Counter-Reformation conformity, an explanation that for a long time proved too attractive to resist. Although critiques of nudity in art did increase in the sixteenth century (even before Michelangelo painted the *Last Judgment*), there are also a number of much earlier complaints about 'indecent' images that express very similar sentiments. Rather than being attributed purely to a changing religious climate, then, Bernadine Barnes pointed out that this growth in criticism may also have had something to do with transformations to mass media and communication that allowed for the far wider distribution of those images that might previously have been seen by only a very select and highly cultured audience.[9] Second, generalised discussions of prohibitions on the naked form in early modern art often fail to take into account the fact that seemingly small differences in context and visibility determined whether an image was condemned or tolerated, and since a level of nudity continued to be accepted in devotional artworks, it is important to clarify the precise limits of what was permissible and what was not. Third, it is too simplistic to reduce the debates concerning the nudity in Michelangelo's *Last Judgment* solely to changing mores and increasingly rigid notions of decorum. Not only does this reveal an anachronistic tendency to see the whole episode as a battle between 'conservative' clerics and libertine artists, but by promoting the idea that Michelangelo's vision was simply out of step with an increasingly austere artistic climate, this can be at the expense of considering precisely why certain aspects of the fresco proved to be so controversial. In sum, whilst the onus is often placed squarely on the changing historical context of the sixteenth century in order to understand why some devotional artworks were critiqued,

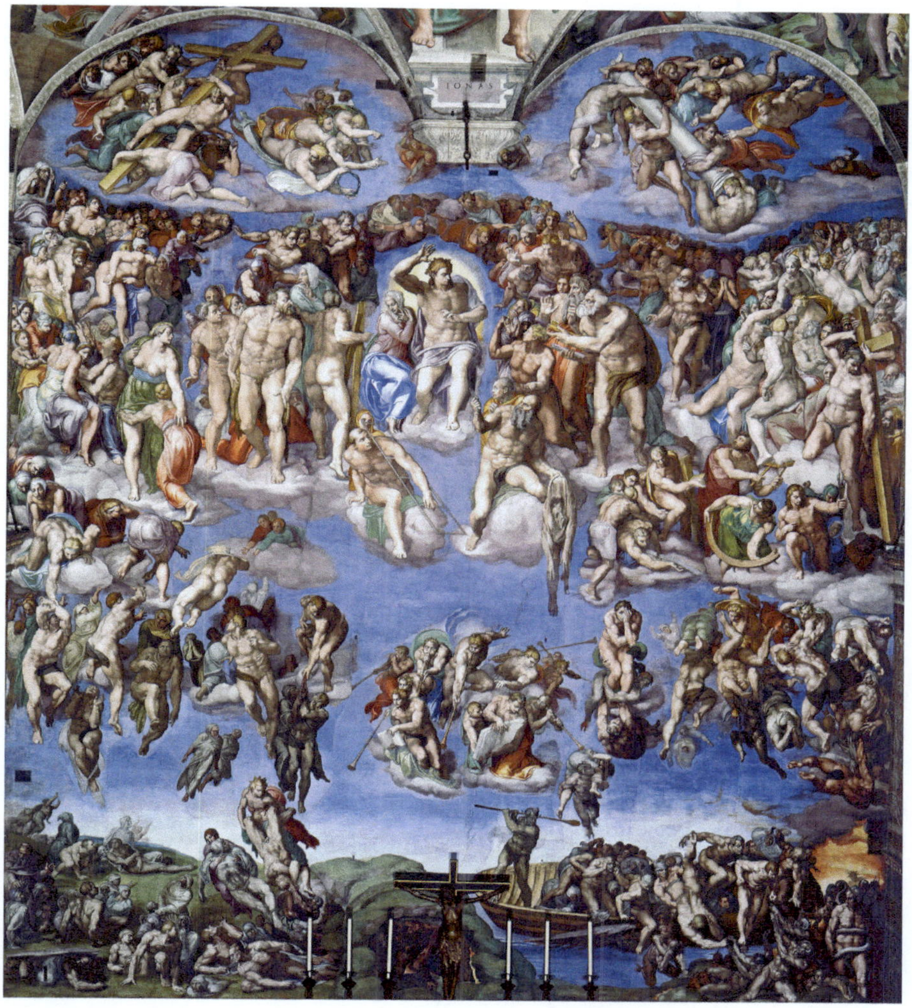

22. Michelangelo, *Last Judgment,* 1541, fresco, Sistine Chapel, Vatican Museums and Galleries, Vatican City (Photo: Bridgeman Images)

this cannot be at the expense of looking carefully at the images themselves in order to understand why this might have been the case.

One might wonder why I am approaching the question of the *Last Judgment* again, given the amount of ink that has been spilled over the whole event (Fig. 22). But the polemics caused by the nudity in the painting were an important turning point in the history of art, sparking renewed attention to the ways in which sacred images might encourage devotion and propagate Catholic belief. It is clear that artists were more aware of the debates surrounding the contested elements of this fresco than they were of the Tridentine decrees on images.[10] These debates had a particular relationship to Venice, from whence some of the most significant early diatribes against the nudity in the *Last Judgment* emanated. This is the subject of the second half of this chapter, where I argue that the censoring of Michelangelo's fresco has been taken as symptomatic of a plight that must have been shared by all artists, namely, that during the freedom-loving Renaissance they could insert sensuous nudes into their works with abandon, but that after the Council of Trent this was reined in as the repressive Counter-Reformation Church took hold.[11] To nuance this argument it is worth considering that one artist argued that those of his profession were obliged to work on profane figures in order to satisfy the requests of their patrons and avoid falling into an abject state of poverty, even if they might rather depict biblical scenes. A recently discovered series of documents demonstrates that this was the opinion of the Bolognese painter Prospero Fontana (1512–97), who argued that the patrons who desired such works would be most effectively dealt with by encouraging them to desist with their requests over time via the confessional, and that the artists who painted lascivious nudes should make an examination of conscience, even if he simultaneously defended the need for artists to learn by studying the nude form from life.[12]

The most famous examples of devotional artworks featuring full-frontal nudity are predominantly from central Italy – Rome and Florence in particular – and they appear to have been scarce in Venice. That this is rarely pointed out might also suggest the lingering associations of the Vasarian canon of art history, and the pre-eminence given to the vicissitudes of Tuscan artists at the expense of their colleagues elsewhere. This is because there is some evidence to suggest that artists active in Venice may have seen things differently. In the previous chapter the data from the Inquisition records there showed that artists were not a particularly heretical group. Moreover, they tended to show careful attention to the decorum demanded by the sites where their religious artworks were to be viewed.[13] Venetian painters might have made famous the genre of the sensual reclining nude, and the very canal façade of the German fondaco at the Rialto was frescoed by Giorgione (c. 1473/4–1510) with full-length naked male and female figures, a programme commissioned in 1508 by the Venetian State, but in general they were careful not to blur the *sacro e profano* to the same extent that Michelangelo and some of his younger compatriots had been accused of doing.[14] Might it not be significant that even an artist as influenced by Buonarroti as Tintoretto was, nevertheless took care to cover the genitalia of the saints in his own *Last Judgment* for the church of Madonna dell'Orto of c. 1559–60, prior to the censorship of Michelangelo's fresco, as well as the later vision of *Paradise* displayed in the non-ecclesiastical context of the Ducal Palace (Fig. 23)?[15] Seen in this light, one can speculate that Vasari's 'bad review' of the Madonna dell'Orto canvas might have been about more than just his infamous dislike for the Venetian's lack of *disegno*, and could have even stemmed from the troubling

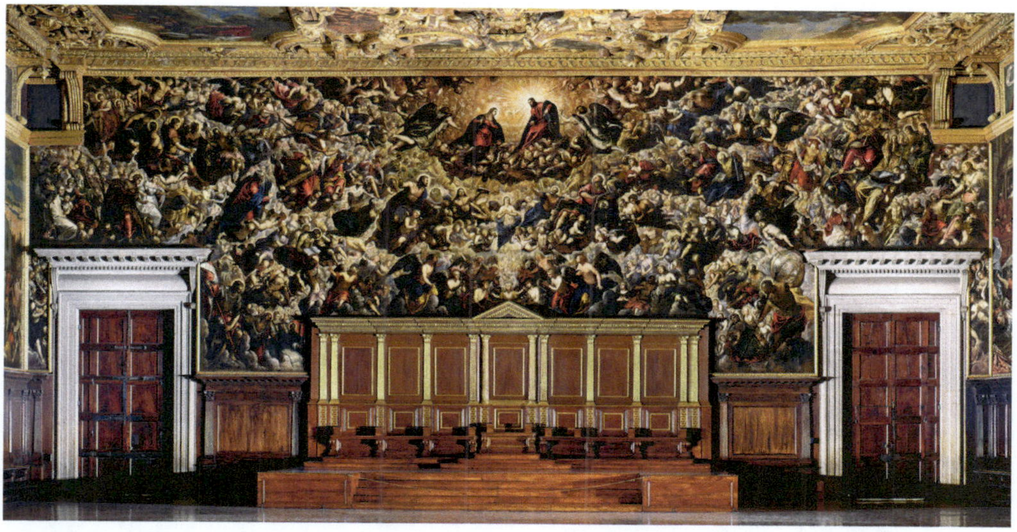

23. Tintoretto and workshop, *Paradise,* 1588–92, oil on canvas, Sala del Maggior Consiglio, Ducal Palace, Venice (Photo: Cameraphoto)

notion that individuals like Tintoretto were rectifying what Michelangelo had misjudged in the Sistine Chapel.[16]

'TRUE IMAGES OF IDOLS'

Before examining the sixteenth-century image polemics regarding the place of nudity in devotional images, it is first necessary to go back in time to the previous century, beginning with an account by a Dominican monk from Ulm, who visited Venice on his way to the Holy Land in the year 1483. Faber's words demonstrate that concerns about nakedness had a long history, and so cannot be attributed solely to Counter-Reformation prudery. Faber's fascination with the ducal monuments that punctuated the walls of the Dominican basilica of Santi Giovanni e Paolo caused him to note in awe that 'even those of the Popes in Rome cannot equal the tombs of the Doges of Venice'.[17] Describing the cenotaph to Doge Mocenigo by Pietro Lombardo and his sons of 1476–80, Faber was struck by the prominence of Hercules, going on to describe the presence of 'naked gladiators with swords and spears in their hands and shields about their necks, but without cuirass or breastplate or helmet, and these really are idols. There are naked boys with wings on, holding the emblems of victory, or else wrestling together, and many such symbols of paganism are inserted among those of our redemption. Simple people think these are images of saints, and they honour Hercules, thinking him Samson, and Venus, mistaking her for the Magdalen.'[18] The warriors arranged on either side of the central section of the Mocenigo monument are not, in fact, unclothed (Fig. 24). But because the muscles of these statues are

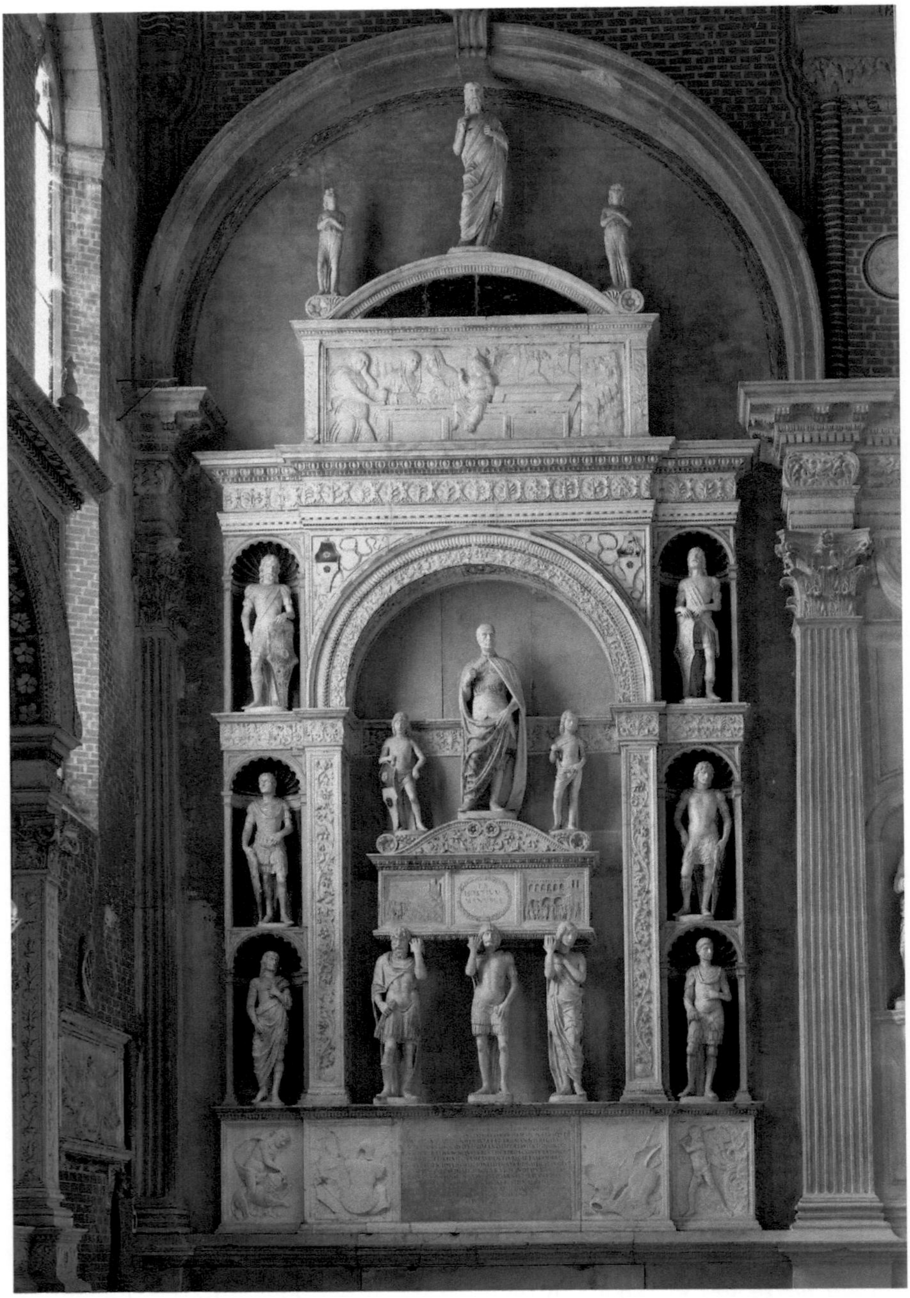

24. Pietro Lombardo and shop, *Monument to Pietro Mocenigo,* 1476-80, Santi Giovanni e Paolo, Venice (Photo: Cameraphoto)

visible underneath their armour, and this armour is really only noticeable if you look carefully at the statues' chests, Faber described them as naked. In his discussion of Michelangelo's *Risen Christ* (1519–21), Leo Steinberg pointed out that the word '*ignudo*' did not always have the same connotations of full-frontal nakedness that we might associate with it today, since even penitents stripped to the waist were commonly referred to as 'nude'.[19] For this reason Faber may not have considered that there was a significant difference between an uncovered or semi-covered form. He also might have confused or conflated the pugilists with something else that he remembered seeing at the basilica, since his description is not particularly precise. The point is that what Faber meant by 'naked bodies' does not necessarily correspond to our own present-day understanding of what this term means, something that is of importance when we invoke it with relation to early modern art.[20]

Faber was evidently surprised by the Venetian tolerance for classical references in a sacred setting. His response was thus different to that of later spectators who found the Mocenigo monument unproblematic. Francesco Sansovino, for example, who was born in Rome but lived most of his life in Venice, provided a straightforward description of it in his 1581 guide to the city as a 'most rich tomb of Istrian stone with seventeen marble figures'.[21] What Faber perceptively realised at Santi Giovanni e Paolo was that the appearance of the secular in the sacred space had the potential to confuse the laity, hence why he described the classical statues as 'true images of idols'. His observation was a prescient one: almost a century later in 1581 the Apostolic Visitation to Venice – tasked with inspecting the city's churches for irregularities – lamented that the equestrian statue of the condottiere Taddeo Volpe of c. 1536 in the church of Santa Marina was mistaken by the faithful for Saint George or Martin, causing them to genuflect and light candles in front of the monument (Fig. 25).[22] The monument was destroyed in 1801 as a consequence of the Napoleonic suppression of the Church, but its appearance is recorded in a 1759 watercolour by Johannes Grevembroch.[23] The Church's defence against accusations of idolatry, one that was reiterated at the Council of Trent, was that the faithful venerated not the image but the prototype to which it referred. For both Faber and the Apostolic visitors, however, the representation of these profane figures had the potential to lead to 'idolatrous' veneration. But because the laity at Santa Marina were mistaken in their identifications, they did not venerate these figures as secular ones. In accordance with the justification of the council, their devotions were directed to the saints whom they believed most closely resembled the figures that they observed.

Idolatry was a concern as old as devotional art itself, but critiques of 'lascivious' images are usually thought to have arisen at the same time as naturalistic sacred art began to obscure the boundaries between the sacred and profane to a greater degree from the mid-fifteenth century onwards, during the Renaissance. Although such complaints certainly grew in number at this period, that they seem to have always been of concern is demonstrated by canon one hundred of the Trullan Synod called by Emperor Justinian II in 692. The assembly denounced pictures that 'offend the eye, corrupt the mind

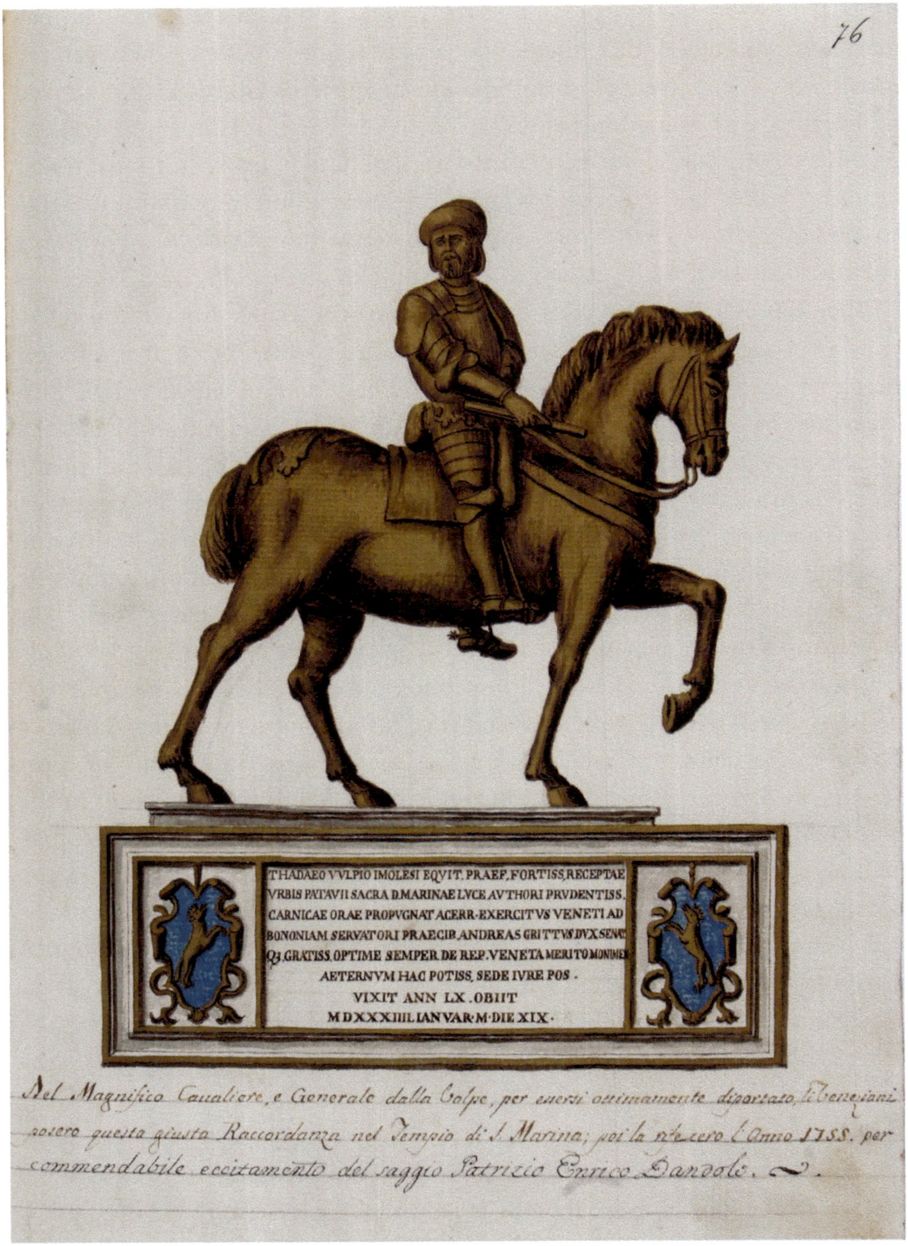

25. Johannes Grevembroch, *Monument to Taddeo Volpe,* 1759, watercolour, Biblioteca del Museo Correr, Venice (Photo: Biblioteca Correr, Fondazione Musei Civici di Venezia)

and kindle base pleasures'.[24] Later in the sixteenth century a series of local councils expressed identical sentiments: the 1528 Council of Sens in Paris condemned lascivious images, ordering that the visiting bishop or vicar should give their approval to any new image before it was displayed in a church; the 1548 Council of Augsburg warned against 'obscene pictures'; as did the 1549 Council of Mainz.[25] Individual clerics castigated artists and patrons for these practices too: at the beginning of the fifteenth century Jean Gerson (1363–1429), chancellor of the University of Paris, complained about naked figures in ecclesiastical decoration, and later in the same century Archbishop Antoninus of Florence (1389–1459) and Girolamo Savonarola (1452–98) did too.[26] Both of these individuals were active in Florence, where sensuously beautiful depictions of the holy figures appear to have become ubiquitous. Antoninus closely anticipated some of the Council of Trent's objections when he condemned sacred images that featured superfluous or apocryphal details, theological inaccuracies, and, in particular, those that might provoke desire.[27] Savonarola similarly railed against provocative paintings, taking particular issue with attractive depictions of the Madonna. He argued that the Virgin Mary would never have been garbed in the kind of fashionable contemporary clothes that Florentine artists liked to paint her in, and that in doing so they showed 'the Virgin Mary dressed like a prostitute'.[28] Savonarola was thus a literalist who called for fidelity to biblical descriptions, in a similar vein to some of the writers on the subject of devotional art whom we will meet later on. In fact, there were probably more artworks destroyed in his bonfire of the vanities of 1497 and 1498 than there ever were by the Catholic Church after the Council of Trent, and the artist who arguably produced the most dazzlingly beautiful depictions of the Virgin Mary of all – Sandro Botticelli (1445–1510) – was said by Vasari to have been an enthusiastic partisan of the Dominican preacher.[29]

The perception that there was a lack of decorum in some devotional imagery was not limited to Florence, and with the advent of the Reformation these complaints began to increase in published material. Luther's enemy, Hieronymus Esmer, defended images against Protestant iconoclasts in his treatise of 1522, but condemned the fact that artists 'make images of the beloved saints so shamelessly whorish and roguish that neither Venus nor Cupid were so scandalously painted or carved by the pagans'.[30] Esmer argued that it would be better if provocative devotional images were burnt, rather than displayed on altars or in churches, although he conceded that the power of images to provoke desire was 'the fault of a perverted world, not of images'.[31] Echoing Savonarola's comment about the 'Virgin Mary dressed as a prostitute', in his *Modus orandi Deum* (first published 1524), Erasmus of Rotterdam likewise laid the blame on those painters who demonstrated a lack of judgment in choosing their models, with the result that 'saints are not depicted in a form which is worthy of them', that images of Christ or Saint Paul were based upon 'some drunken rascal', and that Saint Agatha or the Virgin Mary were on occasion modelled after 'a lascivious little whore'.[32] In Italy, two Venetian-born reformers expressed similar views on the existences of such 'abuses' little more than a decade apart. The reforming bishop of Verona, Luigi Lippomano (1500–59), issued a handbook of Catholic teachings for the laity in the vernacular that admitted that 'lascivious paintings' and 'dishonest sculptures' had the potential to give rise to feelings of concupiscence rather than devotion.[33] Appearing in 1553, it was anticipated by a work in a similar format authored by Gasparo Contarini in 1542. Contarini took a particularly dim view of those who 'use pictures and images of the saints to set off the skill of the artist', giving rise to 'vain or even base delight'.[34] Although Contarini is usually associated with the *spirituali* – the implications of which were discussed in the previous chapter – his judgment on unnecessarily distracting artistry was one that would be oft repeated as the Cinquecento progressed: the creation of a devout and convincing sacred image was to be the aim of the artist. 'Showing off' or distracting the viewer with lascivious or irrelevant details impeded this objective.

The debates about the appropriate representation of the naked form gained traction from the early sixteenth century onwards, reached a swell mid-century, and then proliferated after the unveiling of Michelangelo's *Last Judgment* and the closure of the Council of Trent, when numerous treatises were published on the topic of decorous devotional art.[35] Following the observations of Barnes, Depasquale recently argued that this boom coincided with developments in the printing industry, which could very well mean that in the ten years following 1541 more appears to have been printed on the subject of art in Italy than had been cumulatively published up until 1540. This led him to hypothesise that 'the critical exchange on nudity in art that appears in the mid and late 1500s is perhaps no less than one would expect to find when the concerns raised in the scanty Quattrocento references to nudity and propriety were amplified and expanded in scale with the discussion of other subjects'.[36] This is an important consideration to bear in mind and one that has been hitherto given scant attention. Combined with the events of the Reformations that engendered a variety of contrasting attitudes regarding the very necessity and appearance of devotional images, as well as the pre-existing concerns relating to the nature of nudity in Renaissance art, the decorum of images became a popular topic. Yet it seems to me doubtful that these debates would ever have been sustained in the same way had Michelangelo not painted the saints totally unclothed in the Sistine Chapel in Rome and had the subsequent reproduction and dissemination of his fresco via printed reproductions not proved to be so very popular. Michelangelo had represented the holy figures in a manner in which they had very rarely been shown previously. This was the driving force behind the censorship of the *Last Judgment*, and it was an aspect of the painting that numerous commentators repeatedly pointed out, whether they positively or negatively embraced Michelangelo's vision.[37] Since the *Last Judgment* became the most 'scandalous' painting of the age, its censorship would prove to be just as important for defining the boundaries of decorum for artists as the decrees of the Council of Trent would.

Many years prior to the eruption of these debates in the sixteenth century, the Venetian State had already become increasingly vigilant about public displays of nakedness in the city, even when this arose from pre-existing penitential traditions. Despite the precedent of Saint Francis of Assisi shedding his clothing at the moment he renounced his fortune, in 1420 the Signori di Notte arrested four members of the Franciscan Order who were found processing through the streets of Venice nude, armed with crosses, and accompanied by a crowd. The friars were released, but in addition to a punishment to be meted out by their ecclesiastical superiors, they were to be warned that such comportment 'greatly displeased' the city authorities.[38] A few years later, in 1438, four male nobles at the church of Santa Maria del Giglio were found to have been whipped in the nude by their confraternity brothers, something that Guido Ruggiero points out would have been a typical practice of expiating sin for such brotherhoods a century and a half earlier. Troubled perhaps by the possibility of homosexuality, now the men were convicted and the Council of Ten made it clear that male nudity in public places, including churches, was a criminal act. The State eventually watered down this ruling, and nakedness was allowed for religious processions, but only provided a license had been granted.[39] This sensitivity to nudity on behalf of the State may also have been reflected in local attitudes towards its inclusion in artworks destined for public display in the churches of Venice. To clarify this, it is worth briefly examining the degree of bare flesh that was tolerated in devotional imagery, by which I refer to adult figures in particular, since the nudity of infants, as well as of angels and putti, was widely accepted both before and after the Council of Trent.[40] At the basilica of San Marco there are a few early examples of full frontal nudity, like the reliefs of Hercules carrying the Ceryneian hind and presenting the Erymanthean boar to Eurystheus (thirteenth century and fifth century, respectively) that were placed on the façade at some point before 1267.[41] In the atrium, the early thirteenth-century mosaics in the Genesis cycle show Adam and Eve nude before the Fall, and Noah is portrayed similarly disrobed in the mosaics recounting his drunkenness and death (Fig. 26). In both of these cases the nudity is a crucial element in the biblical event depicted and was in keeping with well-established iconographies. However, later mosaic programmes dating to the late sixteenth and seventeenth centuries inside the church appear to have covered genitalia even in those scenes where a case could have been made for its inclusion, such as the cycle of *Susanna and the Elders* for which Tintoretto produced the cartoons, or in the group of the damned shown being swallowed by the Leviathan, based upon a 1606 design by Maffeo da Verona (Fig. 27).[42] A direct warning against lust, the 'concupiscence of the flesh' is contained in the inscription below, and even though the figures themselves are sensual, their veiling points to a recognition amongst artists and patrons that the nude figure had to be

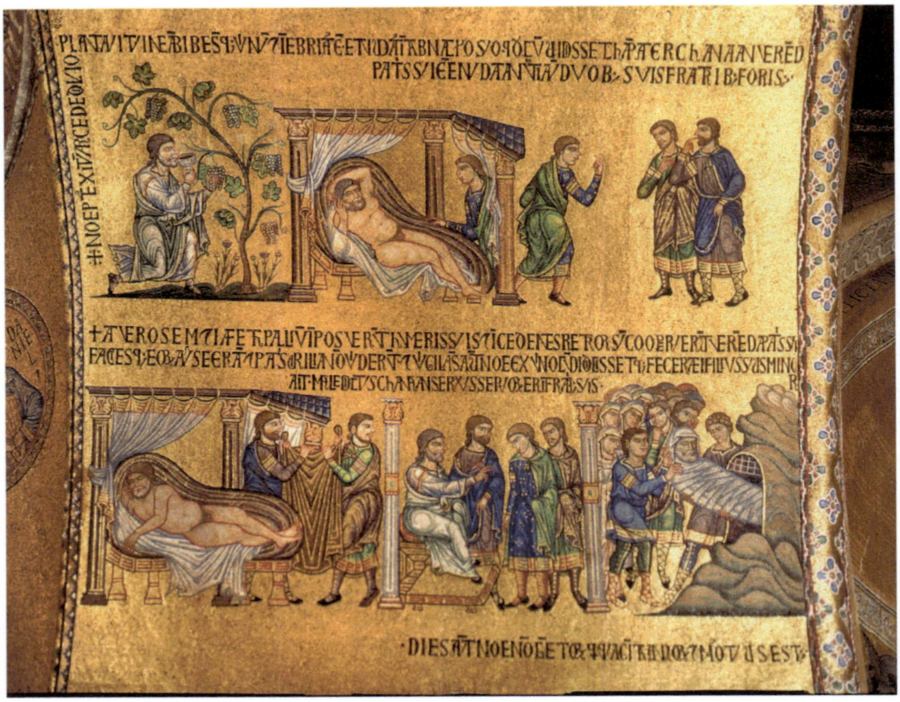

26. *Cycle of Noah,* c. 1230s–40s, mosaic, Basilica di San Marco, Venice (Photo: Cameraphoto Arte Venezia/Bridgeman Images)

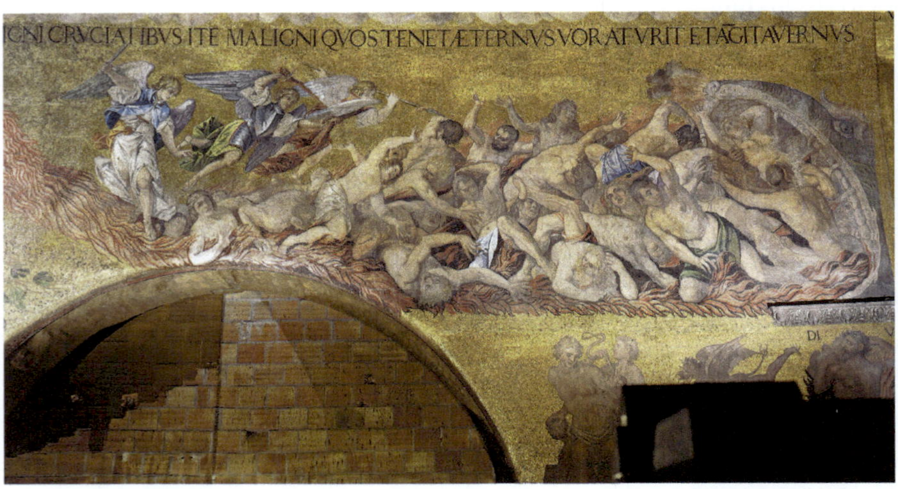

27. Cartoon by Maffeo da Verona (1606), execution by Luigi Gaetano, *The Damned,* 1613–19, mosaic, Basilica di San Marco, Venice (Photo: Scala/Art Resource, New York)

approached with sensitivity to prevailing notions of decorum.[43] It would also seem to reverse a situation that had been gaining ground since the early 1400s onwards when artistic innovations meant that holy figures were sometimes even shown nude in direct contradiction to scripture. Jill Burke pointed out that despite its obvious derivation from the Bible, which allowed for total nudity only in the prelapsarian state, in this period Adam and Eve began to be

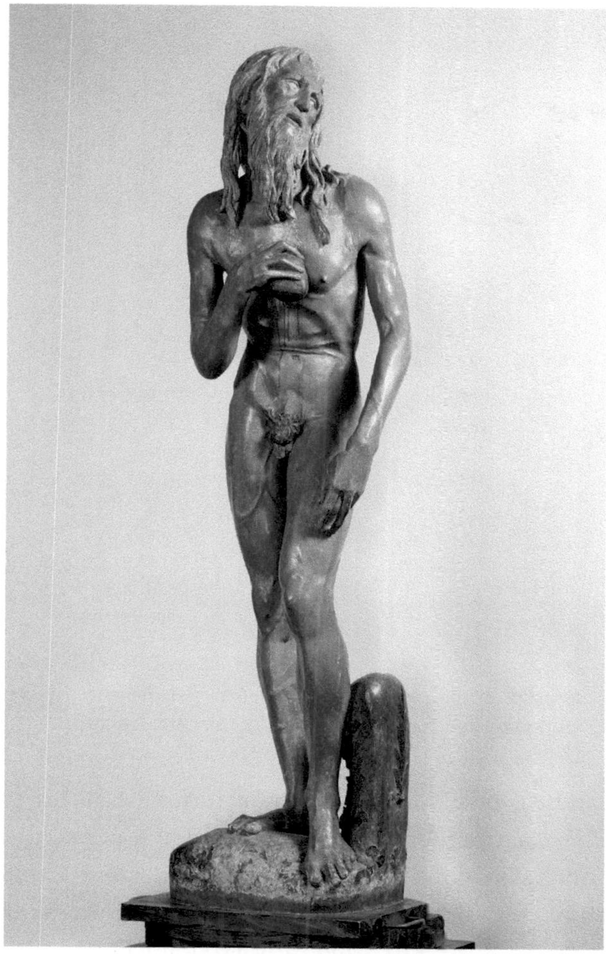

28. Attributed to Donatello and Bertoldo di Giovanni, *Saint Jerome*, c. 1460–70, polychromed wood, Pinacoteca Comunale, Faenza (Photo: Scala/Art Resource, New York)

depicted naked after the Fall, most famously in Florence with Masaccio's (1401–1428/29) *Expulsion from Paradise* of 1426 for the Brancacci Chapel.[44]

One interesting early sculpted precedent for the nudity of Michelangelo's saints in the Sistine Chapel is an extraordinary wooden statue attributed to Donatello (c. 1386–1466) of the ascetic Jerome, shown in the process of mortifying his flesh, blood streaming from his chest as he strikes it with a rock (Fig. 28). Until 1866 the statue was located in a chapel dedicated to the saint in the Franciscan church of San Girolamo in Faenza, although the pubic area may well have been covered with a fabric loincloth at different points in its history.[45] This seems to have been the case with Brunelleschi's (1377–1446) nude figure of Christ (c. 1410–15) for Santa Maria Novella in Florence according to Philipp Fehl, who believes that the artist intended for it to be draped.[46] Jerome's own writings on his time spent in the desert would suggest

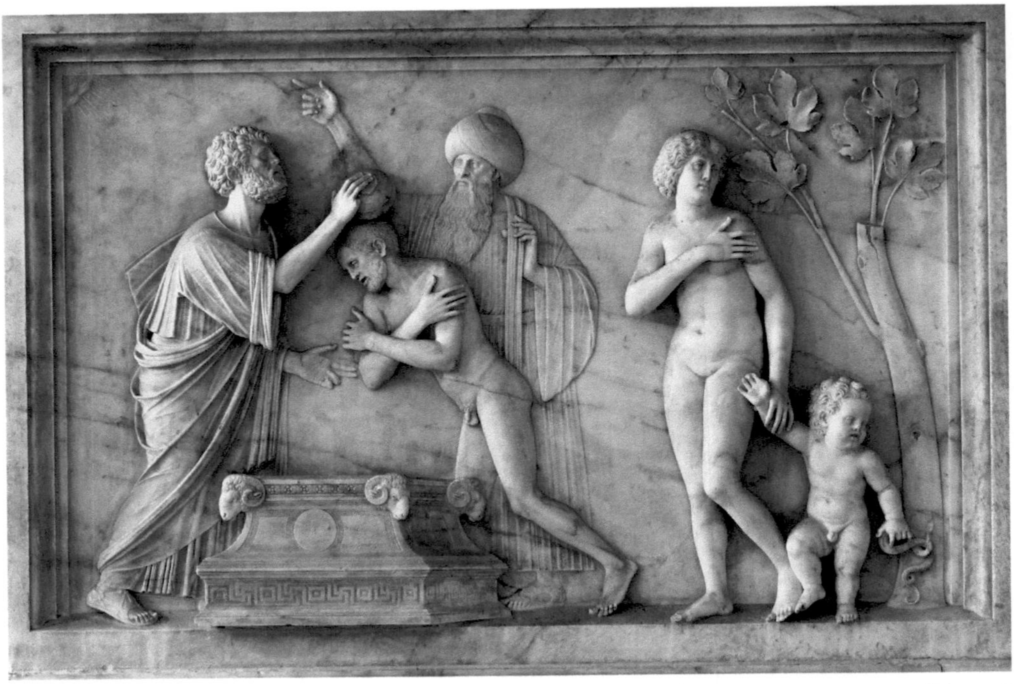

29. Tullio and Sante Lombardo, detail of *The Baptism of Anainus,* Monument to Giovanni Mocenigo, 1522, Santi Giovanni e Paolo, Venice (Photo: Cameraphoto)

that he was clothed, but Donatello's radical treatment of his tortured body could be justified on account of the saint's ideas on nudity as a sign of renunciation of the worldly, as pointed out by Stephen Campbell.[47] I am not aware of any equivalent to the total nudity of this statue in a Venetian church, although in the late 1400s and early 1500s unclothed figures, although still rare, occasionally appeared on the tombs and monuments created by the Lombardo workshop and their contemporaries, which is telling in light of the earlier cited comments of Faber at Santi Giovanni e Paolo. At this same church a relief on the tomb of Doge Giovanni Mocenigo by Tullio (c. 1455–1532) and Sante Lombardo (1504–60) depicts the baptism of the naked Anainus by Saint Mark with his companions, as well as two nude winged Ephebes, who support the epitaph at the lower centre of the monument (Fig. 29).[48] The monument to Pietro Bernardo on the retro-façade of the Frari by Tullio and Sante Lombardo features two small bas-reliefs from the second campaign of works on the tomb in the 1550s. They show a nude Adam and Eve located on either side of the epitaph that derive from an engraving of Marcantonio Raimondi (c. 1480–1534), best known for producing the infamous *I modi.*[49] Far more dramatic in terms of their carnality are the life-sized statues of a naked Neptune and Mars also at the Frari, which adorn either side of the memorial by Giambattista Bregno (c. 1467 to after 1518) to Benedetto Pesaro (Fig. 30).[50] One final example of an unusual nude statue in a Venetian church is a figure of Saint Lawrence by Jacopo Fantoni (1504–40) for San Salvador, dated to 1530

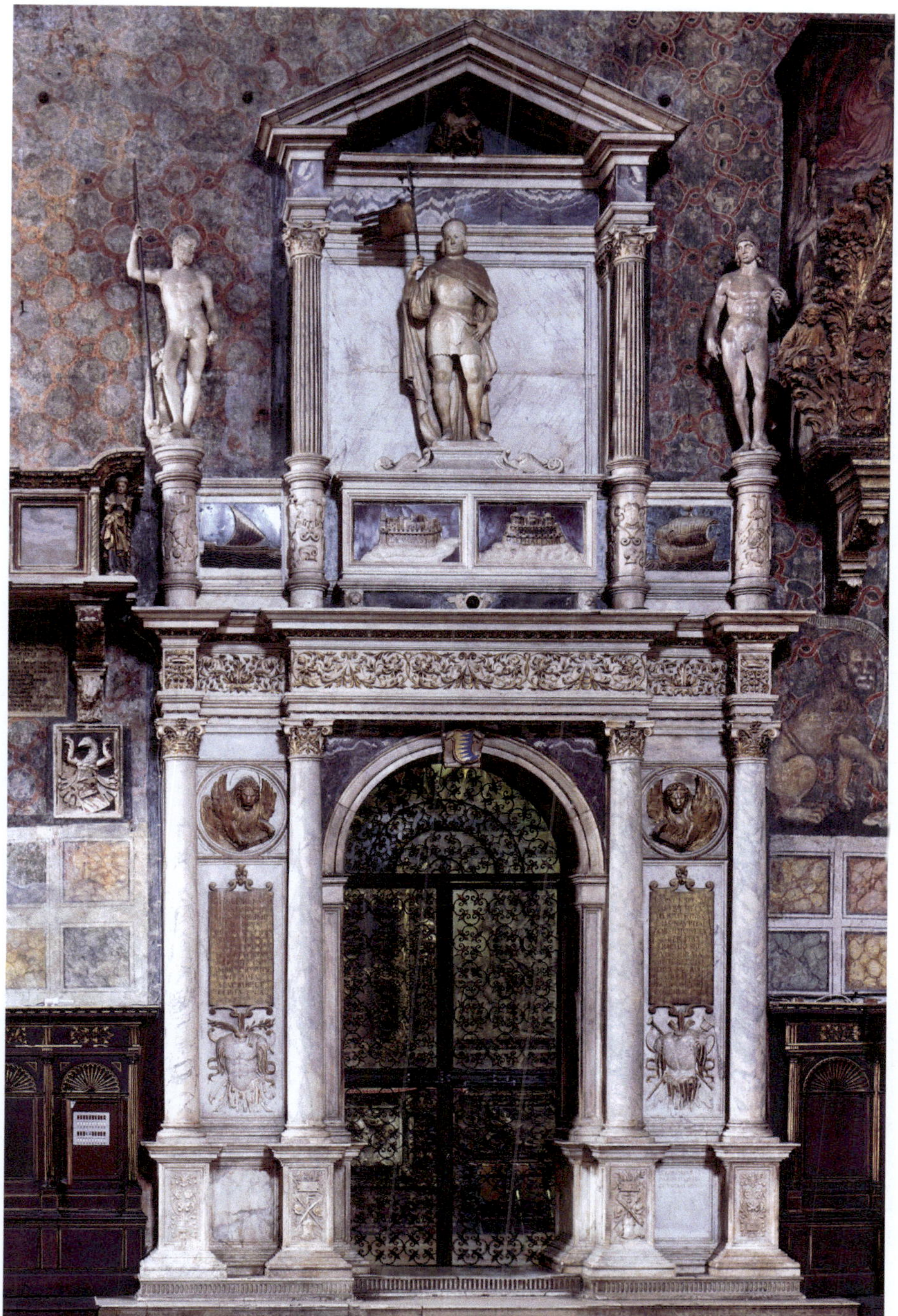

30. Giambattista Bregno and shop, Baccio da Montelupo, *Monument to Benedetto Pesaro*, c. 1508, Santa Maria dei Frari, Venice (Photo: Cameraphoto)

(Fig. 31). Situated in a niche to one side of the interior lateral entrance to the edifice, the pendant statue also depicts a semi-nude saint: the penitent Jerome, his groin covered with a loincloth, accompanied by his lion, a work attributed to Fantoni's rival, Danese Cattaneo (1512–72).[51] Unlike the well-established

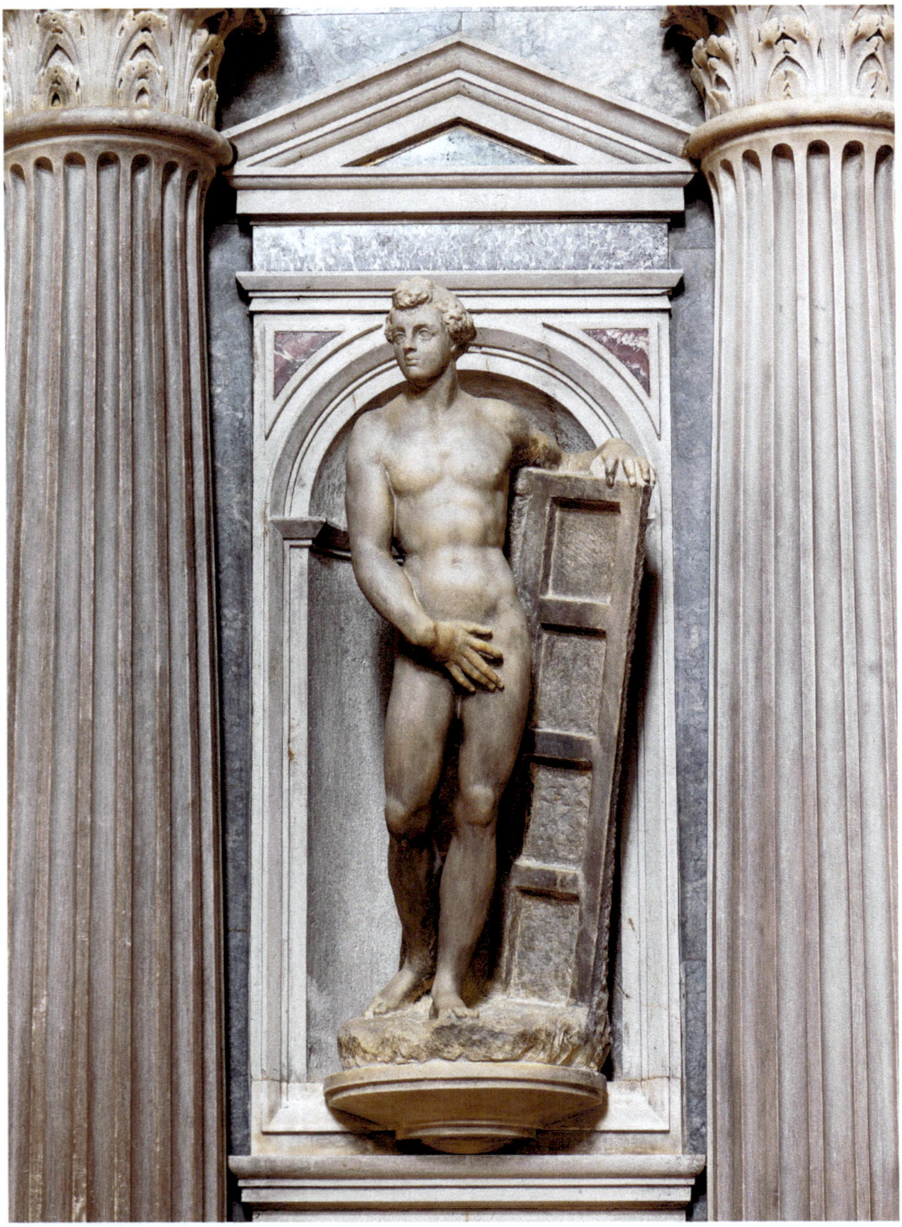

31. Jacopo Fantoni, *Saint Lawrence,* 1530, marble, San Salvador, Venice (Photo: Cameraphoto)

iconography of Danese's saint, Anne Markham Schulz has pointed out that the nudity of Lawrence in Fantoni's statue is anachronistic for an upright free-standing figure of the saint, since in this pose he is usually depicted dressed in his deacon's vestments. The crudely rendered right hand of the saint bends in an impossible angle to cover the genitalia. Schulz has argued that this gargantuan hand must be a later replacement, but it is also possible – in the absence of evidence to the contrary – that Lawrence was once even more naked than we see him today, the hand modified at a later stage to preserve a modicum of modesty.[52] Rather than the body of the saint being a vehicle through which spiritual ideas can be communicated to the viewer, Fantoni's Lawrence appears much more an exposition of the sculptor's interest in depicting a nude figure, perhaps in competition with Cattaneo. This rings true if we consider other works attributed to Fantoni, like the three bas-reliefs commissioned by the Scuola Grande di San Rocco for the staircase of their confraternity building in 1531 that include a completely nude Neptune, as well as two nudes of the Old Testament figures of David and Goliath. Commenting on the figure of the Philistine, Schulz exclaims that it 'is represented in so audacious and shocking a view that even Titian's *Goliath* from S. Spirito seems tame by comparison'.[53] Although no evidence has been found to suggest that Fantoni came to the attention of the authorities in Venice for creations like these, he is believed to have been the sculptor responsible for the wooden statue of Taddeo Volpe in Santa Marina, the very same work that years after his death caused the concern of the Apostolic Visitation.

To sum up, there are just a handful of examples of secular nudes in Venetian churches, and there appears to be only a couple of images (the bas-reliefs at the Frari and the Marcian mosaics) of biblical figures deprived of any form of loincloth or covering. Apart from the examples in San Marco, the works I have cited are all from monastic churches, and particularly in the case of the Franciscans at the Frari and the Dominicans at Santi Giovanni e Paolo, this permissiveness can be explained by the fact that they were the prime choices for burials, and thus for the kinds of monuments commemorating illustrious secular figures associated with the Venetian State that might reasonably include such imagery.[54] It is telling that Patriarch Lorenzo Priuli, who was intent on making his diocese a model of post-Tridentine reform, legislated against elaborate and offensive wall tombs at the end of the sixteenth century in Venice, although his powers as a pastoral visitor extended only to the city's parish churches.[55]

Although closer attention was paid to the decorum of the unclothed body throughout the course of the Cinquecento, at the same time representations of the nude in devotional art were often powerfully imbued with multivalent spiritual meanings. In a post-Freudian world we might deny that this could ever negate the erotic charge of bare flesh, but too great an insistence on the 'sexiness' of nakedness can be equally as reductive as the earlier denial of the sensuousness of some Renaissance works of art, as has been persuasively pointed out by Tom Nichols.[56] Examples like the figure of Jerome attributed to Donatello eloquently demonstrate that nakedness did not just provide an opportunity for artists to depict sensual bare flesh but was tied to theological concepts relating to the nature of the body and the soul, and because of this it could be tolerated. Steinberg masterfully demonstrated that the appearance of the genitalia of Christ in devotional art reflected the theology of the incarnation, reminding the viewer that he became man and took on human form. Images of the nude Christ-child were widely diffused by the fourteenth century, as were some images of Christ without a loincloth at the Crucifixion.[57] The pious King Philip II of Spain was the owner of Benvenuto Cellini's (1500–71) marble statue of the naked crucified Christ, for example, gifted to him by Francesco I de' Medici and originally intended for the sculptor's tomb.[58] The complete nudity of Christ at the moment of his death was scripturally accurate on account of the casting of lots for his clothes, even if, as Steinberg put it, the theologian and the moralist might agree that a loincloth is needed when depicting the holy body, 'not to conform to his [Christ's] own nature, but in concession to ours – so that lewd ogling not be encouraged'.[59] The depiction of a number of biblical episodes, as well as the iconographies of saints including Jerome, Sebastian, or Mary Magdalen, required a level of nakedness that communicated ideas relating to shame, chastity, renunciation of the flesh, and the repudiation of vice.[60] Old Testament heroines like Judith were sometimes shown with a bare breast, in imitation of the chastity of the goddess Diana.[61] Later in the sixteenth century, south of the Alps the poor and outcast were commonly depicted semi-nude to denote both their deprived state and their closeness to the Kingdom of God.[62] More importantly, the Council of Trent did not outlaw the representation of the naked body, but warned against images that were deemed to be 'lascivious' or that featured a 'beauty exciting to lust', terms that left a degree of leeway for how they were to be interpreted. Since the lascivious denotes the obscene, this was different to an outright interdict on the unclothed form (even if the two were often conflated) and explains why these representations continued.[63]

'THE INVENTOR OF FILTHS'

Even if nudity could be tolerated on theological grounds, some depictions of the naked body on public display were nevertheless believed to carry the risk of prurience, and this was why it was believed that anything potentially 'lascivious' should be carefully managed, so as not to misguide the viewer and lead them into sin.[64] This carnal reaction supposedly happened in the early sixteenth century with Fra Bartolomeo's (c. 1472–1517) lost painting *Saint Sebastian Greeted by an Angel*, one that Vasari tells us had to be removed from public display in the church of San Marco in Florence and placed in the friar's chapter house, since the 'comely and lascivious' naturalism with which the saint's image had been rendered was causing the female members of the laity to sin upon sight of it.[65] The painting was sold by the convent in 1529 and entered the collection of King François I of France before 1532 – perhaps the real reason for its removal – but regardless of this, the tall tale caught the attention of later

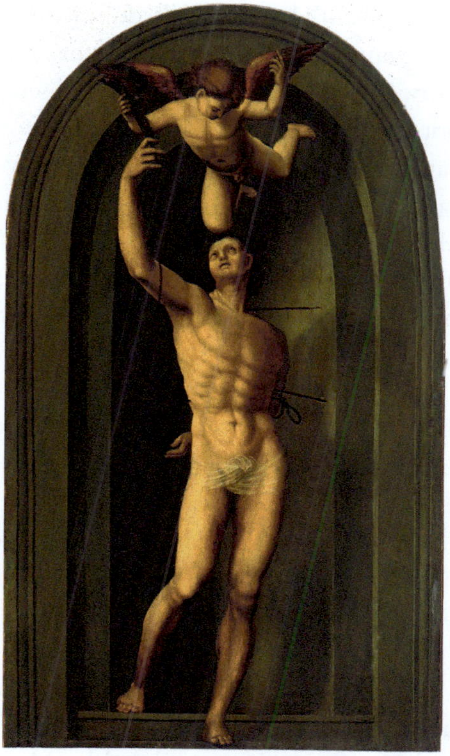

32. Zacchia il Vecchio after Fra Bartolomeo, *Saint Sebastian Greeted by an Angel,* copy of original dating to 1514, 1520s, oil on wood, San Francesco, Fiesole (Photo: AKG Images/ Rabatti & Domingie)

commentators, and in 1585 Gian Paolo Lomazzo similarly referred to it as an example of a lascivious painting (Fig. 32).[66] The fact that a contemporary copy of the lost image survives, albeit almost half the size of the original, and that it was much later proudly displayed in the church of San Francesco in Fiesole, shows that even if Vasari's account was to be trusted, there was nonetheless some variance in what might be tolerated from one place to another.[67]

Whether Vasari's account of the impact of Fra Bartolomeo's painting on the laity was apocryphal or not, the copy of the painting points to why it caused such a stir: the pose of Sebastian was based upon Sansovino's marble statue of a nude Bacchus (now in the Bargello, Florence), and the saint's loincloth is so transparent that his body appears almost completely nude, something that Beverly Louise Brown describes as an unprecedented depiction of a saint for this period.[68] The debacle also illustrates that certain images were thought to be so capable of provoking a base reaction that they disrupted the very justification for having edifying images of the saints on public display in the first place. A similar strain of thought runs through responses to Michelangelo's art. In 1549, the Florentine diarist Antonio Marucelli grimly described the unveiling of Nanni di Baccio Bigio's copy of Michelangelo's *Saint Peter's Pietà* in the church of Santo Spirito in Florence in the following terms: 'it is said that the original is by the inventor of filths, who saved his art but not devotion, Michelangelo Buonarroti. All the modern painters and sculptors, by imitating similar Lutheran caprices, paint or sculpt nothing for the holy churches but figures to bury faith and devotion, but I hope that one day God will send his saints to throw idolatries like these to the ground'.[69] The diarist has been described as a 'savagely puritan Catholic of the Counter-Reformation', but his comments were not poles apart from those of Contarini, resulting from a conviction that Renaissance artists were placing physical beauty and artistic virtuosity above all else.[70] The diarist's desire for the destruction of the statue would be partially fulfilled over four centuries later, when in 1972 the arms and nose of the Virgin Mary belonging to the original statue in Saint Peter's basilica were hacked off by one Laszlo Toth during an iconoclastic attack.[71]

Due to biblical precedents such as the account of the worship of the golden calf in the Book of Exodus, statues tended to be more often associated with idolatry than paintings. Although the diarist did not describe precisely what upset him so about Bigio's copy, given his incensed reaction he may have been similarly enraged by the nude *Crucifixion* of c. 1493 attributed to Michelangelo that hung above the high altar in the same church of Santo Spirito.[72] His anger with the *Pietà* probably related to its divergence from scriptural sources and iconographic tradition. The Virgin Mary sculpted by Michelangelo between 1498 and 1500 was a young, beautiful maiden, rather than the older woman that she would have been at the time of her son's death. This related to a spiritual 'truth' concerning the Madonna's virginity, but that this may have been lost on the more literal-minded observers of the statue is demonstrated by the fact that Michelangelo eventually provided a justification for his choice to his biographer Ascanio Condivi.[73] After the unveiling of the *Last Judgment*, tensions surrounding Michelangelo's iconographic novelties grew, and it thus seems significant that a 1604 engraving of the *Pietà* by Lucas Kilian (1579–1637) depicted the Madonna as an older woman, 'correcting' what had become one of the most famous aspects of Michelangelo's statue (Fig. 33).[74] Later in the seventeenth century, the Venetian painter Palma il Giovane was given instructions in the name of the Countess Camilla Ruggeri Brami that the Virgin Mary he was to paint should be beautiful, but that she should be shown at 'about fifty years of age' in a canvas of the *Lamentation* to be placed in the countess's chapel at the cathedral of Reggio Emilia.[75]

The opinions of the engaged Florentine diarist cannot be easily dismissed as the rantings of an unusually orthodox member of the laity. In 1527 the penis of the nude statue of Michelangelo's *Risen Christ* of 1519–21 in Santa Maria sopra Minerva was vandalised by the Dominican friars attached to the church, leading to the covering of the genitals with a bronze loincloth (Fig. 34).[76] Notwithstanding this, the statue became a popular cult image, and the right

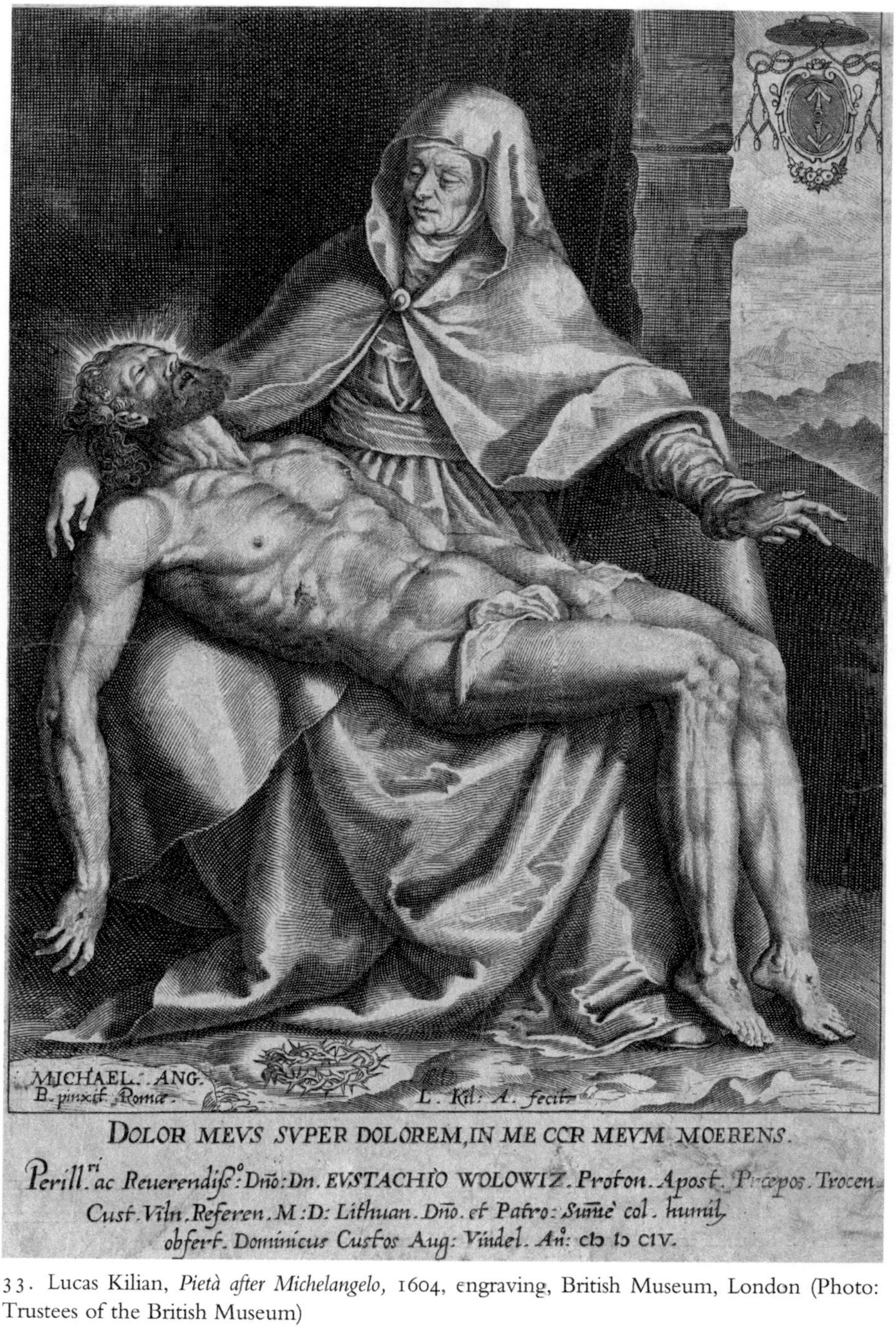

33. Lucas Kilian, *Pietà after Michelangelo,* 1604, engraving, British Museum, London (Photo: Trustees of the British Museum)

foot of Christ was also eventually covered in bronze (to protect it from damage), having become the focus of the devotions of the laity who knelt to kiss and touch it.[77] Even though the total nudity of Michelangelo's Christ symbolised his humanity and his unfallen nature, presenting the viewer with his sinless form, the sensuous aspects of the life-sized statue were evidently too

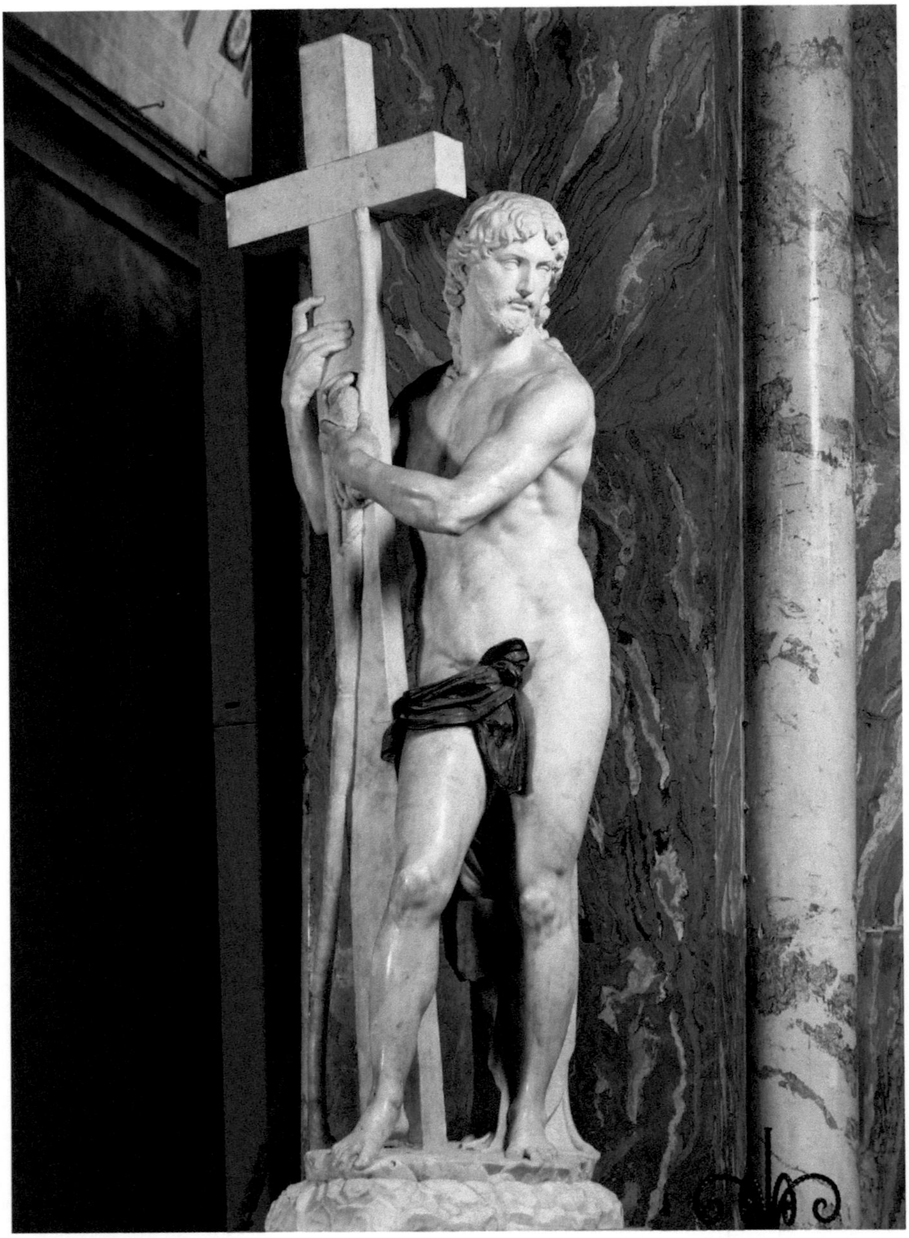

34. Michelangelo, *Risen Christ,* 1519–21, marble, Santa Maria sopra Minerva, Rome (Photo: Bridgeman Images)

much for those viewers who took it upon themselves to veil the offending body.[78] The earlier cited comments of Erasmus, Esmer, and later Contarini (the latter of whom may have been inadvertently passing judgment on Michelangelo) suggest that there was an underlying suspicion that for some artists depicting nudity in devotional art provided a convenient pretext for creating images that debased rather than edified. Even though the lumpy bodies of the saints depicted by Michelangelo in the *Last Judgment* would seem to be deliberately designed to deflect a sensual response, this made little difference to the opponents of the fresco, many of whom had never even seen the painting in real life.[79] That Michelangelo was aware of these kinds of reactions, even prior to the completion of the fresco, is demonstrated by a sonnet of 1534 to Tommaso dei Cavalieri where he cast his detractors as hypocritical fools, unable to understand the purity of his ideas on beauty due to the coarseness of their own minds.[80] Years later, in an open letter of 1582 to the Florence Academy of artists by the sculptor Bartolomeo Ammannati (1511–92), which famously described his own remorse at having created the secular *ignudi* for the fountain of Neptune in Florence's Piazza della Signoria, Ammannati defended the pure intentions of his contemporary. The final line of his letter stated that it had been Buonarroti who had told him that 'good Christians always made good and beautiful figures'.[81]

But these good and beautiful figures engendered visceral reactions that suggest a gulf between the intent of the artist and the way in which his message was interpreted. To cast Michelangelo's detractors simply as hopeless philistines or reactionary prudes is to suggest that the theological meanings that his works presented went far beyond their intellect. This is perhaps too easy an assumption to make. Even if the significance of the nude form of the *Risen Christ* had been widely comprehended, this does not mean that the censorship would not have happened regardless. After all, the attack on the genitalia was purportedly the work of the Dominican friars, an order renowned for their theological sophistication. Here, the veiling of the genitalia was a way of attempting to regulate the emotions that the unclothed body might give rise to. Such official action may also have had something to do with placating the kind of vigilante attacks on images elsewhere that had the potential to lead to social disorder. Given that iconoclasm in France provided the very impetus for the Council of Trent's decrees on sacred images in the first place (to be explored in the next chapter), this should not be disregarded as a plausible motivation. The later additions of the bronze veil and the bronze foot of the *Risen Christ* can thus be seen as a way of encouraging certain responses, by simultaneously dissuading an overt interest in the groin and demarcating a particular zone of the statue suitable for the adorations of the devout. That these seemingly contradictory reactions were caused by the same image confirms Michelangelo's own opinion that the austere beauty of well-wrought artworks was capable of inspiring 'great reverence and fear'.[82]

The question of whether or not genitalia should be depicted even when this was scripturally accurate was brought to prominence by the polemics unleashed by Michelangelo's decision to do just this in his fresco of the *Last Judgment*. The original brief from Pope Clement VII (r. 1523–34) had been to paint 'the resurrection' of the blessed on the day of Judgment. The Latin Creed refers to the resurrection of the flesh (*carnis resurrectionem*), and this was understood in a literal sense, the fresco presenting the majority of the saints completely nude in a variety of different poses, although care was taken to completely clothe the Virgin Mary and to envelop Christ with a veil that shields his groin.[83] As far as I am aware, there are few, if any, extant painted precedents for depicting the saints in this manner. In sculpture, first Donatello's (c. 1435–40) and later Michelangelo's (c. 1501–4) statues of the Old Testament King David had shown him nude, but neither were ever displayed in a church. The comparisons made between the *Last Judgment* and the *Resurrection of the Flesh* in Luca Signorelli's San Brizio chapel in the cathedral of Orvieto (1499–1502) fail to take into account that although this fresco similarly features a number of completely bare bodies, in the scene of *The Elect* the genitals of those invited into heaven are veiled with strategically placed coverings.[84] They also do not carry saintly attributes, as so many of Michelangelo's figures do, since the saints required a particular attention to decorum that in this case trumped scriptural accuracy. A later example is the fresco cycle of Pontormo at San Lorenzo, but as we have seen this received a resoundingly negative reception and was eventually destroyed.

The censorship of Michelangelo's fresco demonstrates that the nudity of the saints came to be perceived as a graver offence than diversion from scripture. This is illustrated by the fact that the anachronistic figures of Charon and Minos in the bottom left of the *Last Judgment* were allowed to remain, mostly uncensored, whilst the figures of Saints Catherine and Blaise were radically transformed.[85] We can gain a sense of their original arrangement with recourse to Niccolò della Casa's engraving, a comparison with the fresco demonstrating that Blaise's head was chipped out, then completely repainted and oriented towards Christ – so that the relationship between the figures of the two saints carried less of a potential whiff of the lascivious – whilst Catherine's stout body was veiled in an iridescent green shift (Fig. 35).[86] That the veiling of the nudity was the primary aim of the changes is made explicit by two receipts recording payments that were sent in 1567 to the heirs of Daniele da Volterra (1509–66), the student of Michelangelo who came to be known as the 'breeches maker'. These invoices note that the transformation to the fresco in 1565 consisted of 'covering the private parts'.[87] Although the first campaigns of censorship are believed to date from between August 1564 to December 1565, years after the work was first unveiled on 31 October 1541, opinion was already divided only a few weeks after the painting made its debut. The Theatine Order were some of the earliest detractors, apparently stating that 'the nudes displaying their goods in such a place is not right',[88] whilst a number of the most eloquent supporters of the fresco hailed from Florence, suggesting that their enthusiasm may also have been linked to their *campanilismo* and a desire to defend the reputation of their illustrious compatriot.[89]

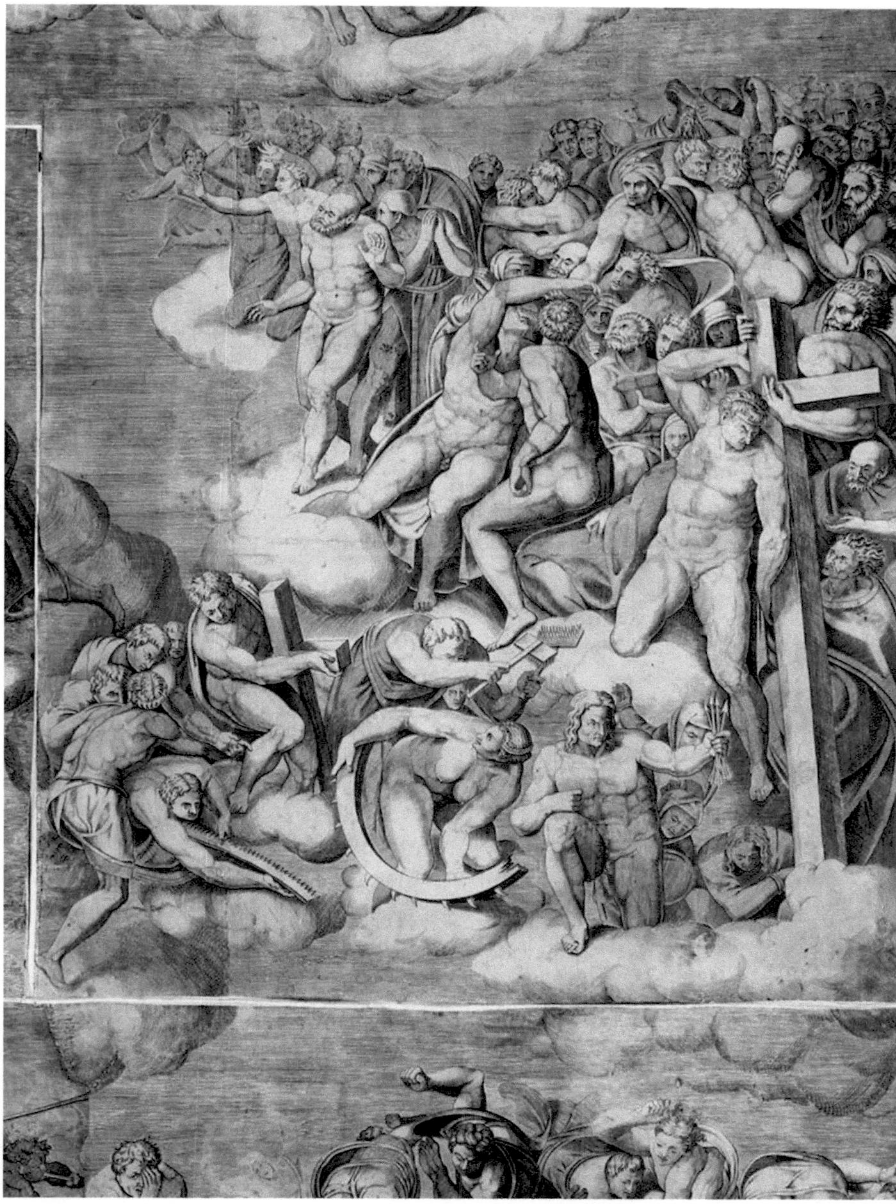

35. Niccolò della Casa after Michelangelo, *Last Judgment Showing Saints Catherine and Blaise,* c. 1543–48, engraving, Metropolitan Museum of New York (Photo: Open Access)

Rather than the *Last Judgment* causing controversy purely because it was out of step with a changing climate, it was more the case that it went so far beyond norms for the representation of the saints, and the juxtaposition of the sacred with the profane, that it caused the reassessment and re-evaluation of these very norms. This supports Paul Hill's observation that 'notions of decorum cannot lie entirely outside artistic production, governing it, but are in turn revised and reconstituted by art itself'.[90] Regardless of this, a changing historical context continues to be proposed as the primary reason why Michelangelo's fresco, one of the crowning achievements of Renaissance art, suffered the ignominy of being tainted by the additions of Volterra's brush. This is partly due to the widespread influence of an inaccuracy repeated in Romeo de Maio's influential book on Michelangelo and the Counter-Reformation, which stated that the *Last Judgment* had been the subject of lively discussion at the Council of Trent, influencing the 1563 decree.[91] John O'Malley provided an important corrective to this assertion by demonstrating that there is no evidence that it ever happened.[92] But although the frescoes were never mentioned at Trent, the decision taken to alter them was nevertheless linked to the subsequent impact of the council, since this was agreed at a meeting of 21 January 1564 by the deputation of cardinals who had been charged by Pope Pius IV (r. 1556–65) with implementing the Tridentine decrees in the city of Rome.[93] The same year Giovanni Gilio da Fabriano's (d. 1584) *Due dialoghi* was printed, presenting an encyclopaedic account of everything wrong with Michelangelo's fresco. Unsurprisingly, the nudity was condemned for numerous reasons. This point had already been made countless times before Gilio's treatise was issued, but amongst his more novel arguments employed against the fresco was his comment that 'a saint would not only have avoided displaying his private parts to others but would not even have looked at them himself'.[94]

In recent times, early modern critics of the fresco are often described as 'conservative' and closely associated with the clergy.[95] Of course, this classification doesn't sit well with the very different climate of the sixteenth century when the heights of ecclesiastical power included elite intellectuals who could equally be classified (anachronistically) as early modern equivalents of 'liberals'. De Maio went as far as to class clerical opponents of the painting as supporting a 'Vatican tradition'. Never mind the fact that the Vatican came into existence only in the twentieth century, but this makes little sense when we consider that the fresco had been commissioned by the pope in the first place.[96] Moreover, the supporters and opponents of the *Last Judgment* did not form distinct enough groups for this to have been a reality.[97] De Maio further stated that Cardinal Morone was a Theatine, and thus a reactionary conservative, when in fact he did not belong to the order, and he had even been persecuted by the Theatine Pope Paul IV (r. 1555–59), as O'Malley pointed out.[98] Yet it is true that some of the more orthodox members of society were deeply perturbed by the painting. For example, Paul IV, born Gian Pietro Carafa, who had been one of the co-founders of the Theatine Order, considered destroying the painting upon ascending to the papacy.[99] The anti-Lutheran polemicist Catarino, O.P, despised the work, and even if he admired the art of Michelangelo, he felt it was indecent to see 'the naked bodies of men and their *pudenda* ... everywhere, on the altars and in the chapels of God'.[100] It is equally true, however (and seldom pointed out), that some clergy partially defended the painting, such as the Inquisitor Aurelio Schellino at Veronese's interrogation of 1573. Responding to the artist's argument that Michelangelo was a worse offender than himself, the Inquisitor pointed out that the nudity in the Sistine Chapel was technically accurate, in contrast to Veronese's imaginative rendition of the Last Supper.[101] Some other clergy even demonstrated a sense of humour over the affair: Don Miniato Pitti of the Olivetans wrote to his friend Giorgio Vasari on 1 May 1545 making light of the 'thousand heresies' in the wall painting.[102]

Shifting political or ideological motivations, in short, cannot alone explain the negative receptions of the *Last Judgment*, since the criticisms of the fresco to some extent defy neat categorisations. Some artists demonstrated mixed reactions to the work. Others, like El Greco, were decidedly unimpressed.[103] One of the reasons invoked as convincing evidence of a shift away from a climate of tolerance and artistic liberty to one of Counter-Reformatory oppression is that the ceiling of the Sistine Chapel also featured nude figures but never garnered the same negative reaction as that meted out to the *Last Judgment*.[104] In fact, Michelangelo's frescoes of 1508–12 had been criticised: according to Vasari, the Flemish Pope Adrian VI (r. 1522–23) considered having them destroyed, decrying the '*bagnio*' of nudes that they featured.[105] Later on, Bishop Cirillo Franco praised Michelangelo's supreme artistic talents, but argued that the vault frescoes would be better suited to 'a gallery, or some garden loggia'.[106] The nudity on the ceiling was also different to that presented in the *Last Judgment*, and it was probably for this reason that Don Miniato compared the 'heresies' of the *Last Judgment* to the ceiling frescoes, which he preferred.[107] First, the genitalia on the ceiling were not as glaringly evident as that depicted on the wall.[108] Second, whereas the ceiling depicted secular *ignudi*, and narrative episodes from the Old Testament in the central compartments – some of which necessitated nakedness – the *Last Judgment* presented iconic representations of the nude saints armed with their attributes.[109] Their nakedness was inescapable, and this was made all the worse by the popularity of reproductions of the fresco, which meant that the nude bodies of the saints could be gawped at in private.[110] Thus, the debates over the *Last Judgment* can be best understood as the culmination of pre-existing disputes about the appropriate limits of artistic license that had been simmering for decades, but also one that was sustained by changes in communication that meant it became a 'casualty of the early revolution in the mass media' as Marcia Hall so aptly put it.[111]

'THE SHAMEFUL NUDITY OF THE HERETICS'

Not only did copies of the *Last Judgment* mean that it became known by a broader audience than initially considered; the printing press meant that polemical opinions about its content could be diffused. Venice played an important role in doing just this: most significantly through the publication of Pietro Aretino's letters on the topic and Ludovico Dolce's treatise *L'Aretino* (1557), which discussed the image at length and expanded upon the opinions that Aretino had presented in his correspondence. Prior to these robustly negative views, the Venetian response had been one of praise, beginning in 1544 with a dedication to Michelangelo penned by Michele Tramezzino that contrasted the imperfect bodies produced by nature with the perfection achieved by Michelangelo.[112] This laudatory tone continued to exist alongside the invectives of Aretino written in the 1540s, one example of this being the Venetian Michelangelo Biondo's 1549 *Della nobilissima pittura*, which pointed to the fame of the *Last Judgment* and its international influence upon other artists, who having been to see the fresco, 'judged it to be the most beautiful and the most famous, in other words the most glorious [work] that has ever been done in the world by any painter'.[113] In the same year the Piacentino Lodovico Domenichi's treatise on 'the nobility of women' appeared in Venice. Here the nudity of Michelangelo's *Last Judgment* was positively conflated with a return to the 'wonderful tradition' of the ancients where women could wander around naked at their leisure.[114] After Aretino's notorious diatribe against the *Last Judgment* appeared in print in 1550, praise took on a notably bawdier turn in a 1552 sonnet of the Venetian playwright Andrea Calmo. Written in dialect, Calmo joked about 'a hundred priests' who 'lovingly admire your figures'.[115] That the nudity of the image became infamous in Venetian artistic circles is illustrated by Veronese's reference to it during his questioning by the Inquisition of 1573.[116] This invocation of Michelangelo's 'errors' as a defence before the Inquisition is intriguing, since Veronese referred to it after being reminded of the obscene use of images in Germany 'and other places infected with heresy'. The artist responded that he knew of this, before shifting the attention away from himself and onto the supposedly graver artistic sins of his Tuscan superior. Might his association between obscene anti-Catholic images and the example of Michelangelo suggest that the fresco had become synonymous with something very different to what its creator had intended?

The Inquisitor's point about the use of images by enemies of the Church was one referenced by Aretino years earlier in a letter of January 1546 to the engraver Enea Vico (1523–67).[117] Here Aretino referred to an engraved copy of the *Last Judgment* by the artist Bazzacco, known as Giovanni Battista Ponchini da Castelfranco (d. c. 1577), a figure whom we will encounter again later on. Aretino advised Vico to produce a censored version of the *Last Judgment* due to his fear that the nudity could cause a scandal amongst Lutherans.[118] Alessandro Nova has pointed out the gradual eroticisation of sight in the graphic sphere in sixteenth-century Italy, and Vico himself was no stranger to nude flesh, having produced plates after Parmigianino's (1503–40) *Mars, Venus and Vulcan* that showed Mars and Venus copulating behind the cuckolded Vulcan's back.[119] The reference to Lutherans is revealing given the availability of the image in printed format, and the potential it provided to lambast the Catholic Church if it fell into the wrong hands. Given Aretino's ecclesiastical ambitions it is not unreasonable to suggest that he may genuinely have been perturbed by how elements of the fresco would be interpreted not only by potential enemies of the Church but also by the average person unfamiliar with the sophisticated tastes of the intended audience.[120] In the 1540s copies of the *Last Judgment* were being produced in quick succession, meaning that they had the potential to travel across borders, where they could fall into the hands of audiences whose reactions would have been far from benevolent.[121] This had already happened with the report commissioned by Pope Paul III (r. 1534–49): the *Consilium de emendanda ecclesia* of 1537, which described the worst abuses present in the Church and called for a purified Catholicism. Although intended as an internal document, it was leaked in 1537 and subsequently translated into German. Luther himself wrote the introduction and annotations to a pirated version, in which he gleefully proclaimed that 'the pope is trailing his poor council around like a cat with kittens . . . so now they have invented a new stratagem, and that is this booklet which so beguilingly proclaims the reformation of the whole church'.[122] In a period when some reformed areas of Europe were ridding their churches of 'idolatries', a similar opportunity to poke fun at the pontiff would have been provided by the naked saints displayed in his own chapel. Aretino pointed this out in his letter to Vico, possibly because the printer may have relished the opportunity to depict the more controversial aspects of the fresco.[123] The nudity in the *Last Judgment* was more forcefully denounced for similar reasons as Aretino by Caterino, who stated that he vehemently detested it, describing the bodies as the 'shameful nudity of the heretics'.[124] Despite the papal patronage of the fresco, Caterino interpreted the nudity of the saints as providing ammunition for a kind of covert attack on the Church, reminiscent of the earlier comment that the artist imitated 'Lutheran caprices'. However unfair this association may have been – especially given Michelangelo's profound piety – that it appears to have stuck is demonstrated by the nature of Veronese's defence to the Inquisition in 1573.

That Caterino and Aretino could have anything in common would be surprising. The former was a theologian and a formidable opponent of Luther; the latter was a prominent man of letters, and an occasional purveyor of erotic literature, infamous for his poison pen. Aretino's increasingly incensed reaction to the *Last Judgment* in a series of public and private letters authored in Venice between 1537 and 1546 is usually understood as resulting from his annoyance that his constant requests for a drawing from Michelangelo were falling on deaf ears.[125] It has also been suggested that Aretino was aware of the shifting religious climate in Venice during the 1540s and so propelled by his desire to ascend the upper echelons of the ecclesiastical hierarchy, he thus decided to make a sham show of his orthodoxy.[126] Barnes built upon both of these hypotheses by pointing out a third motivation: Aretino's shrewd understanding of the changing audience for his letters in the years spanning their publication, and an awareness that they were being read not just by the literati to whom they were mainly addressed, but also by the literate, whom Barnes believes probably shared the criticisms of the fresco associated with the clergy and, through them, the lower classes.[127] That this particular divide existed is signalled by Domenichi's comment that the nudity of the *Last Judgment* was lauded by the cognoscenti, and condemned by the 'ignorant peasants ... who are brought to shame in looking at the most beautiful parts of each sex'.[128]

The motivations concerning the drawing and the changed audience would explain why Aretino went from contentedly situating himself as one of the intellectual elite who comprehended Michelangelo's genius in the early correspondence to the populist man of the people outraged by Michelangelo's impudence in the last two letters, famously stating that 'as a baptised man, I am ashamed of the licence, so unallowable to the spirit, that you have taken in expressing these ideas'.[129] Aretino's dramatic change in tone, in comparison to the fulsome praise of the earlier correspondence, is usually framed as evidence of his insincerity. Yet he did not necessarily have firm, or at least complete visual knowledge of the painting prior to his final two vitriolic letters of 1545 and 1546. The praise contained in the preceding writings was vague and dispensed in generalised terms. Even after this date Aretino only knew the *Last Judgment* through copies – he never went to Rome to see it – and the earliest known complete reproduction of the image by Giulio Bonasone (c. 1510–c. 1576) appeared in 1546, the same year he wrote to Vico after having seen Bazzacco's engraving.[130] Thus, having viewed the contested iconographic elements of the fresco for himself, Aretino may have delighted in the opportunity to indirectly criticise the papacy not only for having commissioned Michelangelo's work in the first place but for having accepted his unorthodox representation of the saints without objection. The other alternative, that he was genuinely shocked by what he saw, seems implausible given that Aretino was an unlikely figure to be scandalised by anything, demonstrated most famously by his erotic poems of c. 1527 that had accompanied Raimondi's sixteen censored engravings based on Giulio Romano's drawings of figures in various sexual positions, known as *I modi*.[131] Particularly in the medium of print – something by this point associated with Protestant visual propaganda – the outrage that this material was greeted with, particularly by agents of the Church, is not to be underestimated. The original

1524 copies were confiscated, and Raimondi was imprisoned. Aretino's *Sonetti lussuriosi* were also censored, with Bishop Giberti possibly encouraging the censorship in his role as datary of the pope.[132] In a strange reversal of roles and possibly as revenge for his earlier treatment at the hands of the clergy, Aretino thus went from being a victim of censorship to suggesting it as a solution for the *Last Judgment*, calling for the pope to follow the example of Gregory the Great, who devoted himself to removing from Rome 'all the prideful statues of idols'.[133]

'EXTREME PERFECTION AND EXTREME INDECENCY'

Although Aretino hailed from Tuscany, writing from his base in Venice he can be said to have fanned the flames that eventually led to the *Last Judgment*'s censorship. They were further stoked in 1557, one year after the death of Aretino, when Dolce's treatise appeared in the same city. The 'shamelessness' of the nude figures in the Sistine Chapel was criticised in similar terms and it was argued that Michelangelo had flouted the rules of decorum by demonstrating insensitivity to the context in which the frescoes were displayed and the saints who were to be represented. What this treatise did not argue was that profane images or depictions of the naked body should cease to exist.[134] As should be expected given his publication of erotica, the voice of Aretino defended such representations 'by way of a pastime' but pointed out that they had to be adapted to place and audience. For an ecclesiastical setting such as the Sistine Chapel, figures that had been 'fully decent and less perfect in their design' would have been preferable to the 'extreme perfection and extreme indecency' of the *Last Judgment*.[135] Unless this distinction between site and audience is appreciated, the extent to which sacred images were controlled after the Council of Trent cannot be properly assessed, since the Tridentine decrees were primarily concerned with the ambit that the Church had clear jurisdiction over: images on display in devotional settings. Strictly defining and separating the different genres of the spiritual and the profane would also have been of growing concern given the increasing eroticism of some mythological imagery during the 1520s in Italy.[136] This means that whilst Aretino may well have had personal motives for his increasing impatience with Michelangelo, the point made about context and audience was one that was widely agreed upon at the time, and it is not necessarily so different from what might be considered appropriate for display in a religious edifice today.[137]

Like Aretino's letters, Dolce's treatise was influential, blazing the way for the minutiae of Gilio's treatise of 1564.[138] Complaints about the fresco had been rumbling on for years, but the Aretine letters and the two treatises meant that its nudity became something of a cause célèbre. Cumulatively, they can be said to have strengthened opinion against the painting by emotively appealing to standards of decorum.[139] To modern viewers the eventual decision taken to censor the genitalia seems a drastic solution, particularly given Michelangelo's fame. The fresco was tampered with, its integrity was called into question, and the 'problematic' aspects of it were erased: cleansed and neutralised in order to cater to the concerns of a reactionary public. But in the midst of the contemporary polemics the censorship is perhaps best understood as a middle way between those who preferred to leave the fresco as it was and the more zealous who advocated for its removal. Vasari himself alluded to the changes as a resolution that ensured the fresco's survival. He described the insertion of Volterra's 'light garments' as a scheme dreamt up by 'cardinals and men of learning', who believed that to destroy the work according to the wishes of Pope Paul IV would have been 'a great sin'.[140] Vasari's account suggests that the decision to do something about the fresco had been decided much earlier during Paul IV's reign, and that 'the business was afterwards finished in the time of Pius IV'. Given the uproar, Michelangelo may not have necessarily disagreed with this if a letter of 1561 penned by Scipione Saurolo is to be trusted. Saurolo was a minor figure in the curia, but the recipient of his correspondence was Carlo Borromeo, who was later a member of the delegation that decided the fate of the fresco. Saurolo asserted that even Michelangelo's great patron, Pope Paul III, had been 'greatly displeased' by the situation in the Sistine Chapel and sought to deal with it by enlarging the chapel on each side of the sacristy.[141] Saurolo went on to say that during the last year of the reign of Paul IV, 'Michelangelo said that he wished to arrange it, since it was a matter of conscience to leave such a thing behind.'[142] To erase the *Last Judgment* completely would have meant admitting that previous popes had erred in allowing the painting in the first place, and would also have smacked of iconoclasm. But since numerous commentators found the genitalia in the *Last Judgment* to be lascivious, not doing anything about it could have put the papacy at odds with the decrees of the Council of Trent, and possibly with popular opinion.[143] In contrast to the delegation's direct orders that anything 'obscene or obviously false' was to be covered up in the Apostolic chapel (and in the diocese of Rome more broadly), the full-frontal nudity on Michelangelo's ceiling remained untouched, and the figures of Minos and Charon in the *Last Judgment* remained, demonstrating that the veiling of the genitalia that began in 1564 might have been more of a half-hearted bow to external pressure than the dawn of a systematic campaign of censorship.[144]

AFTERMATH

Visual and documentary evidence suggests that artists active in the late sixteenth and seventeenth centuries were well aware of the events surrounding

Michelangelo's *Last Judgment*. This is hardly surprising given his fame, but it helps to put the impact of the Tridentine decrees on images into perspective. Not only did Veronese directly refer to the iconography of the *Last Judgment*, but El Greco apparently offered to replace the painting with his own new and improved version upon arriving in Rome after his sojourn in Venice in 1570.[145] In his personal annotations to Vasari's adulatory comments on the painting, El Greco wrote that 'you don't mean to say that you can't paint better than this?'[146] In the years after the censorship, diverse artists in Italy issued their own 'corrected' versions of the painting that demonstrated knowledge of where it had purportedly erred.[147] For example, in a retrospective study by Federico Zuccaro dated to the mid 1590s, his brother Taddeo was shown as a young man intent on copying the lower left section of the fresco prior to Volterra's interventions. The controversial genitalia, however, were rendered indistinct.[148] The Bergamese artist Giovanni Battista Moroni (1520/24–79) – who had been present in Trent at the time of the council – was working on a version of the *Last Judgment* for the church of San Pancrazio in Bergamo that drew inspiration from Michelangelo at the time of his death in 1579.[149] The upper zone, believed to have been finished by Francesco Terzi (1523–91), showed the figures judiciously clothed, an iconographic decision possibly influenced by the fact that one Monsignor Porro, who had visited the church in 1575, had criticised the nudity of the angels in Francesco Zanchi's frescoes at the altar of the Blessed Sacrament, commissioned by the same Scuola that later employed Moroni.[150] Back in Venice, the vast 1588 *Paradiso* completed for the Sala del Maggior Consiglio in the Ducal Palace by Jacopo and Domenico Tintoretto (1560–1635) depicted the nudity of the Elect respectfully shrouded, as did Tintoretto's earlier *Last Judgment* in Madonna dell'Orto (Fig. 36).[151]

In the next chapter it will be shown that orders to remove 'lascivious' artworks from the churches of Venice were exceedingly rare at the end of the sixteenth century, which suggests a level of pre-existing sensitivity (or self-censorship) amongst artists in the city as to what was appropriate for specific locations and audiences. The long-term impact of the polemics surrounding the *Last Judgment* was that it became unusual for the genitalia of the saints to be depicted in devotional settings, and when this did happen it was usually greeted with condemnation. This is well illustrated by an episode that took place in the town of Castelfranco Veneto in 1554, when the censorship of the nudity in Giovanni Battista Ponchini's 1551 altarpiece *Christ Descending into Limbo* was commanded by the visiting bishop of Crete, Francesco Verdura. The parish priest was ordered, upon pain of excommunication and the payment of a twenty-five-ducat fine, to cover the altarpiece until the figures were adjusted by the painter (Fig. 37).[152] That Ponchini was the artist responsible for the painting is telling. He had previously authored the image of the *Last Judgment* referred to in shocked terms by Aretino in his letter to Enea Vico.

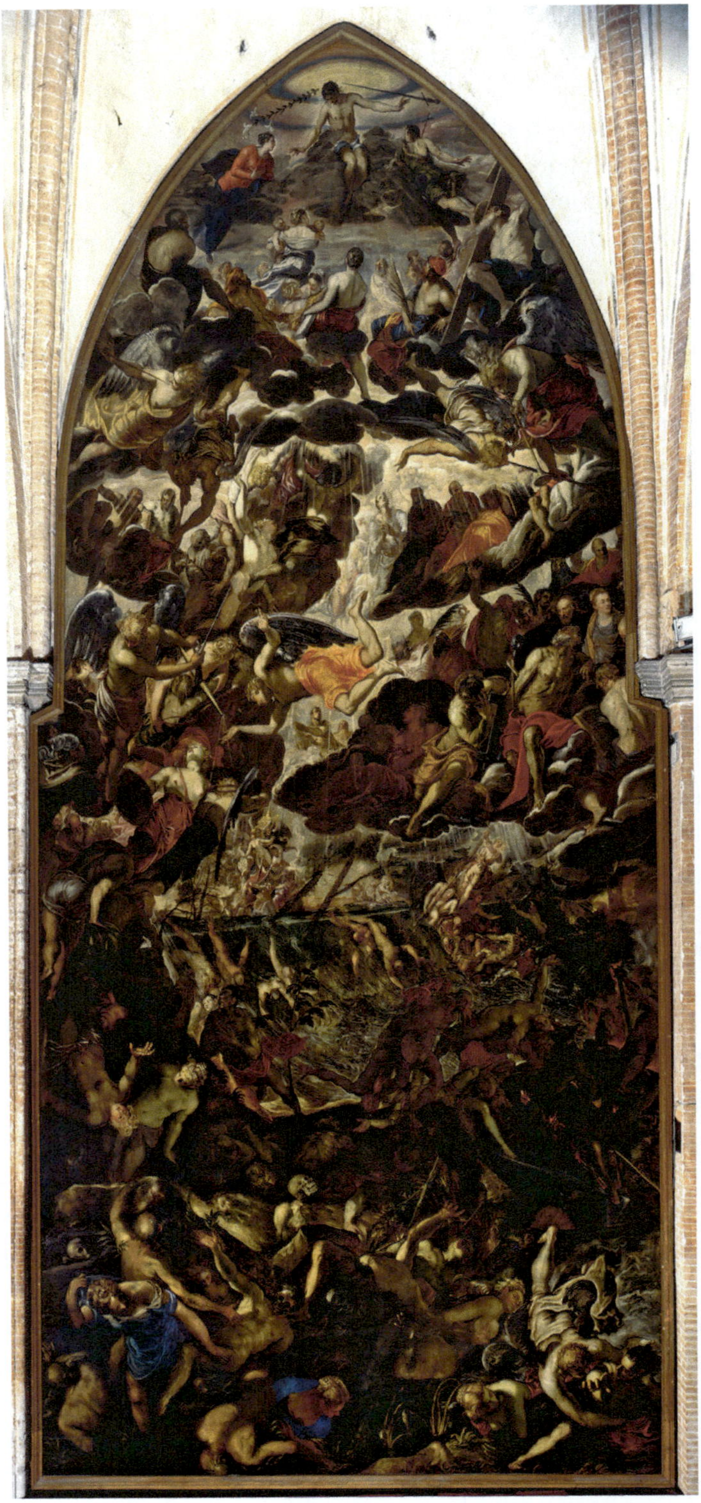

36. Tintoretto, *Last Judgment,* c. 1559–60, oil on canvas, Madonna dell'Orto, Venice (Photo: Cameraphoto)

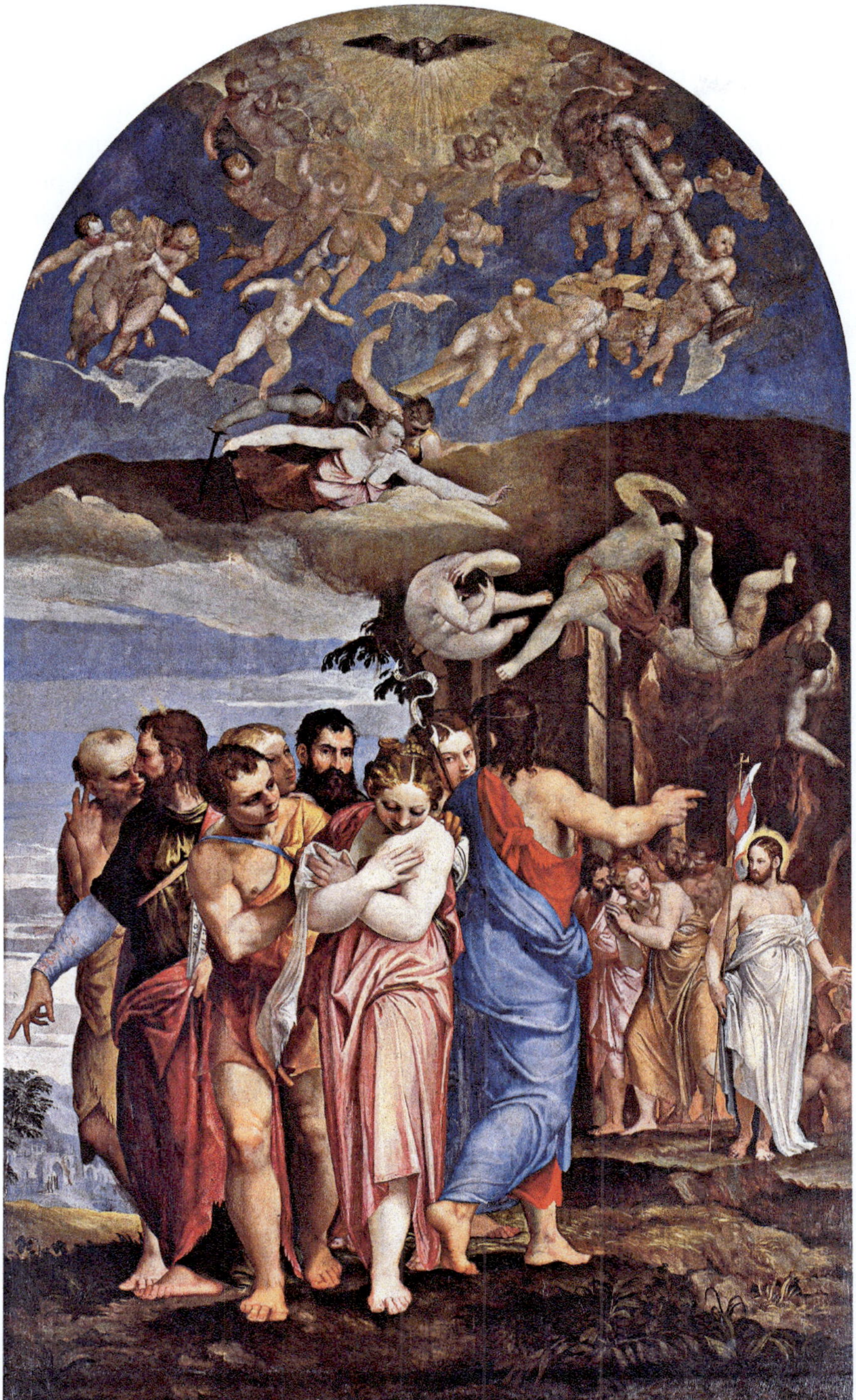

37. Giovanni Battista Ponchini, *Christ Descending into Limbo,* 1551, oil on canvas, Santa Maria Assunta e San Liberale, Castelfranco (Photo: HIP/Art Resource, New York)

The Castelfranco altarpiece demonstrated clear knowledge of the Sistine Chapel fresco, most obviously through the various gymnastics of the nudes, and the angels shown carrying the instruments of the passion. Depicted naked, the bare porcelain flesh of the statuesque Eve must have acted as a foil to the clothed male figures that surround her, alarming the visiting bishop and suggesting Ponchini's proclivity for the transgressive.[153] The artist had become a priest in 1550, but just a few years later, in 1553, he was denounced for sodomy and heresy, accusations that were found to be baseless. Even if his Castelfranco altarpiece was deemed to be inappropriate, the artist went on to paint the thoroughly orthodox subject of the 'Triumph of the Faith over Heresy' for the Ducal Palace, and he was still receiving commissions in 1572, when he was the parish priest of Creola.[154] Ironically, it was not Ponchini but the bishop who ordered the censoring of his work who ended up being imprisoned in Rome in 1558 by the Inquisition after a series of accusations of heresy, his freedom being granted only upon the death of Pope Paul IV a year later.

The events surrounding Ponchini's altarpiece provide an interesting precedent in the Veneto for the changes made to Michelangelo's fresco, and since the altarpiece directly alluded to the *Last Judgment*, the censorship provides further evidence that the older artist's innovations were interpreted by some as having presented a bad example to his imitators. Dolce's *L'Aretino* argued that artists like Raphael and Titian were eminently more attentive to the decorum of place and audience than Michelangelo had been. By comparison he was made to appear something of an intellectual snob.[155] This was a snub to some extent confirmed by Michelangelo himself, who had supposedly distinguished between cerebral Italian painting suited to the cognoscenti and mediocre Flemish painting, which was emotive in nature, but appealed to women, especially the very old and the very young, monks and nuns, and to 'certain noblemen who have no sense of true harmony'.[156] This kind of accusation was rarely aimed at Venetian artists. Tintoretto, for example, was known for his popular appeal, something of growing importance in the latter half of the sixteenth century, after the Council of Trent had reasserted the communicative power of the sacred image. In his 1648 *Considerationi*, the Bolognese writer Virgilio Malvezzi argued that the colouring of Robusti's paintings appealed to the common person, even if Raphael was by far the greater artist.[157]

To conclude, Michelangelo's *Last Judgment* might have stimulated a reassessment of the boundaries of the decorum for sacred images, but the nude form was far from being banished from the church interior. That artists active in Venice had never been particularly inclined to depict holy figures totally nude in ecclesiastical settings in the first place suggests that the contemporary mores did not necessarily present an insurmountable barrier to their artistic expression. Sensuous depictions of the saints continued, albeit more so for domestic settings rather than sacred ones, and there were plenty

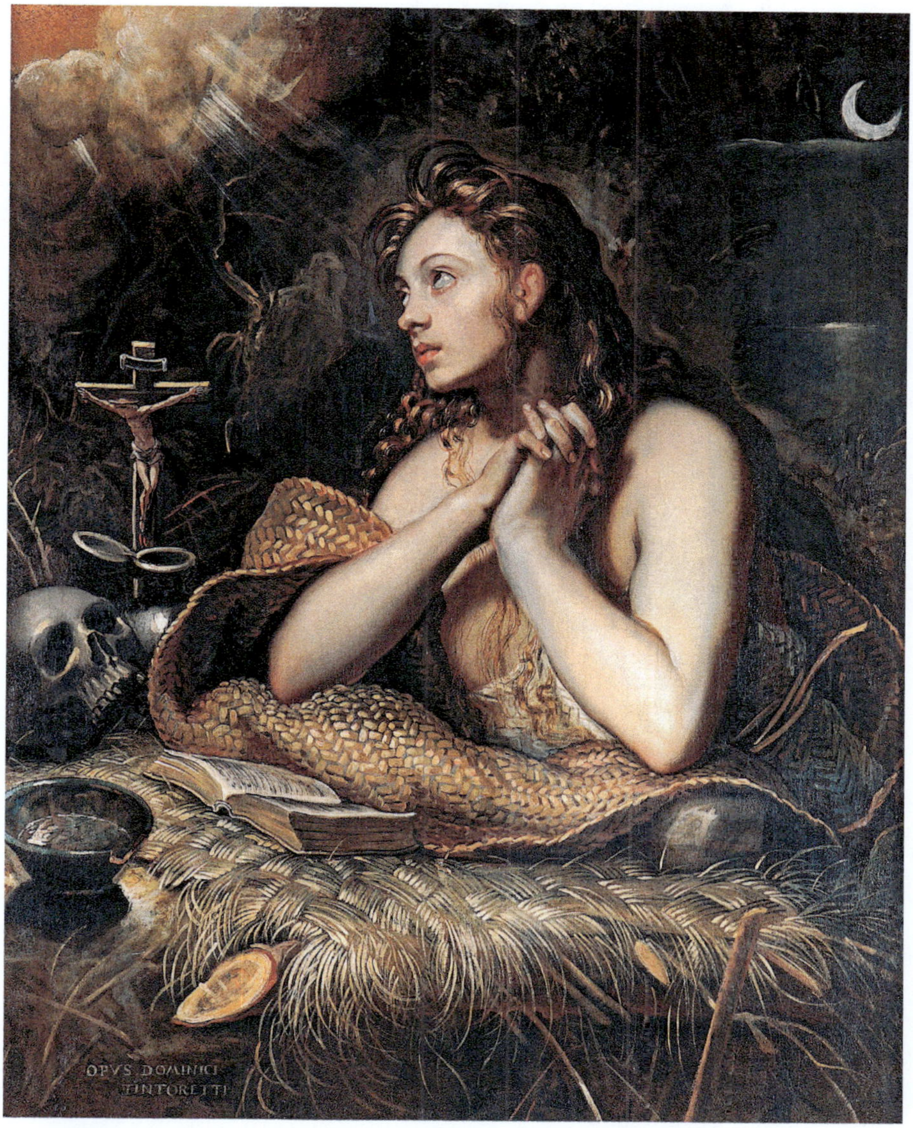

38. Domenico Tintoretto, *The Penitent Magdalen,* c. 1598–1602, oil on canvas, Musei Capitolini, Rome (Photo: GL Archive/Alamy Stock Photo)

of secular nudes in the seventeenth century too. Although we know nothing of the appearance of 'certain privately owned paintings depicting women in lascivious poses' found in the nuns' cells at San Sepolcro in Venice in 1620, that Patriarch Giovanni Tiepolo (1570–1631, r. 1619–31) ordered their removal shows that he considered them base enough to present a risk to nuns' souls.[158] Domenico Tintoretto grew so attached to a painting of the Magdalen by his own hand, possibly the ravishing *Penitent Magdalen* of c. 1598–1602 now in the Capitoline Museum, that he was incensed when his father Jacopo sold it to a merchant, if Ridolfi is to be believed (Fig. 38).[159]

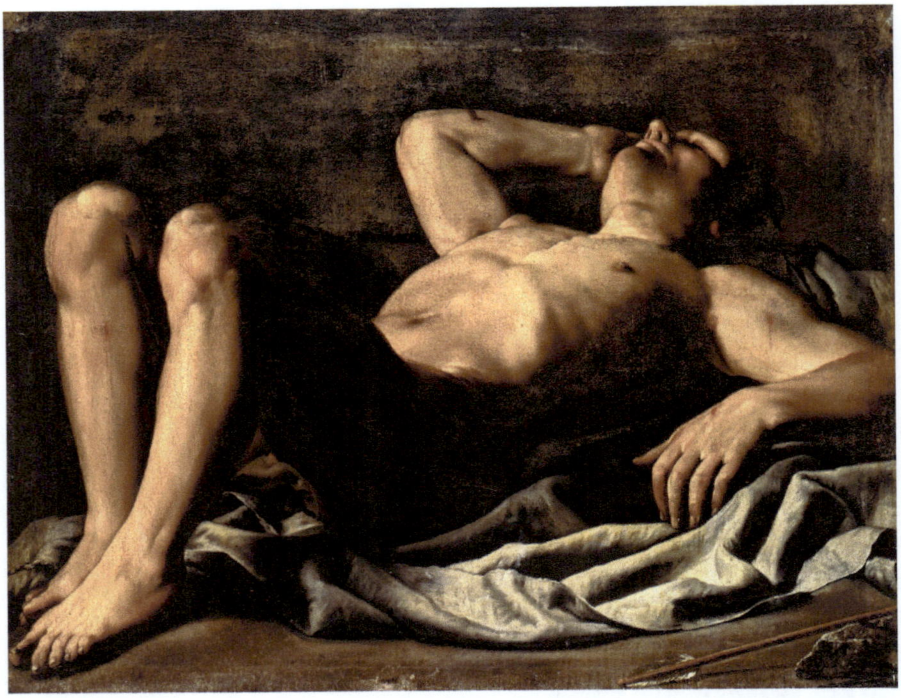

39. Marcantonio Bassetti, *Saint Sebastian,* 1620s, oil on canvas, Private Collection (Photo: Private collection)

A second case in point is the Veronese painter Marcantonio Bassetti's (1586–1630) Caravaggesque *Saint Sebastian* of c. 1620, held in a private collection. The popularity of Sebastian was in part due to his status as a plague-saint, yet for artists it also provided the opportunity to depict an idealised nude, something that Bassetti seems to have relished. Here he painted Sebastian as a foreshortened figure lying undressed on the ground, the only thing identifying him as the saint being an arrow that lies by his side and a second that pierces his arm (Fig. 39).[160] A different version of a similar theme by Bassetti shows Sebastian sprawled naked, the modesty of his perfect sensual body only just covered, as the homely figure of Saint Irene removes an arrow from his leg.[161] Bassetti's interest in the nude form as the principal subject matter of painting is alluded to in a letter of 1616 sent from Rome to Palma il Giovane where he promised to work hard, as 'we have initiated our academy, drawing figures in various poses with brushes and colours'.[162]

Even long after the Council of Trent the expurgation of images deemed to be obscene from devotional settings was mostly haphazard. What might have been considered acceptable for decades could suddenly be subject to fits of puritanism that saw images removed or veiled, and two later examples from Venice eloquently demonstrate this: in 1757 the guardian of the church of the Redentore complained to the Provveditori al Sal about the scandal of thirteen of the paintings in the niches of the temple, arguing that here in 'the house of the Lord, where everything should inspire devotion and sanctity ... objects of abuse and scandal dominate'.[163] Even though the originals of 1619 had been completed by the artist Paolo Piazza (1560–1620), himself a member of the Capuchin Order that officiated at the Redentore, in 1758 it was reported in the Senate Hall that the artist Giuseppe Angeli had been ordered to 'reform' the chiaroscuro paintings and to render them 'more devout and edifying'.[164] In this case, reform of the visual was specifically referred to in the context of censoring nudity and it was approved by the Venetian State at the behest of the Capuchins. Similarly, even though Tullio Lombardo's altarpiece of the *Coronation of the Virgin* (1499–1501) for the church of San Giovanni Crisostomo was one of the rare occasions when the 1581 Apostolic Visitation praised an artwork, elements of his ducal tombs came to be viewed less positively in the nineteenth century.[165] John Ruskin took issue with the virtues on the monument to Doge Andrea Vendramin (Fig. 40), describing them as 'dressed like heathen goddesses, and totally devoid of expression, though graceful and well-studied merely as female figures'.[166] He even argued that the effigy of the doge demonstrated such 'utter coldness of feeling, as could only consist with an extreme of intellectual and moral degradation'.[167] In 1819, some years before Ruskin's account was published, Tullio Lombardo's *Adam* (Fig. 41) and the accompanying statue of Eve (attributed to Francesco Segala) were removed from the Vendramin tomb on account of the fact that 'the two statues are nude, and thus indecent to the sanctity of the site'.[168] The original home of the monument was Santa Maria dei Servi, near the east end of the church, but it had been shifted into the high altar of the Santi Giovanni e Paolo in 1816 after the Servite complex was suppressed. The placement of the figures in the most hallowed area of the edifice apparently offended Patriarch Francesco Milesi (r. 1815–19), who harangued the prior of the Dominican convent, Emmanuele Lodi, to do something about them, so they were removed and replaced with the statues of the warriors. Adam and Eve languished first in the courtyard of Lodi, moving then to the Palazzo Vendramin-Calergi, where Eve remained after Adam was sold at auction in Paris. If anything, the location of the statues in the presbytery of Santi Giovanni e Paolo would only have strengthened the theological point that their presence alluded to: humanity was fallen, but it was redeemed through Christ, who was believed to be whole and present during the sacrifice of the mass on the high altar. The import of this relationship must have been considered secondary to considerations of decorum by the patriarch who wanted them removed, but there is a certain irony in the fact that this censorship happened not during the Counter-Reformation but during the far more prudish nineteenth century, over 300 years after Felix Faber had first stood in the same church, awed and surprised by the naked 'idols' of the Lombardo tomb monuments.

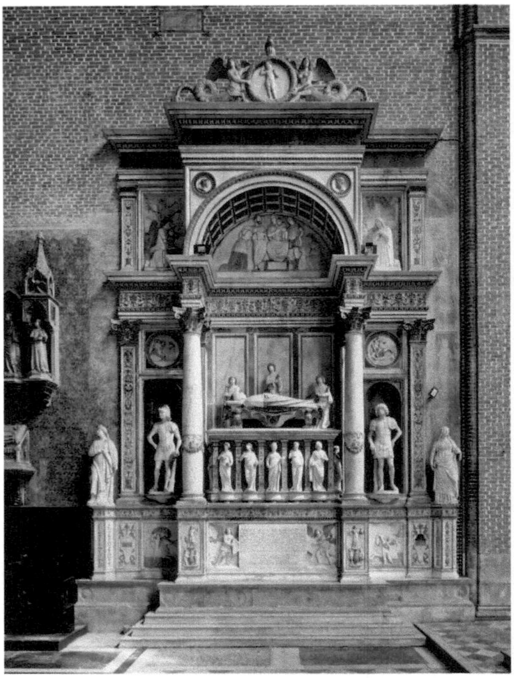

40. Tullio Lombardo, *Monument to Andrea Vendramin,* c. 1490–1500, Santi Giovanni e Paolo, Venice (Photo: Cameraphoto)

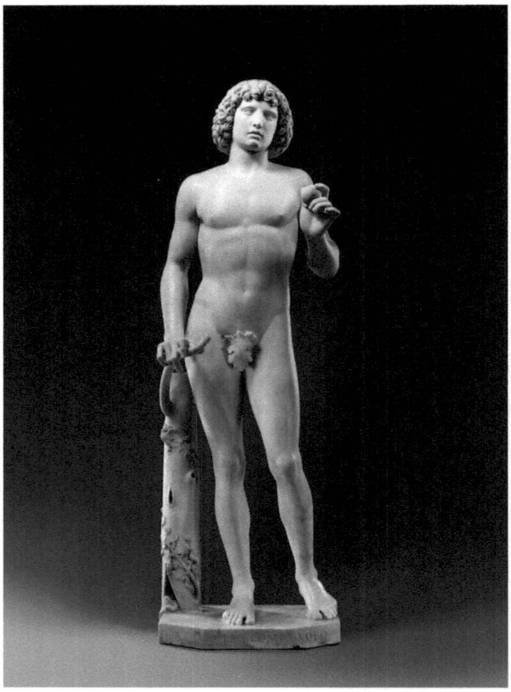

41. Tullio Lombardo, *Adam,* c. 1490–95, marble, Metropolitan Museum of Art, New York (Photo: Open Access)

NOTES

1 Thanks to Julian Gardner for alerting me to this source. Vincenzo Joppi, 'Contributo secondo alla storia dell'arte nel Friuli ed alla vita dei pittori e intagliatori friuliani', in *Monumenti Storici publicati dalla R. Deputazione Veneta di storia patria*, 4, miscellanea (Venice: Fratelli Visentini, 1890), 37. See also Augusto Gentili, 'San Marco nelle immagini del Cinquecento: problemi di iconologia contestuale', in *San Marco: aspetti storici e agiografici*, ed. Antonio Niero, Proceedings of the International Conference, Venice, 26–29 April 1994 (Venice: Marsilio, 1996), 303–12.

2 The hypothesis of Gentili, 'San Marco nelle immagini del Cinquecento', 304.

3 Vasari, *Lives of the Painters, Sculptors and Architects*, vol. 1: 900.

4 For an interrogation of the terminology and its implications, see Robert W. Gaston, 'How Words Control Images: The Rhetoric of Decorum in Counter-Reformation Italy', in *The Sensuous in the Counter-Reformation Church*, ed. Marcia B. Hall and Tracy E. Cooper (Cambridge: Cambridge University Press, 2013), 74–90. Also useful is the introduction to D'Elia, *The Poetics of Titian's Religious Paintings*.

5 Michael Baxandall, *Giotto and the Orators: Humanist Observers of Painting in Italy and the Discovery of Pictorial Composition, 1350–1450* (Oxford: Clarendon Press, 1971), 10; Gaston, 'How Words Control Images: The Rhetoric of Decorum in Counter-Reformation Italy', 75.

6 The most famous example of this tendency is Romeo De Maio, *Michelangelo e la Controriforma* (Rome: Laterza, 1978). Despite some notable inaccuracies (see note 98 below and main body text), De Maio's book had gone through three editions by 1990 and was widely cited for years afterwards. More recently, Melinda Schlitt stated that fresco stood 'at the fulcrum of a cultural shift in which stylistic paradigms were used to support ideological and political agendas that were often contrary to artistic ideals and motivation', whilst Hall suggested that a partial explanation for Michelangelo's miscalculation could be explained by the fact that 'between the time the fresco was commissioned and designed, and its unveiling on 31 October 1541, a cultural shift of enormous magnitude had been taking place'. Melinda Schlitt, 'Painting, Criticism, and Michelangelo's "Last Judgment" in the Age of the Counter-Reformation', in *Michelangelo's 'Last Judgment'*, ed. Marcia B. Hall (Cambridge: Cambridge University Press, 2005), 115; Hall, *The Sacred Image in the Age of Art*, 100.

7 The interpretation propounded by De Maio, *Michelangelo e la Controriforma*. See previous note. For the various interventions of Volterra and the successive campaigns of censorship, see, in particular, Fabrizio Mancinelli, Gianluigi Colalucci, and Nazzareno Gabrielli, *Michelangelo: il Giudizio Universale*, Art Dossier, no. 88 (Florence: Giunti, 1994), 7, 19–23; Fabrizio Mancinelli, Gianluigi Colalucci, and Nazzareno Gabrielli, 'The "Last Judgment": Notes on Its Conservation History, Technique, and Restoration', in *The Sistine Chapel: A Glorious Restoration*, ed. Pierluigi de Vecchi and Carlo Pietrangeli (New York: Harry N. Abrams, 1999), 236–55.

8 A reassessment of some long-standing beliefs regarding the censorship of the nude is provided by Thomas Depasquale, 'Epilogue Two: Michelangelo's "Last Judgment" and the Reception of the Nude in Counter-Reformation Italy', in *The Renaissance Nude*, ed. Thomas Kren, Jill Burke, and Stephen J. Campbell, Exhibition Catalogue, J. Paul Getty Museum, Los Angeles, 30 October 2018–27 January 2019, Royal Academy of Arts, London, 2 March–2 June 2019 (Los Angeles: J. Paul Getty Museum, 2018), 367–73. Also useful is Bette Talvacchia, 'The Word Made Flesh: Spiritual Subjects and Carnal Depictions in Renaissance Art', in *The Sensuous in the Counter-Reformation Church*, ed. Marcia B. Hall and Tracy E. Cooper (Cambridge: Cambridge University Press, 2013), 49–73.

9 See Bernadine Ann Barnes, 'Aretino, the Public and the Censorship of Michelangelo's Last Judgment', in *Suspended License: Censorship and the Visual Arts*, ed. Elizabeth C. Childs (Seattle,: University of Washington Press, 1997), 59–61. Discussed also by Depasquale,

'Epilogue Two: Michelangelo's "Last Judgment" and the Reception of the Nude in Counter-Reformation Italy', 368.

10 Apart from the obvious stylistic influence of Michelangelo's painting on other artists, in the sixteenth century painters including Vasari, Veronese, El Greco, and Giovanni Paolo Lomazzo all commented on the work. In the seventeenth century this continued with the writings of Karel van Mander, Vicente Carducho, Francisco Pacheco, Giovanni Pietro Bellori, and Salvator Rosa. For contemporary and later reactions to the *Last Judgment*, see Paola Barocchi, ed., *La vita di Michelangelo nelle redazioni del 1550 e del 1568*, vol. 3 (Milan: Riccardo Ricciardi, 1962), 1254–73; André Chastel, *Art of Italian Renaissance*, trans. Linda Murray and Peter Murray (London: Alpine Fine Arts Collection, 1985), 188–207.

11 This view is common to many of the art historians described in the introduction who held generally negative opinions about art after the Council of Trent, usually focusing on examples from Rome and Florence. For the 'erotic revolution', see James Turner, *Eros Visible: Art, Sexuality and Antiquity in Renaissance Italy* (New Haven, CT: Yale University Press, 2017).

12 Ilaria Bianchi, *La politica delle immagini nell'età della Controriforma: Gabriele Paleotti teorico e committente* (Bologna: Editrice Compositori, 2008), 63–64, 73. Fontana's comments are contained in an account that Bianchi dates to after 1578. The documents, contained in the Archivio Isolani of Bologna, are dated to c. 1580–81 by Giulia Daniele, *Prospero Fontana "Pictor Bononiensis" (1509–1597). Catalogo ragionato dei dipinti* (Rome: De Luca editori d'Arte, 2022), 66.

13 Pointed out also by Humfrey, who noted that some of the criticisms of writers such as Gilio were associated not only with the *Last Judgment*, but with the kind of mannerism that developed in Central Italy, and 'abuses' that Venetian painters tended to avoid. Peter Humfrey, 'La pala d'altare veneta nell'età delle riforme', in *La pittura nel Veneto: il Cinquecento*, ed. Mauro Lucco, vol. 3 (Milan: Electa, 1999), 1136–37.

14 For Giorgione's frescoes at the Fondaco, see, most recently, Tom Nichols, *Giorgione's Ambiguity* (London: Reaktion Books, 2020), 167–80.

15 This observation is at odds with Gentili's attempt to read a hidden, heterodox message in the *Last Judgment*, apparent evidence of Tintoretto's adherence to a larger movement of 'European evangelism'. This is based on the fact that the scales of the archangel Michael appear to be without plates (thus useless for weighing souls). According to the author it follows that this signifies a possible rejection of the role of good works in salvation despite the prominence given to the allegorical figure of charity towards the height of the painting, just below the figure of Christ, who looks down at her. Augusto Gentili, 'Tintoretto in contesto tra politica e religione', in *Jacopo Tintoretto*, ed. Miguel Falomir, Proceedings of the International Symposium, 26–27 February 2007, Museo Nacional del Prado, Madrid (Madrid: Museo Nacional del Prado, 2009), 20.

16 Vasari, *Lives of the Painters, Sculptors and Architects*, vol. 2: 511–12. Centuries later, Ruskin compared Michelangelo's painting unfavourably to Tintoretto's *Paradiso* in the Ducal Palace. He wrote that the 'dark carnality of Michael Angelo's has fostered insolent science, and fleshy imagination'. See John Ruskin, *The Relation between Michael Angelo and Tintoret: Seventh of the Course of Lectures on Sculpture Delivered at Oxford, 1870–71* (London: Smith, Elder, 1872), 40. Humfrey first recognised that Tintoretto might have been aware of critiques of Michelangelo's *Last Judgment* when he produced the painting for Madonna dell'Orto. Peter Humfrey, 'Venezia 1540–1600', in *La pittura nel Veneto: il Cinquecento*, ed. Mauro Lucco, vol. 2 (Milan: Electa, 1998), 511–12. Ilchman was the first to note that Tintoretto avoided gratuitous nudity in his version of the subject. Ilchman, 'Tintoretto as a Painter of Religious Narrative', 87–91, 94, note 80. Ridolfi tells us that Tintoretto had also painted a *Last Judgment* for the Sala dello Scrutinio in the Ducal Palace, destroyed by fire in 1577. Ridolfi, *Le maraviglie dell'arte*, vol. 2: 25.

17 David Chambers and Brian Pullan, eds., *Venice: A Documentary History, 1450–1630*, reprint of the 1992 edition (Toronto: University of Toronto Press in association with the Renaissance Society of America, 2001), 198.

18 Chambers and Pullan, *Venice*, 199. For the original Latin text, see Felix Faber, *Fratis felicis fabri evagatorium in terrae sanctae, Arabiae et Egypti peregrinationem*, ed. Conrad D. Hassler, vol. 2 (Stuttgart: Societatis literariae stuttgardiensis, 1843), 424–26. For the Mocenigo tomb, see the catalogue entry of Anne Markham Schulz in Giuseppe Pavanello, ed., *La Basilica dei Santi Giovanni e Paolo: Pantheon della Serenissima* (Venice: Marcianum Press, 2013), 142–49, cat. 28.

19 Leo Steinberg, *The Sexuality of Christ in Renaissance Art and in Modern Oblivion*, 2nd ed. (Chicago: University of Chicago Press, 1996), 146. Vasari also described Michelangelo's *Crucifixion of Saint Peter* in the Pauline chapel as 'a nude figure of rare beauty', even though the genitals were covered with a loincloth. Vasari, *Lives of the Painters, Sculptors and Architects*, vol. 2: 696.

20 For changing connotations of the nude and nudity, see, in particular, Jill Burke, 'The European Nude, 1400–1650', in *Splendor, Myth and Vision: Nudes from the Prado*, ed. Thomas J. Loughman, Kathleen M. Morris, and Lara Yeager-Crasselt, Clark Art Institute, Williamstown, Massachusetts, in association with Museo Nacional del Prado Madrid (New Haven, CT: Yale University Press, 2016), 16–49.

21 Francesco Sansovino, *Venetia città nobilissima et singolare, descritta in XIIII. Libri* (Venice: Giacomo Sansovino, 1581), 18v. Francesco's attitude may well have been influenced by the work of his father, the Florentine sculptor Jacopo Sansovino, whose mastery of the mythological nude was renowned.

22 Faber may even have witnessed similar behaviour when he visited Santi Giovanni e Paolo. For the statue at Santa Marina, see Silvio Tramontin, 'La visita apostolica del 1581 a Venezia', *Studi Veneziani* 9 (1967): 522; Anne Markham Schulz, 'The Life and Works of Jacopo Fantoni, Venetian Sculptor', *Nuovi studi* 19 (2013): 111–12. When Fynes Moryson visited Venice in the late sixteenth century, he listed the statue of 'Tadeo della volpe of Imola' as one of the 'must-see' artistic treasures of the city. Fynes Moryson, *An itinerary written by Fynes Moryson … containing his ten yeeres travell through the twelve dominions of Germany, Bohmerland, Sweitzerland, Netherland, Denmarke, Poland, Italy, Turky, France, England, Scotland, and Ireland* (London: J. Beale, 1617), 83.

23 'BMC, MS Gradenigo 228/3, J. Grevembroch, Monumenta veneta ex antiquis ruderibus, III' (1759), fol. 76. See also Schulz, 'The Life and Works of Jacopo Fantoni', 111, 118, note 19.

24 David Freedberg, 'Johannes Molanus on Provocative Paintings: De historia sanctarum imaginum et picturarum, Book II, Chapter 42', *Journal of the Warburg and Courtauld Institutes* 34 (1971): 243. In the thirteenth century, Bishop William Durandus wrote that the Greeks depicted figures from the navel upwards, 'to remove all occasion for foolish thoughts'. For an analysis, see Steinberg, *The Sexuality of Christ in Renaissance Art and in Modern Oblivion*, 28.

25 Giovanni Domenico Mansi, *Sacrorum conciliorum nova et amplissima collectio*, vol. 32 (Paris: H. Welter, 1901), 1200 (Sens), 1321 (Augsburg), 1414–15 (Mainz). These precedents were noted in the discussion of lascivious images of Federico Borromeo, *Sacred Painting; Museum*, ed. and trans. Kenneth S. Rothwell, Introduction and notes by Pamela M. Jones (Cambridge, MA: Harvard University Press, 2010), 57. The decree of Sens is analysed by O'Malley, 'Trent, Sacred Images, and Catholics' Senses of the Sensuous', 32.

26 For Gerson, see Blunt, *Artistic Theory in Italy, 1450–1600*, 117.

27 Antoninus's comments appear in his *Summa theologica*, written while he held the bishopric between 1446 and 1459. Creighton Gilbert, 'The Archbishop on the Painters of Florence, 1450', *Art Bulletin* 41, no. 1 (1959): 75–76.

28 See Marcia B. Hall, 'Savonarola's Preaching and the Patronage of Art', in *Christianity and the Renaissance: Image and Religious Imagination in the Quattrocento*, ed. Timothy Verdon and John Henderson (Syracuse, NY: Syracuse University Press, 1990), 499–500, 516, note 19; Alexander Nagel, 'Art as Gift: Liberal Art and Religious Reform in the Renaissance', in *Negotiating the Gift: Pre-modern Figurations of Exchange*, ed. Gadi Algazi, Valentin Groebner, and Bernhard Jussen (Göttingen: Vandenhoeck & Ruprecht, 2003), 352–53.

29 Vasari, *Lives of the Painters, Sculptors and Architects*, vol. 1: 539. For the comparison with image destruction in the sixteenth century, see Depasquale, 'Epilogue Two: Michelangelo's "Last Judgment" and the Reception of the Nude in Counter-Reformation Italy', 373, note 15. It has been often reported that Botticelli tossed some of his own paintings into the flames, but this appears to be apocryphal. Interestingly, a Venetian merchant was said to have unsuccessfully bid 20,000 gulden for the contents of Savonarola's last bonfire, but this is reported by an unreliable source. See David Freedberg, 'The Structure of Byzantine and European Iconoclasm', in *Iconoclasm: Papers Given at the Ninth Spring Symposium of Byzantine Studies, University of Birmingham, March 1975*, ed. Anthony Bryer and Judith Herrin (Birmingham: Centre for Byzantine Studies, 1977), 171.

30 Mangrum and Scavizzi, *Karlstadt, Emser, and Eck on Sacred Images*, 86. Disussed by Thomas Kren, 'Epilogue One: Reformation and beyond in Northern Europe', in *The Renaissance Nude*, ed. Thomas Kren, Jill Burke, and Stephen J. Campbell, Exhibition Catalogue, J. Paul Getty Museum, Los Angeles, 30 October 2018–27 January 2019, Royal Academy of Arts, London, March 2–2 June 2019 (Los Angeles: J. Paul Getty Museum, 2018), 361.

31 Mangrum and Scavizzi, *Karlstadt, Emser, and Eck on Sacred Images*, 86.

32 Erwin Panofsky, 'Erasmus and the Visual Arts', *Journal of the Warburg and Courtauld Institutes* 32 (1969): 208–9. Erasmus's comments bring to mind Giulio Mancini's much later accusations in his *Considerazioni sulla pittura* that Caravaggio's model for the Virgin Mary in his altarpiece of the *Death of the Virgin* was based upon a 'a dirty whore'. Frances Gage, 'Caravaggio's Death of the Virgin, Giulio Mancini, and the Madonna Blasphemed', in *Caravaggio: Reflections and Refractions*, ed. Lorenzo Pericolo and David M. Stone (Farnham: Ashgate, 2014), 83–104.

33 Luigi Lippomano, *Confirmatione et stabilimento di tutti li dogmi catholici* (Venice, 1553), 183r–v. See also Gaston, 'How Words Control Images: The Rhetoric of Decorum in Counter-Reformation Italy', 82. For Lippomano and the genesis of his treatise, see Emily Michelson, 'Luigi Lippomano, His Vicars, and the Reform of Verona from the Pulpit', *Church History* 78, no. 3 (2009): 584–605.

34 Contarini provided his thoughts on the veneration of saints and of images in the *Articuli orthodoxae professionis*. This was written at the behest of Cardinal Morone as a catechism for the academicians of Modena. The text appeared with the title *Catechesis sire Christiana instructio* in Contarini's collected works of 1571. See Gasparo Contarini, *Gasparis Contareni cardinalis opera* (Farnborough: Gregg, 1968), 544; Gleason, *Gasparo Contarini*, 289.

35 See Ruth S. Noyes, '"Aut numquid post annos mille quingentos docenda est Ecclesia Catholica quomodo sacrae imagines pingantur?": Post–Tridentine Image Reform and the Myth of Gabriele Paleotti', *Catholic Historical Review* 99, no. 2 (2013): 243.

36 Depasquale, 'Epilogue Two: Michelangelo's "Last Judgment" and the Reception of the Nude in Counter-Reformation Italy', 368.

37 A number of the critiques are collected in Barocchi, *La vita di Michelangelo*, vol. 3: 1250–97; De Maio, *Michelangelo e la Controriforma*, 17–30; Chastel, *Art of Italian Renaissance*, 188–207, 278–83.

38 Guido Ruggiero, *The Boundaries of Eros: Sex Crime and Sexuality in Renaissance Venice* (New York: Oxford University Press, 1985), 141, 196, note 136.

39 Ruggiero, *The Boundaries of Eros*, 141.

40 With the exception of the treatise of Molanus, who disagreed with images of the nude Christ-child, exclaiming, '[W]hat sort of edification can there be in this nakedness?' See Freedberg, 'Johannes Molanus on Provocative Paintings', 239.

41 The date and provenance of the second relief is disputed. For an analysis, see Lenia Kouneni, 'From Antiquity to Byzantium in Late Medieval Italy: Hercules on the Façade of San Marco', in *Herakles Inside and Outside the Church: From the First Apologists to the Quattrocento*, ed. Arlene L. Allan, Eva Anagnostou-Laoutides, and Emma Stafford (Leiden: Brill, 2020), 219–47.

42 Maria Andaloro et al., *San Marco: Basilica patriarcale in Venezia: i mosaici, le iscrizioni, la Pala d'oro* (Milan: Fabbri, 1991), 82, 138–39. A oil on canvas cartoon by Maffeo da Verona for the mosaic survives in the museum of San Marco. For the mosaic programmes in this period, see Diana Gisolfi, *Paolo Veronese and the Practice of Painting in Late Renaissance Venice* (New Haven, CT: Yale University Press, 2017), 209–10; Otto Demus, *The Mosaics of San Marco in Venice* (Chicago: University of Chicago Press, 1984), vol. 2: 22–24. Demus was unsure whether the Susanna cycle continued a pre-existing iconography. For Tintoretto's mosaic designs, see Rodolfo Pallucchini and Paola Rossi, *Tintoretto: le opere sacre e profane* (Milan: Alfieri, 1982), vol. 1: 237, cat. B; Roland Krischel, 'Tintoretto and the Sister Arts', in *Tintoretto*, ed. Miguel Falomir, English ed., Exhibition Catalogue, Museo Nacional del Prado, Madrid, 30 January–13 May 2007 (Madrid: Museo Nacional del Prado, 2007), 133–34. Stringa noted that the mosaics represented 'the example of the chastity of Susanna'. Giovanni Stringa, *Venetia città nobilissima, et singolare; descritta già in XIIII.libri da M. Francesco Sansovino* (Venice: Altobello Salicato, 1604), 39v.

43 For the inscriptions, see Andaloro et al., *San Marco*, 138–39.

44 Jill Burke, 'Nakedness and Other Peoples: Rethinking the Italian Renaissance Nude', *Art History* 36, no. 4 (2013): 718.

45 See Stephen Campbell's catalogue entry in Kren, Burke and Campbell, eds., *The Renaissance Nude*, 288–89.

46 Philipp Fehl, 'The Naked Christ in Santa Maria Novella in Florence: Reflections on an Exhibition and the Consequences', *Storia dell'arte* 45 (1982): 161.

47 Kren, Burke and Campbell, eds., *The Renaissance Nude*, 289. For the penitence of Jerome, see also Steinberg, *The Sexuality of Christ in Renaissance Art and in Modern Oblivion*, 195–96.

48 Anne Markham Schulz, *The Sculpture of Tullio Lombardo* (London: Harvey Miller, 2014), 93–102. On page 99 Schulz notes that in Venetian funerary sculpture there is nothing comparable to these naked Ephebes.

49 The figures are shown in the prelapsarian state. Schulz, *The Sculpture of Tullio Lombardo*, 113. See also Anne Markham Schulz, 'Il problema della scultura tarda di Tullio Lombardo', *Prospettiva*, nos. 115–16 (2004): 46.

50 Anne Markham Schulz, *The History of Venetian Renaissance Sculpture ca. 1400–1530* (London: Harvey Miller, 2018), vol. 1: 301–2. Commenting on Baccio da Montelupo's (1469–c. 1536) statue of Mars, Schulz also noted the explicit sexuality of this figure.

51 For the attributions, see Schulz, 'The Life and Works of Jacopo Fantoni', 109–10.

52 Schulz, 'The Life and Works of Jacopo Fantoni', 110.

53 Schulz, 'The Life and Works of Jacopo Fantoni', 111.

54 That the government in Venice exercised considerable control over churches in Venice but was significantly more lenient concerning the design and scale of ducal tombs was pointed out by Benjamin Paul, 'The Venetian Doges and Their Tombs in the Early Modern Period: Observations on Self-Representation in a Republic', in *The Tombs of the Doges of Venice: From the Beginning of the Serenissima to 1907*, ed. Benjamin Paul, Proceedings of the International Conference, 30 September–1 October 2010, Centro Tedesco di Studi Veneziani & the Fondazione Cini (Rome: Viella, 2016), 19.

55 Kathryn B. Hiesinger, 'The Fregoso Monument: A Study in Sixteenth-Century Tomb Monuments and Catholic Reform', *Burlington Magazine* 118, no. 878 (1976): 287. See also Martin Gaier, 'Il mausoleo nel presbiterio: patronati laici e liturgie private nelle chiese veneziane', in *Lo spazio e il culto: relazioni tra edificio ecclesiale e uso liturgico dal XV al XVI secolo*, ed. Jörg Stabenow, Proceedings of the Study Day, Kunsthistorisches Institut, Florence, 2003 (Venice: Marsilio, 2006), 153–80.

56 Tom Nichols, 'Too Sexy for the Nude. Review of Patricia Lee Rubin, "Seen from Behind: Perspectives on the Male Body and Renaissance Art", James Grantham Turner, "Eros Visible: Art, Sexuality and Antiquity in Renaissance Italy", Jill Burke, "The Italian Renaissance Nude"', *Oxford Art Journal* 43, no. 3 (2020): 469–76.

57 Steinberg, *The Sexuality of Christ in Renaissance Art and in Modern Oblivion*, 135–39, 147–49.

58 See Michael W. Cole, *Cellini and the Principles of Sculpture* (Cambridge: Cambridge University Press, 2002), 106–10; Holmes, *The Miraculous Image in Renaissance Florence*, 258.

59 Steinberg, *The Sexuality of Christ in Renaissance Art and in Modern Oblivion*, 146. This would concur with the sentiments of Esmer and Vasari described in notes 31 and 80, respectively.

60 The Old Testament episode of Susanna and the Elders increased in popularity during the late sixteenth and early seventeenth centuries, for example. See Patricia Simons, 'Artemisia Gentileschi's "Susanna and the Elders" (1610) in the Context of Counter-Reformation Rome', in *Artemisia Gentileschi in a Changing Light*, ed. Sheila Barker (London: Harvey Miller, 2017), 41. For images in Venice, see Seidel, *Venezianische Malerei zur Zeit der Gegenreformation*, 175–89.

61 See Anne Markham Schulz, 'Two New Works by Antonio Minello', *The Burlington Magazine* 137, no. 1113 (1995): 808, note 26.

62 See Tom Nichols, 'Images of Almsgiving and Poverty in Venetian Art of the Sixteenth Century', in *Armut und Armenfürsorge in der italienischen Stadtkultur zwischen 13. und 16. Jahrhundert: Bilder, Texte und soziale Praktiken*, ed. Philine Helas and Gerhard Wolf (Frankfurt: Peter Lang, 2006), 363–65; Tom Nichols, 'Secular Charity, Sacred Poverty: Picturing the Poor in Renaissance Venice', *Art History* 30, no. 2 (2007): 160. In his discussion of Tintoretto's *Pool of Bethesda* for the church of San Rocco, Nichols notes that the nudity of the figures is to some extent a standard manifestation of their worldly poverty (one of four conditions of nudity recognised by the medieval Church). Nichols, *Tintoretto: Tradition and Identity*, 270. John Florio's Italian-English dictionary of 1611 translated the word '*nudo*' as 'nude, naked, bare, discovered. Also poore, beggarly and deprived of.' Burke, 'The European Nude, 1400–1650', 20.

63 For the changing connotations of the word lascivious in the sixteenth century, see Turner, *Eros Visible*, 20–21.

64 That these restrictions on nudity did not apply to the Christ-child is illustrated by the numerous paintings of the Madonna and Child, the Presentation of Christ in the Temple, and the Adoration produced in and around Venice by artists including Cima da Conegliano, Giovanni Bellini, Jacopo and Francesco Bassano, and Veronese. This continued after the Council of Trent. For example, Marco del Moro's altarpiece the *Circumcision* (c. 1565–70) completed for the Jesuit church of the Madonna dell'Umiltà featured the Christ-child partially covered by a sheer loincloth, his genitals visible underneath as the circumcision is completed by the high priest.

65 Vasari, *Lives of the Painters, Sculptors and Architects*, vol. 1: 676. The episode is discussed by Freedberg, *The Power of Images*, 346–48. Vasari also recounts that Fra Bartolomeo contributed to Savonarola's bonfire of the vanities by bringing along his studies of the nude to be burnt. Vasari, *Lives of the Painters, Sculptors and Architects*, vol. 1: 672.

66 Giovanni Paolo Lomazzo, *Trattato dell'arte della pittura, scoltura et architettura* (Milan: Paolo Gottardo Pontio, 1585), 366. Lomazzo cannot have seen the painting, as pointed out by Janet Cox-Rearick, 'Fra Bartolomeo's St. Mark Evangelist and St. Sebastian with an Angel', *Mitteilungen des Kunsthistorischen Institutes in Florenz* 18 (1974): 350–51.

67 Cox-Rearick, 'Fra Bartolomeo's St. Mark Evangelist and St. Sebastian with an angel', 332, note 9. The painting was a gift from Alice Rosenberg and Odgen Steinhardt. The precise date of this exchange is unknown, but when Cox-Rearick viewed it the painting hung above the main door of the church.

68 Beverly Louise Brown, 'Between the Sacred and Profane', in *The Genius of Rome, 1592–1623*, ed. Beverly Louise Brown, Exhibition Catalogue, Royal Academy of Arts, London, 20 January–16 May 2001 (London: Royal Academy of Arts, 2001), 284–86.

69 A translation of the passage into English, which I have slightly adapted, was first provided by Anthony Hughes, 'Authority, Authenticity and Aura: Walter Benjamin and the Case of Michelangelo', in *Sculpture and Its Reproductions*, ed. Anthony Hughes and Erich Ranfft (London: Reaktion Books, 1997), 35. The passage was analysed also by Firpo, *Gli affreschi di Pontormo a San Lorenzo*, 61–62. For the most recent discussion of the text and the identity of the diarist, see Maratsos, *Pontormo and the Art of Devotion in Renaissance Italy*, 159–60.

70 Hughes, 'Authority, Authenticity and Aura: Walter Benjamin and the Case of Michelangelo', 35.

71 For the episode, see Freedberg, *The Power of Images*, 409–11, 420.

72 Vasari, *Lives of the Painters, Sculptors and Architects*, vol. 2: 649.

73 Ascanio Condivi, *The Life of Michelangelo*, ed. Hellmut Wohl, trans. Alice Sedgwick Wohl (Oxford: Phaidon, 1976), 24.

74 See Grażyna Jurkowlaniec, 'Masterpieces, Altarpieces, and Devotional Prints: Close and Distant Encounters with Michelangelo's Vatican Pietà', ed. Salvador Ryan, *Religions* 10 (2019): 16–17; Claudia Echinger-Maurach, 'Models for Sculptures in Print: Michelangelo's "Samson and Two Philistines" in Lucas Kilian's Engravings', in *Sculpture in Print, 1480–1600*, ed. Anne Bloemacher, Mandy Richter, and Marzia Faietti (Leiden: Brill, 2021), 337–61. Produced in Augsburg, from where Kilian hailed, the print was dedicated to the protonotary Apostolic Eustachy Wollowicz, who later became Bishop of Vilnius. Strangely, no comment is made in either article on the older appearance of the Madonna. Echinger-Maurach notes that Kilian may have come into contact with replicas of the *Pietà* in Venice, where he stayed from 1601 to 1603.

75 Mason Rinaldi, *Palma il Giovane: l'opera completa*, 104, cat. 228.

76 Michael Hirst, *Michelangelo: The Achievement of Fame, 1475–1534* (New Haven, CT: Yale University Press, 2011), 175, 331, note 30. First reported in Pirro Ligorio, 'Libri dell'antichità' (ms. Canon Ital. 138, Bodleian Library, Oxford, n.d.), 6r. Ligorio complains that during the papacy of Clement VII, 'the virile member' of 'the most beautiful statue of our saviour' was hacked off and then covered by the friars. Ligorio described this act as demonstrating a lack of respect both to the patron and to Christ himself. That a single friar destroyed the genitalia '*per scrupolo*' is later reported by Gaspare Celio, *Memoria fatta dal signor Gaspare Celio dell'habito di Christo: delli nomi dell'artefici delle pitture, che sono in alcune chiese, facciate, e palazzi di Roma* (Naples: Bonino, 1638), 65–66.

77 Steinberg, *The Sexuality of Christ in Renaissance Art and in Modern Oblivion*, 147. The foot would have been the easiest point of the statue for the laity to reach, but it might also have been chosen for theological reasons since the veneration of the cross on Good Friday involves parishioners kissing the crucifix.

78 The groin had been covered by 1600, when the work was illustrated in the guidebook of Girolamo Francini. The statue was left in its uncensored state for most of the late twentieth century, until the year 2000 when one of its seventeenth-century coverings was restored so as not to offend visiting pilgrims. Stephen J. Campbell and Michael W. Cole, *A New History of Italian Renaissance Art*, 2nd ed. (London: Thames & Hudson, 2017), 436.

79 See Nagel, *Michelangelo and the Reform of Art*.

80 For an analysis, see Depasquale, 'Epilogue Two: Michelangelo's "Last Judgment" and the Reception of the Nude in Counter-Reformation Italy', 369. Vasari later followed suit, arguing in his *vita* of Fra Angelico that those censors who police representations of the saints 'reveal the unsoundness and corruption of their own minds'. Vasari, *Lives of the Painters, Sculptors and Architects*, vol. 1: 409. Vasari also pointed out that Michelangelo's love for depicting the human body was guided 'not with lascivious and disgraceful thoughts, as he proved in his way of life, which was very frugal'. Vasari, *Lives of the Painters, Sculptors and Architects*, vol. 2: 739.

81 Bartolomeo Ammannati, *Lettera di messer Bartolomeo Ammannati scultore, e architetto fiorentino, scritta agli accademici del disegno l'anno 1582* (Florence: Sermartelli, 1582), unnumbered folios. This sentiment was close to that of Cardinal Federico Borromeo, who criticised aspects of

the *Last Judgment*, but concluded that Michelangelo was a devout man, describing his kindness to the poor. Borromeo, *Sacred Painting; Museum*, 51.

82 See the third dialogue of Francisco de Hollanda, *Four Dialogues on Painting*, trans. Aubrey F. G. Bell (London: Oxford University Press, Humphrey Milford, 1928), 65–66. Discussed also by Marcia B. Hall, ed., *Michelangelo's 'Last Judgment'* (Cambridge: Cambridge University Press, 2005), 34.

83 John W. O'Malley, 'The Council of Trent (1545–63) and Michelangelo's "Last Judgment" (1541)', *Proceedings of the American Philosophical Society* 156, no. 4 (2012): 388.

84 Patrick Preston, 'The Critical Reception of Michelangelo's 'The Last Judgement': The Theological Context', *Reformation & Renaissance Review* 7, nos. 2–3 (2005): 337–38. The comparison is also made by Hall, *The Sacred Image in the Age of Art*, 99. Michelangelo likely visited Orvieto in 1501. See Patricia Lee Rubin, *Seen from behind: Perspectives on the Male Body and Renaissance Art* (New Haven, CT: Yale University Press, 2018), 198–99. Rubin writes that the chapel 'is overwhelming in its presentation of epic nudity, no longer reserved for the damned and their diabolic tormentors but also granted to the elect', but the covering of the genitalia in the *Crowning of the Elect* and the *Resurrection of the Flesh* is never mentioned. The same thing happens with the author's analysis of Bronzino's *Portrait of Cosimo I as Orpheus* where the insistence on the 'intentionally exposed buttocks' fails to take into account that this part of Cosimo's anatomy is in fact veiled, as pointed out also by Nichols, 'Too Sexy for the Nude', 472.

85 Minos was supposedly a portrait of the pope's master of ceremonies, Biagio da Cesena. Cesena, having viewed the work when it was almost complete, opined that the quantity of nudity meant that it was more suited to a bathhouse or tavern than to the honoured place it occupied. Vasari, *Lives of the Painters, Sculptors and Architects*, vol. 2: 692. Doubt was cast on this widely reported episode by Leo Steinberg, 'A Corner of the "Last Judgment"', *Daedalus* 109, no. 2 (1980): 211–12. As Steinberg argues, 'the story is historically improbable, chronologically inconsistent, psychologically obtuse, theologically unsound; and what is worse, it dims the reality of the painting'.

86 In the original fresco Blaise appeared with an irate expression clapping his currycombs over the head of the stout, naked Catherine, 'suggesting some kind of sadistic activity, or even sodomy', as Barnes observed (first suggested by Stendhal). Barnes, 'Aretino, the Public and the Censorship of Michelangelo's Last Judgment', 59, 72–73. Stendhal's suggestion is vigorously refuted by Steinberg, 'A Corner of the "Last Judgment"', 214, 266, note 44. For the dating of Della Casa's engraving see note 121 below.

87 Volterra's work was incomplete upon his death, and campaigns continued into the eighteenth century. Mancinelli, Colalucci, and Gabrielli, *Michelangelo*, 20, 22; Mancinelli, Colalucci, and Gabrielli, 'The "Last Judgment": Notes on Its Conservation History, Technique, and Restoration', 238. See also Peter M. Lukehart, 'Painting Virtuously: The Counter-Reform and the Reform of Artists' Education in Rome between Guild and Academy', in *The Sensuous in the Counter-Reformation Church*, ed. Marcia B. Hall and Tracy E. Cooper (Cambridge: Cambridge University Press, 2013), 180.

88 Letter of 19 November 1541 from Nicolo Sernini to Cardinal Ercole Gonzaga. See Chastel, *Art of Italian Renaissance*, 188–89. I have cited the more literal translation of Schlitt, 'Painting, Criticism, and Michelangelo's "Last Judgment"', 121.

89 For the Florentine defenders of the painting (including Anton Francesco Doni, Niccolò Martelli, and Vasari), see Schlitt, 'Painting, Criticism, and Michelangelo's "Last Judgment"', 122–24. Other sixteenth-century Florentines including Raffaello Borghini, Paolo Mini, and Benedetto Varchi also reserved superlatives for Michelangelo's achievement. See Barocchi, *La vita di Michelangelo*, vol. 3: 1263, 68.

90 Paul Hills, 'Decorum and Desire in Some Works by Tintoretto', in *Decorum in Renaissance Narrative Art: Papers Delivered at the Annual Conference of the Association of Art Historians, London, April 1991*, ed. Francis Ames-Lewis and Anka Bednarek (London: Department of the History of Art, Birckbeck College, 1992), 125.

91 De Maio, *Michelangelo e la Controriforma*, 39. The sequence of events is described in note 4 of the 2019 annotated version of Steinberg, 'A Corner of the "Last Judgment"', 332.

92 O'Malley, 'The Council of Trent', 391, 396.

93 O'Malley, 'The Council of Trent', 396. 'The pictures in the Apostolic Chapel are to be covered, as [is to be done] in other churches [of Rome] if they display anything obscene or obviously false, according to the decree of the council.' The congregation included Carlo Borromeo and Gabriele Paleotti. First cited by Ludwig von Pastor, *The History of the Popes, from the Close of the Middle Ages: Drawn from the Secret Archives of the Vatican and Other Original Sources*, ed. Ralph Francis Kerr, vol. 12 (London: Kegan Paul, Trench, Trübner, 1914), 618, note 1. Pastor believed representations like Michelangelo's must have influenced the decrees at Trent. Since it preceded O'Malley's corrective to the claims of De Maio (see note 98), Treves's article on the collaborations between Volterra and Michelangelo suggested that the latter knew about Trent's decision regarding the fate of the fresco before his death on 18 February 1564. What *is* possible is that the artist knew of the decision of the delegation of cardinals and recommended his friend Daniele, knowing that he would complete the alterations as sensitively as possible. Letizia Treves, 'Daniele Da Volterra and Michelangelo: A Collaborative Relationship', *Apollo* 154, no. 474 (2001): 43.

94 Giovanni Andrea Gilio, *Dialogue on the Errors and Abuses of Painters*, ed. Michael Bury, Lucinda Byatt, and Carol M. Richardson, trans. Michael Bury and Lucinda Byatt (Los Angeles: Getty Research Institute, 2018), 184. The treatise is also contained in Paola Barocchi, ed., *Trattati d'arte del Cinquecento: Fra Manierismo e Controriforma* (Bari: Laterza, 1960), vol. 2: 3–115. For Gilio, see Blunt, *Artistic Theory in Italy, 1450–1600*, 111–14; Scavizzi, *The Controversy on Images from Calvin to Baronius*, 93–102; Vincenzo Caputo, 'Gli "abusi" dei pittori e la "norma" dei trattatisti: Giovanni Andrea Gilio e Gabriele Paleotti', *Studi rinascimentali* 6 (2009): 99–110.

95 For later scholars who variously accepted or challenged De Maio's analysis, see Bernadine Ann Barnes, *Michelangelo's Last Judgment: The Renaissance Response* (Berkeley: University of California Press, 1998), 78–80; Schlitt, 'Painting, Criticism, and Michelangelo's "Last Judgment"', 121.

96 De Maio, *Michelangelo e la Controriforma*, 17–18.

97 That 'connoisseurs and the religious did not form mutually exclusive groups' is discussed also by Barnes, *Michelangelo's Last Judgment*, 80.

98 De Maio concedes that Morone was a friend of Michelangelo. See De Maio, *Michelangelo e la Controriforma*, 38; O'Malley, 'Trent, Sacred Images, and Catholics' Senses of the Sensuous', 47, note 37.

99 Vasari, *Lives of the Painters, Sculptors and Architects*, vol. 2: 595.

100 Chastel, *Art of Italian Renaissance*, 202.

101 'Don't you know that in painting the universal judgment, clothes, or similar things, are not required, and that amongst those figures there is nothing which is not of the spiritual, there are no jesters, nor dogs nor weapons, nor similar buffooneries?' The most accurate transcript of the interrogation in the original Latin and Italian is provided by Maria Elena Massimi, *La Cena in casa di Levi di Paolo Veronese: il processo riaperto* (Venice: Marsilio, 2011), 179–81.

102 Chastel, *Art of Italian Renaissance*, 190.

103 Francisco Pacheco believed that the *Last Judgment* was overrated (1649). Veronese (1577) argued before the Inquisition that it featured iconographic novelties far worse than his own (although his true thoughts on the painting are not documented). El Greco (1570) offered to replace the fresco with a new and improved version. See note 145 below and Barocchi, *La vita di Michelangelo*, vol. 3: 1268, 1270.

104 Preston, 'The Critical Reception of Michelangelo's "The Last Judgement"', 338. Preston appears to have been unaware of Pope Adrian VI's reaction when he stated with reference to the later *Last Judgment* that 'the outcry thirty years later is prima facie strange' when compared with the tolerance for the ceiling.

105 Vasari, *Lives of the Painters, Sculptors and Architects*, vol. 2: 106.

106 John Shearman, *Mannerism* (Harmondsworth: Penguin Books, 1967), 167–68. Cirillo's letter dates to 1549 and was published in 1567.

107 That the ceiling was superior to the *Last Judgment* was a view expressed also by Lomazzo (1590) and later by Bellori (1672). Barocchi, *La vita di Michelangelo*, vol. 3: 1268–69, 1272.

108 The wall has continued to make an impression in recent times: on the occasion of the restoration of the *Last Judgment* in 1994 one staff writer for the Religious News Service noted with surprise that 'Pope John Paul II was not embarrassed by the huge numbers of naked bodies of both sexes displayed in Michelangelo's monumental painting.' Schlitt, 'Painting, Criticism, and Michelangelo's "Last Judgment"', 143.

109 An opposite conclusion to my own, one that argues the nudity was not the most offensive element in the painting (despite extensive evidence of contemporary opinions to the contrary), does so on the basis of the ceiling nudes being 'far more disturbing'. Antonio Forcellino, *The Sistine Chapel: History of a Masterpiece*, trans. Lucinda Byatt (Cambridge: Polity Press, 2022), 206.

110 Barnes pointed out that although half of the Sistine Chapel was nominally open to the laity, evidence shows that one had to be an invited guest of the papal court to be granted access. It was only on rare occasions that the wider public were allowed inside the chapel. Barnes, 'Aretino, the Public and the Censorship of Michelangelo's Last Judgment', 69.

111 Hall, *The Sacred Image in the Age of Art*, 99.

112 Barocchi, *La vita di Michelangelo*, vol. 3: 1259. This appeared in the *Roma triumphans* of Flavio Biondo. See also Caterina Furlan, 'La "fortuna" di Michelangelo a Venezia nella prima metà del Cinquecento', in *Jacopo Tintoretto nel quarto centenario della morte*, ed. Paola Rossi and Lionello Puppi, Proceedings of the International Conference, Università Ca'Foscari, Venice, 24–26 November 1994 (Padua: Il poligrafo, 1996), 23.

113 Barocchi, *La vita di Michelangelo*, vol. 3: 1259.

114 Barocchi, *La vita di Michelangelo*, vol. 3: 1262–63.

115 Barocchi, *La vita di Michelangelo* vol. 3: 1259–60.

116 'Inside the pontifical chapel, Michelangelo painted Our Lord Jesus Christ, his mother and Saint John, Saint Peter, and the celestial court, all of which (after the Virgin Mary) are depicted nude, in various poses with little reverence.' Massimi, *La Cena in casa di Levi di Paolo Veronese*, 180–81.

117 Chastel, *Art of Italian Renaissance*, 200. Nothing is known about this lost image. In a discussion on engravings, Vasari commented positively on the phenomenon, but observed that 'many plates have been badly executed through the avarice of the printers, eager more for gain than for honour'. Vasari, *Lives of the Painters, Sculptors and Architects*, vol. 2: 94. Of the *Last Judgment*, he noted that 'so many copies of it, both large and small, have been printed' (vol. 2: 691). Barnes noted that the uncensored versions of the painting were much more popular than the censored ones, despite Aretino's advice to Vico that a censored image would prove profitable. One can speculate that there might even have existed versions of the image that further exaggerated the nudity of the saints which were later destroyed. Barnes, 'Aretino, the Public and the Censorship of Michelangelo's Last Judgment', 77–78.

118 The letter was later published in the *Third Book of Letters*. See also Barnes, *Michelangelo's Last Judgment*, 80; Boschloo, *The Limits of Artistic Freedom: Criticism of Art in Italy from 1500–1800*, 45.

119 Alessandro Nova, 'Correggio's "Lascivie"', in *Renaissance Love: Eros, Passion, and Friendship in Italian Art around 1500*, ed. Jeanette Kohl, Marianne Koos, and Adrian W. B. Randolph, trans. Adrian W. B. Randolph (Berlin: Deutscher Kunstverlag, 2014), 129. For Vico's image, see Freedberg, *The Power of Images*, 362–63; Turner, *Eros Visible*, 189–91.

120 Already in 1537 Aretino had alluded to the discussions surrounding the youthfulness of Michelangelo's Virgin Mary for the St Peter's *Pietà* and had pointed out that she appeared much younger than her son. Ettore Camesasca, ed., *Lettere sull'arte di Pietro Aretino (1526–1542)*, Edizioni del Milione, vol. 1 (Milan, 1957), 102.

121 The earliest copies of the *Last Judgment* were those of Marcello Venusti, who began work the same year the painting was unveiled. His labours progressed slowly, but on 5 August 1542 the section with Charon's boat was complete. Venusti's painted copy, now in the Capodimonte Museum, was completed in 1549. The earliest engraving is Della Casa's, which has a very complex history and was first published by Antonio Salamanca in Rome commencing around 1543. It has been suggested that reproductions of specific sections of the fresco were issued between 1543 and 1548, but that the first complete reproduction by Della Casa appeared only in 1548. If the date of 1546 attributed to Giulio Bonasone's print is correct, then it would qualify as the earliest that depicted the fresco in its entirety. Bonasone's print proved incredibly popular and it preserved the nudity of the original fresco even in those editions dating to post-1564. The plates were modified to reflect the censorship only in their last known state, which is believed to have been in the seventeenth century. See the analysis of Bernadine Barnes, *Michelangelo in Print: Reproductions as Response in the Sixteenth Century* (London: Taylor & Francis Group, 2010), 99–106. For copies of the painting, see also De Maio, *Michelangelo e la Controriforma*, 70–79.

122 Stephen D. Bowd, 'Review of Marco Cavarzare, "Adhortatio ad concordiam. By Isidoro da Chiara [Temi e testi, vol. 63]"', *Catholic Historical Review* 96, no. 1 (January 2010): 129.

123 'Take care to finish this holy and praiseworthy enterprise, so that the scandal that may be caused by the license of Michelangelo's art among the Lutherans on account of the small respect paid to natural shame disclosed by the figures in the abyss and in heaven may be avoided.' Chastel, *Art of Italian Renaissance*, 200.

124 To relate contested aspects of devotional painting to heresy became a relatively common slur in the late sixteenth century according to Chastel, *Art of Italian Renaissance*, 199.

125 For the first two laudatory letters written whilst Michelangelo was working on the frescoes, see Camesasca, *Lettere sull'arte di Pietro Aretino*, vol. 1: 64–66, 112–13. These date to 16 September 1537 and 20 January 1538, respectively. For the third letter of April 1544 where Aretino describes being deeply moved by the painting, see Ettore Camesasca, ed., *Lettere sull'arte di Pietro Aretino (1543–1555)*, Edizioni del Milione, vol. 2 (Milan, 1957), 15–16. In April 1545 Aretino wrote again to Michelangelo, but did not mention the *Last Judgment*. Camesasca, *Lettere sull'arte di Pietro Aretino*, vol. 2: 62–63. In October 1545 Aretino reminded Titian to lose himself in the contemplation of the *Last Judgment* whilst in Rome. Camesasca, *Lettere sull'arte di Pietro Aretino*, vol. 2: 106–7. The infamous vitriolic letter against the *Last Judgment* is dated to 6 November 1545; see Chastel, *Art of Italian Renaissance*, 190–95. For the published version addressed to Alessandro Corvino, see Camesasca, *Lettere sull'arte di Pietro Aretino*, vol. 2: 175–77. This letter did not appear in print until 1550 where all references to the longed-for drawing were removed and it was addressed to Alessandro Corvino. For the debates over the dating of the final letters, and whether the letter to Vico precedes or postdates the invective, see Barnes, 'Aretino, the Public and the Censorship of Michelangelo's Last Judgment', 67–68.

126 De Maio, *Michelangelo e la Controriforma*, 21–23; Sergio Ortolani, 'Pietro Aretino e Michelangelo', *L'arte* 25 (1922): 25. As pointed out by Barnes, since Aretino harboured similar ambitions in the early 1530s, this cannot alone account for his sharp change in tone. Barnes, 'Aretino, the Public and the Censorship of Michelangelo's Last Judgment', 63.

127 Barnes, 'Aretino, the Public and the Censorship of Michelangelo's Last Judgment', 76.

128 Barocchi, *La vita di Michelangelo*, vol. 3: 1262–63.

129 Chastel, *Art of Italian Renaissance*, 190.

130 See note 121.

131 Chastel raised the possibility that Aretino might have had a sudden attack of prudery or at least have shared some of the worries of the Roman censors. Chastel, *Art of Italian Renaissance*, 199. For a detailed account of the scandal, see Bette Talvacchia, *Taking Positions: On the Erotic in Renaissance Culture* (Princeton, NJ: Princeton University Press, 1999), 3–19.

132 A letter of 1527 by Aretino refers to the '*querele Gibertine*', suggesting the intervention of Gian Matteo Giberti. See Talvacchia, *Taking Positions: On the Erotic in Renaissance Culture*, 13–14; Nagel, *The Controversy of Renaissance Art*, 223–32.

133 Camesasca, *Lettere sull'arte di Pietro Aretino*, vol. 2: 177. See also Chastel, *Art of Italian Renaissance*, 194; Barnes, *Michelangelo's Last Judgment*, 82.

134 Raimondi's woodcuts were partly defended in the treatise because he 'did not put them on public display in the city squares of the churches'. Mark W. Roskill, *Dolce's Aretino and Venetian Art Theory of the Cinquecento* (Toronto: University of Toronto Press in association with the Renaissance Society of America, 2000), 164–65.

135 Roskill, *Dolce's Aretino*, 165. Here the text echoed not only the comments of Cirillo about the context in which images were viewed, but Alberti's point made in *De pictura* (1435) that 'the parts of the body that are ugly to see' should be covered. See Depasquale, 'Epilogue Two: Michelangelo's "Last Judgment" and the Reception of the Nude in Counter-Reformation Italy', 372.

136 For examples, see Nova, 'Correggio's "Lascivie"'.

137 Catarino also argued that 'these nude bodies are indecent when seen on altars and in the sanctuaries of God'. Chastel, *Art of Italian Renaissance*, 202. With reference to the personification of lust in the *Last Judgment*, Steinberg pointed out that 'even today, motifs of this sort would probably be unacceptable in a public building, sacred or secular'. Steinberg, 'A Corner of the "Last Judgment"', 167.

138 For the influence of the treatise, see appendix A of Roskill, *Dolce's Aretino*, 63–73.

139 For example, in Dolce's treatise it was argued that it was 'none too commendable' that such immodesty might be viewed by the eyes of 'infants, mothers and girls'. Roskill, *Dolce's Aretino*, 167. That opinion hardened as a result of these texts, even if some commentators defended the work, was noted by Barnes, *Michelangelo's Last Judgment*, 124–25. Nagel pointed out that Aretino's criticisms ultimately prevailed. Nagel, *Michelangelo and the Reform of Art*, 195.

140 'It was said by the Cardinals and by men of judgment that it would be a great sin to spoil them, and they found a way out of it, which was that Daniello should paint some light garments to cover them.' Vasari, *Lives of the Painters, Sculptors and Architects*, vol. 2: 595.

141 Chastel, *Art of Italian Renaissance*, 204. In contrast to Pope Paul IV, Vasari emphasised the artistic license granted to Michelangelo by Pope Paul III, who 'allowed him to continue the work as ordered by Clement, without changing anything in the inventions and the general conception that had been laid before him, thus showing respect for the genius of the great man'. Vasari, *Lives of the Painters, Sculptors and Architects*, vol. 2: 690–91.

142 Saurolo also noted that twenty years after its unveiling threats against the painting 'continued to be expressed'. Chastel, *Art of Italian Renaissance*, 204. Like his friend Ammanati, Michelangelo's later letters and poetry show that the artist questioned his legacy and demonstrated uncertainty about his own salvation. According to Vasari he refused payment for his later works on Saint Peter's, embarking on the project 'for the love of God'. Vasari, *Lives of the Painters, Sculptors and Architects*, vol. 2: 698–99, 713.

143 That the common person was offended by nudity is suggested by Marucelli's account of Baccio Bandinelli's *Adam and Eve* of 1549–51 for Santa Maria del Fiore, which he condemned as 'filthy, swinish marble figures', describing how they were 'by the whole city greatly blamed, as was the Duke [who] brought such a thing into the cathedral before the altar where the Most Holy Sacrament of the Body and Blood of the Blessed Jesus Christ is laid, so that great agitation was aroused in some people'. Maratsos, *Pontormo and the Art of Devotion in Renaissance Italy*, 159. Both sculptures were expediently replaced and then converted into a Bacchus and Ceres.

144 O'Malley pointed out that 'there is no instance of any other painting in Rome being defaced as a result of it'. O'Malley, 'The Council of Trent (1545–63) and Michelangelo's "Last Judgment" (1541)', 397.

145 'The occasion having arisen to cover some of the figures of the *Judgment* . . . he ventured to say that if the whole work had been torn down, he would have made one with honesty and decency, not inferior to that masterpiece of painting.' El Greco's opinion was said to have so annoyed the other painters in Rome that he had to leave for Spain. Giulio

Mancini, *Considerazioni sulla pittura*, ed. Adriana Marucchi and Luigi Salerno (Rome: Accademia nazionale dei Lincei, 1956), vol. 1: 230–31. Mancini's work was written between 1614 and 1621, according to Salerno.

146 See George A. Rodetis, 'El Greco's Statements on Michelangelo the Painter', *Journal of Aesthetic Education* 31, no. 3 (1997): 26, 35. Rodetis points out that due to El Greco's cultural background as an icon painter in Crete he may have been predisposed to dislike the nudity of the *Last Judgment*. See also Xavier de Salas, 'Miguel Angel y El Greco', in *El Greco y el arte de su tiempo: las notas de El Greco a Vasari* (Madrid: Real Fundacíon de Toledo, 1992), 33–52.

147 For other prints and paintings that were influenced by Michelangelo's painting, see Barnes, *Michelangelo's Last Judgment*, 124–33. In Antwerp Michelangelo's painting had a notable influence, and images of the same episode featuring nudity were displayed in sacred and secular settings, although as noted by De Clippel, 'the situation became more delicate after the Council of Trent and after the censorial intervention in Michelangelo's fresco'. Karolien De Clippel, 'Smashing Images: The Antwerp Nude between 1563 and 1585', in *Art after Iconoclasm: Painting in the Netherlands between 1566 and 1585*, ed. Koenraad Jonckheere and Ruben Suykerbuyk (Turnhout: Brepols, 2012), 61.

148 Lukehart, 'Painting Virtuously: The Counter-Reform and the Reform of Artists' Education in Rome between Guild and Academy', 178–80.

149 The painting was completed by Francesco Terzi. See Pietro Della Lucia, *Giovan Battista Moroni: itinerari bergamaschi*, I quaderni del Museo Bernareggi (Milan: Silvana Editoriale, 2004), 62, no. 18; Ekserdjian, *The Italian Renaissance Altarpiece*, 400.

150 Della Lucia, *Giovan Battista Moroni*, 62, no. 18.

151 All of the contestants for the competition of c. 1579–82 for the Ducal Palace *Paradiso* did the same. See Jean-Pierre Habert, ed., *Il 'Paradiso' di Tintoretto: un concorso per Palazzo Ducale*, Exhibition Catalogue, Musée du Louvre, Paris, 9 February–8 May 2006, Museo Thyssen-Bornemisza, Madrid, 6 June–27 August 2006, Palazzo Ducale, Venice, 9 September–3 December 2006 (Milan: Continents Editions, 2006); Gisolfi, *Paolo Veronese and the Practice of Painting in Late Renaissance Venice*, 178–84. Tintoretto also completed a Last Judgment for Philip II of Spain, now lost. Linda Borean, 'Documentation', in *Tintoretto*, ed. Miguel Falomir, English ed., Exhibition Catalogue, Museo Nacional del Prado, Madrid, 30 January–13 May 2007 (Madrid: Museo Nacional del Prado, 2007), 444; Pallucchini and Rossi, *Tintoretto: le opere sacre e profane*, vol. 1: 260.

152 Bishop Verdura was present at the Council of Trent from May 1562 until December 1563, in the period that included the formulation of the decree on images. Jaynie Anderson, 'A Precedent for the Tridentine Decree on Religious Imagery: An Early Restoration of Giambattista Ponchini's "Castelfranco Altarpiece"', *Arte Veneta* 28 (1975): 239–41; Hochmann, *Peintres et commanditaires à Venise (1540–1628)*, 273–74.

153 The changes ordered appear to have been made to Eve amongst the patriarchs, and the two figures who emerge from Limbo next to Christ. In a seventeenth-century account of the orders of the zealous bishop the painting was attributed to Veronese. Marco Vincenzo Coronelli, *Viaggi* (Venice: Gio. Battista Tramontino, 1697), vol. 1: 66.

154 Firpo and Biferali, *Immagini ed eresie nell'Italia del Cinquecento*, 80–81.

155 'If Michelangelo does not want anyone to understand his inventions, apart from a small number of intellectuals, then I, who am not one of the intellectual few in question, leave thinking about them to him.' Roskill, *Dolce's Aretino and Venetian Art Theory of the Cinquecento*, 166–67.

156 Hollanda, *Four Dialogues on Painting*, 15–16.

157 Virgilio Malvezzi, *Considerationi con occasione d'alcuni luoghi delle vite d'Alcibiade e di Coriolano* (Bologna, 1648), 92; Philip Sohm, *Pittoresco: Marco Boschini, His Critics, and Their Critiques of Painterly Brushwork in Seventeenth- and Eighteenth-Century Italy* (London: Cambridge University Press, 1991), 57; Boschloo, *The Limits of Artistic Freedom: Criticism of Art in Italy from 1500–1800*, 57.

158 Mary Laven, *Virgins of Venice: Broken Vows and Cloistered Lives in the Renaissance Convent* (London: Viking Penguin, 2002), 212, note 17.
159 Carlo Ridolfi, *Le maraviglie dell'arte: ovvero le vite degli illustri pittori veneti e dello stato* (1648), ed. Detlev von Hadeln (Berlin: G. Grote, 1914), vol. 2: 67. The painting was not included in the Pallucchini & Rossi Tintoretto catalogue, but cat. A9 (vol. 1) on a different painting noted that the Capitoline work was signed by Domenico. Various theories exist as to which of the *Penitent Magdalenes* Ridolfi's account relates to since Domenico produced more than one. See Michiaki Koshikawa, 'La "Maddalena penitente" della Pinacoteca Capitolina di Domenico Tintoretto', in *Jacopo Tintoretto nel quarto centenario della morte*, ed. Paola Rossi and Lionello Puppi (Padua: Il Poligrafo, 1996), 115–18. The author believes that the most likely candidate is indeed the Capitoline Museum painting. See also Alain Tapié, ed., *Baroque vision Jésuite: du Tintoret à Rubens*, Exhibition Catalogue, Musée des Beaux-Arts de Caen, 12 July–13 October 2003 (Paris: Somogy, 2003), 150–51, cat. 6.
160 Sold at Sotheby's, Old Master Paintings Evening Sale, Lot 32, 2005. Bassetti trained in Venice, was a close friend of Palma il Giovane, and moved to Rome in around 1615. Here he was influenced by the innovations that had been forged by Caravaggio and worked closely with Carlo Saraceni, returning to the lands of his birth in c. 1620. For a biography, see Ridolfi, *Le maraviglie dell'arte*, vol. 2: 241–42; Rodolfo Pallucchini, *La pittura veneziana del Seicento* (Venice: Alfieri, 1981), vol. 1: 123–26. Representations of Sebastian were particularly adaptable. The sculptor Alessandro Vittoria suggested that his bronze statue of the saint in San Francesco della Vigna in Venice could work equally well as Marsyas. Campbell and Cole, *A New History of Italian Renaissance Art*, 549.
161 For this painting, see *Parcours: catalogue guide du Musée des Beaux-Arts de Marseille* (Marseilles: Musées de Marseille, 1990), 170–71.
162 Catherine Whistler, 'Life Drawing in Venice from Titian to Tiepolo', *Master Drawings* 42, no. 4 (2004): 373.
163 The Provveditori underlined the need for the censorship due to the status of the church as a public votive temple, even if they had approved the project in the first place. See Antonio Niero, 'Un episodio controriformistico di arte veneziana: l'epurazione "post-mortem" del Capp. P. Paolo Piazza', *Arte Veneta* 28 (1975): 296–97. The episode is noted also by Davide Portogruaro, *Il tempio del Redentore e il convento dei Cappuccini di Venezia* (Venice: Libreria Emiliana Editrice, 1930), 38, note 2.
164 Paolo Piazza had produced thirty-two of these '*sagome*' on wood, thirteen of which were described as '*inoneste*' in the supplication of the state. In the upper part of the nave were depictions of the prophets, and in the lower order were the sibyls, the Evangelists, and Doctors of the Latin Church. Father Massimo of Verona, another Capuchin painter, had painted twelve further images of the apostles at the base of the cupola in around 1674. The hope was to eventually replace the paintings with statues, but this never happened. Subsequently white-washed, photographs showing glimpses of the remaining fictive paintings can be seen in Portogruaro, *Il tempio del Redentore e il convento dei Cappuccini di Venezia*, 15–19.
165 Described as '*insignis*'. Tramontin, 'La visita apostolica del 1581 a Venezia', 525.
166 John Ruskin, *The Stones of Venice: The Fall*, vol. 3 (Smith, Elder, 1853), 88.
167 John Ruskin, *The Stones of Venice: The Foundations*, vol. 1 (London: J. Wiley, 1851), 29. See also Schulz, *The Sculpture of Tullio Lombardo*, 9.
168 The tomb was originally located in Santa Maria dei Servi and was moved to the Dominican basilica in 1816. Schulz, *The Sculpture of Tullio Lombardo*, 48–49; Schulz, *The History of Venetian Renaissance Sculpture ca. 1400–1530*, vol. 1: 235. The episode is recounted in BM, MSS. IT. C1. VII. 2283 (= 9121), Francesco Fapanni, Chiese claustrali di Venezia, 1884, 69r–v, 79–80. The account on pages 79–80, taken from the unpublished diaries of Cicogna, recommended that the statues should be given to the Accademia di Belle Arti in Venice.

CHAPTER THREE

THE LIMITS OF ENFORCEMENT

Artistic Censorship in Venice

In the previous chapter it was demonstrated that the kind of nudity in devotional images that was on view in Florence and Rome never caught on to the same extent in Renaissance Venice. The censorship of so-called lascivious statues or paintings also happened quite randomly, often taking place centuries after these works had first been put on public display. The evidence examined so far would thus seem to support the Jesuit historian John O'Malley's assertion that after the Council of Trent, the Church 'pursued no consistent or broadly enforced policy regarding music, painting, sculpture, or architecture'.[1] O'Malley's argument is in contradiction to that of the art historian Alexander Nagel, who instead stated that censorship became 'a threat to be reckoned with, a programmatic threat', and that artists 'had to learn how to play a new game of cat and mouse'.[2] In the next chapter, which examines the pastoral visitations of the austere Patriarch Lorenzo Priuli at the end of the sixteenth century in Venice, the paucity of image censorship will lend further credence to O'Malley's analysis. Nevertheless, the impact of successive visitations from 1581 to 1604 on the churches of Venice was significant in some areas, and this means that these inspections do present a sort of 'programmatic campaign' to enforce post-Tridentine standards for ecclesiastical furnishings and decorations in the city, only at no point did this involve severe or extensive censorship of pre-existing images. Although the 1563 decrees on images forged at the Council of Trent invested bishops with the power to police the decorum of artworks displayed in the churches of their diocese (suggestive of the new climate of censorship that Nagel refers to) this never happened consistently in Venice, and there were important structural reasons as to why this was the case. Campaigns tended to be far more haphazard than programmatic, as the expurgation of 'lascivious' images demonstrates, and often the exhortations concerning images of local synods were flouted or consistently overlooked even by their own ecclesiastical authors.

In this chapter I examine the nature of institutional artistic censorship in late sixteenth-century Venice by exploring the means available for controlling the arts and the extent of their efficacy in the city. This includes an analysis of the Tridentine decrees, the decisions of synods, and the activities of the Inquisition, all of which had different levels of jurisdiction over the appropriateness of sacred images. I also offer some thoughts on the impact of some of the most widely cited contemporary treatises on devotional art and architecture. If taken literally, a number of these sources suggest that censorship must have been far more widespread than was actually the case after the Council of Trent. For example, some of the treatises were published in successive editions and so were presumably widely read, but it is important to remember that unless there is evidence to show that their ideas were put into practice by an artist, a patron, or a powerful ecclesiastic intent on reforming the devotional images in his diocese, they had no enforceable authority over these groups. Yet they are sometimes selectively or superficially quoted to suggest that painters had compromised control over the appearance of their output, with the more sensationalist accounts suggesting that they were labouring under a climate of enforced obedience to the requirements of a 'Counter-Reformation' Church that left meagre room for invention or innovation.[3] Whilst these texts provide evidence of a certain censorial mindset – one that is inevitably far removed from today's attitudes concerning artistic freedom –one should be very wary of taking them at face value as evidence of what actually happened. Nor should they be understood in isolation from the actual images and architecture produced in the same years, which often present a very different picture of the real boundaries of what was and was not now acceptable for the devotional image.

THE DECREES OF THE COUNCIL OF TRENT

The great historian of the Council of Trent, Hubert Jedin, argued that the Tridentine decrees demonstrate that Church reform was never revolutionary, acting instead as a synthesis between the conservation of the old and the necessity of the new.[4] This is borne out by the decrees regarding sacred images of the twenty-fifth and final sessions of the meeting on 3–4 December 1563, which depended upon the Second Council of Nicaea for the general justification of devotional representations as objects worthy of veneration insofar as they referred to the prototype represented, as well as by the *sententia* (opinion) of the French colloquy of Saint-Germain-en-Laye (1562), which was at certain points quoted verbatim or closely paraphrased in the decrees.[5] In the first section of the Tridentine image decrees, charges of idolatry were rejected, and the legitimacy, usefulness, and 'great profit derived from all sacred images' were asserted.[6] This positive endorsement of images was justified on the basis of the potential that they had to remind viewers of the beneficence of Christ, and the holy lives of the saints, causing them to 'adore and love God, and to cultivate piety', and to order their own lives in imitation of the saintly exemplars depicted. In the second section of the decrees, it was stated that abuses were to be eradicated. The uneducated were to be taught that no divinity resided in the image, and that nothing suggestive of false doctrine, or that presented a serious theological error, was to be tolerated. As pointed out by Giuseppe Scavizzi, 'false doctrine' referred to the representation of Protestant ideas or those in direct opposition to Catholic belief, which as we saw in Chapter 1 was unsurprisingly rare in Catholic countries.[7] The decrees on images came under the same heading as the interrelated issues of the veneration of relics and the invocation of saints, and it was stated that with regard to all three of these practices, all superstitions were to be removed, any association with 'filthy lucre' was to be abolished, and lasciviousness was to be avoided.[8] No figures that demonstrated 'a beauty exciting to lust' were to be tolerated. The person responsible for ensuring that all of this was carried out was the bishop, who was charged with overseeing that nothing profane, indecorous, or disorderly was allowed in the churches of his diocese. Finally, any unusual image was to be approved by him prior to it going on display, suggestive of an increased level of clerical control, an important aspect of the Tridentine decrees to which I will return.

In sum, these decrees encouraged artists to produce sacred images that were free from what the Church regarded as false dogma, and any kind of lasciviousness. These images were to be emotionally stimulating, but the faithful were not to be misled by superstitious beliefs concerning their powers. It is worth reminding ourselves that these were not particularly onerous guidelines for artists and patrons to follow. That sacred images should be appropriate to both setting and audience must have been a notion that most artists were aware of, even before this was formally decreed at Trent. That the destruction of sacred images was wrong, that they were useful and to be encouraged, had already been stated centuries earlier in the midst of the Byzantine image controversies. Although these relatively brief statements have understandably elicited great interest from art historians, both Jedin and later O'Malley have demonstrated the extent to which images were a non-issue at the Council of Trent until the eleventh hour.[9] Had it not been for the influential French delegation led by Cardinal Charles de Guise, it was entirely possible that the matter might never have made it onto the council's agenda at all, and it had been the opinion of the papal legates that this was a topic that could be best clarified in the catechism, or occasion a straightforward reassertion of the Nicaean decree.[10]

It might seem odd considering the drastic impact of iconoclasm in reformed areas of Europe that this was not considered of more urgent importance at the council. Not only was the question of images considered to already be a settled one by many of the delegates at Trent, but the majority of them initially hailed from Italy, Spain, and Portugal, areas that were unaffected by iconoclasm. This situation was very different in war-torn France, where outbursts of image destruction had been taking place since the 1520s. A series of local synods and colloquies had been held there during the course of the sixteenth century in order to reach some kind of agreement with the Protestant Huguenots on the question, but to no avail.[11] So when De Guise arrived in Trent in November 1562, his delegation was insistent that a resolution on images should be agreed upon.[12] The legates were initially unconvinced, especially given that the council operated under the twin headings of reform and doctrine, ones that did not easily accommodate the image question. But when the council had to be brought to a swift conclusion owing to the illness of the pope in late November 1563, and the possibility that if he died it might take years to convoke another conciliar meeting, De Guise demanded that a decree be formulated. They agreed, and he became the chairman of a committee responsible for images, as well as other matters, such as indulgences, fasts, and the venerations of saints and relics.[13] The decrees on images were presented to the council at the General Congregation in the afternoon of 2 December. They went undebated, and were then solemnly approved in session twenty-five. In the short passage on formulating the decrees on purgatory, relics, and the veneration of images, it was noted that this material had already been covered in other councils.[14] On 14 November, Carlo Borromeo (one of the papal legates) reported that because of this it had been decided to pursue these issues along the lines not of dogma but of reform, by concentrating on 'removing abuses'.[15] Since the document on images had been put together in great haste, Jedin argued that it must have been based upon a prior text that was readily available: the *sententia* from Saint-Germain. Five of the Sorbonne theologians who had helped draw it up in the first place were present in Trent, hence this was the reason the decrees followed similar wording to the earlier text authored in France.

The sequence of events that led to the promulgation of the decrees regarding images in such great haste demonstrate that they were never part of a grand plan engineered by the Catholic Church to control the visual arts and enforce censorship. Neither the legates nor the pope's confidant and advisor, Cardinal Morone, demonstrated any marked enthusiasm for the French proposal concerning images, and although we have seen that complaints about artistic license in devotional representations had been rumbling on for decades, the impetus behind the Church's statements on this matter at Trent stemmed not from these debates over decorum but from the reality of Protestant iconoclasm. The decrees were not intended to target artists such as Michelangelo, as De Maio asserted, and there is no record of any specific artist or artwork being mentioned in the conciliar record.[16] To suggest otherwise is purely speculative. O'Malley argued that the Church 'steered a virtually hands-off course in stated policy' with regard to the arts, and the lack of consensus about what sacred images should look like beyond adhering to the generalised pronouncements made at Trent is attested to not only by the stylistic eclecticism of late sixteenth-century painting but by the diverse patronage activities of the upper clergy that demonstrated varying levels of tolerance for what might be accepted as appropriate.[17]

Beyond the specifications relating to images, a number of other Tridentine decrees are just as important to consider in terms of their impact on sacred art and architecture. The decrees on images may even have been given excessive attention by art historians at the expense of some of the other decisions forged at Trent. For example, the decrees of session thirteen of 11 October 1551 concerning the dogma of the real presence of Christ in the eucharist and of transubstantiation, and of session twenty-two of 17 September 1562 (which incorporated the decrees of session thirteen) that decreed the sacrificial nature of the mass, had a sustained impact in Venice, as will be shown in the next chapters.[18] The theology of purgatory that was decreed in the same session as those on images was significant because this had suddenly become a very popular subject by the end of the century. The same can be said about the council's assertion of the importance of the saints and their relics. This may be related to the increasingly heroic depictions of their lives and martyrdoms in the same period, as well as the concern of the visitations for the correct labelling and division of documented relics from those with a less convincing provenance. More generally, the Council of Trent placed great emphasis on the sacraments and the ritual of the mass. Ceremony was to be encouraged because it meant that the minds of the faithful could be 'excited, by those visible signs of religion and piety, to the contemplation of those most sublime things which are hidden in this sacrifice'.[19] Even though the adaptability of the spoken low mass meant that it was given priority over the solemn mass in the Roman Missal of 1570, the emphasis on the 'majesty of the great sacrifice' and the endorsement given to the use of 'mystic benedictions, lights, incense, vestments' at Trent seem almost to anticipate the sensory appeal of the Baroque, and it was the polar opposite to attitudes in Protestant Europe.[20] Zwingli held that the mass was the worst idol of all, and that true religion could not allow mediation through matter.[21] In England, Hugh Latimer's sermon to convocation in 1536 targeted the cult of saints, images, lights, relics, pilgrimages, and purgatory, denouncing those who believed images should be gilded, dressed in silk garments, or have candles lit before them.[22]

The Council of Trent's proscriptions could never have been realised without the cooperation of the bishops, so the decrees also contained important details regarding their role in ensuring that all of this was carried out. Not only were they to inspect unusual images before they went on display, but during their visitations they were to overrule secular patrons, who were ordered not to 'meddle with the visitation of the ornaments of the church'.[23] Theoretically, this presented a significant shift, by making private patrons subservient to the desires of the bishop. The Jesuit Order had attempted to limit concessions made to donors in their churches, and in 1581 a letter to the rector of San Giovannino in Florence stated that those who wished 'to have burial rights [*ius sepulturae*] or found "*cappellanie*" [endow a chapel] should not think of it, because the Company cannot give it to them'.[24] Although this ideal was noble in theory, it often proved impossible to uphold in practice. Compromises with generous patrons were inevitable, especially when funds were dependent on acquiescing to their demands. At the mother church of the same order, the Gesù in Rome, Cardinal Alessandro Farnese (1520–89) had control over the choice of architects, as well as the painters and sculptors for the tribune area, and his name is emblazoned on Giacomo della Porta's (c. 1532–1602) façade.[25]

The decrees had also asserted that bishops were to play a pivotal role in ensuring that churches of their dioceses were adequately maintained and decorated. This was referred to in the image dictates, as well as in the earlier seventh session of the council where they had been ordered to 'provide by suitable legal remedies that whatever needs repairs, be repaired'.[26] In session twenty-one, bishops were also instructed to ensure the restoration of parish churches in a state of disrepair, and if resources were insufficient, patrons who benefitted from the church should be compelled to pay, or as a last resort the parishioners were to be approached for funds.[27] A badly kept or decayed church could sometimes be a sign of errant or ineffective clergy. In 1565 during the visitation of the diocese of Modena, one church was found so neglected that the eucharist conserved in the tabernacle had decayed due to the dirt, and in other places sacred edifices had become home to hens and wild animals, a cause of local scandal.[28] By contrast, a clean, orderly, and well-decorated church could demonstrate the piety and efficient management of the diocese, which was one of the reasons why successive patriarchs were so keen to insist upon such high standards for the appearance of the churches of Venice.

VENICE AND THE COUNCIL OF TRENT

The approach of Venice to the spectre of a great council can be summed up as initial interest in the idea, followed by definite listlessness, concluding with a marked enthusiasm for the final stage of the council from 1562 to 1563. Jedin argued that Venice was something more than one of the most honourable Italian States for the council, but was also its '*piazza finanziaria*, its economic and cultural centre, its magnet'.[29] The conciliar decrees formally came into force on 17 September 1564 with the synod of Patriarch Giovanni Trevisan, and they were read aloud in the cathedral of San Pietro di Castello where the city's clerics vowed to respect them. The same ceremony was repeated for the doge and the Venetian government, which meant that the Tridentine dictates were instituted as laws of the Republic early on.[30] Some years previous to this, in the late 1530s, Venice had even been ready to host the council in Vicenza, causing Jedin to observe that the Tridentine Council was very nearly a Venetian Council or, more precisely, a Vicentine one.[31] Some initial preparations were made, and the papal legates visited the city on 12 May 1538, but nothing came of the plan, and a year later it was suspended. By the time the council eventually commenced on 13 December 1545 in the city of Trent, in the southernmost area of the Holy Roman Empire, the Venetians had lost much of their early enthusiasm for the idea.[32] This was probably due to the fact that attempts to convene the meeting had been frustrated time and time again, and because the Serenissima disapproved of Emperor Charles V's war against the Schmalkaldic League on account of the obstacles it presented to a commercial relationship with Germany. Since the war was supported by the council, when hostility was manifested towards Southern Germany in July 1546, Doge Francesco Donà opined that 'this will be a great disturbance'.[33] The majority of the bishops of Venice's dominions found an excuse not to attend the first period of the Council of Trent, arguing that their age and poverty made the journey impossible, surely an exaggeration given the relative geographical proximity.[34] But particularly in the third and final period of the council under Pope Pius IV, Venice was well represented by the patriarchs of Venice and Aquileia, Giovanni Trevisan and Daniele Barbaro, together with a majority of the most important bishops of the terraferma, as well as the ambassadors Matteo Dandolo and Nicolò da Ponte, who later became doge in 1578.[35] Da Ponte was an important patron of Tintoretto, as was Antonio Milledonne, who attended the council as secretary to the ambassadors. Ridolfi tells us that Da Ponte had an image of the Council of Trent by the artist in his own home.[36] By the time of the third phase of the council, Venice's earlier indifference had been replaced with a far more eager approach to the proceedings.[37] The coadjutor Bishop of Famagusta, the Venetian-born Girolamo Ragazzoni, gave a passionate speech to his colleagues in the final session. He announced that because the delegates had 'proscribed all superstition and avarice, and all irreverence in the celebration of the mass ... [and] removed sensual songs and music from the temples of the Lord ... [g]reat ecclesiastical offices will in future be filled by those in whom virtue prevails over ambition ... and bishops will remain in the midst of their flocks'.[38]

Even if their successes may have been variable, Venetian patriarchs of the late sixteenth and early seventeenth centuries were notably dedicated to initiating the Tridentine decrees, evinced through Trevisan's foundation of a patriarchal seminary in 1580 for the education of the clergy, and the convocation of three synods during his tenure, a stance that was continued and expanded upon by his successors.[39] As Deborah Walberg noted, 'by the end of the sixteenth century the religious face of Venice outside the ducal chapel had been transformed into a reflection of the demands and precepts of the Counter-Reformation church in Italy in most respects'.[40] The Venetian State was nevertheless wary of the centralising impulses of the Holy See and the challenge to their empire's relative ecclesiastical independence and stability that outside interference might present. Venice was in the habit of taxing their clergy,[41] electing their own patriarchs (with a preference for laymen),[42] granting the laity agency in electing their parish priests,[43] and insisting that lay patricians, the three *Savi dell'eresia*, sat alongside the clerical members of the Inquisition. There were also effectively two churches in Venice: that of the cathedral of San Pietro oriented towards Rome and headed by the patriarch, and that of the Marcian basilica that was officiated by the *primicerio*, who answered directly to the doge (*princeps in ecclesia, princeps in republica*) rather than the pope. The latter was precisely the kind of autonomous local Church that was at odds with the standardisation required by the post-Tridentine movement.[44] But just as Venice was wary of the encroachment of Rome regarding its ecclesiastical structures and historic privileges, so too was the Holy See sceptical about the Republic's ability to enact Tridentine reform without any external oversight. The row over jurisdiction eventually erupted with the Interdict placed on the city in 1606 by Pope Paul V (r. 1605–21), but signs of the troubles to come were already manifested some years earlier at the beginning of the 1580s, when Patriarch Trevisan sided with the Senate in opposing Borromeo's plan for the city to be subject to an Apostolic Visitation.[45] In contrast to a pastoral visit, which was conducted on the authority of a bishop in his diocese, or in the case of Venice by its patriarch, an Apostolic Visit was carried out by external agents and was intended to satisfy a higher ecclesiastical power, in this case the pope. These visits increased exponentially in the immediate decades following the Council of Trent, and they were perceived by the papacy as an effective tool for enacting reform, culminating in the 1624 institution of the Congregation for Apostolic Visitation.[46] The initial reaction from Venice to Borromeo's suggestion that they might benefit from such a visit was one of anger and ridicule, and it was met with howls of protest. Trevisan pronounced the city to be 'more religious than ten Milans', whilst the doge Nicolò da Ponte was of the opinion that the

Ambrosian archbishop was, without a doubt, 'the strangest brain in Italy'.[47] In the barrage of critiques that followed, the Senate argued that Borromeo's 1580 visits to Brescia (a Venetian territory) had left the faithful confused, thus having a detrimental rather than a positive impact on religious life there.[48] In private correspondence Borromeo had completely dismissed the aged patriarch, who was now in his late seventies, as 'not of ill will, but a man of insignificance, who will achieve nothing of importance', which seems unfair given Trevisan's demonstrable record of attempting to instigate Tridentine reforms and the fact that his own pastoral visits were under way by this point.[49] After drawn-out negotiations, the Apostolic Visitation did eventually take place on terms acceptable to the Venetians. The visits to the city's churches (with the exception of San Marco) and male convents was led by the Bishop of Verona, Agostino Valier (1531–1606, r. 1565–1606),[50] together with the Apostolic Nuncio, Lorenzo Campeggi (1547–85), whilst the nunneries, the state of which had been a particular point of contention between Venice and the Holy See, were instead to be inspected by the patriarch.[51] Compromises might have been achieved between Rome and Venice, but Trevisan nonetheless had to suffer the embarrassment of an interrogation by the two visitors, something that had not taken place in the same way in other Apostolic Visits, according to Paolo Prodi, and one in which the patriarch appeared 'almost in the guise of an accused offender'.[52]

Although one factor in Venetian resistance to the Apostolic Visit was doubtless related to the lax state of their monasteries and convents, their attitude also stemmed from a belief that they were more than capable of enacting Tridentine reforms independently, and that their city was *more* pious than other places, including even Rome, an idea inherent in the myth of Venice as a divinely blessed and serene Republic without a pagan past.[53] Anti-Roman feeling unsurprisingly grew around the time of the Interdict, and the Servite friar Paolo Sarpi penned his hostile account of the Council of Trent that was first published in London in 1619.[54] Sarpi's polemics should not be taken as indicative of a fixed Venetian viewpoint, however. Richard Mackenney found little evidence of diverging opinions between Venetian patricians and Roman churchmen during Inquisition tribunals, causing him to wonder whether Sarpi disguised 'rhetoric as history' in order to exaggerate the differences between the outlook of the Venetian State and the Roman Church.[55] For example, in contrast to Sarpi's later view of Trent, the secretary of the Council of Ten, Antonio Milledonne, authored one of the earliest accounts of the council that was diffused in manuscript form already in the 1580s.[56] Having attended the council in person, his factual chronicle was positive in tone, and as we have seen there was a level of enthusiasm in terms of realising the reforming aims of Trent in its initial aftermath. Perhaps most importantly, the anti-Roman feeling that was sometimes manifested in Venice should not be misconceived as secularism.[57] As Bernardo Giustiniani argued in 1480, for Venetian cardinals, 'Venice was their mother, Rome their godmother.'[58] If Venice demonstrated hostility towards Rome, it was not because of scant regard for religion, and it is also not that unusual since political obstacles meant that it took a long time for Tridentine decrees to be accepted in France, and even in Catholic Spain.[59]

IDEALS VERSUS REALITY IN POST-TRIDENTINE TREATISES

In the years following the Council of Trent, a glut of treatises about the decorum of devotional images and architecture appeared. Their publication reached a peak from the 1560s to the 1590s, but they remained popular well into the seventeenth century.[60] A number of the most well-known examples were authored by high-ranking churchmen such as Johannes Molanus (rector of Louvain University and a canon of St Peter's),[61] Cardinal Gabriele Paleotti (archbishop of Bologna),[62] and Cardinals Carlo[63] and Federico Borromeo (archbishops of Milan).[64] Since the Tridentine decrees on images were general in nature and provided scarce practical advice on how precisely images might be reformed, the authors of these particular treatises attempted to come up with detailed guidelines that might be of use to patrons, artists, and architects, but that were primarily intended for other priests and bishops whose role in enforcing the decrees was ordered by Trent. For example, we know that both Carlo Borromeo and Paleotti had read the popular *De picturis et imaginibus sacris* of Molanus, which helped shaped the format of their own offerings on interrelated subjects: Borromeo's *Instructiones fabricae et supellectilis ecclesiasticae* of 1577 and Paleotti's *Discorso intorno alle imagini sacre et profane* of 1582.[65] The very existence of these writings demonstrates that the role and appearance of devotional imagery and architecture was given renewed focus in the late sixteenth century, and that it elicited a level of interest amongst readers, especially since Molanus's work was published in successive editions.[66]

These treatises have been given considerable attention by scholars, particularly from the 1960s onwards when a number of them were republished and translated.[67] Yet we still know relatively little about their reception amongst other ecclesiastics and artists, and their direct influence upon the latter was most likely slight, even if they may have shared some of the authors' concerns.[68] With the exception of some well-known examples, such as Carlo Borromeo's employment of the architect Pellegrino Tibaldi, or Paleotti's championing of the painter Prospero Fontana and enthusiasm for Federico Barocci, it is unclear how familiar artists or patrons might have been with the arguments presented in these texts. In the absence of evidence that demonstrates a convincing relationship between the two, there is a risk of formulating a tenuous link. Attempts have been made to tie Paleotti closely to the stylistic revolution of the Carracci in Bologna, for example, yet Agostino Carracci (1557–1602) produced a series of erotic engravings that were censured by Pope Clement VIII, and in 1579 he dedicated a sacred image to Paleotti of the kind his treatise would condemn, at which point drafts of the *Discorso* were already in circulation in Bologna. This shows that he flagrantly ignored, or was at the very least unaware of, the very artistic norms that Paleotti sought to establish.[69]

The direct impact of these treatises in Venice seems to have been minimal, with the exception of Carlo Borromeo's manual on sacred architecture and decoration. This work was surely known by both Priuli and the patriarch of Aquileia Francesco Barbaro (1546–1616, r. 1593–1616), and its impact will be discussed in more detail in the next chapter.[70] Yet apart from Dolce's *Aretino* of 1557, none of the treatises on devotional art that tend to be most frequently cited today were published in Venice, and they did not necessarily have a great influence on artists outside of the dioceses where their authors were incumbent as bishops. For instance, in the Introduction it was noted that Paleotti explicitly stated in his *Discorso* that he had little interest in playing the censor in places where pictorial customs might be different to those of Bologna, and Borromeo had a similar disclaimer in his own treatise.[71] These tolerant sentiments would appear at odds with Borromeo's zeal as an Apostolic Visitor, as well as Paleotti's later unsuccessful attempt to greatly expand the institutional censorship of sacred images by the Catholic Church through the establishment of an 'index' of forbidden images, similar to that which existed for books, and to entrust its functions to a congregation of cardinals to be tasked with outlawing the 'abuses' in devotional art that he believed remained widespread.[72] His plans were set out in a text of 1596, the *De tollendis imaginum abusibus novissima consideratio*, which was distributed amongst members of the papal court and select cardinals and prelates. It garnered some powerful support, yet also strident criticism from clergy in the very orbit of the Inquisition, and was thankfully never adopted.[73] That Paleotti lamented how the practices he had denounced years ago continued unabated tells us that the majority of artists and patrons paid little heed to such instructions, illustrating the gulf that clearly existed between textual instruction and artistic reality. Something of a frustrated reformer by the end of his life, Paleotti's critiques also demonstrate that for some churchmen the Tridentine decrees were considered not to have gone far enough in laying down the rules for image reform, or at the very least had not been enforced with sufficient rigour. This opinion was far from being universally shared, and the influential Silvio Antoniano (1540–1603) penned an aghast rebuttal to Paleotti's proposal.[74] After the publication of his earlier *Discorso* Paleotti had been sought out by Antoniano as something of an expert on orthodox iconography, and the pair were in correspondence regarding Scipione Pulzone's *Assumption* for the Bandini chapel in San Silvestro al Quirinale in 1583, and then again in 1595 for the frontispiece of Paleotti's

De bonus senectutis, which was printed that same year.[75] Like the prelates at Trent, Antoniano's response to Paleotti's *De tollendis imaginum abusibus* shows that he considered the image question to be a settled one and that he believed Paleotti's proposals were over the top and unnecessary.[76]

The writings of figures like Gilio (whom we met in the previous chapter), Molanus, or Paleotti thus present an approach to sacred art that remained idealistic and was rarely realised consistently. We need look no further than the vast majority of contemporary devotional images to find evidence of this, since many would have failed to conform to their rigorous standards. Because the stipulations that these writers dispensed regarding particular iconographies were extremely detailed, and on occasion contradictory, it is possible to find images that in some areas are in keeping with their requirements, yet can be discounted in others.[77] What the treatises do provide fascinating evidence of is a distinct outlook regarding the appropriate role and appearance of sacred art, as well as efforts to go beyond the decrees of Trent in attempting to reform it. Given their theological expertise, the *trattatisti* desired a sacred art that was faithful to both the venerable traditions of the Church and the biblical sources, one that 'conforms to scriptural truth' as Carlo Borromeo put it.[78] Their clerical status also explains why they were relatively silent on the issue of style, beyond recommending that images should be emotive and beautiful, because their talents lay in explicating the sources for what they believed to be historically accurate norms for sacred art. The keenness of these writers to correct erroneous visual interpretations of scripture and the lives of the saints is one of the reasons why they were mostly invoked pejoratively by modern art historians until relatively recently. This negative assessment is hardly surprising because the approach of the *trattatisti* threatens to render the hallowed category of art subservient to the requirements of religion. The successive editions and international reception of a treatise such as Molanus's demonstrates that his efforts to clarify the theological basis for specific iconographies were met with an interested audience, perhaps furnishing patrons and some artists with the sort of detailed knowledge that might assist them in confidently commissioning and producing decorous devotional images. At the same time, it is also true that these writers could be extremely pedantic, whether it be the minutiae of Gilio's objections to the *Last Judgment* or Molanus's exhaustive iconographic clarifications. The latter argued, for example, that to show Saint Helen with a crown was technically incorrect, for she was an empress not a queen, and as such should be shown as an older woman, tall in stature and holding a cross.[79] Molanus also devoted several different chapters to the iconography of Saints Peter and Paul, and he spent pages airing the various arguments regarding the vexed question on whether Paul should be shown to the right-hand side of Peter, or if the other way around was more appropriate.[80]

Yet it would also be wrong to assume that these authors were philistines or that the limitations on artistic freedom that they believed to be prudent had uniformly negative results. During Paleotti's archbishopric in Bologna there was a surge in both the production of and quality of sacred art; there were greater opportunities for women artists than elsewhere in Italy; and Paleotti was eager to employ a talented artist like Barocci to complete the altarpiece *Madonna and Child with Saints Francis and Petronio* in his family chapel, a commission that was eventually fulfilled by Lavinia Fontana (1552–1614) as the *Assumption of the Virgin*.[81] Paleotti confirmed the power of art and the power of its language in his *Discorso*, arguing: 'for there is no one so stupid and senseless that he does not feel great pleasure from beautiful pictures', and he elevated its role to that of meeting a universal need.[82] Federico Borromeo (1564–1631), the cousin of Carlo and heir to his Ambrosian archbishopric, whose *De pictura sacra* appeared in 1624, had studied with Paleotti in Bologna and owned a collection of around 172 paintings. Forty-eight per cent of these works were of devotional themes, with the remainder consisting of landscapes, still lifes, garland paintings with the Virgin and Child, portraits, classical scenes and those of undisclosed subjects.[83] A great lover of art, Federico founded the Ambrosiana in Milan in 1607 as a diocesan tripartite institution consisting of a library, art collection, and academy; he helped create a new genre of panting – that of the Madonna and Child surrounded by a garland of flowers – and he sponsored Flemish landscape artists including Pieter Brueghel the Younger (1564/65–1637/38) and Paul Bril (1554–1626).

For individuals like Federico Borromeo or Paleotti, second-rate artists would not have been capable of achieving the emotional impact that they desired of devotional images.[84] As noted by Pamela Jones, Borromeo recounted with pride that 'I have had my room ornamented with paintings, and I have made sure that all of them are excellent; there is not one vulgar or cheap thing.'[85] When he began writing his treatise, Paleotti took the time to consult numerous experts that included the architect Domenico Tibaldi (1541–83), as well as the painter Prospero Fontana. And even though there are only a few examples of artists showing a definite awareness of the precepts presented in some of these texts, this is not to say that the debates that they raised would not have been of interest to them. For example, Gilio's *Dialogue on the Errors and Abuses of Painters* objected to the thieves at Christ's crucifixion being depicted bound by ropes instead of nails, a seemingly minor visual quibble.[86] But the Spanish painter and official artistic 'censor' of Seville, Francisco Pacheco, was so perturbed by the similar question of whether Christ should be shown nailed to the cross with three nails or four in the seventeenth century, that he sought out the advice of the poet-scholar Francisco de Rioga. Pacheco settled on four, and once this visual precedent was set, Jonathon Brown demonstrated that this was observed with 'unswerving dedication' by the next generation of Sevillian painters.[87]

WHICH SACRED IMAGES SHOULD BE CENSORED?

Building upon the exhortations of Trent to avoid the lascivious, some of the *trattatisti* believed that particular biblical episodes would be better avoided by artists altogether, or at least depicted with the utmost attention to decorum due to the potential for abuses that they presented. Molanus disapproved of depictions of Bathsheba being seduced by David, or Salome dancing, and even ones of the naked Christ-child, but he endorsed images of Susanna because he thought that she reminded viewers of the virtue of temperance.[88] Federico Borromeo had a different opinion, writing, 'I therefore cannot praise the nude figure of Susanna in pictures like that [that is, paintings displayed in a public church], even if the biblical narrative calls for it.'[89] Even if Molanus condemned the display of images that might give rise to 'dangerous error' amongst the uneducated laity, judging it vital that humble souls should not be offended or scandalised by what they saw, his concerns about possible iconoclasm meant that he warned strenuously against private authorities attempting to take it upon themselves to correct abuses in devotional works, ordering them to temper their zeal with discretion.[90] He also thought that the vast majority of sacred paintings did not present any serious abuses.[91] Anachronistic details and harmless apocryphal elements could be tolerated in religious art, although it would be better if in the future artists tried to avoid them.[92] An event that was probable, but not absolutely verifiable, could also be acceptable, as long as its probability was agreed by a competent person or widely accepted by the populace.[93]

So although none of these writers believed that what they considered to be falsehoods should be depicted, they demonstrated varying degrees of tolerance for artistic freedom and for elements that, although not central to the narrative, were capable of delighting the viewer and engaging them in pondering the image at hand. Federico Borromeo used the example of a little puppy being edited out of one of his favourite paintings by Titian, the *Adoration of the Magi* (c. 1557–60), to argue against 'issuing condemnations that are *too* rigid or severe, as a contemporary of ours recently did'.[94] The dog has now been restored to its rightful place in the painting, and is shown cocking its leg in the general direction of the alighting crowd (Fig. 42), perhaps why the member of his cousin Carlo's household that decided on the censorship saw to it that the offending canine was painted over.[95] Federico's account was confirmed by technical analysis during the restoration of the work, which demonstrated extensive overpainting in the area where the dog can now be seen, previously covered by dark and incongruous vegetation. Describing the censor as an

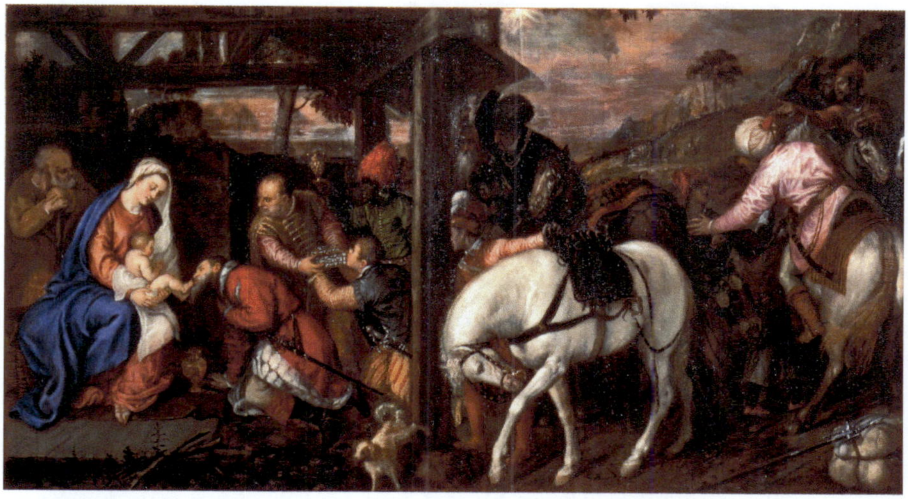

42. Titian, *Adoration of the Magi*, c. 1557–60, oil on canvas, Pinacoteca Ambrosiana, Milan (Photo: Veneranda Biblioteca Ambrosiana/Mondadori Portfolio/Bridgeman Images)

'inflexible', 'austere', and 'hard-hearted' man, Federico claimed that Titian himself was exasperated by the episode, writing that he 'is reported to have sighed and groaned that it was hardly surprising to him that men ignorant of art ordered the figure to be obliterated'.[96]

SHOULD IMAGES BE DESTROYED?

For all the writers here mentioned, the most serious image abuse of all was considered to be deliberately offensive or polemically anti-Catholic imagery. In Chapter 1 it was mentioned that Molanus and Paleotti believed portraits of known heretics should be prohibited and that their destruction was merited.[97] There is no example on Priuli's visitation of the destruction of a devotional image being ordered due to impropriety, despite the importance that was given to this in the late sixteenth century, and as we shall see in the next chapter, the few orders to remove images were usually because they were considered to be completely beyond repair. The appropriate process for the destruction of sacred images was described by the Bishop of Torcello, Antonio Grimani (1557–1628, r. 1587–1618), in his synod of April 1592. Grimani decreed that altars were to be adorned with 'honourable and decent images', but that if over the passage of time said images had become damaged, consumed, corroded, or deformed, then they should be burnt and the ashes buried. This was to be done with the utmost caution and out of the sight of the public. The same procedure was to be applied to altarpieces and other ornaments and furnishings that 'due to their age were rendered useless'.[98]

Similar to the actions of Priuli in Venice, even in Rome where Pope Clement VIII frequently ordered either the removal or editing of the offending areas of figures deemed to be too sensual, he commanded the destruction of an image only once, and for a different reason. The painting of Pope Leo the Great in the basilica of Santa Maria Maggiore was destroyed due to the apocryphal nature of the miracle that related to the arousal of the pope and his subsequent invocation to the Madonna via the miracle working icon of the *Madonna salus populi romani*.[99] In the treatises the destruction of Catholic sacred images was considered undesirable in light of Protestant iconoclasm, and the displacement of anything particularly problematic was advised. Having said that, the long history of Jewish communities being accused of image desecration meant that on the eve of the expulsion of Jews in 1557 in Bologna it was decided to whitewash some sacred images in the homes where Jews had been compelled to reside, and in 1625 Pope Urban VIII (r. 1623–44) ordered his cardinal vicar to proceed with the removal of sculpted and painted images of the Virgin Mary, Christ, and the saints from houses in the Roman ghetto and their substitution with marble tiles or simple letters inscribed with the names of the owners of the houses.[100] In these cases the removal or covering of devotional images was deemed preferable to the perceived risk that they could be vandalised. Punishments for image violations could be extremely severe: two young Jewish men found guilty of throwing stones at an image of the Madonna in 1611 were whipped through the streets of Rome, whilst an older pair condemned for partaking in the same crime were also sentenced to ten years on the galleys.[101] One's stance on sacred images was also tied to identity. Catherine Infante's work on cultural encounters in early modern Spain has demonstrated both how some exiled Moriscos were impressed by the Protestants, approving of their rejection of idolatry, and how Catholics in turn tended to view Protestants and Muslims as united in their contempt for icons.[102]

For Catholics, not having images at all could be a sign of a lack of religious fervour. A series of documents in the patriarchal archive of Venice dating to the late 1580s show that the city's teachers were subject to interrogation, amongst other things, about what they read, whether or not they knew anyone who consulted prohibited books, and if they kept images both in their homes and in their schools of Christ, the Madonna, and the saints.[103] Orthodox attitudes towards images were drummed into children at the schools of doctrine, which became a significant feature of post-Tridentine religious life in Venice.[104] Patriarch Priuli's popular catechism, which was still being reissued in the nineteenth century, reminded its readers to pay daily reverence to images and defended the Church's stance on the issue.[105] He recommended that parish catechism schools, in common with those founded in other parts of Italy, should give out little images printed on cards as prizes for those children who performed well, with the truly excellent being rewarded with 'painted or framed images'.[106]

The endorsement of the ownership of devotional images and the avoidance of their destruction means that what happened in Italy was thus very different to events on the global missions, where non-Christian images were often ruthlessly suppressed. At the same time as the power of the devotional image was being reasserted in Catholic areas of early modern Europe and Protestant iconoclasm was being condemned, Saint Francis Xavier (1506–52) was encouraging Indian children to smash 'idols' as part of his evangelising activities in South-East Asia. Whilst living amongst the Paravas in Cape Comorin, Xavier recounted that the infants 'run at the idols, upset them, dash them down, break them to pieces, spit on them, trample on them, kick them about, and in short heap on them every possible outrage'.[107] The zeal of the children extended to reporting their own parents for idolatrous worship, causing Xavier to approvingly comment that 'their hatred for idolatry is marvellous'.[108] In Peru, 'idolatry inspections' were sporadically carried out from the mid-seventeenth century to the 1750s, a practice that led to the destruction of *huacas* (ancestral remains/pre-Christian ritual sites) and the erection of crucifixes instead.[109] Four years after becoming the first bishop of Mexico City in 1528, the Franciscan Juan de Zumárraga proudly claimed that he had destroyed 500 temples and 20,000 idols.[110] But the *trattatisti* here examined were obviously not moral relativists. For them idols existed to be smashed down. It is doubtful that many of them would have perceived the irony in the actions of the Catholic missionaries against the backdrop of iconoclasm in Europe. Molanus referred positively to the destruction of pagan statues in Rome by Gregory the Great, as well as referencing the instructions to the Israelites contained in the book of Deuteronomy (7:5) that ordered them to 'break down their altars, smash their sacred stones, cut down their Asherah poles and burn their idols in the fire'.[111]

THE VIRTUOUS IMAGE MAKER

Following Vasari's championing of the Dominican Fra Angelico (1395–1455) as the ideal Christian painter due his great piety, Paleotti dedicated a whole chapter of his treatise to successful artists who were also 'numbered among saints and the blesseds, or renowned for the exemplary goodness of their lives'.[112] Likewise, Federico Borromeo praised the sculptor Annibale Fontana (1540–87) not only for his artistic talents but for his moral qualities and for acting 'with kindness and generosity not toward princes or other human beings, as some men do, but toward God himself'.[113] Just as Michelangelo had purportedly said that the artist who depicts Christ should be 'of blameless life, even if possible a saint, that the Holy Spirit may inspire his understanding', so too it was believed that the pious individual was better equipped to produce moving devotional artworks.[114] The exaltation of the virtuous image maker can thus be seen as an advocation for self-censorship, since it was thought that a good Christian could avoid impious mistakes by the sheer force of their religious conviction.

Artists were reminded of their vocation to create devout images in a variety of different ways. In Milan, Carlo Borromeo recommended calling mass meetings of artists to inform them of their obligations, suggesting that bishops should ensure that no painter or sculptor produced any sacred image prior to consulting the parish priest.[115] In Rome, members of the Accademia di San Luca (whose cardinal-protectors included first Federico Borromeo and then Paleotti) were addressed by a Jesuit priest in 1598 who encouraged them to make 'virtuous and praiseworthy things and to flee from any lascivious or indecent [things]'.[116] The founding documents of the academy made the academicians' aims for sacred art and their pious sympathies clear, by banning blasphemers from membership, for example.[117] Some years earlier in 1563, the members of the Università dei pittori in Rome were admonished that if they did not create virtuous images of Christ, the Virgin Mary, and the saints, their works would be destroyed and they would be punished.[118] There is little evidence that this ever happened, though.[119] Finally, in 1593 Pope Clement's cardinal vicar, Girolamo Rusticucci, issued an edict 'for altars and for their paintings' that ordered artists to present preparatory drawings for devotional works for official approval, a decree that was reissued in 1603.[120] Again, whether this ever enforced with much consistency is unclear, particularly since we would expect more drawings for altarpieces to exist if it had been. Two of Caravaggio's altarpieces – *The Death of the Virgin* and the first version of *The Inspiration of Saint Matthew* – were rejected by their patrons, suggesting that a preparatory drawing had never been officially approved in the first place.[121]

The statements pronounced at the Accademia di San Luca were interpreted by Anthony Blunt as evidence of the austere new climate for artistic production.[122] Although they might appear both to anticipate and to have been influenced by Trent, it is worth remembering that they also took their cue from older confraternal and guild traditions. For example, in 1506 the Florentine guild of Doctors and Apothecaries (to which painters at this point belonged) ordered that the members were not to create figures of 'our Lord or our Lady or any saint, male or female, in any location . . . that is used to piss or do other bad things'.[123] A century earlier in 1406 the statutes had been amended to oblige painters to attend mass at Santa Maria Nuova at least twice a month as members of the Confraternity of Saint Luke.[124] In Venice, the rulebook of the *Arte dei Pittori* suggests that such a provision was applicable only to the *gastaldo* and his companions. Chapter 50 of the confraternity rules stipulated that they should attend mass 'according to our orders' and that they were to be fined for absenteeism, unless there had been some rightful impediment that rendered attendance impossible.[125] A few years before the similar order given to the painters of Florence, in 1500 the Signoria of Venice ordered that the *Gastaldi* of the painters' confraternity should ensure that saints or crucifixes were not depicted in 'shameful places' such as latrines, which became chapter 56 of the guild regulations. Every painter in the city was to be made aware of this, and punishment for violations was to consist of a fifteen-lire fine, a month in prison, and a permanent ban on membership to the Scuola.[126] Even more significantly, a record of 25 February 1665 in the *mariegola* of the Scuola del Santissimo Sacramento in the parish of Sant'Agnese in Venice stipulated that the Council of Ten had ordered that in every one of the city's churches during the exposition of the eucharist, or for any festivity or ceremony, decorations of paintings or sculptures must not be profane, but should consist of sacred and devout histories, that encourage 'reverence and veneration'. Anyone who ignored this order was to be subject to the most serious penalties. The commandment of the Ten was to be exposed in every sacristy of the city, as well as being registered in the chapters of the confraternities of the Blessed Sacrament.[127]

SYNODS

One of the ways in which the Church in Venice sought to make expectations for sacred images clear was through diocesan synods, which of course predated the Council of Trent, but as with visitations, were convened more regularly after it.[128] Even before this, various patriarchs had taken steps to crack down on the production of 'immoral' printed illustrations: in 1497 Patriarch Tommaso Donà threatened the printer Luc'Antonio Giunta the Elder with excommunication unless he modified his edition of Ovid's *Metamorphoses* that featured nude figures, and in 1510 Patriarch Antonio Contarini issued a decree to bookmen that prohibited all illicit illustrations and dictated that he was to see any scriptural commentary prior to its publication.[129] Sacred images displayed in churches were a different matter to published material, of course, and from the final decade of the sixteenth century onwards the synods began to consistently reassert elements of the Tridentine decrees on images, as well as add their own advice about aspects of the decoration of the ecclesiastical space and the appearance of painted and sculpted representations that was, in theory at least, more stringent than the Tridentine image decrees. The first synods to be held post-Trent were the three convocated in 1564, 1571, and 1578 by Patriarch Trevisan. His aim was above all to improve the education and behaviour of the city's clergy, and he said nothing at all about images.[130] But after the decrees of the 1581 Apostolic Visitation were issued, this became a constant fixture in all of the synods held in the Venice diocese between 1592 and 1653, after which date interest in the issue appears to have waned. The 1581 general rules to be applied in all of Venice's churches decreed that altars had to be decorated with an 'honorific icon', and they had six months in which to do this.[131] The fifth decree stated that in cases where altars had not been adorned in the subscribed form, an interdict was to be placed on the space and no masses were to be celebrated.[132] The Torcellan synod of Grimani of 1592 went into far greater detail on the theme of sacred images, dedicating a whole chapter to the topic.[133] Grimani's dictates have been little examined by scholars, but they must have influenced the contents of Patriarch Priuli's 1594 Venetian synod. Grimani began by noting that 'there are still many things to be warned about concerning sacred images', ordering that paintings were to be pious, beautiful, and venerable.[134] They were to demonstrate 'religious decorum' and a 'saintly aspect' and were to be far from every vain beauty, lasciviousness, or obscenity that could offend the eyes of the beholder. Nothing profane, dishonest, false, or contrary to scripture was to be depicted, nor should histories that had not been approved by the Church. 'Ugly animals', beasts, dogs, and other similar [creatures] were not to appear on the walls of the church or in altars, unless the episode in which they appeared was the nativity. Profane and indecent animals were to be amended, and to avoid any further indecencies, images or altarpieces were not to be painted without advice from the priest. If this did not happen, it was the priest rather than the artist who was to be charged with amending the offending image at his own expense under pain of suspension.[135] No 'unusual' images were to be displayed; new ones were to be blessed according to the special form given by the pope; and the clergy was to teach the populace about the appropriate reverence paid to images in accordance with the Tridentine decrees.[136]

Patriarch Priuli held two synods, in September 1592 and November 1594.[137] Like Grimani, the second of these included a distinct chapter on images.[138] Here the contents of the Tridentine decrees were referred to at length, and painters and sculptors were advised to create works in conformity with ecclesiastical tradition and historical 'truth'. Just as Grimani had done, Priuli warned against depicting beasts or animals that were not required by the episode to be depicted, as well as stipulating that new images were to be approved before going on public display either by the patriarch or by those who had been entrusted with this role.[139] Moreover, saints were not be dressed with profane clothes or vain ornaments, and altars were not to be adorned with multiple images of the same saint, unless this was required by the narrative to be represented. The saints were never to be portrayed with the features of living men or women, a practice that had been vehemently denounced by numerous *trattatisti* and already by Savonarola in his Lent sermon of 1496.[140] Priuli's solution for images that transgressed his rules was that they should be burnt by the sacristan, even if – as the examination of his visitation records presented in the next chapter makes clear – it was extremely rare that anything was ever removed for these reasons, let alone deliberately destroyed.[141] His only remark about the altar in the church of San Trovaso where Tintoretto's *Temptation of Saint Anthony Abbot* was displayed was that it was 'decently decorated'.[142] This was despite the fact that the saint was a portrait of the donor, Antonio Milledonne, and that one of the temptresses of

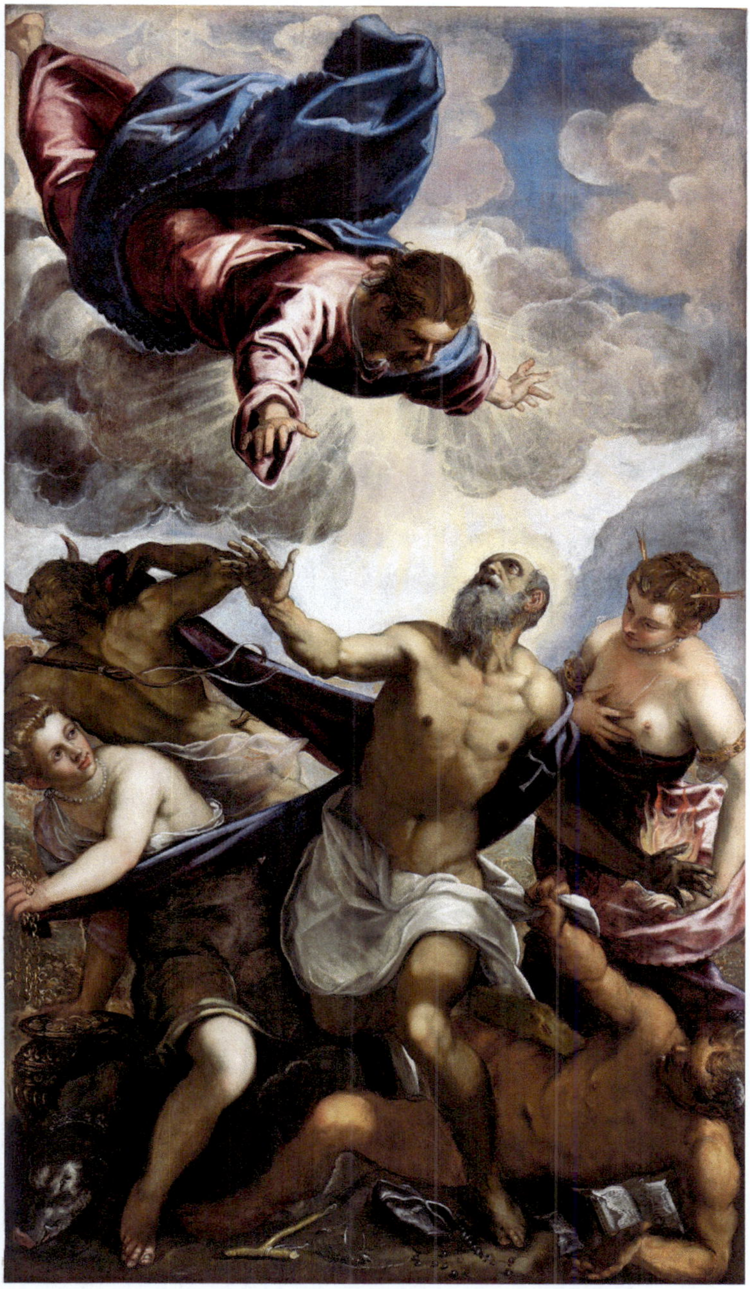

43. Tintoretto, *The Temptation of Saint Anthony Abbott,* c. 1577, oil on canvas, Santi Gervasio e Protasio (San Trovaso), Venice (Photo: Cameraphoto)

Anthony was shown conspicuously bare-breasted, her presence illustrating the saint's triumph over worldly vices (Fig. 43). The inclusion of portraits in sacred images, whether as an onlooker or as saints, was a well-established and popular practice in Venice and its territories. Yet the overt prominence of patrons in devotional images did occasionally arouse complaint and even vandalism. The

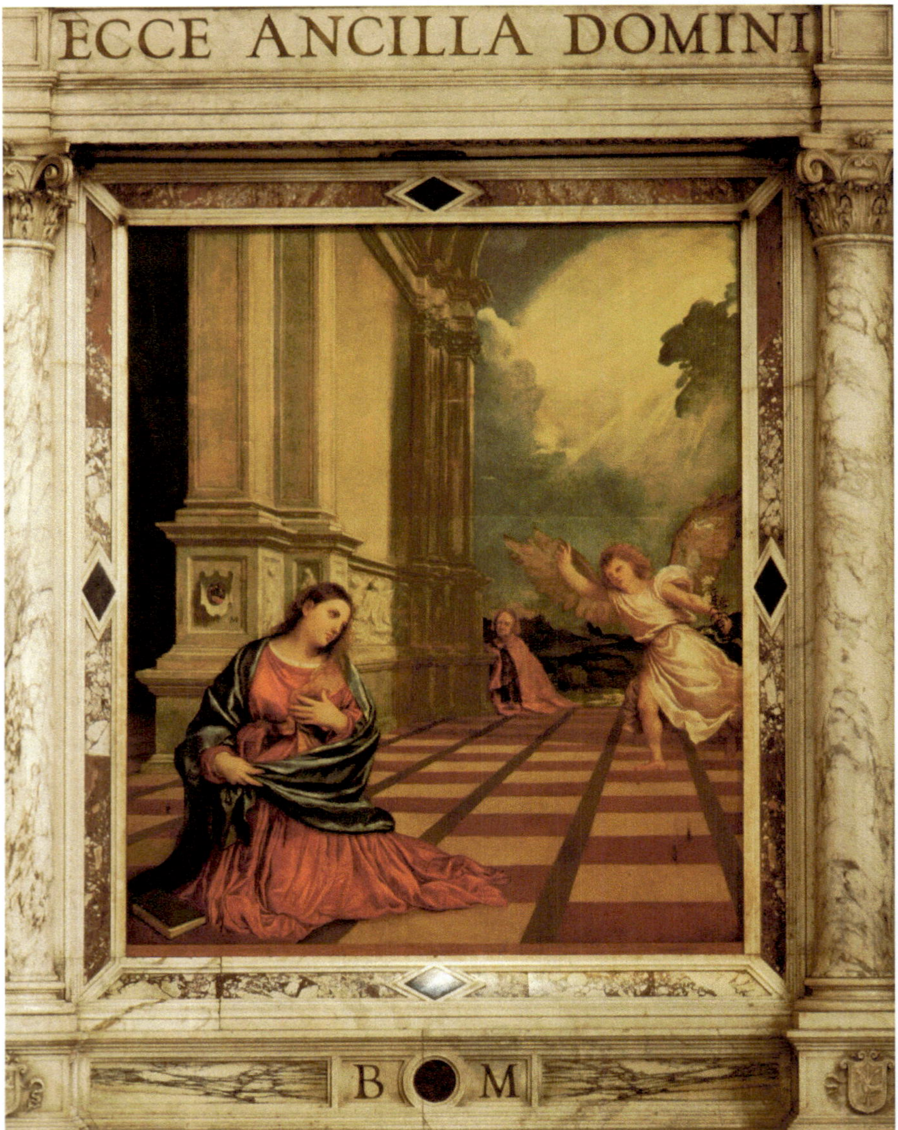

44. Titian, *The Annunciation,* 1520, oil on wood, Cattedrale di San Pietro Apostolo, Treviso (Photo: Dario Grimaldi/Bridgeman)

portrait of the donor, the canon Broccardo Malchiostro, in Titian's 1520 *Annunciation* for the cathedral of Treviso was defaced in 1526, and the statement of one of the witnesses recalled overhearing a fellow cleric recount that the work made him feel 'thoroughly contaminated, because one is making reverence to that figure and not to the image of the Madonna' (Fig. 44).[143]

The inclusion of portraits in devotional works had the potential to be vainglorious and distracting for the viewer. The Venosan-born Bartolomeo Maranta's (1500–71) *Discorso* of c. 1559–71 on Titian's *Annunciation* painted for San

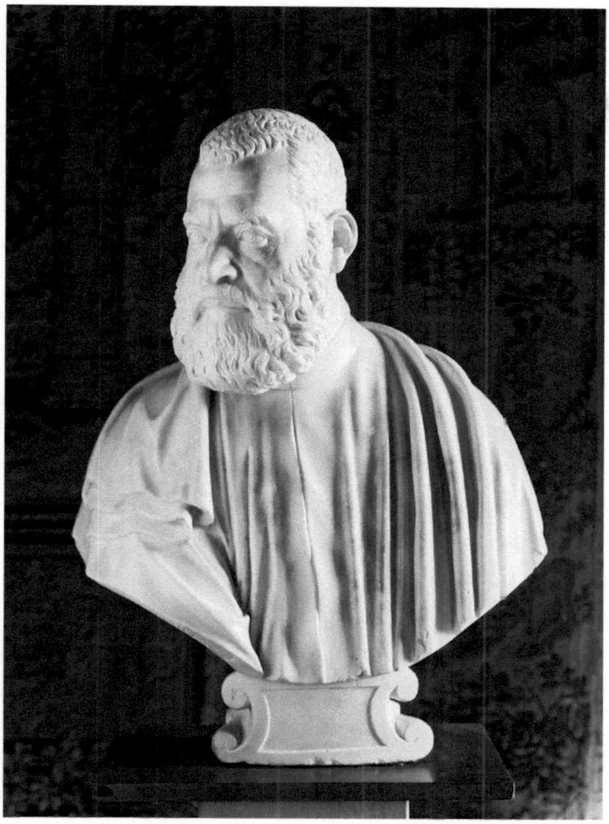

45. Alessandro Vittoria, *Benedetto Manzini,* c. 1560, marble, Galleria Franchetti, Ca d'Oro, Venice (Photo: Cameraphoto)

Domenico Maggiore in Naples argued that the sight of portraits of men of ill-repute dressed up as saints did little to inspire devotion, pointing to the hypocrisy of such representations.[144] Yet such likenesses could also attest to the piety of the individual portrayed, as well as their special dedication to a particular saint.[145] First Thomas Martin and later Xavier Salomon have pointed out the strong resemblance between the parish priest Benedetto Manzini (portrayed in a portrait bust by Alessandro Vittoria, Fig. 45) and the figure of Saint Geminianus depicted on Veronese's organ shutter (c. 1560) for the church of San Geminiano in Venice.[146] By the time the Priulan visit inspected the church in 1593, Manzini (1500–70) was long dead, but as shown in the next chapter, this particular church passed its visitation with flying colours, and was subject to the fewest recommendations of any parish inspected. That these kinds of portraits persisted in Italy, particularly in the domestic sphere, is attested to by examples like Artemisia Gentileschi's (1593–1654) self-portrait as Saint Catherine of Alexandria (c. 1615–17), or Palma il Giovane's moving self-portrait in the guise of a monk of c. 1606, once in the Bardisian Collection and recently sold at auction.[147] Palma, who as we shall see, was an extremely popular artist towards the end of the century in Venice and garnered praise for his works from successive visitations, used portraits liberally in his sacred paintings, and he even appears to have portrayed himself as a bystander who looks directly out at the viewer in the *Burial of the Beheaded Saints Tiburzio and Valeriano* for the Foscari Chapel at the church of San Nicola da Tolentino in Venice (c. 1620).[148]

Priuli's synodal instructions ordered that all images were to be inspected before being displayed in churches, even though the Council of Trent had ordered that this was to be done only for 'unusual' examples. There is no documentary evidence to suggest that this happened, and if it did its ineffectiveness is demonstrated by the later synod of Patriarch Gianfrancesco Morosini of June 1653.[149] Here it was ordered that prior to constructing altars, tabernacles, baptisteries, and reliquaries, as well as the creation of paintings and all such similar things, a model of said project was to be presented to the patriarch or to the vicar general. This was to be done for three reasons: in order to avoid 'the infinite errors and abuses that occur on a daily basis', because after such things had been made it was 'almost impossible to reform them', and since in this way money would not be wasted on works that were not in conformity with the accepted rules.[150] Demonstrating a censorial mindset not far from that of the elderly Paleotti, Morosini's synod also decreed that the visitors from each *sestiere* were to inspect every church in their district of the city once a month to ensure these and the other rules and constitutions established by the synod were being properly observed, as well as those of Morosini's predecessors and above all by the dictates established by the Apostolic Visitation, which the inspectors were always to have at hand, and which were by now over seventy years old. Once a month anything that had yet to be executed was to be reported to the patriarch or the vicar general, as well as estimations about what might be necessary and expedient in order for these changes to be made. In sum, the synods of the late sixteenth and seventeenth centuries demonstrate that the upper clergy of Venice and its lagoon not only were keen to enforce the Tridentine decrees concerning images but also were willing to go beyond the directives of the council to ensure the display of decorous devotional images in the parishes of the city. At the same time, patriarchs such as Priuli were often far more tolerant of the same artistic practices that they had condemned in their synods when confronted with them in the course of their visitations, once again demonstrating the distance between ideal and practice that must have contributed to the situation bemoaned by Morosini almost ninety years after the decrees on images had been agreed at the Council of Trent.

PUNISHMENTS

Encouraging artists to self-censor their output was a significant method for regulating images, albeit certainly not a foolproof one. This is why more direct and coercive means were also suggested to discourage the creation of anything potentially controversial. As has been noted, Fontana lamented that some artists would prefer religious themes to profane ones, but that economic constraints meant that artists were obliged to fulfil such commissions, rather than suffer falling into an 'unhappy state of misery' due to their poverty.[151] This is fascinating in light of Lavinia Fontana's activity as a painter of mythological nudes, and no doubt Prospero's assertions should be taken with a pinch of salt because they may have been intended to please his pious patron Paleotti, who annotated the text.[152] Prospero's solution that this unsatisfactory situation might be remedied through the sacraments is a striking one. It is perhaps an exaggeration to claim that this was 'a sly and well-argued escamotage ... in order to circumvent the rules and do as he pleased', as one scholar did recently, and I would interpret Prospero's opinions as reconciling the pedagogic necessity of artists to continue studying the nude with the spiritual context of his time, shown in his awareness that works that provoke 'scandal' should be avoided 'since this would be committing a sin'.[153] Federico Borromeo considered the crime of selling sensual images almost worse than the act of buying them. He argued that the purchasers of such 'lascivious figures' should be encouraged to understand the 'ruin and disgrace' such works could cause, but if they persisted, and gave 'their vices lasting nourishment', then excommunication might be the only adequate punishment left.[154] The apparent reluctance of some artists to paint profane works places them in a similar rank to two Florentines who experienced fits of remorse relating to their authorship of 'lascivious' artworks: Ammannati (described in the previous chapter) and the Florentine painter Francesco Furini (1603–46), who became a priest in his middle age, and on his deathbed apparently ordered that the erotic female nudes that brought him such fame were to be burnt.[155] Later, the French painter Philippe de Champaigne (1602–74) outright refused to paint nudes, demonstrating a piety that was 'equal to the popes' in the words of Mâle.[156]

As has been shown, these examples demonstrate that in the aftermath of the debacle over the *Last Judgment* there was a reaction against nudity, one that was accentuated through the Tridentine image decrees, and the gusto with which the problem was debated in numerous written sources.[157] Molanus believed that artists who indulged in the making of deliberately offensive or lascivious works should be excommunicated, although neither Agostino Carracci nor Giulio Romano before him, met this fate for their sensual engravings.[158] Carlo Borromeo's chapter on sacred images in the *Instructiones* ordered that rectors who consented to the display of unusual or offensive images were to be penalised, and that those painters or sculptors whose works departed from the prescribed rules were to be subject to a 'heavy punishment or fine'.[159] It is unclear to what extent this threat was ever put into practice in his diocese when it was brought into force with the Fourth Provincial Council of 1576.[160]

In the case of Ponchini's Castelfranco altarpiece, it had been the clergy, not the artist, who were threatened with excommunication and a fine if the offending painting was not shielded from public view and then reformed. What seems to be clear is that these kinds of punishments were intended for those abuses considered to be of the very gravest nature. For the most part, artistic traditions like the practice of representing the saints with the features of a living person or drawing upon sources like the *Golden Legend* for popular iconographies were too deeply rooted to be swiftly transformed, and there were often economic reasons that ensured their continuation. For example, from 1587 onwards Bishop Agostino Valier was the head of the Congregation of the Index that compiled the Clementine Index of 1596 that outlawed all Vernacular Bibles.[161] Yet during his earlier visitation to the churches of Venice he passed no negative comment on those images that made reference to these sources.[162] Similarly, and as noted by Martin Gaier, Patriarch Lorenzo Priuli introduced significant changes for burial practices in Venice beginning with his 1592 synod. Yet the instructions Priuli left for his own interment at the church of San Pietro di Castello were in contradiction to some of the very reforms that he had been so keen to enact.[163] Finally, despite rallying against nudity in devotional settings, even the 1598 decorations for the funerary ceremony for Paleotti in the cathedral of San Pietro in Bologna featured a fictive statue of the virtue of truth in the guise of a 'beautiful nude woman with an apple in her right hand'.[164]

INQUISITION

Veronese's 1573 interrogation by the Inquisition is the lens through which the impact of religious reform on Venetian art has been most frequently examined, as discussed in the Introduction to this book in connection with Fig. 1. This is unsurprising given that the painting in question survives, as does the record of the interrogation, affording a unique example of a Renaissance artist defending and discussing his creation before the Holy Office. Yet in many ways this book endeavours to shift the focus away from this episode, precisely because it was so unusual that it cannot be understood as representative of the experience of the vast majority of contemporary Venetian artists. The Inquisition was concerned with eliminating heresy, but because few devotional images were ever suspected of heretical content, the records of the Venetian Inquisition that cover the period from 1541 to 1797 appear to present only three other examples of direct image 'abuse', all of which dated from the Cinquecento. These are the confiscation of fifteen Flemish paintings at Rialto in 1561 that included 'dishonest' images, the unsolved crime of the graffiti on the walls of the offices of the Inquisition that depicted phalluses urinating into chalices in 1566, and an altarpiece in Verona that supposedly featured the portrait of a priest admiring his mistress in the guise of Saint Apollonia of 1587 – a case that was dismissed due to lack of evidence.[165] With the exception of Veronese, then, there appears to be no other case of an individual being called before the Inquisition in late sixteenth-century Venice due to the content of an image that they had created, although there are examples of artists being interrogated for their religious beliefs, as detailed in Chapter 1. New cases may of course come to light, but on the basis of the existing evidence Depasquale recently concluded that 'the record of the Inquisition should probably be treated as testimony against, not in support of, the notion of a vigorous response to images by the Counter-Reformation officialdom'.[166]

The activities of the Inquisitions in policing images differed from one place to another. In Spain and in Spanish territories, for example, the Holy Office theoretically wielded far greater control over visual representations than in Venice.[167] In Naples, images were included in the category of 'sacrilege, offense to saints, images and holy places,' even if from 1564 to 1740 there were only sixteen secondary charges ever issued relating to this full gamut of crimes.[168] One of the reasons why Veronese's *Last Supper* for the Dominican convent of Santi Giovanni e Paolo was investigated by the Holy Office was that it was situated in the refectory of a monastery. The remit of the patriarch's pastoral visitations in Venice did not include monastic houses, and they were subject to an inspection only on the occasion of the 1581 Apostolic Visitation. Nevertheless, Patriarch Trevisan would have been present at Veronese's tribunal, accompanied by the Inquisitor Fra Aurelio Schellino, a Dominican from Brescia; the three *savi sopra l'eresia* (although usually only two were present), Giacomo Foscarini, Nicolò Venier, and Alvise Zorzi; and, finally, the Apostolic Nuncio, Giovanni Battista Castagna, who was archbishop of Rossano.[169]

On the one hand, the very fact that Veronese was called before the Inquisition demonstrates the concern authorities had for the decorum of sacred images in this period and shows that artists were now subject to some level of censorship. On the other, the fact that this was so rare that this case appears to be unique demonstrates that these tactics were seldom used. Veronese's interrogation does not seem to have been a particularly important event in the grand scheme of the artist's life and was never mentioned by his biographers, who may have been unaware of the event or wished to defend his reputation from any suspicion of scandal.[170] In its aftermath, he was subject to no further admonishments by the Holy Office, and his output continued to consist primarily of religious works, even if it has been noted that he ceased to create the joyful feast scenes that had been popular prior to the interrogation.[171] As we shall see, Veronese's paintings were singled out for praise in the course of Priuli's visitations in the 1590s, and in 1714 his *Temptation of Saint Anthony* (1552–53) for the cathedral of Mantua was described as an 'excellent painting' by the bishop inspecting the edifice.[172] Finally, when Veronese's ceiling for the new Jesuit church of Santa Maria dell'Umiltà had been completed in 1564, featuring a central scene of the Assumption, together with two scenes of the Annunciation and the Adoration of the Shepherds, it was rapturously praised by the Company of Jesus, who wrote that 'one finds the ceiling of our church painted and complete, the results are very good and all the city has come to see it, amazed by its beauty', demonstrating that Veronese was generally sensitive to issues of decorum and was perceived as a highly talented religious painter (Fig. 46).[173]

The most believable reconstruction of the events surrounding Veronese's *Last Supper* is as follows. It was commissioned by one Fra Andrea de'Buoni, of whom little is known, to replace a Last Supper by Titian that was destroyed by fire in 1571.[174] The painting was completed by 20 April 1573, the date of the inscription that appears on the staircase in the painting. Due to the huge size of the canvas and its location in a refectory (quite different in terms of audience to the public setting of a church), Veronese explained that he added additional figures that are not described in the biblical narrative in order to fill the space, which we can presume was upon the instruction of his patron. We know from the surviving contract of 6 June 1562 for Veronese's much fêted *Marriage Feast at Cana* for the Benedictines at San Giorgio Maggiore that it had been stipulated that the painting had to completely cover the end wall of the refectory, and that it was to be filled with as many figures as could be effectively accommodated.[175] It is not known how the Santi Giovanni e Paolo painting came to the attention of the Inquisition, whether it was specifically denounced by someone who objected to it, or if it was noticed by the Inquisitor Schellino, himself a Dominican. Prior to the interrogation of Veronese on 18 July 1573, the prior of Santi Giovanni e Paolo had been called before the Inquisition and had been ordered to make the artist transform the small dog in the foreground into a figure of Mary Magdalen, thus changing the subject matter to a 'Feast in the House of Simon'. As noted in the transcript, Veronese had painted scenes of this episode for a number of refectories already, something that was perhaps taken into consideration.[176] Yet Veronese was unwilling to make such a change, and so he was summoned to appear before the tribunal in the *chiesetta* of Saint Theodore adjacent to San Marco (now the chapel), where he was questioned. The painting was not present at the interrogation, but it had clearly been pored over, the Inquisitor referencing figures such as the man whose 'nose is bleeding' that are difficult to individuate without a privileged view of the work. In the course of his questioning, Veronese clearly stated that the painting was of a Last Supper, demonstrating some confusion, however, over where the event described in the Gospels had taken place. After the interrogation, Veronese was ordered to improve his painting in three months' time at his own expense. Significantly,

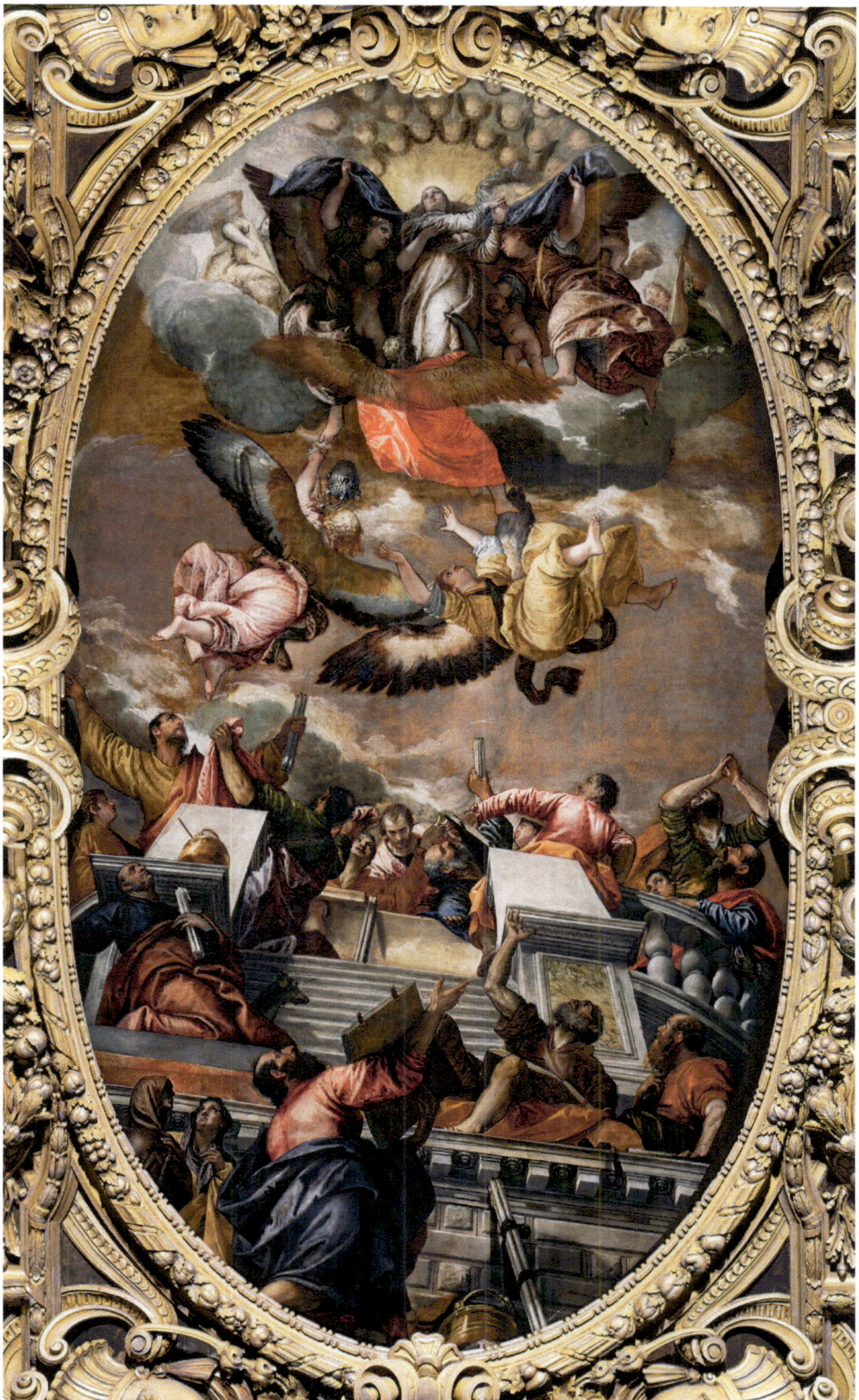

46. Veronese, *The Assumption,* c. 1564, oil on canvas, Santi Giovanni e Paolo, Chapel of the Rosary, formerly in Santa Maria dell'Umiltà, Venice (Photo: Cameraphoto)

the remark that the changes should be consistent with the episode of the Last Supper was struck off, and as noted by Edward Grasman this suggests that the new inscription referring to the banquet in the house of Levi was a resolution that was agreed between the relevant parties, rather than the often cited triumph of artistic freedom (or perhaps laziness) that saw Veronese having the gumption to outsmart the religious authorities.[177] The addition of the inscription was an intelligent resolution, because the biblical description of the event in Luke 5:27–29 ('Levi made him a great feast in his own house; and there was a great company of publicans, and of others, that were at the table with him) both corresponded to and licensed Veronese's artistic vision, meaning that no other changes had to be made.[178] Subsequently, the painting was accepted as a 'Feast in the House of Levi' by all who saw it from the time of this adjustment to the discovery of the transcript detailing the episode in 1867.

Unsurprisingly, the interrogation of Veronese has sparked a range of hypotheses, from Veronese the quasi-heretic to Veronese the mouthpiece of Renaissance artistic liberty.[179] Even though interrogation and painting survive, we do not know the tone of the artist's voice when he replied to the questions of the Inquisition, or whether he was nervous or indeed defiant in his behaviour. Scholars have veered between looking at the historical context to provide clues as to why the painting came to the Inquisition's attention and focusing purely on the iconography of the image itself, an approach that has spawned some imaginative interpretations, to put it mildly. For example, despite the fact that the artist explicitly stated that his canvas was a 'Last Supper, that Jesus Christ had with his apostles in the house of Simon', this has been no barrier to art historians arguing that it actually presents a completely different subject matter altogether, the most recent attempt provided by Maria Elena Massimi's otherwise valuable book, which argues that the painting is in reality a 'Feast in the House of the Pharisee', an episode recounted in Luke 11:37–54.[180] Richard Cocke believed that the painting was not a 'Last Supper' but a 'Feast in the House of Simon', on the basis of Veronese's reference to the 'house of Simon'.[181] These hypotheses beg the obvious question as to why – if the painting did not in fact represent the Last Supper – was this not explained to the Inquisition immediately. Prior to the technical analysis of the painting carried out during its restoration from 1979 to 1983 that confirmed that there were no substantial corrections or changes to the canvas (aside from those consonant with the creative process, and the later inscription), Emerich Schaffran even argued that the pentimenti around a female figure of the Magdalen were still to be seen in the area of the dog, testament to the ability of some scholars to imagine elements in the painting that simply did not exist.[182]

In terms of the historical context, resistance to reform at Santi Giovanni e Paolo as it was transformed from a conventual Dominican convent to an observant one in the decades subsequent to the Council of Trent may have caused Veronese's canvas to be carefully scrutinised.[183] The institution had become something of a thorn in the side of the Church in Venice and was beset by all kinds of problems in the early 1570s.[184] It thus seems fitting that the magnificence, verging on decadence, presented in the *Last Supper* was carried out at the behest of the brothers of Santi Giovanni e Paolo. Although this historical context is important, the very fact that some scholars still cannot agree on which biblical event the painting was intended to depict eloquently demonstrates precisely why the Inquisition found Veronese's *Last Supper* problematic in the first place. Of all the artist's religious paintings, this one departs the furthest from scripture, presenting Christ's final dinner with his disciples as a celebration, a convivial banquet rather than a sombre meal. Ruskin, for example, found Veronese's iconographic vagueness insupportable, pronouncing the painting to be 'nothing but a confused meeting of very mixed company'.[185] The array of figures anachronistic to the Gospel account in the painting meant that it could well have qualified as the kind of 'unusual image' that according to the Tridentine decrees should have been approved by the bishop prior to being put on display. The artist's perceived lack of attention to the scriptural sources was the key concern of the Inquisition in their line of questioning. It also explains the resolution of the changed title, since the lesser-known feast in the house of Levi could conceivably include the 'drunk buffoons, Germans, dwarves and other such scurrilities' that were out of place in a Last Supper scene. Although Veronese clarified that he had deliberately placed the festivities outside the inner sanctum where Christ was situated, the Inquisitor got to the crux of the Church's concerns when he referred to the events of the Protestant Reformation: 'Do you not know that in Germany and other places infected with heresy that they are in the habit of filling their paintings with obscenities, and with the same love of invention they insult and denigrate the Holy Church and teach evil doctrines to the idiots and ignorant?'[186] The intended audience for Veronese's painting had never been the 'idiots and ignorant', but the friars who would have looked at it whilst they ate. A painting for a church had to take into account the spectatorship of a broader range of viewers, but Veronese had responded to the brief for a refectory setting in a different way, assuming the ability of the learned Dominicans to accurately interpret the episode depicted. Despite this, for the Inquisition Veronese's free artistic licence was not just in bad taste, considering the theological importance of the episode, but carried with it the suspicion of heresy. This may have related more to the state of affairs at Santi Giovanni e Paolo and the inferred influence of the patrons on the appearance of Veronese's painting than the artist's own religious convictions, which do not appear to have been in question.

The Inquisition did not destroy the painting, nor did they insist that it be adequately transformed to represent the episode of the Last Supper. Recently, some scholars have underlined the process of negotiation that the judicious use of an inscription provided by clarifying the subject matter in a way that rendered it intelligible, providing an acceptable compromise for both the artist and authorities.[187] As an example, then, the case of Veronese's interrogation demonstrates a relatively pragmatic approach taken to reforming art, something also illustrated by the vicissitudes of three of Tintoretto's paintings for the Scuola Grande di San Marco: *The Discovery of the Body of Saint Mark*, *The Removal of the Body of Saint Mark*, and *Saint Mark Assisting a Saracen*.[188] Given the vicinity of this confraternity building to Santi Giovanni e Paolo, Grasman hypothesised that the decision of the *confratelli* to return the paintings that had been hanging in the chapter room to Tommaso Rangone on 10 August 1573 (Rangone being the *Guardian Grande* of the confraternity that had commissioned them in the first place) may have stemmed from a desire to avoid a confrontation with the Inquisition similar to that which had befallen Veronese.[189] The dating indeed suggests that this decision may have been more than coincidental, especially since the canvases had been hanging in the Scuola for some years. But it may have equally stemmed from growing annoyance with Rangone's shameless self-promotion, since he appears with an almost humorous regularity as an active participant to Saint Mark's miracles (Fig. 47). Tintoretto's penchant for flattering his patrons had already caused a disagreement with the members of the Scuola del Sacramento at the church of San Felice (Fig. 48).[190] After the head of the confraternity changed in 1560, Tintoretto was ordered to remove the portraits in the *Last Supper* that he had completed just one year earlier, although whether this ever happened is unclear.[191] After receiving the Scuola di San Marco paintings in September 1573, Tintoretto offered to remove the prominent figure of the patron, even though Rangone had paid for them himself, rather than drawing upon confraternity funds.[192] The extent to which Veronese's contemporaries were even aware of his Inquisitorial questioning is hard to say with any certainty. But if the solution adopted by Tintoretto is anything to go by, artists in Venice do not appear to have been labouring in fear of the Holy Office for the more unusual aspects of their creations. Despite promising to make the required changes, there is no evidence that Tintoretto ever altered the paintings in any way. Doing nothing at all seems to have worked out without any unfortunate consequences. Rangone appears just as prominent as he was before the debacle, and the works were returned to their original location, to the best of our knowledge without complaint.

To conclude, this chapter commenced with two very different statements from scholars regarding the censorship of art after the Council of Trent. What I have attempted to demonstrate is that although new methods for controlling the decorum of sacred images arose and were referred to more frequently in the aftermath of the Council of Trent, they were never enforced systematically.

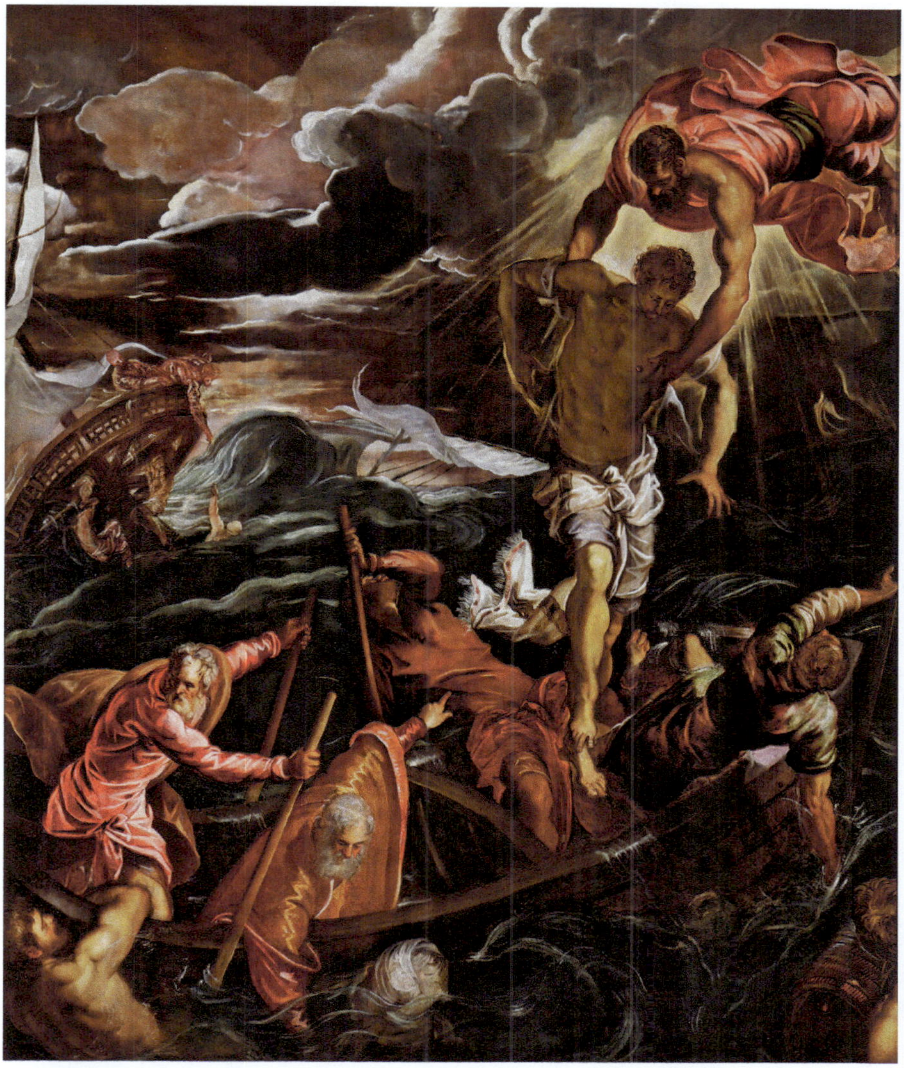

47. Tintoretto, *Saint Mark Assisting a Saracen,* 1562–66, oil on canvas, Gallerie dell'Accademia, Venice, formerly in the Scuola Grande di San Marco (Photo: Cameraphoto)

In large part this is because there do not seem to have been that many images that broke the rules set out in the Tridentine decrees. The debacle surrounding the *Last Judgment* had already impressed upon artists the requirement to be attentive to the use of nudity in their devotional output. Even when artworks presented elements that had been specifically warned against by the synods in Venice (the presence of incongruous animals or the portraits of secular figures as saints), it was highly unusual that they were censored or even commented upon by visiting patriarchs. This would seem to support the observations of a number of historians of Catholic Reform, most recently Celeste McNamara, that 'scholars who focus primarily on the bishops' decrees risk assuming, along with

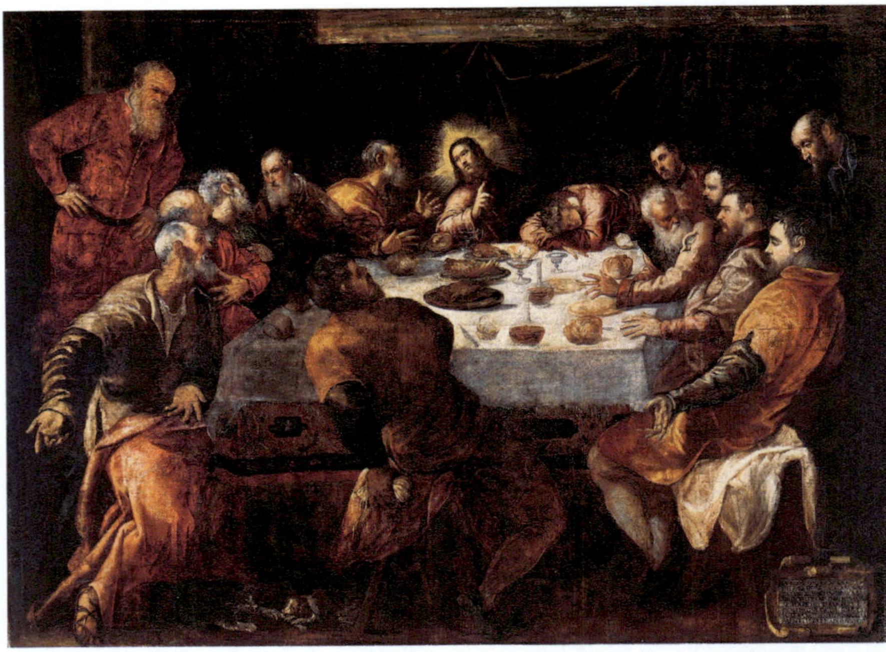

48. Tintoretto, *The Last Supper,* 1559, oil on canvas, church of Saint François-Xavier, Paris, formerly in the chapel of the Blessed Sacrament, San Felice, Venice (Photo: Bridgeman Images)

the bishops, that their decrees led directly to meaningful change'.[193] A number of the texts explored in this chapter presented high ideals for devotional art, but it was the more pragmatic approach to image reform that won out, in accordance with the general stipulations of the Council of Trent on the matter. This is eloquently summed up in Antoniano's arguments against Paleotti's proposal to institutionally expand the censorship of images: 'I do not deny that some abuses have crept in, but not such a great number nor in so many places; the universal practice of the Church is correct.'[194]

NOTES

1 O'Malley, 'Trent, Sacred Images, and Catholics' Senses of the Sensuous', 28.

2 Nagel, *The Controversy of Renaissance Art*, 6. Doubt was cast on Nagel's assertions by Depasquale, 'Epilogue Two: Michelangelo's "Last Judgment" and the Reception of the Nude in Counter-Reformation Italy', 367–68.

3 The tendency towards superficial citation of these texts was pointed out years ago by Paolo Prodi with reference to Gabriele Paleotti's 1582 *Discorso intorno alle imagini sacre et profane*. See Paolo Prodi, *Il cardinale Gabriele Paleotti (1522–1597)*, Uomini e dottrine, 7 (Rome: Edizioni di storia e letteratura, 1959), vol. 2: 527. Highlighted also by Noyes, 'Post-Tridentine Image Reform and the Myth of Gabriele Paleotti', 284.

4 Hubert Jedin, *La conclusione del Concilio di Trento (1562–1563): Uno sguardo retrospettivo a quattro secoli di distanza* (Rome: Editrice Studium, 1964), 134. More recently, McNamara pointed out that 'Trent sought to renew established traditions and expectations rather than create new ones.' McNamara, *The Bishop's Burden*, 9.

5 As noted first by Hubert Jedin, 'Entstehung und Tragweite des Trienter Dekrets über die Bilderverehrung', *Theologische Quartalschrift* 116, nos. 1–2 (1935): 175. See also Hubert Jedin, 'Genesi e portata del decreto Tridentino sulla venerazione delle immagini', in *Chiesa della fede, Chiesa della storia* (Brescia: Morcelliana, 1972), 340–90. Also of use are Scavizzi, *The Controversy on Images from Calvin to Baronius*, 70–75; O'Malley, 'The Council of Trent (1545–63) and Michelangelo's "Last Judgment" (1541)'; O'Malley, 'Trent, Sacred Images, and Catholics' Senses of the Sensuous'.

6 For the image decrees, see Waterworth, *Canons and Decrees of the Council of Trent*, 232–26; Tanner, *Decrees of the Ecumenical Councils*, vol. 2: 774–76. In some places Waterworth's translation is more literal than Tanner's, but the latter has the advantage of placing the English translation side by side with the Latin. See note 8.

7 Scavizzi, *The Controversy on Images from Calvin to Baronius*, 77.

8 The original Latin reads '*omnis denique lascivia vitetur*', which Tanner translates as 'all sensual appeal must be avoided', rather than 'all lasciviousness must be avoided', which is the translation of Waterworth. Tanner, *Decrees of the Ecumenical Councils*, vol. 2: 776; Waterworth, *Canons and Decrees of the Council of Trent*, 235–36.

9 See note 5.

10 The sequence of events is eloquently summarised by O'Malley, 'The Council of Trent (1545–63) and Michelangelo's "Last Judgment" (1541)', 392–96; O'Malley, 'Trent, Sacred Images, and Catholics' Senses of the Sensuous', 33–35.

11 The first was the Council of Sens in Paris, the second was the 1561 Colloquy of Poissy where images were sharply debated between Huguenot and Catholic leaders (to no avail), and the third was the Colloquy of Saint-Germain-en-Laye, called by an increasingly desperate Queen Catherine de' Medici in 1562. The debate between Protestants and Catholics immediately broke down over the first item on the agenda: the veneration of images. See O'Malley, 'Trent, Sacred Images, and Catholics' Senses of the Sensuous', 32–33; Scavizzi, *The Controversy on Images from Calvin to Baronius*, 70–78

12 As O'Malley points out, 'Almost from the moment of his arrival at Trent, the French cardinal became the most powerful and insistent voice there demanding that the council issue a decree on images.' O'Malley, 'Trent, Sacred Images, and Catholics' Senses of the Sensuous', 36.

13 O'Malley, 'The Council of Trent (1545–63) and Michelangelo's "Last Judgment" (1541)', 394.

14 *Concilium tridentinum: diariorum, actorum, epistularum, tractatuum nova collectio* (Freiburgi Brisgoviae: Herder, 1901), vol. 9: 1069, note 367.

15 *Concilium tridentinum: diariorum, actorum, epistularum, tractatuum nova collectio*, vol. 9: 1069, note 1.

16 De Maio, *Michelangelo e la Controriforma*, 39.

17 O'Malley, 'Trent, Sacred Images, and Catholics' Senses of the Sensuous', 28.

18 For session thirteen, see Waterworth, *Canons and Decrees of the Council of Trent*, 75–85. For session twenty-two, see Waterworth, 152–62. In addition, chapter VII of the second decrees on Reformation of session twenty-four (11 November 1563) instructed the clergy to ascertain if the laity understood the divine nature of the Blessed Sacrament before receiving it. See Waterworth, 213–14. The importance of this decree, and those on the Eucharist more generally, was noted by Humfrey, 'La pala d'altare veneta nell'età delle riforme', 1134.

19 Chapter V 'on the solemn ceremonies of the Sacrifice of the Mass' of session twenty-two. Waterworth, *Canons and Decrees of the Council of Trent*, 156.

20 The low mass was better suited to the demands of saying mass in rural areas, and it proved to be very useful on the global missions. However, its prevalence meant that the 'sensory dimensions of the liturgy' were curtailed. See Uwe Michael Lang, *The Roman Mass: From Early Christian Origins to Tridentine Reform* (Cambridge: Cambridge University Press, 2022), 354–55.

21 Eire, *Reformations: The Early Modern World, 1450–1650*, 233–34.

22 Eamon Duffy, *The Stripping of the Altars: Traditional Religion in England c. 1400–c. 1580*, 2nd ed. (New Haven, CT: Yale University Press, 2005), 389–90.

23 See chapter III on Reformation in session twenty-four. Waterworth, *Canons and Decrees of the Council of Trent*, 210.

24 Pietro Pirri, 'L'architetto Bartolomeo Ammannati e i Gesuiti', *Archivum Historicum Societatis Iesu* 12 (1943): 18, note 34.

25 For the relationship between the Jesuit Order and Farnese, see, above all, chapters 6 and 7 of Bailey, *Between Renaissance and Baroque*.

26 Chapter VIII on Reformation in session seven (3 March 1547). Waterworth, *Canons and Decrees of the Council of Trent*, 62.

27 Chapter VII on Reformation in session twenty-one (16 July 1562). Waterworth, *Canons and Decrees of the Council of Trent*, 149–50.

28 '"La chiesa sta malissimo" Giovanni Morone e le cure di una diocesi post-Tridentina', *Rivista di Storia della Chiesa in Italia*, no. 1 (2013): 142.

29 Hubert Jedin, 'Venezia e il Concilio di Trento', *Studi Veneziani* 14 (1972): 152–54.

30 Cecilia Cristellon and Silvana Seidel Menchi, 'Religious Life', in *A Companion to Venetian History, 1400–1797*, ed. Eric Dursteler (Leiden: Brill, 2013), 387. Prior to this, on 22 July 1564, the Venetian Senate had already adopted the Tridentine decrees and declared them binding throughout the Serenissima. See Jarrod Michael Broderick, 'The Supremacy of Faith: Venetian Spirituality and Tridentine Doctrine in the Sala Capitolare at the Scuola Grande di San Rocco', *Studi Veneziani* 85–86 (2022): 81–82.

31 Jedin, 'Venezia e il Concilio di Trento', 137.

32 In the late fifteenth century German travellers passing through Verona on their north-bound journey home considered Trent the beginning of Germania. See R. Po-chia Hsia, *Trent 1475: Stories of a Ritual Murder Trial* (New Haven, CT: Yale University Press, 1992), 8.

33 Jedin, 'Venezia e il Concilio di Trento', 142.

34 Of the seventy-eight dioceses that came under the dominions of Venice, only twenty-one bishops participated in the first period of the council, and the two patriarchs of Venice and Aquileia (Girolamo Querini and Giovanni Grimani) were notably absent. Jedin, 'Venezia e il Concilio di Trento', 140.

35 Jedin, 'Venezia e il Concilio di Trento', 144–45. Jedin attributed Venice's sudden interest in the council to the fact that a Venetian, Bernardo Navagero, had become pontifical legate. The key Venetian contribution to proceedings at Trent was a petition in favour of Greek Orthodox marriage practice, an issue of importance for the Serenissima, considering the nature of her dominions. See Jedin, 'Venezia e il Concilio di Trento', 150–51; Antonio Niero, 'Riforma Cattolica e Concilio di Trento a Venezia', in *Cultura e società nel Rinascimento tra riforme e manierismi*, ed. Vittore Branca and Carlo Ossola (Florence: Leo Olschki, 1984), 88–89.

36 See Anna Pallucchini, 'L'abbozzo del "Concilio di Trento" di Jacopo Tintoretto', *Arte Veneta* 24 (1970): 93–102. Pallucchini attributed the hand of Tintoretto to an oil sketch of the council in a private collection, but this attribution is not universally accepted.

37 A collection of documents relating to the Tridentine decrees are held in BM, MSS. Lat. IV (2318–19), Acta Concilii Tridentini. For the decrees regarding images, see 2319, fols. 74r–75v.

38 J. H. Elliott, *Europe Divided, 1559–1598* (New York: Harper & Row, 1969), 149.

39 See Silvio Tramontin, 'Gli inizi dei due seminari di Venezia', *Studi Veneziani* 7 (1965): 363–77. The Ducal Seminary attached to St Mark's was established in 1579. The two institutions attempted to improve the education and training of the clergy, which up until this point had mostly been the responsibility of parish schools. For an analysis of the synods of 1564, 1571, and 1578, see Antonio Niero, 'L'"honestas vitae clericorum" nei sinodi di Giovanni Trevisan patriarca di Venezia', in *Il Concilio di Trento e la riforma tridentina: atti del convegno storico internazionale, Trento, 2–6 settembre 1963*, 2 vols. (Rome: Herder, 1965), vol. 2: 745–48. For Trevisan, see Niero, *I patriarchi di Venezia*, 92–98.

40 Deborah Walberg, 'Patriarch Giovanni Tiepolo and the Search for Venetian Religious Identity in the Waning of the Renaissance', in *Celebrazione e autocritica: la Serenissima e la ricerca dell'identità veneziana nel tardo Cinquecento*, ed. Benjamin Paul (Rome: Viella; Venice: Centro tedesco di studi veneziani, 2014), 236.

41 See Aldo Stella, 'La proprietà ecclesiastica nella Repubblica di Venezia dal secolo XV al XVII', *Nuova rivista storica* 42 (1958): 50–77.

42 The preference for laymen is noted in Cozzi, *Il doge Nicolò Contarini*, 222, note 2. After the difficult tenure of the Dominican Patriarch Girolamo Querini (1524–54) up until 1619 the office was awarded to noble laymen, rather than a candidate from the Mendicant orders. One exception to this is the Benedictine Trevisan, probably because of his well-known patriotism. Venice maintained the right to nominate the patriarch until the beginning of the Seicento. See also Paolo Prodi, 'The Structure and Organisation of the Church in Renaissance Venice: Suggestions for Research', in *Renaissance Venice*, ed. John Hale (London: Faber & Faber, 1973), 415–16.

43 The parish priest (*piovan*) of a collegiate church was elected by the laity, and the other titular priests were elected by the chapter. Once elected, the nomination would be approved by the patriarch, a system that was formally approved throughout the Cinquecento by Popes Leo X, Clement VII, Paul IV, Pius IV, and Sixtus V. Nicholas Davidson, 'The Clergy of Venice in the Sixteenth Century', *Bulletin of the Society of Renaissance Studies* 2 (1984): 20. See also Prodi, 'The Structure and Organisation of the Church in Renaissance Venice', 419–21; Anthony Wright, 'Republican Tradition and the Maintenance of "National" Religious Traditions in Venice', *Renaissance Studies* 10, no. 3 (1996): 405–16.

44 Walberg, 'Patriarch Giovanni Tiepolo and the Search for Venetian Religious Identity in the Waning of the Renaissance', 234–35.

45 Tramontin, 'La visita apostolica del 1581 a Venezia'. See also Giovanni Soranzo, 'Rapporti di S. Carlo con la Repubblica Veneta', *Archivio Veneto* 27, nos. 53–54 (1940): 1–40.

46 See Tramontin, 'La visita apostolica del 1581 a Venezia', 453, notes 1 and 2. Pope Clement VIII had already created a congregation of cardinals to oversee such visits in 1592. See Grace Theresa Harpster, 'Evaluating the Altarpiece: Image Decorum in Post-Tridentine Apostolic Visitations', *Religions* 14, no. 615 (2023): 2.

47 For the quote from Trevisan, see Tramontin, 'La visita apostolica del 1581 a Venezia', 458, note 21. For Da Ponte, see Gino Benzoni, 'Una città caricabile di valenza religiose', in *La Chiesa di Venezia tra riforma protestante e riforma cattolica*, ed. Giuseppe Gullino (Venice: Studium cattolico veneziano, 1990), 40.

48 Soranzo, 'Rapporti di S. Carlo con la Repubblica Veneta', 22, note 2.

49 Soranzo, 'Rapporti di S. Carlo con la Repubblica Veneta', 20, 31. For Trevisan's visits from 1560 to 1590, see APV, Archivio 'segreto', Visite pastorali, Visitationes ecclesiarum Venetiarum per reverendissimum dominum dominum Ioannem Trevisanum patriarca Venetiarum in anno Domini MCCCCCLXI. 1560 ad 1590 and Visite pastorali a monasteri femminili, Monialium visitationum sub reverendissimo domino Ioanne Trivisano patriarcha Venetiarum. 1560–1589.

50 Valier was closely associated with Borromeo and wrote a biography of him that was published in 1586. Valier was an experienced Apostolic Visitor who had already inspected the dioceses of Istria and Dalmatia. For a list of his visits, see the documentation held in the Curia Vescovile di Verona: https://siusa.archivi.beniculturali.it/cgi-bin/pagina.pl?TipoPag=comparc&Chiave=5396&RicProgetto=ev (accessed 17 May 2023).

51 For visitations to the nunneries see previous note 49, and note 9 of chapter 4. The records of the parish inspections are held in the Archivio Storico del Patriarcato in Venice, whilst those of the conventual houses are kept in the Vatican Archive and are in a poor state of repair. Partial transcriptions of the latter are provided by Remigio Ritzler, 'Gli atti della visita apostolica del 1581 ai conventi di S. Maria Gloriosa e di S. Nicoletto dei frati minori conventuali in Venezia', *Miscellanea Francescana* 69 (1969): 153–86; Paola Modesti, 'I cori

nelle chiese veneziane e la visita apostolica del 1581: il "barco" di Santa Maria della Carità', *Arte Veneta* 59 (2004): 38–65. Mackenney appears to have been unaware of the full extent of the visits, incorrectly asserting that the Frari and San Zanipolo were never visited. Mackenney, *Venice as the Polity of Mercy*, 272.

52 Prodi, 'The Structure and Organisation of the Church in Renaissance Venice', 416, 427, note 38. The lack of attention to the peculiarities that this document presents is criticised by Prodi with relation to the analysis of Silvio Tramontin, 'La figura del vescovo secondo il concilio di Trento ed i suoi riflessi veneziani nell'interrogatorio del Patriarca Trevisan', *Studi Veneziani* 10 (1968): 423–56.

53 The longevity and international appeal of the myth of Venice was examined by Grubb, 'When Myths Lose Power'.

54 Anti-Romanism was obviously strong during the Interdict and under the dogeship of Leonardo Donà (r. 1606–12) more generally. See Bouwsma, *Venice and the Defense of Republican Liberty*, 233–34, 337, 509–10; Gaetano Cozzi, 'I rapporti fra Stato e Chiesa', in *La Chiesa di Venezia tra riforma protestante e riforma cattolica*, ed. Giuseppe Gullino (Venice: Studium cattolico veneziano, 1990), 11–36.

55 Mackenney, *Venice as the Polity of Mercy*, 255.

56 Antonio Milledonne, *Dell'Historia del Sacro Concilio di Trento: scritta da Antonio Milledoni segretario del Consiglio de X di Venetia in detto Concilio. Libri due* (Venice, n.d.). For Milledonne, see Pietro D'Arduino, *Vita di Antonio Milledonne secretario del Conseglio di X. Da altro Secretario Scritta* (Venice, 1618); Massimo Galtarossa, 'Vita d'Antonio Milledonne Secretario del Consiglio di X (1522–1588): contributo sulla concezione del "servito" burocratico a Venezia', *Studi Veneziani* 39 (2000): 239–52. The Marciana Library holds annotations by Paolo Sarpi of Milledonne's manuscript (MSS. It. V 115 (= 5829)).

57 Noted also by Mullett (amongst others), who points out that the Venetian stance is not to be mistaken for the kind of secularism that later prevailed in much of Europe during the Enlightenment. Michael A. Mullett, *The Catholic Reformation* (London: Routledge, 1999), 146.

58 Cozzi, 'I rapporti fra Stato e Chiesa', 17. Bernardo Giustiniani (1408–89) was nephew of the first patriarch of Venice, Lorenzo Giustiniani, and one of the most influential patricians of the second half of the Quattrocento.

59 See also Mackenney, *Venice as the Polity of Mercy*, 246. Mackenney notes that although Venice may seem an exceptional case study since it remained Catholic whilst simultaneously resisting the claims of Rome, 'the experience of the Venetians in this confessional era, was, in an important sense, typical of many other European societies'.

60 Noyes, 'Post-Tridentine Image Reform and the Myth of Gabriele Paleotti'. Not all the titles listed by Noyes dealt solely with the reform of images, but to different extents they all explored this theme.

61 Johannes Molanus, *De picturis et imaginibus sacris* (Louvain: Wellaeus, 1570). For Molanus, see also Freedberg, 'Johannes Molanus on Provocative Paintings'. Molanus's text was published in the aftermath of the iconoclastic fury that swept the Low Countries in the 1560s. It was republished in 1581 and enjoyed significant success from the sixteenth to eighteenth centuries, with repeat editions being published in Louvain, Douai, Antwerp, and Lyon.

62 Gabriele Paleotti, *Discorso intorno alle imagini sacre e profane* (Benacci: Bologna, 1582). Paleotti wrote his treatise in response to Trent's requirement that bishops oversee the display of sacred art in their diocese. Written in the vernacular, of the five books planned, only the first two were ever completed. The text was then published in Latin at Ingolstadt in 1594. For the man and his treatise, see, above all, the scholarship of Paolo Prodi. In addition to his introductions for the 1990 and 2002 Italian editions of Paleotti's discourse, as well as the 2012 English edition, also of relevance are Prodi, *Il cardinale Gabriele Paleotti (1522–1597)*, vol. 2: 517–62; Paolo Prodi, 'Ricerche sulla teorica delle arti figurative nella riforma cattolica', *Archivio italiano per la storia della pietà* 4 (1965): 121–212; Prodi, *Ricerca sulla teorica delle arti figurative nella Riforma Cattolica*; Paolo Prodi, *Arte e pietà nella Chiesa tridentina*

(Bologna: Il Mulino, 2014). The 1965 article that appeared in the *Archivio italiano* was also published as an advance offprint in 1962, and then again in 1984 as a separate volume, which is the one I cite here. Also relevant are Scavizzi, *The Controversy on Images from Calvin to Baronius*, 131–40; Pamela M. Jones, 'Art Theory as Ideology: Gabriele Paleotti's Hierarchical Notion of Painting's Universality and Reception', in *Reframing the Renaissance: Visual Culture in Europe and Latin America, 1450–1650*, ed. Claire Farago (New Haven, CT: Yale University Press, 1995), 127–39; Bianchi, *La politica delle immagini nell'età della Controriforma.*

63 Carlo Borromeo, *Instructionum fabricae et suppelletilis ecclesiasticis* (Milan: P. Pontium, 1577). The treatise was the result of instructions given in Borromeo's diocesan synods that arose out of inconsistencies encountered in the course of pastoral visitations carried out in the Ambrosian diocese. Now most commonly referred to as the *Instructiones*, the text is best understood as a practical guide to ecclesiastical architecture, furnishings, and vestments that provides advice on everything from the site, plan, and orientation of a church to the organisation of the chapels, the tabernacle, the balustrades, and the choir, as well as a concise chapter on sacred images. See the notes in Evelyn Carole Voelker, 'Carlo Borromeo's Instructiones fabricae et supellectilis ecclesiasticae, 1577. A translation with commentary and analysis' (doctoral thesis, University of Syracuse, 1977). Also of use are Blunt, *Artistic Theory in Italy, 1450–1600*, 127–31; Aurora Scotti, 'Architettura e riforma cattolica nella Milano di Carlo Borromeo', *L'arte* 5 (1972): 54–90; Scavizzi, *The Controversy on Images from Calvin to Baronius*, 121–31; Robert Sénécal, 'Carlo Borromeo's Instructiones fabricae et supellectilis ecclesiasticae and Its Origins in the Rome of His Time', *Papers of the British School at Rome* 68 (November 2000): 241–67; Richard Schofield, 'Carlo Borromeo and the Dangers of Laywomen in Church', in *The Sensuous in the Counter-Reformation Church*, ed. Marcia B. Hall and Tracy E. Cooper (Cambridge: Cambridge University Press, 2013), 187–205.

64 Federico Borromeo, *De pictura sacra: libri due* (Milan: Mediolani, 1624). This treatise was similar in structure to that of Gilio and Paleotti, dispensing advice concerning what was and was not appropriate for religious art. Federico's *Musaeum* of 1625 (only published recently) provided a description, or 'walking tour' of his public art collection housed at the Ambrosiana in Milan. Borromeo, *Sacred Painting; Museum.* See also Pamela M. Jones, 'Federico Borromeo as a Patron of Landscapes and Still Lifes: Christian Optimism in Italy ca. 1600', *Art Bulletin* 70, no. 2 (1988): 261–72; Jones, *Federico Borromeo and the Ambrosiana.*

65 On 22 April 1579 Paleotti wrote to Carlo Borromeo to tell him that he would not need to borrow his personal copy of Molanus's work since he was now in possession of his own. Prodi, *Il cardinale Gabriele Paleotti (1522–1597)*, vol. 2: 531, note 15.

66 Noyes, 'Post-Tridentine Image Reform and the Myth of Gabriele Paleotti', 261.

67 See the important volumes of Barocchi, *Trattati d'arte del Cinquecento: Fra Manierismo e Controriforma.* A few further examples: the English translation of Carlo Borromeo's tract appeared in 1977; a French translation of Molanus appeared in 1996; and English editions of Borghini's *Il Riposo* (2007), Federico Borromeo's *De pictura sacra/Musaeum* (2010), Paleotti's *Discorso* (2012), and Gilio's *Dialogo* (2018) appeared in the first two decades of the 2000s.

68 Paleotti, *Discourse on Sacred and Profane Images*, 26. Argued for also by Bailey, *Between Renaissance and Baroque*, 15.

69 See Anton Boschloo, *Annibale Carracci in Bologna: Visible Reality in Art after the Council of Trent*, 2 vols., Kunsthistorische Studiën van Het Nederlands Instituut Te Rome (The Hague: Government Publ. Office, 1974). For counterarguments to Boschloo's analysis, see Noyes, 'Post-Tridentine Image Reform and the Myth of Gabriele Paleotti', 247–49; Locker, *Art and Reform in the Late Renaissance*, 11. Noyes also points to Ludovico Carracci's depictions of saints with the faces of contemporary figures in the *Madonna dei Bargellini* altarpiece.

70 Noted by Hochmann, *Peintres et commanditaires à Venise (1540–1628)*, 277.

71 Voelker, 'Carlo Borromeo's Instructiones fabricae et supellectilis ecclesiasticae,' 22–23.

72 For a transcription of the text, see Prodi, *Ricerca sulla teorica delle arti figurative nella Riforma Cattolica*, 94–110.

73 For the supporters of the text, see Prodi, *Ricerca sulla teorica delle arti figurative nella Riforma Cattolica*, 80–82.

74 Prodi, *Ricerca sulla teorica delle arti figurative nella Riforma Cattolica*, 111–14. Here I quote Prodi's English translation of Antoniano in Paleotti, *Discourse on Sacred and Profane Images*, 25–26.

75 For the correspondence between Antoniano and Paleotti, see Prodi, *Ricerca sulla teorica delle arti figurative nella Riforma Cattolica*, 91–93; Noyes, 'Post-Tridentine Image Reform and the Myth of Gabriele Paleotti', 252–55.

76 Paleotti, *Discourse on Sacred and Profane Images*, 26.

77 Peter Humfrey's analysis of Palma il Giovane's *Beheading of Saint John the Baptist* of c. 1610 for the church of the Crociferi in Venice provides a pertinent example of this, since the painting includes both secular portraits in the guise of saints and anachronistic saints who have no direct relationship to the episode depicted. On the other hand, the lively martyrdom scene might well have been endorsed by the authors of the treatises. See Humfrey, 'La pala d'altare veneta nell'età delle riforme', 1137. For the altarpiece, see Mason Rinaldi, *Palma il Giovane: l'opera completa*, 127, cat. 432. For the objections of the *trattatisti*, see Johannes Molanus, *Traité des saintes images*, ed. François Boespflug, Olivier Christin, and Benoit Tassel (Paris: Les Éditions du Cerf, 1996), book 2, chapter 37; Paleotti, *Discourse on Sacred and Profane Images*, 214; Voelker, 'Carlo Borromeo's Instructiones fabricae et supellectilis ecclesiasticae', 229.

78 Voelker, 'Carlo Borromeo's Instructiones fabricae et supellectilis ecclesiasticae', 228.

79 Molanus, *Traité des saintes images*, book 3, chapter 34.

80 Molanus, book 2, chapter 46. See also chapters 21–24 of book 3. Molanus likely went to such pains to clarify the placement of the two saints as a rebuttal to reformers such as Luther who had sought to diminish the primacy of Peter, something that Molanus described as a 'new and heretical' idea.

81 In a letter of 23 February 1586 by Paleotti to the secretary of the Duke of Urbino, Francesco II della Rovere, the cardinal inquired about Barocci's availability after having been offered his services. Bianchi, *La politica delle immagini nell'età della Controriforma*, 179. See also Stuart Lingo, *Federico Barocci: Allure and Devotion in Late Renaissance Painting* (New Haven, CT: Yale University Press, 2008), 144. Lingo points to the education and culture of commentators like Paleotti following the reminder of John Shearman. For the Bolognese art market, see Caroline P. Murphy, 'The Market for Pictures in Post-Tridentine Bologna', in *The Art Market in Italy, 15th–17th Centuries*, ed. Marcello Fantoni, Louisa C. Matthew, and Sara F. Matthews-Grieco (Modena: F. C. Panini, 2003), 41–53. As Murphy points out (p. 46), 'Although Tridentine reform is sometimes viewed as stifling the creativity of Italian artists, the evidence suggests that, in the case of Bologna, the impact of Tridentine policies as applied by Gabriele Paleotti and his successors can be said to have had an extremely positive effect on the Bolognese art market.'

82 Paleotti, *Discourse on Sacred and Profane Images*, 111–12.

83 Jones, *Federico Borromeo and the Ambrosiana*, 53.

84 'All the arts and sciences and disciplines are like that: when practiced by persons of great experience and skill, they are greatly esteemed, whereas if those engaging in them are inadequate and inexpert, they remain abject and vile.' Paleotti, *Discourse on Sacred and Profane Images*, 72–73.

85 Jones, *Federico Borromeo and the Ambrosiana*, 64.

86 Gilio, *Dialogue on the Errors and Abuses of Painters*, 121–22.

87 Brown, *Painting in Spain, 1500–1700*, 102.

88 Freedberg, 'Johannes Molanus on Provocative Paintings', 240–41; Brown, 'Between the Sacred and Profane', 277–78; Simons, 'Artemisia Gentileschi's "Susanna and the Elders"

(1610) in the Context of Counter-Reformation Rome', 48. Images of Susanna were even recommended as a cure for the temptations of carnal acts. See Steven F. Stowell, 'Purging the Eye. Images and the Cure for Lust in Catholic Reformation Italy', in *Renaissance Religions: Modes and Meanings in History*, ed. Peter Howard, Nicholas Terpstra, and Riccardo Saccenti (Turnhout: Brepols, 2021), 220.

89 Borromeo, Sacred Painting: Museum, 35. Patricia Simons argued that even 'the most central and censorial of authorities' approved of depictions of the episode of Susanna and the Elders (the intent being that the viewer should sympathise with the plight of the heroine and condemn the voyeurism of the elders), but Federico Borromeo's opinion presents an exception to this rule. Simons, 'Artemisia Gentileschi's "Susanna and the Elders" (1610) in the Context of Counter-Reformation Rome', 49.

90 Molanus, *Traité des saintes images*, book 2, chapters 23, 24. In chapter 25 it is made clear that the very worst abuses are those that one finds amongst 'the heretics', or images that blaspheme against Catholics and the Church, such as depictions of the pope as the anti-Christ. These should never be displayed in public.

91 Molanus, *Traité des saintes images*, book 2, chapter 52.

92 Molanus, *Traité des saintes images*, book 2, chapters 19, 28.

93 Molanus, *Traité des saintes images*, book 2, chapter 30–32. Borromeo also wrote in favour of 'probable' elements being cautiously included in sacred paintings, arguing that they 'can carry persuasive force, be highly amusing, and convey the pleasure that every novelty brings'. Borromeo, *Sacred Painting; Museum*, 13.

94 Borromeo, *Sacred Painting; Museum*, 31. It is possible that Federico refers to Paleotti's infamous proposal of 1596.

95 The painting was previously owned by Carlo Borromeo and was originally painted for Cardinal Ippolito d'Este. For its provenance and restoration, see the catalogue entry of Luisa Arrigoni, *Restituzioni 2006. Tredicesima edizione. Tesori d'arte restaurati*, ed. Carlo Bertelli, Exhibition Catalogue, Gallerie di Palazzo Leoni Montanari, Vicenza, 25 March–11 June 2006, Pincoteca di Brera, Milan and Gallerie dell'Accademia, Venice, October–November 2006 (Vicenza: Banca Intesa, 2006), 286–90, cat. 52.

96 Federico pleaded that 'surely room could have been made in the painting for the little animal'. Borromeo, *Sacred Painting; Museum*, 31–33.

97 Paleotti, *Discourse on Sacred and Profane Images*, 118; Molanus, *Traité des saintes images*, book 2, chapter 58. There was talk of burning lascivious artworks in honour of Pope Clement during the jubilee year of 1600. See Brown, 'Between the Sacred and Profane', 278.

98 Giuseppe Cappelletti, *Storia della Chiesa di Venezia dalla sua fondazione sino ai nostri giorni*, vol. 6 (Venice: Tipografia Armena di S. Lazzaro, 1850), 680. The procedure was also described in Borromeo's Fourth Provincial Council of 1576. Voelker, 'Carlo Borromeo's Instructiones fabricae et supellectilis ecclesiasticae', 241–42. That sacred images should be retained appropriately, kept free of dirt and so on, was also encouraged by Molanus, *Traité des saintes images*, book 2, chapter 43.

99 This was the only occasion for which such harsh action was taken during Clement's visitations. As Mansour notes, even though the image would not have depicted any nudity, it referred 'to the sexual sinfulness and self-mutilation of a sanctified pope – at a time when Clement was striving to present a devout image of the papacy'. Mansour, 'Censure and Censorship in Rome, c. 1600', 149–50.

100 Simona Feci, 'Guardare e vedere al di là del muro: immagini sacre e iconoclastia ebraica a Roma in età moderna', in *Le Inquisizioni cristiane e gli ebrei: tavola rotonda nell'ambito della conferenza annuale della ricerca, Rome 20–21 December 2001*, ed. Giuseppe Galasso (Rome: Accademia nazionale dei Lincei, 2003), 415, 417, 424–25. Measures were also taken to cover images in the Ghettos of Cremona in 1580 and Mantua in 1613. Katherine Aron-Beller, 'The Inquisition, Professing Jews, and Christian Images in Seventeenth-Century Modena', *Church History* 81, no. 3 (2012): 584. For accusations of image desecration by Jews in late fifteenth-century Mantua and Florence, see chapters 2 and 4 of Dana E. Katz,

The Jew in the Art of the Italian Renaissance (Philadelphia: University of Pennsylvania Press, 2008).

101 Feci, 'Guardare e vedere al di là del muro', 422–23.

102 Catherine Infante, *The Arts of Encounter: Christians, Muslims, and the Power of Images in Early Modern Spain* (Toronto: University of Toronto Press, 2022), 12–13.

103 The 1564 bull of Pope Pius IV (*In sacrosancta beati Petri*) required teachers to profess their Catholic faith before the bishop or a relevant representative. APV, Sezione antica, *Attestazioni per le professioni di fede richieste agli insegnanti*, b. 1, fasc. 2 (1587–88). These documents have been examined by Vittorio Baldo, *Alunni, maestri e scuole in Venezia alla fine del xvi secolo* (Como: New Press, 1977); Paul F. Grendler, *Schooling in Renaissance Italy: Literacy and Learning, 1300–1600* (Baltimore: Johns Hopkins University Press, 1991), chap. 2.

104 See Paul F. Grendler, 'The Schools of Christian Doctrine in Sixteenth-Century Italy', *Church History* 53, no. 3 (1984), 319–31.

105 Lorenzo Priuli, *Dottrina christiana, divisa in tre parti, da insegnarsi nella Città e Diocese di Venezia ... E per ordine di Mons. Ill. e Reverendiss. Marco Gradenigo Patriarca di Venezia* (Venice: Alvise Valvasense, 1728), 19–20, 67.

106 Lorenzo Priuli, *Regole della Compagnia della dottrina Cristiana per le scole delle donne. Fatte d'ordine di Monsig. Illustriss. & Reverendiss. Sig. Cardinal Priuli Patriarca di Venetia* (Treviso: Girolamo Righettini, 1634), 121.

107 Henry James Coleridge, *The Life and Letters of St. Francis Xavier* (London: Burns and Oates, 1872), vol. 1: 154.

108 Coleridge, *The Life and Letters of St. Francis Xavier*, vol. 1: 153.

109 R. Po-chia Hsia, *The World of Catholic Renewal 1540–1770* (Cambridge: Cambridge University Press, 1998), 169.

110 Eire, *Reformations: The Early Modern World, 1450–1650*, 479.

111 Gilio's treatise similarly described the smashing of the statue of Venus when Saint Helen arrived in Jerusalem. See Gilio, *Dialogue on the Errors and Abuses of Painters*, 122; Molanus, *Traité des saintes images*, book 1, chapters 1–3. See also book 2, chapter 57. Demonstrating a greater degree of tolerance, Molanus argued in chapter 60 that the pagans did produce some moral and edifying images, and that these could serve a use.

112 Paleotti, *Discourse on Sacred and Profane Images*, 78–81. In his life of Fra Angelico, Vasari argued that 'those who work at religious and holy subjects should be religious and holy men; for it is seen, when such works are executed by persons of little faith who have little esteem for religion, they often arouse in men's minds evil appetites and licentious desires'. Vasari, *Lives of the Painters, Sculptors and Architects*, vol. 1: 408–9. Discussed by Nova, 'Correggio's "Lascivie"', 123.

113 Borromeo, *Sacred Painting; Museum*, 49–51.

114 Hollanda, *Four Dialogues on Painting*, 65. In his commentary on the painter Pietro Cavallini, Paleotti noted that he 'was not only a master artist but highly devout and a great friend of the poor. As he grew older, he gave himself with such spirit to religion, leading a truly exemplary life, that he was regarded as a saint'. Paleotti, *Discourse on Sacred and Profane Images*, 80.

115 Voelker, 'Carlo Borromeo's Instructiones fabricae et supellectilis ecclesiasticae', 238–39, note 2.

116 Lukehart, 'Painting Virtuously', 169.

117 Detlef Heikamp, ed., *Scritti d'arte di Federico Zuccaro* (Florence: Leo Olschki, 1961), 25. This was also a standard feature of confraternity regulations. Chapter 21 of the regulations of the Scuola del Santissimo Sacrament at the church of Sant'Agnese in Venice banned any person that used any 'ugly and dishonest word'. BMC, MS.CI. IV025, Mariegola della Scuola del Santissimo Sacramento in Sant'Agnese, fol. 14.

118 Lukehart, 'Painting Virtuously', 161, 68.

119 Lukehart, 'Painting Virtuously', 168. Here it is pointed out that little is known about any legal action taken against painters in Rome.

120 Brown, 'Between the Sacred and Profane', 277. Like Pope Clement, Rusticucci was very keen on ridding church interiors of nudity; for examples, see Bianchi, *La politica delle immagini nell'età della Controriforma*, 216.

121 The *Death of the Virgin* (c. 1604–6) was then snapped up for the collection of the Duke of Mantua on the advice of Rubens. That the rejection of Caravaggio's altarpieces may have been connected with 'the fact that he did not draw' is considered by David Ekserdjian, 'Bad Reception and the Renaissance Altarpiece', *Mitteilungen Des Kunsthistorischen Institutes in Florenz* 63 (2021): 34.

122 Blunt, *Artistic Theory in Italy, 1450–1600*, 120.

123 Scott Nethersole, *Art of Renaissance Florence: A City and Its Legacy* (London: Laurence King, 2019), 69.

124 Nethersole, *Art of Renaissance Florence*, 70–71.

125 BMC, MS.CI. IV163, Mariegola dell'Arte dei Pittori, fol. 17v. Similar rules set out the terms of the agreement with the clergy at the church of San Luca, where funds were set aside to keep the confraternity's oil lamp burning before their altar, and for a mass to be said every first Monday of the month (chapter 22, fol. 7v), as well as obliging those that were commanded to do so by the *banca* of the confraternity to attend the funeral of defunct brothers, since this was 'a humane thing, and also a demonstration of true charity' (chapter 36, fols. 11v–12r). Absenteeism was to be fined. The original statues of the confraternity were drawn up in 1271. The new statutes dated to 1436 are contained in the copy of the *mariegola* dating from 1676. See Valentina Sapienza, 'L'arte dei pittori a Venezia tra Quattro e Cinquecento: una comunità? Alla ricerca di un'identità tra pratiche di mestiere e apprendistato', in *Comunità e società nel commonwealth Veneziano*, ed. Gherardo Ortalli, Ermanno Orlando, and Oliver Jens Schmitt (Venice: Istituto Veneto di Scienze, Lettere ed Arti, 2018), 203 and note 19; Elena Favaro, *L'Arte dei pittori in venezia e i suoi statuti* (Florence: Leo Olschki, 1975).

126 BMC, MS.CI. IV163, Mariegola dell'Arte dei Pittori, fols. 19v–20r.

127 BMC, MS.CI. IV025, Mariegola della Scuola del Santissimo in Sant'Agnese, fol. 43. The record begins by describing the importance of giving honour to the divine cult in churches, but that appearances must be 'modest and reverent, that excite one to respect', and that they should 'focus the minds to a saintly resignation and composure'. The introduction of 'inappropriate profanities' fails to move the soul, but works 'only to excite the eyes'.

128 For the early synods, see Cappelletti, *Storia della Chiesa di Venezia*, vol. 6: 5–376.

129 Grendler, *The Roman Inquisition and the Venetian Press, 1540–1605*, 72. In Rome at the beginning of the seventeenth century, the Master of the Sacred Palace mandated that every printed image was to be approved before publication. For this and related bibliography, see Noyes, 'Post-Tridentine Image Reform and the Myth of Gabriele Paleotti', 241.

130 Cappelletti, *Storia della Chiesa di Venezia*, vol. 6: 377–500.

131 Cappelletti, *Storia della Chiesa di Venezia*, vol. 6: 519, 524.

132 Cappelletti, *Storia della Chiesa di Venezia*, vol. 6: 525. For examples of the level of freedom families could exercise in decorating their chapels in Venice, see Hochmann, *Peintres et commanditaires à Venise (1540–1628)*, 305–8.

133 Cappelletti, *Storia della Chiesa di Venezia*, vol. 6: 681–82.

134 Cappelletti, *Storia della Chiesa di Venezia*, vol. 6: 681.

135 Cappelletti, *Storia della Chiesa di Venezia*, vol. 6: 681.

136 Cappelletti, *Storia della Chiesa di Venezia*, vol. 6: 681–82.

137 For the first synod of September 1592, see Cappelletti, *Storia della Chiesa di Venezia*, vol. 6: 749–892. For the second, see Cappelletti, vol. 6: 906–84. A partial French translation of the 1594 (given as 1592) chapter on images is provided by Hochmann, *Peintres et commanditaires à Venise (1540–1628)*, 275–76.

138 Cappelletti, *Storia della Chiesa di Venezia*, vol. 6: 918–20.

139 Cappelletti, *Storia della Chiesa di Venezia*, vol. 6: 919. Commented upon also by Hochmann, *Peintres et commanditaires à Venise (1540–1628)*, 275. Borromeo's chapter on images contained a similar warning regarding the representation of animals. His ideas had been instituted by the 1576 Provincial Synod. Voelker, 'Carlo Borromeo's Instructiones fabricae et supellectilis ecclesiasticae', 229, 241.

140 Cappelletti, *Storia della Chiesa di Venezia*, vol. 6: 919–20; Rudie van Leeuwen, 'The Portrait Historié in Religious Context and Its Condemnation', in *Pokerfaced: Flemish and Dutch Baroque Faces Unveiled*, ed. Katlijne van der Stighelen, Hannelore Magnus, and Bert Watteeuw (Turnhout: Brepols, 2011), 111–15.

141 See Chapter 4. Similar conclusions to my own are discussed with relation to the Southern Netherlands by van Leeuwen, 'The Portrait Historié in Religious Context and Its Condemnation'. A ban on portraits of the living 'on the main paintings of the altars' was dictated at the third provincial council of Mechlin in 1607 and then ratified at the episcopal synod of Antwerp in 1610, which expanded the ban to altarpiece predellas. Visitation reports show the ban was often violated. In Seville, the 1603 synod banned portraits from images on altars and in their vicinity. Alfonso Rodríguez G. De Ceballos, 'La repercusión en España del decreto del Concilio de Trento acerca de las imágenes sagradas y las censuras al Greco', *Studies in the History of Art* 13, no. El Greco: Italy and Spain (1984): 157.

142 See Marie-Louise Lillywhite, 'Artistic Liberty and Its Limits: Tintoretto's Temptation of Saint Anthony Abbot for Antonio Milledonne', in *Jacopo Tintoretto: Identity, Practice, Meaning*, ed. Marie-Louise Lillywhite, Tom Nichols, and Giorgio Tagliaferro (Rome: Viella, 2022), 212. That the figure of Saint Geminianus depicted on Veronese's organ shutter (c. 1560) at the church of San Geminiano in Venice was a portrait of the parish priest Benedetto Manzini has been argued by Xavier F. Salomon, '"A ruby among many pearls": The Lost Church of San Geminiano in Venice and Its Sixteenth-Century Decoration', in *David Bowie's Tintoretto: Angel Foretelling the Martyrdom of Saint Catherine of Alexandria*, ed. Benjamin van Beneden and Nicola Jennings (London: Colagni Foundation, 2017), 66. The likeness between Vittoria's extant bust of Manzini and Veronese's painting was first noticed by Thomas Martin, *Alessandro Vittoria and the Portrait Bust in Renaissance Venice: Remodelling Antiquity* (Oxford: Clarendon, 1998), 119.

143 Giuseppe Liberali, 'Lotto, Pordenone e Tiziano a Treviso: cronologie, interpretazioni ed ambientamenti inediti', *Istituto Veneto di Scienze, Lettere ed Arti* 33, no. 3 (1963): 97, doc. 27; Hope, 'Altarpieces and the Requirements of Patrons', 551–54. The episode is extensively analysed by Elsje van Kessel, *The Lives of Paintings: Presence, Agency and Likeness in Venetian Art of the Sixteenth Century* (Berlin: De Gruyter, 2017), 81–114.

144 The passage points out that Titian had completed such portraits in the past, in order to please his patrons. See Kessel, *The Lives of Paintings*, 108.

145 For other examples, see Marie-Louise Lillywhite, 'Artistic Liberty and Its Limits', 228.

146 The two scholars disagree on whether Manzini is Saint Geminianus (Salomon) or Severus (Martin). See Martin, *Alessandro Vittoria and the Portrait Bust in Renaissance Venice*, 119; Salomon, '"A ruby among many pearls"', 66. For other examples of donor portraits by Veronese, see Stefania Mason, 'La "presenza" dei committenti nei dipinti di Paolo Veronese', in *Paolo Veronese: l'illusione della realtà*, ed. Bernard Aikema and Paola Marini, Exhibition Catalogue, Palazzo della Gran Guardia, Verona, 5 July–5 October 2014 (Milan: Electa, 2014), 153–63.

147 Stefania Mason Rinaldi, 'Novità, ritrovamenti e restituzioni a Jacopo Palma il Giovane', *Arte Veneta* 36 (1982): 152–53; Mason Rinaldi, *Palma il Giovane: l'opera completa*, 146, cat. 565. The painting was sold at the Dorotheum Auction House in Vienna on 9 June 2020, lot 78. Mason hypothesised that Palma was shown as a member of the Crociferi, but the colour of the vestments does not match those used by the order at this point in their history. See Marie-Louise Lillywhite, 'Family Values & Artistic Alliances in Seventeenth-Century Venice: The Wife and Daughters of Palma Il Giovane', *Master Drawings* 59, no. 2 (2021): 224–25, 239, note 82.

148 Mason Rinaldi, *Palma il Giovane: l'opera completa*, 131, cat. 462.
149 Cappelletti, *Storia della Chiesa di Venezia*, vol. 6, part 2: 94–165. A second synod was convened by Morosini in April 1667.
150 Cappelletti, *Storia della Chiesa di Venezia*, vol. 6, part 2: 138.
151 Bianchi, *La politica delle immagini nell'età della Controriforma*, 63–64, 73.
152 For the ways in which the ideas of Fontana on images relates to those of Paleotti, see Bianchi, *La politica delle immagini nell'età della Controriforma*, 64–68.
153 See Daniele, *Prospero Fontana "Pictor Bononiensis"* (1509–1597). *Catalogo ragionato dei dipinti*, 66.
154 Borromeo, *Sacred Painting; Museum*, 55–57.
155 Filippo Baldinucci (1625–96), *Notizie dei professori del disegno da Cimabue in qua*, vol. 4 (Florence: Studio per edizioni scelte, 1974), 641. See also Maria H. Loh, '"La Custodia degli Occhi": Disciplining Desire in Post-Tridentine Italian Art', in *The Sensuous in the Counter-Reformation Church*, ed. Marcia B. Hall and Tracy E. Cooper (Cambridge: Cambridge University Press, 2013), 105.
156 Mâle, *L'art religieux de la fin du XVIe siècle, du XVIIe siècle et du XVIIIe siècle*, 2–3.
157 Paleotti, for example, had planned to write a whole further book of his treatise on the theme of lascivious images. See the planned chapter headings for the third book, which was never completed. Paleotti, *Discourse on Sacred and Profane Images*, 332–33.
158 Molanus, *Traité des saintes images*, book 2, chapter 42; Voelker, 'Carlo Borromeo's Instructiones fabricae et supellectilis ecclesiasticae', vol. 1: 59.
159 Voelker, 'Carlo Borromeo's Instructiones fabricae et supellectilis ecclesiasticae', 228.
160 Voelker, 'Carlo Borromeo's Instructiones fabricae et supellectilis ecclesiasticae', 228, 238–40. The First Provincial Council of 1565 also stipulated that transgressors should be punished. The Fourth Council recommended 'a heavy fine' for artists who broke the rules, whilst the clergy who had consented to the display of such works were to be fined and may have also faced excommunication according to the discretion of the bishop.
161 Grendler, *The Roman Inquisition and the Venetian Press, 1540–1605*, 256, 256.
162 Such as Tintoretto's *Assumption* of c. 1553–55 for Santa Maria dei Crociferi (the first version of which is now in the Cathedral of Bamberg). See Douglas-Scott, 'Prohibition of Text and License of Image: Painters and the Vernacular Bible in Counter-Reformation Venice', 244; Allison Sherman, *The Lost Venetian Church of Santa Maria Assunta dei Crociferi: Form, Decoration, Patronage*, ed. Carlo Corsato (London: Independent Publishing Network, 2020), 99–106.
163 The eventual tomb was completed in perfect conformity with post-Tridentine norms. See Gaier, 'Il mausoleo nel presbiterio: patronati laici e liturgie private nelle chiese veneziane', 179–80; Martin Gaier, 'Il patriarca e il suo vicario: Lorenzo Priuli, Giovanni Mozanega e la questione dei monumenti sepolcrali nella chiesa post-tridentina', in *La chiesa di San Pietro di Castello e la nascita del patriarcato di Venezia*, ed. Gianmario Guidarelli, Michel Hochmann, and Fabio Tonizzi (Venice: Marcianum Press, 2018), 217.
164 Bianchi, *La politica delle immagini nell'età della Controriforma*, 17–18.
165 Fehl and Perry, 'Painting and the Inquisition at Venice: Three Forgotten Files'.
166 Depasquale, 'Epilogue Two: Michelangelo's "Last Judgment" and the Reception of the Nude in Counter-Reformation Italy', 367.
167 In Spain, the Florentine sculptor Pompeo Leoni was tried by the Inquisition in 1558 for Lutheranism and sentenced to one year's reclusion in a monastery. The artisan Esteban Jamete was investigated for his ownership of a Protestant print and was subsequently excommunicated. He was also so badly injured as a result of the Inquisition's torture that he could no longer work as a sculptor or carver. For these and other cases, see Fernando Marías, 'Censuring Public Images: A Woodcut in the Inquisition Trial of Esteban Jamete', in *The Early Modern Hispanic World: Transnational and Interdisciplinary Approaches*, ed. Kimberly Lynn and Erin Kathleen Rowe, trans. Consuelo López-Morillas (New York: Cambridge University Press, 2017), 293–318.

168 Tedeschi and Monter, 'Toward a Statistical Profile of the Italian Inquisitions', 146.

169 The identities of the individuals who made up the tribunal were not listed on the document, but the most plausible reconstruction is provided by Edward Grasman, 'On Closer Inspection: The Interrogation of Paolo Veronese', *Artibus et Historiae* 30, no. 59 (2009): 128–29.

170 Borghini was the first to describe the painting during Veronese's lifetime as 'a large canvas, containing a feast held by one of the apostles'. Borghini, *Il Riposo*, 562. Ridolfi referred to the subject of the painting as 'that narrated by Saint Luke in the house of Levi the money lender'. Ridolfi, *Le maraviglie dell'arte*, vol. 1: 314.

171 Noted by Paul H. D. Kaplan, 'Veronese's Last "Last Supper"', *Arte Veneta* 41 (1987): 51. The desire for these paintings may also have waned.

172 Geraldine A. Wojno Kiefer, 'Mid-sixteenth Century Veronese Painting in the Duomo of Mantua', *Antichità viva* 26 (1987): 41. Veronese was also a popular artist with the clergy of Venice; see Xavier F. Salomon, 'Francesco degli Arbori's Chapel in Murano and Its Decoration by Paolo Veronese', in *Veronese in Murano: Two Venetian Renaissance Masterpieces Restored* (New York: Frick Collection, 2017), 46–51; Lillywhite, 'The Decoration of the Church of San Giacomo dall'Orio in Venice', 119.

173 Lillywhite, 'The Decoration of the Jesuit Church of the Madonna dell'Umiltà in Venice', 166. The letter dates to 1564.

174 The patron was first noted by Ridolfi, *Le maraviglie dell'arte*, vol. 1: 314. Vasari had noted Titian's painting prior to its destruction. Vasari, *Lives of the Painters, Sculptors and Architects*, vol. 2: 792. For Titian's lost painting, see Brian T. D'Argaville, 'Titian's "Cenacolo" for the refectory of SS. Giovanni e Paolo Reconsidered', in *Tiziano e Venezia: atti del convegno internazionale di studi. Venice, 1976* (Vicenza: Neri Pozza, 1980), 161–67.

175 The contract left the invention up to Veronese. It was highly praised by Vasari. See the analysis of Gisolfi, *Paolo Veronese and the Practice of Painting in Late Renaissance Venice*, 115–16.

176 Massimi, *La Cena in casa di Levi di Paolo Veronese*, 179–80. Veronese was asked what other '*cene*' he had painted and he listed versions for the refectory of Santi Nazaro e Celso in Verona (1556, now in the Galleria Sabauda, Turin), for the refectory of the Servites in Venice (c. 1570–72, now in the Musée National du Château of Versailles), for that of the Hieronymites of San Sebastiano (c. 1568–70, now in the Pinacoteca di Brera, Milan), and for the fathers of the Maddalena in Padua (1570–73, lost). All of these were scenes of the Feast in the House of Simon. He also listed his feast scene for Benedictines on the island of San Giorgio Maggiore (1562–63, now in the Louvre), but was reminded that this was not in fact a '*cena*' (it depicted the *Marriage Feast at Cana*). In addition to these examples, Veronese also painted a *Feast in the House of Gregory the Great* (1572) for the Servite sanctuary of Monte Berico in Vicenza, which in still in situ. For this, see Terisio Pignatti and Filippo Pedrocco, *Veronese* (Milan: Electa, 1995), vol. 1: 287–88, cat. 193. For the other feast scenes, see vol. 1: 136, cat. 101 (Turin); 287, cat. 192 (Versailles); 275, cat. 179 (Brera); 250–52, cat. 149 (Louvre). Veronese produced a *Supper at Emmaus* (c. 1559), also in the Louvre (153, cat. 100), and a second *Marriage Feast at Cana* (c. 1571–72) for the Cuccina family, now in the Gemäldegalerie, Dresden (280–82, cat. 185). For the lost work in Padua, see Hans H. Aurenhammer, 'Et ne ho fatto una in Padoa ai Padri della Maddalena": Una Cena perduta (e quasi dimenticata) del Veronese', *Venezia Cinquecento* 11, no. 21 (2001): 121–40.

177 Grasman, 'On Closer Inspection: The Interrogation of Paolo Veronese', 127.

178 FECIT D[OMINVS]. CO[N]VI[VIVM]. MAGNV[M]. LEVI // LVCAE CAP[VT]. V. (Levi prepares a great banquet for Christ, Luke Chapter V).

179 For an extensive discussion of these authors, see Massimi, *La Cena in casa di Levi di Paolo Veronese*, 20–25, with notes.

180 Maria Elena Massimi, 'La cosiddetta "Cena in casa di Levi" di Paolo Veronese: descrizione preliminare all'identificazione del soggetto come "Cena in casa del fariseo"', *Venezia*

Cinquecento 14, no. 27 (2005): 123–68; Massimi, *La Cena in casa di Levi di Paolo Veronese*. See also Salomon, 'Review of "La Cena in casa di Levi di Paolo Veronese. Il processo riaperto" by Maria Elena Massimi'.

181 Simon's feast precedes Judas's betrayal and the apostles' final meal in the Gospels of Matthew and Mark, hence why Veronese was confused. The location of the Last Supper is recorded in the Bible merely as a 'a large room upstairs' belonging to a man, that was 'furnished and ready'. Cocke's argument was based on the fact that the 'Last Suppers' that Veronese listed at his interrogation were all versions of the *Feast in the House of Simon*, plus the *Marriage Feast at Cana*. Cocke had not examined the transcript carefully since in the first instance where Veronese clarified the subject matter of the Santi Giovannni e Paolo painting he used the words '*cena ultima*', but later in the transcript he was asked to list his other '*cene*', which refers to feasts, or literally 'dinners', and not specifically to the Last Supper. Richard Cocke, 'Venice, Decorum and Veronese', in *Nuovi studi su Paolo Veronese*, ed. Massimo Gemin (Venice: Arsenale Editrice, 1990), 241–55.

182 Giovanna Nepi Scirè, ed., *Il restauro del Convito in casa di Levi di Paolo Veronese*, vol. 11, Quaderni della Soprintendenza ai Beni Artistici e Storici di Venezia (Venice: Stamperia di Venezia, 1984), 16; Emerich Schaffran, 'Der Inquisizionsprozess gegen Paolo Veronese', *Archiv für Kulturgeschichte* 42, no. 2 (1960): 190.

183 First Kaplan and later Grasman have suggested that the Inquisitor Schellino was eager to impress the new Apostolic Nuncio and to demonstrate that Venice was committed to enforcing the dictates of the Council of Trent, particularly in the aftermath of Venice's peace treaty with the Ottoman Empire of 7 March 1573. Paul H. D. Kaplan, 'Veronese and the Inquisition: The Geopolitical Context', in *Suspended License: Censorship and the Visual Arts*, ed. Elizabeth C. Childs (Seattle: University of Washington Press, 1997), 100–105; Grasman, 'On Closer Inspection: The Interrogation of Paolo Veronese', 129–31.

184 The laxity of observance at the convent was noted first by Gino Fogolari, 'Il processo dell'Inquisizione a Paolo Veronese', *Archivio Veneto* 5, no. 7 (1935): 325–86. See also Massimo Gemin, 'Riflessioni iconografiche sulla Cena in casa di Levi', in *Nuovi studi su Paolo Veronese*, ed. Massimo Gemin, Proceedings of the International Conference, Università di Venezia, 1988 (Venice: Arsenale Editrice, 1990), 367–70; Kaplan, 'Veronese and the Inquisition: The Geopolitical Context', 100–101; Grasman, 'On Closer Inspection: The Interrogation of Paolo Veronese', 130. The final author rejects the idea that heresy at the monastery had much to do with the questioning of the artist (see previous note).

185 John Ruskin, *Guide to the Principal Pictures of the Academy of Fine Arts at Venice* (London: Hazell, Watson and Viney, 1877), parts 2, 54.

186 Massimi, *La Cena in casa di Levi di Paolo Veronese*, 180. Consistent with this concern for a possible Teutonic influence is the fact that Veronese was also asked about the presence of German soldiers in the painting. That Swiss soldiers from Graubünden appear to have been housed at the monastery and were responsible for the fire of 1571 is described by Grasman, 'On Closer Inspection: The Interrogation of Paolo Veronese', 131.

187 Hall, 'Introduction', 4.

188 Pallucchini and Rossi, *Tintoretto: le opere sacre e profane*, vol. 1: 183–85, cats. 243–45.

189 Grasman, 'On Closer Inspection: The Interrogation of Paolo Veronese', 132–33.

190 Stefania Mason, 'Tintoretto the Venetian', in *Tintoretto: Artist of Renaissance Venice*, ed. Robert Echols and Frederick Ilchman, Exhibition Catalogue, Palazzo Ducale, Venice, 7 September 2018–6 January 2019, National Gallery of Art, Washington, 24 March–7 July 2019 (New Haven, CT: Yale University Press, 2018), 49–50. The documents were found by Pallucchini and Rossi, *Tintoretto: le opere sacre e profane*, vol. 1: 179. cat. 225.

191 As noted by Pallucchini/Rossi and Mason (see previous note), the two portrait figures are still visible on the outskirts of the table. A third seated figure can be seen in X-radiographs, but it is unclear whether this was an earlier *pentimento*.

192 On 8 September 1573 the artist 'offered to said guardian and his *vicario* to finish [the canvases] to perfection by removing the figure of the excellent Ravena and replacing him with another figure'. For a transcription of the document, see Borean, 'Documentation', 430. See also Humfrey, 'Venezia, 1540–1600', 511; Mason, 'Tintoretto the Venetian', 50–53.

193 McNamara, *The Bishop's Burden*, 11.

194 Paleotti, *Discourse on Sacred and Profane Images*, 26.

CHAPTER FOUR

A REFORM IN QUANTITY

Patriarch Lorenzo Priuli's Visitations

In the previous chapter, the standards that sacred images were theoretically to abide by from the late sixteenth century onwards were explored. In this chapter the reality of how these standards were enforced and the results that this had in Venice are examined through the prism of Patriarch Lorenzo Priuli's inspections of the city's parish churches, which took place between 1591 and 1598.[1] The evidence presented by these records demonstrates that the visitations were simultaneously generative and destructive. On the one hand, the restoration of old or damaged images, altars, or buildings was of concern for Patriarch Priuli. He rarely requested that images should be removed, and, on the contrary, he was overwhelmingly more likely to advise their multiplication. Numerous significant architectural and decorative interventions took place in Venetian churches in the late Cinquecento, and although not all of this is attributable to the impact of these visits, they clearly played an important role in stimulating renovations. On the other hand, these transformations were simultaneously destructive, since the visitation had no hesitation in ordering the stripping away of older altars or furnishings if they were thought to be deficient or considered in some way moribund. More often than not, this was because they were judged to be incompatible with the rules established by the guidelines of the 1581 Apostolic Visit, or because they presented a visual or physical impediment to the site of the eucharist, which contained within a magnificent tabernacle, which was now to be the pièce de résistance of the church interior. Whilst the changes in this ambit were often eagerly realised by the increasingly popular and influential eucharistic confraternities of the Blessed Sacrament in Venice, they nevertheless provide early modern evidence of Leo Steinberg's observation that 'nothing endangers a work's survival more than a recent aversion of taste'.[2]

One limitation of sixteenth-century visitation records for the art historian is that they rarely mention the identity of artists or the subject of specific images outright. Patriarch Priuli never provided the name of an artist, and it was unusual that he detailed the iconography of artworks either.[3] Priuli tended to state whether or not he approved of whatever he was looking at, providing a judgment on the appearance of each altar as he walked around the church, as well as drawing some conclusions on the overall state of the edifice. However, by cross-referencing descriptions of altars and chapels with information contained in near contemporary guides to the city (such as Francesco Sansovino's 1581 *Venetia città nobilissima et singolare*, with its expanded editions of 1604 and 1663), it is sometimes possible to deduce what the visitors were seeing and the probable authorship and subject of the images that they singled out for praise or condemnation. Policing images was never Priuli's overarching priority, and there are relatively few examples of him ordering their removal or destruction. Particularly when the visits concern the state of the clergy, they should be examined in light of the fact that their intent was to search for problems, which could then be corrected, rather than 'praise success stories', as the historian Carlos Eire put it.[4] Yet during his visits relating to the fabric and decoration of the parish churches Priuli regularly complimented what he saw, most often relating to how the site of the Blessed Sacrament had been visually celebrated, how relics were displayed, or the form and appearance of altars, altarpieces, and chapels. In terms of understanding the ideal that Priuli had in mind when he visited a church, what he endorsed and encouraged was just as important as what he disliked or sought to change. Consistencies in what he deemed to be laudable allow us to appreciate something of his tastes and preferences, as well as his understanding of the potential power of images in fostering devotion. In sum, the records of Priuli's visitations are documents of clear importance for exploring how standards for devotional art and architecture were implemented and enforced after the Council of Trent and the Apostolic Visit to Venice of a few years previous. Even if these kinds of reforms were never completely uniform in nature – the preferences of one patriarch might differ somewhat from those of the next – the transformations that took place in the wake of these inspections show that in some areas they had a cumulative impact on the appearance of the Venetian parish church from the late sixteenth century onwards.

VISITATIONS IN VENICE

Pastoral visitations had been held sporadically in Venice prior to 1563, the year that bishops were exhorted by the Council of Trent to complete them at the very least biannually.[5] The primary aims of these inspections were defined by the council as ensuring the maintenance of good morals and the extirpation of heresy, as well as encouraging people to live in a state of faith, peace, and innocence.[6] We have seen in the previous chapter that the decrees also referred to the responsibilities of a bishop regarding the maintenance of holy sites in his diocese. Commencing with the Apostolic Visit, subsequent pastoral visits in Venice were far more concerned with the arrangement and appearance of the liturgical space than they had been previously. The Priulan visits exemplify this tendency. Rather than the investigation of the clergy being the primary focus of the visit, accompanied perhaps by a few comments on the state of the church buildings, the reports were divided into two separate sets of documents, and both were carried out with exhaustive rigour.[7] This gives some sense of the heavy workload brought on by the council's insistence on more frequent visits and helps to explain why the aim of a cycle of visits every few years was very rarely achieved, even if they did take place far more often henceforth.[8] In addition to his parish visits, Priuli also investigated the nunneries of Venice and proved to be a strict enforcer of rigid enclosure rules.[9] He even wrote a treatise on the subject, his meticulous *Orders & admonitions concerning Visitors to Convents and the Maintenance of Enclosure.*[10]

The dispute between the Holy See and Venice occasioned by the spectre of an Apostolic Visitation was discussed in the previous chapter. Since such visits were carried out to satisfy papal authority, their orders were not easily ignored, and however fraught the seemingly endless negotiations regarding the visit proved to be, after it had taken place the rules it established went on to have a decisive impact in Venice. The resulting reform document – the *Decreta e hortationes* – drawn up by the two visitors, Bishop Agostino Valier of Verona and the Papal Nuncio Lorenzo Campeggi, was read aloud to the city's clergy in the sacristy of the church of San Salvador on 11 August.[11] The 'general rules' to be applied in each Venetian church consisted of norms for the appearance and location of the tabernacle, baptismal fonts, relics, altars, sacristies, and the fabric of the building more generally, which were then condensed into a list of twelve general terms to be followed.[12] The decrees for each individual church were consigned to the relative parish priests over the next few months, and these were later consulted by Priuli, who referred to their orders on his own visits, as did subsequent patriarchs.[13] As a faithful servant to both Rome and his homeland, Priuli made his intentions to newly enforce the decrees of the earlier Apostolic Visit clear in 1592, the year that he ordered its dictates to be reissued and republished in Venice.[14]

In common with other late sixteenth-century visits, Priuli's inspections proceeded according to a consistent formula, and they were events of great pomp and ceremony befitting his elevated rank. For example, at the church of San Tommaso Apostolo (San Tomà) it was recorded that the parish chapter received the patriarch 'honorably', with the sound of the organ, bells, and music greeting the retinue as they entered the church. Once inside, they were met with the spectacle of each altar illuminated by lamps and candles.[15] The patriarch would first celebrate mass, often attended by huge crowds of the laity, and a sermon would be provided by a preacher, the favoured choice being one Paulo Tolosa.[16] The patriarch would then make a beeline for the tabernacle where the Blessed Sacrament was reserved, and some initial comments on the state in which it was maintained and the dignity of the site and receptacle chosen for it were noted down. The eucharist was then adored, accompanied by the singing of the *Pange lingua*, and the burning of incense. At this point the populace would usually be blessed and sometimes confirmations would take place.[17] With the first element of the visit concluded, the inspection proper began. It usually commenced at the baptismal font, followed by a look at the holy oils, the relics, the high altar, and the site of the Blessed Sacrament (subject to a second set of more detailed observations and recommendations). Next came each of the individual altars and chapels, comments on the structure and maintenance of the church in general, and the contents of the sacristy. The vestments and altar furnishings were then inspected, as were the documents relating to bookkeeping.[18] Finally, it was usually stipulated that one or two wooden confessionals were to be constructed; flooring was to be fixed where it was damaged; walls whitewashed where necessary; and windows or openings that compromised the privacy of the church were to be closed. Cadavers were to be removed from wall tombs, and if the church had a cemetery then this was to be fitted with gates. The clergy and members of the confraternities were frequently lectured by the patriarch in the sacristy, where they were exhorted to help the needy and provide exemplars of morality in their personal conduct.[19] The individuals tasked with noting down the recommendations did so diligently, and the records for most of the churches are detailed and well organised. Each one concludes with a summary of the patriarch's orders. These lists would have been useful both for subsequent visitations, as well as for the parish clergy charged with implementing the decreed changes.

The general order of proceedings presented by the Priuli visitation took its cue from the Apostolic Visit. Yet Priuli tended to make far more fastidious and extensive recommendations than this delegation, particularly relating to the appearance and organisation of the liturgical space. At the church of San Giacomo dall'Orio, for instance, the 1581 visitors made only six brief orders, whereas Priuli made eighteen detailed ones, with further sub-orders contained within a number of them.[20] He also visited far more sites than his successors Patriarchs Matteo Zane (1545–1605, r. 1600–5) and Francesco Vendramin (1555–1619, r. 1605–19), inspecting sixty-four parishes, compared to thirty-nine by Zane and eighteen by Vendramin.[21] In fact, with the exception of the

Apostolic Visit, which inspected sixty-nine parishes (plus the churches of the male religious orders), Priuli's record of number of parishes visited remained unbeaten until those of the mid 1700s undertaken by Patriarch Francesco Antonio Correr (1676–1741, r. 1734–41).[22] Priuli was accompanied on his pastoral visitations by the patriarchal vicar, the Cypriot Giovanni Mozanega, and the 'reverend visitors' from each relevant sestiere of the city.[23] On those occasions when the patriarch could not attend in person, due to illness or pressing engagements, it was the vicar and the district inspectors who carried out the visitation, which is what happened at eight different churches.[24]

THE PATRIARCH'S PREFERENCES

Unlike his contemporaries in other places, it was very unusual that Priuli censored artworks because of their perceived indecency. He did this only twice, at the parishes of Sant'Angelo Raffaelle and Santi Ermagora e Fortunato (San Marcuola). At the first of these, it was ordered that since the paintings in the high altar chapel included 'some figures of women uncovered', they were to be expurgated as soon as possible, because they encouraged 'lasciviousness' more than devotion. Despite his disapproval of these elements, Priuli judged the high altarpiece at the church to be 'very honourable'.[25] In a similar vein, at San Marcuola Priuli ordered that the 'profane German figures' were to be removed from the ciborium used to take the eucharist to the sick. They were to be replaced by devout ones, the appearance of which the parish priest could decide for himself. No other information was given as to the nature or appearance of these offending details.[26] Since there were numerous paintings in Venetian churches that featured some degree of nudity, the paucity of Priuli's dictates that they should be altered or removed is different to the approach of someone like Pope Clement VIII, whose visitations to the churches of Rome were carried out near contemporaneously to Priuli's in Venice, between the years 1592 and 1596. Acting out of a much more extensive definition of decorum, the pope was deeply distressed at the slightest hint of anything potentially sensual, even declaring that the fully dressed figure of Mary Magdalen in Scipione Pulzone's (d. 1598) *Lamentation* be changed to have 'a more devout and modest appearance' (Fig. 49).[27] This dictate seems to have been ignored by the Jesuit Order at the Gesù, and it is unclear whether Pulzone's altarpiece of the *Seven Archangels* at the same church was later replaced as a direct result of the pope's objections (he also desired that these angels should be more decently covered), or because the chapel of the Angels had simply changed hands.[28]

Priuli did order the removal of images at other points during his visits, usually because they were deemed to be antiquated and irreparably damaged, which is what happened in four instances: at the churches of Sant'Eufemia,

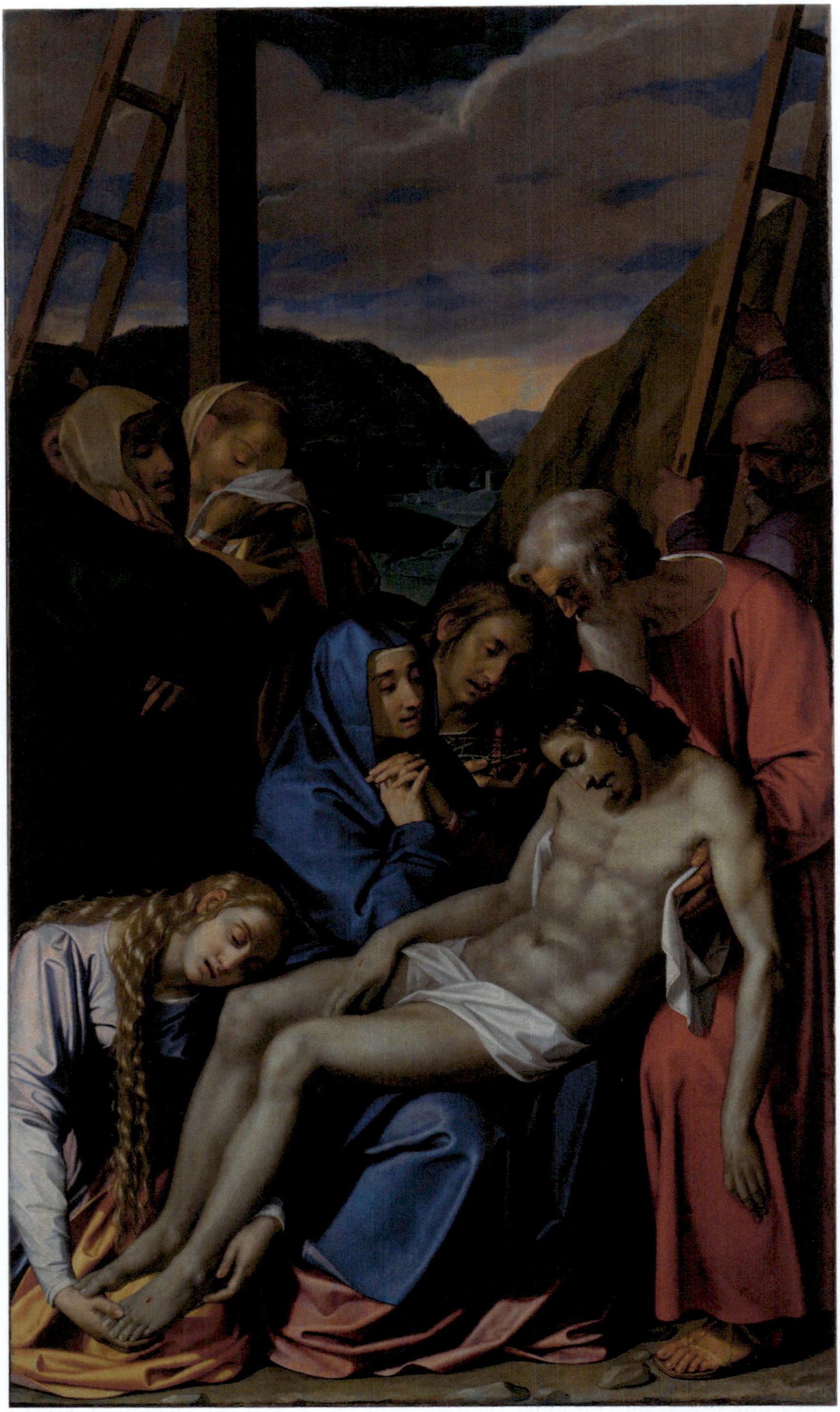

49. Scipione Pulzone, *Lamentation,* 1593, oil on canvas, Metropolitan Museum of Art, New York (Photo: Open Access)

Santa Fosca, San Martino, and Santa Margherita.[29] At the last of these, the parish priest was accused of ignoring the orders of the Apostolic Visitation to provide a new high altarpiece, and he was given a year to arrange a replacement work. Priuli judged the offending image to be too old and small and is reported as having been 'greatly amazed' that during the ten years that had lapsed since the last visit an 'honourable' altarpiece had never been commissioned.[30] We know nothing about the subject or artist of this altarpiece, but perhaps it depicted Saint Margaret of Antioch, to whom the church and this altar were dedicated. We do know that at the time Priuli visited the church it would have had a very rich sanctuary, one covered with gold mosaics.[31] These were later destroyed when, as Giustiniano Martinioni wrote in 1663, the high altar 'was torn to the ground due to its old age and remade in a modern form'.[32] The resident eucharistic confraternity (the Scuola del Santissimo Sacramento) had taken possession of the sanctuary and began extensive building works in the space beginning in 1603, which eventually included crowning the high altar with a marble tabernacle, shifting the choir stalls into the chancel, and reassembling Tintoretto's paintings of *The Last Supper, Christ Washing the Apostles Feet*, and *The Agony in the Garden* in their new location.[33] Over on the island of the Giudecca, at the church of Sant'Eufemia, Priuli decreed that the canvases of the eponymous saint that were ranged around the body of the church had to be taken down without delay since they were torn. The paintings were described as illustrating 'the life and miracles of Saint Euphemia and her companions', and in the summary of orders Priuli detailed that new canvases were to be made to replace these damaged ones.[34] In other cases it appears Priuli was more concerned with the age of paintings. This probably had less to do with their style than the fact that they had become dirty or damaged over the passage of time. For example, at the altar of the Madonna at Santa Fosca, the 'old canvas' above the altarpiece was to be removed and replaced with a crucifix or, failing that, some other 'honourable figure'.[35] Although referring not to an image but to decorative elements more broadly, at the baptistery of San Maurizio it was felt that the 'old and indecent ornament' had to be replaced.[36] The same fate was dictated for the 'old altarpiece' of Saint Martin on display in the church of the same name, and the baptistery was now to be shifted into the chapel where this painting had been displayed.[37] Ideally, baptisteries were now to be embellished with images of the baptism of Christ in the river Jordan, so a representation of Martin would have been incongruous in this new location. At both Santa Marina and Angelo Raffaele, Priuli also ordered that images were to be moved away from the baptistery. At the former, a secular portrait of a former priest was judged to be better suited to display in the sacristy.[38] At the latter, the canvas of the *Pietà* was to be removed and replaced with a more fitting scene of Christ's baptism.[39] Inspired by the advice of Borromeo, who wrote that the altar of a baptistery chapel should feature a representation of John baptising Christ on the wall above it, and that the ciborium that covered the font should include statues of the same scene, the addition of such images at the baptismal font was one repeated by the patriarch in numerous other churches throughout Venice.[40]

There are also a few moments in Priuli's visits where he wanted new altarpieces to be commissioned but gave no information about what was wrong with the pre-existing ones, something that almost certainly would have been discussed in greater detail orally. At San Severo, the altar of San Gallo was deemed 'very indecent and inconvenient'. It was to be remade in the appropriate form with a new altarpiece.[41] At San Bartolomeo, Priuli wished for significant adjustments to be made to the high altar that included the creation of a new altarpiece that had to be ample enough in size to appropriately fill the space. His wish was acted on swiftly: the visit took place on 30 November 1592, and by 1593 *The Martyrdom of Saint Bartholomew* had been completed by the artist Palma il Giovane (Fig. 50).[42] As an arbiter of standards of decorum then, we will see that Priuli was far stricter when this concerned the appearance, materials, and locations of altars, chapels, and tabernacles than he ever was with images. Since it was only in the Seicento that guidebooks to Venice began to systematically list the majority of artworks on display in the churches of the city, we know very little about the style or authorship of the works that the patriarch wanted to be removed when they are not mentioned in the documentation of the parish. They were probably of compromised artistic value due to their poor state of repair, and if they had been by a significant artist or considered of special worth, then an order would have most likely been given to better accommodate or renew them.

From what is possible to garner from the visitation records it appears that Priuli approved of works of near contemporary artists displayed in churches or chapels that had recently been restored, rebuilt, or updated. It is telling that the freshly completed church of San Geminiano in Piazza San Marco (destroyed in 1807), once one of the city's architectural and artistic jewels, was subject to the fewest structural recommendations of any church inspected by the visitation.[43] Decorated with paintings and sculptures by the leading artists of the day, including Alessandro Vittoria, Veronese, and Tintoretto, the altars were all described as being 'of the appropriate form and honourably kept'.[44] The high altar survives in the church of the Knights of Malta in Venice, and is decorated with porphyry, serpentine, and roundels of *verde antico* (Fig. 51).[45] Since Priuli tended to encourage the use of opulent materials, one can imagine him approving of the precious stones incorporated into the structure. Although this visit was carried out by the patriarchal vicar and not by Priuli himself, the delegation would have been well versed in his preferences, and given the central location of this church it was bound to have been well known by the

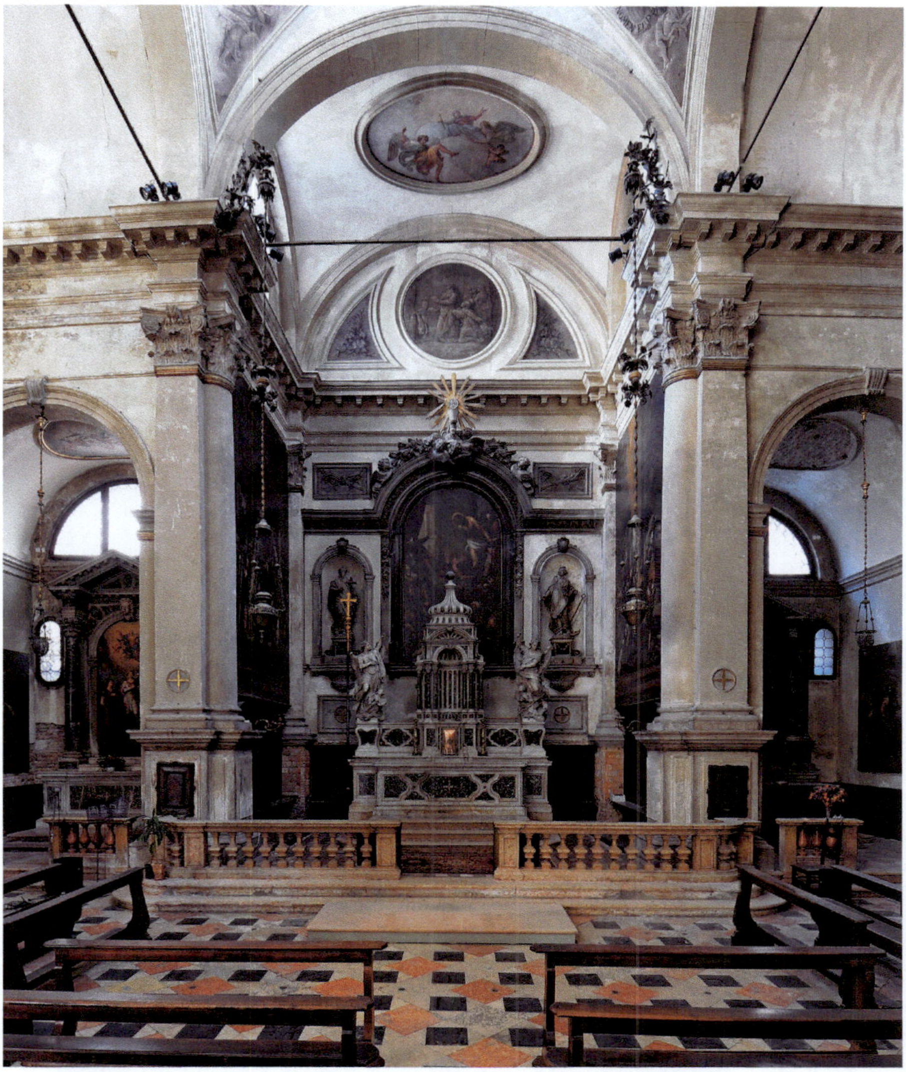

50. High Altar of San Bartolomeo with *The Martyrdom of Saint Bartholomew* by Palma il Giovane (Photo: Francesco Turio Bohm)

patriarch. Priuli's visits were confined to the parishes, but the Apostolic Visitors had also been impressed by the works of the pre-eminent architects of the day, reserving high praise for Palladio's churches of San Giorgio Maggiore and the Redentore.[46] Presumably, the more recent the church was, the more likely it would have been constructed and decorated in line with contemporary norms for sacred edifices, meaning that there was less chance that the visitors would have to make extensive orders in order for it to be brought up to date.

On two occasions in particular, Priuli had glowing praise for decorative programmes that had been commissioned by the clergy. At San Polo he described the chancel as having been found 'very well and very nobly built

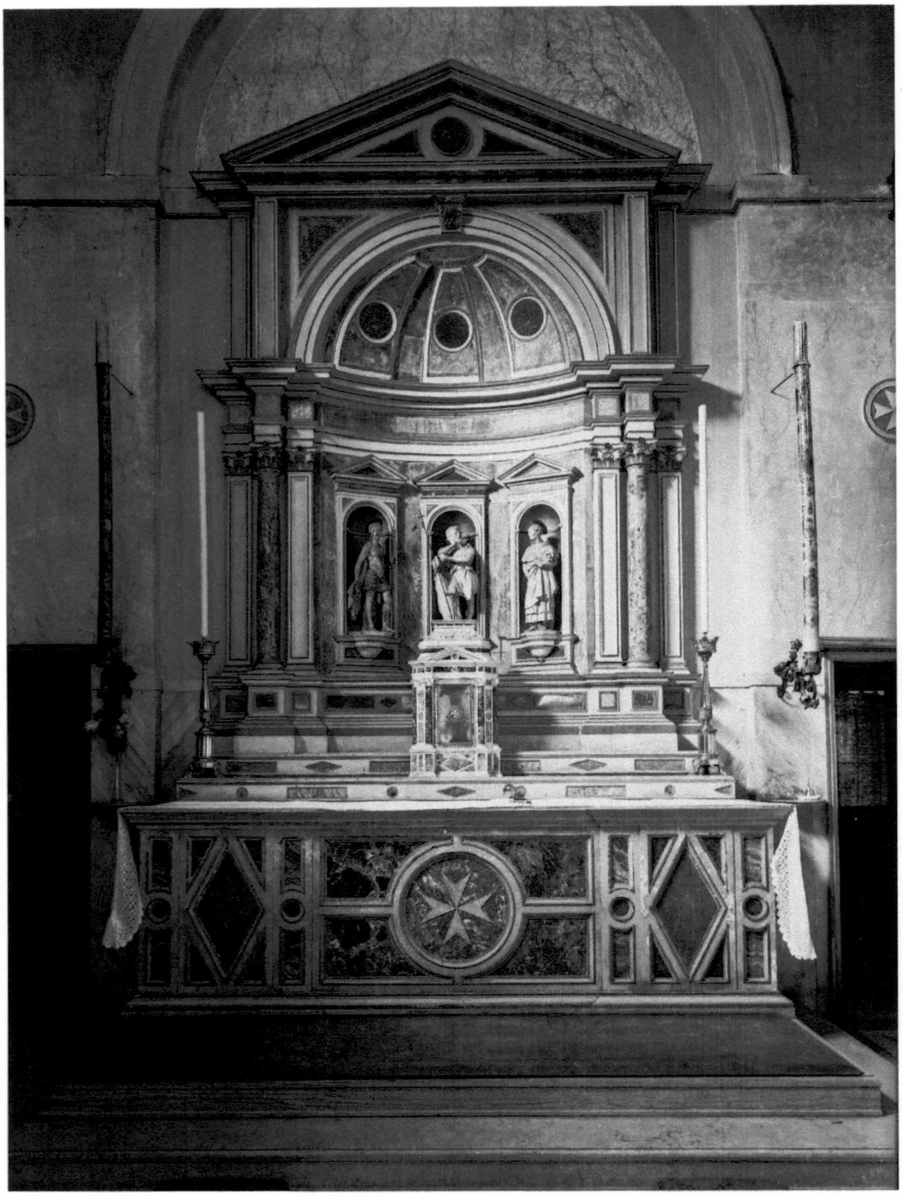

51. Cristoforo del Legname and Bartolomeo Bergamasco, *High Altar of San Geminiano*, San Giovanni di Malta, Venice (Photo: Alinari Archives, Florence)

with a very ornate high altar. For which I commend and laud the good memory of the deceased Reverend priest who did such a good work. The altar is consecrated, and decently decorated'.[47] The patron in question was one Antonio Gatto, who embellished the renovated chancel with two bronze statues of Saint Paul (c. 1590–92), by Agostino Rubini, and of Anthony Abbot (c. 1586–90), a work by Alessandro Vittoria, as well as the high altarpiece *The Conversion of Saint Paul* by Palma il Giovane and two paintings

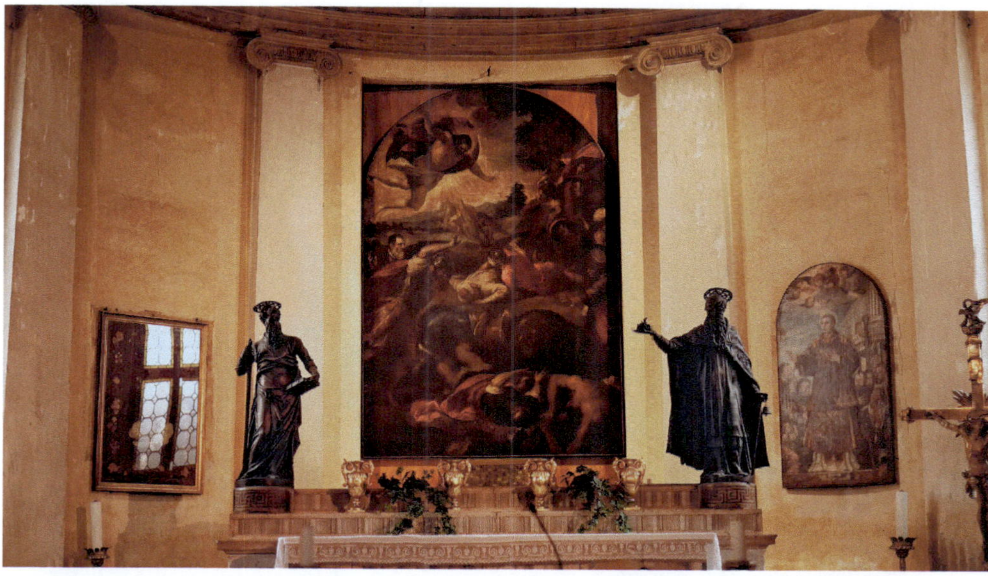

52. High Altar of San Polo with *The Conversion of Saint Paul* by Palma il Giovane and the statues of Saints Paul (left) by Agostino Rubini and Anthony Abbot (right) by Alessandro Vittoria, Venice (Photo: Sebastiano Giannesini/with permission of the Patriarchal Curia of Venice)

of the temptation and liberation of Saint Anthony (c. 1591), as well as Gatto's own funerary monument (Fig. 52).[48] Likewise, at the nearby church of San Giacomo dall'Orio where the parish priest Giovanni Maria da Ponte also embarked on an ambitious programme of patronage, Priuli praised the baptistery chapel, which had been paid for by Da Ponte, as being 'very well decorated and maintained' (Fig. 53).[49] So too had the earlier Apostolic Visit approved of this chapel, and although this delegation rarely commented on paintings, they also lauded Palma's canvases of Old and New Testament episodes for the sacristy, which were commissioned by Da Ponte as well.[50] In an echo of Priuli's pointed praise for the beneficence of Gatto, when Patriarch Zane inspected San Giacomo dall'Orio in 1604 he deemed the baptistery as 'nobly built of marble' and 'very well kept', providing him with the occasion to commend for his piety and diligence the priest under whose aegis it had been built.[51] These visitations often ordered that baptisteries should be removed from sites where their dignity was compromised by the vicinity of other altars or the pulpit, and ideally they wanted the font to be freestanding and situated in distinct chapels that were enclosed by gates. They certainly did not approve of the earlier altar-font typology that was widely diffused in Venice during the Cinquecento. These objects, a phenomenon that appears to have been uniquely Venetian, resembled normal altars but had stone fonts beneath the moveable wooden *mensa*.[52] They were judged to be incompatible with Tridentine norms by the Apostolic Visitation, and from the reaction of

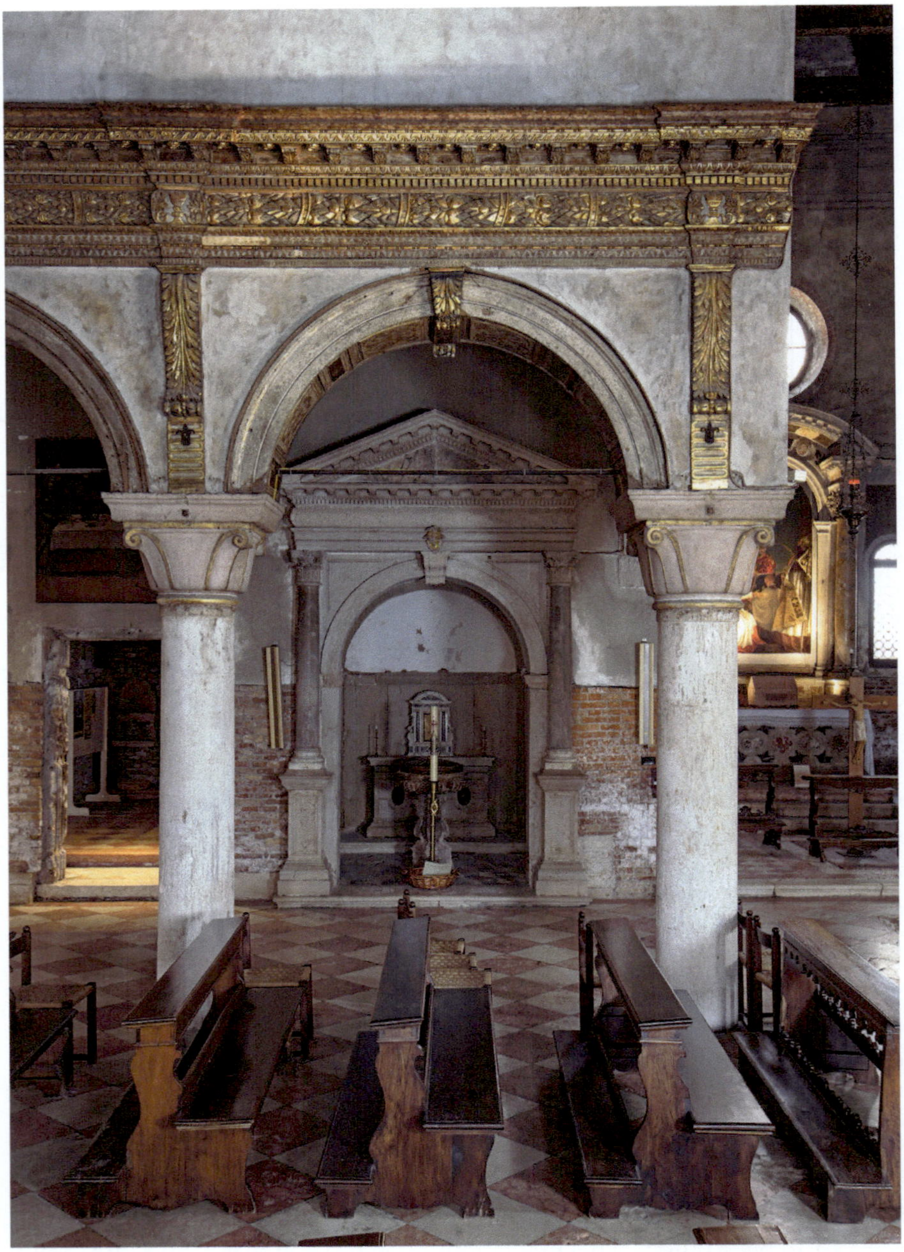

53. Baptistery of San Giacomo dall'Orio, Venice (Photo: Francesco Turio Bohm)

three different visitors to the San Giacomo dall'Orio baptistery it is clear that this chapel was much closer to what they had in mind. Not only was the font of the correct form, but the chapel would have been a far more lavish affair in the sixteenth century than it is today. Sansovino commented upon its rich gilding and stucco work, which was later lost, and the space was also furnished with a painting, the *Baptism of Christ*, attributed to Palma il Giovane.[53] What

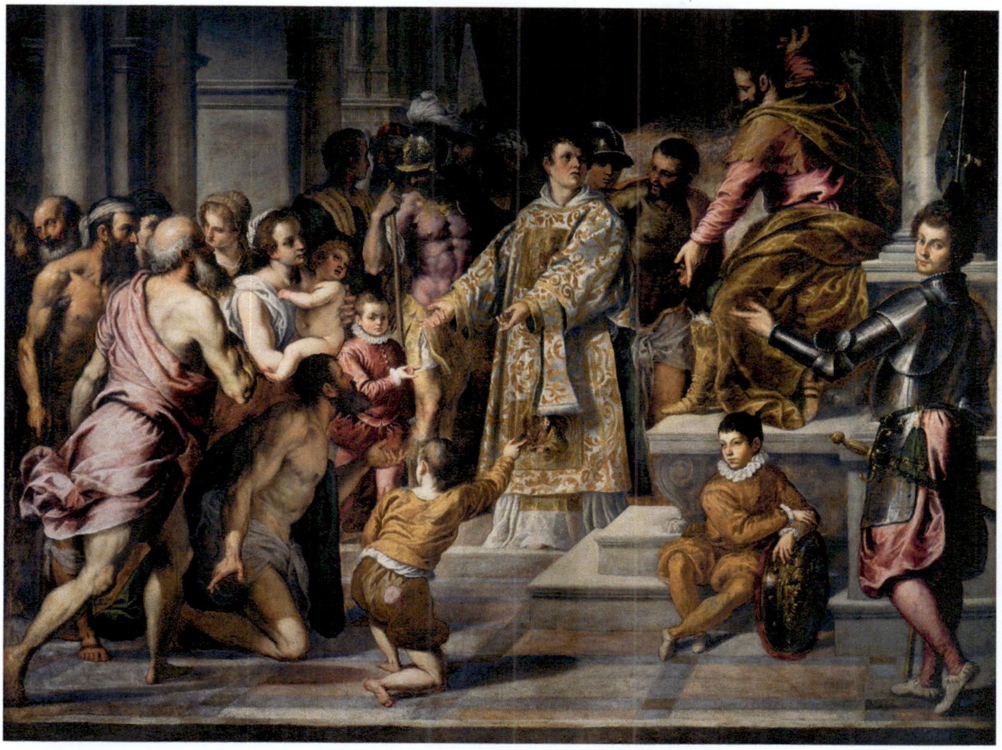

54. Palma il Giovane, *Saint Lawrence Presenting the True Riches of the Church to the Emperor*, c. 1582, oil on canvas, San Giacomo dall'Orio, Venice (Photo: Cameraphoto)

had been witnessed by the visitation at San Giacomo in October of 1592 may have been remembered when the parish of San Maurizio was inspected on 18 May 1593. Here, it was ordered that the baptistery was to be embellished with 'paintings of gold', as well as the standard canvas of John the Baptist.[54]

Just as Priuli had a penchant for recently completed renovation projects, so too did he appear to appreciate the works of contemporary artists such as Palma il Giovane, and ones who had recently deceased, such as Veronese (d. 1588). Possibly influenced by the judgment of the Apostolic Visit regarding the old sacristy paintings by Palma, at the same church of San Giacomo it was noted approvingly that the chapel of Saint Lawrence was very well decorated. This space was arrayed with two lateral paintings on either side of the chapel: *Saint Lawrence Presenting the True Riches of the Church to the Emperor* and *The Martyrdom of Saint Lawrence* (c. 1582) by Palma (Figs. 54 and 55). The high altarpiece was the work of Veronese, and depicted Saints Lawrence, Jerome, and Prospero (c. 1573–81). Here Priuli appreciated that the space had been 'well decorated' thanks to the beneficence of the Malipiero family, and when Zane visited in 1604 he described the chapel 'as decorated with many beautiful and devout paintings'.[55] Not only did Priuli also laud the redecoration of the San Polo chancel, which at the time featured three paintings by Palma, but his successor

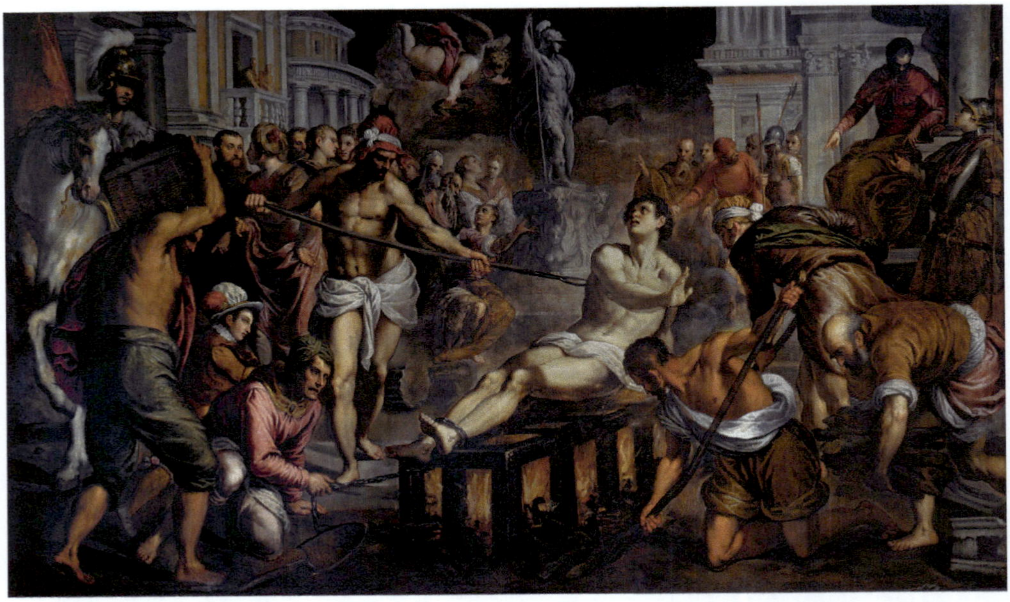

55. Palma il Giovane, *The Martyrdom of Saint Lawrence*, c. 1582, oil on canvas, San Giacomo dall'Orio, Venice (Photo: Cameraphoto)

Zane deemed Palma's canvases for the high altar of San Bartolomeo to be 'very beautiful and devout', which was one of his stock phrases for images that he deemed to be of particular note. Exactly the same wording had been used by Zane at San Giacomo dall'Orio for paintings by Palma, and we have seen that the creation of the new high altarpiece at San Bartolomeo had been directly ordered by Priuli, which may have been a further reason why Zane was keen to praise the new paintings.[56] The critical reception of Palma in more recent times has been mixed, but that his works were complimented by successive visitations demonstrates that he was perceived as creating images that corresponded to the contemporary climate for devotional art in Venice during the late sixteenth and early seventeenth centuries.[57] Palma was one of the leading artists in Venice by the time of the visit of Priuli, and on more than one occasion his shop was tasked with completing the new paintings and altarpieces ordered and encouraged by the ecclesiastical authorities.[58]

In contrast to Veronese's troubles with the Inquisition, on at least three occasions Priuli praised the spaces where the painter's works were almost certainly on display. One example is the artist's aforementioned altarpiece in the chapel of Saint Lawrence at San Giacomo; a second is *The Apparition of the Virgin Mary to Saint Luke* (Fig. 56) still in location at the church of San Luca; and a third is the lateral painting of *The Falling of the Manna* at Santi Apostoli that was completed by Veronese's heirs. At San Luca, Priuli deemed the high altar and chapel to have been 'built with great splendour', and that the Scuola del Sacramento who shared rights to the space with the parish chapter had with

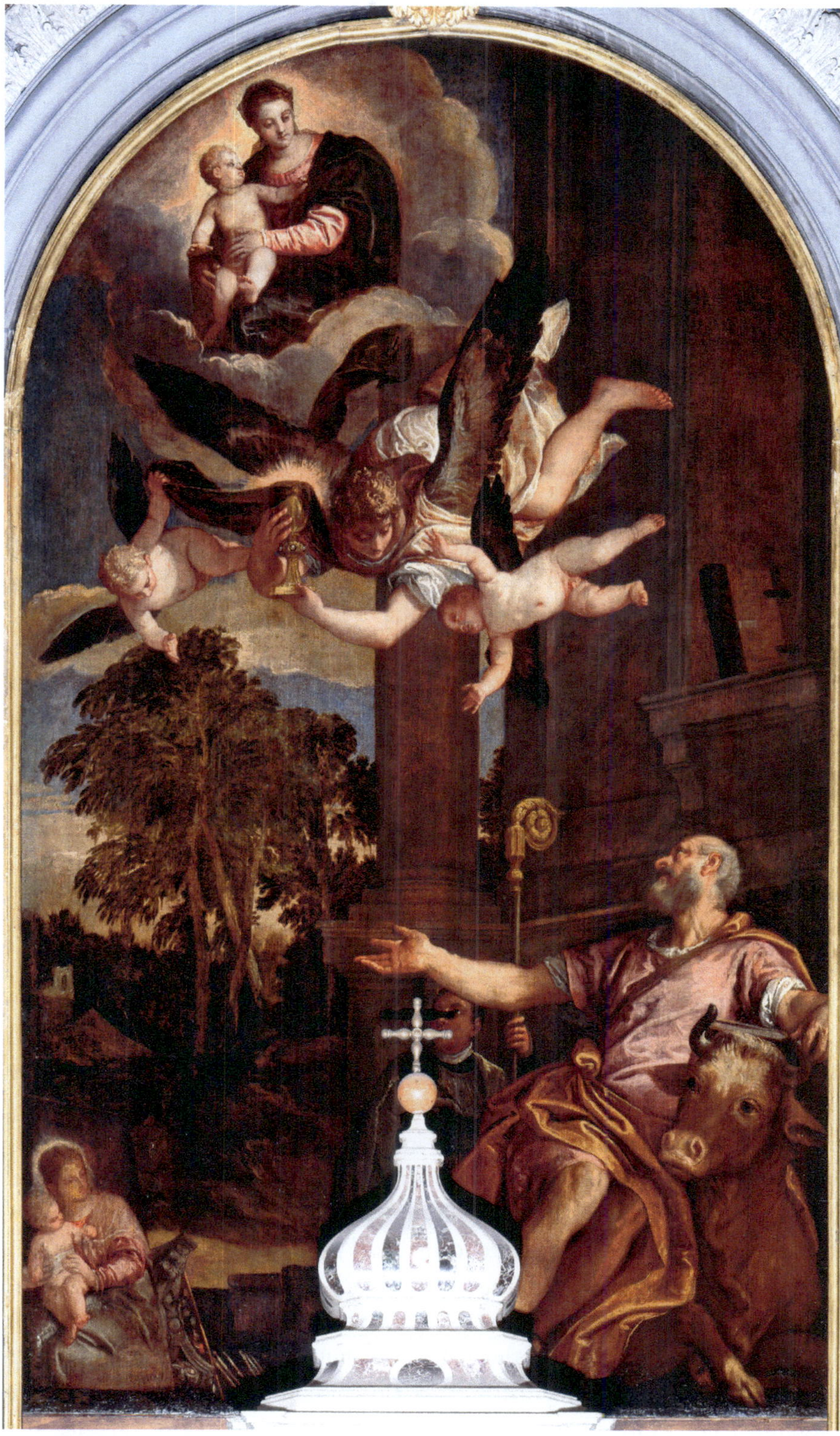

56. Veronese, *The Apparition of the Virgin Mary to Saint Luke*, c. 1581, oil on canvas, San Luca, Venice. (Photo: Cameraphoto)

'great piety decorated said altar, and chapel very nobly'.[59] The space had been renewed by the confraternity in 1581, and Veronese's altarpiece has been dated to the same year.[60] At the church of Santi Apostoli Priuli praised the high altar chapel as being 'nobly decorated'.[61] When Zane visited in 1604 he concurred with this judgment, the records describing the chapel as being 'beautiful, and everywhere decorated with attractive and devout paintings'.[62] The painting by the Veronese family is still displayed on the right wall of the chapel, and it is accompanied by a second lateral painting, *The Last Supper* by Cesare da Conegliano, dated to 1583.[63] The precise dating of *The Falling of the Manna* is unknown, and it was first mentioned in Giovanni Stringa's 1604 additions to Francesco Sansovino's earlier guidebook of 1581. Yet it may well have already been in place by November 1592 on the occasion of Priuli's visit since Veronese died in 1588 and the patriarch explicitly referred to the chapel being decorated. Just as the Apostolic Visit had approved of the old sacristy cycle in San Giacomo dall'Orio where episodes from the Old and New Testaments were arranged so that connections between the two could be made by the viewer, here at Santi Apostoli the manner in which a scene of Christ's final supper was arranged opposite the episode from Exodus when the Israelites were nourished by the heavenly food may have been particularly appealing to the patriarch. Such an arrangement was clearly didactic, seeking to stress the fulfilment of the Old Testament in the New, and with its obvious eucharistic emphasis it was in harmony with the use of the space by the confraternity of the Blessed Sacrament and the presence of the tabernacle on the high altar of the church.[64]

Other paintings that Priuli positively commented upon during the course of his visits can be identified as Cima da Conegliano's (1459/60–1517/18) marvellous *Incredulity of Saint Thomas* of 1504–5 for the oratory of the Scuola dei Mureri (Masons) at San Samuele (now in the Gallerie dell'Accademia, Fig. 57)[65] and the high altarpiece of the church of San Barnaba, attributed to Dario Varotari (1539–96).[66] Seated upon a raised marble plinth, in this painting the titular saint of the church is shown garbed in his bishop's attire, raising one hand in benediction as he looks directly out to the viewer, accompanied by angels and a crowd of saints below that include Peter and Claire. Stringa noted that the high altar had recently been rebuilt in the 'modern manner', and Priuli deemed it as being 'decorated with all the necessary things', remarking on the 'very honourable altarpiece' that adorned it.[67] In a number of cases Priuli also commented positively on paintings about which we know little. For example, at the altar of the cross at San Nicolò dei Mendicoli and the high altar of San Silvestro the patriarch praised the altarpieces, but their subject and authorship were only described for the first time by Boschini in 1664 as the *Finding of the Cross by Saint Helena* by Giovanni Battista Zelotti (c. 1526–78) and the *Apotheosis of Saint Sylvester, with the Virgin Mary and God the Father* by

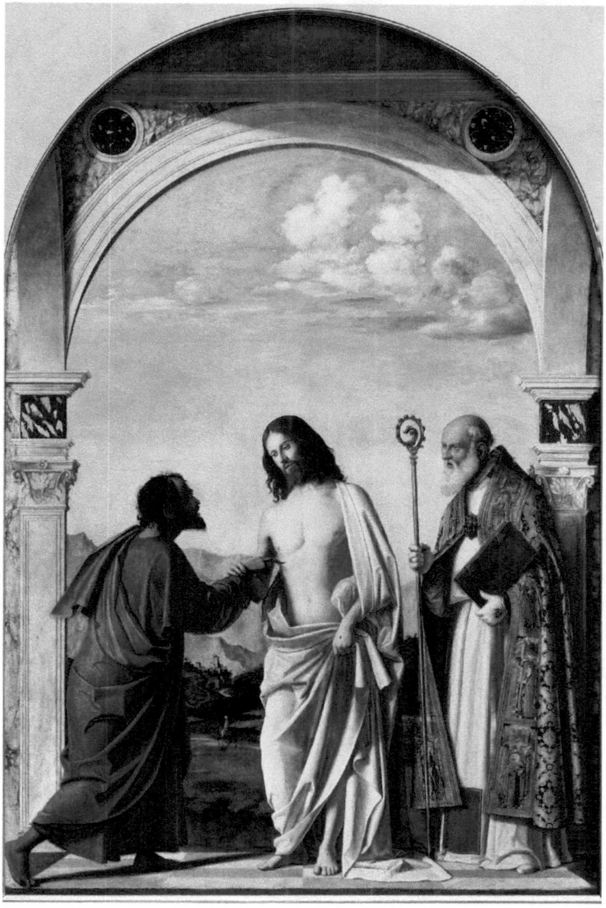

57. Cima da Conegliano, *The Incredulity of Saint Thomas with Saint Magnus of Oderzo*, c. 1504–5, tempera and oil on panel, Gallerie dell'Accademia, Venice (Photo: Cameraphoto)

Giovanni Battista Lorenzetti (c. 1588–1668).[68] Lorenzetti was only a few years old by the time Priuli was making his visits, meaning either that Boschini's attribution was incorrect or that a different painting arrayed the altar at San Silvestro when Priuli visited. Zelotti, on the other hand, died in 1578, so it is plausible that the patriarch viewed the same altarpiece listed first by Boschini that is now on display in the nearby church of Angelo Raffaelle.[69]

Most tellingly, at the famously poor parish of San Nicolò dei Mendicoli it was described how the patriarch 'had taken great pleasure in seeing all of the church gilded and decorated with beautiful paintings and surrounded by walnut benches. He exhorted the populace, and particularly the heads [*gastaldi*] of said confraternities, to reduce the work to perfection in conformity with the design that has been begun'.[70] The document further noted that the confraternities active in the church had 'spent a great amount of money decorating it'. The patriarch was evidently delighted that the church had been decorated thanks to the beneficence of the confraternities, since he was keen to

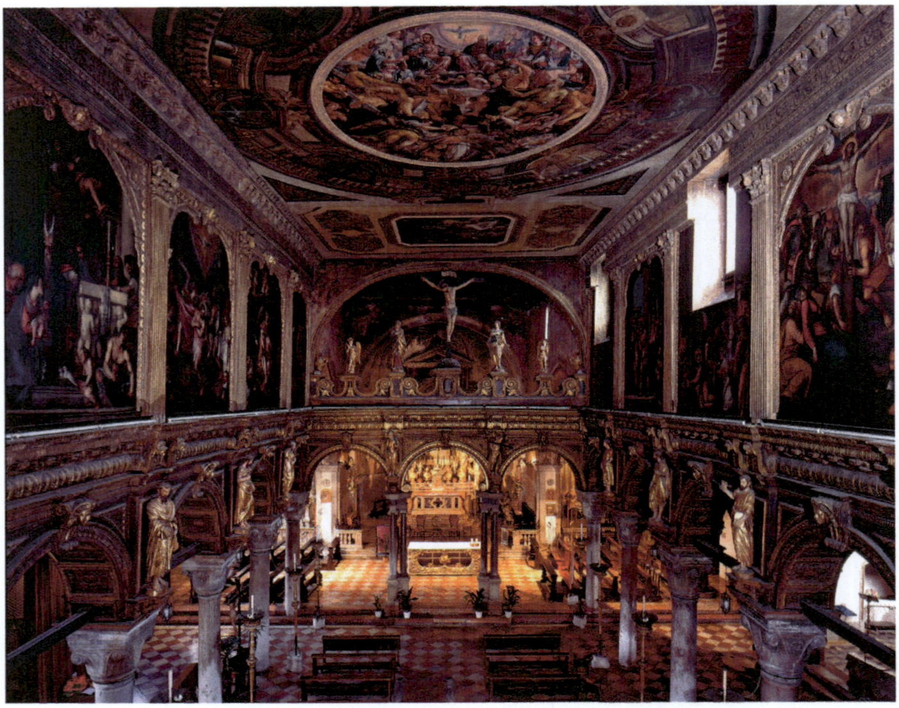

58. Interior of San Nicolò dei Mendicoli, Venice (Photo: Cameraphoto)

encourage this kind of parish-based collective patronage.[71] The 'beautiful paintings' that he liked so much were likely to have been those painted by Veronese's nephew, Alvise dal Friso, also known as Luigi Benfatto (1544–1609): *The Adoration of the Shepherds*, *The Adoration of the Magi*, *The Presentation of Christ in the Temple*, *Christ Supported by an Angel in Gethsemane*, and *The Kiss of Judas*.[72] These works were part of the narrative cycle of canvases that illustrated the life, passion, and resurrection of Christ ranged around the upper nave of San Nicolò dei Mendicoli (Fig. 58). Dal Friso's paintings were on the left side of the nave, and they were later accompanied by further paintings on the opposite side: *Christ Presented to Herod* (artist unknown); three works attributed to Antonio Vassilacchi (otherwise known as Aliense, 1556–1629), *The Flagellation*, *Christ and Veronica on the Road to Calvary*, and *The Crucifixion*; as well as a *Deposition* (artist unknown) and Palma's *Resurrection*. The central ceiling painting in the nave is *The Apotheosis of Saint Nicholas*, by Francesco Montemezzano (1555–c. 1600), accompanied by two episodes from the life of the saint (Nicholas ordering the felling of a tree inhabited by demons, Nicholas banishing the storm) on either side of it, works attributed to Leonardo Corona (1552–96) and believed to have been completed by 1591.[73] Thomas Worthen opined that most of this cycle was concluded by the time of Patriarch Zane's visit in 1604, but suggested that it had yet to have been begun by the time of Priuli's inspection.[74] Stefania Mason dated Dal Friso's works to the first years of the 1590s, and the rest of the cycle to the beginning of the seventeenth century, assigning a late date of c. 1610 to Palma's *Resurrection*.[75] Following the dating of Mason, Priuli's reference to '*quadri di pittura*' would strongly suggest that at least some of the paintings were in place at this point, whilst his exhortation to complete the project points to the fact that the rest of the nave decoration was indeed incomplete.[76] A document published by Valentina Sapienza demonstrates that some of the paintings were definitely in situ by November 1589, so Priuli would have seen them when he visited the site.[77] His positive appraisal of the ongoing works at San Nicolò was matched by Patriarch Zane, and by Patriarch Vendramin in 1612 too. Zane pronounced that the church was decorated with 'devout and attractive paintings', whilst Vendramin was more precise, noting the presence of the 'beautiful paintings' that were situated below the ceiling and above it.[78] Priuli's reference to 'seeing all of the church gilded' most probably referred to the *soazoni*, or richly gilded woodwork that formed a kind of entablature that encased the nave arches and crossing, and was further decorated with painted statues of the apostles.[79] Worthen described how these structures had the advantage of imbuing a church with an opulent, rich appearance for a relatively low cost, and they enjoyed a brief vogue in Venice from the 1560s to 1610. It was the Scuole del Sacramento that paid for the *soazoni* in every church for which the documentation survives, and they became popular precisely when the Catholic Reformation was at its most intense in the city. This caused Worthen to persuasively argue that this parochial decoration was far more characteristic of Tridentine Venice than the better-known Palladian Basilica of San Giorgio. He likened their emergence to the earlier patriarchate of Giovanni Trevisan, being 'both reformist and Venetian, and wholly independent of Rome'.[80] Be that as it may, notwithstanding his greater papal sympathies so too were these kinds of decorative programmes endorsed by Priuli, and by later ecclesiastics in Venice.

A REFORM IN QUANTITY

Priuli's encouragement for freshly completed decorative programmes brings us to a further aspect of his visits: in terms of visual decorations, more was certainly better than less, and new was certainly preferable to old. Before continuing, then, it is worth pausing for a moment to consider how this first tendency was diametrically opposed to the attitudes of Protestant Reformers like John Calvin in Geneva or Ulrich Zwingli in Switzerland. All of the sacred images and ritual objects in the churches of Zurich were systematically removed and destroyed in the summer of 1524. After two weeks nothing remained. The city had been cleansed of popish superstitions and idolatry, and as such the Reformation could flourish.[81] Like Zwingli, for Calvin sacred images constituted an oppression. They should be eliminated not just because their existence was in contradiction to the second commandment, but because they inevitably led to idolatry, presenting an insurmountable obstacle to the laity accessing the true word of God.[82] Andreas Karlstadt similarly came to believe that images were an abomination, stating that 'pictures are loathsome. It follows that we also become loathsome when we love them.'[83] But for post-Tridentine Catholics, such as the laypeople belonging to the confraternities of the eucharist in Venice, nothing could have been further from the truth, and their approach to the visual was much closer to the later declaration at the Council of Trent that 'great profit is derived from all sacred images'. They tended to feel great affection for the kinds of pictures abhorred by Calvin, Zwingli, and Karlstadt: they paid for them, they lit candles and prayed before them, and they were surrounded by devotional imagery on a daily basis, not just when they were at church, but in their homes and on the streets of Venice too.[84] Priuli's drive to encourage the liberal use of images in churches was matched by similar exhortations for domestic spaces. Silvio Antoniano, whom we met in the previous chapter, powerfully endorsed the use of sacred images in homes in a number of chapters of his *Tre libri dell'educazone christiana dei figliuoli*, published in Verona in 1584. He exhorted fathers to retain 'many holy pictures in their homes' not only because they moved the viewer to devotion, but because this way children could learn how to honour sacred images appropriately.[85]

Just as it has been persuasively argued that the progress of the Swiss Reformation can be effectively revealed by following the trail of iconoclastic destruction that it left in its wake, so too might the progress of the Catholic Reformation in Venice be gauged in opposite terms by looking at just how many new devotional works of art were created and commissioned.[86] The proponent of this first point, Carlos Eire, asserted that 'few other aspects of the Reformation lend themselves as well for studying the way in which theology inspires action, as this war on idolatry'.[87] Margaret Aston's study of iconoclasm in England similarly underlined the paramount importance of how the destruction of sacred images was a key element in a spiritual revolution designed to promote the primacy of the word, as part of what one scholar called a 'verbal victory over the visual'.[88] This not only transformed ritual and worship, but was also a sensory revolution, since the losses of bells and organs affected the ears, just as image removal affected the eyes. Instead of destroying images, Catholics commissioned more of them, and rather than laying their overarching emphasis on the word, their rituals harnessed multiple senses, and a special emphasis was placed on sight and the role of imagery in contemplating the divine.[89] This is not to suggest a simple binary of attack and counter-attack, or to suggest that Catholics were merely responding to Protestant objections by going out of their way to do the opposite, even if it might sometimes seem that way. For one thing, documents like the visitations examined here almost never mention the Reformation or Protestant 'heresies'. Priuli's aim in encouraging the use of images can be attributed to the fact that he thought that they helped rather than hindered worship, contributing to the splendour of the church interior and, by extension, demonstrating the devotion of the parish laity and clergy who had commissioned them. For a Swiss Protestant a beautiful church was one cleansed of images, reliquaries, altars, or holy water fonts so that one could focus on the word of God.[90] For a Catholic like Priuli, all of these elements were to be encouraged. Rather than a reform achieved by eliminating images as done by the Northern Reformers or being overly zealous in ordering the removal or editing of supposedly problematic ones as Pope Clement had done, the visual reforms that Priuli encouraged constituted a move towards greater quantity and coverage. This became a hallmark of the decoration of many churches at the end of the century in Venice. At the Gesuati, Stringa commented positively on the fact that 'there are other large canvases around the church, in such a way that there is not a place, or space that can be seen empty, and almost all of them have been painted by excellent masters'.[91] He made a similar observation at San Giovanni Elemosinario, extolling the 'marvellous adornment' of the interior with such a quantity of beautiful paintings, large and small, painted by diverse artists of the day, that no space was left bereft of decoration.[92] Last, at San Polo, Stringa described approvingly how 'there are many other pictures throughout this church that occupy all its empty spaces in such a way that there is not a place that is not covered by them'.[93]

A kind of horror vacui can also be sensed in Priuli's approach to ecclesiastical decoration. At the church of San Nicolò dei Mendicoli, the patriarch lauded the plans for the cycle of paintings that decorated the interior in places that might otherwise have remained bare, in this case at the height of the nave aisles. At San Giuliano (San Zulian), a cycle of paintings depicting the passion of Christ were also arranged around the heights of the walls of the nave, above the altars, and they were completed in the late sixteenth century too, around the same time as that of San Nicolò (Fig. 59).[94] Even though the interior of this church now benefits from artificial illumination, said paintings are barely visible in the dark surroundings. Yet when he visited the site in 1593, Priuli deemed the church to be 'honourably decorated', suggesting that coverage, rather than necessarily visibility, was an important element in his aesthetic criteria.[95] Rather than focusing on the individual details of images, Priuli was interested in the overall impact of a richly decorated church interior. On a number of other occasions he ordered paintings to be commissioned to fill vacant spaces and altarpieces to be hung in those altars that were without one.[96] If found damaged, altar decorations were to be repaired, or better accommodated if necessary.[97] At Sant'Eufemia, Priuli deemed the high altar

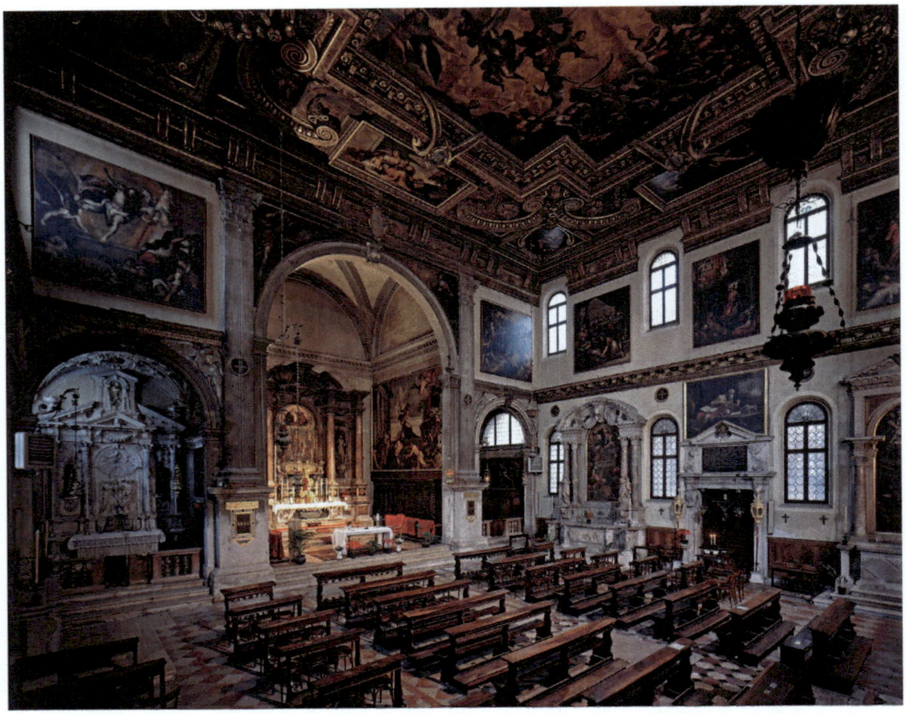

59. Interior of San Giuliano, Venice (Photo: Cameraphoto)

chapel of the Blessed Sacrament to be pleasing, noting the presence of multiple paintings there (Fig. 60).[98] Boschini was the first to list the subject matter of the works many years later as an Ascension of the Virgin Mary with Saints, accompanied by the two lateral canvases of the Last Supper and the Falling of the Manna, which he attributed to the heirs of Veronese (usually Alvise dal Friso). These may have been the same paintings viewed by Priuli.[99] At Santa Marina, Priuli decided that the body of the church could be reduced to perfection by having canvases arranged in the areas 'that are currently empty',[100] and at Santa Trinità (Santa Tèrnita), where the ceiling had begun to be painted and the walls were being decorated with canvases, he exhorted the parish priest to encourage the *contrada* and the confraternity of the Blessed Sacrament to continue the work of decorating the church with paintings, so that it 'appears more beautiful'.[101] Moreover, at San Simeone e Guida (San Simeone Piccolo) the chapel of the Blessed Sacrament was to be whitewashed, then decorated with paintings,[102] as was the chapel of Saint Joseph at Santa Maria Formosa.[103] At San Benedetto, Priuli instructed the confraternity of the Blessed Sacrament to paint the walls of their chapel, or to provide some kind of wooden cladding, so that it was sufficiently decorated,[104] and at Santa Margherita the Scuola del Sacramento were ordered to commission a new painting for their chapel.[105] On one occasion Priuli even gave detailed instructions regarding the iconography of a new altarpiece. This happened at San Simeone Profeta (San Simeone Grande) where he specified that this new work

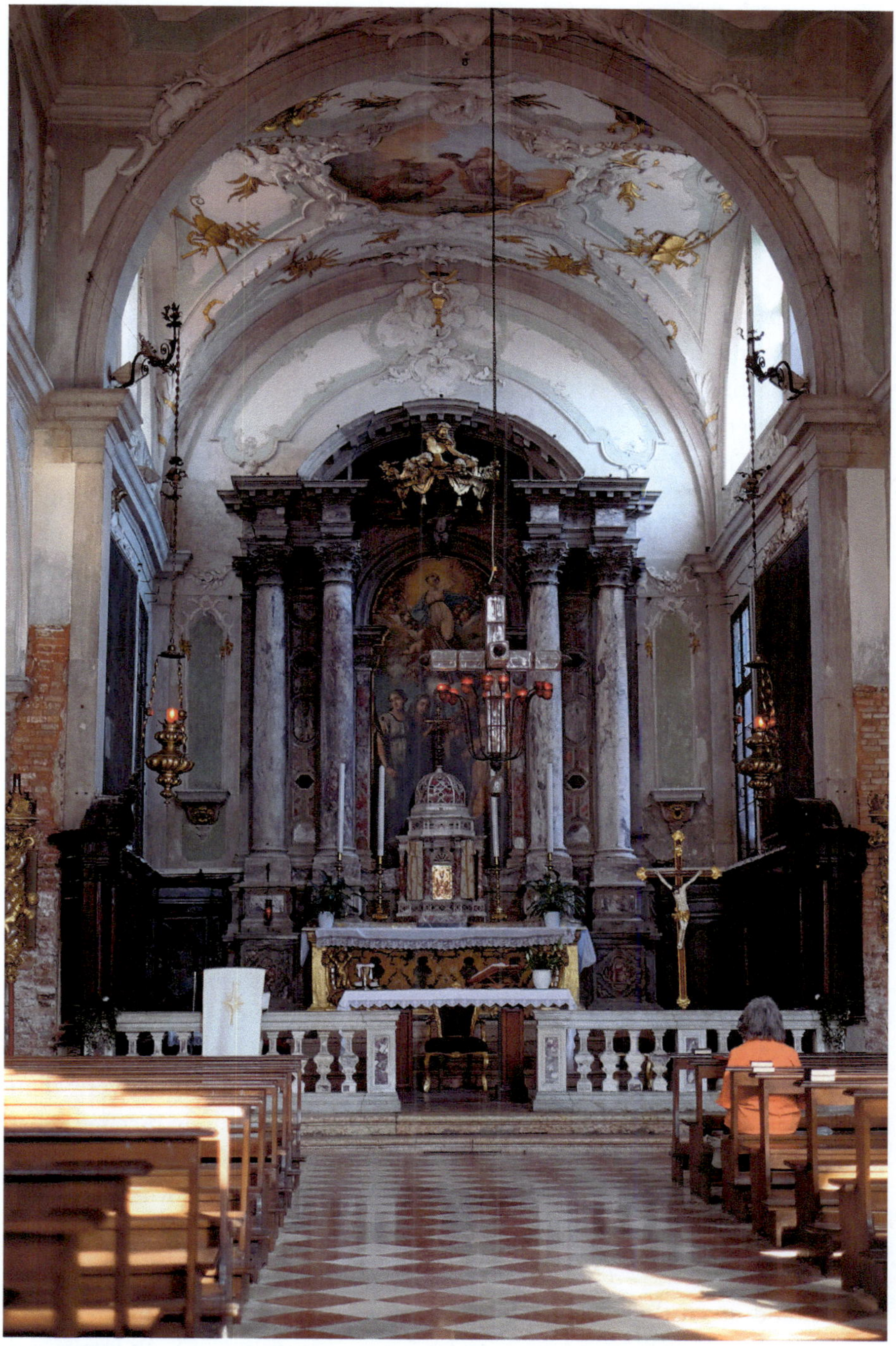

60. High altar of Sant'Eufemia, Giudecca (Photo: Sebastiano Giannesini/with permission of the Patriarchal Curia of Venice)

was to be placed between the two windows where the relics of Saint Simon were to be found at the high altar, and that it was to depict the Presentation of the Madonna in the Temple, with a figure of the titular saint of the parish to be included in the scene. In the summary of the orders, Priuli dictated that the painting should instead represent a '*purification*' – the subject of the eventual replacement altarpiece of c. 1610–11 that was painted by none other than Palma il Giovane.[106] On one occasion, however, Priuli found the quantity of images decorating an altar distracting. At San Luca the patriarch disapproved of the number of images of the Virgin Mary above the eponymous altar, since one was considered adequate.[107] He also showed limited patience for the crowding of altars with votives offered by the laity. Priuli often recommended that these should be removed and placed on the walls nearby or, in poorer parishes, melted down and then recycled to create the necessary liturgical items for the celebration of the mass.[108]

In 1604 Stringa wrote in his description of the church of San Polo that 'in all Christendom there are no churches more ornate and embellished than those of Venice'.[109] The richly embellished ducal chapel of San Marco acted as an exemplar for the kind of incrustations of decoration that were to be found in Venetian churches, and this inclination became ever more widespread in the late Cinquecento.[110] Stefania Mason argued that the reaction to the earlier Apostolic Visit in Venice led to the city 'reasserting the sincerity and strength of her faith, as demonstrated by the piety of her people and the religiosity of her ruling class'.[111] In line with this observation is the fact that the final two decades of the century saw numerous parishes embark on extensive programmes of restoration or rebuilding, as well as the commissioning of extensive cycles of paintings. In Stringa's introduction to his updated version of Sansovino's guide, it was described how in the twenty-three years since the publication first appeared, more than a third of Venice's sacred and secular sites had been renovated.[112] Priuli clearly approved of these kinds of projects – after all, he was instrumental to the costly renovations at San Pietro di Castello – and his instructions helped to accelerate them. Since all reformers have an ideal in mind, the evidence would thus suggest that his prerogative was for the buildings of his diocese to be ever more richly decorated, and that he divested this responsibility to the parish confraternities and clergy who were then responsible for realising his recommendations. Priuli very rarely dictated what would be the most suitable subject matter for altarpieces or paintings, and he certainly never recommended specific artists,[113] but he did very occasionally request that plans for the rebuilding of high altars be submitted for his approval before works began.[114] Thus, in terms of his approach towards decoration and images, and given the fact that he was not a particularly rigid censor of the latter, Priuli's visitations can be said to have been generative in both intent and results. This contrasts to the actions of later patriarchs, particularly those of the nineteenth century, such as Giovanni Ladislao Pyrker (1772–1847, r. 1820–27) and Jacopo Monico (1778–1851, r. 1827–51), who tended to be far more iconoclastic, the latter ordering the removal of 'superfluous ornaments, and other things that are more an embarrassment than an embellishment'.[115]

Despite describing himself as having a 'great predilection for masterpieces of art', Pyrker disliked those more 'popular' image cults that involved the dressing of devotional statues of the Madonna and saints with precious clothes and jewels, or the crowding of altars with images, and he issued numerous decrees to eliminate these potentially superstitious practices during his pastoral visits of 1821.[116] These actions, together with his attempts to move towards a greater seriousness in the celebration of the divine cult, including placing limitations on music and the sounding of bells, even caused him to be compared to Martin Luther in a series of popular Venetian poems.[117]

THE EUCHARIST

Prior to the visits of Priuli, the tendency to encourage the visual aggrandisement of the eucharist through the creation of elaborate tabernacles, where the consecrated host was reserved, can be seen in the Apostolic Visitation records, and it had been famously championed by Archbishop Carlo Borromeo in his own diocese of Milan. Borromeo was partly inspired by important precedents in the Veneto, yet even compared to these illustrious examples, Priuli stands out for the great detail of his instructions concerning the eucharist. Devotion to this sacrament was already popular in Venice, given the pre-existing number of confraternities of the Blessed Sacrament, and their richly decorated chapels, the presence of which distinguished the city from other Italian centres, like Rome, for example.[118] Even if the elaborate ornamentation of these confraternal spaces was unusual, honouring the site of the eucharist and spending significant sums in order to achieve this aim was not. Already in the twelfth century, Abbot Suger of Saint Denis in Paris expressed his belief that the most important materials should be reserved for this sacrament, writing that 'every costlier or costliest thing should serve, first and foremost, for the administration of the Holy Eucharist'.[119] Suger's conviction is well illustrated by the beautiful sardonyx communion chalice originally studded with rubies and sapphires that he commissioned for Saint Denis, now in the National Gallery of Washington. The object is a visual witness to his belief that the 'the dull mind rises to truth through that which is material'.[120] We can well imagine Priuli agreeing with Suger, as might the many Venetians who belonged to confraternities of the Blessed Sacrament. Although these confraternities were not solely a Venetian phenomenon, there were more of them in the city than in other places, and they got going there earlier than in many other parts of Italy.[121] For example, a confraternity dedicated to ensuring that the eucharist was given appropriate reverence existed in Venice as early as 1385 at the church attached to the convent of Corpus Domini.[122] Be that as it may, the proliferation of the Scuole del Sacramento, not just in Venice but in Italy more broadly, was essentially a sixteenth-century phenomenon, with sixty-six such confraternities founded in

Venice during the century.[123] Although the movement predated the Reformation by some years, it was further stimulated by Reformation debates concerning the eucharist; the activities of Catholic Reformers like the co-founder of the Theatines, Saint Gaetano da Thiene (1480–1547), who was born in Vicenza, or Bishop Gian Matteo Giberti in Verona; and the expansion of devotional practices like the *Quarant'ore* (continuous prayer of forty hours' duration before the exposed eucharist.)[124] In 1539 Pope Paul III gave eucharistic confraternities papal approval, whilst Trent's promulgations on this sacrament, and the attention it was paid by successive visitations, were all factors that provided an impetus for confraternities to make their devotional spaces as visually impressive as possible.

Confraternities such as those dedicated to the Blessed Sacrament in Venice played a vital role in establishing local religious identity at a time when their existence coincided with the more universal aims of the post-Tridentine Church. Deborah Walberg has pointed to the importance of Giulio Strozzi's 1624 poem *La Venezia edificata,* a text that attributed Venice's profound piety to devotion to the Virgin Mary (something it shared with many other places), but also to the frequent celebration of the eucharist, and the rich altars at which the host was honoured.[125] Thus, Priuli's efforts in this area can be understood as both encouraging deeply felt local spiritual practices as well as responding to norms associated with the Catholic Reformation more broadly that were then bolstered by the Apostolic Visit.[126] Due to this, his proposed changes met with a fertile reception from the parish confraternities that had rights over the majority of the chapels where the tabernacles containing the eucharist were displayed. By 1581 Francesco Sansovino stated that every single parish in Venice had a Scuola del Santissimo Sacramento, and they proved to be indefatigable patrons of the arts.[127] They were intent on decorating not just the chapels under their care, but in some cases also the area around their *banco*, or desk and bench where they conducted their meetings.[128] The extent of their patronage caused Maurice Cope to observe that if one adhered to the characterisation of Venice as a secular state wary of Tridentine reform, then the city should have logically been one of the last, not the first places to construct and decorate chapels dedicated to the Blessed Sacrament.[129] Whilst it is true that evidence from Inquisition trials testifies that membership of the Scuole del Sacramento was associated with orthodoxy, it is also the case that Venetian devotion to the eucharist could be harnessed for more polemical aims, which is what happened during the 1606 Interdict when the Corpus Domini procession was staged in defiance of the pope.[130] The English ambassador, Sir Henry Wotton, observed that the feast was celebrated 'with the most sumptuous procession that ever had been seen here, wherein the very basins and ewers were valued in common judgment at 200,000 pounds sterling, besides many costly and curious pageants'.[131] If by way of such an event the Catholic piety of the city was to be impressed upon the spectator, it did not convince everyone. Appalled by one particularly polemical float, which showed the collapsing Church supported by the doge, Saint Dominic, and Saint Francis, a Jesuit spy, Giacomo Lambertengo, concluded that it was 'a miserable spectacle'.[132] In this case, the procession that honoured the eucharist – the sacrament that was so vigorously promoted in the post-Tridentine world – was instead deployed to assert the Serenissima's resistance to the jurisdictional overreach of the Counter-Reformation papacy.

Years prior to these events, in 1542, Bishop Giberti had been the first to insist that the tabernacle was to be placed on the high altar in the cathedral of Verona, part of the Venetian land empire.[133] Carlo Borromeo later did the same in the diocese of Milan, and recommended the practice in his influential *Instructiones fabricae*, with such prescriptions then formalised by Pope Gregory XIII in the 1584 *Rituale sacramentorum romano*.[134] Of local significance were also the visits of the Bishop of Treviso, Giorgio Corner (1524–78), who had attended the Council of Trent and began his diocesan visits swiftly after its conclusion. Corner dictated changes to the location of the eucharist, the visibility of the high altar (where the sacrament was now to be reserved), and the decorum of tabernacles that were to become standardised elsewhere towards the end of the century.[135] The Tridentine mass increased the amount of times that the host was elevated by the priest, a change in liturgical practice that meant the viewer came into repeated visual contact with the consecrated host.[136] Even when mass was not being celebrated, the fashion for ever larger and more imposing tabernacles would have reminded the spectator of the significance of the object that they contained. These tabernacles functioned both as a receptacle that contained the consecrated sacrament to be taken to the sick or housebound (one of the primary duties of the eucharistic Scuole) and as a focus for prayer and meditation. In Venice it was usual for the chapels of the Blessed Sacrament to be separate from the high altar, a local variant that was mostly respected by the 1581 Apostolic Visitation. Patriarch Trevisan explained that whilst in conventual churches the tabernacle was situated on the high altar – in accordance with the opinion of Borromeo – this was not the case in Venice's parishes, because they were gifted with the presence of the Scuole del Santissimo Sacramento and their 'beautiful, honourable, well-kept and reverent altars'.[137] Not only that, but Trevisan argued that these pious laypeople had 'adorned churches, as one can see, in all of the city, so that when one removes the sacrament from their altars made with great expense, one runs the risk of cooling the soul of these good, and devout persons, so that they would not then make those expenses, that they do out of reverence for the divine cult'.[138] Trevisan had pragmatic reasons for avoiding changes that might cause such pious projects to dwindle, but his worries would seem to have been unfounded. This is illuminated by the fact that Priuli ordered the transferral of the tabernacle into the high altar on nine occasions,[139] whereas the Apostolic Visitors only ordered this twice, at the parishes of Angelo Raffaelle and San Giovanni in Bragora.[140] The subsequent visitations of Zane demonstrate that Priuli's orders were quickly realised in five of the nine churches that he visited at the beginning of the Seicento, whilst two of these parishes were never inspected either by Zane or by his successor Patriarch Vendramin.[141] Only at one site, the church of Sant'Antonin, does it appear that the instructions of the visit were ignored, which is probably because they were lengthy, involving significant building works at the high altar, and because the visit wished for the space to be shared with the relics of Saint Sabba.[142] Priuli's exacting standards meant that he was more likely than the earlier inspection to judge the space in which the eucharist was consigned to be in some way inadequate. But if anything, his decisions seem to have caused the decorative programmes and building projects of these confraternities to have increased in scope and cost, rather than to diminish as Trevisan had feared.

Nothing appears to have given Priuli more pleasure in the course of his visits than a sumptuously decorated and well-maintained area for the Blessed Sacrament, one that was fitted out with an impressive tabernacle, ideally as large and richly ornamented as possible. The patriarch paid scrupulous attention to numerous details relating to the care of the eucharist, advising that the key used to open the tabernacle should be gilded and kept on a loop of silk, for example, or that the interior of said tabernacle should be carefully lined with silk. In doing so, he was paying obedient heed to the practical instructions of Borromeo, as well as the precepts of the Apostolic Visit.[143] Materials that either were in the immediate vicinity or may have come into contact with the communion wafer were to be of the highest quality the parish could reasonably afford, and chapels that were humid, small, with unimpressive tabernacles and scarce decoration were targeted with a wealth of proposals and instructions. San Bartolomeo illustrates this well, since the church was criticised for having a wooden tabernacle that was too small and lacking in any ornaments.[144] The Scuola del Sacramento were ordered to see to it that a large, honourable tabernacle of gilded wood, lined with white silk and placed on the high altar, was fashioned without delay.[145] The church was the parish of the German community in Venice, whose *fondaco*, or meeting house, was just a few steps away. The diffusion of Protestantism amongst the Germans in Venice has been well documented. There was nothing much out of the ordinary in Priuli's orders for the parish, but the various confraternities instigated his wishes swiftly and efficiently, perhaps to disassociate themselves from any rumours of heterodoxy, but maybe also because Mozanega, the patriarchal vicar and thus a man of significant power and influence, also held the title of perpetual vicar of San Bartolomeo di Rialto.[146] By the time that Stringa's observations on the church were published in 1604, the high altar was described as having 'a very beautiful and rich tabernacle of marble, decorated with little columns and other small canvases, and detailed stonework of many colours, with the four Evangelists in four niches, six angels, and a resurrected Christ at the top, all made out of bronze and in relief, of a height of half a *braccio*, something that gives a beautiful view to the spectator'.[147] The Scuola had gone above and beyond the patriarch's recommendations, and Stringa also commented on the general improvement to the state of the church in the year he visited, mainly because the high altar and all the other altars had been renewed and rebuilt in stone '*alla moderna*'. Of these, he judged the high altar to be particularly beautiful and of notable expense.[148] The tabernacle that replaced the one viewed by Priuli would have certainly met with the patriarch's firm approval, and it was singled out for praise by Zane, who described it as 'a very beautiful and honourable tabernacle' in the same year that Stringa's text was published.[149] Gilded wood, as a cheaper alternative to more expensive materials, was often recommended for new tabernacles, but Priuli seems to have preferred the use of the more costly and durable stone. At San Marcuola he praised the 'very noble' tabernacle of the high altar, noting that it was fashioned from stone, with columns of marble.[150] Priuli also lauded the chapel of the Blessed Sacrament at San Moisè, describing it as having been found in a most honourable state.[151] Although the patriarch made no mention of the materials of the tabernacle, we know from the Apostolic Visitation that it was a marble one.[152]

Even if Priuli complimented numerous chapels of the Blessed Sacrament, this did not mean that any of them escaped from at least a few nuggets of his plentiful advice. For example, at San Zulian, site of the magnificent sacrament chapel adorned with Girolamo Campagna's (1549/50–1625) marble bas-relief, *Dead Christ Supported by Angels* (Fig. 61), it was recorded that to his great satisfaction, the patriarch found the chapel 'nobly built and adorned, and the altar, and tabernacle, in which the Blessed Sacrament is retained, is with much honour decorated and maintained'.[153] Nevertheless, since the site of this tabernacle was not particularly capacious, it was deemed necessary to provide 'a smaller ciborium, with which [the sacrament] could ordinarily be reserved for greater commodity and decency'.[154] At San Gregorio, Priuli was pleased with both the 'most noble' tabernacle of the high altar as well as the ciborium. However, since the interior of the latter was damaged, it was to be reworked and inlaid with gilded silver so that no fragment of the host could enter in the crevices. It was also to be fitted with a lid to ensure that it could be securely closed.[155] Even though the tabernacle itself was 'very honourable', it was still deemed imperfect in some areas. This could only be remedied by procuring 'figures, that were to be placed around it' (presumably small statues or images), and by fitting it with a door that could be locked shut in a more secure manner. In addition, the tabernacle was to be fitted out with a baldachin cover above it of gilded leather (*corame*) that was larger than the present example; the

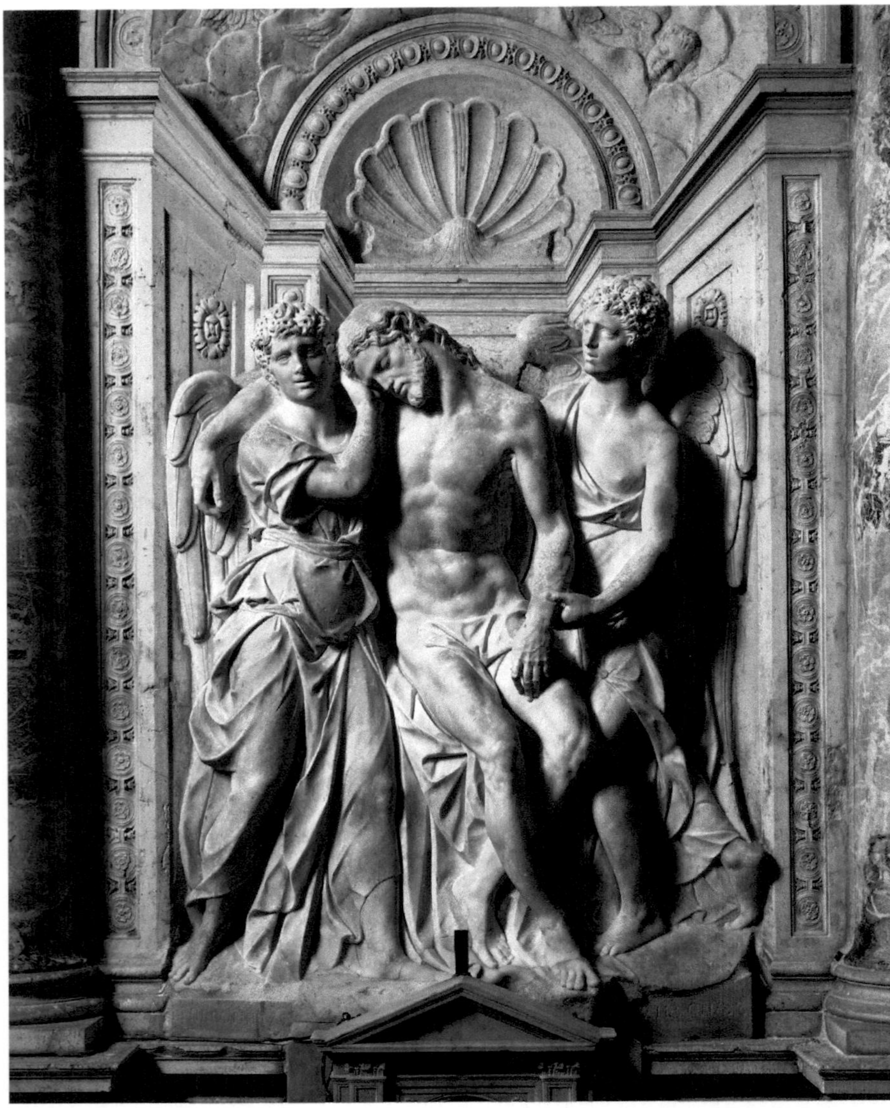

61. Girolamo Campagna, *Dead Christ Supported by Angels,* 1579, marble, Chapel of the Blessed Sacrament, San Giuliano, Venice (Photo: Cameraphoto)

altar mensa was to be protected with a tablecloth; and the small space (*armaruolo*) under the tabernacle was to be used only for objects pertinent to the use of the altar, and was to be kept under lock and key.[156] Priuli was particularly struck by the high altar chapel of San Luca, controlled by the Scuola del Santissimo Sacramento, as well as that of San Marziale, where 'everything was found to be in a laudable form', as were the decorations made in both the altar and the chapel.[157] At Santa Marina, everything at the Blessed Sacrament chapel was found to be in such an excellent state that the parish priest was complimented for his diligence in honouring the eucharist, as were the priest and

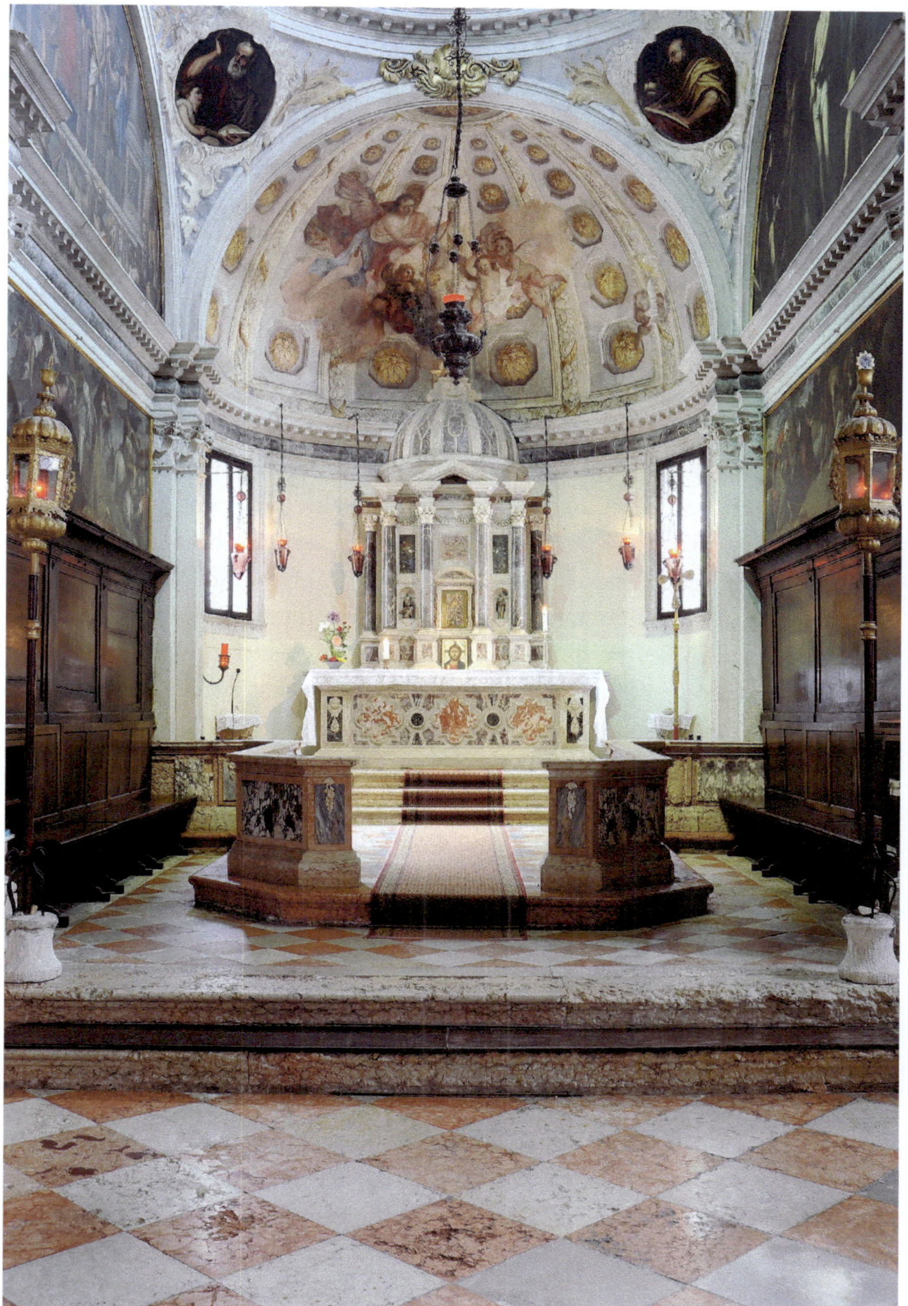

62. Chapel of the Blessed Sacrament, San Giacomo dall'Orio, Venice (Photo: Francesco Turio Bohm)

confraternity members at Sant'Agnese for the same reason.[158] Finally, at San Giacomo dall'Orio it was recorded that the patriarch very much liked the chapel of the Blessed Sacrament, but he still encouraged the resident Scuola del Sacramento to enlarge and redecorate the chapel anew (Fig. 62). The parish priest, Da Ponte, was to assist them in this noble aim, and the projected costs were to be forwarded to the patriarch for his consultation.[159] The resulting chapel of the sacrament is one of the loveliest in Venice, and it was mostly complete by the time of Zane's 1604 visit, which praised the 'beautiful architecture' of the imposing stone and marble tabernacle, as did Stringa's guide of the same year, which described this object as being of 'extraordinary beauty'.[160]

In paying so much attention to the eucharist, Priuli did not neglect other aspects of importance for the devotional interior, such as the display and care given to relics. He ordered the separation of authentic remains from those of a more dubious provenance, and he offered advice on how they could be best displayed to encourage greater reverence.[161] Although not a relic as such, at San Silvestro Priuli was angered that a ring supposedly once belonging to Saint Thomas Becket had been taken away from the altar dedicated to him inside the church, and that it was currently being held in a private house. He ordered the *gastaldo* and members of the governing body of the Scuola dei Barilleri e Mastelleri (barrel and bucket makers), whose confraternity was dedicated to the saint, to appear before him to explain themselves and to make provisions for a safer location within the church for the ring that could be locked.[162] Moreover, at the church of San Polo he was saddened to find no relics at all, exhorting the priest to procure some, since 'a church that is so honourable, should not be without such a treasure'.[163] Yet the advice Priuli gave regarding the eucharist was still distinctly more copious than his directives for relics ever were, suggesting that by the twilight of the Cinquecento the former had almost become of greater significance than the latter in Venice. The events surrounding the recommendations of the Priuli visitation for the precious relics of the body of Saint Sabba at Sant'Antonin shed some light of this state of affairs. When the patriarchal vicar and the inspectors visited the church in 1593, a new chapel paid for by the procurator Francesco Tiepolo in the left nave was being prepared for the saintly remains, but was at this point incomplete.[164] The visitors wanted the high altar to be partially rebuilt in line with its recommendations, and so it was ordered that once these works had terminated, both the relics and the Blessed Sacrament had to be moved into the high altar chapel. The sacrament chapel was too close to a public road to be allowed to remain in its current location, and once it was shifted into the chancel a 'new, honourable, and proportionate' tabernacle was also to be constructed, which could happen only once said works at the high altar were concluded.[165] On 12 November 1595 the Tiepolo chapel had been consecrated by Priuli himself, and the Zane visitation of a few years later noted that it had been 'reduced to perfection'.[166] Even though Zane reasserted the instructions of the previous visitation that both the body of Sabba and the Blessed Sacrament should be in the high altar, which was dedicated to the saint,[167] we know from the 1620 inspection of Patriarch Giovanni Tiepolo that this never happened. Perhaps unsurprisingly given his surname, this patriarch instead deemed the present location to be a 'more decent' site for the remains than the high altar.[168] In this particular instance, it had made sense to resist the exhortations of the Priuli visitation. Not only did the Tiepolo family have a historic connection to Saint Sabba, whose relics were brought to Venice by Crusaders in 910, but the chapel was conceived as a kind of elaborate reliquary for his remains, containing a stone casket crowned with two marble angels below the altarpiece of the apotheosis of the saint by Palma, with paintings on the lateral walls by the same artist that depicted Sabba's miracles, as well as the arrival of his remains into Venice.[169] Even though the Scuola del Sacramento at Sant'Antonin paired itself with the ancient confraternity of San Sabba in 1609, a dedicated space in the church where the saint could be appropriately honoured must have seemed far preferable to moving his remains onto a high altar, which now had to be shared with the confraternity of the Blessed Sacrament, and which also had to accommodate a sizeable tabernacle.[170] At the moment that the decorations of the Tiepolo chapel were terminated, it would have made even less sense for the relics to be moved, when the casket and paintings all pointed to their presence there, and so they stayed in the location desired by Francesco Tiepolo for centuries, until 1965, when they were returned to the Holy Land and finally placed in the Orthodox Monastery of Mar Saba in Bethlehem, which had been founded by the saint himself.

COOPERATION AND RESISTANCE

Just as noble families like the Tiepolos had rights to a significant number of altars and chapels in Venice, so too did lay confraternities. Since these groups funded the decoration and maintenance of these spaces, any transformation desired by the patriarch was to a great extent reliant on both their cooperation and that of the clergy. The Scuole del Sacramento in Venice were particularly distinctive in this regard because they avoided priestly interference in their organisation and governance, as pointed out by Worthen.[171] Because of this, they differed from similar organisations elsewhere, even if ecclesiastical authorities became more closely associated with their activities after the Council of Trent. During the debates surrounding the Apostolic Visitation of 1581, some members of the Venetian Senate argued that the altars of the city's Blessed Sacrament confraternities were not to be inspected at all since this would constitute an infringement of their historic self-determination. Since these confraternities were dependent on the churches in which they were active but independent in the sense that they were mostly funded, maintained, and governed by the laity, it was pointed out that they had never before been subject to ecclesiastical oversight.[172] Worthen observed that 'the decorative undertakings of the scuole del Sacramento were the most striking examples of parochial piety in sixteenth-century Venice'.[173] This is all the more interesting given that membership was open to all parishioners (including women), and because confraternities were often poor.[174] There must have been enough well-off individuals to fund some of the more ambitious projects, but it may also have been the case that as membership swelled, smaller donations from a larger number of donors could compensate for the lack of one, or just a few, particularly generous patrons.[175] In 1604 at the aforementioned church of San Nicolò dei Mendicoli, the parish priest Salomon Lando recorded that the four confraternities of the parish, 'in all their poverty, in around twenty-six years have spent twelve or thirteen thousand ducats in beautifying the church and maintaining the altars'.[176] Unlike the very different funding systems of the main religious orders, parishes in Venice varied greatly in wealth, and they were often reliant on the alms of their parishioners, something that could have an evident impact on rebuilding projects.[177] In these particular cases the clergy was sometimes at the mercy of their parishioners, rather than the reverse.[178]

That the Scuole del Sacramento realised so many of the new standards relating to the eucharist encouraged by visitations does not imply that this was merely a case of the dominant ecclesiastical elite enforcing Tridentine reform upon the people of the parish. Such an assumption would deny the confraternity members any agency, and it would be at odds with evidence that has explored aspects of popular support for reform elsewhere in the Veneto.[179] Clearly, the ideals that figures like Priuli espoused aroused some level of sympathy amongst the laity, and sometimes the lay people even anticipated them. At San Marziale, the Scuola del Sacramento had requested that a gilded tabernacle should be placed on the high altar already in 1573, since its present site was 'old, dark, in disorder, and not of the dignity that is appropriate'.[180] This justification used very similar language to that later employed by Priuli himself in the course of his visits, and as we have seen he was complimentary about the high altar of the church when he visited it in October 1591.[181] The support of these confraternities should not come as a surprise, then, when one considers that most of Priuli's directives involved them aggrandising their ritual spaces within the parish. The motivations behind this kind of patronage were multiple, something eloquently testified to by an account of the Scuola Grande della Carità in 1538. After having received Titian's painting *The Presentation of the Virgin in the Temple*, and deciding to proceed with new decorations for their meeting house, it was noted in the confraternity records 'how necessary and appropriate to mortal men is the adornment of the tabernacle of omnipotent God and of the most glorious protectress, mother of Charity, our Holy Lady Mary, cannot be expressed with words ... As a result, they [the adornments] not only increase devotion but kindle the souls of the many, who, all the more willingly and with good heart, may hasten to enrol in the aforesaid confraternities and congregations'.[182] The competitive nature of the patronage of the Scuole is well established, but attempts to reveal the more worldly aims of the guilds should not diminish from the fact that piety was the primary factor that propelled their activities.[183] In 1614 the Scuola del Sacramento at San Samuele recorded their desire to restore their altar for 'the honour and glory of our Lord Jesus Christ and the benefit of our souls', reminding us that the act of embellishment was the kind of 'good work' that also testified to parochial piety and generosity.[184] Priuli sometimes directly appealed to this piety: at San Simeone Piccolo he stated that the confraternity of the Madonna would be content to pay to accommodate the holy relics at their altar 'in honour of God, as well as the Blessed Mary and Saints'.[185]

By the latter years of the sixteenth century no parish would have wanted to retain an outdated or shabby chapel of the sacrament when other churches were commissioning ever more ornate ones. The aforementioned Scuola del Sacramento at San Samuele wrote wistfully about how they not yet been able to restore their altar, even though nearly every other similar confraternity in the city had managed to 'accommodate and embellish the altars, chapels and places where they meet in their churches', a lament repeated every few years until 1632, when their new altar was finally consecrated.[186] Stringa also mused on the decorative ambitions of the eucharist confraternities in his discussion of the chapel of the Holy Sacrament at San Simeone Grande at the beginning of the seventeenth century. Lost in admiration for the marvellously embellished ceiling of their altar in the church, he reflected that 'it was a marvel, that not only this [church], but almost all the churches of this city, have these decorations, and through holy competition, each one of them makes the effort to do as such for the honour and glory of the Lord. And all of this is done at the expense of the Scuola del Santissimo Sacramento, which are to be found in every church'.[187] What Stringa termed 'holy competition' collectively contributed to the beauty of Venice's churches, and this material splendour could be interpreted as tangible evidence of the religion of the city itself and its collective moral values: a conviction that the account from Botero at the beginning of this book alluded to.

As mentioned previously, the patriarch and his delegation met regularly with the clergy and confraternities in the sacristy during the visits, and on a number of occasions the brethren of guilds were directly instructed to assist with the decoration of the church.[188] At San Maurizio, for example, the visitation described how thanks to the diligence of the parish priest three of the chapels had been renovated and necessary vestments provided. Since San Maurizio was not a collegiate church, it had limited funds, including a miserable annual budget for buildings works of only one and half ducats. Thus, the visitation directed the priest to call on the parishioners for greater assistance in order to ensure the perfection of the rest of the building, and it was ordered that the Scuola degli Albanesi should take responsibility for restoring the nave towards the campo, and that they had been directly exhorted by the visitors to do so.[189] Ideally, then, confraternities were to act in concert with the clergy, and priests were to rally the Scuole and laity in assisting with the renovation of their parish.[190] Since parish priests in Venice were elected by the parishioners, and the procurators who administered parish funds were also laymen, these groups had to work in close consultation with one another. This does not necessitate that these relationships were necessarily harmonious; often no love was lost between the laity and the clergy (and vice versa), but Priuli's comments do provide some insights into how visual reforms could be negotiated between these groups.[191] One interesting case study of a breakdown in the relationship between the various parties is illustrated by the records of the same Scuola del Sacramento at San Samuele, where the fraternity members and clergy were at loggerheads for decades. This was the result of a feud that commenced in 1603 when the priests and chapter had an altar built in the area reserved for the Scuola's *banco*. The Scuola had obediently moved their bench due to ongoing works on the paving of the church and were horrified when the clergy ignored the terms of an agreement of 1525 that gave them rights over the space. The case was referred to the patriarch, then sent to Rome, and eventually the patriarchal vicar made a site visit, reviewed the documentation, and judged in favour of the confraternity. The Scuola were so irate that they referred to this debacle for years afterwards in their rulebook (especially because it was so long and expensive to resolve), eventually deciding in 1613 that they wished to elect two 'defenders', whose role was to protect the confraternity's jurisdiction in the parish. The funds of the Scuola were also robbed on more than one occasion, leaving them almost penniless. In 1614 it was suggested that the numerous 'disorders and inconveniences' that had befallen the Scuola might be in part the fault of the confraternity management, since 'everything proceeds with little care and charity'.[192]

In just the same way as the priests at the impoverished San Nicolò were dependent on the generosity of confraternities for realising ambitious decorative projects, in a number of cases the largesse of a single parish priest was essential for exactly the same reason. At San Geminiano, the cleric Benedetto Manzini was crucial for the completion of the new church in the sixteenth century, something pointed out by the architect Jacopo Sansovino's son, and he even paid for the organ, which cost over 600 ducats.[193] Like Manzini, well-off clergy such as Antonio Gatto at San Polo,[194] Giovanni Maria da Ponte at San Giacomo dall'Orio,[195] and Bartolomeo Borghi at San Pantalon were all similarly important for the embellishment of their churches in the late Cinquecento.[196] All of these priests were remembered visually in their parishes: likenesses of Da Ponte and Borghi were included in paintings by Palma il Giovane and Veronese, respectively (Figs. 63 and 64), whilst portrait busts of

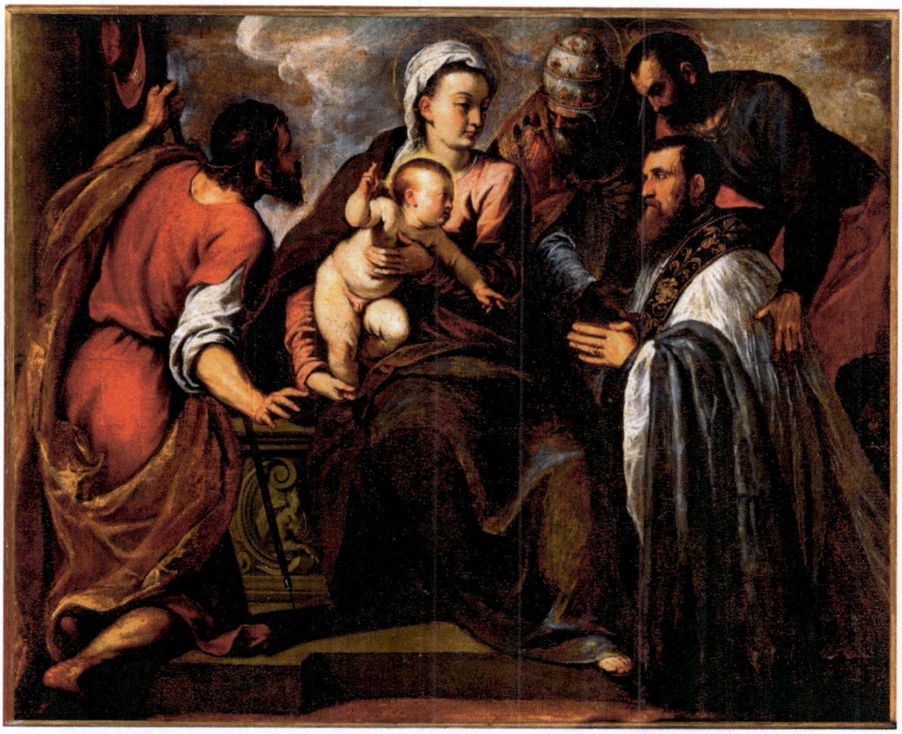

63. Palma il Giovane, *Giovanni Maria da Ponte, Assisted by Saints Sylvester and James, Is Presented to the Virgin by Saint Mark,* c. 1577–81, oil on canvas, San Giacomo dall'Orio, Venice (Cameraphoto)

Manzini (Fig. 45) and Gatto were once to be seen in San Polo and San Geminiano. Just as parishioners felt a sense of local pride in the embellishment of their devotional spaces, so too were these priests often very attached to the sites that they had helped to decorate, and some had a keen interest in the visual arts. In his life of Tintoretto, for example, Ridolfi described how the parish priest of Santa Fosca, one Monsignor Melchiori, was a 'protector of painters', who owned an important collection of artworks.[197] The wills of Gatto and Da Ponte, whose renovation efforts were lauded by successive visitations, also speak to an abiding affection for their parish churches. Gatto's will touchingly referred to San Polo as 'my beloved and dear wife', leaving further monies for the edifice as 'a sign of the most sincere love I have always held for her',[198] and at San Giacomo, Da Ponte left to the chapter 'everything that I have done in my church', which aside from his patronage of chapels and paintings, included vestments, altar furnishings, and the earnings from real estate on the terraferma.[199] Finally, besides paying for his own chapel at San Paternian, the will of the priest Pietro Filomaso attests that he had also funded the rebuilding of the rest of the church, 'for the glory of God'.[200] Preoccupied about the future of the edifice after his death, he dictated that if some calamity should affect his church, such as a fire, then the funds that he

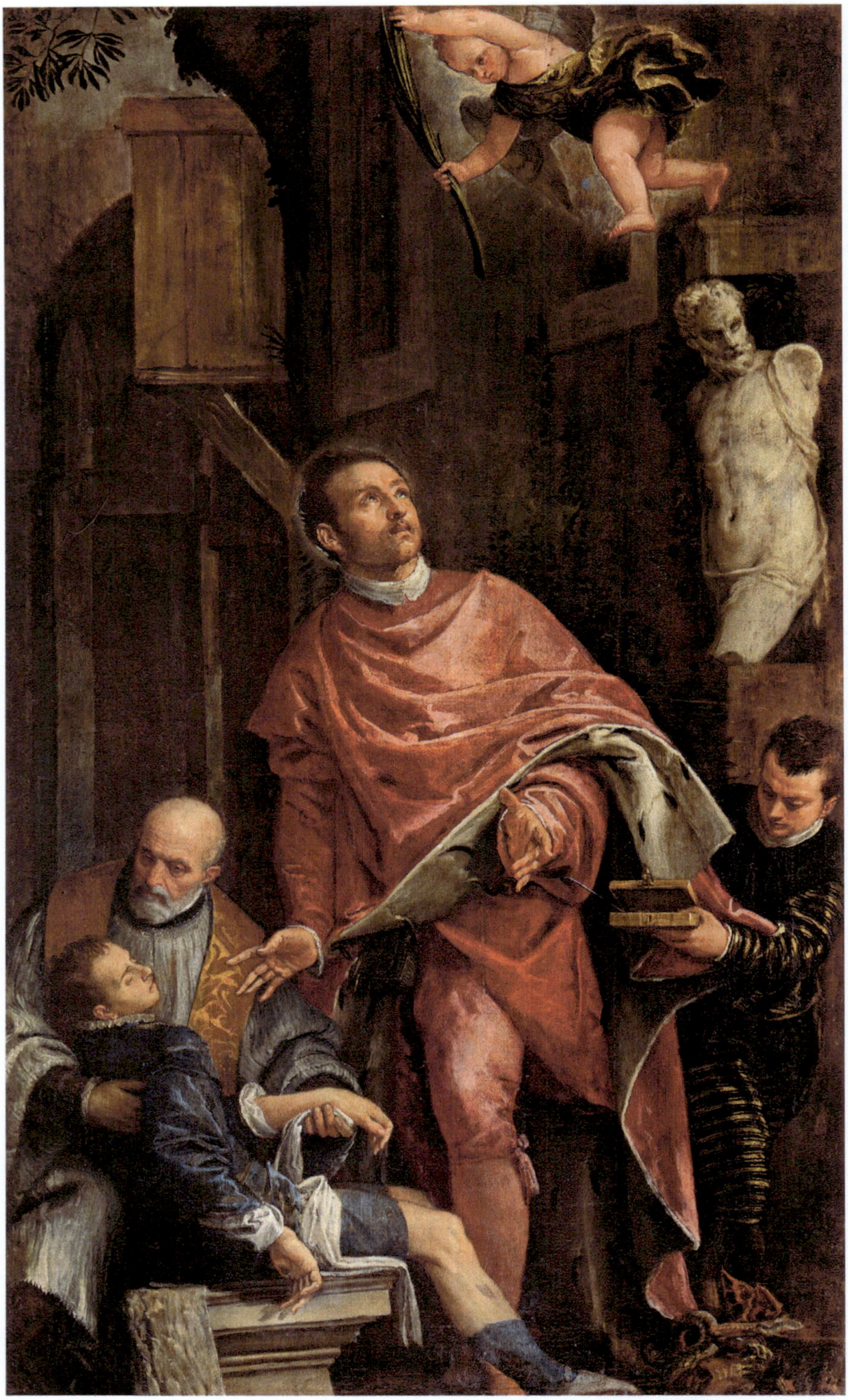

64. Veronese, *Conversion of Saint Pantaleon with Bartolomeo Borghi Who Tends to the Poisoned Youth,* 1587–88, oil on canvas, San Pantalon, Venice (Photo: Cameraphoto)

had left for other purposes should be diverted to the structure until restorations were complete.[201]

Examples of cooperation between parishioners and the will of the Priuli visitation tend to be easier to locate than examples of resistance. This is partly because his most copious orders concerned the eucharist, and the city's Scuole del Sacramento had already begun making changes to their chapels that were in harmony with these requirements. One of the most obvious ways in which the changes required by the visitations could be resisted was by simply ignoring them. This was difficult to do when interdicts had been placed on altars and chapels until such time as changes deemed non-negotiable were realised; however, since much of Priuli's advice was dependent upon funds being raised, or confraternities and the clergy leaping into action, it could also be tacitly avoided. This was what the Jesuits appear to have done at the Gesù in Rome when faced with the pope's objections to Pulzone's paintings, and there are instances of the same tactics being used in Venice. Even though subsequent visits would theoretically consult the preceding recommendations to ensure that they had been fulfilled – Priuli visits are full of remonstrations that the orders of the Apostolic Visit had yet to be actioned – they didn't always advise precisely the same changes. At San Giacomo dall'Orio, the Apostolic Visitation had ordered that the wooden altar of the crib should be demolished, but Priuli was more lenient since alms left at the altar were a source of income for the parish. He ordered that it be moved elsewhere, and it was eventually demolished only in 1764.[202] Since it is not easy to discern what the average layperson thought about these changes (although the *mariegole*, or rulebooks, do offer some useful insights), it is also hard to know to what extent unwillingness to make certain changes was symptomatic of 'resistance' to the will of the visitation or stemmed rather from apathy, laziness, or just a lack of funds. At San Giacomo, in the face of the decorative ambitions of the Scuola del Sacramento, who described their desire to 'multiply, as much as is possible', their efforts to 'decorate and adorn the church of San Giacomo dall'Orio in every way, carried out in honour of God', the path of least resistance was taken and all of the Scuola's desires for expansion were met.[203] Furthermore, in the parishes of San Giovanni in Bragora, San Provolo, San Canciano, and perhaps also at San Moisè, the confraternities dedicated to the titular saints of these churches ceased to exist completely, and they were absorbed into the new confraternities dedicated to the Blessed Sacrament.[204]

CATHOLIC ICONOCLASM?

The loss of some of the older confraternities as those of the eucharist proliferated throughout Venice brings us to the next point to be made about the impact of these visitations: in ordering so many extensive changes to the parishes of his diocese, did Priuli's inspections have an iconoclastic impact?[205] Of course, this stemmed from a very different set of beliefs to those that led to the transformation of the church interior that took place in varying degrees of intensity in Protestant areas of Europe. Priuli wanted more, not fewer sacred images, and he was certainly averse to ordering their destruction. He believed in the inherent value not just of devotional artworks but of magnificent, richly decorated churches too. The changes that Priuli ordered at each parish he visited were driven by a belief that they would improve the appearance and function of the liturgical space, rendering it more 'honourable' and 'noble', two words that are used liberally throughout the visits. Yet if we recall Steinberg's warning about the potential damage wreaked by gustatory changes with which this chapter commenced, it is worth also considering the destructive results behind the extensive restorations and renovations to so many of Venice's parish churches after the Council of Trent. This was first noted by Antonio Niero, who pointed out that even though the Apostolic Visit encouraged new architectonic forms, the changes wrought by the decisions to move tabernacles to the high altar often led to significant and disruptive structural modifications to the presbytery, causing the loss of older wooden ciboriums and the displacement of silver altarpieces.[206] Moreover, the general rules of the Apostolic Visit meant that many altars and tabernacles had to be remade in order to conform to the official standards, and even if this could sometimes take a long time to achieve, it did bring about long-lasting change.[207] Destruction could sometimes go hand-in-hand with a visitation. The local populace in Bergamo had been scandalised by the decision of the 1575 Apostolic Visit headed by Carlo Borromeo to destroy the tombs of illustrious men and remove their military insignia.[208] The act of one Ludovico Moneta, who entered the chapel of the *condottiere* Bartolomeo Colleoni during the night and removed all his emblems, was perceived as a gross violence against his memory, and had displeased the Signoria.[209] With events such as this in living memory, it is little wonder that the Serenissima was so hostile to Borromeo's proposal of an Apostolic Visit to Venice. Yet there was a degree of hypocrisy in their reaction to the events in Bergamo, since the redrawing of the city lines there upon the orders of the Venetian State in 1561, as well as those of Brescia in 1516, had resulted in the complete destruction of important churches and monasteries in both of these cities.[210]

During the course of Priuli's visits he ordered the widening of chapels; the rearrangement of altars, baptisteries, and relics; the destruction and replacement of any of these if deemed old or unsuitable in some way;[211] the removal of wall tombs or *depositi*; the transferral of confraternities into different areas of the church;[212] and, on one occasion, the unification of two saints or devotions into one altar.[213] In some instances this led to the almost complete loss of local variants for liturgical architecture, such as the aforementioned altar-font, which all but disappeared from the Venetian parish church.[214] We have also seen that the Priuli visits were more intent on stipulating that the tabernacle should be placed on the high altar than were the Apostolic Visits, and compared to the 1581 delegation Priuli's visitation was also more prone to ordering the removal of the choir and its transferral into the high altar. The Apostolic Visit only ordered this once, at the church of San Nicolò dei Mendicoli, compared to five times by the Priuli visits.[215] None of these actions had been decreed by the Council of Trent, and there were important earlier precedents for the placement of both the tabernacle on the high altar and the retro-choir fitted behind the high altar, but they are understood as very much being in the 'post-Tridentine spirit', since the visitations that took place after the council attempted to implement these changes more systematically. Centuries later, events surrounding the Second Vatican Council followed a similar trajectory. In its wake, not only were tabernacles often removed from the sanctuary and shifted to side chapels (reversing the post-Tridentine norms and ironically returning to a practice that had been favoured by the Venetians centuries earlier), but the ancient *ad orientem* high altars were effectively made obsolete. In older churches this sometimes led to the unsightly presence of two altars in the chancel: the pre–Vatican II typology, often too precious to destroy, and a few steps in front of it a newer altar that allowed the priest to face the congregation (one sees this at the Frari in Venice, for example). For its opponents, these changes were iconoclastic, and came to be termed 'wreck-ovation'. But as was the case with the Council of Trent, they had never been directly dictated by Vatican II, but came to be realised 'in its spirit', inspired by changes in liturgy that emphasised a more active participation of the laity during the celebration of the mass.[216]

Be that as it may, there is one important difference between reactions to ecclesiastical architecture and decorations post–Vatican II compared to post-Trent. Whilst the former council has been attributed an iconoclastic bent that sought to strip away ornament and decoration, stipulating, for example, that the number of images placed in a church 'should be moderate', the latter is often linked to the eventual rise of the Baroque.[217] The emphasis that Priuli placed on the ever more magnificent decoration of the city's churches resulted from an outlook that to some extent defined itself in opposition to the opinions not only of reformers such as Calvin or Zwingli, but of those who had once been active in Venetian territories. Vittore Soranzo, the Bishop of Bergamo (c. 1500–58) who was condemned by the Inquisition shortly before his death, had purportedly shown distaste for images of the saints during his pastoral visits, breaking two images according to eyewitness accounts, and preferring those churches with minimal decoration.[218] Witnesses also claimed that prior to his exile, Bishop Pier Paolo Vergerio (1498–1565) was an iconoclast, who had destroyed images of the saints in his diocese of

Capodistria.[219] Priuli's very different emphasis on the magnificence of churches was continued by patriarchs in the seventeenth century. Zane often affirmed the earlier judgments of Priuli when he visited the churches of Venice, and Giovanni Tiepolo, who was patriarch from 1619 until his death in 1631, was very keen to visually promote obscure Marian dedications and the cults of Venetian *beati*, and he used his own funds to do so.[220] After having renounced the patriarchate in 1644, Federico Cornaro (1579–1653, r. 1631–44) commissioned arguably the most spectacular Baroque space anywhere on earth: the Cornaro chapel in Santa Maria della Vittoria, Rome, featuring Bernini's (1598–1680) *Ecstasy of Saint Theresa*.[221] Earlier in the Cinquecento, Pietro Cataneo's architectural treatise published in Venice in 1554 encouraged spending on sacred edifices based on the biblical precedent of the Temple of Solomon, whilst Palladio argued that temples should be so pleasing to the eye that 'nothing more beautiful could be imagined', so that 'those who enter there, may be astonished, and remain in a kind of ecstasy in admiring their grace and beauty'.[222] The authors of the treatises examined in the previous chapters shared these sentiments. Molanus had advised that it was a good thing for images of saints to covered with gold or silver, or decorated with crowns or precious vestments, and he encouraged the liberal use of candles, the latter being an aspect of Catholic worship that was universally despised by Protestant polemicists.[223] Gilio's dialogue urged the reader to 'consider what Lutheran churches must be without paintings',[224] and, closer to Venice, the 1605 instructions on the restoration and decoration of churches in the diocese of Aquileia, written by its patriarch, Francesco Barbaro, stated that 'the more the church is majestic, the more it should be amply decorated'.[225] In Venice this applied even to those parish churches of more modest means, as the earlier cited observations of Stringa make clear.

CONCLUSIONS

En route to his pilgrimage to Jerusalem in the year 1494, Canon Pietro Casola described how even in comparison to Rome, which he had visited, he had never found 'in any city so many beautiful and ornate churches as there are in Venice. It would take too long to name them all.'[226] Casola had been awestruck by what he encountered, observing that 'the poorest parish church of Venice is more ornate than the finest in Milan. Almost all the Venetian churches – the parish churches I mean – have a beautiful choir and an organ, and no expense is spared to decorate them; everything is gilded, and they are well served. This makes me think strongly that the Venetians must be greatly aided by God in their affairs, because they are very solicitous with regard to divine worship in all their churches'.[227] Casola expressed these thoughts years before the Reformations or the Council of Trent. The impulse to render the city's churches as ornate as possible existed prior to these events, but as we have seen, the changes advised by the visitations relating to decorative improvements in the parish churches were often realised relatively swiftly, suggesting that Venetians were enthusiastic protagonists in visual reform. Patriarch Zane's 1604 *Ad Limina* report on the state of the churches and clergy in Venice declared that with regard to the city's church buildings, he had found them 'all to be splendidly and generously appointed, so that it seems that nothing can be added to them and there is no more to be desired'. Some years earlier, during the Apostolic Visitation, Valier and Campeggi were similarly impressed by some of the aspects that had wowed Casola and would later be praised by Zane, and reports were sent to Rome commenting positively on the amount of vestments and the candlelit altars in the parishes, causing them to conclude that 'one could not desire a greater signal of piety in this part of the exterior cult'.[228] Some years later in 1596, Priuli, despite having been a layman at the time of his election to the patriarchate, was elevated to the cardinalate. Doubtless his extensive experience as an ambassador abroad, including embassies to Spain and war-torn France, had impressed upon him the need to instigate Tridentine reform.[229] In the ambit of devotional art and architecture this is eloquently illustrated not just by Priuli's ambitious plans for the cathedral of San Pietro di Castello, but through his visitations: the methodical, detailed, and consistent manner in which they were carried out attests to a determined and rigorous reformer. It should thus come as no surprise that the suggestion of sanctity hung over him during the latter years of his life, and in death too.[230]

Earlier in the Cinquecento, the proto-Lutheran Alessandro Caravia had praised the Scuola del Santissimo Sacramento of Venice in his 1541 *Sogno di Caravia* as exemplars of a genuine and humble piety. This was contrasted in the text to the worldly self-promotion of the ostentatious Scuole Grandi and, in particular, to the Scuola Grande di San Rocco, which had spent so much on 'columns carved in the newest manner' for their meeting house.[231] But by the end of the century, these same eucharistic confraternities were resolute in their grand decorative ambitions, updating their chapels with lavish embellishments and crowning their altars with intricately wrought tabernacles. The records of the Priuli visitation show the extent to which these efforts were given robust institutional backing by the Venetian Church. Taken as a trio, the post-Tridentine visits of the Apostolic Visitation, Patriarch Priuli, and Patriarch Zane, spanning a period of just over twenty years, from 1581 to 1604, shed light on how the ideas of the Catholic Reformation concerning devotional art, architecture, and furnishings were instituted in Venice, and they go some way to explaining the expansive programmes of restoration and redecoration of the city's churches that took place in the later decades of the sixteenth century, since the appropriate appearance and maintenance of holy sites was an important priority for such visits, as it was for the parish laity. The excellence of local artistic and architectural traditions and the professed faith of the Venetians to the eucharist meant that there were already firm foundations in the city that enabled it to make an important and wide-ranging contribution to post-Tridentine visual culture. This chapter has sought to understand the institutional framework through which this was encouraged in the latter decades of the Cinquecento. In the next part of the book, the ultimate power invested in the hands of artists to make visible some of the most contested beliefs of the age will be explored, underlining how those who hailed from in and around Venice developed existing iconographies as they restlessly experimented with the potential of the sacred image.

NOTES

1 APV, Archivio 'segreto', Visite pastorali, Visitationes ecclesiarum. Liber primus (hereafter Visite Priuli).

2 Steinberg, *The Sexuality of Christ in Renaissance Art and in Modern Oblivion*, 184.

3 APV, Visite Priuli, fol. 48v. For the oratory of the carpenters at San Samuele it was noted that the altarpiece was titled *Christ's Circumcision at the Temple*. Noted also by Michel Hochmann, who gave the location as San Tomà. Hochmann, *Peintres et commanditaires à Venise (1540–1628)*, 272. There are a few further examples referred to in the course of this chapter. Visitations in Venice appear never to have systematically provided this kind of information, but some later visits occasionally include it. Examples are the visits of Patriarch Giovanni Badoer in the late Seicento and early Settecento and the 1821 visits of Patriarch Giovanni Pyrker. Doubtless there are a few other exceptions. See APV, Visite pastorali, Visitationes Baduarii, 1690–1698; I, fol. 67v (a list of 'other objects' drawn up by the parish priest at San Geminiano that details a number of moveable paintings in the church, including a 'Madonna and Child by the hand of Bellini'), and Bruno Bertoli and Silvio Tramontin, eds., *La visita pastorale di Giovanni Ladislao Pyrker nella diocesi di Venezia (1821)* (Rome: Edizioni di storia e letteratura, 1971), 181–82. Pyrker references artworks on a number of occasions, and his visits include a detailed description of the paintings in the church of San Bartolomeo.

4 Eire, *Reformations: The Early Modern World, 1450–1650*, 603.

5 The earliest surviving visitation records of parishes in Venice date to between 1461 and 1558 and consist of material relating to visits made by six different patriarchs divided into twenty-two files. For a description of the archival material, see https://siusa.archivi.beniculturali.it/cgi-bin/siusa/pagina.pl?TipoPag=unita&Chiave=309325&RicProgetto=evve (consulted 16 June 2023).

6 Canon III of the decree on reform of session twenty-four (11 November 1563). Tanner, *Decrees of the Ecumenical Councils*, vol. 2: 761–63.

7 Following the example of the Apostolic Visit, which had also divided the material in this way. APV, Visite Priuli, Supplemento alle visite Priuli. 1591 ad 1598. Not every parish that was subject to a visitation appears in the *supplemento*, presumably because there was nothing seriously amiss that had to be investigated. Of the sixty-four parishes that Priuli inspected, fifty appear in the *supplemento*. As well as attestations regarding the state of the parish clergy, the majority include the paperwork that had been requested by Priuli (inventories, accounts, details of bequests, etc.). Only two churches were subject to repeat visitations: San Cassiano and San Marziale.

8 The final church visited by Priuli for his initial round of visits was San Severo, inspected on 14 October 1593. The supplementary material was complete by 1598, and Patriarch Matteo

Zane's visits began a few years after this, commencing with the visit to San Biagio on 13 July 1603.

9 APV, Archivio 'segreto', Visite pastorali a monasteri femminili, Visite de monache. 1592–1596. These visits were analysed by Laven, *Virgins of Venice: Broken Vows and Cloistered Lives in the Renaissance Convent*. The nunneries were visited only a few times in the history of the Serenissima. Conflicts between Priuli and the Venetian State regarding jurisdiction over the Marcian basilica's twin institution of the convent of Santa Maria delle Vergini arose often during his tenure as patriarch. Sperling, *Convents and the Body Politic in Late Renaissance Venice*, 214–15, 229–31.

10 Lorenzo Priuli, *Ordini, & auuertimenti, che si deuono osservare ne' Monasteri di Monache di Venetia. Sopra la visita e la clausura* (Venice: Giovanni Antonio Rampazetto, 1591).

11 See Cappelletti, *Storia della Chiesa di Venezia*, vol. 6: 501–29; Tramontin, 'La visita apostolica del 1581 a Venezia', 495.

12 Cappelletti, *Storia della Chiesa di Venezia*, vol. 6: 514–24.

13 Tramontin, 'La visita apostolica del 1581 a Venezia', 495, note 55.

14 Priuli's cardinal vicar noted the difficulties of enforcing the norms established by the Apostolic Visitation in his preface to the synod of 1592. Noted first by Gaier, 'Il patriarca e il suo vicario: Lorenzo Priuli, Giovanni Mozanega e la questione dei monumenti sepolcrali nella chiesa post-tridentina', 211–12.

15 APV, Visite Priuli, fol. 55r.

16 Tolosa was described as a cleric regular. He preached at the churches of San Marcuola, San Geremia, San Tomà, San Silvestro, and San Giovanni in Bragora, where his sermon was praised for its 'great doctrine and religion'. The Capuchins were also a very popular choice, as was the Jesuit Don Flaminio Beringucci, who preached at Santi Apostoli, San Giacomo dall'Orio, San Moisè, and San Polo. At the church of San Giovanni Decollato there was no preacher, since the site was too small to accommodate the crowds that might attend. At San Luca, the patriarch visited the church privately due to its small size. APV, Visite Priuli, fols. 359r (San Giovanni Decollato), 111r (San Luca).

17 Depending on the time of day, Priuli would occasionally celebrate mass and adore the sacrament, and then return again to conclude the visit. For example, at San Cassiano he went to the patriarchal palace for lunch and came back in the afternoon. The church may have required particular attention due to the testimonies of clergy and laity recounting the sexual abuse of, violence to, and rape of women in the parish, described in detail in the *supplemento*. San Cassiano was subject to a second visitation on 23 September 1598, the first having taken place on 8 November 1592. APV, Visite Priuli, fol. 307v; Supplemento alle visite Priuli, number 11. Priuli sometimes also managed to visit multiple churches in one day. At San Severo it was noted that the parishes of Giovanni Nuovo and San Provolo had been inspected on the same day. APV, Visite Priuli, fol. 560r

18 A huge amount of new paperwork was required from each parish after the Council of Trent. This included keeping records of baptisms, holy communions, confirmations, marriages, deaths, any bequests, accounts more generally, masses for the dead, and the names and details of all clergy in each parish. The visit also required the compilation of inventories of relics, vestments, and altar furnishings, but unfortunately not images. Priuli almost always had to instruct parish priests to retain records that were missing, and often they were admonished for allowing people other than the priest to write in the book of baptisms or deaths, or for not keeping these records properly and forgetting to include crucial information like the names of the godparents.

19 For example, at San Simeone Piccolo the members of the confraternities were exhorted to take communion frequently and to attend 'to the cult of God in the ornaments of the church', but to a greater extent to the purity of their own souls. At San Trovaso the priest and chapter were treated to a long sermon on their responsibilities, and the importance of living an 'innocent and pure life'. At Sant'Eufemia the patriarch spoke with the members of the confraternity of the Soccorso and exhorted them to help the poor and to procure a

doctor who could attend to the sick. APV, Visite Priuli, fols. 341r (San Simeone), 227r (San Trovaso), 156v (Sant'Eufemia).

20 APV, Archivio 'segreto', Visite apostoliche, Visita apostolica, fol. 70v (hereafter Visita apostolica); Visite Priuli, fols, 281v–82v.

21 There are thirty-eight churches listed in the records of Zane's visits. See APV, Archivio 'segreto', Visite pastorali, Visite parochiali Zane 1601 ad 1604 (hereafter Visite Zane). His visit to San Barnaba is separate to this and can be found in APV, Archivio 'segreto', Visite pastorali, Santa Barbara, fasc. 20. Priuli's inspection also covered the Ospedale di SS. Giovanni e Paolo.

22 Correr visited sixty-seven sites, some of which were on the mainland, plus thirty-six oratories. APV, Archivio 'segreto', Visite pastorali, Visitationes ecclesiarum, Correr 1735–1742.

23 For Mozanega, see Gaier, 'Il patriarca e il suo vicario'. Gaier notes the important influence of Mozanega on the reforms of Priuli, but in my opinion he overstates his case on page 213 when he argues that the real 'agent of the interests of the Holy See in Venice was not the patriarch Priuli but his vicar general'.

24 San Vidal, Santa Maria Formosa, Santa Maria del Giglio, San Geminiano, San Maurizo, San Fantin, San Basso, and Sant'Antonin. With the exception of Sant'Antonin and Santa Maria Formosa, all of these churches were in the sestiere of San Marco, so Priuli may well have been aware of their state of repair already.

25 APV, Visite Priuli, fol. 179v. A command repeated in the list of orders for the church (fol. 182r), where it is decreed that the offending figures should be 'covered with paintings in such a way that there is no scandal' (i.e., painted over). Near contemporary guides provide no clues about the subject of these paintings, and in any case the church was completely rebuilt in the early Seicento, leaving 'no vestiges' of the earlier church in the words of Giustiniano Martinioni, *Venetia città nobilissima, et singolare, Descritta in XIIII. Libri* (Venice: Steffano Curti, 1663), 244r. This painting may be identifiable as Aliense's *Serpent of Bronze*, which is still present on the right-hand side wall of the later high altar chapel. The work features a prominent female figure whose upper chest is uncovered. We do not know the original location of the painting in the church, but it bears a date of 1588, so it would have been in situ by the time of Priuli's visit on 30 September 1591. For the date, see Paolo Bordignon, 'Antonio Vassilacchi detto l'Aliense. Biografia e catalogo delle opere' (MA thesis, Università Ca' Foscari, 2015), 112–13, cat. 10. Priuli's order is noted also by Matile, *'Quadri laterali' im sakralen Kontext*, 144–45.

26 APV, Visite Priuli, fols. 122r, 125r. At San Leonardo (fol. 133r) Priuli also ordered that a '*figura Todesca*' above the altarpiece of the Madonna should be removed.

27 Bailey, *Between Renaissance and Baroque*, 210–11; Mansour, 'Censure and Censorship in Rome, c. 1600', 146–47.

28 Bailey, *Between Renaissance and Baroque*, 211–14, 242–47; Mansour, 'Censure and Censorship in Rome, c. 1600', 145–46. As Bailey points out on page 212, since the print by Hieronymus Wierix that is likely based on Pulzone's picture survives, 'his angels can hardly be seen as scantily clad, unless bare feet are offensive'.

29 APV, Visite Priuli, fols. 156v, 158v (Sant'Eufemia, Body of the Church); 212r, 214r (Santa Fosca, Altar of the Madonna); 391v–392r (San Martino, Baptistery); 372r, 374r (Sant'Agnese, Altar of San Vidal); 197v, 200r (Santa Margherita, High Altar).

30 APV, Visite Priuli, fol. 197v. The Apostolic Visit described the altar as having a mediocre altarpiece, a judgment that was applied to a number of other altars in the church. APV, Visita apostolica, fol. 91v.

31 Sansovino, *Venetia città nobilissima et singolare, descritta in XIIII. Libri*, 88v; Worthen, 'Tintoretto's Paintings for the Banco del Sacramento in S. Margherita', 728.

32 Martinioni, *Venetia, città nobilissima, et singolare*, 245.

33 Worthen, 'Tintoretto's Paintings for the Banco del Sacramento in S. Margherita', 728, 731. The paintings were taken down from above the *banco* in the south aisle between December

1652 and April 1653. The new high altar was first described by Martinioni, *Venetia, città nobilissima, et singolare*, 245. Paola Modesti states that Priuli ordered the removal of the choir and quotes instructions that he ordered it to be shifted into the high altar, but she confuses Santa Margherita with the documents relating to San Marziale. Modesti, 'I cori nelle chiese veneziane e la visita apostolica del 1581', 45, 55, note 23.

34 Serious damage was also recorded at the altar of San Vidal at Sant'Agnese, which was described as in a most indecent state. Here the visit dictated that the 'dirty' and 'burnt' *tavola* above the altar mensa was to be removed. This likely refers to something other than a painting, since Priuli used the words *quadro* and *immagine* for images, and *palla* to distinguish altarpieces. APV, Visite Priuli, fol. 372r, 374r.

35 Said altarpiece was also to be 'better accommodated'. At the same church Priuli ordered the high altarpiece to be 'renewed' in the orders, but what exactly he intended by this is unclear. He also wanted the canvases above said high altarpiece to be more securely attached to the wall. APV, Visite Priuli, fols. 211v–212r, 214r.

36 APV, Visite Priuli, fols. 449v, 451r. Since Priuli was otherwise occupied, this visit was conducted by the *vicario* accompanied by the '*reverendi visitatori*' of the sestiere. Priuli would have been subsequently informed about what they encountered, as noted on fol. 450v. He met with the parish priest on Monday 7 June 1593, the visit having taken place on Tuesday 18 May 1593.

37 APV, Visite Priuli, fols. 389v, 391v–392r. Priuli only refers to the altarpiece in the summary of orders.

38 APV, Visite Priuli, fols. 398r, 399r. The space was to be filled with some other 'devout figure' and the other painted figures in the baptistery were to be better accommodated according to the judgment of the parish priest.

39 APV, Visite Priuli, fols. 179v, 182r–v. It is likely this painting was placed elsewhere in the church.

40 Voelker, 'Carlo Borromeo's Instructiones fabricae et supellectilis ecclesiasticae', 249, 255.

41 APV, Visite Priuli, fols. 560r, 561r.

42 APV, Visite Priuli, fol. 330r. Mason Rinaldi, *Palma il Giovane. l'opera completa*, 118, cats. 355–58. The high altarpiece and the two accompanying paintings by Palma, *The Baptism of the King of Armenia* and *The Beating of Bartholomew*, were commissioned by the Scuola dei Remeri, who shared rights to the high altar space with the Scuola del Sacramento. The latter commissioned a large *Serpent of Bronze* from Palma, dated to c. 1595–1600. Aspects of the building works appear to have been planned previous to Priuli's visit, since it is mentioned that 'in this chapel the choir will be made'. A reconstruction of the high altar took place again in 1769, but the paintings remained in the same place. See Gianmario Guidarelli, 'La ricostruzione seicentesca della chiesa di San Bartolomio a Venezia', in *Da Longhena a Selva: un'idea di Venezia a dieci anni dalla scomparsa di Elena Bassi*, ed. Martina Frank, Università Ca' Foscari, Università Iuav di Venezia, Accademia di Belle Arti di Venezia, 9–11 December 2009 (Bologna: Archetipolibri, 2011), 39. For the church, see also Natalino Bonazza, Isabella di Lenardo, and Gianmario Guidarelli, eds., *La chiesa di San Bartolomeo e la comunità tedesca a Venezia* (Venice: Marcianum Press, 2013).

43 APV, Visite pastorali, Priuli, fol. 467r–v. The visit offered only three orders regarding the baptistery in this summary, which was to be moved. Proper record-keeping at the parish was also insisted upon. For this church, see Alvise Zorzi, *Venezia scomparsa* (Milan: Electa, 1977), vol. 2: 332–37; Kristin Love Huffman and Iara Dundas, 'Finding San Geminiano: "A Ruby among Many Pearls"', *Journal of the Society of Architectural Historians* 79, no. 1 (2020): 6–16; Salomon, '"A ruby among many pearls"'.

44 APV, Visite Priuli, fol. 465v.

45 As does a second altar, that of the Blessed Sacrament, now at the Villa Pisani at Stra. Zorzi, *Venezia scomparsa*, vol. 2: 334; Joachim Strupp, 'The Sculptured Altarpiece in Renaissance Venice, ca. 1460–1530' (doctoral thesis, University of St. Andrews, 1993), 116, note 96.

46 Modesti, 'I cori nelle chiese veneziane e la visita apostolica del 1581', 55, note 21.

47 APV, Visite Priuli, fols. 297v–298r. The statues and paintings remain in situ, but the chapel itself was transformed by the neoclassical interventions of Davide Rossi between 1799 and 1804.

48 The works began in April 1586 and were completed by Gatto's executors by January 1595. For Gatto's high altar, see Emma Jones, 'Priestly Patronage in Late Renaissance Venice: Antonio Gatto's *cappella maggiore* in San Polo', in *Carvings, Casts & Collectors: The Art of Renaissance Sculpture*, ed. Peta Moture, Emma Jones, and Dimitrios Zikos (London: V&A Publishing, 2013), 218–35; Emma Jones, 'The "cappella maggiore" of San Polo and Its Late Sixteenth-Century Reconstruction', in *La chiesa e la parrocchia di San Polo: spazio religioso e spazio pubblico*, ed. Gabriele Matino and Dorit Raines (Rome: Viella, 2021), 231–64. There are also two further paintings by Palma in the high altar, the *Delivery of the Keys to St Peter* and *St Peter Sending St Mark to Preach the Gospel at Aquileia*, both dated to 1625 by Mason Rinaldi, *Palma il Giovane: l'opera completa*, 132, cats. 473–74.

49 Priuli did not mention Da Ponte's input here in the same way as he did for Gatto at San Polo, but he would have been aware of it, not least because Da Ponte's coat of arms crowns the entrance to the chapel. Lillywhite, 'The Decoration of the Church of San Giacomo dall'Orio in Venice', 120.

50 Tramontin, 'La visita apostolica del 1581 a Venezia', 525; Lillywhite, 'The Decoration of the Church of San Giacomo dall'Orio in Venice', 122.

51 APV, Visite Zane, no. 15; Lillywhite, 'The Decoration of the Church of San Giacomo dall'Orio in Venice', 120.

52 Thomas Worthen, 'Architecture & Sacraments in Venetian Parish Churches', paper presented at the Annual Conference of the Renaissance Society of America, New York City, 27–29 March 2014. To my knowledge the Venetian altar-font has only been examined by Worthen, who generously shared this unpublished conference paper with me shortly before his death.

53 Sansovino, *Venetia città nobilissima et singolare, descritta in XIIII. Libri*, fol. 74r–v.

54 APV, Visite Priuli, fols. 449v, 451r.

55 APV, Visite Priuli, fol. 280v; Visite Zane, no. 15. See also Lillywhite, 'The Decoration of the Church of San Giacomo dall'Orio in Venice', 133–34.

56 APV, Visite Zane, no. 6.

57 See Mason Rinaldi, *Palma il Giovane: l'opera completa*, 58–63. Examining the well-received altarpiece *The Virgin and Child with Five Saints* by Palma for the Cornaro chapel in San Nicolò da Tolentino, Barcham points out that it was neither 'pictorially innovative nor emotionally moving' but that it was 'nonetheless thoroughly well-done.' William L. Barcham, *Grand in Design: The Life and Career of Federico Cornaro, Prince of the Church, Patriarch of Venice and Patron of the Arts* (Venice: Istituto Veneto di Scienze, Lettere ed Arti, 2001), 253.

58 Examples include San Bartolomeo, San Polo (where Palma went on to create further paintings for the chancel in the 1620s, perhaps due to his earlier success at the site), San Simeone Profeta (see note 106), and San Tomà, At the latter Priuli ordered that the altar dedicated to the Madonna belonging to the Scuola dei Calegheri be moved to another part of the church since the choir was to be remade. By the time Zane visited in July 1604 the altar of the confraternity was described as being dedicated to Saint Anianus, but it had yet to be consecrated. Zane did not mention the altarpiece by Palma, *The Healing of Anianus by Saint Mark,* but it has been dated to c. 1593. See APV, Visite Priuli, fols. 57v, 62r, Visite Zane, no. 35. Mason Rinaldi, *Palma il Giovane: l'opera completa*, 136, cat. 505.

59 APV, Visite Priuli, fols. 111v, 112r.

60 Pignatti and Pedrocco, *Veronese*, vol. 2: 430–31, cat. 321; Seidel, *Venezianische Malerei zur Zeit der Gegenreformation*, 114. First mentioned by Stringa, *Venetia, città nobilissima, et singolare*, 93r.

61 APV, Visite Priuli, fol. 317v.

62 APV, Visite Zane, no. 3.

63 Stringa, *Venetia, città nobilissima, et singolare*, 141r; Terisio Pignatti, *Veronese* (Milan: Alfieri, 1976), vol. 1: 213, cat. A328. The lateral canvases were once accompanied by the high altarpiece of the apostles by Cesare da Conegliano, as noted by Marco Boschini, *Le minere della pittura* (Venice: Francesco Nicolini, 1664), 432.

64 Zane deemed said tabernacle to be 'very beautiful, and honourably made'. APV, Visite Zane, no. 3.

65 Priuli notes that the altar is dedicated to Saints Thomas and Magnus of Oderzo, and that it has 'a painted altarpiece that is very beautiful'. APV, Visite Priuli, fol. 48r.

66 Attributed incorrectly to Tintoretto by Stringa, and to Damiano Mazza by Martinioni. Boschini was the first to attribute the work to Varotari. Stringa, *Venetia, città nobilissima, et singolare*, 180r; Martinioni, *Venetia, città nobilissima, et singolare*, 246; Boschini, *Le minere della pittura*, 368. I have found no good reproduction of this image, and the permanent exhibition in the church renders photography challenging. A black and white photograph can be viewed online at the *Catalogo generale dei Beni Culturali*: https://catalogo.beniculturali.it/detail/HistoricOrArtisticProperty/0500138079B (accessed 6 July 2023).

67 APV, Visite Priuli, fol. 139v.

68 APV, Visite Priuli, fols. 171v–172r (San Nicolò), 74v (San Silvestro). Boschini, *Le minere della pittura*, 326, 254. The first described as having 'an altarpiece that is very beautiful', the second with a 'very honourable altarpiece'.

69 Its presence here is noted by Stefania Mason and Andrea Gallo, *Chiesa di San Nicolò dei Mendicoli: arte e devozione* (Venice: Marsilio, 1995), 45.

70 APV, Visite Priuli, fol. 171v.

71 The remodelling of the church by the parish confraternities of the Blessed Sacrament, the Visitation, the Cross, and Saint Nicholas began in 1578. Worthen, 'Soazoni, or the Venetian Reformation of San Nicolò dei Mendicoli', 254.

72 In 1592, the year following Priuli's visit, Dal Friso's *Baptism of Christ* was paid for. Worthen, 'Soazoni, or the Venetian Reformation of San Nicolò dei Mendicoli', 259. For the decorative cycle in the nave, see Juergen Schulz, *Venetian Painted Ceilings of the Renaissance* (Berkeley: University of California Press, 1968), 74, 75, cat. 17; Mason and Gallo, *Chiesa di San Nicolò dei Mendicoli: arte e devozione*, 4–6, 25–45.

73 There were once further paintings in the ceilings of the naves, including the *Gloria* of Saint Nicholas by Alvise dal Friso, designed by Veronese. For this, see Hans Dieter Huber, *Paolo Veronese. Kunst als soziales System* (Munich: Wilhelm Fink Verlag, 2005), 194–96. For Veronese's heirs at San Nicolò, see Gisolfi, *Paolo Veronese and the Practice of Painting in Late Renaissance Venice*, 216. Other losses include a number of paintings once displayed in the parish that are now to be found in other places. See Mason and Gallo, *Chiesa di San Nicolò dei Mendicoli: arte e devozione*, 27, 29, 45.

74 Worthen, 'Soazoni, or the Venetian Reformation of San Nicolò dei Mendicoli', 259.

75 Mason Rinaldi, *Palma il Giovane: l'opera completa*, 130, cat. 449. Hans Dieter Huber believed Dal Friso's works on the walls of the nave were carried out even earlier, between 1578 and 1581. Huber, *Paolo Veronese. Kunst als soziales System*, 194.

76 Mason noted Priuli's comment about the paintings, arguing that it contradicts Stringa, who didn't mention the cycle in his updates to Sansovino. This leads her to suppose that either the cycle was not yet in situ, or Stringa had not visited the site in person. Mason and Gallo, *Chiesa di San Nicolò dei Mendicoli: arte e devozione*, 28.

77 Valentina Sapienza, '(Intorno a) Leonardo Corona (1552–1596): Documenti, fonti e indagini storici-contestuali' (doctoral thesis, Università Ca' Foscari, 2012), 151, note 482. This evidence was overlooked by Worthen's 2014 study on the church.

78 APV, Visite Zane, no. 27. For Vendramin, see Mason Rinaldi, *Palma il Giovane: l'opera completa*, 130, cat. 449.

79 A *soazone* is a cornice or entablature, most often made from wood. In Venice references to *soazoni* generally include the cladding of the arches and the entablature above them, as noted by Worthen, 'Soazoni, or the Venetian Reformation of San Nicolò dei Mendicoli',

257. The decorative programme at San Nicolò began in 1578, and had already made considerable headway by the time Sansovino described the church as 'in large part restored a few years ago' in 1581. Sansovino, *Venetia città nobilissima et singolare, descritta in XIIII. Libri*, 87v.

80 Worthen, 'Soazoni, or the Venetian Reformation of San Nicolò dei Mendicoli', 270–72.

81 Eire, *Reformations: The Early Modern World, 1450–1650*, 231–32.

82 For Calvin and idolatry, see Carlos M. N. Eire, *War against the Idols: The Reformation of Worship from Erasmus to Calvin* (Cambridge: Cambridge University Press, 1986), 195–233; Scavizzi, *The Controversy on Images from Calvin to Baronius*, 9–61.

83 Contained in Karlstadt's *On the Removal of Images* of 1522, where he also refuted the notion that images function as the 'bibles of the illiterate'. See Mangrum and Scavizzi, *Karlstadt, Emser, and Eck on Sacred Images*, 20.

84 See Edward Muir, 'The Virgin on the Street Corner: The Place of the Sacred in Italian Cities', in *Religion and Culture in the Renaissance and Reformation*, ed. Steven E. Ozment (Kirksville, MO: Sixteenth Century Journal Publishers, 1989), 25–40; Maya Corry, Deborah Howard, and Mary Laven, eds., *Madonnas & Miracles: The Holy Home in Renaissance Italy*, Exhibition Catalogue, the Fitzwilliam Museum, Cambridge, 7 March–4 June 2017 (London: Philip Wilson, 2017).

85 Silvio Antoniano, *Tre libri dell'educazione christiana dei figliuoli* (Verona: Sebastiano dalle Donne, 1584), 54v. See also Margaret A. Morse, 'Creating Sacred Space: The Religious Visual Culture of the Renaissance Venetian "casa"', *Renaissance Studies* 21, no. 2 (2007): 158.

86 Eire, *Reformations: The Early Modern World, 1450–1650*, 236.

87 Eire, *War against the Idols*, 7.

88 Margaret Aston, *Broken Idols of the English Reformation* (Cambridge: Cambridge University Press, 2015); Camille, *The Gothic Idol*, 347–48.

89 In Catholic societies 'seeing' was accepted as the only reliable source of knowledge. See Muir, 'The Virgin on the Street Corner: The Place of the Sacred in Italian Cities', 29. Muir cites the work of Peter Burke and David Gilmore's anthropology of Mediterranean societies.

90 Eire, *War against the Idols*, 152.

91 Stringa, *Venetia, città nobilissima, et singolare*, 187r.

92 Stringa, *Venetia, città nobilissima, et singolare*, 154v.

93 Stringa, *Venetia, città nobilissima, et singolare*, 152r. Worthen notes that these paintings likely filled the aisles. Worthen, 'Soazoni, or the Venetian Reformation of San Nicolò dei Mendicoli', 266–67, note 46.

94 Sapienza dates the San Zulian cycle to the ninth decade of the Cinquecento, with some of the last works being completed between 1587 and 1588. Sapienza, '(Intorno a) Leonardo Corona (1552–1596)', 150; Valentina Sapienza, *La chiesa di San Zulian a Venezia nel Cinquecento: dalla ricostruzione sansoviniana alle grandi imprese decorative di fine secolo* (Rome: École française de Rome, 2018), 123–24. Mason dates the cycle to the 1580s. Mason and Gallo, *Chiesa di San Nicolò dei Mendicoli: arte e devozione*, 29. Worthen points out that although both the San Zulian and San Nicolò paintings were completed around the same time, it is not clear which came first, but he nevertheless hypothesises that this was probably the San Nicolò cycle. Worthen, 'Soazoni, or the Venetian Reformation of San Nicolò dei Mendicoli', 276.

95 APV, Visite Priuli, fol. 412v. With the exception of the high altar, described as being 'ugly' and without decorations. Tommaso Rangone had the rights over this space. See Deborah Howard, *Jacopo Sansovino: Architecture and Patronage in Renaissance Venice* (New Haven, CT: Yale University Press, 1975), 84–87.

96 That each altar was to have an image had been stipulated by the Apostolic Visit. Cappelletti, *Storia della Chiesa di Venezia*, vol. 6: 519.

97 This order was made on numerous occasions. Examples of advised restorations include Priuli's order at San Lio that the altarpiece at the altar San Michele should be repaired

where broken; at San Pantalon he instructed that the alabaster altarpiece with figures in relief at the altar of the Blessed Sacrament should be polished; and at San Giovanni Crisostomo he instructed that the canvases in the high altar should be fitted with frames, because this would make them appear 'more noble'. APV, Visite Priuli, fols. 220r, 221v (San Lio); 188v, 191r (San Pantalon); 520r, 522r (San Giovanni Crisostomo).

98 APV, Visite Priuli, fol. 153v. He also approved of the 'large, and very noble' tabernacle, the altarpiece, and the presence of wooden benches.

99 The current altarpiece that is attributed to one Bartolomeo Giorda cannot be the same one described by Boschini since it presents iconographic differences at odds with his description. See Boschini, *Le minere della pittura*, 401. Of these, only the *Last Supper* was attributed to Dal Friso by Ridolfi, *Le maraviglie dell'arte*, vol. 2: 142.

100 APV, Visite Priuli, fols. 398r–v, 399r.

101 APV, Visite Priuli, fols. 564v–565r, 566r. See also note 190.

102 APV, Visite Priuli, fols. 339v–340r. The chapel is first described by Boschini as being adorned with the *Flagellation* by Antonio Foller. Above the sacristy he notes the *Deposition* 'with the Maries and some portraits', which may well have been commissioned by the Scuola del Sacramento, as well as the *Dead Christ* by Palma above the door of the tabernacle, and the *Last Supper* by Alvise dal Friso. Boschini, *Le minere della pittura*, 509–10. Mason dates the Palma painting to c. 1600. Mason Rinaldi, *Palma il Giovane: l'opera completa*, 132–33, cat. 480.

103 APV, Visite Priuli, fols. 487v, 490r.

104 APV, Visite Priuli, fols. 419r–v, 423r. Priuli referred to the confraternity providing '*qualche spaliera*', which denotes some kind of wooden cladding. Worthen notes the use of the term '*spalliere over soazze*' in the *mariegola* of the Scuola del Sacramento at San Severo to refer to this. Worthen, 'Soazoni, or the Venetian Reformation of San Nicolò dei Mendicoli', 257, note 16.

105 APV, Visite Priuli, fols. 197r, 200r. The missing painting 'towards the sacristy' was one of two painted by Andrea Vicentino: *The Multiplication of the Loaves and Fishes* and *Moses Striking the Rock*. He was paid for the first of these in 1590. See Worthen, 'Tintoretto's Paintings for the Banco del Sacramento in S. Margherita', 729.

106 APV, Visite Priuli, fols. 94r, 96r. For the canvas of Palma, which includes a prominent portrait of what must have been the parish priest at its centre and two donor portraits in the bottom foreground, see Mason Rinaldi, *Palma il Giovane: l'opera completa*, 132, cat. 479.

107 APV, Visite Priuli, fol. 113r. Priuli's synod of 1594 dictated that altars were not to be adorned with multiple images of the same saint. See Chapter 3, note 120.

108 This happened in numerous parishes. At San Fantin, for example, the visitation thought that the silver votives left for the Madonna could be used to make two new chalices and patens, whilst at Sant'Agnese Priuli gave permission for various objects, including silver votives, to be used to help make the 'many things' that the church was lacking. APV, Visite Priuli, fols. 458r, 459r (San Fantin); 373r (Sant'Agnese). For a useful catalogue with images of the kinds of liturgical objects referred to in documents such as visitations, see Salvatore Baviera and Jadranka Bentini, *Mistero e Immagine: L'Eucaristia nell'arte dal XVI al XVIII secolo*, Exhibition Catalogue, Chiesa abbaziale di San Salvatore, Bologna, 20 September–23 November 1997 (Milan: Electa, 1997), 233–72.

109 Stringa, *Venetia, città nobilissima, et singolare*, 152r.

110 Worthen analysed how both San Marco and the contemporary renovations of the Ducal Palace may have functioned as a decorative example at San Nicolò dei Mendicoli. See Worthen, 'Soazoni, or the Venetian Reformation of San Nicolò dei Mendicoli', 272–77. Prior to this, the example of San Marco for the decoration of Venetian parishes in the sixteenth century had been observed by Paul Hills, 'Piety and Patronage in Cinquecento Venice: Tintoretto and the Scuole Del Sacramento', *Art History* 6 no. 1 (1983): 37.

111 Mason, 'Images of Christ for Venetian Piety and Devotions in the Light of the Council of Trent', 296.

112 Unnumbered introductory pages. Stringa, *Venetia, città nobilissima, et singolare.*

113 We cannot rule out the possibility artists may have been discussed in person, although this is never mentioned in the documentation.

114 This happened at San Moisè and Sant'Aponal. At San Zulian, the priest was to ensure that before a ruined building close to the church was rebuilt, a model was to be made, and an estimate of the costs procured from the appropriate workers. At Santa Sofia, Priuli advised that the display of relics should emulate what had been done at Santa Marina. This example was to serve as its model. See APV, Visite Priuli, fols. 287v, 290v (San Moisè); 263v, 266v (Sant'Aponal); 412r, 415r (San Zulian), 503v, 505r (Santa Sofia).

115 See Bruno Bertoli and Silvio Tramontin, *Le visite pastorali di Jacopo Monico nella diocesi di Venezia (1829–1845)* (Rome: Edizioni di storia e letteratura, 1976), 31ff.

116 Bertoli and Tramontin, *La visita pastorale di Giovanni Ladislao Pyrker nella diocesi di Venezia (1821)*, 193.

117 Bertoli and Tramontin, *La visita pastorale di Giovanni Ladislao Pyrker nella diocesi di Venezia (1821)*, lxv, cxiii, cxv–cxvi.

118 Stefania Mason, 'Venetian Painting in the Late Sixteenth and Early Seventeenth Centuries', in *Venice: Art & Architecture*, ed. Giandomenico Romanelli, vol. 2 (Cologne: Köneman, 1997), 534.

119 Elizabeth Basye Gilmore Holt, ed., 'The Book of Suger, Abbot of St-Denis, on What Was Done under His Administration', in *A Documentary History of Art* (New York: Doubleday Anchor Books, 1957), vol. 1: 31.

120 Holt, 'The Book of Suger, Abbot of St-Denis', vol. 1: 25.

121 Cope, *The Venetian Chapel of the Sacrament in the Sixteenth Century*, 2, 265. Note 1 of page 265 details that by comparing near contemporary guidebooks to Rome and Venice it appears that at the end of the seventeenth century about one church in forty in Rome had a chapel of the sacrament (or a high altar treated as such), compared to about one church in every two and a half in Venice. For these confraternities, referred to also as *venerabile*, see Mackenney, *Venice as the Polity of Mercy*, 196–206.

122 Hills, 'Piety and Patronage in Cinquecento Venice', 31. Pages 32–33 provide an eloquent summary of the aims and practices of the Scuole del Santissimo Sacramento. Similar kinds of confraternities existed in Northern Europe even before the establishment of the feast of Corpus Domini in 1264. See Cope, *The Venetian Chapel of the Sacrament in the Sixteenth Century*, 271. The important differences between the confraternity at Corpus Domini in Venice and the parish-based Scuole del Sacramento that began to be established in the city during the early Cinquecento is pointed out by Worthen, 'Tintoretto's Paintings for the Banco del Sacramento in S. Margherita', 711, note 20. That the utmost reverence should be paid to the eucharist, and that it should be retained in a tabernacle with a lamp before it, was a preoccupation of the much earlier constitutions of Patriarch Tommaso Donà of c. 1495–1503. Vuillemin Pascal, 'Une reforme de l'interieur . . . : les constitutions pastorales du patriarche de venisa Tommaso Dona (1492–1504). Presentation, examen et édition', *Studi Veneziani* 54 (2007): 76–77.

123 The earliest documented Scuola del Sacramento in Venice was that of San Zulian, founded in 1502. Worthen, 'Tintoretto's Paintings for the Banco del Sacramento in S. Margherita', 710. See also Mackenney, *Venice as the Polity of Mercy*, 196–202. Mackenney argues that since fifty-six of these were founded before the first session of Trent in 1545 and only eleven after it, this should be taken as strong evidence that the confraternities had little do with Catholic reform. However, the falloff in foundation rates probably has more to do with the fact that by mid-century almost every single parish in the city now had such a confraternity, meaning there was no necessity for further ones to be established. By the end of the sixteenth century in Milan, 556 of the 763 parishes in the city had a fraternity dedicated to the eucharist. Padre Pietro Tacchi Venturi, *Storia della Compagnia di Gesù in Italia*, vol. 1, part 1 (Rome: Civiltà Cattolica, 1931), 226.

124 The impact of Thiene is noted by Niero, 'Riforma Cattolica e Concilio di Trento a Venezia', 91–92. Thiene founded a company of the Blessed Sacrament in Verona already in 1517. Cope, *The Venetian Chapel of the Sacrament in the Sixteenth Century*, 272. The practice of the *Quarant'ore* appears to have begun in Milan in the late 1520s.

125 Deborah Walberg, 'Tradition and Propaganda in the Venetian Madonna Della Pace', *Ikon* 9 (2016): 10. Giulio Strozzi, *Venezia edificata* (Venice: Pinelli, 1624), 140, canto 14, no. 35.

126 Similar points were made also by Niero, 'Riforma Cattolica e Concilio di Trento a Venezia', 91–96; Mason, 'Venetian Painting in the Late Sixteenth and Early Seventeenth Centuries', 534.

127 Sansovino, *Venetia città nobilissima et singolare, descritta in XIIII. Libri*, 103v. With the exception of San Marco, as noted by Gastone Vio, *Le Scuole Piccole nella Venezia dei dogi: note d'archivio per la storia delle confraternite veneziana* (Costabissara: A. Colla, 2004), 21.

128 Worthen, 'Tintoretto's Paintings for the Banco del Sacramento in S. Margherita'.

129 Cope, *The Venetian Chapel of the Sacrament in the Sixteenth Century*, 3.

130 In 1560 an apothecary's decision to cease attending his parish Scuola was used as evidence against him at an Inquisition tribunal. Mackenney, *Venice as the Polity of Mercy*, 263.

131 Logan Pearsall Smith, *The Life and Letters of Sir Henry Wotton* (Oxford: Clarendon Press, 1907), vol. 1: 350.

132 Edward Muir, *Civic Ritual in Renaissance Venice* (Princeton, NJ: Princeton University Press, 1981), 230.

133 Giberti, *Constitutiones*, 30.

134 Cope, *The Venetian Chapel of the Sacrament in the Sixteenth Century*, 17. This location was made obligatory also by Pope Paul V's *Rituale Romanum* of 1614. See Nagel, *The Controversy of Renaissance Art*, 206.

135 Corner's significance is noted also by Humfrey, 'La pala d'altare veneta nell'età delle riforme', 1135. For his visits, see Giuseppe Liberali, *Documentari sulla Riforma Cattolica pre e post-tridentina a Treviso (1527–1577): La diocesi delle visite pastorali*, vols. 7 and 8, parte prima (Treviso: Seminario vescovile, 1976).

136 Andrew R. Casper, 'Display and Devotion: Exhibiting Icons and Their Copies in Counter-Reformation Italy', in *Religion and the Senses in Early Modern Europe*, ed. Wietse de Boer and Christine Göttler (Leiden: Brill, 2013), 52. See also chapter 9 on Tridentine reforms to the mass in Lang, *The Roman Mass*.

137 Tramontin, 'La visita apostolica del 1581 a Venezia', 523–34.

138 Tramontin, 'La visita apostolica del 1581 a Venezia', 534.

139 San Lio, San Leonardo, Santa Maria Formosa, Sant'Agostino, Sant'Antonin, Santo Stefano Confessore (San Stin), San Canciano, San Biagio, and San Tomà. APV, Visite Priuli, fols. 219r (San Lio), 131r (San Leonardo), 487r (Santa Maria Formosa), 351r (Sant'Agostino), 495r (Sant'Antonin), 403r (Santo Stefano Confessore), 251v–252r (San Canciano), 163r (San Biagio), 55v (San Tomà). At San Giovanni in Bragora the transferral of the eucharist to the high altar was imminent (see following note). At San Paternian, a public *bottega* was placed close to the window of the sacrament chapel. Thus, the priest was to find some masters who could judge the thickness of the chapel's wall and how secure the Blessed Sacrament was in its current site. If it was judged to be 'in danger', or 'indecent', then the move to the high altar was to be completed in consultation with the confraternity (431r–v). Conversely, at Santa Maria del Giglio the visitation ordered the Blessed Sacrament to be moved off the high altar, and into the chapel that was reserved for it (439r).

140 Tramontin, 'La visita apostolica del 1581 a Venezia', 524, note 241, 529, 532. By the time of Priuli's visit in 1591 the tabernacle of Angelo Raffaele appears to have been shifted into the chancel. At the Bragora the sacrament was still conserved in a small *altarino* attached to the right pilaster of the high altar, but it was noted that 'the patriarch has understood that in a few days the Blessed Sacrament will be transported into the high altar'. APV, Visite Priuli, fols. 179r–v (Angelo Raffaele), 83v (Bragora).

141 Sant'Agostino and San Stin were never visited by either Zane or Vendramin, and Sant'Agostino was in any case reconstructed beginning in 1639. At San Lio Zane made no comment on the high altar or location of the Blessed Sacrament. Since he did not reassert Priuli's request, which he often did for other things, it seems likely the change had already been made. APV, Visite Zane, no. 17.

142 APV, Visite Priuli, fols. 495r, 497r. The visit ordered the widening of the high altar and the provision of a stone altar. The space was to be surrounded by columns and a gate, or '*porticella*', that could be closed. Zane reasserted the orders of Priuli. APV, Visite Zane, no. 2.

143 Voelker, 'Carlo Borromeo's Instructiones fabricae et supellectilis ecclesiasticae', 160–63; Cappelletti, *Storia della Chiesa di Venezia*, vol. 6: 514–15. The Torcellan synod of Grimani, as well as Priuli's own two synods, dictated similar things. Cappelletti, vol. 6: 601–2, 763–66, 930–34.

144 APV, Visite Priuli, fols. 329r, 332r.

145 See APV, Visite Priuli, fol. 329r. The Priuli visitation did the same at numerous other churches. For example, even though the tabernacle was deemed 'quite well decorated' at San Fantin, it was judged to be too small and so a new one was to be made. At San Lio, Priuli objected to the chapel being 'on the left hand side of the church', ordering that the tabernacle was to be moved to the high altar and a new one of the maximum size that could conveniently be accommodated in the altar be acquired, noting that the confraternity of the Blessed Sacrament had promised to make this purchase and 'do other things that will be necessary for the divine cult'. APV, Visite Priuli, fols. 457r (San Fantin), 219r (San Lio).

146 Michele Cassese, 'I tedeschi luterani a Venezia e il loro rapporto con la parrocchia di San Bartolomeo (dal'500 alla fine della repubblica)', in *La chiesa di San Bartolomeo e la comunità tedesca a Venezia*, ed. Natalino Bonazza, Isabella di Lenardo and Gianmario Guidarelli (Venice: Marcianum Press, 2013), 249–68; Gaier, 'Il patriarca e il suo vicario', 211.

147 Stringa, *Venetia, città nobilissima, et singolare*, 95v.

148 Stringa, *Venetia, città nobilissima, et singolare*, 95r.

149 APV, Visite Zane, no. 6.

150 APV, Visite Priuli, fol. 121r. The tabernacle may have recently been completed, since Stringa described the high altar as having been newly rebuilt 'in a lovely manner'. Stringa, *Venetia, città nobilissima, et singolare*, 139v. Tintoretto had painted the *Last Supper* (1547) and the *Washing of the Feet* (1548–49) for the *banco* of the Scuola del Sacramento at San Marcuola. See Worthen, 'Tintoretto's Paintings for the Banco del Sacramento in S. Margherita', 719–20, 731–32.

151 APV, Visite Priuli, fols. 287r–v. The altar and chapel were found so well decorated that the patriarch took the opportunity to encourage the parish to persevere in paying honour to the cult of the Blessed Sacrament.

152 Noted first by Hills, 'Piety and Patronage in Cinquecento Venice', 37. The space was also adorned with the Tintoretto workshop's lateral painting of *The Washing of the Feet* (c. mid 1580s).

153 APV, Visite Priuli, fol. 411r. For the elaborate decoration of the chapel, which included rich stucco work on the ceiling by Ottaviano Ridolfi, and paintings by Palma, Leonardo Corona, and the workshop of Veronese, see Stefania Mason Rinaldi, 'La cappella del SS. Sacramento in San Zulian', *Atti del Istituto Veneto di Scienze, Lettere ed Arti* 134 (1976): 439–56; Sapienza, *La chiesa di San Zulian a Venezia nel Cinquecento*, 33–77.

154 APV, Visite Priuli, fol. 411r. The ciborium is ordinarily chalice-shaped and is used for distributing holy communion and reserving the consecrated host in the tabernacle. The pyx is a box used for taking the eucharist to the sick. See www.newadvent.org/cathen/03767a.htm (accessed 10 July 2023). During his visits Priuli also routinely ordered the purchasing of *corporali* (the eucharistic altar cloth), the *pianetta* (vestment necessary for the eucharistic celebration), as well as new liturgical objects if the existing ones were inadequate (see note 108).

155 APV, Visite Priuli, fols. 529r–v, 532r.
156 Borromeo had advised against having any kind of cupboard below the tabernacle, even if used for retaining church furnishings. Voelker, 'Carlo Borromeo's Instructiones fabricae et supellectilis ecclesiasticae', 162.
157 APV, Visite Priuli, fol. 112r (San Luca), 205r–v (San Marziale). The latter was decorated with Aliense's *Resurrection* (1586) and Domenico Passignano's *Crucifixion*. See Cope, *The Venetian Chapel of the Sacrament in the Sixteenth Century*, 289.
158 APV, Visite Priuli, fols. 397r (Santa Marina), 371r (Sant'Agnese).
159 APV, Visite Priuli, fols. 280r, 281v. See Worthen, 'The Altar and the "banco" of the Scuola del Sacramento in San Giacomo dall'Orio'; Lillywhite, 'The Decoration of the Church of San Giacomo dall'Orio in Venice', 137.
160 APV, Visite Zane, no. 15. Stringa, *Venetia, città nobilissima, et singolare*, 163v–64.
161 Priuli usually ordered an inventory of relics if one had yet to be drawn up. If of a suitable size, these relics were to be placed in labelled crystal containers and then arranged in a cabinet with a gilded sign reading '*Reliquie Sanctorum*' to denote the contents. In doing this he was following the norms set out by the Apostolic Visitation, the guidelines of the 1592 Torcellan synod, as well as the advice of Borromeo. Cappelletti, *Storia della Chiesa di Venezia*, vol. 6: 517–19, 666–71; Voelker, 'Carlo Borromeo's Instructiones fabricae et supellectilis ecclesiasticae', 207–10.
162 APV, Visite Priuli, fols. 71r, 73v–74r, 79r.
163 APV, Visite Priuli, fols. 297v, 300v–301r. Santi Apostoli also had no relics (fol. 317v).
164 APV, Visite Priuli, fols. 495v–496r, 497r. The priest was to ensure that this chapel was 'reduced to perfection' as soon as possible, and the translation of the saint's remains was to take place only once patriarchal approval had been granted. For the chapel, see Stefania Mason Rinaldi, 'Il libro dei conti della famiglia Tiepolo per la Capella di S. Sabba in S. Antonin', *Atti dell'Istituto Veneto di Scienze, Lettere ed Arti* 135 (1976–77): 193–212.
165 APV, Visite Priuli, fols. 495r, 497r.
166 Mason Rinaldi, 'Il libro dei conti della famiglia Tiepolo per la Capella di S. Sabba in S. Antonin', 211. APV, Visite Zane, no. 2.
167 APV, Visite Zane, no. 2. Zane did not include this exhortation in the summary of orders for the parish, so it was perhaps not to be taken as seriously as some of the changes deemed to be non-negotiable.
168 APV, Archivio 'segreto', Visite pastorali, Visita pastorale del patriarca Giovanni Tiepolo, I, no. 11.
169 For Palma's paintings here, see Mason Rinaldi, *Palma il Giovane: l'opera completa*, 117, cats. 342–48.
170 For the fusion of the two confraternities, see Mackenney, *Venice as the Polity of Mercy*, 204.
171 Worthen, 'Tintoretto's Paintings for the Banco del Sacramento in S. Margherita', 710.
172 Tramontin, 'La visita apostolica del 1581 a Venezia', 477–78.
173 Worthen, 'Tintoretto's Paintings for the Banco del Sacramento in S. Margherita', 710.
174 Worthen, 711, note 25. Worthen notes that women could be members but that they could never hold office. Direct evidence is rarely given for this assertion, but the confraternity at San Samuele detailed that anyone from the parish could be admitted to the fraternity for devotional reasons, including 'brothers and sisters of any age male or female', as long as they obeyed the rules set out in the *mariegola*. BMC, MS.CI. IV016, Mariegola della Scuola del Santissimo in San Samuele, fol. 2v.
175 San Nicolò dei Mendicoli is a case in point. The records of the Apostolic Visit show that the parish was a large one, with 3,500 residents, but the clergy had an annual income of only thirty-seven and a half ducats, and only ninety-five ducats from four bequests. Fifty ducats annually were reserved for the building. At San Simeone Grande, a parish of a similar size (3,000 residents), with exactly the same amount of clergy, the income was 180 ducats, with forty-six ducats for the building, and twelve bequests that totalled 170 ducats annually. In both cases housing was provided exclusive of these amounts. Clergy often had

other sources of income in addition to these sums. Tramontin, 'La visita apostolica del 1581 a Venezia', 512–13.

176 Worthen, 'Soazoni, or the Venetian Reformation of San Nicolò dei Mendicoli', 254.

177 A point made also by Howard, *Jacopo Sansovino*, 77. Artists may also have worked for poorer Scuole for reduced fees. We know that Tintoretto did this frequently, charging the confraternity of the linen-weavers just twenty ducats for their altarpiece. Nichols, *Tintoretto: Tradition and Identity*, 130, 182.

178 See the examples in note 190. See also Christopher F. Black, *Italian Confraternities in the Sixteenth Century* (Cambridge: Cambridge University Press, 1989), 235. Black notes that at San Marziale the priest appealed to the Scuola dedicated to San Marcilian for financial assistance with the organ repairs in 1575 and the decoration of the sacristy in 1603 and 1642.

179 For seventeenth-century Padua, for example, see Celeste McNamara, 'What the People Want: Popular Support for Catholic Reform in the Veneto', *Catholic Historical Review* 102, no. 3 (2016): 492–516. See also Black, *Italian Confraternities in the Sixteenth Century*, 75. Black argues that relationships between clergy and laity were 'complex and inconsistent', and that rather than a one-direction acculturation process imposed by the dominant elite over popular culture and religion, the two groups could influence one another.

180 Noted by Hills, 'Piety and Patronage in Cinquecento Venice', 38.

181 See body text and note 157.

182 Rosand, *Painting in Cinquecento Venice*, 89, 234. Discussed by Black, *Italian Confraternities in the Sixteenth Century*, 250, 251–52.

183 See, for example, Manfredo Tafuri, *Venezia e Il Rinascimento: religione, scienza, architettura* (Turin: Einaudi, 1985), 125–54; Peter Humfrey, 'Competitive Devotions: The Venetian Scuole Piccole as Donors of Altarpieces in the Years around 1500', *Art Bulletin* 70 (1988): 401–23.

184 BMC, MS.CI. IV016, Mariegola della Scuola del Santissimo in San Samuele, fol. 41v. Similar sentiments were expressed by other confraternities; see Marie-Louise Lillywhite, 'The Decoration of the Church of San Giacomo dall'Orio in Venice', 118.

185 APV, Visite Priuli, fol. 339v.

186 BMC, MS.CI. IV016, Mariegola della Scuola del Santissimo in San Samuele, fols. 41v, 55v.

187 Stringa, *Venetia, città nobilissima, et singolare*, 163r. In 1604 Patriarch Zane also credited the generosity of the eucharistic confraternities in Venice for their contribution to 'the splendour and magnificence of the churches'. Chambers and Pullan, eds., *Venice: A Documentary History*, 193.

188 Later in seventeenth-century Padua, Bishop Gregorio Barbarigo took the time to have open audiences with the laity during his visitations. See McNamara, 'What the People Want', 495.

189 The clerical income was thirty-four ducats annually and there were four bequests totalling eighty-one ducats. APV, Visite Priuli, fol. 450v; Tramontin, 'La visita apostolica del 1581 a Venezia', 511.

190 Some examples: at San Cassiano Priuli exhorted the priest to encourage the parishioners to assist with the raising of the paving; at Santa Trinità the priest was to encourage the *contrada* and the Scuola del Sacramento to continue the work of decorating the church and to persuade the confraternity at the chapel of Sant'Anastasio to make a new altar and altarpiece; at San Silvestro the priest and church procurators were to do 'everything possible' to ensure that the high altar was replaced with a new one; at Sant'Agnese the confraternities were encouraged to assist with the decoration of the altars and the church. APV, Visite Priuli, fols. 308v, 311r (San Cassiano); 564v, 566r (Santa Trinità); 76v (San Silvestro); 373v (Sant'Agnese). Stringa noted that the church of Santa Trinità had recently been renewed, and that the relics of Sant'Anastasio were placed in a 'beautiful chapel', suggesting that the changes advised by the visitation had been completed. Stringa, *Venetia, città nobilissima, et singolare*, 110v.

191 For interactions between parish priests and confraternities, see Black, 'The Development of Confraternity Studies over the Past Thirty Years', 20.

192 BMC, MS.Cl. IV016, Mariegola della Scuola del Santissimo in San Samuele, fols. 19v–24r, 27r, 38r–v, 40v.

193 Howard, *Jacopo Sansovino*, 81–82. In the early Cinquecento the parish priest Matteo Eletti had also tried to raise funds for San Geminiano.

194 See note 48.

195 See note 49.

196 Borghi commissioned at least four altarpieces and a number of other works for his church from 1585 onwards. He appears as a protagonist in one of the altarpieces: Veronese's *The Conversion of Saint Pantaleon* (1587–88). See Adriano Aymonino, 'La Pala di San Pantalon: immagine devozionale e manifesto politico', *Venezia Cinquecento* 15, no. 30 (2005): 159–200. The various benefices and titles held by these priests are detailed in Lillywhite, 'The Decoration of the Church of San Giacomo dall'Orio in Venice', 119. Manzini, Gatto, and Da Ponte were all canons of San Marco, as was Don Filomaso at San Paternian (see note 200). For other examples of clerical patronage in Venice, see Louisa Matthew, 'Clergy and Confraternities', in *Artistic Centers of the Italian Renaissance: Venice and the Veneto*, ed. Peter Humfrey (New York: Cambridge University Press, 2007), 92–150; Sherman, *The Lost Venetian Church of Santa Maria Assunta dei Crociferi: Form, Decoration, Patronage*, 61–63.

197 Ridolfi, *Le maraviglie dell'arte*, vol. 2: 57. The author could not resist pointing out that this famous collection included a 'singular portrait' by Ridolfi himself.

198 Jones, 'Priestly Patronage in Late Renaissance Venice: Antonio Gatto's *cappella maggiore* in San Polo', 223.

199 Lillywhite, 'The Decoration of the Church of San Giacomo dall'Orio in Venice', 120. MSM, *Mariegola della Scuola del Santissimo in San Giacomo dall'Orio*, fol. 41v.

200 With the exception of the chapels of Saint Mark and the Blessed Sacrament, and fifty ducats received from the Scuola of Santa Caterina for part of the building of the wall where their altar was placed. APV, Visite Priuli, Supplemento alle visite Priuli, number 34, fol. 552r. The will is dated 22 July 1591. For Filomaso's bequest to his parish, containing ample information on the renovation of the high altar at the end of the seventeenth century, see APV, Parrocchia di San Paternian, Venezia, Commissarie, Commissaria del R. mo pievano don Pietro Filomuso.

201 APV, Visite Priuli, Supplemento alle visite Priuli, number 34, fol. 562r. With the exception of one *'D[onna] elena'* who should receive the funds left to her regardless. Boschini mentions a chapel in the church with a painting 'of a priest' by Baldassare d'Anna. This could possibly be connected with Filomaso. Boschini, *Le minere della pittura*, 129.

202 Lillywhite, 'The Decoration of the Church of San Giacomo dall'Orio in Venice', 141. Zane made no recommendations for the altar. The significance of the episode was noted also by Modesti, 'I cori nelle chiese veneziane e la visita apostolica del 1581', 41.

203 Lillywhite, 'The Decoration of the Church of San Giacomo dall'Orio in Venice', 137, 141.

204 Vio, *Le Scuole Piccole nella Venezia dei dogi: note d'archivio per la storia delle confraternite veneziana*, 21. For an example of protest against the eucharist confraternities on the island of Sant'Erasmo, see Martin, *Venice's Hidden Enemies*, 193–94.

205 Nagel explored what he termed 'soft iconoclasm' in Italy, arguing that anti-image impulses were redirected back into the art. See section three of Nagel, *The Controversy of Renaissance Art*.

206 Niero, 'Riforma Cattolica e Concilio di Trento a Venezia', 91. For silver altarpieces, see Antonio Niero, 'Notizie di archivio sulle pale d'argento delle lagune venete', *Studi Veneziani* 2 (1978): 257–91. Niero did not include the example of San Marcuola, where a 'silver altarpiece that had been removed from the high altar' was described as present in the sacristy. The visitation ordered that a better solution should be found for it, and that it was to be 'diligently cared for'. Priuli had also ordered that the silver altarpiece at San

Pietro di Castello should be restored where necessary, suggesting that Niero's claim cannot be applied to Priuli's visit. APV, Visite Priuli, fol. 122r.

207 For altars before the Council of Trent, see Gianmario Guidarelli, 'Gli altari nel Rinascimento prima del Concilio di Trento', in *L'Altare: recenti acquisizioni storiografiche e prospettive di ricerca*, ed. Bert Daelemans, Proceedings of the XVII International Liturgical Conference, Bose, 30 May–1 June 2019 (Magnano: Edizioni Qiqajon, 2021), 119–37.

208 For Borromeo in Bergamo, see Angelo Giuseppe Roncalli, *Gli atti della visita apostolica di San Carlo Borromeo a Bergamo (1575)*, 2 vols. (Florence: Leo Olschki, 1936–57).

209 The events are summarised by Hochmann, *Peintres et commanditaires à Venise (1540–1628)*, 268–69.

210 For the *spianate*, see Andrea Bayer, 'Bergamo and Brescia', in *Artistic Centers of the Italian Renaissance: Venice and the Veneto*, ed. Peter Humfrey (Cambridge: Cambridge University Press, 2007), 306, 309. Borromeo had also been Apostolic Visitor to Brescia in 1580. See Angelo Turchini, Giovanni Donni, and Gabriele Archetti, *Visita apostolica e decreti di Carlo Borromeo alla Diocesi di Brescia*, 6 vols. (Brescia: Brixia sacra, 2003–7).

211 A few examples: at San Giovanni in Bragora the two *'altaroli'* of the Cross and the Blessed Sacrament (decorated with Cima da Conegliano's painting of *Constantine and Saint Helena* and Alvise Vivarini's *Resurrection*, respectively) were to be demolished, and the eucharist was to be moved into the high altar; at San Vio the altar of Saint Matthew belonging to the Barbarigo family was deemed 'very old and indecent', so it was to be demolished and the family were to fund a new one, together with a new altarpiece; at Sant'Antonin the baptistery was to be moved to the head of the nave, and the altar currently in this space was to be displaced. APV, Visite Priuli, fols. 85r (San Giovanni in Bragora), 537v (San Vio), 495v (Sant'Antonin). For the Bragora paintings, see Peter Humfrey, 'Cima da Conegliano, Sebastiano Mariani, and Alvise Vivarini at the East End of S. Giovanni in Bragora in Venice', *Art Bulletin* 62, no. 3 (1980): 350–63.

212 This most often involved the Scuole del Sacramento, which had to follow the transferral of the tabernacle into the presbytery. At San Leonardo the confraternity dedicated to the titular saint was to move to the high altar. This was already dedicated to the saint, but the congregants had been worshipping at a second altar behind the choir, which was to be moved elsewhere. APV, Visite Priuli, fol. 132v.

213 At San Simeone Piccolo the two altars dedicated to the 'Angel and to San Francesco di Paola' were to be removed and united into one altar. Their relative confraternities were also to be unified and hold their devotions at the altar on alternate days. They were also expected to pay for the costs. APV, Visite Priuli, fol. 340r.

214 One example in the church of San Lio survives. Worthen, 'Architecture & Sacraments in Venetian Parish Churches'.

215 Sant'Agnese, Sant'Angelo, San Marziale, San Moisè, and San Tomà. Worthen, 'Soazoni, or the Venetian Reformation of San Nicolò dei Mendicoli', 256, note 13, 271; Modesti, 'I cori nelle chiese veneziane e la visita apostolica del 1581', 45, 55, 57, notes 23, 47, 48.

216 See Duncan G. Stroik, 'Church Architecture since Vatican II', *Jurist* 75 (2015): 5–34; John F. Baldovin, 'The Constitution on Sacred Liturgy', in *The Oxford Handbook of Vatican II*, ed. Catherine E. Clifford and Massimo Faggioli (Oxford: Oxford University Press, 2023), 148–68.

217 Chapter 7 of the constitution on the sacred liturgy (4 December 1963). See www.vatican.va/archive/hist_councils/ii_vatican_council/documents/vat-ii_const_19631204_sacrosanctum-concilium_en.html (accessed 16 July 2023).

218 Firpo, *Artisti, gioiellieri, eretici*, 317–18.

219 Vergerio argued that he had objected to some images on the grounds that they were badly designed, superstitious, and in some cases indecent. Schutte, *Pier Paolo Vergerio: The Making of an Italian Reformer*, 174–75.

220 Deborah Walberg, 'The Writings and Artistic Patronage of Patriarch Giovanni Tiepolo (1570–1631): A Preliminary Investigation', *Studi Veneziani* 62–64 (2011): 193–224;

Sherman, *The Lost Venetian Church of Santa Maria Assunta Dei Crociferi: Form, Decoration, Patronage*, 273–77.

221 Barcham, *Grand in Design: The Life and Career of Federico Cornaro, Prince of the Church, Patriarch of Venice and Patron of the Arts*. Barcham attributes Cornaro's tastes not to any great piety but to his careerism and ambition.

222 Pietro Cataneo, *I quattro primi libri di architettura* (Venice: House of Aldus, 1554), 35v–36v; Andrea Palladio, *The Four Books of Architecture (1570)*, introduction by Adolf K. Placzek (New York: Dover, 1965), 82. Leon Battista Alberti had made similar points in the previous century, arguing, 'I would deck it out [the temple] in every part so that anyone who entered it would start with awe for his admiration at all the noble things.' Leon Battista Alberti, *On the Art of Building in Ten Books (1443–52)*, trans. Joseph Rykwert, Neil Leach, and Robert Tavernor (Cambridge, MA: MIT Press, 1991), 194.

223 Molanus, *Traité des saintes images*, book 2, chapters 40, 41. Freedberg, 'The Structure of Byzantine and European Iconoclasm', 171–72.

224 Gilio, *Dialogue on the Errors and Abuses of Painters*, 229.

225 See Hochmann, *Peintres et commanditaires à Venise (1540–1628)*, 276–77. Not all Venetians agreed with this stance. In 1544 the apothecary Francesco Locadel had requested that no symbols should be placed in the sacrament chapel that he had left monies for at San Zulian, save for an image of Christ on the tabernacle door. As we have seen, his request was completely ignored. Mason Rinaldi, 'La cappella del SS. Sacramento in San Zulian', 339–440.

226 Margaret M. Newett, ed., *Canon Pietro Casola's Pilgrimage to Jerusalem in the Year 1494* (Manchester: Manchester University Press, 1907), 137.

227 Newett, *Canon Pietro Casola's Pilgrimage to Jerusalem in the Year 1494*, 138.

228 For Zane, see Chambers and Pullan, eds., *Venice: A Documentary History*, 193. For the Apostolic Visit, see Tramontin, 'La visita apostolica del 1581 a Venezia', 493.

229 As demonstrated by Priuli's *Relazioni* (ambassadorial reports read to the Senate upon returning from an embassy). See Albèri, *Le relazioni degli ambasciatori veneti al senato durante il secolo decimosesto*, vol. 4: 405–49; Eugenio Albèri, *Le relazioni degli ambasciatori veneti al senato durante il secolo decimosesto*, vol. 5, series 1 (Florence: Società editrice fiorentina, 1861), 229–72.

230 Niero, *I patriarchi di Venezia*, 106. Priuli's body was allegedly found incorrupt when it was exhumed in 1624.

231 Nichols, *Tintoretto: Tradition and Identity*, 187–88.

PART II

CHAPTER FIVE

THE BODY OF CHRIST

In a surreal drawing of the 1620s by Palma il Giovane, the crucified Christ is depicted emerging from a chalice (Fig. 65). Accompanied by two plump, winged putti at its base, Christ is sustained by the presence of two further angels above who gently support him as blood flows from the wound in his side.[1] Images of the crucified Christ in a communion vessel were commonly found in the rulebooks, or *mariegole*, of eucharistic confraternities in Venice as well as in an urban context, one example of this being the relief on the façade of the sacrament chapel at the parish church of San Polo.[2] In Palma's drawing, and in a second very similar sketch in the Museo Correr in Venice, the outlines of the figures have been pricked, suggesting that the drawing may have been used for a print (which does not survive) or some other liturgical use, perhaps the embroidery for a vestment or a tabernacle door.[3] Whatever its precise function, this is an image that cogently visualises eucharistic dogma: that the bread and wine are transformed into the body and blood of Christ at the moment of transubstantiation, that Christ is whole and present in the eucharist, and the idea of the mass as a sacrifice. It is thus a deeply theological image, and this is important to keep in mind if we consider that David Freedberg recalled that in the late 1960s, when he commenced his pioneering investigations into the effects of iconoclasm on art in late sixteenth-century Antwerp, it was Michael Baxandall who asked him more than once why he thought theology had any influence on painting at all.[4] Like Baxandall, Charles Hope has argued that altarpieces were much more about the devotional practices associated with

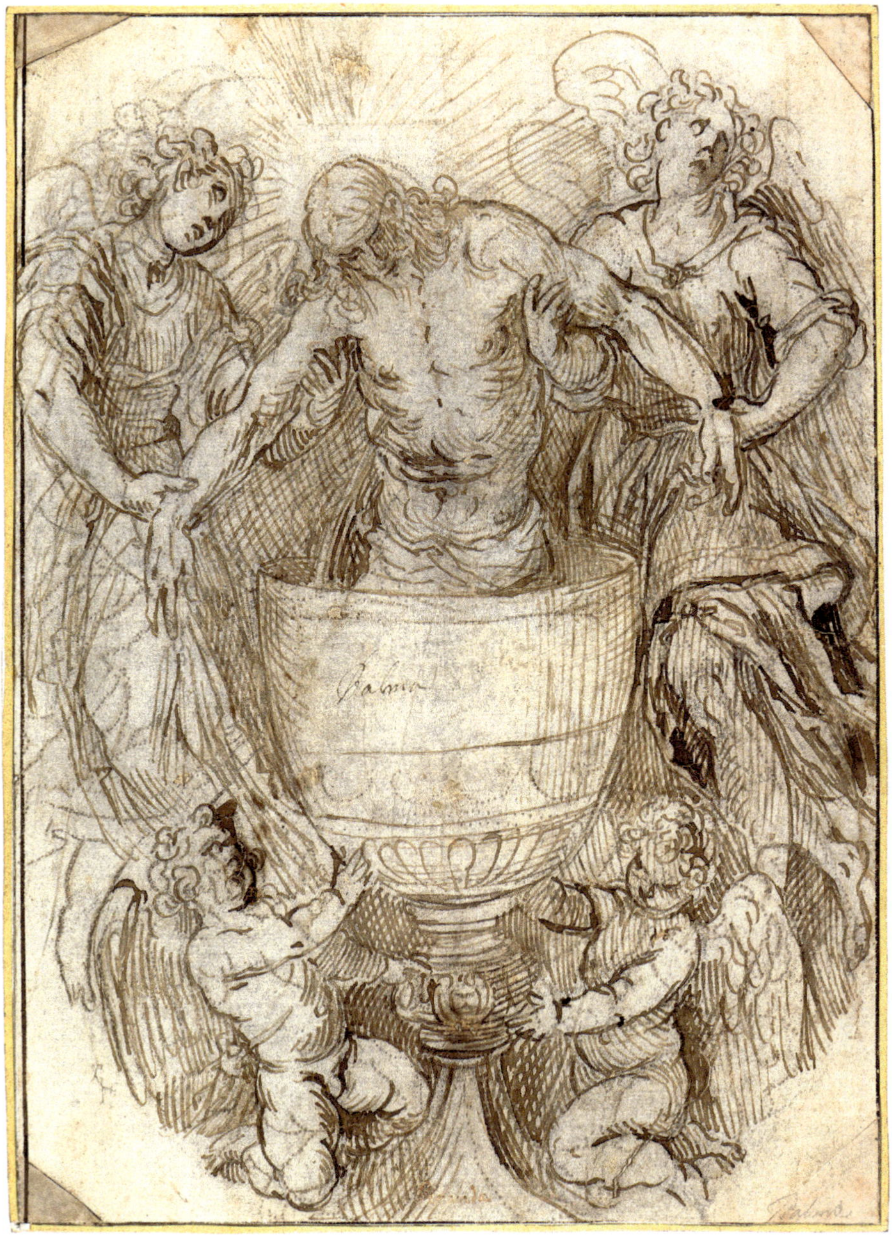

65. Palma il Giovane, *Christ in a Chalice Supported by Angels,* 1620s, pen and ink with chalk, National Gallery of Scotland, Edinburgh (Photo: National Galleries of Scotland, William Finlay Watson Bequest 1881)

them than they were a reflection of theological ideas or doctrines. Although this may hold true for many examples, in particular, the category of the altarpiece, it is also the case that from the mid-sixteenth century onwards doctrine and image became closely intertwined.[5] After all, the contemporary controversies surrounding images were profoundly theological in nature. This is not to suggest that artists were merely beholden to theology, and that their devotional output was a straightforward explication of the most important religious issues of the day.[6] As we shall see, the potential of the theme of the body of Christ for novel artistic expression and experimentation might have attracted artists to depicting it in the first place. And although sacred images were linked to the *actions* of religious communities, as Hope emphasised, this does not mean that the theology of the eucharist would have been too abstruse for the average Venetian to comprehend. The *mariegole* of the confraternities of the Blessed Sacrament, for example, clearly elucidated the dogmas that underpinned their devotional activities, and such *scuole* were popular with a broad cross-section of society. Not only did numerous artists in Venice work on repeated occasions for the Scuole del Santissimo Sacramento (Tintoretto being the most famous example of this), but their families also supported them financially.[7] In fact, in most cases a modern-day viewer is at a greater disadvantage when attempting to make sense of the iconography in Palma's drawing than an early modern Catholic would have been.

THE HOST

The drawing by Palma il Giovane was part of a rich tradition of eucharistic imagery in Venice that made visible the body of Christ on a symbolic and figurative level.[8] Majestic tabernacles, often inset with paintings or small sculptures; representations of the host, glowing in its monstrance or floating above a chalice; and the dead Christ, suffering and supported by angels all proliferated in the latter half of the Cinquecento. Over 300 years earlier, in the wake of both the Fourth Lateran Council of 1215, which established the doctrine of transubstantiation and obliged Christians to partake in the eucharist at least once a year, and the establishment of the feast of Corpus Domini in 1264, the host became an image of singular importance to Christians.[9] Yet it was not until the second half of the sixteenth century in Venice that we see a demonstrable increase in the quantity of altarpieces with explicitly eucharistic themes or subject matters.[10] The resulting artistic experiments to be discussed here point to both how images could further particular ideas and how they were stimulated by them in the first place.

To begin with representations of the host, Richard Trexler's study of the Florentine Interdict of 1376–78 pointed out that for some medieval Christians it was thought that 'continued staring at the host was equivalent to communion itself'.[11] Going to mass was referred to as 'going to see the body of Christ' and worshippers were known to move between multiple masses to view the elevation as many times as possible. This longing for visual access to the fleeting moment when the priest raised the communion wafer and its miraculous transformation into the body of Christ that was believed to take place might

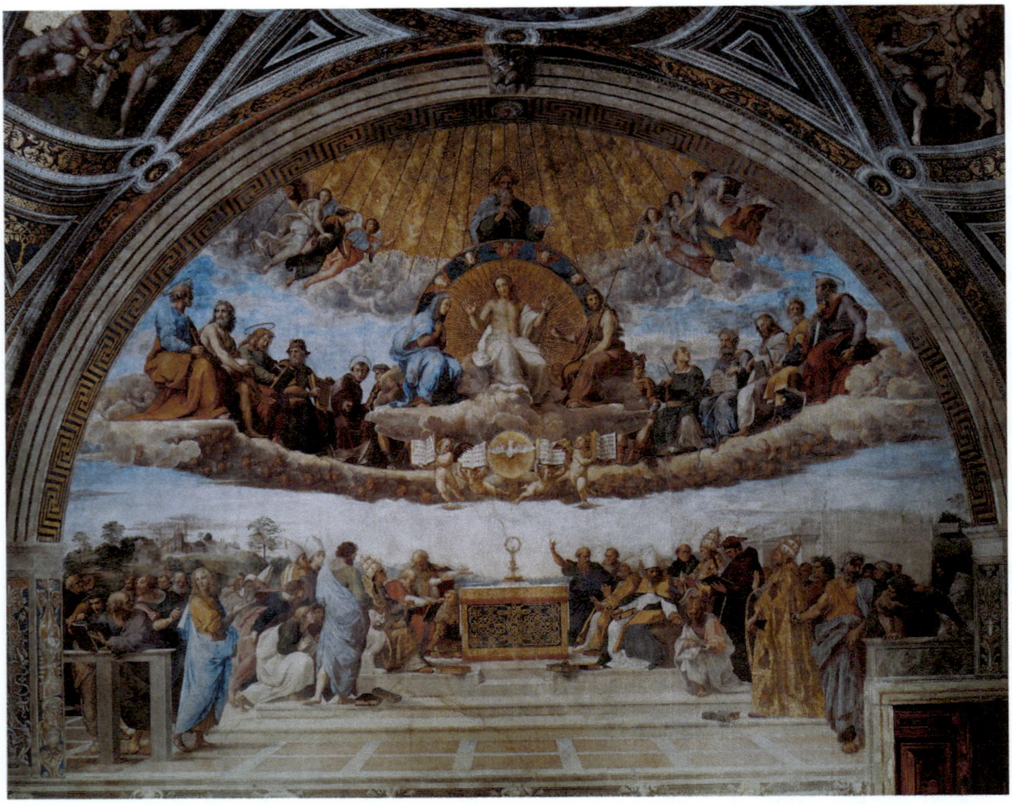

66. Raphael, *Disputation of the Sacrament,* 1509–10, fresco, Stanza della Segnatura, Vatican Museums and Galleries, Vatican City (Photo: Alinari/Bridgeman)

have on some level been satisfied by depictions of the host that could enhance these transient sightings. Michael Camille was surely right when he pointed out that the 'notion of the "real presence" in eucharistic practice must have deeply influenced people's perception of images, for here a visible thing was itself capable of becoming and not just signifying its prototype'.[12] Images could work to propagate the significance of the eucharist, amplifying the realness of the body of Christ and making visually manifest something that could not be seen: his mystical presence in the consecrated host. Given that these representations accelerated in the sixteenth century, this core Catholic belief would have been drummed into the consciousness of the viewer, if anything by the sheer number of images that referenced it.

Raphael's fresco the *Disputation of the Sacrament* of 1509–10 in the Apostolic Palace provided an early representation of the host framed in its monstrance, one that likely served as inspiration for later artists in Venice such as Palma il Giovane, who had studied in Rome during his youth (Fig. 66). Brescia and Bergamo, those two important artistic centres that were part of the Venetian *stato da terra*, but artistically oriented also to Milan, were early locations for the development of some of the most compelling eucharistic imagery of the

Renaissance, spurred on by the activities of the Blessed Sacrament confraternities in these places.[13] A processional standard of c. 1544–45 commissioned by one such fraternity at the Brescian church of Saints Faustinus and Jovinus (the latter known locally as Giovita) illustrates this. The work of Romanino (c. 1484/87–1561), who was born in Brescia and completed his artistic education in Venice and Milan, the standard depicted on one side *The Mass of Saint Apollonius* and on the reverse *The Resurrection* (Figs. 67 and 68).[14] The first of the paintings recounts the local legend that the Brescian Bishop Apollonius, who upon finding himself without the necessary liturgical objects to celebrate mass one night, prayed for assistance together with the deacons Faustinus and Jovinus. The two patron saints of Brescia can be seen by Apollonius's side, after having been miraculously liberated from their imprisonment under Emperor Hadrian. Their prayers are answered and in Romanino's painting the glowing host in its intricate gold monstrance is held aloft by two incense-swinging angels as the bishop greets the apparition that descends from the heavens. The reverse of the standard shows Christ levitating above his tomb as dawn breaks across the shadows of the land below, rays of light illuminating his head in a similar manner to the divinely lit, levitating host on the reverse.

The scene of the *Mass of Saint Apollonius* represents a local miracle of the kind that had been popular throughout the Middle Ages. Romanino's painting places a firm emphasis on the host, rather than the other items – tablecloth, chalice, candles – detailed in the 1490 *Legenda de sancto Faustino e Jiovita*.[15] Scholars have argued that the early explosion in eucharistic paintings in Brescia may have been stimulated by accounts of the desecration of the host and the infiltration of heretics in the areas around the city both just before and after the Reformation took hold.[16] In this sense, representations of the eucharist could be harnessed to prove the fallacy of the other side's arguments, to sharply distinguish 'Catholic identity from heretical error'.[17] As Christopher Black has argued, confraternities played an indirect role in doing this: providing an antidote to heterodoxy by promoting the eucharist and other sacraments, teaching Christian doctrine, and advocating for the significance of good works.[18] Their artistic patronage could play a similar role by envisioning key beliefs and concepts, particularly those that had been brought into question by the Reformations. The output of both Romanino and his contemporary Alessandro da Bonvicino (otherwise known as Moretto da Brescia, c. 1498–1554) is a pertinent example of this because they worked for the confraternities of the Blessed Sacrament on numerous occasions, most famously together in the chapel of the Santissimo Sacramento at the church of San Giovanni Evangelista in Brescia.

Moretto was responsible for some of the most imaginative and emotive sacramental imagery of all of the sixteenth century, surely inspired in some part by the visionary quality of some of his contemporary Lorenzo Lotto's works

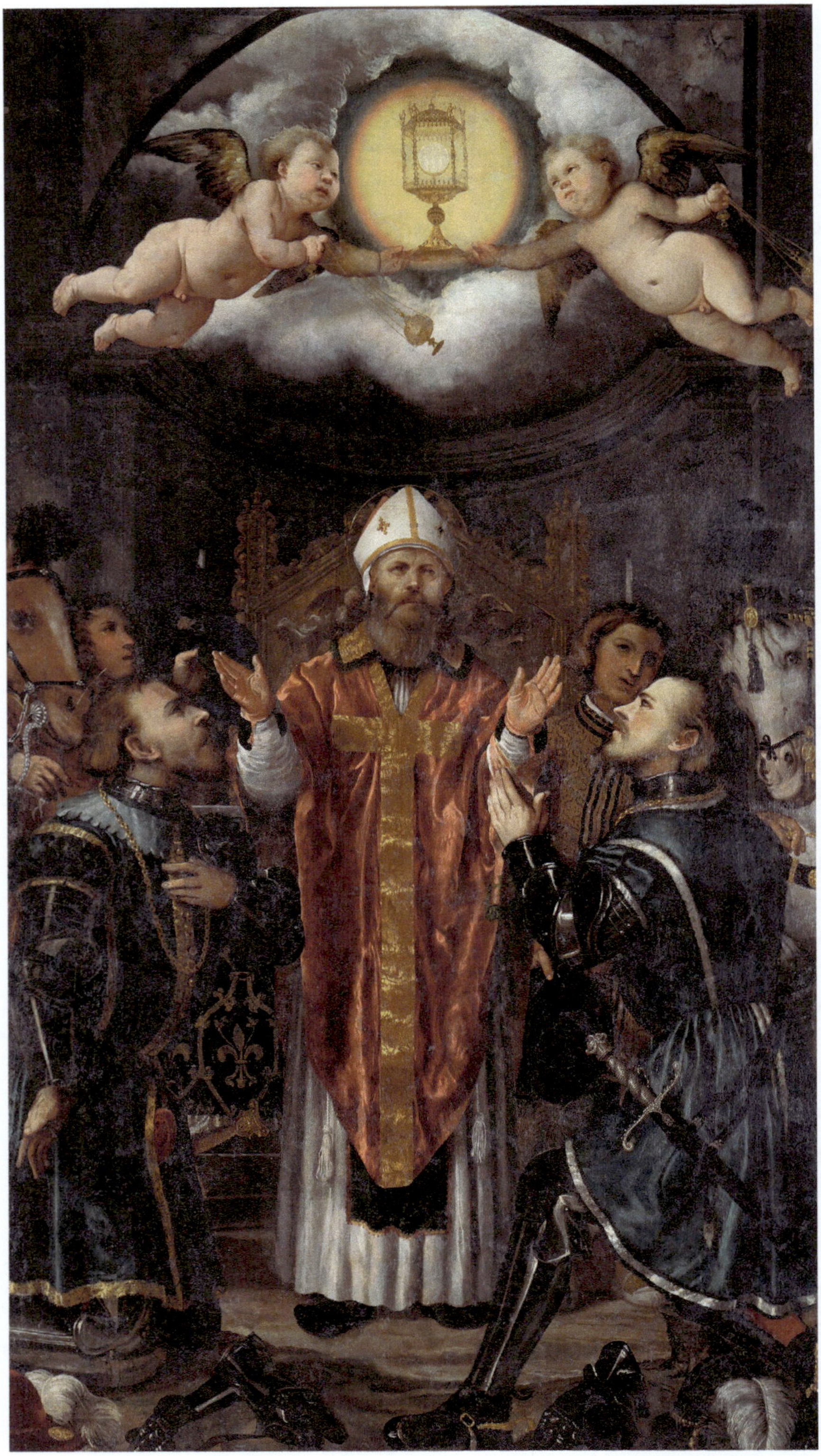

67. Romanino, *The Mass of Saint Apollonius,* c. 1544–45, oil on canvas, Santi Faustino e Giovita, Brescia (Photo: Fotostudio Rapuzzi)

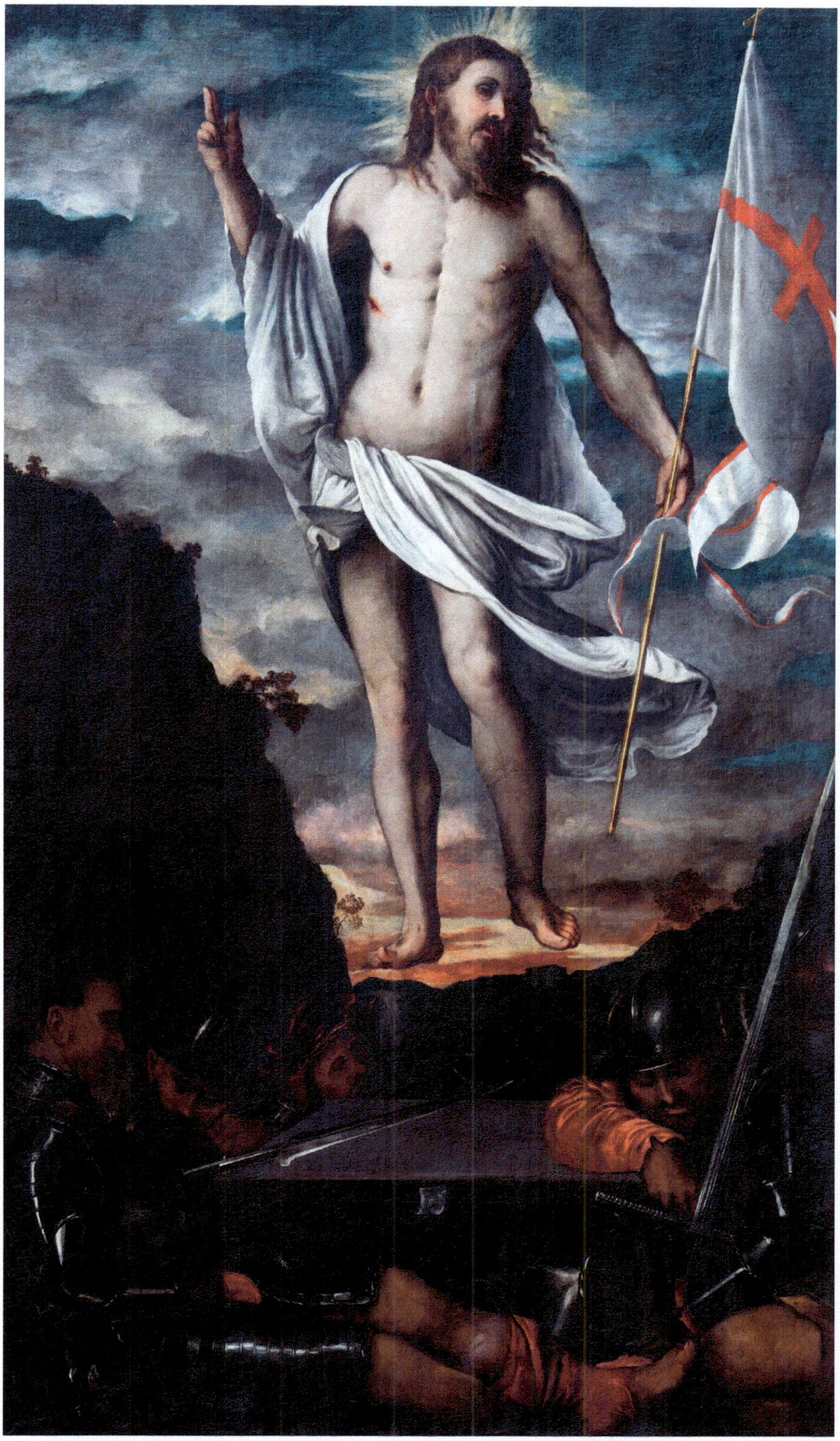

68. Romanino, *The Resurrection,* c. 1544–45, oil on canvas, Santi Faustino e Giovita, Brescia (Photo: Alamy)

that treated similar themes.[19] Here one is reminded of Lotto's frescoes for the Suardi chapel that were analysed in Chapter 1, or the 1522 Bergamese *Ponteranica Polyptych*, the upper panel of which shows the blood from the wounds of the crucified Christ dramatically spurting into a chalice below. Two paintings illustrate Moretto's talents in this area well: the unnerving *Dead Christ with an Angel* of 1550, which will be discussed later on, and the *Eucharistic Christ between Saints Bartholomew and Roch* of c. 1545 for the parish church of Saint Bartholomew in Castenedolo (Fig. 69).[20] This extraordinary altarpiece shows the eucharistic Christ twice: as a crucified outline imprinted in the host at the centre of the altar and as a vision above it that is witnessed by the kneeling saints. Christ is depicted borne aloft by a cloud, framed by a burst of golden light (not unlike the sunburst design of monstrances used to transport the host), with his wounded hands open and the crown of thorns floating above his head as his sidelong gaze confronts the viewer. He is accompanied on either side by the objects of the passion – the column, ropes, and branches of the flagellation and the cross, spear, and hyssop stick of the crucifixion – the miraculous force of the arrival suggested by the gust of wind that blows his beard to one side, threatening to extinguish the candles below. Here it is the host that offers the potential for transcendental experience, the realism of Moretto's painting presenting the supernatural as a visual reality.

Back in Venice, depictions of the host being adored appeared later than they had in Brescia or Bergamo. To the best of my knowledge one of the earliest painted examples is Palma il Giovane's *Holy Sacrament with the Four Evangelists* of c. 1577–81 that adorns the ceiling of the old sacristy in the parish church of San Giacomo dall'Orio (Fig. 70). Part of a cycle of paintings that conflate Old and New Testament episodes of eucharistic significance, in the ceiling image the glowing host in its monstrance is displayed upon an altar. It is accompanied by the Evangelists below, who are shown with their bestial attributes, their presence denoting the scriptural basis for eucharistic dogma. Commissioned by the incumbent parish priest, Giovanni Maria da Ponte, whose coat of arms can be seen between the feet of Saints Mark and John, the decorations were singled out for special praise by the Apostolic Visitation of 1581. During the day as one enters the sacristy the light hits the communion wafer at the centre of this image, illuminating the outline of the crucifixion within it. Upon leaving the space, the final image that one encounters is the *Deposition*, where the dead Christ is carried to his tomb by Joseph of Arimathea and Nicodemus (Fig. 71). The considered placement of these paintings between entry and exit points attempts to make visible the mystery of the eucharist: that it is the literal body and blood of Christ at the same time as it appears as the bread, or wafer, of communion. In an earlier article on this cycle I speculated that there was no clear precedent for Palma's iconography in Venice, but that he was probably familiar with Raphael's *Disputation* from his sojourn in Rome.[21] Yet Palma

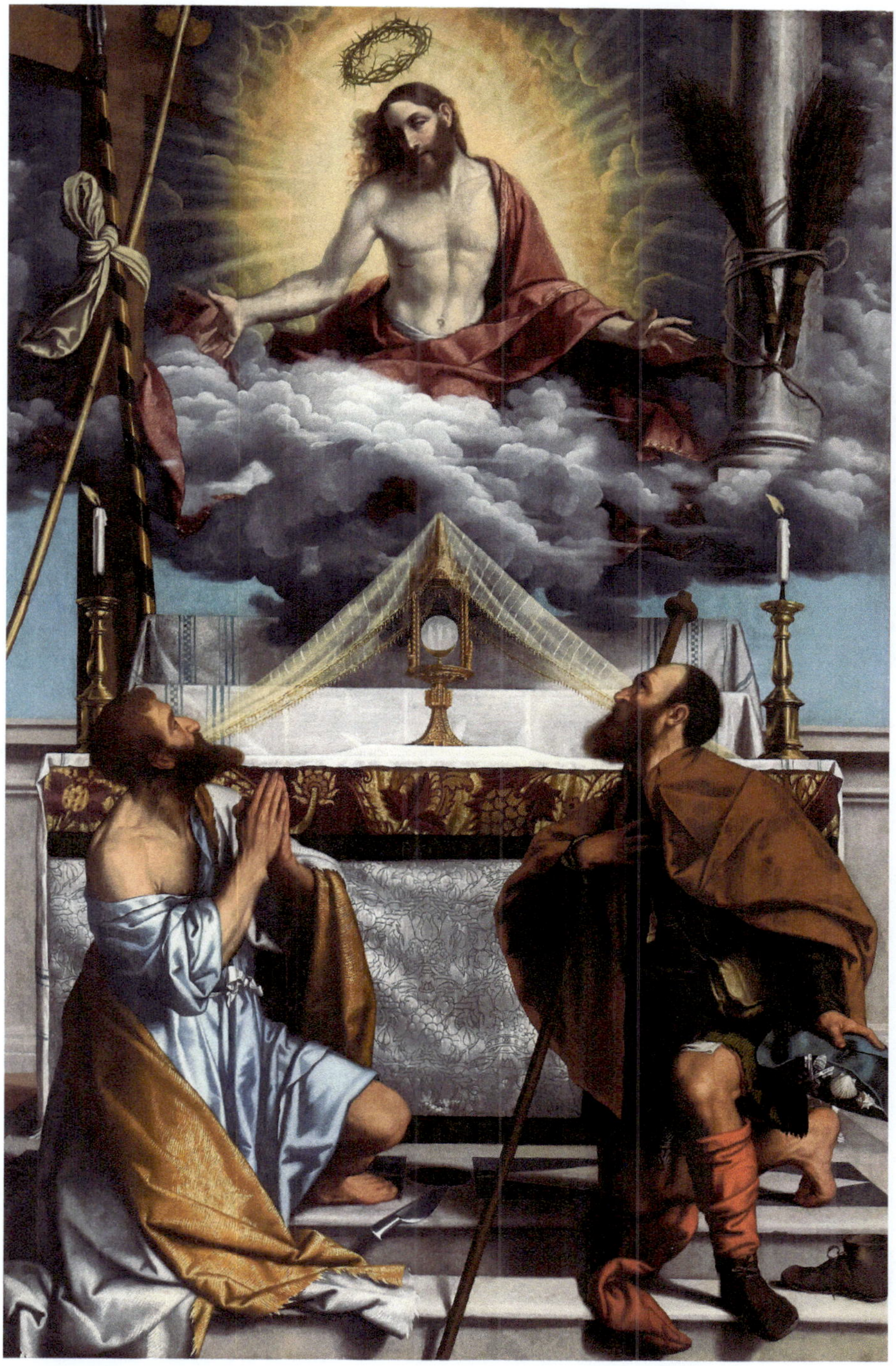

69. Moretto, *Eucharistic Christ between Saints Bartholomew and Roca,* c. 1545, oil on canvas, San Bartolomeo, Castenedolo (Photo: Mario Bonotto/Scala/Art Resource, New York)

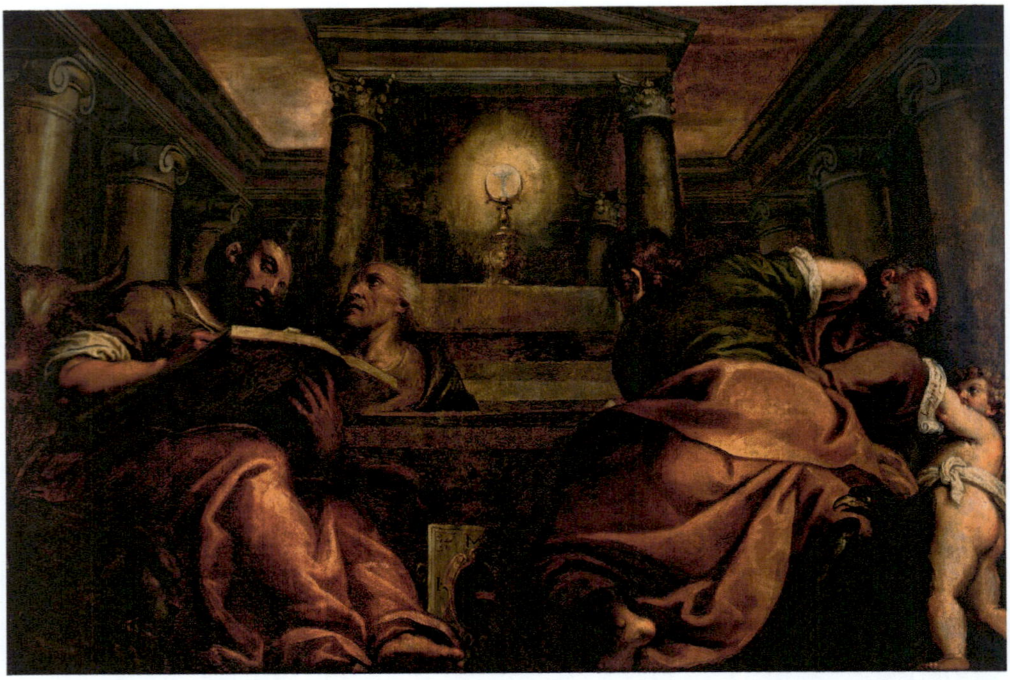

70. Palma il Giovane, *The Holy Sacrament with the Four Evangelists,* c. 1577–81, oil on canvas, San Giacomo dall'Orio, Venice (Photo: Cameraphoto)

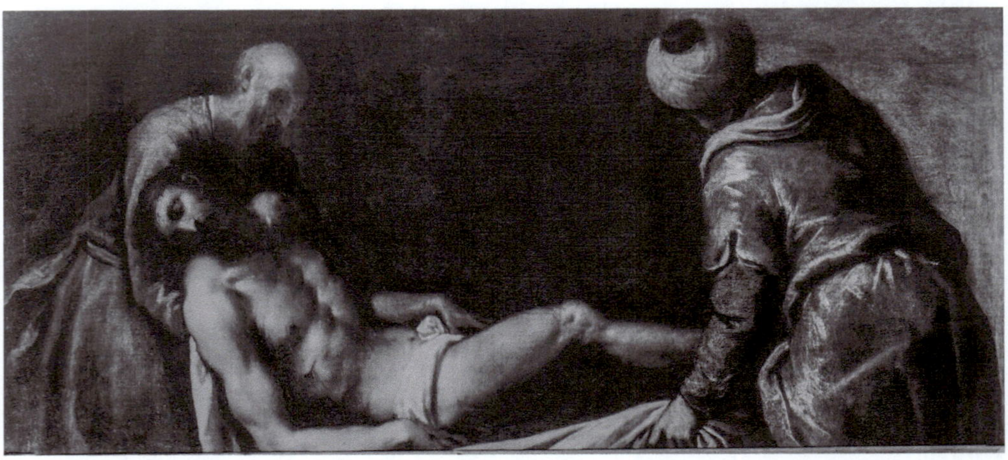

71. Palma il Giovane, *Deposition,* c. 1577–81, oil on canvas, San Giacomo dall'Orio, Venice (Photo: Francesco Turio Bohm)

would have also known about the experiments of Brescian and Bergamese artists with sacramental imagery, since Ridolfi records that he was greatly impressed by Romanino's lost painting of the *Lamentation* for the chapel of the sacrament at the church of San Faustino, where the aforementioned standard for the Scuola was located.[22] What is more, Palma's paternal family hailed from Serinalta, near Bergamo, and his workshop went on to produce works for numerous churches in and around both centres.[23]

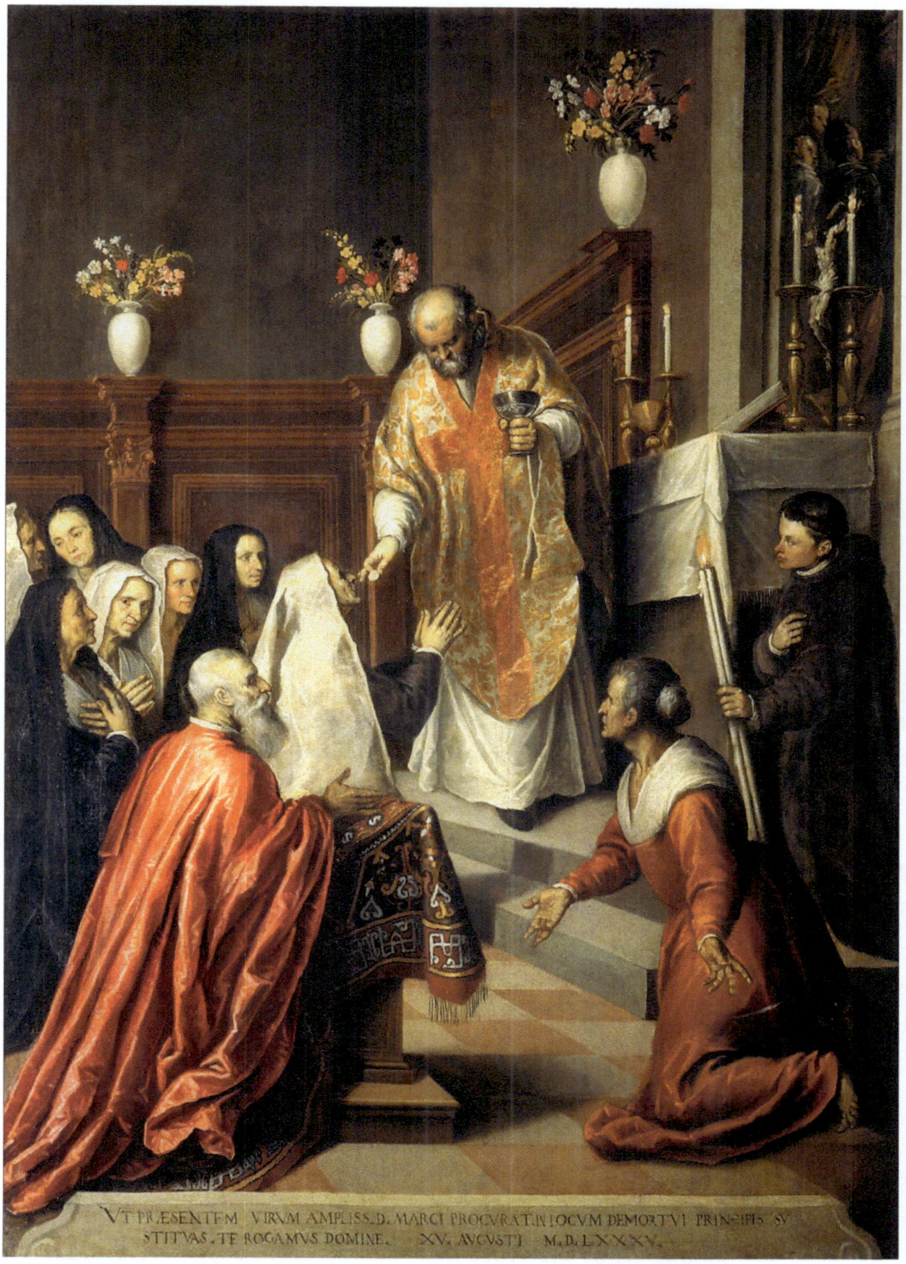

72. Palma il Giovane, *Father Priamo Balbi Administers the Host to Pasquale Cicogna and the Ospizio Widows*, 1585–88, oil on canvas, Oratorio dei Crociferi, Venice (Photo: Cameraphoto)

Depictions of the host in its monstrance were uncommon in Venice until Palma's painting, and even after it more usual were images of the dispensing of the eucharist by the clergy. This can be seen in Palma's *Priamo Balbi Administers the Host to Pasquale Cicogna and the Ospizio Widows* of 1585–88 for the oratory of the Crociferi in Venice (Fig. 72) or, for outside of Venice, in Veronese's

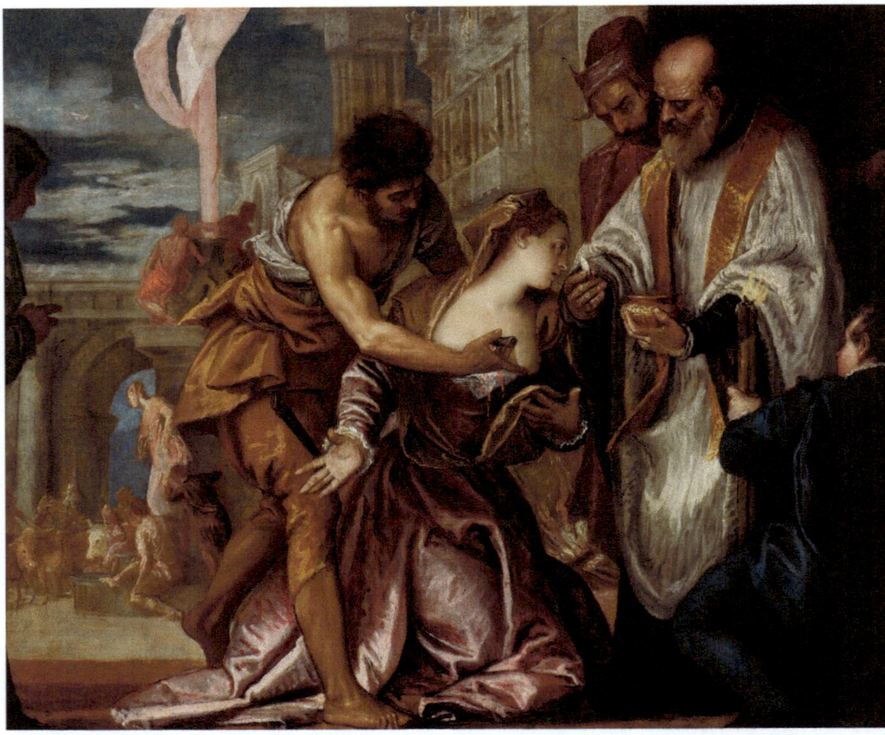

73. Veronese, *The Martyrdom and Last Communion of Saint Lucy*, c. 1585–86, oil on canvas, National Gallery of Art, Washington (Photo: Open Access)

Martyrdom and Last Communion of Saint Lucy of c. 1585–86 for the church of Santa Croce in Belluno (Fig. 73).[24] Here, in the same moment as a knife pierces Lucy's breast she receives communion. She fixes her sights not on her executioner but firmly on the host held in front of her. As blood seeps down her bodice and her eyes well with tears, her departure from this life is marked by her partaking of the sacraments, a reminder to the spectator of the redemptive powers of the viaticum.[25] Widely diffused in Venice were instead representations of the chalice with the communion wafer suspended either above or before it. The 1577–78 sculpted altarpiece ensemble for the chapel of the sacrament at San Zulian features a chalice and host at its summit below Girolamo Campagna's moving relief *The Dead Christ Supported by Angels* (Fig. 61), and numerous *mariegole* belonging to the Scuole del Sacramento deployed an identical iconography.[26] In a beautifully illuminated folio of the San Giacomo dall'Orio rulebook, the chalice and host are shown together, underlining the dual aspect of the latter as simultaneously the flesh and blood of Christ (Fig. 74).[27] A mosaic of 1611–17 designed by Aliense for the basilica of San Marco shows the host above a jewel-studded chalice at the centre of an altar. In this mosaic, *The Communion of the Apostles under Both Species*, Christ is shown twice, distributing the eucharist in its two forms on either side of the

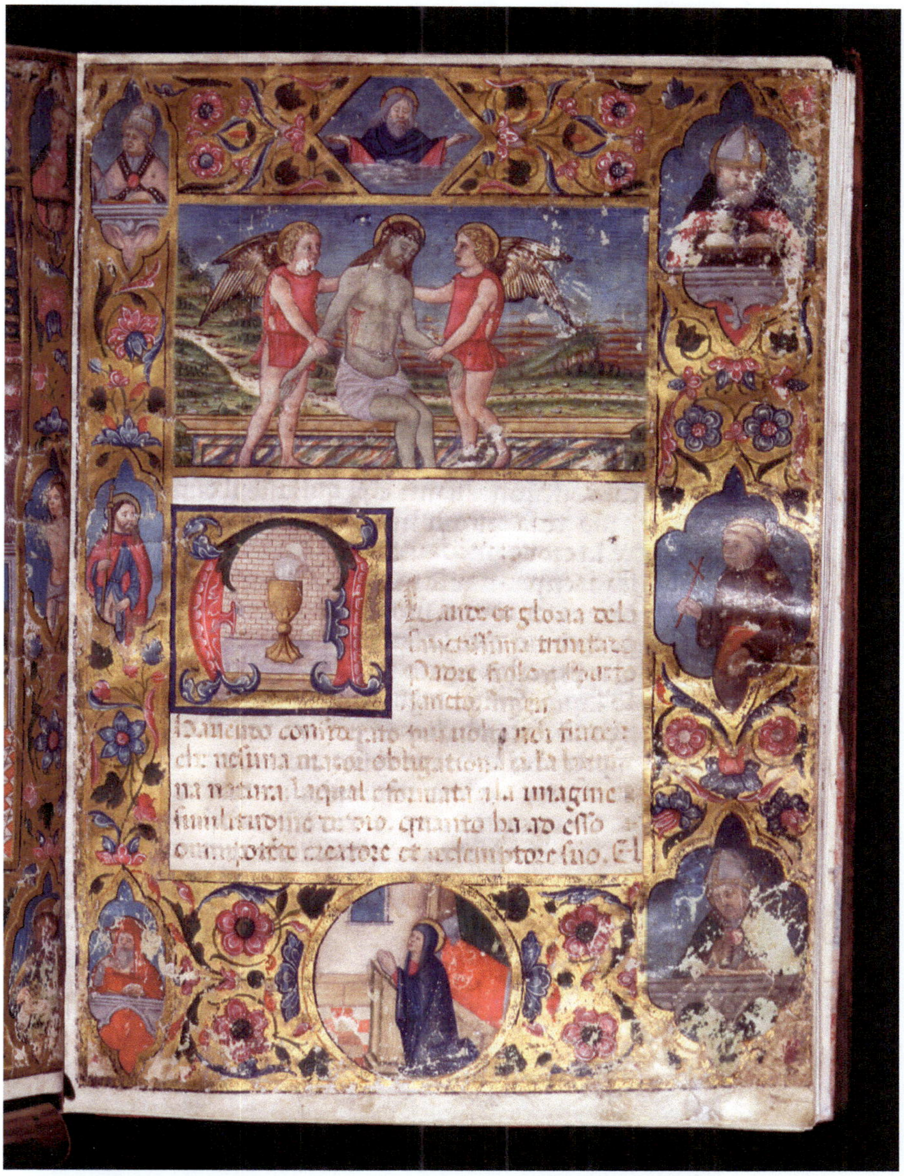

74. Illustration from the *Mariegola della Scuola del Santissimo Sacramento in San Giacomo dall'Orio,* Museum of the Basilica of San Marco, Venice (Photo: Archivio Fotografico della Procuratoria di San Marco/by kind permission of the Procuratoria di San Marco)

mensa, the inscription underlining the mystical nature of the heavenly bread (Fig. 75).[28]

Liberated from its monstrance, images of the chalice and host as an allegory for faith became more and more popular in Venice, and by the seventeenth century they were widespread. In the *mariegola* of the Scuola del Santissimo of San Zulian one illustration of the three theological virtues depicts the allegorical figure of Faith blindfolded, shown holding a chalice with the host floating

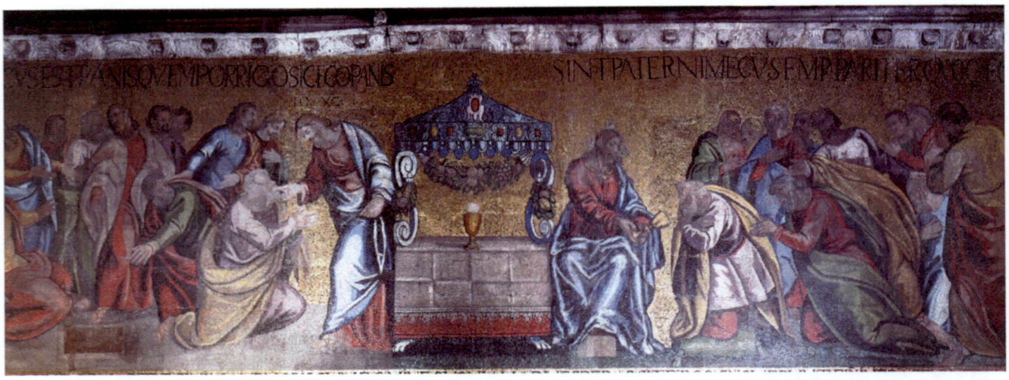

75. Cartoon by Antonio Vassilacchi, execution by Lorenzo Ceccato, *The Communion of the Apostles under Both Species,* 1611–17, mosaic, Basilica di San Marco, Venice (Photo: Archivio Fotografico della Procuratoria di San Marco/by kind permission of the Procuratoria di San Marco)

above it (Fig. 76).[29] The accompanying inscription reads '*sola fides sufficit*'. In this particular context, faith is interpreted as the virtue upon which belief in the eucharist depends. The crowning sculpture of the façade of the Redentore, commissioned in 1673 and attributed to Giusto le Court (1627–79), shows a near identical figure: Faith armed with a cross, the chalice, and the host, denoting the piety of the city that was believed to have delivered them from the plague of 1577.[30] In Cesare Ripa's popular illustrated emblem book of 1603, the *Iconologia*, Ripa, following Saint Paul, defined the two cornerstones of faith as 'believing in the Crucified Christ, and in the sacrament on the altar'.[31] In the San Zulian *mariegola* illustration aspects of Ripa's description of 'Christian faith' (to be depicted as a woman, armed with a cross and chalice) is conflated with the 'Catholic faith', which was instead to be shown as a woman with a helmet, holding a lit candle in her right hand and an open book with the old law and the new together in the other, described as 'the principle sum of that in which one must believe'.[32]

THE ANGELIC PIETÀ

The crucified Christ supported by two angels, an iconography generally referred to in broad terms as the Angelpietà, was one with a rich tradition in Venice. One of Giovanni Bellini's (1435–1516) many paintings of the subject, dating to c. 1480–85 and now in Berlin, depicts the beautiful, iconic body of Christ as if asleep, the warmth of his complexion hinting that blood still flows in his veins (Fig. 77).[33] One angel lifts up Christ's hand, making visible the wound of the crucifixion, whilst the second appears to whisper words of solace in his ear. A pink shroud that encased the crucified body has been unrolled, functioning as a frame from behind which the celestial figures appear. There is a touching contrast between the heaviness of Christ's limbs and the slim wrists

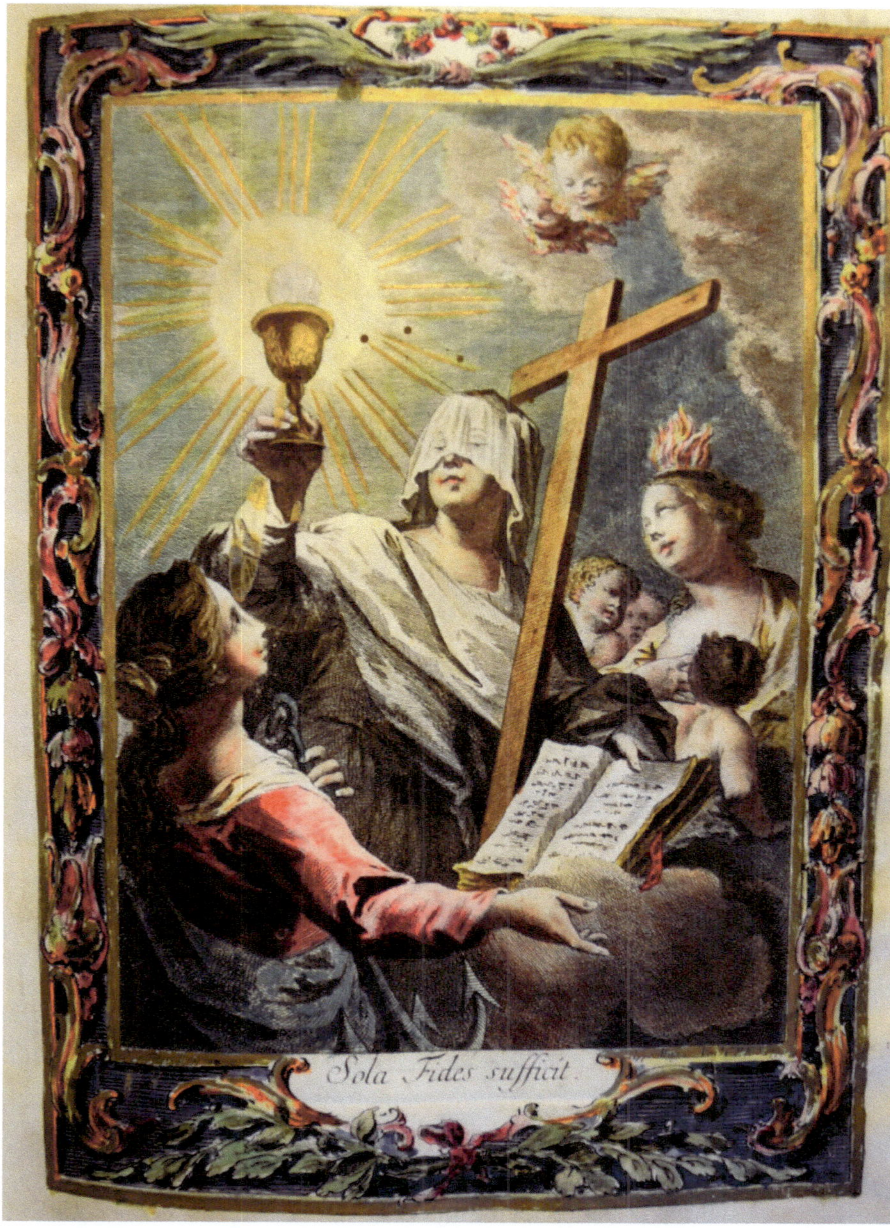

76. Illustration from the *Mariegola della Scuola del Santissimo Sacramento in San Zulian,* Biblioteca Correr, Venice (Photo: Sebastiano Giannesini/Biblioteca Correr, Fondazione Musei Civici di Venezia)

and delicate embrace of the two angels, who appear completely human were it not for their technicolour wings, tinged with pink and green feathers, and their superhuman strength.

The angels were implicated in eucharistic imagery because they were believed to descend from the heavens to be invisibly present at the moment of transubstantiation. The ordinary of the mass spoken by the celebrant

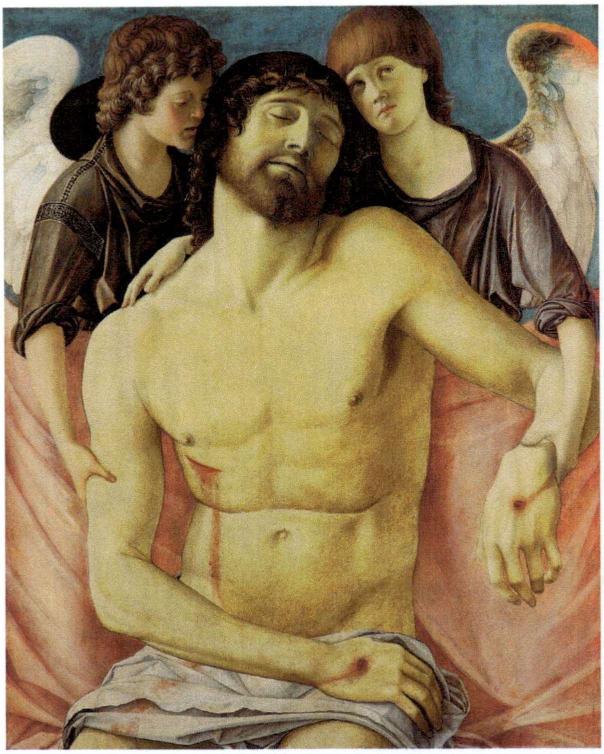

77. Giovanni Bellini, *Christ Supported by Angels,* 1480–85, tempera on wood, Gemäldegalerie Staatliche Museen zu Berlin (Photo: Open Access)

exhorted God to accept the eucharistic gifts 'borne by the hands of your holy Angel to your altar on high'. Although angels were held to be a constant companion to the Christian throughout their life, the dedication of these celestial beings to the Blessed Sacrament was such that they were thought to be constantly accompanying and adoring the consecrated host wherever it may be. Patriarch Giovanni Tiepolo's *Discorso et considerationi sopra il Santissimo Sacramento dell'Altare* of 1618 featured a chapter on the 'the continual assistance and reverence of the angels to the Blessed Sacrament of the body of Christ'.[34] Tiepolo cited a number of miracles to claim that the angels attended Corpus Domini processions, replenished church candles so that they were always lit in the presence of the eucharist, and were even known to play their celestial music in acts of nocturnal adoration, such was the delight that they took in honouring the body of Christ.[35] In this sense, the angels played an active role in reinforcing Catholic beliefs. Against the backdrop of the Reformations, their cult was enthusiastically reasserted by the Church, culminating in the institution of the feast of the Holy Guardian Angels by Pope Paul V in 1608, made universal by Clement X (r. 1670–76) in 1670.[36]

The Angelpietà was both a particularly compassionate kind of image, confronting the viewer with the essentials of the wounded body in the same

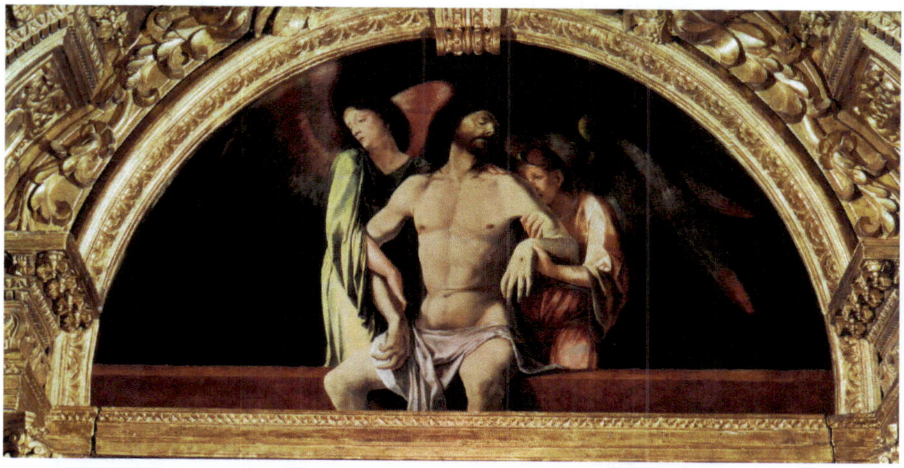

78. Lorenzo Lotto, *Upper Register of the Santa Cristina al Tiverone Altarpiece*, c. 1504–6, oil on panel, Santa Cristina, Quinto di Treviso (Photo: Scala/Art Resource, New York)

way as the *Man of Sorrows* (from which it derived), and on occasion a hopeful one. Operating outside of time and space so that the beholder can concentrate on the essentials of the eucharistic image, the iconography plays with the moments between life, death, and resurrection, in some cases suggesting that the angelic companions will awaken Christ to fulfil the promise of his rebirth. In the late sixteenth century the Angelpietà enjoyed great popularity with artists in Northern Italy, and it was painted many times by both Veronese and Palma il Giovane. Its plainly eucharistic symbolism meant that it was well adapted for the decoration of sacrament chapels and liturgical objects used for the mass, as well as for domestic devotions.[37] The Scuola del Santissimo Sacramento at the parish of San Samuele, which in 1525 described the host in their *mariegola* as the 'heavenly bread of the angels, with which we are spiritually nourished', decorated one of the folios with an illumination of Christ at the tomb supported by two angels, as did a vignette from the aforementioned folio from the San Giacomo dall'Orio rulebook, and many others like it.[38]

The Angelpietà was also to be found on the upper registers of altarpieces and polyptychs. Giovanni Bellini's *Saint Vincent Ferrer* polyptych for Santi Giovanni e Paolo in Venice of 1464–68 is an example of this, later quoted in Lotto's altarpiece for the parish of Santa Cristina al Tiverone outside Treviso (c. 1504–6, Fig. 78). Lotto's affective variation on the theme was featured also at the summit of the *Recanati Polyptych* of 1506–8 (Fig. 79) where an angel present at the lamentation pulls themself around the arm of the dead Christ. The emotive potential of this pre-existing iconography corresponded to the Council of Trent's dictum that sacred images could cause the beholder to 'cultivate piety'. It was the possibility of a compassionate response, one that Marcia Hall argued was assisted by the sensuous aspects of Venetian colour,

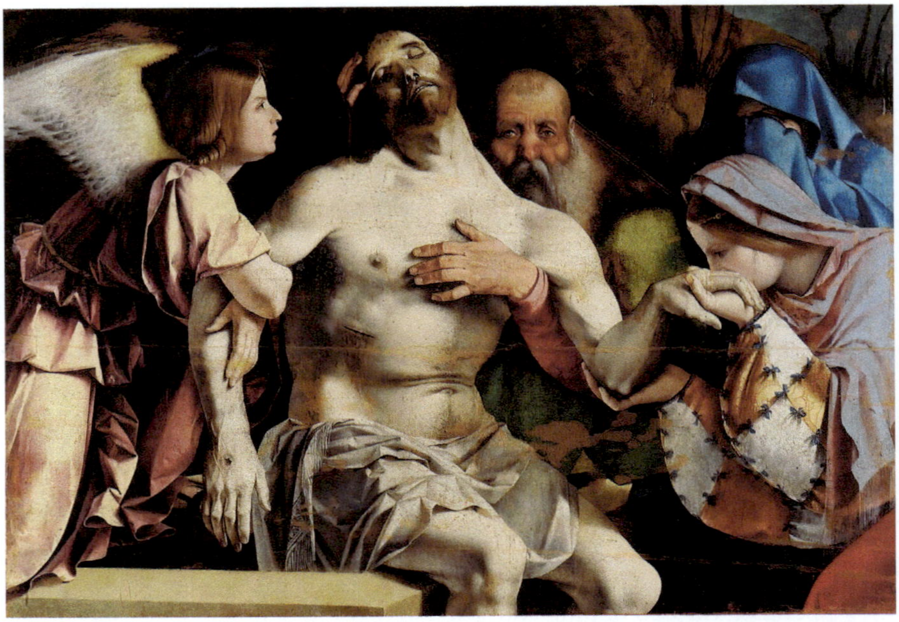

79. Lorenzo Lotto, *Lamentation* (upper register of the Recanati Polpytych), 1506–8, oil on panel, Museo Civico Villa Colloredo Mels, Recanati (Photo: Artefact/Alamy Stock Photo)

that may have attracted the city's artists to the theme, knowing that they were treating a subject matter that had proved equally compelling to artists of the previous generation such as Giovanni Bellini. Veronese, a master at engaging the spectator in the act of attentive looking, deliberately left the nature of the moment depicted unresolved in his c. 1587–89 *Christ Supported by Angels* (Fig. 80).[39] One wonders whether Christ is alive or dead. From his hands and chest dribbles of blood emerge and his body has a ghastly pallor, the contrast accentuated by the lustrous fabrics that partially envelop him and the coal-black backdrop of the composition. From Christ's head the light of his divinity pulsates, and his posture is not completely slumped as it is in other versions of the theme by the artist. Indeed, it appears to faintly stir.[40] Rather than the last vestiges of life, Veronese chooses to depict the beginning of a new one. These are the pair of angels described in Luke 24:4–7 that rolled back the stone from Christ's tomb and announced his resurrection to the Marys. Rather than mourners, the angels appear to awaken Christ, beckoning him towards the first steps of the resurrection.[41] The light illuminating the group from above is suggestive of daybreak making its way into the tomb as the stone that encloses it is rolled away.

In Veronese's painting the angels offer solace to Christ, in a similar way as to how they were believed to fill the invisible world of the dying person, floating above the deathbed, encouraging the individual to resist the wiles of the devil as their soul made its passage from this life to the next.[42] On other occasions

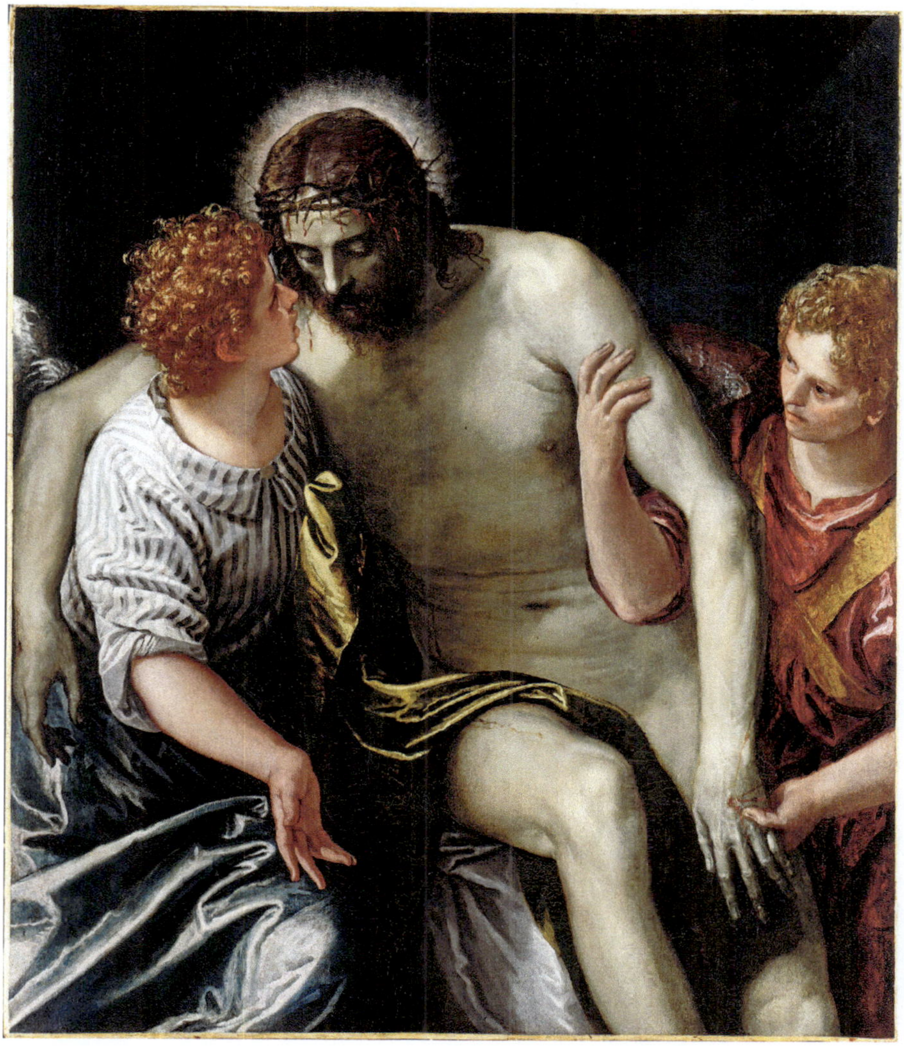

80. Veronese, *Christ Supported by Angels*, c. 1587–89, oil on canvas, Staatliche Museen zu Berlin (Photo: Staatliche Museen zu Berlin, Gemäldegalerie/Jörg P. Anders; Public Domain Mark 1.0)

they are depicted in the midst of a vortex of grief. Here one thinks of the three, perfect crystalline tears of Antonello da Messina's (c. 1430–79) crying angel in the Prado (1475–76), or the screams of Christ's two companions in a lost relief made in Padua in the late fifteenth century (Fig. 81), one that recalls the lamenting angels of Donatello's relief *Dead Christ with Angels* of 1447–49 in the Santo, a work that seems to have established the iconography in Northern Italy.[43] The expressions of these angelic figures invite a meditative mood, something also seen in Moretto's *Ecce Homo Accompanied by an Angel*, which must be one of the most alarming paintings of all of the sixteenth century (Fig. 82). In the narrow staircase of the praetorium Christ is seen in an unusual

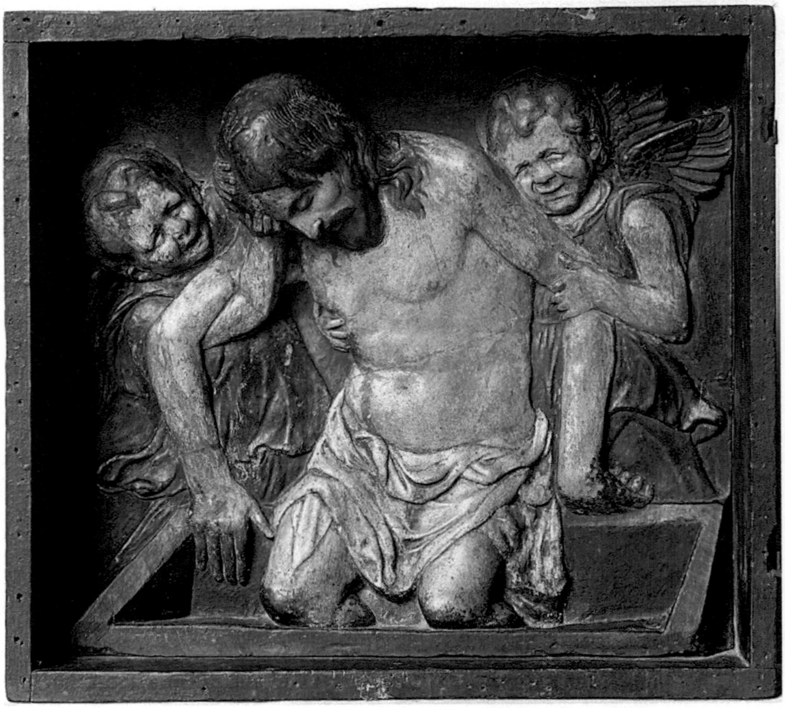

81. *Dead Christ with Angels,* 1486–1500, painted terracotta, Skulpturensammlung und Museum für Byzantinische Kunst, Staatliche Museen zu Berlin (lost since 1945) (Photo: Open Access)

position, leaning against a wall. He is crowned with the thorns and his hands are bound. Naked aside from his loincloth, his skin is a deathly grey. A moment of rest between his torture and his final crucifixion, the cross that he has carried lies resting at his feet. Behind him an angel holds up a tunic, framing the body of Christ that is presented to the viewer. Every non-essential detail has been eliminated and the palette has been restricted to the essentials, mostly silvers and greys, with some earthen browns and reds. Cleansed of any superfluous element the most unsettling element of this painting is made unavoidable: the expressions of the two protagonists. The angel is about to weep, their face crumpled in grief, while Christ looks out at the viewer with his lips pursed and his black eyes caught in an unforgettably accusatory gaze. Commissioned by the confraternity of the Holy Cross for their chapel in the cathedral of Brescia, a plausible source for the iconography is the *L'arte dell'unione* by the Capuchin monk Giovanni da Fano. Printed in Brescia in 1536 and again in 1548, it describes the setting of a 'palazzo', where the bound and humiliated Christ meets an angel, one who expresses 'great anguish and melancholy' at his fate.[44] Embodying the penitential themes associated with the commissioning confraternity, it also anticipates the emotive experiments of Venetian artists with both the iconography of the *Ecce Homo* and the Angelpietà.

In keeping with its early promotion of the cult of Corpus Domini, Venice and its territories was home to an abundant quantity of images that related to

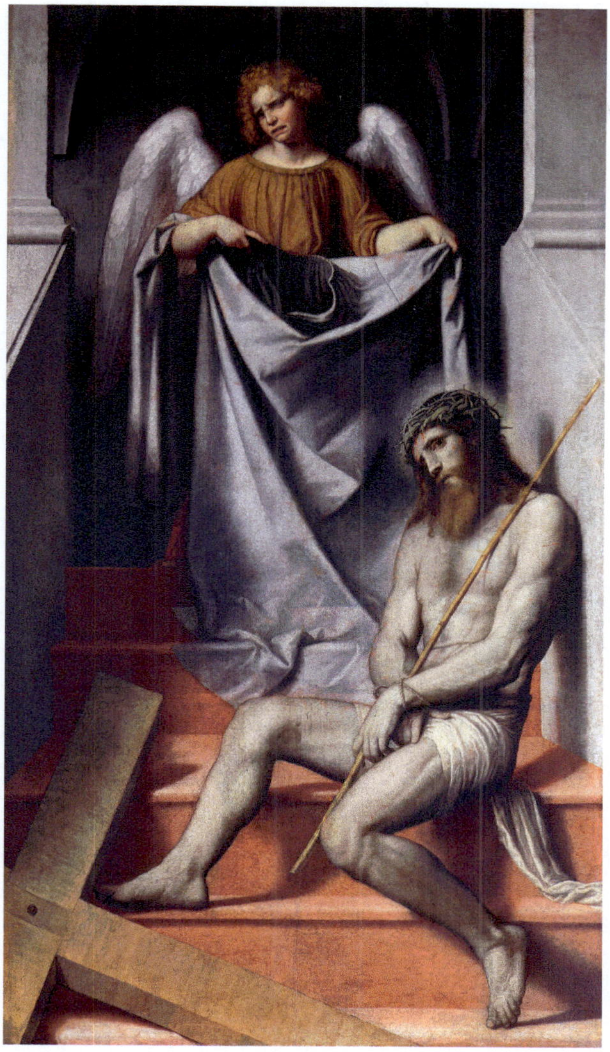

82. Moretto, *Ecce Homo accompanied by an Angel,* 1550–54, oil on canvas, Pinacoteca Tosio Martinengo, Brescia (Photo: A. Dagli Orti/© NPL – DeA Picture/Bridgeman Images)

the eucharistic Christ, and this extended to the civic context of the Ducal Palace, renewed after the fires of 1574 and 1577. In Tintoretto's *Dead Christ with the Saints and Doges Pietro Lando and Marcantonio Trevisan* of c. 1582 for the Sala del Senato, the role of the five winged apparitions is to present the flayed, bloody body of Christ to the viewer (Fig. 83). Tintoretto's painting was a substitute for the original by Titian, destroyed in 1574. We know that this was to depict the Virgin Mary with Christ, and that it was intended also to relate to the Corpus Domini, since Doge Trevisan had been elected shortly after this feast. We do not know how Christ and his mother were depicted in Titian's work (whether Christ was shown as a child or dead in the Virgin's arms), but there were no administering angels detailed in the relevant document.[45] In the painting by Tintoretto they instead play a central role, opening out

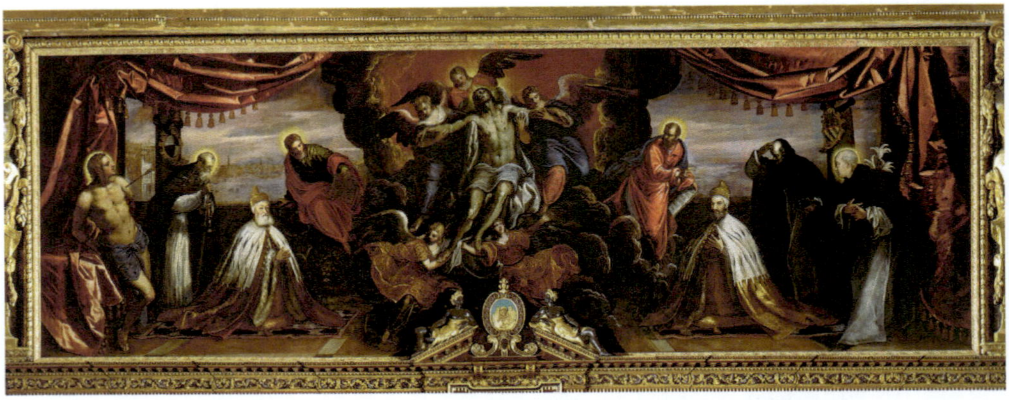

83. Tintoretto, *Dead Christ with the Saints and Doges Pietro Lando and Marcantonio Trevisan*, c. 1582, oil on canvas, Sala del Senato, Ducal Palace, Venice (Photo: Cameraphoto)

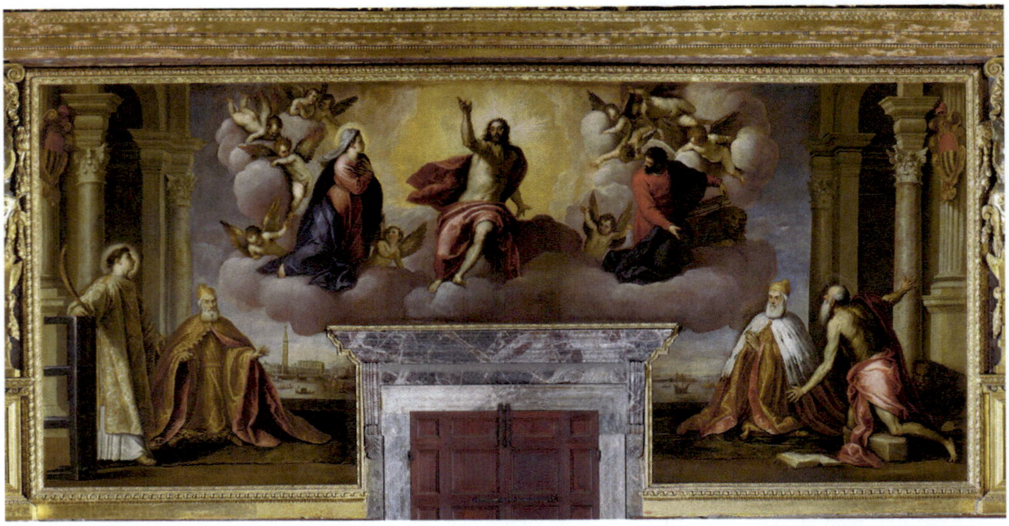

84. Palma il Giovane, *Christ in Glory with the Saints and Doges Lorenzo and Girolamo Priuli*, c. 1583–87, oil on canvas, Sala del Senato, Ducal Palace, Venice (Photo: Cameraphoto)

Christ's arms and supporting his feet as if he has just been removed from the cross.[46] Alighting on a bilious cloud of black smoke and orange light, the visionary aspect of the scene is emphasised by the curtains, drawn open to present us with a view of Venice in the distance, the doges and attendant saints solemnly poised as they bear witness to the vision.[47] Tintoretto's *Dead Christ* was symbolically linked to both the ceiling image directly above it by Tommaso Dolabella (c. 1570–1650) and the painting at the other end of the room by Palma il Giovane. Palma's *Christ in Glory with the Saints and Doges Lorenzo and Girolamo Priuli* deployed a very similar composition to its pendant of the Tintoretto canvas, the scene presenting the perfected body of Christ at its centre: revitalised, radiant, and triumphant (Fig. 84).[48] The

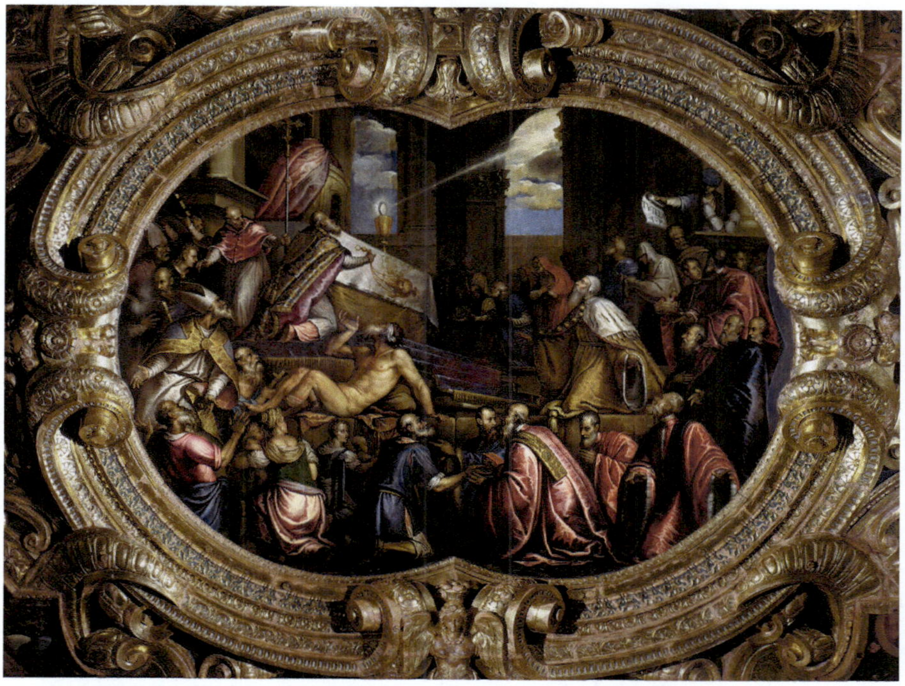

85. Tommaso Dolabella, *Votive Mass for the Cessation of the Plague*, c. 1595, oil on canvas, Sala del Senato, Ducal Palace, Venice (Photo: Cameraphoto)

positioning of these three paintings underlines the links between the sacrifice on the cross, the mass, and the promise of the resurrection, but they clearly emphasise also the devotion of the doges to the eucharist and the divine consecration of city and state by Christ himself.[49]

Dolabella's *Votive Mass for the Cessation of the Plague* of c. 1595 is particularly interesting in this regard. Although there is some debate over precisely which event is represented, the most convincing reconstruction posits that it refers to the plague that struck Candia (or Crete) in 1591 (Fig. 85). As pointed out by Giorgio Tagliaferro, the scene unites disparate figures in a single location and so provides an allegory for the invocation for the end of the plague rather than representing a precise historical event.[50] Immediately to one side of the altar, Patriarch Lorenzo Priuli has been identified as the figure swinging the incense burner as Doge Pasquale Cicogna meditates on the host from the bottom of the altar steps. Displayed upon the altar in front of the tabernacle, the host is suspended above the chalice, a nimbus of white light appearing around it at the moment it is struck by the heavenly ray that breaks through the clouds outside, signifying the miracle that the crowd's prayers have been answered. The populace is entrusted to the saving protection of the eucharist by Lorenzo Vitturi, the Bishop of Candia, and in the foreground one of the crowd is the recipient of charity from a senator, poised in the act of pressing a coin into his palm. Partaking in the eucharist was believed to augment acts of charity as the communicant was theoretically brought into contact with the love demonstrated by Christ when he instituted the sacrament.[51] It is significant that the figure of the nude man afflicted by the plague is afforded a prominence that, on the one hand, functions to illustrate the aim of the votive mass and, on the other, evidences his likeness to Christ, his diseased body located directly below the resplendent host that will heal him.[52] If on the wall below Tintoretto shows Christ's crucified body, flayed and bloodied (Fig. 83), here the host symbolises the sacrifice of that act for the benefit of humanity. The huddled horde made up of the clergy (the Church), the doge and various senators (the state), as well as women, children, the naked, and the needy (the populace) denote the potency of the host as a potential social unifier, 'the source of human community' as Eamon Duffy argued in his study of eucharistic devotion in late medieval England.[53]

THE TABERNACLE

More than any other object, the tabernacle provides a telling barometer of eucharistic devotion.[54] In the previous chapter the great attention paid to the appearance and dignity of the tabernacle by clergy and confraternities in Venice was demonstrated. Acutely intertwined with this was the size, appearance, and materiality of the tabernacle, in which those consecrated communion wafers that had not been consumed at the mass were to be reserved. The Council of Trent had said little on the subject, insisting only on the ancient tradition of reserving the eucharist in the sacrarium at session thirteen of 1551.[55] Over twenty years later, at a point when elaborate high altar tabernacles were already growing in popularity, Borromeo's 1577 *Instructiones* dedicated a distinct chapter to the theme.[56] He recommended that tabernacles should be made with precious materials: gilded plates of silver or bronze or the 'more costly kinds of marble'; that they could be octagonal, hexagonal, square, or round in form; and that at their summit there should be an image of Christ (shown either resurrected or displaying his wounds) and a further one on the door.[57] The whole was to be embellished with sculpted reliefs of Christ's Passion. In keeping with the desire of Borromeo to pay material homage to the container for the body of Christ, during the course of the sixteenth century in Italy tabernacles were transformed from the elaborate stone wall-receptacles that had flourished in the Quattrocento into ever more dominating architectonic features of the church interior.[58] In some cases they even displaced the need for an altarpiece or replaced existing ones entirely,[59] and they reached ever more outlandish proportions in the seventeenth century in Venice as the Baroque tabernacles in the chancels of San Lorenzo,[60] Santi Giovanni e Paolo,[61] and San Nicola da Tolentino attest (Figs. 86, 87, and 88).[62]

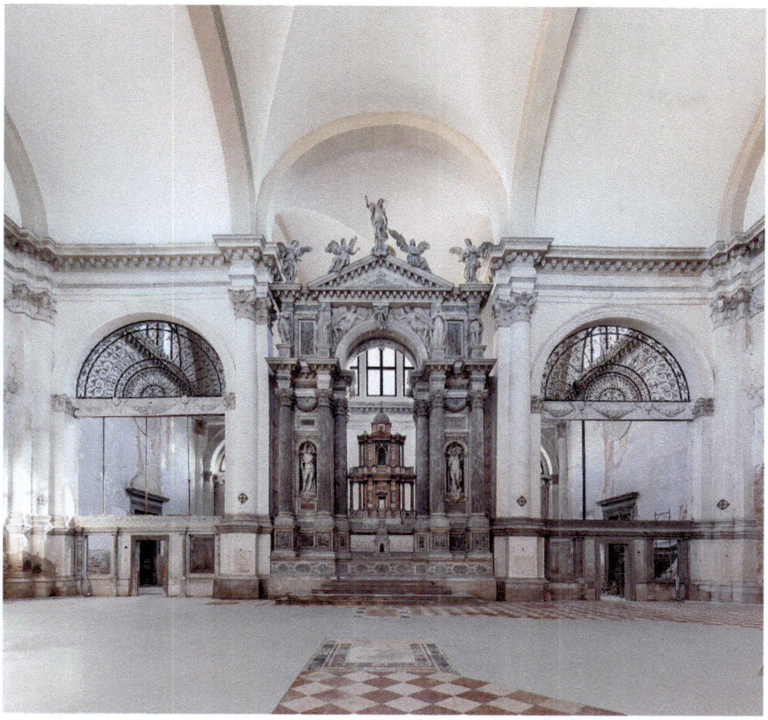

86. Girolamo Campagna, *Tabernacle,* 1618, San Lorenzo, Venice (Photo: Ocean Space)

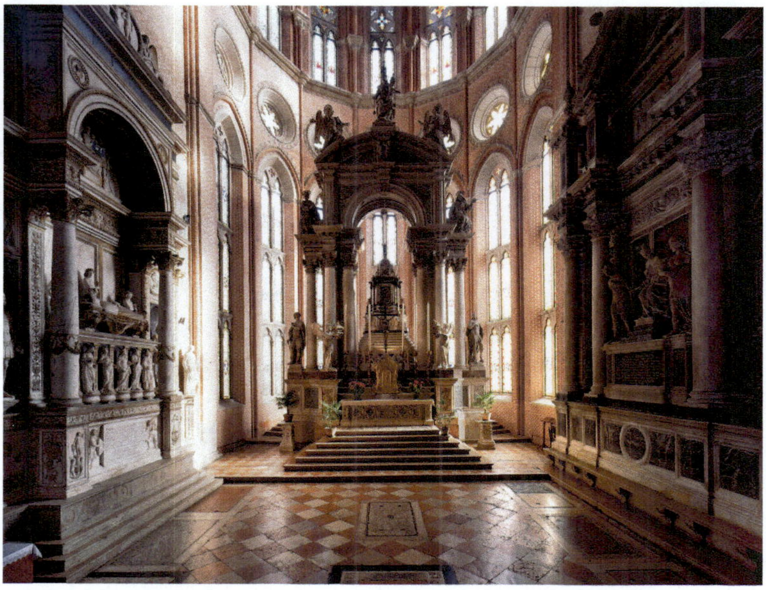

87. Matteo Carneri and Baldassare Longhena, *High Altar,* 1620–52 (tabernacle), 1653–56 (triumphal arch), Santi Giovanni e Paolo, Venice (Photo: Cameraphoto)

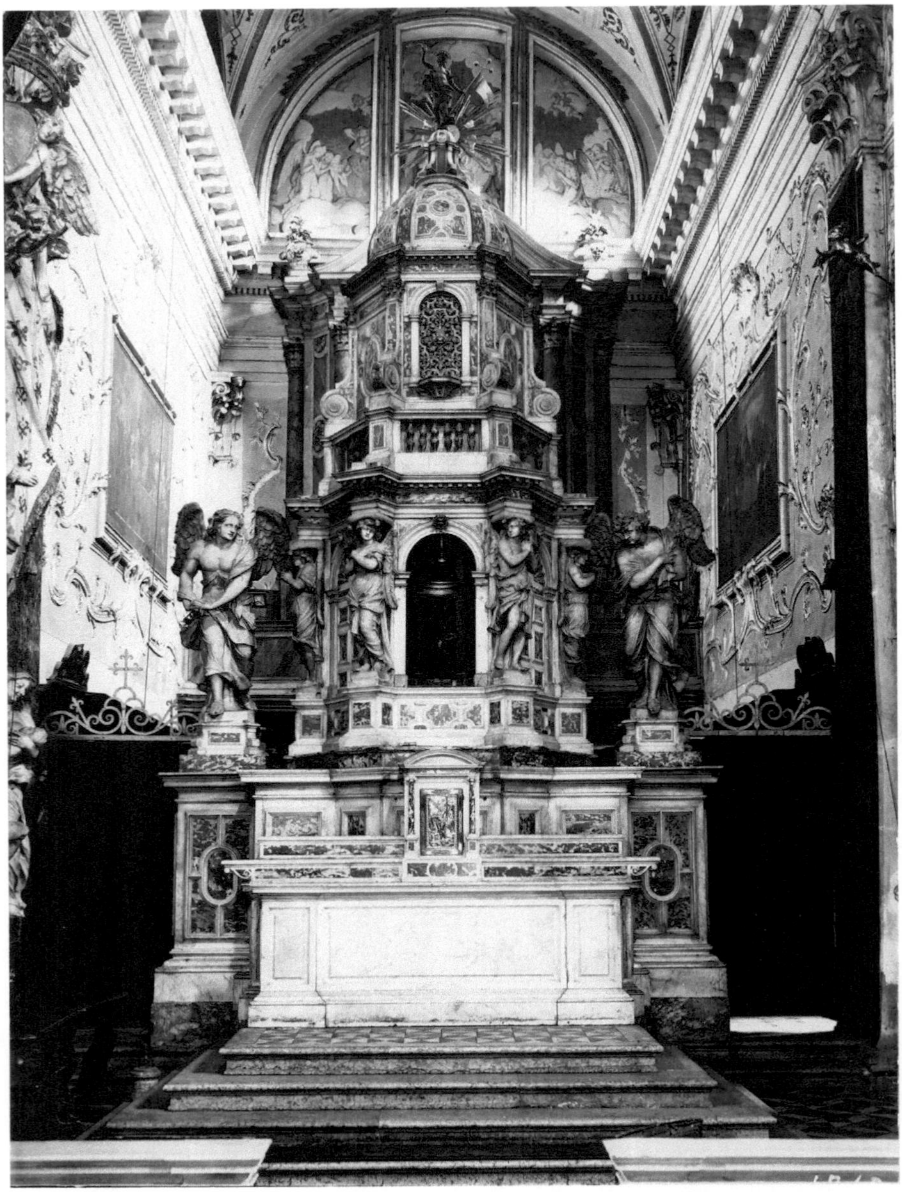

88. Baldassare Longhena, *Tabernacle,* 1661–72, San Nicola da Tolentino, Venice (Photo: Fondazione Giorgio Cini, Fototeca dell'Istituto di Storia dell'Arte, Venice)

Already at the dawn of the Seicento, Giovanni Stringa commented on the craze for elaborate ciboriums in Venice, opining that 'it is a most noble thing to see so many marble tabernacles decorated with bronze ornaments around the city in recent years, not without great expense, to the honour and glory of the divine cult'.[63] His observation is borne out by the sheer quantity of tabernacles and high altars that were renovated between 1581 – the date of Sansovino's guide to Venice – and Stringa's 1604 additions to this text. These transformations were given resolute institutional backing by the Church in Venice, as the visitations of Patriarch Priuli demonstrate. Although the more durable marble or stone 'temple-like' tabernacles swiftly became the norm in the city, prior to this, gilded wooden tabernacles inset with painted images had enjoyed something of a vogue in the late sixteenth century, albeit a short-lived one since the wood was more prone to decay and so they almost always ended up being replaced.[64]

The two most important and renowned examples of this type in Venice were the wooden tabernacles of the Jesuit church of the Madonna dell'Umiltà (c. 1580) and the Capuchin votive basilica of the Redentore (1589–90). Although rendered from marble rather than wood, the tabernacle of the Benedictine convent of San Zaccaria that features paintings dated to 1595–1604 by Palma il Giovane affixed to each of its four sides is an important relation to this typology and remains in situ.[65] Those of the Umiltà and the Redentore were embellished with paintings by the most popular artistic workshops of the day: those of Veronese, the Bassano, and Palma. The structures themselves do not survive but fragments of the original painted decoration do. In their original splendour ciboriums such as these were subtler than their later more bombastic iterations, dependent on the iconographic connections between their inset images for meaning rather than just the magnificence of their materials or sheer dimensions. For example, as the visitor enters the church of San Zaccaria they are greeted with the first of the four sides of the tabernacle that displays Palma's painting of *Christ Supported by Angels*, likely the first time in over a century that the theme appeared painted on a high altar.[66] Processing around and behind the tabernacle, the viewer witnesses the two passion scenes of *The Crowning of Thorns* and *The Scourging at the Pillar* on each of the two tabernacle sides, culminating in the *Resurrection of Christ* on the reverse: a glorious pendant to the moment of Christ's suffering in the tomb depicted on the front. Here, an ambulatory runs around the perimeter of the high altar, an aspect of the site's specificity that informed the design of a tabernacle that could be viewed and meditated upon from multiple vantage points.

In keeping with Borromeo's advice, Palma's decorations for the San Zaccaria tabernacle focused on Christ's Passion, the iconography that was clearly the most pertinent for such structures. At both the Umiltà and the Redentore the decorative programme for the tabernacles included episodes not just from the Gospels but from the Old Testament too, something that Maurice Cope picked up on, arguing that these pairings suggested a highly theologically literate audience.[67] This iconographic sophistication can also be attributed to the fact that the clergy were often closely involved in the design of tabernacles, something to be expected considering their spatial vicinity to these objects during the mass as well as their theological expertise. This was the case at San Giorgio Maggiore, the Redentore, and Santi Giovanni e Paolo, to name but a few examples. Abbot Alabardi at San Giorgio is the most likely candidate for the idea behind Campagna's high concept altarpiece-tabernacle of *The Evangelists Supporting a Globe with the Trinity* (1591–93); at the Redentore the replacement tabernacle of the late seventeenth century was based on a 1679 design by one Father Giuseppe da Vincenza of the Capuchin Order; and at San Nicola da Tolentino we know that the sculptor Baldassare Longhena (1598–1682) had difficulties with modifications to the project demanded by the Theatines.[68]

Decorated wooden tabernacles appear to have cropped up in Tuscany significantly earlier than in Venice. Perhaps some precocious examples once existed in the lagoon city too, but given both the extent of late sixteenth-century renovations to Venetian churches and the fact that the early printed guides did not systematically detail the presence of these objects in the same way as Stringa did at the beginning of the Seicento, we know nothing about them. One early Tuscan example dated to c. 1524–26 is that of the monastery of Santa Maria di Rosano. The painted decoration of the ciborium is attributed to Giovanni di Lorenzo Larciani (1484–1527) and the gilded woodwork to Nanni Unghero (c. 1490–1546). This tabernacle, which takes the form of a tempietto structure surmounted by a dome and lantern, is decorated with four panels on each of the sides depicting angels in various attitudes of reverence, a fifth of Christ shown with his blood flowing into a chalice, and the *sportello* depicting the baptism in the river Jordan (a later substitute for the original).[69] Some decades later, Giorgio Vasari designed a number of important wooden tabernacles, including that of 1566 for the high altar of Santa Croce in Florence paid for by Duke Cosimo I, which still survives in a modified form.[70] In Venice, the high altar tabernacle of the Madonna dell'Umità appears to have been one of the first recorded freestanding painted wooden ciboriums in the city. The fruit of generous lay donations by the city's noblewomen, it adorned the church from the early 1580s until the end of the eighteenth century, by which point its paintings had been sold off by the Benedictine nuns of San Servolo, who had taken control of the site in 1615 after the expulsion of the Jesuits during the Interdict.[71]

The history of the Umiltà tabernacle, with which we will conclude this chapter, demonstrates that the Jesuit Order was partially responsible for stimulating a fashion for conceptually sophisticated high altar tabernacles in Venice, a tendency that later reached its apotheosis with the magnificent example by Campagna for the Benedictines of the Cassinese Congregation at San Giorgio. As two of the principle new religious orders tied to Catholic Reform, both the Jesuits and the Theatines were significant for their promotion of the use of elaborate high altar tabernacles in the Veneto.[72] Indeed, the Jesuit painter and architect Giuseppe Valeriano (1542–96) complained about the superfluous costs incurred by such wooden tabernacles in point seven of his *memoriale* on the deficiencies of his order's building projects, pointing out their close association with the Company of Jesus when he complained that they were commonly thought to be 'something invented and introduced by us'.[73] Ideally, the sanctified hosts retained in the tabernacle were to be easily accessible for the clergy, particularly in the event of the priest finding the freshly consecrated hosts to be insufficient to satisfy all the communicants. Placing the tabernacle on an altar (rather than in a distant closet or in a sacrament house) with access from the front provided a practical solution to this problem, meaning that the officiating priest need not leave the altar to fetch supplies.[74] Although this resolution took far longer to catch on in other places, it became a standard one through the course of the sixteenth century in Italy. But as the dimensions of these objects swelled, in some cases ladders had to be kept in their vicinity in order to facilitate access to the raised part of the structure where the host was retained.[75] This problem was eventually resolved by placing the actual enclosure for the host at the base of the structure surmounting the altar. In cases like the 'skyscraper' tabernacles at Santi Giovanni e Paolo or the Tolentini in Venice, the majority of the tabernacle's architecture was for show, denoting the significance of the host that was retained in this area of the church. Saint Gaetano da Thiene, founder of the Theatines, initiated the exposition of the host during the *Quarant'ore* and at the Tolentini the giant tabernacle would have provided a suitably majestic backdrop for the devotion, held here between the last day of carnival and Palm Sunday at the church.[76] The part of the tabernacle where the wafers were actually kept and that was routinely used by the clergy was relatively small, and in the case of Santi Giovanni e Paolo situated on the reverse and invisible to the layperson.[77] Valeriano suggested that the excessive size of some tabernacles, intended to give the utmost honour to the body of Christ, was even leading to an opposite state of affairs. Such were their colossal dimensions that they had inadvertently provided a welcoming home to stray cats, who clambered inside the structures to give birth, their kittens emerging just as mass was being said and disrupting the celebration with their miaowing![78]

Valeriano also lamented excessive expenditure on paintings, ornaments, and other '*cose impertinenti*' in Jesuit churches, but his objections were in vain, and lavish tabernacles proved to be very popular indeed. For example, when the *tramezzo* was removed from Santa Maria Novella in Florence, an anonymous letter of c. 1565 noted approvingly that the change 'makes it seem larger and much more beautiful'.[79] It was true that projects like the Umiltà tabernacle would have required a team of skilled craftspeople, including carpenters, gilders, painters, and sometimes sculptors too and thus could incur significant financial outlays. In the case of the Umiltà, the overall design and execution of the work can be attributed to the Florentine Jesuit carpenter and wood-carver Bartolomeo Tronchi (1529–1600), who provided 'in-house' labour that should have theoretically helped to cut down on costs.[80] Tronchi worked extensively on such wooden tabernacles for the Jesuits throughout Italy, most famously on the sumptuous example at San Giovannino in Florence completed in 1585 (now lost). Valeriano had even written that the Archbishop of Florence castigated the rector of the Jesuit college at the time, Pietro Blanca, for the magnificence of the San Giovannino tabernacle.[81] Otherwise, it was a success, widely admired and apparently even visited incognito by the Grand Duchess and Duke.[82] Tronchi was already in high demand some years before this: a letter of 30 November 1577 sent from Mario Beringucci, the Provincial in Venice, to Everardo Mercuriano, General of the Jesuits, requested that Tronchi be transferred in order to assist them with realising his 'beautiful design' for their new tabernacle. Jerónimo Nadal (1507–80), who was in Venice at the time, united himself in these pleas, requesting that Tronchi stay for four months in order 'to guide and help to make the tabernacle' according to his design.[83] The finished product ended up costing 1,000 ducats, but even if some Jesuits like Valeriano objected, these appear to have been widely considered monies well spent, especially when they were funded through alms.[84] The tabernacle was extolled by the Jesuits as a 'beautiful and perfect work', typical of the kind of language that they used to praise the appearance of these expensive new objects once they were completed.[85] Their opinion was shared by other commentators, however, and in 1581, by which point the tabernacle was complete, Sansovino mentioned it as 'a thing truly worthy, not just of this church, but of this holy city'.[86] By the 1590s the fame of the high altar of the Umiltà had been firmly established, with a foreign visitor to Venice, Fynes Moryson, recording it as 'one of the fairest in the city'.[87]

Although the tabernacle no longer exists, to some extent it is possible to reconstruct its original appearance using guides and archival documents.[88] Placed at the height of the ciborium was Francesco Bassano's *Nativity* with depictions of the Old Testament figures of Moses, Aaron, and Melchizedek on either side. Veronese's *God the Father* was below this, and his *Christ the Redeemer* decorated the tabernacle portal. A further lunette by Veronese featuring two angels was placed between these works.[89] On either side of the tabernacle door were the two canvases by Veronese that survive: *The Preaching of John the Baptist* (Fig. 89) and *Christ and the Centurion*. Finally, two further extant paintings produced by Palma, the rather beautiful *Elijah and the Angel* and *Christ and Zacchaeus* (Figs. 90 and 91), completed the decoration. Exactly where they were situated is unclear, but it seems most likely that they were 'behind' Veronese's paintings as Boschini described, meaning that they were ranged around the structure in a manner similar to the arrangement for the tabernacle at the Redentore.[90]

Nicola Locatelli pointed out that all the scenes decorating the Umiltà tabernacle had a eucharistic subtext, even if the design eschewed the

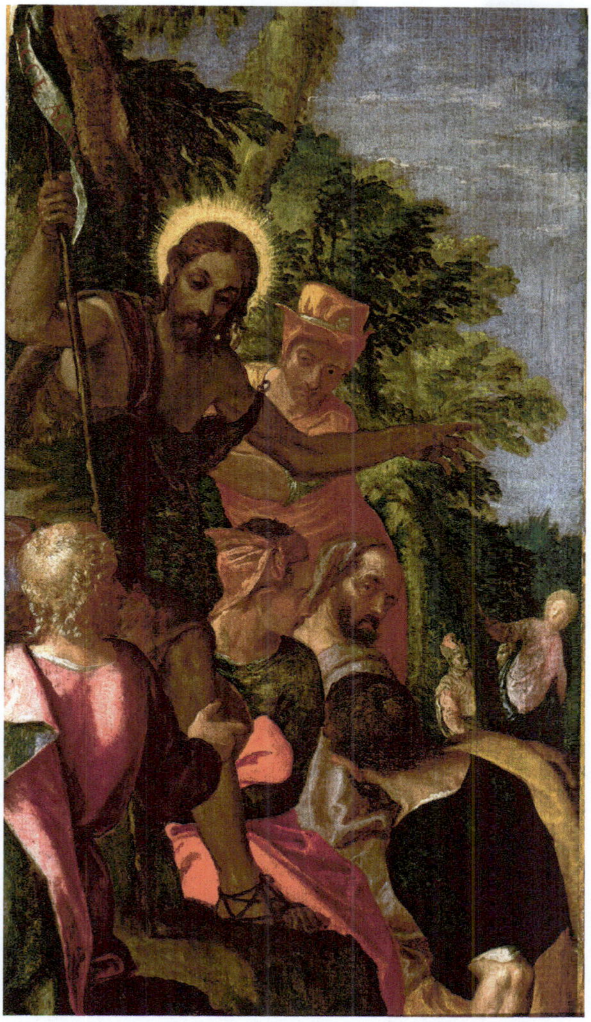

89. Veronese, *The Preaching of John the Baptist*, c. 1580, oil on canvas, Private Collection, Milan (Photo: Cameraphoto)

straightforward passion imagery favoured by Borromeo.[91] Eucharistic themes aside, Stefania Mason's reading argued that it was the words spoken by the centurion to Christ – 'I am not worthy' – that provided the key to understanding the meaning behind the tabernacle decoration.[92] The centurion depicted in Veronese's painting believed that he was unfit to host Christ (Matthew 8:5–13); so too did John the Baptist demonstrate his humility by recognising his unworthiness to untie his cousin's sandal (John 1:27). Palma's image of Christ and Zacchaeus refers to the same virtue, since Zacchaeus the tax collector expressed his humility by hiding in the sycamore tree and promising to give away his earthly possessions (Luke 19:1–10).[93] Last, the Old Testament figure of Elijah went to the desert after having killed the prophets of Baal and prayed for death, saying, 'Take my life; I am no better than my ancestors'

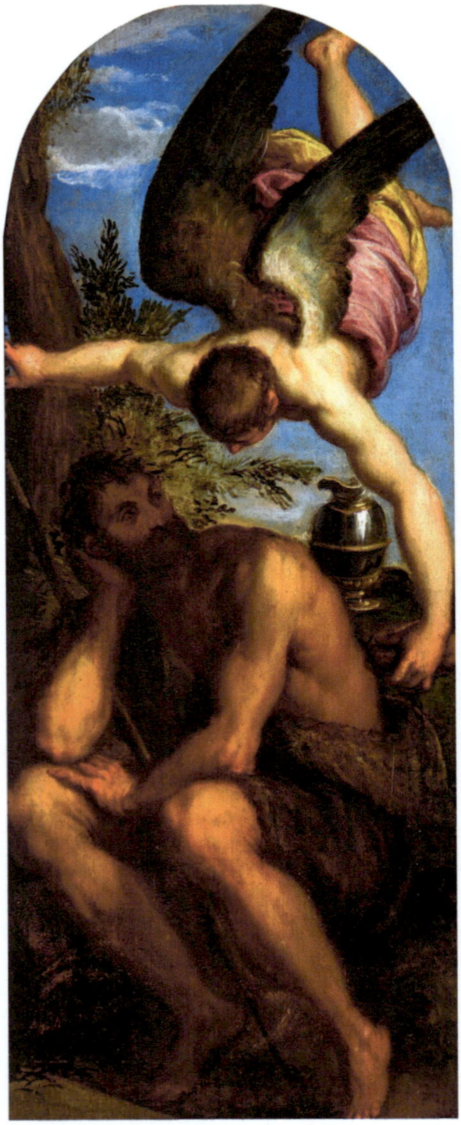

90. Palma il Giovane, *Elijah and the Angel,* c. 1580, oil on canvas, Fitzwilliam Museum, Cambridge (Photo: The Fitzwilliam Museum, Cambridge)

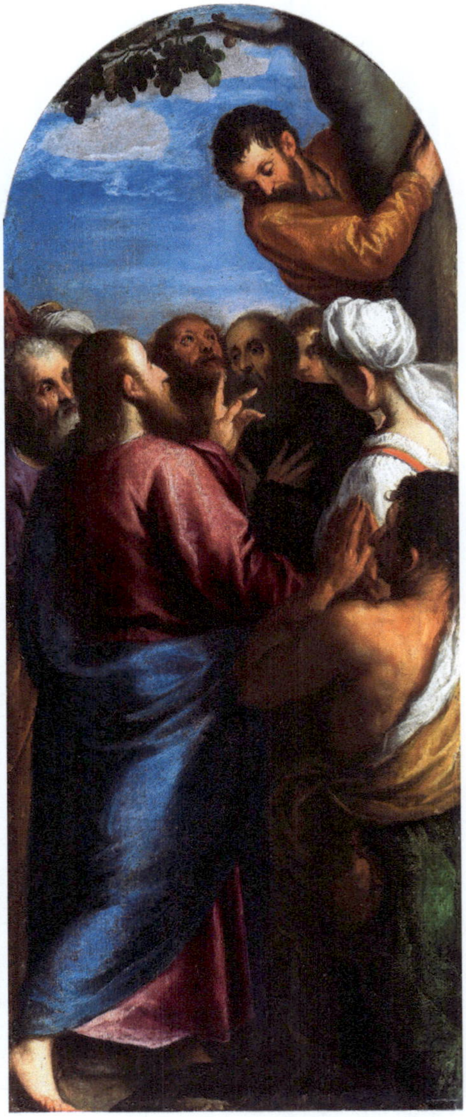

91. Palma il Giovane, *Christ and Zacchaeus,* c. 1580, oil on canvas, Fitzwilliam Museum, Cambridge (Photo: The Fitzwilliam Museum, Cambridge)

(1 Kings 19:4). Humility thus informed the choice of these scenes painted by Veronese and Palma, demonstrating the paramount importance of this virtue for the Jesuit Order and reflecting the dedication of their church to the Virgin of Humility.

There is one final theme that the decorative programme of the tabernacle expressed, and that was conversion. In one of Veronese's paintings John is shown preparing 'the way of the Lord' as he preaches to an attendant crowd of the baptism of repentance for the remission of sins. Both the centurion and the tax collector Zacchaeus depicted by Veronese and Palma were converted after their encounter with Christ, and Elijah exhorted the King Ahab to worship God instead of the idols of Baal.[94] Conversion would have had a special resonance at the Umiltà. Those being converted at the Pia casa dei Catecumeni heard mass at the church until 1596, when their own oratory a few minutes' walk away was completed. Founded in 1557 and dedicated to the Christianisation of Muslims and Jews, the Jesuits were amongst the governors of the institute of the Catecumeni, and the catechumens often received instruction at their house.[95] Their special relationship to the church also appears to have been reflected in Marco del Moro's (c. 1536–86) altarpiece of the *Circumcision* (c. 1565–70), once situated in the nave and now in the Accademia of Venice, where men with turbans and kippahs are shown reverently attending the delicate operation.[96]

The juxtaposition of the paintings on the Umiltà tabernacle was unusual and far more sophisticated than in other places, closely related to the local specificities of site and audience. The nature of this commission as a Jesuit one is significant since the order were unusually tuned in to the role of images in abetting conversion through their global missionary activities. The Jesuit José de Acosta wrote to his fellow missionaries in Peru in the late 1570s that 'priests must be convinced that the use of holy water, images, rosaries, beads, candles, palms and other items of which the Holy Church approves and makes frequent use, are extremely profitable for the recently converted'.[97] The involvement of Nadal, who pushed for the tabernacle at the Umiltà to be completed by the talented Tronchi, is surely significant given that he was the brains behind the *Evangelicae historiae imagines* (first published in 1593). This annotated and illustrated Gospel featured a set of images that were likely the first in history to be reproduced on all four continents, according to Jean Michel Massing, and the book enjoyed huge success as part of the order's evangelising activities.[98] In keeping with the pedagogic talents of the Jesuits, it is tempting to speculate that the Umiltà tabernacle might even have functioned as a kind of teaching aid for the catechumens, who were closely involved with the ministry of the Company of Jesus at the end of the sixteenth century in Venice. The decoration of objects such as these required the spectator to make theological connections between the inset images in order to comprehend the meanings of the programme as a coherent whole. Venetians would have been accustomed to doing this because pairings of episodes from the Old and New Testament were common in the city, particularly from the 1570s onwards. These typologies were most often to be found in confraternity buildings and sacrament chapels, most famously by Tintoretto at the Scuola Grande di San Rocco. Influenced by the popularity of the medieval *Biblia pauperum*, they insisted on the predictive relationship of the Old Testament to the New, particularly with

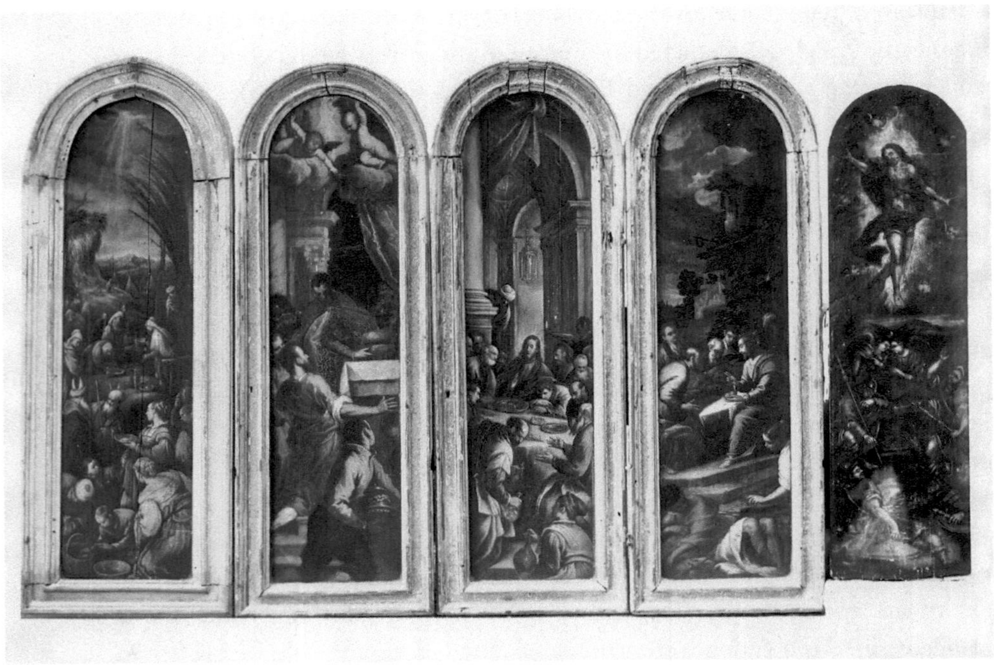

92. Francesco Bassano, *The Falling of the Manna*, *King David and Ahimelech*, *The Last Supper*, *The Supper at Emmaus*, and *The Resurrection*, c. 1585–91, Redentore, Venice (Photo: Fondazione Giorgio Cini, Fototeca dell'Istituto di Storia dell'Arte, Fondo Pallucchini)

regard to episodes like the Falling of the Manna that were understood as foreshadowing the institution of the eucharist at the Last Supper. For example, the first tabernacle of the Redentore (c. 1585–91) featured some exquisite painted scenes by Francesco Bassano that included depictions of *The Falling of the Manna*, *King David and Ahimelech*, *The Last Supper*, *The Supper at Emmaus*, and *The Resurrection* (Fig. 92).[99] In this way, passages from the Old Testament were visually harnessed to bolster Catholic belief relating to the eucharist. This particular example was deigned to be one 'of the most beautiful in the city' according to Stringa, the didacticism of these scenes complementing the co-ordinated programme of Christological altarpieces in the nave of the Redentore.[100]

To conclude, in this chapter and in the ones that follow we will see how older iconographies were often powerfully recast and reinvented by early modern artists in the age of the Reformations. This was first shown in Chapter 1 with Lorenzo Lotto's *Christ the Vine*, which reimagined aspects of the iconography of the Tree of Jesse to create something new and unforgettably arresting, and it continued with the emotive images of Christ's body produced by Lotto's compatriots throughout the course of the sixteenth century. Whether a depiction of Christ comforted by angels in the blackness of his tomb, or his crucified outline depicted in the communion wafer, these were themes that left ample room for the imagination of the artist to set to work, rendering an invisible world visible to the beholder. At the same time, as the design of churches was altered so that everything was made to converge on the high altar tabernacle, and as retro-choirs grew in popularity so that the laity were granted a new level of visual access to the presbytery from the moment they crossed the threshold, as noted by Paul Davies, they were 'drawn into the space by means of the perspective, only for the way to be barred by a bronze door, which hid the object of devotion from view'.[101] Overexposure was believed to devalue the sacred: if one could see everything constantly, then it could lose its mystique, and thus its power. So the transubstantiated host enclosed within the darkness of the tabernacle was hidden, its presence attested to by the lamps that would have been hung before it and the decorated images that adorned its gargantuan enclosure. Images were a substitute for the fleeting glimpses of the host at mass, but they could also tease. Tabernacles might have grown in size and splendour, immediately visible from the moment of entering into the church, but without passing into the sanctuary reserved for the clergy it is not always possible to individuate the details of their decoration, left tantalisingly in view, but distant enough to be out of complete visual reach. This space between revealing and veiling encouraged an imaginative kind of looking, one that could lead the viewer to complete the images in the mind's eye, and thus draw them into active contemplation on the nature of the body of Christ.

NOTES

1 Hans Tietze and Erika Tietze-Conrat, *The Drawings of the Venetian Painters in the 15th and 16th Centuries* (New York: J. J. Augustin, 1944), 202, cat. 896.

2 For examples, see Cope, *The Venetian Chapel of the Sacrament in the Sixteenth Century*, 631–32; Mason, 'Images of Christ for Venetian Piety and Devotions in the Light of the Council of Trent', 296–97; Lyle Humphrey, 'From Column to Chalice: Passion Imagery in Venetian Mariegole ca. 1320–1550', in *New Perspectives on the Man of Sorrows*, ed. Catherine R. Puglisi and William L. Barcham, Studies in Iconography: Themes and Variations (Kalamazoo: Medieval Institute Publications, Western Michigan University, 2013), 239–48.

3 This use was first suggested in Peter Humfrey et al., eds., *The Age of Titian: Venetian Renaissance Art from Scottish Collections*, Exhibition Catalogue, Royal Scottish Academy Building, Edinburgh, 5 August–5 December 2004 (Edinburgh: National Galleries of Scotland, 2004), 265, cat. 118. For the Correr drawing, see Tietze and Tietze-Conrat, *The Drawings of the Venetian Painters in the 15th and 16th Centuries*, 222, cat. 1179; Terisio Pignatti and Giandomenico Romanelli, *Drawings from Venice: Masterworks from the Museo Correr, Venice* (London: Trefoil Books in association with the Drawing Center, New York, 1985), 52, cat. 6; Baviera and Bentini, *Mistero e Immagine: l'Eucaristia nell'arte dal XVI al XVIII secolo*, 164–65, cat. 46. A third variation on the subject was sold at Sotheby's in London on 9 April 1970, lot 20. This is noted in Catherine R. Puglisi and William L. Barcham, eds., *Passion in Venice: Crivelli to Tintoretto and Veronese: The Man of Sorrows in Venetian Art*, Exhibition Catalogue, Museum of Biblical Art, New York, 11 February–12 June 2011 (London: Museum of Biblical Art, 2011), 142–43, cat. 57. The latter have suggested that the drawings might have been utilised by a carpenter or sculptor for a relief or the top of a standard.

4 Freedberg, 'Art after Iconoclasm', 21.

5 Hope, 'Altarpieces and the Requirements of Patrons'. See also Peter Humfrey, 'Some Thoughts on Writing a History of Venetian Altarpieces', in *New Interpretations of Venetian Renaissance Painting*, ed. Francis Ames-Lewis (London: Bickbeck College, 1994), 13. Humfrey agrees with Hope's overall thesis, but thinks that he 'goes too far in seeming to dismiss the possibility that the doctrinal element may often be present as a subplot'.

6 An interesting discussion on the limitations of understanding devotional images, as some pioneering medieval historians had done, as neatly serving 'the ends of religious persuasion and edification' is provided by Andrew Chen, *Flagellant Confraternities and Italian Art, 1260–1610: Ritual and Experience* (Amsterdam: Amsterdam University Press, 2018), 24–25.

7 Two examples: Palma's eldest daughter Giulia planned to leave money to her local confraternity in her will of 1644, as did the second wife of the painter Aliense in 1609, who wished to be accompanied to her burial in San Zaccaria by her parish Scuola del Santissimo Sacramento. ASV, Notarile, Testamenti, b. 227–30, n. 275 (Giulia); b. 222, n. 960 (Giacomina Vassilacchi).

8 See Cope, *The Venetian Chapel of the Sacrament in the Sixteenth Century*, 631–32; Mason, 'Images of Christ for Venetian Piety and Devotions in the Light of the Council of Trent', 295–96; Humphrey, 'From Column to Chalice: Passion Imagery in Venetian Mariegole ca. 1320–1550', 239–48. Depictions of the Man of Sorrows are termed 'a quintessentially Venetian sacred subject' in Puglisi and Barcham, *Art and Faith in the Venetian World: Venerating Christ as the Man of Sorrows*, 291.

9 Camille, *The Gothic Idol*, 215. Camille speculates that the host may even have overtaken veneration of the cross.

10 Noted by Humfrey, 'La pala d'altare veneta nell'età delle riforme', 1143–45.

11 Richard C. Trexler, *The Spiritual Power: Republican Florence under Interdict* (Leiden: Brill, 1974), 126–27.

12 Camille, *The Gothic Idol*, 217.

13 For art in Brescia and Bergamo under Venetian rule, see, in particular, Alessandro Nova, 'La pittura nei territori di Bergamo e Brescia nel Cinquecento', in *La pittura in Italia: Il Cinquecento*, ed. Giuliano Briganti (Milan: Electa, 1988), 1:105–24; Bayer, 'Bergamo and Brescia'; Barbara Maria Savy, *Manducatio per visum: temi eucaristici nella pittura di Romanino e Moretto*, Pittura del Rinascimento nell'Italia Settentrionale, Quaderni 2 (Cittadella: Bertoncello Artigrafiche, 2006).

14 Pier Virgilio Begni Redona, 'Pitture e sculture in San Faustino', in *La chiesa e il monastero benedettino di San Faustino Maggiore in Brescia*, ed. Gianni Mezzanotte (Brescia: Editrice La Scuola, 1999), 171–75; Alessandro Nova, *Girolamo Romanino* (Turin: Allemandi, 1994), 321–23, cat. 95; Campbell, *The Endless Periphery*, 310–11, note 76. An earlier painting of the same miracle had been painted by Romanino for the confraternity of the Blessed Sacrament at Santa Maria in Calchera. Here, Saint Apollonius celebrates the mass with an image of the Pietà in the background. This presents a variation on the legend whereby the two saints Faustinus and Jovinus were invoked in the bishop's prayers and arrived armed with the objects required for the mass. See Campbell, 209.

15 Noted by Nova, *Girolamo Romanino*, 322.

16 See Valerio Guazzoni, *Moretto: il tema sacro* (Brescia: Grafo edizioni, 1981), 46–49. More recently by Campbell, *The Endless Periphery*, 207–11. Campbell points out that Innocenzo Casari's eyewitness account of the 1513 sack of Brescia by French troops concentrated particularly on their desecration of the eucharist. Later in 1527, the chronicle of Pandolfo Nassini recounted the presence of more than 1,500 Germans and heretics in the area.

17 Eire, *Reformations: The Early Modern World, 1450–1650*, 407. Eire's reference was to eucharistic miracles that could be deployed in the face of the Protestant challenge.

18 Black, *Italian Confraternities in the Sixteenth Century*, 77.

19 For the artistic influences of the painters discussed here, active in Brescia and Bergamo, see, most recently, Valerio Guazzoni, 'Un secolo di pittura fra Brescia e Bergamo: l'età

rinascimentale', in *Lotto, Romanino, Moretto, Ceruti: maestri della pittura a Brescia e Bergamo*, ed. Davide Dotti, Exhibition Catalogue, Palazzo Martinengo Cesaresco, Brescia, 21 January–11 June 2023 (Cinisello Balsamo: Silvana Editoriale, 2023), 13–21.

20 See Guazzoni, *Moretto: il tema sacro*, 49–51; *Alessandro Bonvicino, il Moretto*, Exhibition Catalogue, Monastery of S. Giulia, Brescia 18 June–20 November 1988 (Bologna: Nuova Alfa, 1988), 153, cat. 76; Baviera and Bentini, *Mistero e Immagine: l'Eucaristia nell'arte dal XVI al XVIII secolo*, 134–35, cat. 33. This painting is dependent upon the earlier *Eucharistic Christ between Saints Cosmas and Damian* of c. 1540 for its compositional schema. Painted for the altar of the confraternity of Corpus Domini for the parish of Marmentino, the two works likely shared the same patron: the archpriest of the duomo of Brescia Donato Savallo.

21 Lillywhite, 'The Decoration of the Church of San Giacomo dall'Orio in Venice', 129–31.

22 Ridolfi, *Le maraviglie dell'arte*, vol. 1: 269. For the painting, see Redona, 'Pitture e sculture in San Faustino', 171.

23 Palma's great-uncle Palma il Vecchio was born there c. 1480. For the Palma clan's links to Bergamo, see David Rosand, 'Palma Giovane and Venetian Mannerism' (doctoral thesis, Columbia University, 1965), 137–38, note 8.

24 For Palma at the Crociferi oratory, see Sherman, *The Lost Venetian Church of Santa Maria Assunta dei Crociferi: Form, Decoration, Patronage*, 159–74; Giorgio Tagliaferro, 'Procurators on the Threshold: Sitters and Beholders in Palma Giovane's Crociferi Entombment', *Artibus et Historiae* 37, no. 74 (2016): 153–76.

25 See Pignatti and Pedrocco, *Veronese*, vol. 2: 489–91, cat. 391.

26 For the decoration of the San Zulian chapel, see the previous chapter. For Campagna's relief, see Wladimir Timofiewitsch, *Girolamo Campagna: Studien zur venezianischen Plastik um das Jahr 1600* (Munich: Wilhelm Fink Verlag, 1970), 235–36, no. 2.

27 MSM, Mariegola della Scuola del Santissimo di San Giacomo dall'Orio, unnumbered folios. For this illustration and other similar examples, see Humphrey, 'From Column to Chalice: Passion Imagery in Venetian Mariegole ca. 1320–1550'. Dating to the sixth century, the earliest representations of this iconography show Christ depicted twice on either side of the altar. The theme was popular in the orthodox Church and was often situated above the altar. See Schiller, *Iconography of Christian Art*, vol. 2: 28–30.

28 'Misticus est panis quem porrigo sic ego panis sint pater ni (hi) mecu[m] semp[er] pariter quoq[ue] tecum.' The second line is a synthesis of chapter 17 of John. See Andaloro et al., *San Marco*, 74. The scene below depicts the *Supper at Emmaus* and is based upon a cartoon of Leandro Bassano of 1617. Both episodes had been present in the older decoration. See Otto Demus, 'Probleme der Restaurierung der Mosaiken von San Marco im XV. und XVI. Jahrhundert', in *Venezia, centro di mediazione tra Oriente e Occidente, secoli XV–XVI: aspetti e problemi*, ed. Hans-Georg Beck, Agostino Pertusi, and M. I. Manoussacas, vol. 2, Civiltà veneziana, Studi 32 (Florence: Leo Olschki, 1977), 638, 642; Demus, *The Mosaics of San Marco in Venice*, vol. 2: 24–25.

29 BMC, Ms. IV164, Mariegola della confraternita del Santissimo Sacramento in San Zulian, unnumbered folios.

30 The documentation relating to the commission was published by Portogruaro, *Il tempio del Redentore e il convento dei Cappuccini di Venezia*, 33–34.

31 Cesare Ripa, *Iconologia overo Descrittione di diverse imagini cauate dall'antichità, & di propria inuentione* (Rome: Lepido Facii., 1603), 149.

32 Ripa, *Iconologia overo Descrittione di diverse imagini cauate dall'antichità, & di propria inuentione*, 150–51. First published in 1593 without illustrations. In the 1603 edition the image of *Catholic Faith* appears on page 151. A personification of faith holding a chalice and cross (without the host) can be seen in Titian and Marco Vecellio's 1575–76 votive painting of Doge Antonio Grimani in the Sala delle Quattro Porte of the Ducal Palace. Veronese's votive painting for Doge Sebastiano Venier in the Sala del Collegio of 1581–82 also shows the kneeling figure of faith holding a chalice at the feet of Christ.

33 The painting is thought to have been the upper register of an altarpiece. Anchise Tempestini, *Giovanni Bellini* (Milan: Fabbri Editori, 1997), 204, cat. 39. For Bellini's images of the dead Christ, see Rona Goffen, *Giovanni Bellini* (New Haven, CT: Yale University Press, 1989), 66–89.

34 Giovanni Tiepolo, *Discorsi et considerationi sopra il Santissimo Sacramento dell'Altare* (Venice: Santo Grillo, et Fratelli, 1618), 583–87.

35 Tiepolo, *Discorsi et considerationi sopra il Santissimo Sacramento dell'Altare*, 586–87. By contrast Tiepolo argued that the angels were made to blush when confronted with a lack of devotion in honouring the eucharist.

36 Alexandra Walsham and Peter Marshall, eds., *Angels in the Early Modern World* (Cambridge: Cambridge University Press, 2006), 23.

37 For a history of the iconography, see Staale Sinding-Larsen, *Christ in the Council Hall: Studies in the Religious Iconography of the Venetian Republic* (Rome: 'L'Erma' di Bretschneider, 1974), 99–108; Cope, *The Venetian Chapel of the Sacrament in the Sixteenth Century*, 55–62; Schiller, *Iconography of Christian Art*, vol. 2: 215–19. Christ supported by an angel became a standard subject for the doors of tabernacles: the door of the tabernacle for the church of Santa Chiara by Aliense depicted Christ supported by angels, as did that of San Giacomo dall'Orio by Maffeo Verona. See Boschini, *Le minere della pittura*, 505, 515–16. The image was also used on paxes. One example of this is a sixteenth-century pax made in the Veneto held in the Museo Correr (inv. CI. X n. 0084).

38 BMC, MS.CI. IV016, Mariegola della Scuola del Santissimo in San Samuele, fol. 17r.

39 Pignatti and Pedrocco, *Veronese*, vol. 2: 486–87, cat. 387. According to Ridolfi the painting was in the collection of Vincenzo Giustiniani in Rome.

40 To this typology also belongs Veronese's other Berlin *Dead Christ with Angels* (Pignatti and Pedrocco, *Veronese*, vol. 2: 487, cat. 388) and that of the Museum of Fine Arts in Boston (Pignatti and Pedrocco, *Veronese*, vol. 2: 505, cat. A7). The Hermitage *Lamentation* depicts Christ accompanied by the Virgin Mary and an attendant angel (once accompanied by a second angelic companion) who beckons towards the source of the light that that is beginning to creep over Christ's lower body (Pignatti and Pedrocco, *Veronese*, vol. 2: 405–6, cat. 293).

41 The subject matter is thus close to Rosso's *Dead Christ* of c. 1525–26. Shearman noted that this painting emphasised 'the expectation of resurrection rather than the recollection of sacrifice'. John Shearman, 'The "Dead Christ" by Rosso Fiorentino', *Boston Museum Bulletin* 64, no. 338 (1966): 148–72.

42 See Peter Marshall, 'Angels around the Deathbed: Variations on a Theme in the English Art of Dying', in *Angels in the Early Modern World*, ed. Alexandra Walsham and Peter Marshall (Cambridge: Cambridge University Press, 2006), 84–85.

43 For Donatello's influence, see Shearman, 'The "Dead Christ" by Rosso Fiorentino', 152.

44 See Guazzoni, *Moretto: il tema sacro*, 52–53; Jane Martineau and Charles Hope, eds., *The Genius of Venice, 1500–1600*, Exhibition Catalogue, Royal Academy of Arts, London, 23 November 1983–11 March 1984 (London: Royal Academy of Arts, 1983), 185–86, cat. 59; *Alessandro Bonvicino, il Moretto*, 175–76, cat. 90.

45 Sinding-Larsen, *Christ in the Council Hall*, 33–34, 107.

46 Stringa noted that the painting showed the dead Christ 'as he was when he was taken down from the Cross'. Stringa, *Venetia, città nobilissima, et singolare*, 230.

47 Sinding-Larsen, *Christ in the Council Hall*, 107–8; Pallucchini and Rossi, *Tintoretto: le opere sacre e profane*, vol. 1: 222, cat. 423.

48 Sinding-Larsen, *Christ in the Council Hall*, 108–19; Mason Rinaldi, *Palma il Giovane: l'opera completa*, 141–42, cat. 532.

49 For the Christological emphasis in the decorative programme, see Sinding-Larsen, *Christ in the Council Hall.* In his study, Sinding-Larsen paid particular attention to the insistence on eucharistic themes in the Ducal Palace decoration of the late sixteenth century. This is an important aspect, but it also true that he gave other concomitant motivations relatively

short shrift. For a discussion, see Giorgio Tagliaferro, 'Il "Mito" ripensato: trasformazioni della pittura tra Lepanto e l'Interdetto', in *Celebrazione e autocritica: la Serenissima e la ricerca dell'identità veneziana nel tardo Cinquecento*, ed. Benjamin Paul (Rome: Viella; Venice: Centro tedesco di studi veneziani, 2014), 193–231.

50 Tagliaferro, 'Il "Mito" ripensato: trasformazioni della pittura tra Lepanto e l'Interdetto', 220–24.

51 A sentiment expressed throughout Tiepolo, *Discorsi et considerationi sopra il Santissimo Sacramento dell'Altare*.

52 As Nichols points out in his analysis of imagery of the poor, 'the fleshy body of the naked beggar could take on a more positive connotation with that of Christ, and by extension with the sacrament of the eucharist'. Nichols, 'Secular Charity, Sacred Poverty: Picturing the Poor in Renaissance Venice', 160.

53 Duffy, *The Stripping of the Altars*, 93.

54 A concise history of the development of the tabernacle in Italy from the Middle Ages to the seventeenth century is provided by Cope, *The Venetian Chapel of the Sacrament in the Sixteenth Century*, 8–25. For a more general survey, see Joseph Braun, *Der christliche Altar in seiner geschichtlichen Entwicklung*, vol. 2 (Munich: Alte Meister Guenther Koch, 1924), 639–47.

55 Waterworth, *Canons and Decrees of the Council of Trent*, 80.

56 Voelker, 'Carlo Borromeo's Instructiones fabricae et supellectilis ecclesiasticae, 1577', 160–63.

57 For the door, Borromeo similarly recommended an image of Christ either resurrected or displaying the wounds of his passion or 'another pious image'. Voelker, 'Carlo Borromeo's Instructiones fabricae et supellectilis ecclesiasticae, 1577', 163.

58 This was the case not just in Italy but also in the Low Countries, where the verticality of imposing sculpted sacrament houses made a clear statement about the religious persuasions of their donors. See Ruben Suykerbuyk and Anne-Laure van Bruaene, 'Towering Piety: Sacrament Houses, Local Patronage and an Early Counter-Reformation Spirit in the Low Countries (1520–1566)', *Nederlands kunsthistorisch jaarboek* 67 (2017): 118–59. For examples of the fifteenth-century tabernacle type, see Alison Wright, 'Tabernacle and Sacrament in Fifteenth-Century Tuscany', in *Carvings, Casts & Collectors: The Art of Renaissance Sculpture*, ed. Peta Wright, Emma Jones, and Dimitrios Zikos (London: V&A Publishing, 2013), 42–57; Paul Davies, 'Framing the Miraculous: The Devotional Functions of Perspective in Italian Renaissance Tabernacle Design', *Art History* 36, no. 5 (2013): 898–921. The influence of Borromeo is noted in most studies of Italian tabernacle design of the late sixteenth century, including by Braun, *Der christliche Altar in seiner geschichtlichen Entwicklung*, vol. 2: 646–47.

59 In Siena cathedral in 1506 Duccio's *Maestà* high altarpiece was replaced with Vecchietta's eucharistic tabernacle. For a discussion, see Allen, *Transforming the Church Interior*, 94.

60 Dated to 1618, the San Lorenzo tabernacle was designed by Campagna and completed by Giovanni Maria da Cannaregio. See Zorzi, *Venezia scomparsa*, vol. 2: 513.

61 The Santi Giovanni e Paolo tabernacle was designed by Baldassare Longhena in the early 1650s and then inserted into the pre-existing triumphal arch of Matteo Carneri. For the complicated history of the high altar, see Paola Rossi, 'Altare maggiore', in *La Basilica dei Santi Giovanni e Paolo: Pantheon della Serenissima*, ed. Giuseppe Pavanello and Matteo De Fina (Venice: Marcianum Press, 2013), 384–87, cat. 135a; Andrew Hopkins, 'Longhena, Lapislazzuli and the Pozzo Brothers: The Tabernacle of the Sacrament for San Daniele in Venice', in *La festa delle arti: scritti in onore di Marcello Fagiolo per cinquant'anni di studi*, ed. Vincenzo Cazzato, Sebastiano Roberto, and Mario Bevilacqua (Rome: Gangemi, 2014), 243.

62 The Tolentini tabernacle was designed by Longhena, and the two adoring angels and six caryatids are the work of Giusto Le Court. The bronze *Christ the Redeemer* was the only work of Francesco Cavrioli completed before his death. The contract with Longhena was

signed in 1661 and the works were completed by around 1672. The appearance of the high altar prior to Longhena's tabernacle is unresolved, but the impetus for the new design came from a donation of 9,000 ducats by Cornelia Badoer (will of 1658) for the transformation of the presbytery, where she was to be buried. See Nicola Ivanoff, 'Una ignota opera del Longhena: l'altare maggiore dei Tolentini', *Ateneo Veneto* 132 (1945): 96–100; Antonio Manno, ed., *La chiesa di San Nicola da Tolentino a Venezia: storia, arte e devozione* (Padua: Il Prato, 2012), 50; Andrew Hopkins, *Baldassare Longhena and Venetian Baroque Architecture*, 2nd revised ed. (New Haven, CT: Yale University Press, 2012), 141–42.

63 Stringa, *Venetia, città nobilissima, et singolare*, 192v. Stringa's comments relate to his praise for the new tabernacle at the church of the Zitelle.

64 Borromeo had conceded that tabernacles could also be made of wood, but he took care to specify that poplar was to be used rather than walnut, since the latter tended to become damp. Voelker, 'Carlo Borromeo's Instructiones fabricae et supellectilis ecclesiasticae, 1577', 160.

65 For the paintings by Palma, see Mason Rinaldi, *Palma il Giovane: l'opera completa*, 487–90, cat. 133; Puglisi and Barcham, *Art and Faith in the Venetian World: Venerating Christ as the Man of Sorrows*, 281–82. One reason why tabernacles inset with paintings appear to have been more popular in conventual rather than parish churches in Venice may be related to the fact that in parishes the tabernacle was usually placed in a chapel that was already richly decorated with eucharistic imagery commissioned by the Scuole del Sacramento, meaning there was less of an exigency for further narrative images on the tabernacle itself. One exception is the parish of San Moisè, which had a tabernacle inset with canvases of the passion. See Stringa, *Venetia, città nobilissima, et singolare*, 95v.

66 Noted by Puglisi and Barcham, *Art and Faith in the Venetian World: Venerating Christ as the Man of Sorrows*, 281.

67 Cope, *The Venetian Chapel of the Sacrament in the Sixteenth Century*, 24.

68 See Tracy Cooper, 'The History and Decoration of the Church of San Giorgio Maggiore in Venice' (doctoral thesis, Princeton University, 1990), 258; Portogruaro, *Il tempio del Redentore e il convento dei Cappuccini di Venezia*, 40–42; Andrew Hopkins, *Baldassare Longhena, 1597–1682* (Milan: Electa, 2006), 141.

69 See Lucia Aquino and Simone Giordani, *Francesco Granacci e Giovanni Larciani all'Oratorio di Santa Caterina all'Antella*, Exhibition Catalogue, Oratorio di Santa Caterina all'Antella, Ponte a Ema, Bagno a Ripoli, 14 September 2013–12 January 2014 (Florence: Edizioni Polistampa, 2013), 116–17, cat. 12. The inscription that runs along the frieze reads 'HIC EST PANIS DE C[A]ELO DESCENDENS [UT] SI QUIS EX IPSO MANDUCAVERIT NON MORIATUR' (John 6:50).

70 See Cope, *The Venetian Chapel of the Sacrament in the Sixteenth Century*, 21, 610; Maddalena Trionfi Honorati, 'Un tabernacolo Ligneo su disegno del Vasari e l'intagliatore Alberto Alberti', *Antichità viva* 14 (1975): 57–61.

71 The convent was suppressed in 1806 and the church was later demolished. For a history of the early Jesuits in Venice, see Mario Zanardi, 'I "domicilia" o centri operativi della Compagnia di Gesù nello Stato Veneto (1543–1773)', in *I Gesuiti e Venezia: momenti e problemi di storia veneziana della Compagnia di Gesù: atti del Convegno di studi, Venezia, 2–5 ottobre 1990*, ed. Mario Zanardi (Padua: Gregoriana, 1994), 97–110. For the decoration of the Umiltà, see Davide Ambrosi, 'La chiesa di Santa Maria dell'Umiltà a Venezia e il suo apparato decorativo. Cenni storici e artistici', *Marcianum* 10 (2014): 129–46; Lillywhite, 'The Decoration of the Jesuit Church of the Madonna dell'Umiltà in Venice, 1560–1606'. For the dispersal of the tabernacle in the eighteenth century, see Stefania Mason Rinaldi, 'Il tabernacolo della chiesa dei "Giesuiti" alla dogana di mare', *Arte Veneta* 36 (1982): 211–16; Marie-Louise Lillywhite, 'New Insights into the Tabernacle of the Jesuit Church of Santa Maria dell'Umiltà in Venice', *Arte Veneta* 70 (2013): 227, 233 notes 14, 15. See also note 89 below.

72 For the influence of the Theatines, particularly in Padua, see Hopkins, *Baldassare Longhena, 1597–1682*, 142.

73 Pietro Pirri, *Giuseppe Valeriano, S.I. Architetto e pittore, 1542–1596*, ed. Raineri C. Colombo (Rome: Institutum historicum S.I., 1970), 389. Valeriano's *'informatione delle fabriche'* was to be discussed at the fifth general congregation of the order in November 1593–January 1594.

74 An increase in the number of laypeople receiving the eucharist in the sixteenth century (which meant that a larger number of consecrated hosts had to be kept in stock) was noted by Braun, *Der christliche Altar in seiner geschichtlichen Entwicklung*, vol. 2: 639–40.

75 Braun, *Der christliche Altar in seiner geschichtlichen Entwicklung*, vol. 2: 641.

76 Manno, *La chiesa di San Nicola da Tolentino a Venezia*, 51. Citing Vincenzo Coronelli (1700).

77 The high altar tabernacle of Santi Giovanni e Paolo was praised as one of the most brilliant and effective manifestations of a sacramental altar by Braun, *Der christliche Altar in seiner geschichtlichen Entwicklung*, vol. 2: 643.

78 Pirri, *Giuseppe Valeriano, S.I. Architetto e pittore, 1542–1596*, 389.

79 See Allen, *Transforming the Church Interior*, 275–76. Allen believes it was probably written by a Venetian who would have been in town for the upcoming Medici wedding. Although there were a few complaints about such transformations, they were mostly greeted positively. At Orsanmichele, the *tramezzo* came to be viewed as an obstacle to the 'beautiful view' of the tabernacle.

80 For Tronchi and his collaborators, see Pietro Pirri, 'L'architetto Bartolomeo Ammannati e i Gesuiti', *Archivum Historicum Societatis Iesu* 12 (1943): 22–24; Lillywhite, 'New Insights into the Tabernacle of the Jesuit Church of Santa Maria dell'Umiltà in Venice', 228–29. A biography of Tronchi is provided in note 51 of Pirri's text. Prior to working in Venice and then Florence, Tronchi was involved in the tabernacles for Jesuit churches in Siena (from 1569), Nola and Naples (from 1570), and Perugia (1575). He spent his final years in Rome, working at the Gesù from 1595 to 1597.

81 Pirri, *Giuseppe Valeriano, S.I. Architetto e pittore, 1542–1596*, 389. The archbishop at the time was Alessandro de' Medici, later Pope Leo XI in 1605. See also Merlijn Hurx, 'Bartolomeo Ammannati and the College of San Giovannino in Florence: Adapting Architecture to Jesuit Needs', *Journal of the Society of Architectural Historians* 68, no. 3 (September 2009): 350.

82 Pirri, 'L'architetto Bartolomeo Ammannati e i Gesuiti', 24.

83 Pirri, 'L'architetto Bartolomeo Ammannati e i Gesuiti', 23, note 51.

84 A series of histories of Jesuit houses in the Veneto likely dating from between 1578 and 1582 noted that at the Umiltà 'three noblewomen want to make the tabernacle which will cost around six hundred scudi'. A history of the house penned by the Jesuit Lodovico Gagliardi (c. 1582) stated that 'the beautiful tabernacle costs more than 1000 ducats'. Zanardi, 'I "domicilia" o centri operativi della Compagnia di Gesù nello Stato Veneto (1543–1773)', 107, note 47. Sacrament houses in the Low Countries could take years to complete and cost prodigious amounts. See Suykerbuyk and Bruaene, 'Towering Piety: Sacrament Houses, Local Patronage and an Early Counter-Reformation Spirit in the Low Countries (1520–1566)', 138–39. Prices for tabernacles in Venice must have varied greatly: Portogruaro reports that the original Redentore tabernacle only cost 140 ducats, a surprisingly low sum considering its probable similarities to the Umiltà tabernacle. Portogruaro, *Il tempio del Redentore e il convento dei Cappuccini di Venezia*, 40.

85 Zanardi, 'I "domicilia" o centri operativi della Compagnia di Gesù nello Stato Veneto (1543–1773)', 107. In Nola, the Jesuits noted that 'everyone who has seen [the new tabernacle] has judged it to be without equal in Naples'; Tronchi's work in Siena was described as *'molto raro'*; the reception of the Florentine tabernacle was described rapturously in the annual letters of 1586–87. See Pirri, 'L'architetto Bartolomeo Ammannati e i Gesuiti', 23–24.

86 Sansovino, *Venetia città nobilissima et singolare, descritta in XIIII. Libri*, 98r–v.

87 Moryson, *An itinerary written by Fynes Moryson ... containing his ten yeeres travell through the twelve dominions of Germany, Bohmerland, Sweitzerland, Netherland, Denmarke, Poland, Italy, Turky, France, England, Scotland, and Ireland*, book II, part 1, 84.

88 My reconstruction uses the two most detailed descriptions: that provided by Boschini in 1664 and a document of 12 October 1685, which was the eyewitness account of Giovanni Battista Rossi (ASV, Santa Maria dell'Umiltà, b. 2, fasc 26b, fol. 48r).

89 Boschini did not describe the two figures of Moses and Melchizedek by Bassano, whilst Rossi failed to mention Veronese's *God the Father* and he did not describe the subject matter of the paintings on the lower level. The last account of the tabernacle was Zanetti's in 1771, by which point the only remaining image was Veronese's *Christ the Redeemer* and 'a few cherubs', the rest having been sold off some decades previously. Some of the paintings were clearly of different sizes and formats to the surviving ones. Boschini, *Le minere della pittura*, 345–46; Anton Maria Zanetti, *Della pittura veneziana* (Venice: Giambatista Albrizzi, 1771), 186; Tapié, *Baroque vision Jésuite. Du Tintoret à Rubens*, 152–53, cat. 7.

90 Rossi suggested that these were below Veronese's paintings, in 'the lower part of the tabernacle'. It would seem that Palma's paintings were ranged around the structure, especially since Rossi described two of them as being 'close to the wall'. Rossi was the only person to mention a further two paintings by Matteo 'Angoli'. Angoli might refer to Matteo Ingoli, who had also worked at San Giacomo dall'Orio restoring Veronese's ceiling for the sacrament chapel. For Ingoli, see Worthen, 'The Altar and the "banco" of the Scuola del Sacramento in San Giacomo dall'Orio', 203.

91 John the Baptist recognised Christ as the Lamb of God, and during the mass the priest records his words at the moment of the consecration of the host (John 1:29); Elijah was brought heavenly bread by an angel during his flight into the desert, recalling the *panis coeli* consumed at communion (1 Kings 19:5–7); whilst the centurion spoke the words 'Lord, I do not deserve to have you come under my roof. But just say the word, and my servant will be healed' (Matthew 8:8–9) that are recited before receiving the host. Locatelli argues that even the scene of *Christ and Zacchaeus* had a eucharistic theme (albeit a more tenuous one in my opinion), since it was widely suggested in the course of the Middle Ages that Christ would have dined in Zacchaeus's house. See Nicola Locatelli, 'Ancora sul tabernacolo della chiesa dell'Umiltà a Venezia', *Arte Veneta* 62 (2006): 106.

92 Mason Rinaldi, 'Il tabernacolo della chiesa dei "Giesuiti" alla dogana di mare', 214.

93 'Here and now I give half of my possessions to the poor, and if I have cheated anybody out of anything, I will pay back four times the amount' (Luke 19:8). The episode may also have held significance due to the dual importance it placed on faith and good works.

94 Locatelli, 'Ancora sul tabernacolo della chiesa dell'Umiltà a Venezia', 107–8. Elijah was understood as foreshadowing John the Baptist, something referred to by the angel who announced John's birth to Zechariah (Luke 1:16–17), and by Christ himself, who stated that his cousin was 'the Elijah who was to come' (Matthew 11:14). Palma's figure of Elijah could function equally well as a John the Baptist. For the significance of the Old Testament figures in the Bassano paintings at the summit of the tabernacle, see Lillywhite, 'New Insights into the Tabernacle of the Jesuit Church of Santa Maria dell'Umiltà in Venice', 229–30.

95 See Bernard Aikema and Dulcia Meijers, 'I Catecumeni: Chiesa e Ospedale di S. Giovanni Battista', in *Nel regno dei poveri: arte e storia dei grandi ospedali veneziani in età moderna, 1474–1797* (Venice: Arsenale Editrice, 1989), 215–23; Locatelli, 'Ancora sul tabernacolo della chiesa dell'Umiltà a Venezia', 107. The numbers of catechumens increased after the 1571 battle of Lepanto and the influx of Turkish prisoners in Venice that it provoked, but in 1563 there were perhaps only fifteen individuals at the institute. These kinds of houses were rare and there appear to have been only four others like it in Italy in the sixteenth century. Brian S. Pullan, 'The Old Catholicism, the New Catholicism and the Poor', in *Timore e Carità: i poveri nell'Italia Moderna*, ed. Franco Della Paruta, Mario Rosa, and Giorgio Politi, Proceedings of the conference 'Pauperismo e assistenza negli antichi stati italiani', 28–30 March 1980, Cremona (Cremona: Libreria del convegno editrice, 1982), 16.

96 The strict division of the sexes that was dictated both at the institute and by the seating arrangements at the Umiltà may also be reflected in the altarpiece, where the men and women are divided on either side of the altar where Christ's circumcision takes place. The links between the circumcision and the sacrament of baptism may also have had relevance for the catechumens, who were preparing to be baptised into the Catholic faith. See Lillywhite, 'The Decoration of the Jesuit Church of the Madonna dell'Umiltà in Venice, 1560–1606', 176–77. For the baptism of the catechumens, see Locatelli, 'Ancora sul tabernacolo della chiesa dell'Umiltà a Venezia', 107–9.

97 Eire, *Reformations: The Early Modern World, 1450–1650*, 471.

98 Jean Michel Massing, 'Jerome Nadal's "Evangelicae Historiae Imagines" and the Birth of Global Imagery', *Journal of the Warburg and Courtauld Institutes* 80 (2017): 161–220.

99 Now displayed in the sacristy. Three of the scenes are lost, including a Pietà. See Stringa, *Venetia, città nobilissima, et singolare*, 188r; Portogruaro, *Il tempio del Redentore e il convento dei Cappuccini di Venezia*, 60; Timofiewitsch, *Girolamo Campagna: Studien zur venezianischen Plastik um das Jahr 1600*, 253–55, no. 12; Cope, *The Venetian Chapel of the Sacrament in the Sixteenth Century*, 114, note 1; Hochmann, *Peintres et commanditaires à Venise (1540–1628)*, 302. Cope assigns the canvases an earlier date of c. 1582.

100 For this phenomenon see Humfrey, 'Co-ordinated Altarpieces in Renaissance Venice: The Progress of an Ideal'.

101 Davies, 'Framing the Miraculous', 909. As noted by Davies, relics and miracle-working images were also rarely on view.

CHAPTER SIX

SANCTITY

The images of saints and angels should be painted by excellent painters, since they should inspire admiration and sympathy.

–Paolo Veronese, quoted by Carlo Ridolfi[1]

In the latter half of the sixteenth century, representations of sanctity in Venice underwent some fundamental changes. Altarpieces featuring images of the dramatic martyrdoms of the saints became far more diffused, as did images exploring the themes of repentance or conversion. Often the virtue of holy women and men was denoted by their engagement in benevolent acts of charity towards the poor and marginalised, acts that evidenced their presumed likeness to God and the necessity of 'good works' in Catholic soteriology. The efficacy of venerating the saints had been called into question by the Protestant Reformations and was closely interlinked with the question of sacred images, not least because the subject matter of altarpieces very often reflected the saintly dedication of the altar in which they were displayed.[2] The Catholic Church conflated sanctity and image-making in the Tridentine decrees of 1563, and it has been argued that it is to these external factors – the negation of saintliness, on the one hand, and the powerful affirmation of it, on the other – that some of the contemporary changes to the depiction of the saints can be attributed.

The saints had always been central to Catholic devotional images, but the second half of the sixteenth century in Venice witnessed a dramatic increase in the sheer number of altarpieces that concentrated on narrative episodes from their hagiographies.[3] By the end of the century, scenes of their martyrdoms could be seen throughout the altarpieces of the city's churches, sometimes replacing the previous *sacra conversazione* typology where they had tended to be shown in thoughtful attitudes of poised reverence rather than in the dramatic throes of a struggle between life and death.[4] Rather than scenes of the miracles or martyrdom of the saints being reserved for the predella, they now became its central concern. This was matched by the fashion for lateral paintings in Northern Italy (*laterali*), since their particular elongated rectangular shape lent itself to the depiction of narrative events and was widely used throughout the churches of Venice for the decoration of the side walls of chapels, often in those of the Blessed Sacrament where a eucharistic scene from the New Testament on one wall would be coupled with a second from the Old Testament opposite it.[5] Alongside these technical developments, the intensification of both images of charity and the martyrdom of the saints was undoubtedly stimulated further by the impact of the Tridentine decrees, agreed upon both by Peter Humfrey in his studies on Venetian altarpieces and more recently by David Ekserdjian in his analysis of the Italian altarpiece more generally, the latter even going so far as to call it 'the one event that is the major agent of change'.[6]

This chapter is about how images of sanctity presented the kinds of 'salutary examples' that Trent had decreed capable of leading the laity to 'order their own lives and manners in imitation of the saints'.[7] In Venice, depictions of the saintly individual often showed them dutifully alleviating the community's most pressing physical and spiritual ills: giving alms to the poor, attending to the sick and diseased, and dispensing the sacraments. The impact of contemporary social ills and concomitant Catholic reform efforts on the content of these images has already been established, most extensively by the scholarship of Tom Nichols; perhaps what has been less considered is how they might have helped to mould attitudes not just towards the marginalised and vulnerable but also towards the clergy.[8] The paintings that will be examined in this chapter presented an ideal of apostolic poverty and selflessness that was removed from the depressing reality of the increasingly institutionalised existence of the marginalised and the wayward behaviour of some of the city's priests. In light of this, one way of understanding these images might be to argue that they are deceptive since the present-day societal malaises that they appear to refer to are rendered beautiful even when they are painted with a degree of realism, thus masking the bleakness of existing social conditions. A different path, and the one that I subscribe to, would be to comprehend that because these representations dealt with episodes from the lives of the saints, by their very nature they had to be both idealised and attractive. Beauty was understood as a potent manifestation of the kind of spiritual perfection that the saints were believed to possess, virtues that were theoretically within the reach of the mortal spectator if they imitated these paragons of goodness keenly enough. The events that such images referred to, usually the preserve of a distant past, involved the artist creating a visual world that was relatable enough to convince the spectator that such episodes were 'real' and might be emulated in the present, yet adequately different to give some sense of the historical time and place in which they were supposed to have happened. Rather than these representations merely bolstering the status quo, it should also be considered that in presenting the viewer with an ideal, however at odds this was with reality, these images might even have worked to set an elevated standard for the treatment of both the city's vulnerable and the laity's rightful expectations of their clergy.

THE TRUE RICHES OF THE CHURCH

Such lofty sentiments were eloquently expressed in two paintings of episodes from the life of Saint Lawrence: Palma's aforementioned canvas *Saint Lawrence Presenting the True Riches of the Church to the Emperor Valerian* in the parish of San Giacomo dall'Orio (Fig. 54) and Bernardo Strozzi's later *Saint Lawrence Distributing the Wealth of the Church to the Poor* of c. 1640 in the nearby Theatine church of San Nicola da Tolentio (Fig. 93). Turning first to the painting by Palma, this was one of two paintings of Saint Lawrence by the artist commissioned from the Malipiero family to decorate their chapel dedicated to the saint, the second depicting Lawrence's martyrdom.[9] Both of these works were lateral paintings that hung on the two walls on either side of Veronese's central altarpiece of *Saints Lawrence, Jerome and Prospero*, a work that originally featured a predella depicting Lawrence's martyrdom (now lost).[10] Having successfully completed the decoration of the old sacristy in San Giacomo dall'Orio, Palma's paintings of Saint Lawrence were an early commission of importance for the artist who would have been keen to establish himself in his hometown after returning from his studies in Pesaro and Rome in the early 1570s. The subject matter must have held a special resonance for the painter since Palma obsessively returned to the theme of Lawrence's martyrdom numerous times in his graphic oeuvre. Ridolfi also tells us that in the artist's youth Palma copied Titian's masterpiece of the same subject (1548–59) at the church of the Crociferi (now in the Gesuiti), an altarpiece that may have been among the first of its kind.[11] It was here that Palma's talent was 'discovered' by Guidobaldo della Rovere, Duke of Urbino, who went on to generously sponsor his artistic education.[12]

In the table of saints most frequently depicted in altarpieces for Venetian churches between the years 1450 and 1530, Lawrence fails to make an appearance, although by 1581 there were at least seven and a half altars

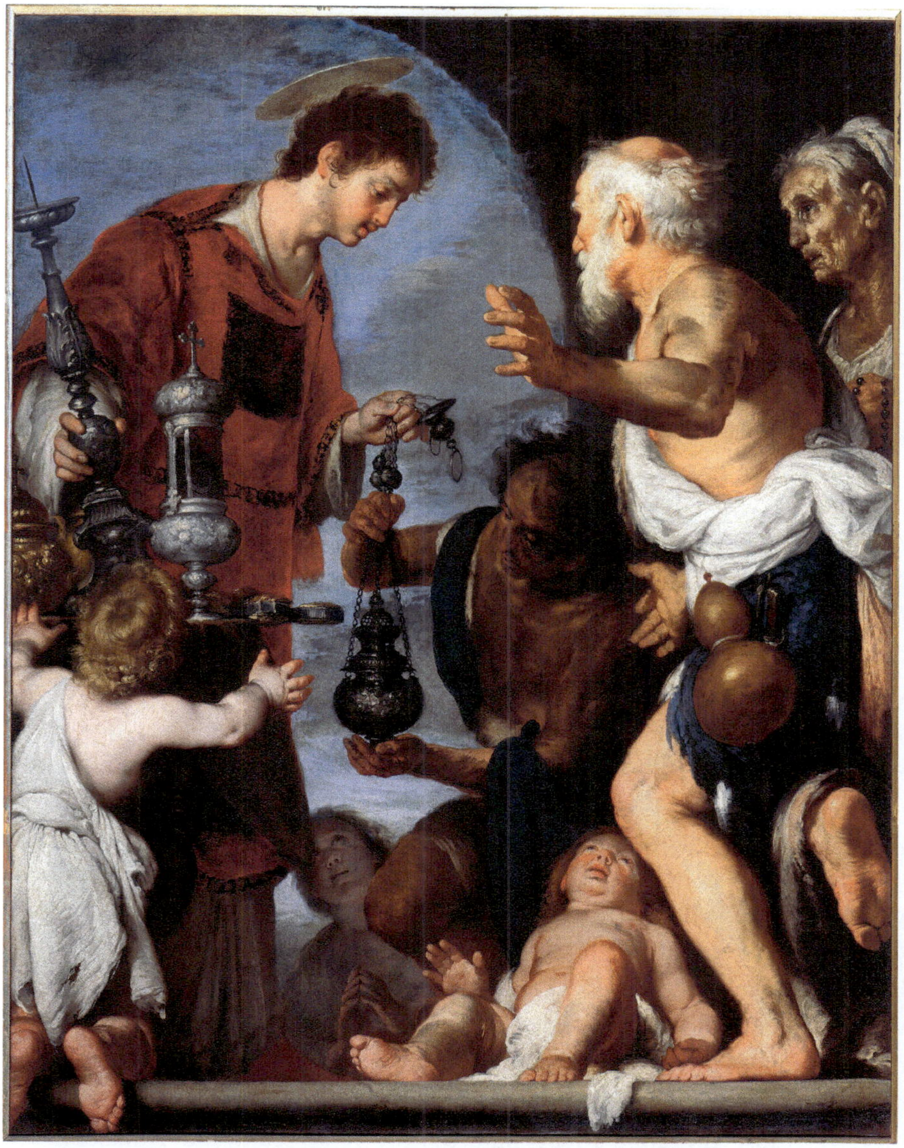

93. Bernardo Strozzi, *Saint Lawrence Distributing the Wealth of the Church to the Poor,* c. 1640, oil on canvas, San Nicola da Tolentino, Venice (Photo: Cameraphoto)

dedicated to him in the city, a respectable number.[13] After Titian's invention at the Crociferi, aspects of Lawrence's demise came to be the go-to episode for altarpieces that focused on him, unlike the saint's presentation of the destitute to the emperor,[14] one of the scenes painted by Palma at San Giacomo, and a choice that was arguably better suited to the horizontal format of a lateral canvas than the vertical thrust of an altarpiece.[15] This is an episode that appears to have been infrequently depicted in Venetian churches before Palma; throughout this chapter we will see how painters including Titian, Jacopo

Bassano, and Veronese placed a new emphasis on scenes from the lives of the saints or the parables of Christ that had been scarcely represented previously, their innovations sparking the imagination of other artists, who often went on to depict exactly the same episodes, ones that responded to contemporary concerns relating to poverty, charity, and the nature of the miraculous. The first of Palma's two paintings for the Lawrence chapel depicts the saint accompanied by a crowd of needy individuals: the aged and disabled, a woman holding her child, and poor men who are shown semi-clothed. In an event said to have taken place during the Christian persecutions of Valerian in the third century, Lawrence had ignored the command to collect the material riches of the Church and to hand them over to the authorities, choosing to interpret the 'true riches' not as the goods that the emperor desired but as those individuals who are close to God in their suffering. Lawrence's subversive defiance triggered his martyrdom, which is shown on the opposite wall. As one of the seven deacons of the city of Rome, Lawrence's duty was to distribute alms to the needy, and he was also ordered by Pope Sixtus II (r. 257–58) to attend to the treasury of the Church. Palma depicted his saint dressed even more beautifully than the emperor, shown akin to a sixteenth-century deacon, garbed in a marvellous white and gold dalmatic. Since one of the aims of post-Tridentine Catholicism was a return to the perceived purity of early Christianity, Palma's depiction of Lawrence's selfless ministry and virtuous stance against the injustices of temporal power provided a paragon of priestly virtue to be imitated. In this sense, it anticipated Veronese's altarpiece of the *Miracle of Saint Pantaleon* of 1587–88, commissioned for the eponymous parish by its priest Bartolomeo Borghi, just a few minutes' walk away from San Giacomo. Emphasising the sacramental duties of the *pievano* to administrate the last rites and to tend to the sick and dying, Borghi is shown cradling the boy who has been poisoned by a snake bite. Forsaking the medicine box proffered by an attendant, the martyr-saint Pantaleon directs his attentions to the heavens, praying for the divine intervention that is about to be granted and that will cause the child to be miraculously resurrected and Pantaleon to convert and be baptised (Fig. 64).[16]

The manner in which Palma chose to portray Lawrence as a youthful deacon, steadfastly defending society's most unfortunate, was in stark contrast to the comportment of the clergy at San Giacomo dall'Orio.[17] The Council of Trent had decreed new responsibilities for priests, involving them more closely in the lives of the laity – particularly with regard to marriage – and delineating an ideal of the *sacerdote* that was 'at once pastor and civil functionary, knowledgeable of his flock but distinct from them', as Cecilia Cristellon put it.[18] Although the parish priest Giovanni Maria da Ponte had been praised by successive visitations for the efforts he had put into redecorating and improving the fabric of the church (personally funding some of these projects and leaving a generous bequest to the parish in his will), the supplement of the visitation of Patriarch Priuli to the parish in 1592 demonstrates that other clerics at San Giacomo were far from the Tridentine ideals, a fact that Da Ponte was reluctant to accept.[19] He believed that his priests were 'exemplary in their behaviour and lifestyle', but the patriarch's inspection revealed that the sub-deacon was in prison, as was one of the seven secular clergy, and that one priest was absent and the deacon was ill, which rendered them unable to participate in the exercise. The assessment of the laity was also at odds with that of Da Ponte. Parishioners were forthright in complaining about one of the priests who socialised in the evenings dressed in the clothes of a layman, was known to enjoy a glass of wine, and had taken into his house first a lame woman and subsequently a widow.[20] The situation at San Giacomo dall'Orio was one that was repeated throughout numerous parishes in the city; indeed, in other places accusations could be far more serious in nature.[21] Given this, Palma's painting of Lawrence could be interpreted as inculcating a rosy view of the diaconate that was dispiritingly divorced from reality given that San Giacomo dall'Orio's own sub-deacon was a criminal. Yet for the laity at San Giacomo who encountered the painting, the acts of the saintly Lawrence might also have functioned as a pressing reminder of the ideals that their clergy were flagrantly abusing, and the image may also have served as a visual accompaniment to the far greater emphasis placed on the responsibilities of Venetian parishes to raise funds for the poor that arose in the sixteenth century. The Poor Law of April 1529 required that a parish committee devoted to this task was to be elected annually, and priests were to habitually appeal to the richer inhabitants of their flock for alms, upon the orders of both the patriarch and the Provveditori alla sanità. Parishioners were to be reminded of the law at every high mass on feast days; a collection box for alms was to be placed in every church; and preachers were exhorted to focus their sermons on charity.[22]

Bernardo Strozzi's (1581–1644) *Saint Lawrence Distributing the Wealth of the Church to the Poor* presents a gesture of munificence towards the needy that might seem in contradiction to its location in the lavishly decorated church of the Theatines in Venice.[23] One of Strozzi's most impressive works, it shows Lawrence distributing the wealth of the Church to the destitute, defying the order to collect it for the emperor. An elderly man and woman react to the generosity of the saint with surprised expressions and outstretched arms. Lawrence appears against the blue sky to proffer an intricately wrought thurible to the kneeling man covered in dirt, who examines it as he emerges from the shadows. The recipients of Lawrence's generosity are intergenerational, and Strozzi evidently relished depicting them with charming realism, from the robust, bearded man to the infant seen from behind with a mop of golden curls. Even if Lawrence's red dalmatic contrasts to the ragged robes in which the poor are arrayed, it is still scruffier than the more refined vestments in Palma's painting. The saint's face is a study in patient concentration and youthful earnestness, and his young age is also suggested by the fact that his vestments are too large for him, revealing his Adam's apple and part of his chest as he leans towards the needy, a few juvenile hairs sprouting from around his jaw and in the place of a moustache, contrasting to the thick, white beard of the older man.

Strozzi surely knew Palma's painting given the vicinity of the church of the Tolentini to San Giacomo. The chestnut waves of hair and rosy cheeks of Lawrence are very similar in the two images, and, like Palma, Strozzi had a personal attraction to Lawrence's hagiography and his cult was strong in Genoa, from where the artist hailed.[24] As a former Capuchin, an order that was dedicated to absolute poverty with a special emphasis on ministering to the sick and outcast, it is significant that Strozzi portrayed the subject matter of Lawrence's act of donation on a number of occasions.[25] In Strozzi's work at the Tolentini the careful gesture of the man who receives the thurible, gently and intently supporting it at its base, communicates his gratitude and understanding of its value. The surprise of the grey-haired, wizened visage of the woman clutching her rosary beads suggests that charitable gestures like Lawrence's are a rarity. The prayers of the young woman in the lower background have finally been answered, her eyes raising themselves to the figure of the saint who looms above, her expression one of piety, almost disbelief. Tom Nichols has highlighted how images commissioned for church settings in Venice developed the visual ideal of the virtuous *povero*, with artists like Tintoretto basing them upon the venerable prototypes of the heroic classical nude.[26] In Palma's painting, the handsome group of indigents are highlighted not only by dint of the artist's brush but by the natural light that streams through the chapel window during the day, beautifully illuminating the semi-nude bodies of the needy. The import of their presence is denoted by the gesture of Lawrence, who bravely beseeches Valerian to consider their worth, but also by the soldier on the far right of the canvas who signals the viewer to the fateful event unfolding. Semi-naked though 'the true treasures of the Church' may be, they are shown as the moral superiors of the emperor in his opulent surroundings.

Nichols has written convincingly about the fact that at the same time as images of the poor increased in Venetian devotional art, the number of the poor being institutionalised also increased. Nourished in part by Tridentine theology, images of charity now began to feature in episodes from the Gospels where it had not been traditional (or scripturally accurate) to ever depict them, such as the *Last Supper* or *Christ and the Adulteress*, innovations of Tintoretto and Jacopo Bassano, respectively.[27] Thus, in the visual realm the poor were more visible, whilst in the public sphere efforts were made to remove them from the streets and squares of Venice and to criminalise vagrancy.[28]

Economic, climactic, and technological transformations in Europe during the age of the Reformations led to a burgeoning quantity of needy individuals, and the solutions for these social-welfare issues have been called one of 'the most significant legacies of the age'.[29] In line with these changes, historians have traced a general hardening of opinion towards the subaltern in the early modern period as destitution became more prevalent, an uncomfortable reminder of the failure of government and the distance between the ideals of Christian Europe and the lives of its inhabitants.[30] Catholics and Protestants were mostly in agreement that the 'deserving poor' had to be in some way distinguished from vagabonds. To the first category belonged those who had fallen on hard times through no fault of their own and were thus rendered unable to work. To the second were those perceived to be lazy swindlers, or even criminals, usually outsiders who supposedly took advantage of the charity of others, thus depriving the truly needy. Having observed reforms to the treatment of the poor in the Netherlands, the 1526 treatise of Spanish Catholic Juan Luis Vives (1493–1540), *De subventione pauperum*, argued that the underserving poor should be forced into work and that foreign beggars had to be driven out of towns. Published in Italian in Venice in 1545, the treatise enjoyed great popularity: in Spain it had a significant impact on legislation, including laws of 1540 that formalised the differentiation between deserving and undeserving poor through the creation of licenses for begging. In Venice, the new poor laws enacted by the State were in the vein of Vives, and they might have been unconsciously influenced by Protestant principles that had been instigated in places like Nuremberg.[31] Yet such ideas were never universally accepted by Catholics. Unsurprisingly, they were vigorously opposed and debated by the Mendicant orders, who had arisen in the Middle Ages and whose itinerant lifestyle and commitment to poverty and serving the needy was dependent upon the donation of alms. A group of friars submitted the new poor laws enacted in 1525 in Ypres to the theologians of the Sorbonne on the basis that a ban on begging was in opposition to divine law, and the Dominican theologian Domingo de Soto in Salamanca rejected the exile of foreign beggars and the compulsory confinement of the poor in a major debate of 1545.[32] Later in the seventeenth century, after the Council of Trent had reasserted the theology of good works, the Bishop of Gubbio, Alessandro Sperelli, argued in *Della pretiosità della limosina* (1666) that it was wrong to divide the 'true' poor from the 'false' poor, a judgment that could only ever be made by God.[33]

So even if there was initially some convergence of thought between Protestants and Catholics on the poor, there were also fundamental differences. For Protestants, the economy of images and pilgrimages was directly implicated in the problem. Money that was spent on idolatry should be channelled into helping the needy, and since works had no impact on salvation, the sacralisation of almsgiving was an empty gesture and one that evaded the problem at hand. Rather than the whole economy of charity being decentralised and tied up with the Church as it had been throughout medieval Europe, figures like Zwingli sought to transform social aid through the establishment of state-run agencies funded through taxes, rather than by parishes, generous donors, or local confraternities. The result of this was the greater secularisation of poor relief and a tighter level of control over who should be able to access assistance. For Catholics, salvation was to be achieved not just through the avoidance of sin but via the active participation in good works, which meant that there still had to be direct opportunities for each individual to contribute to the alleviation of social ills so that they might accumulate the merit required for entry into paradise. The wealth of lay confraternities in places like Venice continued aspects of the older charitable activities that focused on the community's deserving poor as the more divisive categories of *povero* gained ground. Alongside this, the new religious orders of the Catholic Reformation in Venice directed their ministries at society's outcasts, including prostitutes, orphans, and the diseased.[34] This could lead to confinement – by the end of the sixteenth century there were three new institutions in Venice dedicated exclusively to combatting prostitution, for example (the Zitelle, Convertite, and the Soccorso) – but for their advocates these places were believed to provide safe refuge for the vulnerable from the dangers of an insidious world.[35]

The emergence of the poor as a central element in Venetian devotional art was thus closely tied to Catholic reform efforts, functioning as a potent reminder to the parishioner of their Christian duty to engage in the corporal acts of mercy and carry out good works if they were to be saved. Rather than depicting the needy as in any way dishonourable or spiritually deprived, they were exalted to a new extent in the paintings that were displayed in the city's churches. This provides a visual correspondent to Eire's argument that Catholics tended to sacralise charity, encouraging the relationship between the almsgiver and receiver rather than separating the two as tended to be the case in Protestant areas of Europe.[36] Sometimes the needy ceased to be represented as subordinate in importance to the central act of the saintly donor, as had been the case for the group of '*poveri vergognosi*' in Lotto's altarpiece of *The Alms of Saint Antoninus* of 1541–42 for Santi Giovanni e Paolo where they are relegated to the bottom strip of the canvas, or in Titian's altarpiece of *Saint John the Almsgiver* of c. 1545 for San Giovanni Elemosinario, where the recipient of John's beneficence lurks in the shadows below the saint's luminous form.[37]

By giving over ever larger swathes of the pictorial space to representing the poor, as Palma had done at San Giacomo dall'Orio, and ennobling them through the divine associations of the classical nude, artists and patrons presented the moral obligation of alleviating material and social poverty, even if some viewers may well have found their escalating numbers threatening. The friars of Ypres, who had objected to the city's new poor laws, argued that if indigents were removed from public view, then the populace would forget all about them and alms would thus dry up. De Soto in Salamanca also believed that it was harder to feel compassion for the needy unless one was directly confronted with their plight.[38] In keeping with De Soto's argument, Nichols pointed out that engagement with images of the dispossessed in Venetian churches might even have become something of an 'ethical imperative'.[39] It was the catechism of the Council of Trent, now the official text for the instruction of all Catholics in their faith, that hammered home the necessity of almsgiving. First published in Venice in 1567, such charity was 'a medicine suited to heal the wounds of the soul' according to the catechism, and it was deemed that 'God will condemn and consign to everlasting fires those who have omitted and neglected the duty of almsgiving, while on the contrary He will praise and introduce into His heavenly country those who have exercised mercy towards the poor.'[40] In the same decade that Palma produced his two paintings of Saint Lawrence, charitable expenditures in Venice swelled.[41] The same has been noted in other places: in Madrid, for example, the rapid increase in almsgiving recorded in wills between 1570 and 1600 has been attributed to the effectiveness of the Tridentine reinvigoration of charity.[42] If estimates for the sixteenth century that at least two-thirds of Venice's population risked being at some point dependent on charity to survive if they were rendered unable to collect an income are accurate, then a majority of people would have had some level of contact with, or direct experience of, what it could mean to be in need.[43] In this light, paintings like Palma's or Strozzi's could encourage charitable acts, and they may even have even functioned as a bulwark against some of the more dehumanising attitudes towards the oppressed, expressing visual solidarity with a plight that to a greater or less extent was shared by a majority of Venice's inhabitants.

Artists themselves often displayed a deep empathy for the plight of the needy and outcast. Jacopo Bassano was one of the most significant painters of the century in this regard, and as noted by Humfrey, he 'expressed himself best in those subject matters that involved a sympathetic representation of the suffering of humanity, of the humility of the common person'.[44] Even if we must be careful about attempting to deduce individual beliefs from formulaic documents like wills, that the family were philanthropically minded is at least suggested by the various testaments of its members. Leaving monies or assets for charitable purposes was a venerable and deeply established practice by the time of Jacopo's demise in 1592, and by this point it was customary for the notary drawing up the testament to inquire about donations to hospitals and other 'pious places'. Tintoretto's will of 30 May 1594 stipulated that the notary had specifically asked him about such donations and it was to be left up to his wife Faustina Episcopi to arrange, but neither her will of 5 June 1612 nor Domenico Tintoretto's of 20 October 1630 left any money to the needy, their primary duty being to their relatives.[45] Whilst this does not preclude the possibility that sums were bequeathed during their lifetimes, by contrast the Bassano family were far more generous, in their wills at least. Jacopo left six ducats for the *poveri bisognosi* in his will of 10 February 1592 (dying three days later) and his son Francesco (1549–92), who perished from suicide on 3 July of the same year, provided monies for the dowries of six young women from Bassano in his testament of 10 November 1587.[46] In his will of October 1621, Francesco's pious brother Gerolamo (1566–1621) requested to be buried in the habit of a Capuchin and left what he could to the Scuola del Spirito Santo and the Scuola di Gesù in his hometown.[47]

The workshop founded by Jacopo's father Francesco da Ponte the Elder (c. 1470/75–1539) endured for at least a century and a half in various iterations, considerably longer than those of his contemporaries.[48] But if Jacopo laboured from his base in Bassano del Grappa, a pastoral satellite of the Serenissima, the success of his and his sons' novel inventions, from cycles of the months and the seasons, biblical parables, and nocturnal representations of Christ's Passion, was both local and international. Not only were the Bassano family well represented in European courtly collections, but the cycle *Twelve Months* was shipped to the Americas from Seville by Bartolomé Carducho (1560–1608) in 1596, and an extant series survives in the cathedral of Lima, having most likely arrived there towards the end of the 1600s.[49] Vasari described Jacopo Bassano somewhat dismissively as a painter of 'little works and animals of every kind'.[50] It has been observed by scholars that the synods of Torcello and Venice in 1592 and 1594 (described in Chapter 3) condemned the anachronistic inclusion of animals in devotional images, a facet of the Bassanos' artistic production that had become something of a trademark if Vasari's summation of his style was anything to go by.[51] This instruction should be best understood as less of an attack on a particular artist than a continuation of the identical instruction of Carlo Borromeo, and the family's paintings enjoyed great success not just with prominent Catholic patrons like the Hapsburgs and Cardinal Federico Borromeo, but with the new orders of the Catholic Reformation, most notably the Jesuits.[52] Altarpieces were repeatedly commissioned from the Bassano clan by the Society of Jesus for some of their most important churches, including Francesco Bassano's 1588 *Adoration of the Trinity by the Saints* that went to the Gesù in Rome, and his *Martyrdom of Saint Catherine* for San Giovannino in Florence, and Jacopo Bassano's *Saints Peter and Paul* for Santa Maria dell'Umiltà of c. 1564. The family also worked extensively for the new institutions that the order had so energetically championed in Venice: Francesco was the author of the high altarpiece *The Presentation of the Virgin in the Temple* (c. 1586) for the

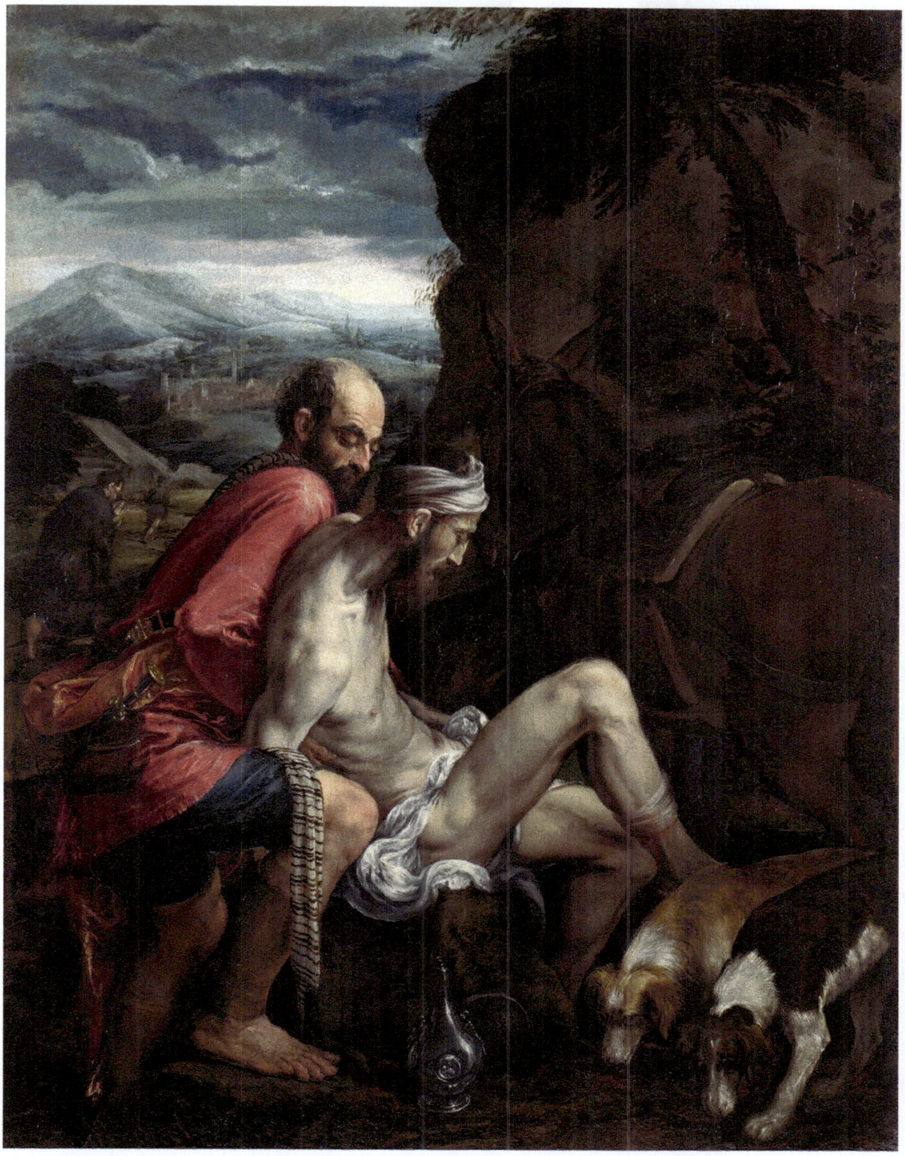

94. Jacopo Bassano, *The Good Samaritan,* c. 1562–63, oil on canvas, National Gallery, London (Photo: National Gallery, London)

Zitelle, and Leandro Bassano painted the high altarpiece *The Baptism of Christ* (c. 1597) for the church of the Catecumeni.[53] Stylistically, the dirty feet of the agrarian actors that populate their paintings and the dramatic chiaroscuro of masterpieces like *The Baptism of Christ* in the Metropolitan Museum of New York anticipated innovations now most famously associated with Caravaggio. Finally, paintings like Bassano's *Good Samaritan*, a parable seldom represented in the Renaissance that Jacopo popularised, insisted on the practical nature of charity and human solidarity (Fig. 94).

THE GOOD SAMARITAN

The *Good Samaritan* of c. 1562–63 depicts the episode recounted by Christ in the Gospel of Luke (10:25–37) in response to the question, 'Who is my neighbour? In the background of the painting dawn breaks and the priest and the Levite who have ignored the desperation of the beaten Jewish man hurry along the road from Jerusalem to Jericho without a backward glance. One of them is absorbed in reading a book, doubtless a devotional text, a motif that appears in Bassano's other versions of the parable, suggesting the futility of study if this is not accompanied by active compassion for one's neighbour. The route to Jericho has been imagined by Jacopo as a marvellously verdant landscape that recalls the views of Monte Grappa around his hometown.[54] In the foreground, the Samaritan gently lifts the wayfarer who has been robbed, stripped of his clothes, and attacked by thieves. His wounds have been bandaged by his compassionate assistant and his modesty covered by a loincloth. The pewter flask containing the oil and wine used to clean his injuries stands in the immediate foreground, as two handsome dogs lick up the blood that has fallen on the earth. Christ-like in his suffering, blood oozes from the scalp and chest of the wounded man, who is to be mounted onto the donkey that will take him to the inn where he can convalesce at the expense of his helper. Jacopo depicts the moment of this difficult manoeuvre onto the animal, as the Samaritan musters his strength in order to lift up the semi-naked man, to restore his autonomy. By transplanting the parable into a recognisably local environment, the selflessness of the Samaritan becomes an encouragement for every person to assist their neighbour, even when those with the most obvious moral responsibility (in this case the fleeing priest) flagrantly ignore their vocation. The sense of contemporary relevance is heightened by the striking realism of the sunburnt Samaritan and his disoriented ward, who may have conceivably been painted from life. The hierarchy of charity in Jacopo's painting is thus very different to works like Titian's *Saint John the Almsgiver*, where the composition is given over to the pious donation of the saint, rather than the recipient in need of succour (Fig. 95). This is understandable considering that Titian's painting was an altarpiece, intended to record the dedication of the church in which it is placed and the saint to be invoked. But in Bassano's image charity is not servile but fraternal. The Samaritan is not a saint, even if his pose seems to have been inspired by the figure of Jerome in the *Crucifixion with Saints* of 1561 now in the Bassanese Museo Civico.[55] Yet he becomes a saviour as he tends to the injured man, the pair cooperating, even communicating, their downward gazes and bent knees mirroring one another as the delicate procedure is enacted.

Not a great deal is known about the provenance of the National Gallery *Good Samaritan*, although it was eventually bought by Sir Joshua Reynolds in

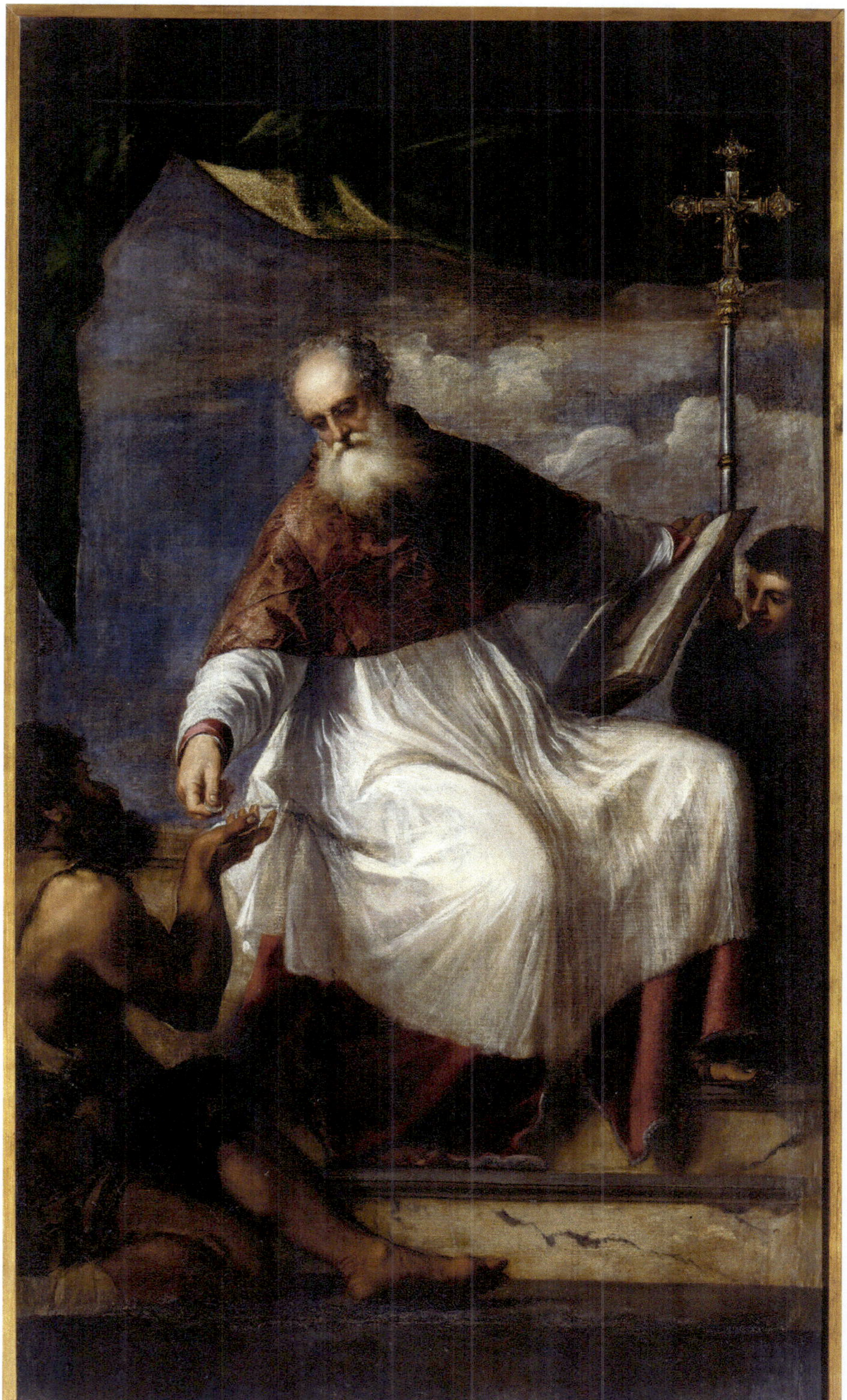

95. Titian, *Saint John the Almsgiver,* c. 1545–50, oil on canvas, San Giovanni Elemosinario, Venice (Photo: Cameraphoto)

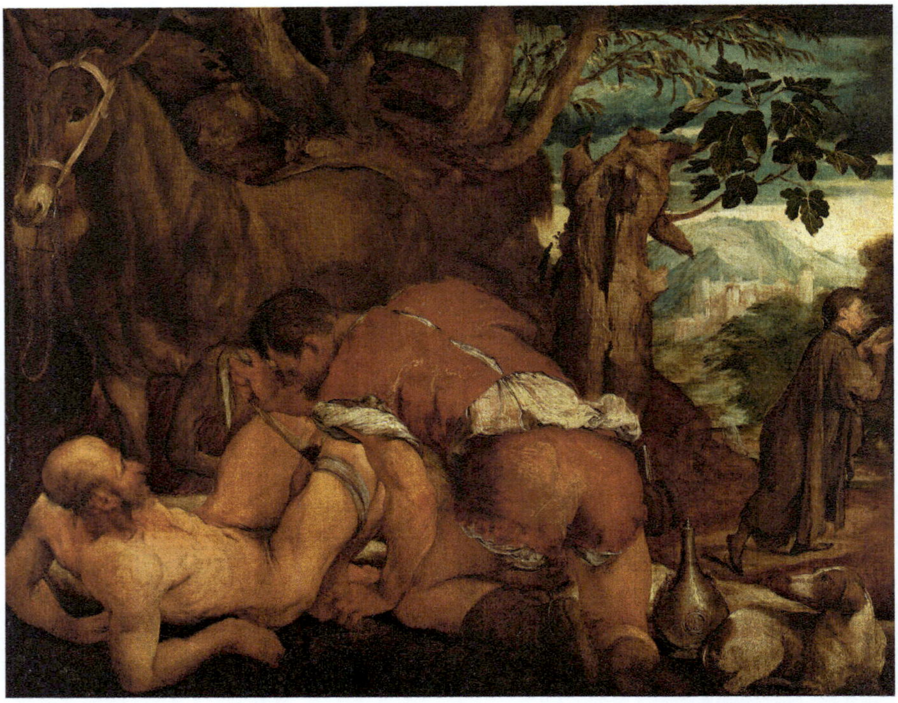

96. Jacopo Bassano, *The Good Samaritan*, c. 1545–50, oil on canvas, Palace of Holyroodhouse, Edinburgh (Photo: Royal Collection Trust/His Majesty King Charles III)

the late eighteenth century, and before this it was present in the Pisani Collection in Venice.[56] The theme was one that Jacopo was evidently attracted to. Not only are details like the eyelashes and beards of the men painted with loving precision, but in the earlier rendition of the parable dating to c. 1545–50, now in the palace of Holyroodhouse, the Samaritan is depicted tending to the wounds of the pitiful injured man, whose outstretched, reclined body is shown completely nude (Fig. 96).[57] Jacopo Bassano may have been one of the earliest Italian artists to depict the episode of the Good Samaritan, and in the years after his paintings appeared it became a popular subject matter with his peers.[58] Veronese produced his own version that drew upon a similar composition,[59] and in the subsequent decades the theme was explored by a host of other artists active in Northern Italy including Palma il Giovane,[60] Marcantonio Bassetti,[61] and Wolfgang Kilian (1581–1662),[62] as well as by Jacopo Bassano's own son Francesco, who were all struck by the older artist's innovation.[63] The compositional schema of Jacopo's paintings of the theme functioned as a point of departure for these artists, but none of them ever matched his sensitivity to the subject or the innovative way in which he had envisioned the sacred narrative. In part this can be attributed to Jacopo's unusual and novel interest in Christ's parables, episodes that were for the most part rarely depicted in devotional art.[64] Furthermore, the rustic actors used in paintings like the *Good Samaritan* provided an effective way of communicating a universal Christian message, a point that was made by Aikema in his penetrating analysis of Jacopo as a moralising artist.[65] In keeping with Aikema's interpretation, the object of the Samaritan's mercy in the two paintings in London and the Royal Collection appear not unlike the mocked Christ: naked, bleeding, and abandoned. Bassano may be making a visual connection to the interrelated parable of the Sheep and the Goats (Matthew 25:31–46), and its exhortation to acts of mercy: 'whatever you did for one of the least of these brothers of mine, you did for me'. This attitude was reflected in the outlook of contemporary orders like the Jesuits for whom Jacopo had worked, and it would have had a powerful resonance in periods of plague and famine. The Company of Jesus made charitable service a requirement in 1541, stipulating that every novice had to complete thirty days of spiritual exercises, thirty of pilgrimage (begging for support), and thirty in a hospital for the poor 'so that by becoming humble and overcoming worldly shame he may set himself apart and lose himself'.[66] The figure with his head in a book in Bassano's earlier *Good Samaritan*, who overlooks his Christian duty, contrasts to a fascinating account by one of the co-founders of the Jesuits – the Portuguese Simão Rodrigues – of his time spent working in the Ospedale degli Incurabili in Venice in the year 1537. Rodrigues recorded how the well-educated Jesuits 'not only abandoned their higher studies to apply themselves to menial work, but also with great care and diligence talked to the beggars about the word of God, and were accustomed to concern themselves deeply, in accordance with the need, with their spiritual welfare'.[67]

Framing Jacopo as an artist sensitive to the charitable aspects of Catholic reform is not to suggest that his achievements can be reduced to inevitable pictorial responses. For one, the sad ordinariness of the plight of some of the protagonists in his devotional works is hardly consoling; it seems to be more the case that they present a moral challenge to the beholder. Since the Samaritans and the Jews despised one another, the subject at hand may also have had a relevance to the religious intolerance and waves of violence triggered by the Reformations. W. R. Rearick believed that Jacopo could have had Lutheran sympathies based on the fact that he worked in Enego for a number of months, a town known for harbouring religious dissidents.[68] And whilst Rearick's suggestions cannot be discounted as a remote possibility, the problems with the 'artist as heretic' narrative have been shown. But casting doubt on the likelihood of this does not mean that Jacopo's art was free from tension or critique. After all, Catholic Reform was initially a self-critical movement, one that sought to cleanse the Church of abuses and minister to the destitute. To what extent these objectives were achieved is debatable, but the Bassano renditions of the *Good Samaritan* communicate the saintliness of everyday charity and humility, the necessity of direct intervention when spiritual hierarchies have abandoned the laity, and the *Imitatio Christi* of the dispossessed – all ideas that were close to the hearts of the century's reformers.[69]

MIRACLES AND MARTYRDOM

Rather different to the unassuming dignity of the virtuous helper in Bassano's *Good Samaritan* are the altarpieces of the marvellous miracles and martyrdoms of the saints that reached new heights of spectacle and emotional drama by the end of the century in Venice. Titian's *Assassination of Peter Martyr* (1526–29), once in Santi Giovanni e Paolo and destroyed by fire in 1867, was an early example of an altarpiece that transformed the iconic depiction of these sacred protagonists into a single narrative scene that presented the viewer with a key episode from the hagiography of the dedicatory saint (Fig. 97).[70] Prior to this, it was unusual in the early Italian Renaissance for martyrdom to be the main subject matter of an altarpiece.[71] Even if Titian's was arguably the first altarpiece in Venice to do this, his innovation neglected to be seriously taken up by other artists until later in the century, a belated shift that may well have been caused by the Tridentine decrees of 1563.[72] In addition to this motivation, martyrdom was a subject that provoked great interest from the mid-sixteenth century onwards. At the behest of Pope Gregory XIII (r. 1572–85), Cesare Baronio produced the revised calendar of martyred saints that was published in 1583, the *Martyrologium romanum*. A few years earlier, in 1578, the Catacomb of the Giordani was discovered in Rome, its paintings providing evidence that early Christians had venerated images and the bodily remains, giving renewed force to the cult of martyrs and their relics.[73] After 1560 the publication of hagiographies also grew exponentially, and accounts of the horrific demises of Catholics on the global missions were eagerly sought out by an international audience. The letters of future saints like Francis Xavier sent from India (1544) and Japan (1549) were translated and published in numerous editions.[74] Like martyrdoms, miracles became a visual theme of paramount importance in Catholic Europe. The saints were believed capable of interceding on humanity's behalf in the world of the living, and for believers their seemingly impossible achievements were convincing evidence not just of their special status but of the veracity of the Roman Church. On the contrary, with the exception of biblical miracles, Protestant reformers rejected the idea of saintly intercession and the miraculous.[75] It is in large part due to this negation that post-Tridentine Catholicism seems to have fashioned itself increasingly in terms of the beliefs and rituals that had been critiqued by the Protestant Reformations, a tendency in the visual arts that reached its apotheosis with the sensuous representations of saintly ecstasies in the seventeenth century.

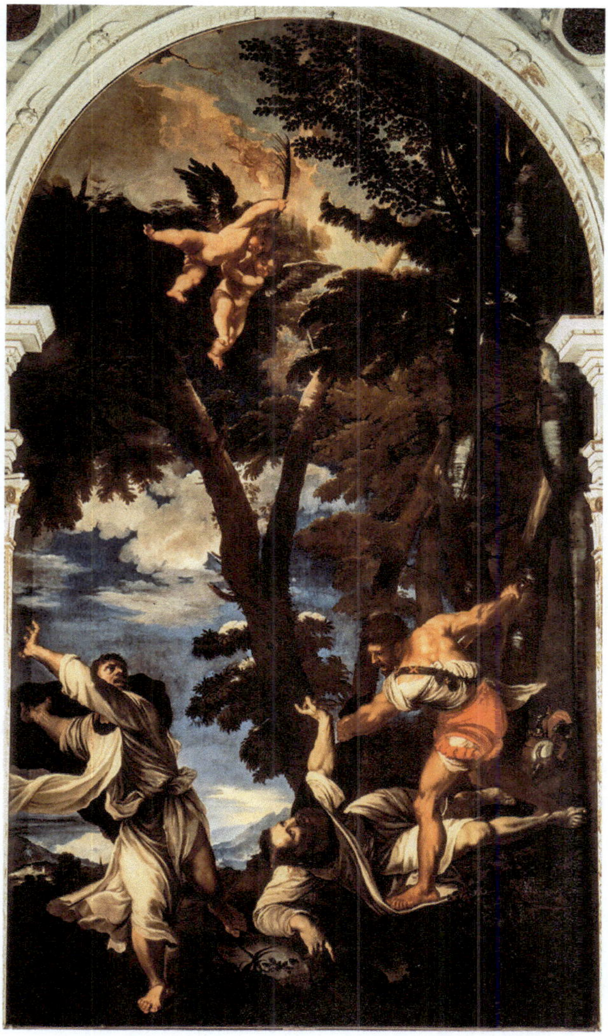

97. Carlo Loth, *Assassination of Peter Martyr* (after Titian), 1691, oil on canvas, Santi Giovanni e Paolo, Venice (Photo: Francesco Turio Bohm)

Prior to Titian's innovatory and much lauded altarpiece, the moment of the Dominican Saint Peter Martyr of Verona's assassination in the countryside of Lombardy had been painted in Venice by the leading artist of the previous generation, Giovanni Bellini (Fig. 98).[76] In his work of c. 1505–7 Peter is shown having fallen to his knees, his eyes serenely closed. His attribute of the axe has already cut through his skull, as the killer Carino (who later converted) brutally pierces the saint's heart. Peter's companion Domenico flees, hotly pursued by a second assassin. The pair have been ambushed from the Cathars, the attackers having pounced from the coppice of trees where the oblivious bystanders are engaged in felling timber, one of whom, located between the two Dominicans, forcefully swings an axe that underlines the violence of

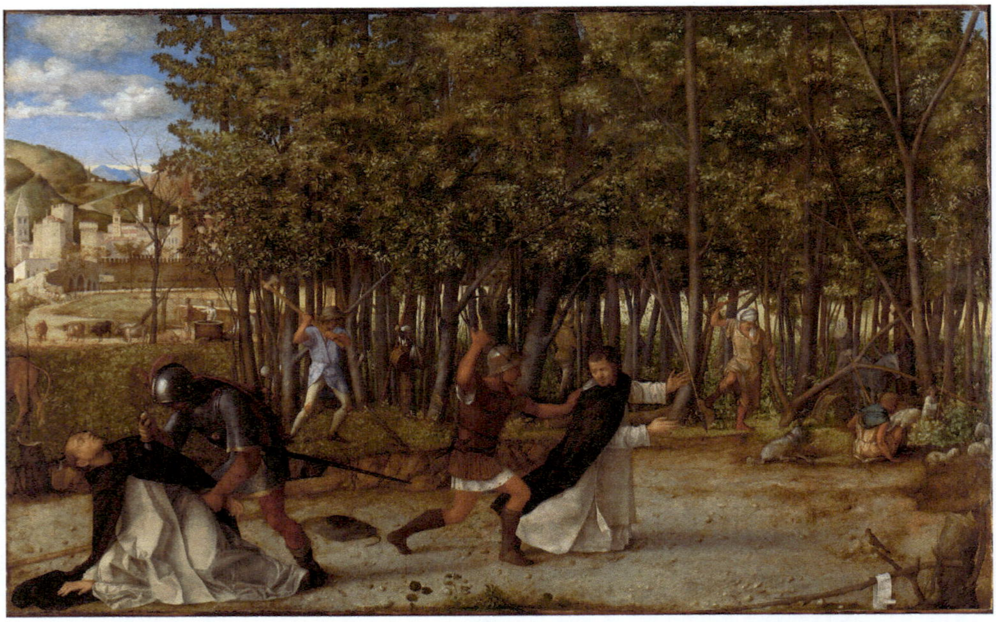

98. Giovanni Bellini, *Assassination of Peter Martyr,* c. 1505–7, oil on wood, National Gallery, London (National Gallery Photo: National Gallery, London)

the unfolding event, the cut tree being an emblem of martyrdom.[77] While in Bellini's painting Peter is already dead, in Titian's altarpiece the moment just before the murder is represented: Peter does not look at his encroaching assassin, but is open-mouthed in wonder as he directs his attention towards the heavens, where two plump putti appear carrying his prize: the martyr's palm, and with it the promise of his salvation. After Titian's work at Santi Giovanni e Paolo, it became more common to see the saints depicted not after or at the time of their murder, but in the brief, final moments before death occurred.[78] This allowed artists to present the apex of the saint's superhuman courage and fortitude in the face of a cruel and painful death, and as the century wore on it was more and more common for these figures to be depicted nonchalantly accepting their fate with placid composure. Veronese was important in this regard, and in his magnificent high altarpiece of c. 1563–66 for the church of San Giorgio in Braida in Verona, one of his delightful putti is shown hurtling gymnastically from the heavens with the crown of victory and the martyr's palm (Fig. 99).[79] At the centre of the composition, George's eyes are steadfastly fixed not on the earthly sphere of his impending mortal torment but on the supernatural one above. Hans Dieter Huber reflected on the weightiness of the lower half of the painting, with the saint almost being pressed to the ground by one of his torturers and the attendant figures bending and peering down on either side, in contrast to the saint's countermovement upwards and the lightness of the heavens above. X-rays of the altarpiece show that the face of George was first envisaged looking

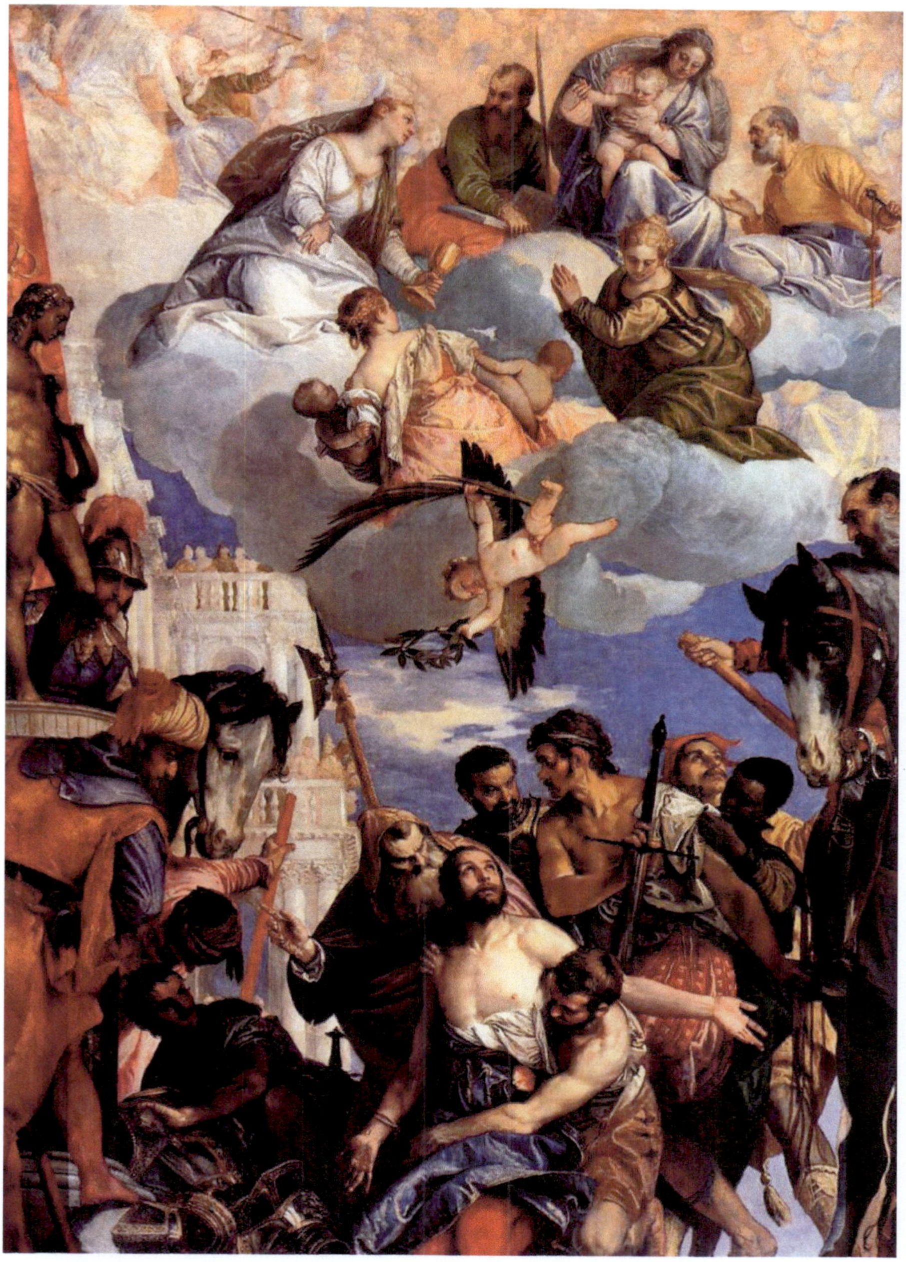

99. Veronese, *Martyrdom of Saint George*, c. 1563–66, oil on canvas, San Giorgio in Braida, Verona (Photo: ARTGEN/Alamy Stock Photo)

toward the statue of the idol Apollo on the left, the subtle change placing a greater emphasis on the saint's redemption and impending entry into the heavens.[80] It is not George's decapitation that is presented but his preparedness for it as he prays that all who called upon his name should be assisted.[81] And rather than salvation being symbolised merely through subtle light effects, as

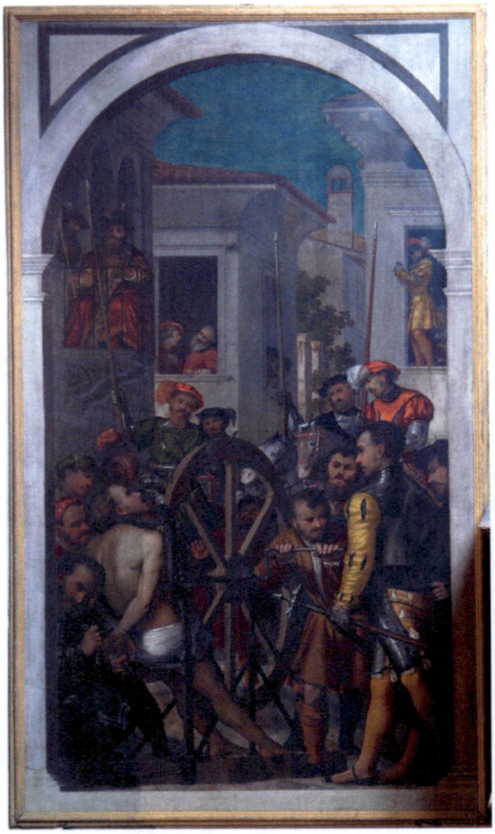

100. Romanino, *Martyrdom of Saint George* 1540, tempera on canvas finished with oil, San Giorgio in Braida, Verona (Photo: Diocesi di Verona)

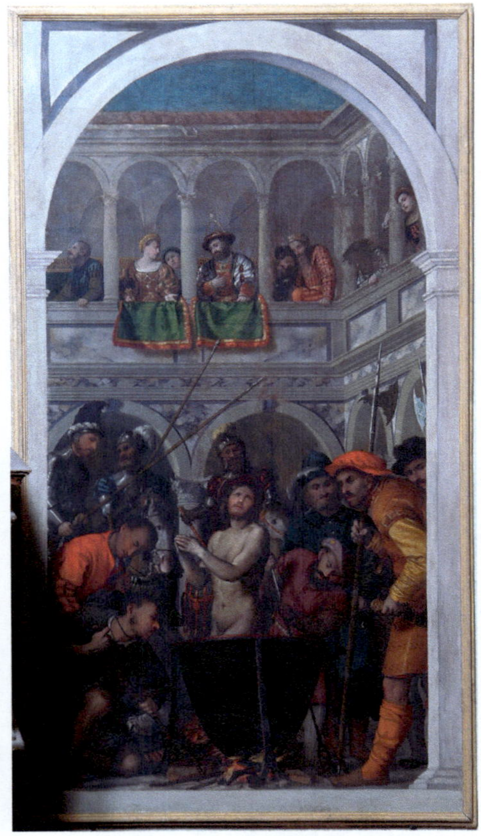

101. Romanino, *Martyrdom of Saint George* 1540, tempera on canvas finished with oil, San Giorgio in Braida, Verona (Photo: Diocesi di Verona)

Bellini appears to have done in his depiction of Peter's martyrdom, here the angels on high, the theological virtues, Saints Peter and Paul, and the Madonna and Child are all shown ready to welcome George into paradise.[82]

As pointed out by Sergio Marinelli, before 1564 there is no mention of any altarpiece in Verona representing a single martyrdom scene, since this was a theme usually reserved for the altarpiece predella.[83] Romanino, however, had painted the organ shutters of San Giorgio in Braida with scenes of the titular saint's martyrdom already in 1540 (Figs. 100 and 101).[84] The internal doors depicted Saint George in a pot of boiling water in one scene and tortured by the lacerations of a wheel spiked with blades in the other. Just as Romanino proved to be an innovator in terms of his eucharistic imagery, so too were his paintings for the church in Verona early examples of the more gruesome kinds of martyrdom scenes that became more common toward the close of the century.[85] Veronese and Romanino were also linked because at Santa Giustina in Padua an altarpiece of the titular saint's martyrdom by Veronese of 1575–76 replaced one of 1513–14 by Romanino, *The Madonna and Child Enthroned, Accompanied by Saints Benedict, Giustina, Prosdocimo, Scolastica and Angels.*[86] At San Giorgio in Braida, the new work by Veronese replaced an altarpiece by Gian Francesco Caroto (1480–1555), *Saint George and the Dragon*, which was at a maximum only three decades old. As noted by Humfrey, in Padua and Verona the pre-existing altarpieces at Santa Giustina and San Giorgio in Braida were evidently believed to be passé by their patrons, who desired something more à la mode for their newly renovated edifices (Fig. 102).[87] The Cassinese Congregation in Padua, who commissioned Veronese's altarpiece, were especially dedicated to Santa Giustina, and she was associated with interceding on behalf of the Holy League at the recent Battle of Lepanto in 1571.[88] Because she was one of the patron saints of the city whose powers had been spectacularly reaffirmed just a few years earlier, it must have seemed appropriate to replace Romanino's older painting that featured a selection of saints with one that focused solely on Giustina, whose relics had been moved to below the high altar of the new basilica in 1562.[89] Like George, the noble virgin Giustina was martyred during the persecutions of Diocletian. The site of the event was traditionally identified as present-day Prato della Valle, adjacent to the basilica dedicated to her, where Veronese's altarpiece was to be displayed. A view of the Santo in the background of the painting denotes the locality of the episode, even if this basilica was constructed many centuries after Giustina's trials had taken place.[90] This inclusion references her special relationship to the city of Padua, home also to the relics of the much-revered Anthony, but it also conveys a fundamental belief about the deaths of martyrs like Giustina: through imitating the death of Christ, they perpetuate his sacrifice and make its message part of a present moment.[91]

Veronese's Paduan altarpiece depicted a miracle associated with the saint, whereby after she was pierced by the executioner's sword she stood in prayer for an hour supplicating Christ to be admitted into heaven. Ridolfi described Giustina's magnanimous action as 'an offering of herself in sacrifice for God', and in the painting she is shown at the summit of a flight of steps, tottering on the brink between life and death.[92] A knife can be seen at the centre of her chest and her skin is drained of colour. But Giustina's eyes are still open and her halo shining as she beholds the heavens above, which explode in a rhapsodic rupture of putti who brandish not only the traditional treasures of martyrdom but a gem-studded golden crown (the crown of her earthly existence lain at her feet), flowers, and rose garlands, as angels are seen playing musical instruments and Christ, accompanied by the Virgin Mary and John the Evangelist, is shown on high. Veronese imagined the heavens where the saints are to be glorified as a space of ethereal sound, light, and spectacular colour. The deaths of Saints George and Giustina were not shown as tragic events because the message to be communicated to the viewer was that they died

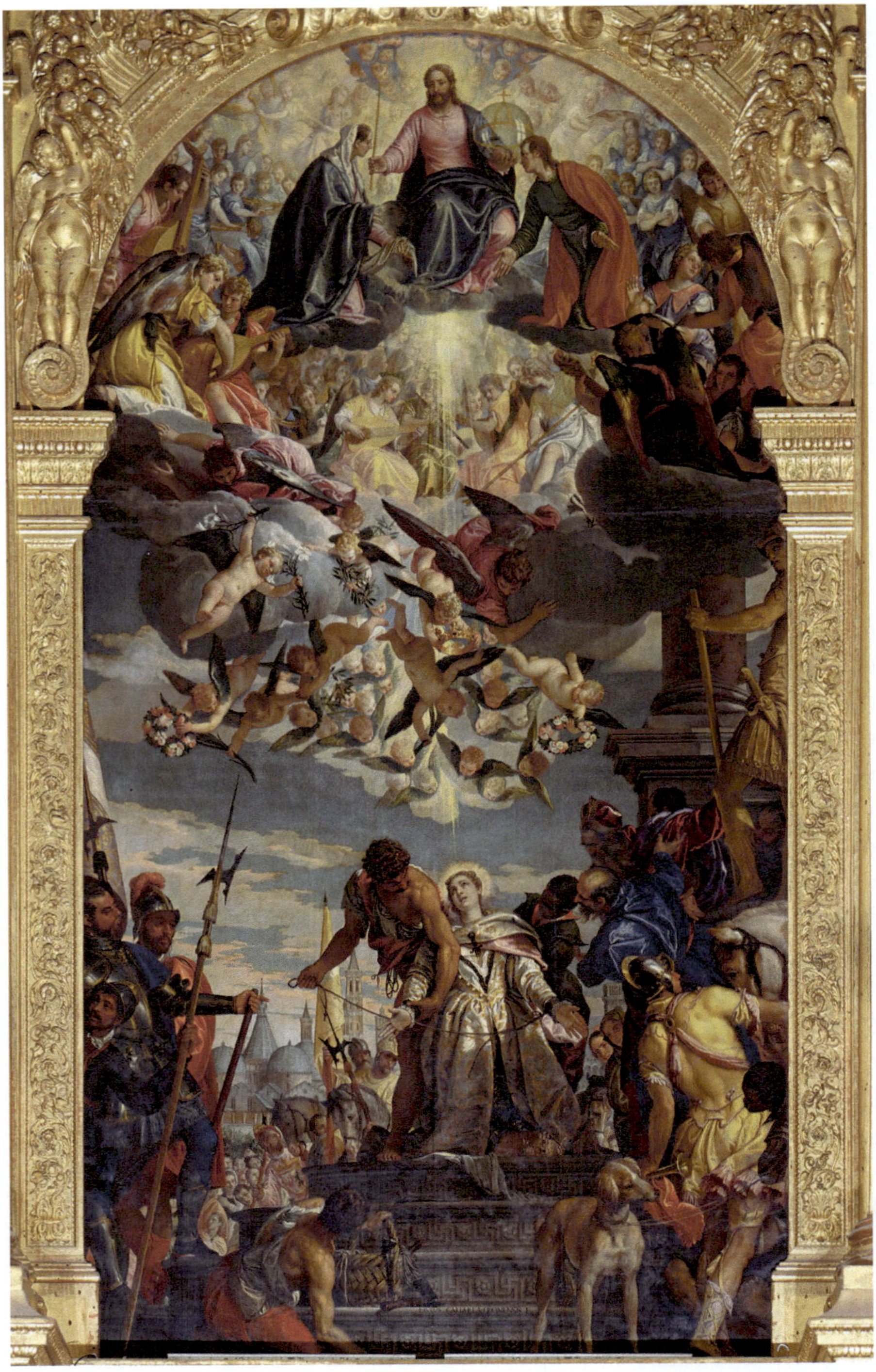

102. Veronese, *Martyrdom of Saint Giustina,* 1575–76, oil on canvas, Santa Giustina, Padua (Photo: By kind permission of Don Giulio Pagnoni, Santa Giustina)

good deaths, and through their loss of life they gained eternity. Since the manner in which an individual confronted the moment of death was understood as indicating the ultimate fate of their soul, the resolute focus of the saints on the world to come presented exemplars for how the spectator might one day approach their own demise.[93]

Veronese's paradise takes up a large proportion of the altarpiece, and a similar division of the pictorial space can be seen in Domenico Tintoretto's *Martyrdom of Saint Stephen* of 1594 for the left transept altar of San Giorgio Maggiore in Venice, within which the saint's relics were contained (Fig. 103).[94] Like Veronese, Domenico shows the first Christian martyr at the heart of the composition, pacifically gazing upward, where the heavens open, as described in Acts 7:54–60. Influenced by the semi-circular arrangement of the crowd in Giulio Romano's altarpiece of the *Martyrdom of Saint Stephen* for the church of Santo Stefano in Genoa (c. 1521), the energetic mob surround Stephen, stoning him with heavy boulders and a storm of smaller rocks, while the light of his halo burns brightly, and he is already armed with the palm of martyrdom. Droplets of blood flow from Stephen's scalp and neck, but he is seemingly immune to human suffering. His prayer to be received by Christ and for his tormenters to be forgiven is witnessed by God the Father and Son, accompanied by the Archangel Michael. On the one hand, the painting celebrates the intercessory powers of prayer, something obviously highly pertinent to its function as an altarpiece, but since Acts 7:57–58 describe the presence of Saul of Tarsus at the event, it also relates to conversion. This is because Saul, the persecutor of the early Christians, was converted on the road to Damascus and eventually martyred as Saint Paul in Rome. Domenico included him in the background of the painting, shown at the centre of the crowd of the Sanhedrin, identifiable by the coat at his feet (Acts 7:58). The message behind his inclusion is hardly subtle: even the sinner can achieve sanctity if they transform their life and submit to the will of God. But this leads to an important point about these kinds of altarpieces, which is that as they were transformed from the iconic to the narrative, no longer were they intended solely for the invocation of the saints depicted, but increasingly they communicated the moralising messages and fundamental beliefs of post-Tridentine Catholic identity.[95]

CONCLUSIONS

All of the paintings discussed presented models of virtuous behaviour that ranged from quotidian acts of charity to superhuman feats of fortitude that rendered the saints seemingly oblivious to the wounds inflicted by their attackers. Although scenes of martyrdom increased in altarpieces, it was also the case that such narrative episodes had previously been more commonly

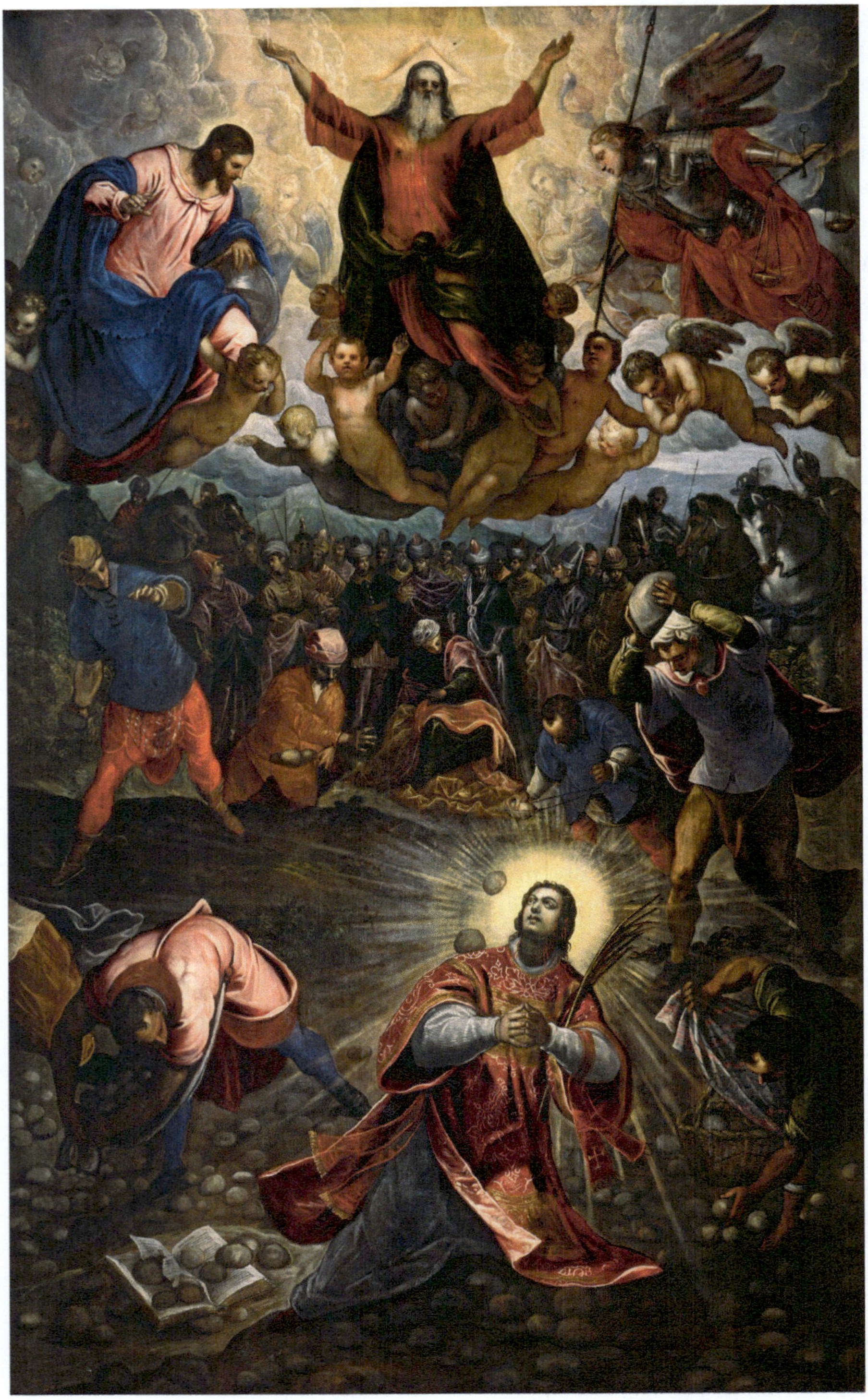

103. Domenico Tintoretto, *Martyrdom of Saint Stephen,* 1594, oil on canvas, San Giorgio Maggiore, Venice (Photo: Cameraphoto)

found in frescoes or, in the case of Venice, most significantly in the mosaics of the basilica of San Marco. A number of these mosaic cycles were renewed in the seventeenth century and were stylistically very different to what had gone before.[96] In a series of Baroque mosaics on the northern vault completed between 1607 and 1624, the terrible torments of the apostles John, James, Andrew, and Thomas were represented, replacing the older thirteenth-century cycle that was in a poor state of repair according to Stringa, and deemed to be of no aesthetic value due to its antiquity.[97] Here, John is shown being tortured in a vat of boiling water; James the Greater is about to be beheaded at the order of King Herod; Andrew's body is stretched out on the X-shaped cross upon which he is crucified; and Thomas's death by a lance that pierces his side is ordered by King Gundaphorus (Figs. 104–107).[98] These are accompanied by two central mosaics: the *Beheading of Saint Paul* and the *Crucifixion of Saint Peter*.[99] Subsequent to what Otto Demus disparagingly termed the 'greatest onslaught' on the mosaics commencing in the 1520s when the pre-existing programmes were rarely repaired and mosaicists were accused of counterfeiting tesserae with cheap paint, successive edicts were issued by the Procuratoria from 1566 onwards with the aim of preserving the original iconographic programme, held to have been designed by the twelfth-century mystic Gioacchino da Fiore.[100] Even though the new *Martyria* programme preserved the general scenario of the medieval cycle, they looked very different and some iconographic changes were inevitably made, ones that match the broader transformations traced in this chapter. To give just a few examples: in the episode of the *Crucifixion of Saint Peter* designed by Palma il Giovane the scene is dramatised by way of representing the moment that the cross is forcefully moved into place with Peter hung upside down upon it (rather than using a static medieval type); although the inscription for the vignette of John's tortures refers to the saint being buried alive, this is suppressed in the scene envisaged by Padovanino, and instead, alongside his trials in boiling oil, the saint is seen celebrating mass as he looks to the heavens to witness the arrival of three angels; finally, Tizianello's rendition of the martyrdom of Thomas incorporates the martyr's reward: the palm and crown carried by the two angels, a motif absent from the older martyrdom scenes in the basilica and one beloved by early modern Venetian painters.[101]

The development of saintly imagery in Venice was undoubtedly stimulated by the contemporary religious climate of the sixteenth century, but it was also strongly indebted to the innovations of earlier artists, in particular, Titian, who had been instrumental in this regard.[102] In the *Martyrdom of Saint Lawrence* he had depicted the saint straining towards the divine light of salvation as he is immolated, the terrifying agony of the procedure suggested by the blackened underside of Lawrence's leg and the manner in which his body is pummelled further into the flames by his assassin.

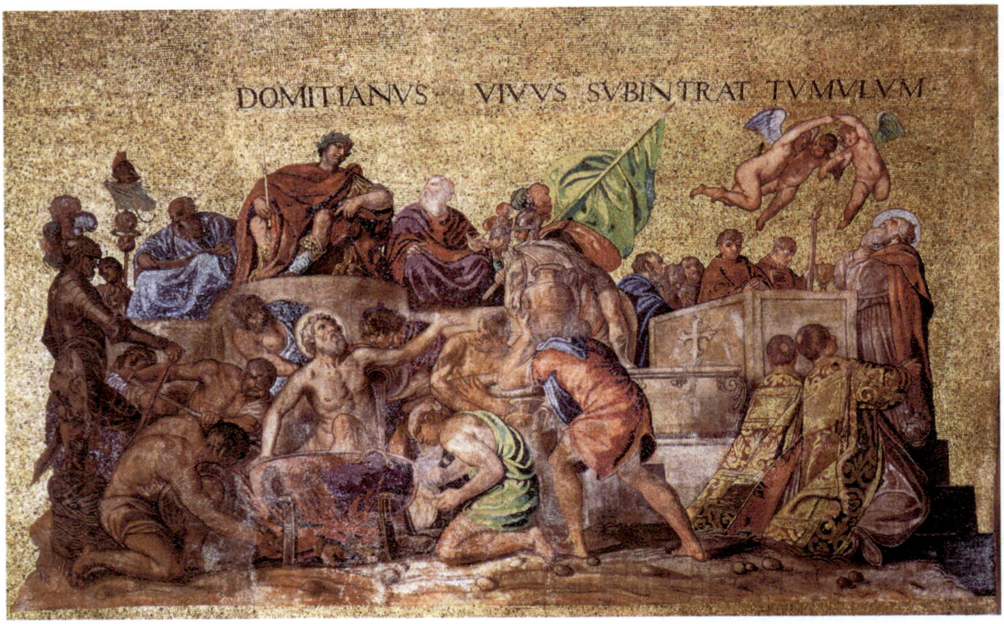

104. Cartoon by Padovanino, execution by Luigi and Girolamo Gaetano, *Martyrdom of Saint John,* 1621, mosaic, Basilica di San Marco, Venice (Photo: Archivio Fotografico della Procuratoria di San Marco/by kind permission of the Procuratoria di San Marco)

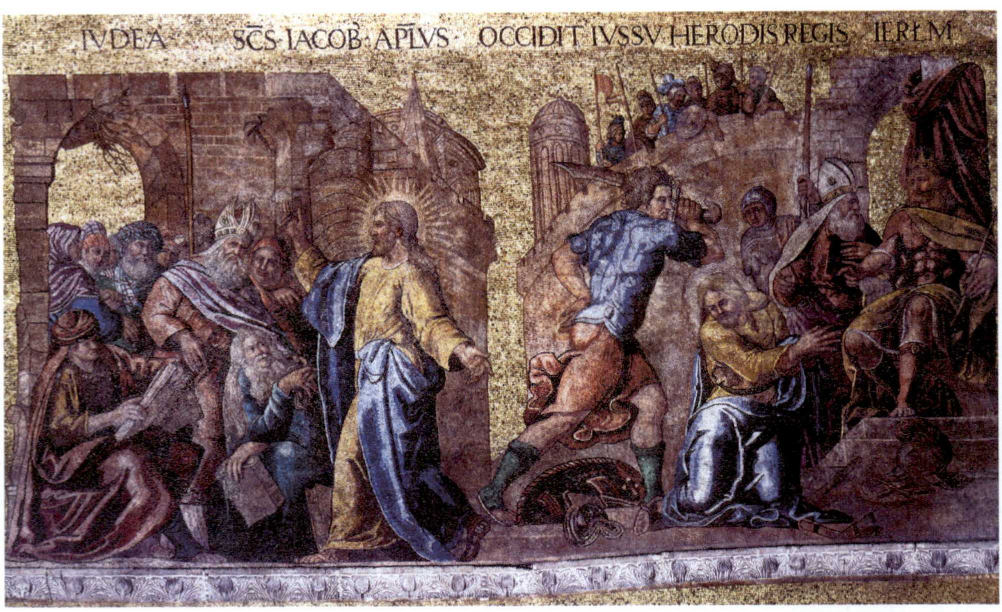

105. Cartoon by Tizianello, execution by Luigi Gaetano and Giacomo Pasterini, *Martyrdom of Saint James,* 1622–23, mosaic, Basilica di San Marco, Venice (Photo: Archivio Fotografico della Procuratoria di San Marco/by kind permission of the Procuratoria di San Marco)

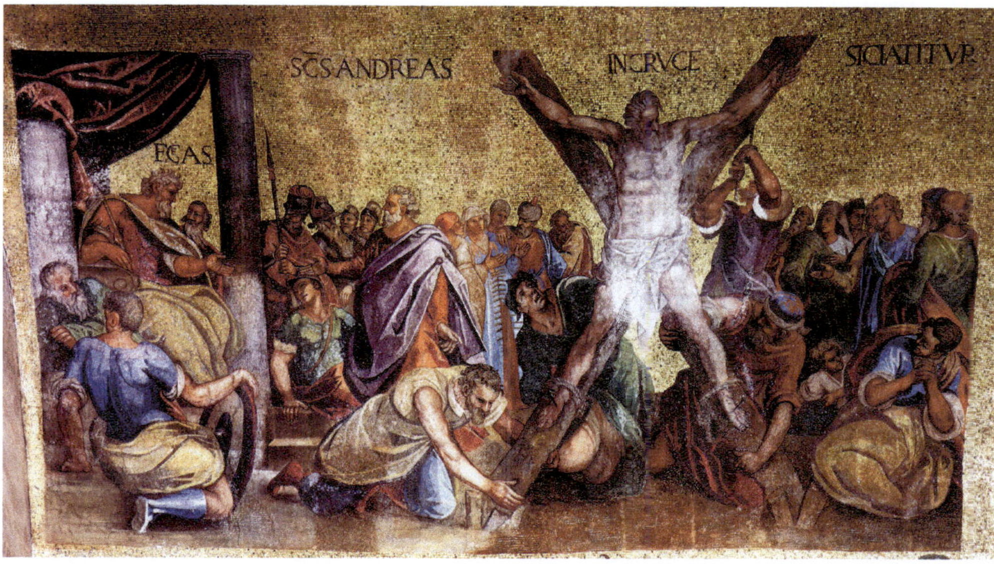

106. Cartoon by Aliense, execution by Luigi and Girolamo Gaetano, *Martyrdom of Saint Andrew,* 1607–20, mosaic, Basilica di San Marco, Venice (Photo: Archivio Fotografico della Procuratoria di San Marco/by kind permission of the Procuratoria di San Marco)

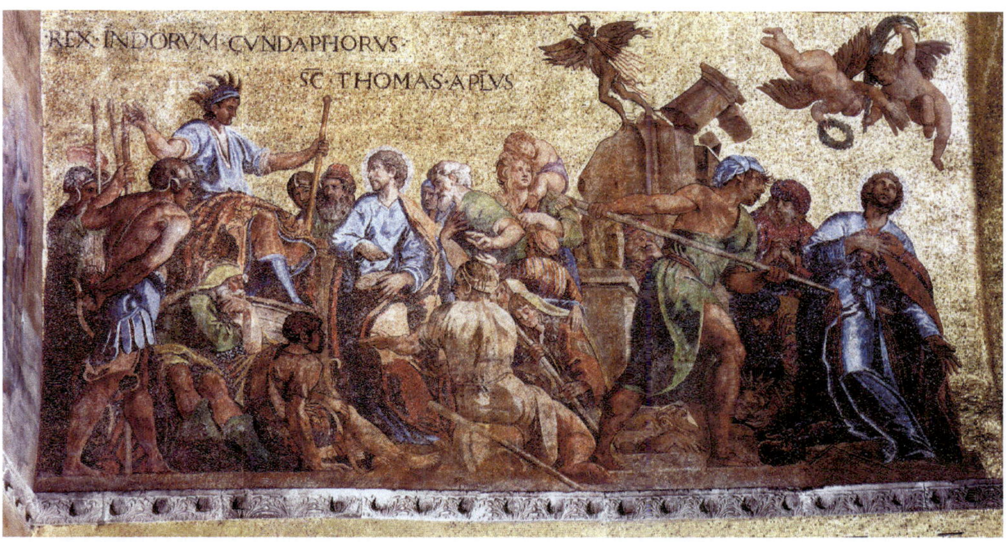

107. Cartoon by Tizianello, execution by Luigi and Girolamo Gaetano, *Martyrdom of Saint Thomas,* 1621, mosaic, Basilica di San Marco, Venice (Photo: Archivio Fotografico della Procuratoria di San Marco/by kind permission of the Procuratoria di San Marco)

Aiming for a response of horror, pity, and ultimately devotion in the spectator, these gorier kinds of martyrdom scenes became widely diffused in Rome toward the end of the century.[103] Here, churches like Santo Stefano Rotundo were embellished with horrifying cycles of the early Christian martyrdoms already in the early 1580s, ones that depicted the trials of the saints so vividly that they apparently moved Pope Sixtus V to tears when he made a visit in 1589.[104] Although this type became gradually more diffused in Venice too, for the most part the typology of the stoic martyr rather than the suffering martyr was preferred.[105] In some ways this was a continuation of Byzantine and medieval martyrdom scenes where the saint is often seen relatively expressionless, but common to both types was the contrast between the heroic pacifism of the victims and the exaggerated gestures and violent cruelty of their murderers. This can be seen in Palma's response to Titian's Crociferi altarpiece in his own *Martyrdom of Saint Lawrence* for San Giacomo dall'Orio where Lawrence is instead shown alert and poised as he meets his grisly fate, perhaps a visual realisation of his infamous instruction to be turned over since he was already cooked on one side (Fig. 55). Like Lawrence, the psychological fortitude of the figure of George, stripped of his armour, and the virgin Giustina, who was famed for her courage, is total. Vanquishing the physical might of the armed oppressors through the force of their prayers, their inner strength and self-control appeared nothing short of miraculous. And if miracles were to become one of the defining aspects of early modern Catholicism, then it was partly as a result of the ways in which these ideas were visualised pictorially that made them seem not just possible, but part of a reality where heaven and earth could collide.

NOTES

1 Ridolfi, *Le Maraviglie dell'arte*, vol. 1: 349. Discussed by Salomon, *Veronese*, 144.

2 See Peter Humfrey, 'Altarpieces and Altar Dedications in Counter-Reformation Venice and the Veneto', *Renaissance Studies* 10, no. 3 (1996): 371–87. Until the Second Vatican Council, every altar had to have in its cavity grains of incense and the relics of three saints, one of whom had to have been a martyr. In early Christian times the mass was celebrated as close to the tomb of a martyr as possible. See Patricia Meilman, *Titian and the Altarpiece in Renaissance Venice* (Cambridge: Cambridge University Press, 2000), 32–33.

3 Humfrey, 'La pala d'altare veneta nell'età delle riforme', 1147.

4 For example, Palma il Giovane's *Beheading of John the Baptist with Saints Lanfranc and Liberius* of 1610 was commissioned by the Scuola dei Varoteri at the church of the Crociferi to replace Cima's *Saint Lanfranc Enthroned with Saints John the Baptist and Liberius* of c. 1515, now in the Fitzwilliam Museum. For this and other examples, see Humfrey, 'La pala d'altare veneta nell'età delle riforme', 1119.

5 For *laterali*, see, in particular, Matile, '"Quadri laterali" ovvero conseguenze di una collocazione ingrata'; Matile, *'Quadri laterali' im sakralen Kontext*.

6 See, for example, Humfrey, 'Altarpieces and Altar Dedications in Counter-Reformation Venice and the Veneto', 371, 374–75. See also Ekserdjian, *The Italian Renaissance Altarpiece*, 370–71, 400–401. Both Humfrey and Ekserdjian are in agreement that the overall number of altarpieces dealing with the martyrdom of the saints increased significantly in the sixteenth century, particularly from the mid-century onward. For the data relating to Venice, see Peter Humfrey, *The Altarpiece in Renaissance Venice* (New Haven, CT: Yale University Press, 1993), 65.

7 Waterworth, *Canons and Decrees of the Council of Trent*, 235.
8 See Nichols, 'Images of Almsgiving and Poverty in Venetian Art of the Sixteenth Century'; Nichols, 'Secular Charity, Sacred Poverty: Picturing the Poor in Renaissance Venice'; Tom Nichols, *The Art of Poverty: Irony and Ideal in Sixteenth-Century Beggar Imagery* (Manchester: Manchester University Press, 2007). Also relevant is Aikema and Meijers, 'L'immagine della "Carità Veneziana"'.
9 See also Lillywhite, 'The Decoration of the Church of San Giacomo dall'Orio in Venice', 133–34.
10 Boschini described it as replete 'with many figures and architecture', and that if the altarpiece was 'splendid, then this is marvellous'. Boschini, *Le minere della pittura*, 514; Lillywhite, 'The Decoration of the Church of San Giacomo dall'Orio in Venice', 146, note 63.
11 See Ekserdjian, *The Italian Renaissance Altarpiece*, 210.
12 Ridolfi, *Le maraviglie dell'arte*, vol. 2: 172–73.
13 Compiled from data that covers 109 of the 137 churches in Venice listed by Marin Sanudo. A half dedication means the altar was dedicated to two saints jointly. See table 3 of Humfrey, *The Altarpiece in Renaissance Venice*, 62–63.
14 Ekserdjian points out that 'it might be tempting to assume that Lawrence was the quintessential one-story saint'. Ekserdjian, *The Italian Renaissance Altarpiece*, 210.
15 The act of Lawrence's donation had been depicted previously in frescoes, an important extant Northern Italian example being those of the Maestro di San Lorenzo in the Oratory of Saints Lawrence and Mark in Vittorio Veneto (first half of the fifteenth century).
16 For the painting, see Bernard Aikema, 'L'immagine devozionale nell'opera di Veronese', in *Nuovi studi su Paolo Veronese*, ed. Massimo Gemin (Venice: Arsenale, 1990), 197–98; Aymonino, 'La Pala di San Pantalon: immagine devozionale e manifesto politico'; Matthew, 'Clergy and Confraternities', 100. Matthew identifies the portrait of Borghi as being that of the saint, whilst the majority of other sources identify Borghi as the figure who embraces the poisoned boy.
17 The Apostolic Visitation noted that the collegiate church of San Giacomo had twelve clergy: the parish priest, the deacon, sub-deacon, three other priests, two younger priests, and four clerics. The events are recounted by Deborah Howard and Laura Moretti, *Sound and Space in Renaissance Venice: Architecture, Music, Acoustics* (New Haven, CT: Yale University Press, 2009), 134–36.
18 Cristellon and Menchi, 'Religious Life', 387.
19 APV, Visite Priuli, Supplemento alle visite Priuli. 1591 ad 1598, number 15, unnumbered folios. For Da Ponte's generosity to his parish, see Chapter 4.
20 The latter arrangement was more acceptable since the widow was forty years of age and 'more ugly than beautiful', according to the local barber. See APV, Visite Priuli, Supplemento alle visite Priuli. 1591 ad 1598, number 15, unnumbered folios, and Howard and Moretti, *Sound and Space in Renaissance Venice*, 136.
21 Such as the situation involving sexual abuse at San Cassiano. See note 17 of chapter 4.
22 See Brian S. Pullan, *Rich and Poor in Renaissance Venice: The Social Institutions of a Catholic State* (Oxford: Blackwell, 1971), 253–54. Pullan believes the law was not fully enforced until 1545 and afterwards.
23 The painting was first recorded in the church by Boschini, *Le minere della pittura*, 379.
24 For Strozzi in Venice, see Pallucchini, *La pittura veneziana del Seicento*, vol. 1: 155–64. For the Tolentini painting, see Ezia Gavazza, Giovanna Nepi Scirè, and Giovanna Rotondi Terminiello, eds., *Bernardo Strozzi: Genova 1581/82 – Venezia 1644*, Exhibition Catalogue, Palazzo Ducale, Genoa, 6 May–6 August 1995 (Milan: Electa, 1995), 244, cat. 73; Manno, *La chiesa di San Nicola da Tolentino a Venezia*, 45–46.
25 For other versions of the same theme by Strozzi, see Gavazza, Nepi Scirè, and Rotondi Terminiello, *Bernardo Strozzi: Genova 1581/82 – Venezia 1644*, 166–67, 180–81, cats. 35, 42.
26 Nichols, 'Secular Charity, Sacred Poverty: Picturing the Poor in Renaissance Venice', 155–60.

27 Nichols, 'Secular Charity, Sacred Poverty: Picturing the Poor in Renaissance Venice', 152, 167, note 50. Humfrey also sees the moral aspects of practical virtue emphasised at Trent reflected in contemporary narrative altarpieces. Humfrey, 'Altarpieces and Altar Dedications in Counter-Reformation Venice and the Veneto', 374–75.

28 Unlike laws passed in many Protestant cities, poor laws in Venice did not completely prohibit begging or secularise poor relief. A poor law of 1522 meant that syphilitics had to be removed from public places and placed in the hospital of the Incurabili. In 1529 the 'idle' male poor were to be banished from Venice or sent to work on the galleys, and in 1574 male vagabondery was to be punished either with five years of the galleys or ten of imprisonment. See Nichols, 'Images of Almsgiving and Poverty in Venetian Art of the Sixteenth Century', 366–67; Nichols, 'Secular Charity, Sacred Poverty: Picturing the Poor in Renaissance Venice', 140. For social welfare in early modern Europe, see Eire, *Reformations: The Early Modern World, 1450–1650*, 704–10. For poverty in Venice, see, in particular, Pullan, *Rich and Poor in Renaissance Venice*.

29 Eire, *Reformations: The Early Modern World, 1450–1650*, 704.

30 Black, *Italian Confraternities in the Sixteenth Century*, 131.

31 This possibility is discussed by Pullan, who nevertheless notes that 'there is no direct and concrete evidence to support such an argument'. Pullan, *Rich and Poor in Renaissance Venice*, 254–56.

32 Black, *Italian Confraternities in the Sixteenth Century*, 140–41; Eire, *Reformations: The Early Modern World, 1450–1650*, 709.

33 Black, *Italian Confraternities in the Sixteenth Century*, 145–46.

34 This was not without precedent, of course. The Jesuits, for example, were inspired by the example of Saint Francis of Assisi, who encouraged friars to identify with outcasts and live with lepers. For the new orders, see Pullan, *Rich and Poor in Renaissance Venice*, 257–70; Brian S. Pullan, 'La nuova filantropia nella Venezia cinquecentesca', in *Nel regno dei poveri: arte e storia dei grandi ospedali veneziani in età moderna, 1474–1797*, ed. Bernard Aikema and Dulcia Meijers (Venice: Arsenale Editrice, 1989), 19–34; Silvio Tramontin, 'Le nuove congregazioni religiosi', in *La Chiesa di Venezia tra riforma protestante e riforma cattolica*, ed. Giuseppe Gullino (Venice: Studium cattolico veneziano, 1990), 77–112.

35 Pullan, 'The Old Catholicism, the New Catholicism and the Poor', 17–18. The institutionalisation of those with leprosy or syphilis was also considered an imperative since these illnesses were believed capable of transmitting themselves via the breath of the diseased and not just through sexual or other contact. See Pullan, *Rich and Poor in Renaissance Venice*, 236, 385–94. The Jesuits were closely involved in the foundation of the Zitelle and they have also been linked to the Soccorso.

36 Eire, *Reformations: The Early Modern World, 1450–1650*, 711.

37 See Nichols, 'Images of Almsgiving and Poverty in Venetian Art of the Sixteenth Century', 360; Nichols, 'Secular Charity, Sacred Poverty: Picturing the Poor in Renaissance Venice', 152–54.

38 Pullan, *Rich and Poor in Renaissance Venice*, 284.

39 Nichols, 'Secular Charity, Sacred Poverty: Picturing the Poor in Renaissance Venice', 163.

40 John A. McHugh and Charles J. Callan, trans., *Catechism of the Council of Trent* (Rockford, IL: TAN Books, 1982), 481, 608.

41 Black, *Italian Confraternities in the Sixteenth Century*, 128. Black provides an analysis of the figures first presented by Pullan in *Rich and Poor in Renaissance Venice*.

42 Carlos M. N. Eire, *From Madrid to Purgatory: The Art and Craft of Dying in Sixteenth-Century Spain* (Cambridge: Cambridge University Press, 1995), 239–40. Eire examines the figures exhaustively and considers all other possibilities before drawing this conclusion.

43 Chambers and Pullan, *Venice*, 297. This poor relief could include the small donations of almsgivers, or larger amounts from institutions or parochial assistance. As noted elsewhere by Pullan, quantifying the percentage of poor in Venice depends on how poverty is defined. The categories of individuals were not always precise in extant documents.

Nevertheless, of those who may have had to resort to charitable assistance, Pullan believes around 20 percent were made up of individuals with precarious and badly paid employment, who would be in serious trouble the moment the price of bread was to rise. Smaller was the second group of the 'structurally poor', who were constantly dependent on assistance for survival. This group included orphans, abandoned children, the elderly, the chronically diseased, and amputees. See Pullan, 'La nuova filantropia nella Venezia cinquecentesca', 19.

44 Humfrey, 'La pala d'altare veneta nell'età delle riforme', 1151. The fundamental study on Jacopo's devotional works remains Aikema, *Jacopo Bassano and His Public*.

45 See Borean, 'Documentation', 448–49. For Faustina's will, see ASV, Notarile, Testamenti, b. 32, n. 349, referenced by Melania G. Mazzucco, *Jacomo Tintoretto & i suoi figli: storia di una famiglia veneziana*, 2nd ed. (Milan: Rizzoli, 2009), 901, note 35. For Domenico's will, see Rosanna Tozzi Pedrazzi, 'Notizie biografiche su Domenico Tintoretto', *Rivista di Venezia* 12 (1933): 316. An extract from the second will by Faustina with a date of 4 August 1613 is included in Giovanni Prosdocimo Zabeo, *Elogio a Giacomo Robusti* (Venice: Tipografia Bernardi, 1813), 58–59.

46 Livia Alberton Vinco da Sesso and Franco Signori, 'Il testamento di Jacopo dal Ponte detto Bassano', *Arte Veneta* 33 (1979): 163; Giuseppe Gerola, 'I testamenti di Francesco il Giovane e di Gerolamo da Ponte', *Bollettino del Museo civico di Bassano* 2 (1905): 104. Both Jacopo and Francesco donated to the 'deserving' poor, and the latter's bequest came with the conditions that the girls should be of respectable parentage and mores. There was little out of the ordinary in this stipulation, and it was similar to the requirements described by Lorenzo Lotto decades previously in his will of 1546. Humfrey, *Lorenzo Lotto*, 179–81.

47 Gerola, 'I Testamenti di Francesco il Giovane e di Gerolamo da Ponte', 113.

48 The workshop lasted from the beginning of the sixteenth century until at least 1655 and involved numerous painters. Carlo Corsato, 'Dai Dal Ponte ai Bassano: l'eredità di Jacopo, le botteghe dei figli e l'identità artistica di Michele Pietra, 1578–1656', *Artibus et Historiae* 37, no. 73 (2016): 195, 197.

49 See Guillermo Lohmann Villena, ed., *La Basílica Catedral de Lima* (Lima: Banca de Credito del Peru, 2004), 253–54. These belonged to the collection of Melchor de Liñán y Cisnero, who was archbishop of Lima from 1676 and later viceroy of Peru. The cycle is on display in the sacristy of the cathedral. One of the paintings in the cycle has been tentatively attributed to the Flemish artist Lodewijk Toeput (Ludovico Pozzoserato), who was present in the workshop of Tintoretto and was influenced by the work of Leandro Bassano. M. A. Katritzky, 'Lodewyk Toeput: Some Pictures Related to the "commedia dell'arte"', *Renaissance Studies* 1, no. 1 (1987): 86–88. Thanks to Delia Moldovan for this reference.

50 Vasari, *Lives of the Painters, Sculptors and Architects*, vol. 2: 796.

51 See previous note and Federico Borromeo's defence of the inclusion of a small dog in Titian's *Adoration of the Magi*. Aikema and Meijers, 'L'immagine della "Carità Veneziana"', 78–79; Rona Goffen, 'Review of "Jacopo Bassano and His Public: Moralizing Pictures in an Age of Reform, ca. 1535–1600" by Bernard Aikema and "The Art of Giovanni Antonio Da Pordenone: Between Dialect and Language" by Charles E. Cohen', *Art Bulletin* 80, no. 1 (March 1998): 187; Aikema, *Jacopo Bassano and His Public*, 159–60.

52 Voelker, 'Carlo Borromeo's Instructiones fabricae et supellectilis ecclesiasticae, 1577,' 229. Jacopo's brother, the priest Girolamo da Ponte, was a friend of Antonio Grandi, a Bassanese hermit that was much admired by the early Jesuits in Venice. Grandi was mentioned in the *Libro secondo* of the workshop in 1529, and both Girolamo and Simão Rodrigues (one of the co-founders of the Jesuits) were mentioned as witnesses to his will. It is possible that through this contact Jacopo came to the attention of the order and was thus in contact with some of the earliest followers of Ignatius of Loyola. See Aikema, *Jacopo Bassano and His Public*, 82; Bernard Aikema, 'Les Jésuites et les arts visuels à Venise: spiritualité, propagande

religieuse et raison d'État du XVIe au XVIIIe siècle', in *Baroque vision Jésuite: du Tintoret à Rubens*, ed. Alain Tapié, Exhibition Catalogue, Musée des Beaux-Arts de Caen, 12 July–13 October 2003 (Paris: Somogy, 2003), 131.

53 See Bernard Aikema and Dulcia Meijers, *Nel regno dei poveri: arte e storia dei grandi ospedali veneziani in età moderna, 1474–1797* (Venice: Arsenale Editrice, 1989), 221, 234–37. The workshop also produced an *Announcement to the Shepherds* for the Zitelle. For the works of the Bassano family for the Jesuits, see Aikema, 'Les Jésuites et les arts visuels à Venise: spiritualité, propagande religieuse et raison d'État du XVIe au XVIIIe siècle'.

54 The painting would have originally been brighter. The copper greens in the foliage, and possibly the grass too, have darkened. The stripes of the scarf worn by the Samaritan have turned from green to brown. Nicholas Penny, *The Sixteenth Century Italian Paintings, Vol. 2: Venice 1540–1600* (London: National Gallery Company, 2008), 16.

55 See W. R. Rearick, 'Vita ed opere di Jacopo dal Ponte, detto Bassano c. 1510–1592', in *Jacopo Bassano c. 1510–1592*, edited by Beverly Louise Brown and Paola Marini, Exhibition Catalogue, Museo Civico, Bassano del Grappa, 5 September–6 December 1992, Kimbell Art Museum, Fort Worth, Texas, 23 January–25 April 1993 (Bologna: Nuova Alfa, 1993), cxii; Penny, *The Sixteenth Century Italian Paintings*, 18.

56 Rearick, 'Vita ed opere di Jacopo dal Ponte, detto Bassano c. 1510–1592', cxxii–cxxiii. See also Penny, *The Sixteenth Century Italian Paintings*, 16–20. An engraving of the painting appeared in the *Raccolta di Centododici Stampe di Pitture della Storia Sacra*, published by Guglielmo Zerletti in 1763. The print asserted that the image had been made after the painting of Jacopo Bassano that was owned by the noble Pisani.

57 As for the National Gallery painting, nothing is known about the nature of the commission, but the format suggests a work for private devotional purposes as noted by Aikema and Meijers, 'L'immagine della "Carità Veneziana"', 74. Rearick speculates that it might be the painting commissioned by Zuanbattista Fontana da Treviso in 1550, but points out the problems with the dating, suggesting other alternatives, including the version in the Pinacoteca Capitolina in Rome and a replica held by the art dealer Piero Corsini in New York. Rearick, 'Vita ed opere di Jacopo dal Ponte, detto Bassano c. 1510–1592', xcii–xciii. For the American painting, see Rodolfo Pallucchini, 'Una "parabola del buon samaritano" di Jacopo Bassano', *Arte Veneta* 41 (1987): 135–38. Another version of this painting signed by Jacopo was once in the Kaiser Friedrich Museum, Berlin, and was destroyed in 1945. For a reproduction, see Rearick, Vita ed opere di Jacopo dal Ponte, detto Bassano c. 1510–1592, cxix. The composition was repeated by Francesco in his painting of the theme in the Kunsthistorisches Museum of Vienna (cxx–cxxi, note 191).

58 For a discussion, see Aikema, *Jacopo Bassano and His Public*, 47–49; Penny, *The Sixteenth Century Italian Paintings*, 16. Aikema noted the likely influence of Netherlandish painters on Bassano and their inclusion of the motif of either priest or Levite absorbed in a devotional text. A painting by Romanino appeared almost simultaneously to the Hampton Court *Good Samaritan*, dated to c. 1544–45 by Nova, *Girolamo Romanino*, 323, no. 96.

59 Pignatti and Pedrocco, *Veronese*, vol. 2: 484–85, cat. 385.

60 Mason Rinaldi, *Palma il Giovane: l'opera completa*, 89, cat. 129. Aside from this painting now in a private collection, there is a drawing by Palma in the British Museum of the parable (1862, 0809.48).

61 Davide Dossi, 'Tra Venezia e Roma: il "Buon Samaritano" di Marcantonio Bassetti conservato a Oxford', *Bollettino d'Arte* 28 (series 7) (2015): 81–86.

62 The German Kilian travelled to Italy at the beginning of the seventeenth century. His engraving after Bassano's *Good Samaritan* (British Museum, 1870, 1008.1172) bears a far closer resemblance to the Holyrood painting than the National Gallery canvas. Dossi, 'Tra Venezia e Roma: il "Buon Samaritano" di Marcantonio Bassetti conservato a Oxford', 82–84. Around 1650–56 David Teniers II also produced a copy after Jacopo's work that is now in the Courtauld Institute.

63 Domenico Fetti also created a number of versions of the parable. There are further surviving copies of Bassano's National Gallery painting: one important version is in the Gallery of the Castle of Prague, attributed to Jacopo Bassano by Alessandro Ballarin and to Francesco by Rearick. The latter also points to the existence of a number of workshop replicas that may be youthful works of Francesco. Rearick, 'Vita ed opere di Jacopo dal Ponte, detto Bassano c. 1510–1592', cxxii–cxxiii, note 202; Alessandro Ballarin, 'Osservazioni sui dipinti veneziani del Cinquecento nella Galleria del Castello di Praga', in *Jacopo Bassano: Scritti 1964–1995*, ed. Vittoria Romani (Cittadella: Bertoncello Artigrafiche, 1995), vol. 1: 31–33.

64 Aikema, *Jacopo Bassano and His Public*, 47–48.

65 Aikema, *Jacopo Bassano and His Public*, 59. Here it was noted that in Jacopo's paintings 'naturalism was never simply employed to purely aesthetic ends but was always an element intended to clarify the significance of a given image'.

66 Pullan, *Rich and Poor in Renaissance Venice*, 266.

67 Pullan, *Rich and Poor in Renaissance Venice*, 265. The account was written forty years later, when Rodrigues was an old man.

68 See the Introduction, note 62. Jacopo may well have been influenced by facets of evangelism in the early part of his career, but this was very different to outright support of Lutheranism.

69 For this reason, based on his work for the Jesuits, Bernard Aikema asked whether Jacopo Bassano and his workshop should rightfully be considered the earliest artists to be associated with the order (which does not mean that their style was in any way informed by a Jesuit 'way of proceeding'). Aikema, 'Les Jésuites et les arts visuels à Venise: spiritualité, propagande religieuse et raison d'État du XVIe au XVIIIe siècle', 131, 136.

70 Palma il Vecchio painted an altarpiece of the same subject matter as Titian's for the church of San Pietro Martire in Alzano Lombardo. Humfrey hypothesises that Palma may have recommended Titian to the Scuola di San Pietro Martire for the commission at Santi Giovanni e Paolo, and soon afterwards been approached by the clergy in Alzano Lombardo in Bergamo, his own region. In the 1540s Bernardino da Asola likewise produced the *Assassination of Peter Martyr*, which drew inspiration from Titian, now in the National Gallery of London, as did Moretto (c. 1530) and Moroni (c. 1560). See Humfrey, *The Altarpiece in Renaissance Venice*, 316–17; Meilman, *Titian and the Altarpiece in Renaissance Venice*, 105–7, 117.

71 Noted by Meilman, *Titian and the Altarpiece in Renaissance Venice*, 32. Martyrdoms were more commonly depicted on peripheral areas like the side panels of a polyptych. Martyrdom cropped up earlier in Northern European altarpieces (there are two examples by Dieric Bouts of c. 1460), and Bosch's *Saint Julia Triptych* of c. 1503 featured a central panel of the martyrdom of the saint. This work may have been present in Venice in the decades preceding the execution of Titian's altarpiece. Meilman, 48, 214, notes 78, 79. For other early examples not considered by Meilman, see the catalogue of Lionello Puppi, *Torment in Art: Pain, Violence, and Martyrdom* (New York: Rizzoli, 1991).

72 Meilman, *Titian and the Altarpiece in Renaissance Venice*, 48–49. One precedent that approximates the later martyrdom altarpieces is Carpaccio's *Martyrdom of the Ten Thousand Christians on Mount Arat* of 1515. Titian already had experience of painting violent deaths at the Scuola del Santo in Padua, where his fresco *The Miracle of the Jealous Husband* of 1511 depicts the murderer poised to deliver the deadly strike to the chest of his wife. For the impact of the Tridentine decrees, see Humfrey, 'Altarpieces and Altar Dedications in Counter-Reformation Venice and the Veneto', 374.

73 For the early Christian revival in Counter-Reformation Rome and the promotion of the cult of the martyrs there, see Steven F. Ostrow, 'The Counter-Reformation and the End of the Century', in *Artistic Centers of the Italian Renaissance: Rome*, ed. Marcia B. Hall (Cambridge: Cambridge University Press, 2005), 270, 276.

74 Eire, *Reformations: The Early Modern World, 1450–1650*, 501. The Jesuits were flooded with thousands of letters from eager novices who wished to be sent on the most perilous and

distant missions of all. Eire, 470. For some examples, see Katherine McAllen, 'Jesuit Martyrdom Imagery between Mexico and Rome', in *The New World in Early Modern Italy, 1492–1750*, ed. Elizabeth Horodowich and Lia Markey (Cambridge: Cambridge University Press, 2017), 156–57.

75 This does not mean that Protestants necessarily ceased to believe in miraculous phenomena, however. For a classic essay on the diffusion of the 'cult of Luther', see R. W. Scribner, 'Incombustible Luther: The Image of the Reformer in Early Modern Germany', *Past & Present*, no. 110 (1986): 38–68.

76 See Rodolfo Pallucchini, *Giovanni Bellini* (Milan: Aldo Martello Editore, 1959), 157–58, cat. 226; Tempestini, *Giovanni Bellini*, 174–75.

77 See Meilman, *Titian and the Altarpiece in Renaissance Venice*, 117.

78 For a history of the martyrdom altarpiece, see Meilman, *Titian and the Altarpiece in Renaissance Venice*, 32–51.

79 See Pignatti and Pedrocco, *Veronese*, vol. 1: 255–56, cat. 153. In 1566 this painting was accompanied by another work of Veronese: *The Healing of St Barnabas*, which was placed under the organ.

80 Huber, *Paolo Veronese: Kunst als soziales System*, 239–41. This change was also more devout, avoiding any suspicion that George could have been tempted by the idol.

81 According to the account in the *Golden Legend*, a heavenly voice affirmed that George's prayer would be answered. See Cocke, *Paolo Veronese: Piety and Display*, 105.

82 Cleaning of Bellini's *Assassination of Saint Peter Martyr* at the National Gallery revealed glimmers of light on the trunks of the trees in the background.

83 Sergio Marinelli, 'La pala per l'altar maggiore di S. Giorgio in Braida', in *Nuovi studi su Paolo Veronese*, ed. Massimo Gemin (Venice: Arsenale Editrice, 1990), 327. Marinelli lists precedents including Titian's *Martyrdom of Saint Lawrence* for the Crociferi in Venice and Giulio Romano's *Martyrdom of Saint Stephen*. In 1564 Domenico Brusasorci painted a *Martyrdom of Saint Barbara* for the eponymous church in Mantua, and in the same year Sigismondo de' Stefani signed and dated a *Martyrdom of Saint Lawrence* for San Giorgio in Braida.

84 See Nova, *Girolamo Romanino*, 307–8, cat. 78.

85 See, for example, Sante Peranda's painting of the *Martyrdom of Saint John the Evangelist* for the Scuola Grande di San Giovanni Evangelista in Venice where the saint is shown immersed in a pot of boiling oil.

86 See Nova, *Girolamo Romanino*, 219–21, cat. 8; Humfrey, 'La pala d'altare veneta nell'età delle riforme', 1119–21.

87 Sergio Marinelli, followed by Humfrey, hypothesised that the Patriarch of Aquileia, Daniele Barbaro, might have played a key role in the decision to replace the altarpiece. He stopped at the church on his return to Venice from the Council of Trent where he witnessed the new apse constructed by Michele Sanmicheli. See Marinelli, 'La pala per l'altar maggiore di S. Giorgio in Braida'; Pignatti and Pedrocco, *Veronese*, vol. 2: 328, cat. 202; Humfrey, 'La pala d'altare veneta nell'età delle riforme', 1147–48.

88 The date of the victory, 7 October, was Giustina's saint's day. Vittoria Romani, '"Picturae opus adiecit Paulus Calliarius Veronensis celebris pictor": la pala dell'altare maggiore di Santa Giustina', in *Magnificenza monastica a gloria di Dio: l'abbazia di Santa Giustina nel suo secolare cammino storico e artistico*, ed. Giovanna Baldissin Molli and Francesco G. B. Trolese (Viella: Rome, 2020), 367.

89 See Massimo Bison, 'Gli spazi del canto: architettura e trasformazioni dei cori abbaziali', in *Magnificenza monastica a gloria di Dio: l'abbazia di Santa Giustina nel suo secolare cammino storico e artistico*, ed. Giovanna Baldissin Molli and Francesco G. B. Trolese (Viella: Rome, 2020), 311.

90 Romani, 'La pala dell'altare maggiore di Santa Giustina', 367. For an identification of the church with Santa Giustina, see Cocke, *Paolo Veronese: Piety and Display*, 107. The Santo was the recognised symbol of Padua by this point and the building bears a closer resemblance to this basilica than it does to Santa Giustina.

91 Puppi, *Torment in Art*, 55.

92 Ridolfi, *Le maraviglie dell'arte*, vol. 1: 317. Despite its size, Ridolfi complained that the altarpiece was 'difficult to enjoy' since it was 'badly served by candles', and its beauty was obstructed by the architectural ornamentation. The altarpiece is surrounded by a monumental frame in the form of a triumphal arch that was carved by the Florentine Giovanni Manetti (begun in 1574) and gilded by the Venetian Giovanni Moretti. Veronese received his first payment on 27 October 1575. See Bison, 'Gli spazi del canto: architettura e trasformazioni dei cori abbaziali', 312; Romani, 'La pala dell'altare maggiore di Santa Giustina'.

93 For the early modern 'art of dying' well, see Eire, *From Madrid to Purgatory*, 24–34.

94 Pallucchini and Rossi, *Tintoretto: le opere sacre e profane*, vol. 2: 253–54, cat. A111.

95 For a discussion of the extent to which saints in polyptychs or *sacre conversazioni* were intended to instruct the viewer in Christian virtues, see Humfrey, *The Altarpiece in Renaissance Venice*, 76.

96 See Demus, 'Probleme der Restaurierung der Mosaiken von San Marco im XV. und XVI. Jahrhundert', 642; Demus, *The Mosaics of San Marco in Venice*, vol. 1: 10–11.

97 Stringa, *Venetia, città nobilissima, et singolare*, 49r.

98 See Andaloro et al., *San Marco*, 115–17; Demus, *The Mosaics of San Marco in Venice*, vol. 1: 219–20.

99 These were based upon drawings by Palma il Giovane of 1623. See Mason Rinaldi, *Palma il Giovane: l'opera completa*, 166, cat. M2.

100 Demus, *The Mosaics of San Marco in Venice*, vol. 1: 8–10.

101 Demus was silent on the inclusion of this motif, which must be a new invention. He also pointed out that the vision of three angels in the scene of John celebrating mass must have surely been a representation of the soul of the saint being carried to heaven in the previous mosaic. Demus, *The Mosaics of San Marco in Venice*, vol. 1: 221–22.

102 In underlining how artists were inspired by aspects of the iconography of Titian's altarpieces, this interpretation is somewhat at odds with recent studies that have seen them as unique solutions that failed to establish new traditions. See Tom Nichols, *Titian and the End of the Venetian Renaissance* (London: Reaktion Books, 2013); Hans Aurenhammer, 'Venetian Painting in the Age of Titian', in *Titian and the Renaissance in Venice*, ed. Bastian Eclercy and Hans Aurenhammer, Exhibition Catalogue, Städel Museum, Frankfurt Am Main, 13 February–26 May 2019 (Munich: Prestel, 2019), 19.

103 For viewer responses, see Puppi, *Torment in Art*, 56.

104 In 1582 the church was decorated with thirty-one martyrdom scenes by Niccolò Cicignani, assisted by Matteo da Siena. See Bailey, *Between Renaissance and Baroque*, 133–52. For the reaction of Sixtus, see the analysis of Puppi, *Torment in Art*, 56.

105 Palma il Giovane and his workshop produced innumerable martyrdom scenes, including the cartoons for the mosaics mentioned in note 99. The goriest depictions have all been dated to the final decades of the Cinquecento onwards and were reserved for beheadings. In the *Beheading of Saint John the Baptist* for the Crociferi (c. 1610), the *Martyrdom of Saint George* in Palermo (c. 1604), and the *Burial of the Beheaded Saints Tiburzio and Valeriano* (c. 1620) for the Tolentini, blood is depicted dramatically spurting from the necks of decapitated corpses.

CHAPTER SEVEN

THE AFTERLIFE

In all of the martyrdom altarpieces discussed in the previous chapter, it is only the saint and the very occasional onlooker who notices the supernatural realm above.[1] In viewing these works, the beholder becomes witness to this heavenly world, one that goes unnoticed by those who are depicted directly engaged in the killings or torture of the protagonists of these paintings, as well as by the passive observers shown in the attendant crowds. In Domenico Tintoretto's *Martyrdom of Saint Stephen*, for example, the opening of the skies causes a gust of wind to disrupt the saint's vestments, but despite the fact that he is the sole figure subject to this unusual climactic variation, his persecutors do not waver in their concentration on the task at hand. It is thus tempting to speculate that these kinds of details might even have had some kind of resonance with regard to the Reformations. Like the Protestants who believed neither in the efficacy of the saints nor in the kind of miraculous phenomena that seemed to abundantly proliferate in the Catholic world, so too did the convictions of those deemed unfaithful in these works mean they could not see, indeed were oblivious to, a mystical reality that was portrayed by artists as close at hand.[2]

The afterlife took on a particular sense of urgency in the sixteenth century framed by the controversies between reformers on salvation, who questioned how and to whom it was granted, as well as its very nature. Illuminated by divine light, a light that signified their impending knowledge of God and entry into paradise, the saints depicted in the paintings of the previous chapter died the death of the minority who were believed to enter heaven directly. Visionary images of the heavens are the subject of the first half of this chapter, where the visceral power of the newly naturalistic imagery used to describe an imagined supernatural realm offered not only a great artistic opportunity but a transcendental one for the spectator. The majority of the faithful departed were believed to be distant from this direct journey, and before entering heaven the sins committed in their lifetime were to be cleansed in the purgatorial fires, the subject of the second section. Although first a medieval concern, representations of purgatory began to rapidly increase from the late sixteenth century onwards, a trend that was stimulated by both the reassertion of this dogma at the Council of Trent and the vigorous denial of its existence by Protestant Reformers. New variations on the theme in Italy, such as altarpieces of the saints freeing souls from the purging fires, were very much tied to the spirit of the age,[3] although it is questionable whether the subject ever gave rise to the same kind of artistic achievement and invention that the beauty of the heavens ever did, purgatory being a challenging concept to render pictorially since it was imagined as being both painful and monotonous (the average soul spent one or two thousand years there before transferring to paradise, according to an estimate of 1583), but also less terrifying than the eternal spectre of hell, for which it could easily be mistaken given that both feature flames.[4] The representations of the saints in the previous chapter offered exemplars of lives lived virtuously, whilst depictions of souls trapped in purgatory instead portrayed the inevitable fate of the majority, albeit one that could be dramatically curtailed in the present through the suffrages offered by the living. The artists who imagined and then depicted the afterlife, whether it be purgatory or paradise, set themselves a considerable artistic challenge in seeking to depict worlds that were unseeable and unknowable.[5] A number of them pulled off this feat admirably, creating some of the most visually compelling paintings of the century.

THE HEAVENS

The more dazzlingly the glories of the heavens were depicted, the more appealing the promise of salvation became. The visions of the world to come tasted by Saints George, Giustina, and Stephen at the moment of their death in the altarpieces of Veronese and Domenico Tintoretto granted the beholder a taste of the beatific vision, or the direct perception of God experienced by the inhabitants of heaven. This was defined by Daniel Arasse in his study of Raphael's visionary altarpieces as 'the moment when man has the intuitive visual revelation of supernatural realities, where two worlds, natural and supernatural, met through the agency of the Christian individual', pointing out that the theme was as old as Christianity itself, but one that acquired significant polemical and imaginative significance during the Counter-Reformation as a tool to resolve the spiritual tensions sparked by both Renaissance and Reformation.[6] Representations of the celestial sphere in altarpieces could also be laden with sacramental implications, reflecting the belief that at the moment of the consecration of the host and chalice during the mass, the space around the altar was miraculously filled with saints and angels, as earthly liturgy fused with the divine liturgy perpetually celebrated in the heavens.[7] In altarpieces prior to the early 1500s this was sometimes denoted by the presence of the angels playing musical instruments, but by the end of the century it became visually explicit and atmospherically credible in a way that made the miraculous appear as a commonplace element in the world of the faithful living. The proliferation of images of the miraculous in the early modern period testified to the presumed veracity of these events, and they may have rendered their beholders more likely to believe in and even experience such phenomena for themselves.[8]

Paradise was a subject approached by all the significant artists of the late Cinquecento in Venice, most obviously due to the famous competition of c. 1582 for the commission of a new painting of the subject for the Sala del Maggior Consiglio of the Ducal Palace to replace Guariento di Arpo's (d. 1368/70) fresco, *The Coronation of the Virgin before the Celestial Hierarchies* (c. 1365), which had been severely damaged during the fire of 1577.[9] The mastery of oil painting in Venice and the ways in which it could be manipulated to create dramatic effects of colour and clarity of light meant that the divine now appeared closer and more realistic than ever. This is not only well illustrated by the examples of Veronese already discussed, but was brilliantly achieved by Titian many years earlier in his altarpiece of the *Assunta* (1516–18) in the Frari, where the celestial world into which the Virgin is assumed is denoted by a brilliant golden cascade of light (Fig. 108).[10] Her feet are cushioned by pillowy clouds, her levitation accompanied by some of the most beautiful putti in the history of art, which must have been modelled on direct study of infants and children. Three of these figures support the cloud on its upward voyage, the chubby leg of one almost touches the head of an apostle, infiltrating the world of the living and disrupting too strict a division between supernatural and earthly spheres. Other putti playfully herald the Virgin with the playing of flutes and a tambourine, pointing to her presence and to that of God the Father above, the embodied throng melting into the transparent, amber-coloured cloud putti who frame the composition at its upper reaches. Titian was one of the first artists to juxtapose these two angelic types, and as Christian K. Kleinbub's study of the Renaissance cloud putto has shown, these figures can tell us much about how artists accommodated the supernatural in naturalistic painting, appearing, as they do, like 'a meteorological event woven within the texture of the physical world'.[11] Bellini had been one of the first to experiment with depicting these nebulous forms in paintings like his

Coronation of the Virgin of c. 1473–76, now in the Museo Civico of Pesaro, and they became sites for artistic experimentation for artists such as Fra Bartolomeo and Raphael, with paintings like the latter's *Sistine Madonna* (c. 1513–14) and the *Madonna di Foligno* (c. 1511–12) demonstrating a deep understanding of the theology of these wispy presences, who, like the formation of clouds, were believed to be rendered material through progressive condensation according to Aquinas, their inclusion serving to encourage the spiritual contemplation of the spectator.[12] In Titian's painting, the meteorological accuracy of the cloud of heaven is also significant and functions as a mechanism for the miraculous revelation, as clouds often do in the Bible.[13] Illuminated by spots of the heavenly light of God's apparition at its billowing heights, engulfed in shadow below as it stretches over the apostles, it works as a bridge between heaven and earth, its very 'realness' enhancing the presumed truth of the episode, an innovation that would appear to have been drawn upon by Lorenzo Lotto in his later altarpiece *Saint Nicholas in Glory* (1527–29) for the nearby Carmelite church of Santa Maria dei Carmini, where the underside of the cloud casts an ominous shadow over the panoramic landscape below, but is immaculately lit by a divine luminescence closest to the ascending Nicholas (Fig. 109).

The pillowy clouds, the embodiment of the angels, the warm golden glow of paradise – all of these elements in Titian's painting worked to make the event depicted seem vibrantly alive, albeit fittingly more gorgeous than reality. Tintoretto, an artist with a talent for dramatising the presence of the sacred, built upon Titian's example in his later *Martyrdom of Saint Paul* (c. 1556) for the church of Madonna dell'Orto by portraying the saint bathed in the rays of golden light that extend from the heavens, much like the glow of the *Assunta* (Fig. 110). Unusually, the emaciated Paul is turned away from the viewer, his face invisible to us. Shown kneeling, he is entranced by the enveloping luminescence that descends from the heavens as his executioner brandishes the sword that is about to deliver the fatal blow to his neck. In Genesis, God creates light and then separates it from the darkness; Christ becomes synonymous with luminance in the Gospels; and the light of the heavens is described throughout the Book of the Apocalypse. Light as theophany, as a mode of encountering the divine, occurs in Augustine's *City of God* and Dante's *Paradiso*, but it was also central to the writings of sixteenth-century Spanish reformers such as Saints Ignatius of Loyola (1491–1556) and Teresa of Ávila (1515–82), as well as the contemporary rise of the devotional practice of the *Quarant'ore*, where the exposed host was theatrically surrounded by a blaze of candles.[14] As pointed out most recently by Martin Kemp in his study of Dante and divine light, in contrast to the austerities of reformers like Calvin, visions of paradise rendered by artists for Catholic audiences became immersively dramatic, particularly in the seventeenth century, beckoning the beholder into their sensuous creations and using 'visual extremes in the service of religious wonder'.[15]

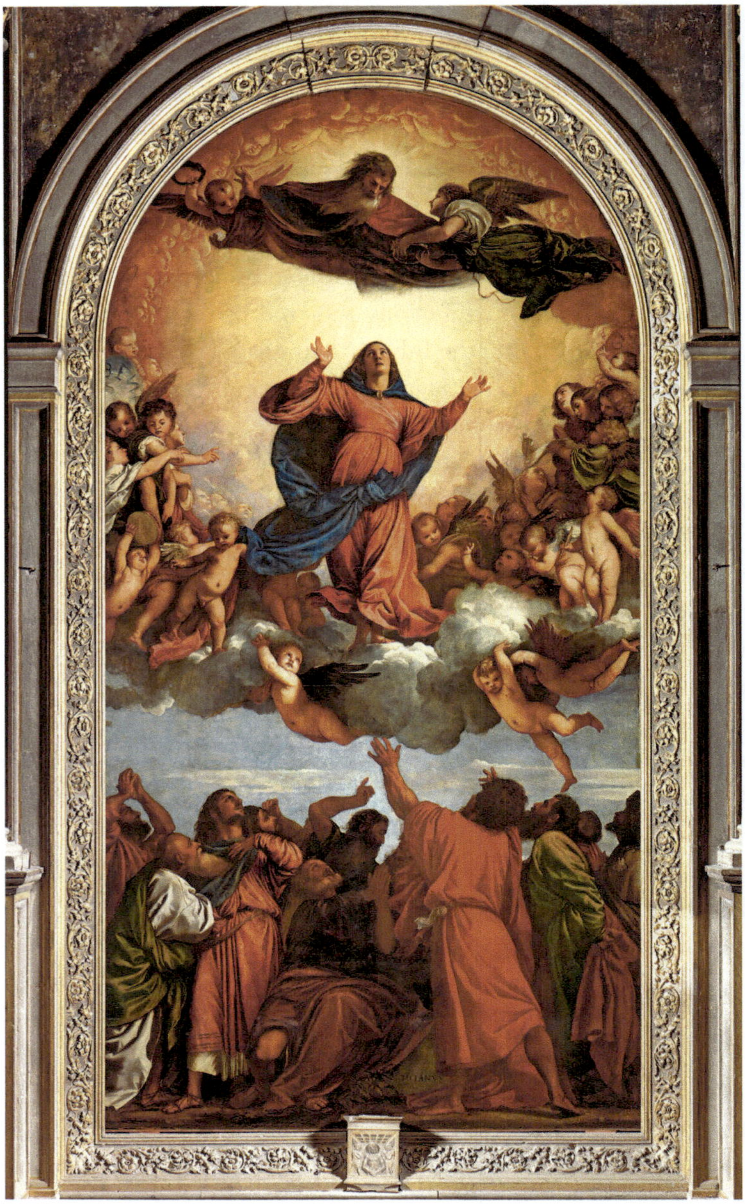

108. Titian, *Assunta,* 1516–18, oil on panel, Santa Maria dei Frari, Venice (Photo: Cameraphoto)

Years after the altarpiece of the *Assunta* had been completed and two years before Tintoretto's Madonna dell'Orto painting, Titian did exactly this: depicting the majesty of the heaven *sotto in sù* in a painting for the Hapsburg Emperor Charles V: the *Gloria* of 1551–54 (Fig. 111).[16] The painting was a deeply important one for Charles. It expressed his hopes for the salvation of his soul and those of his kin; it demonstrated his fidelity to the fundamentals of

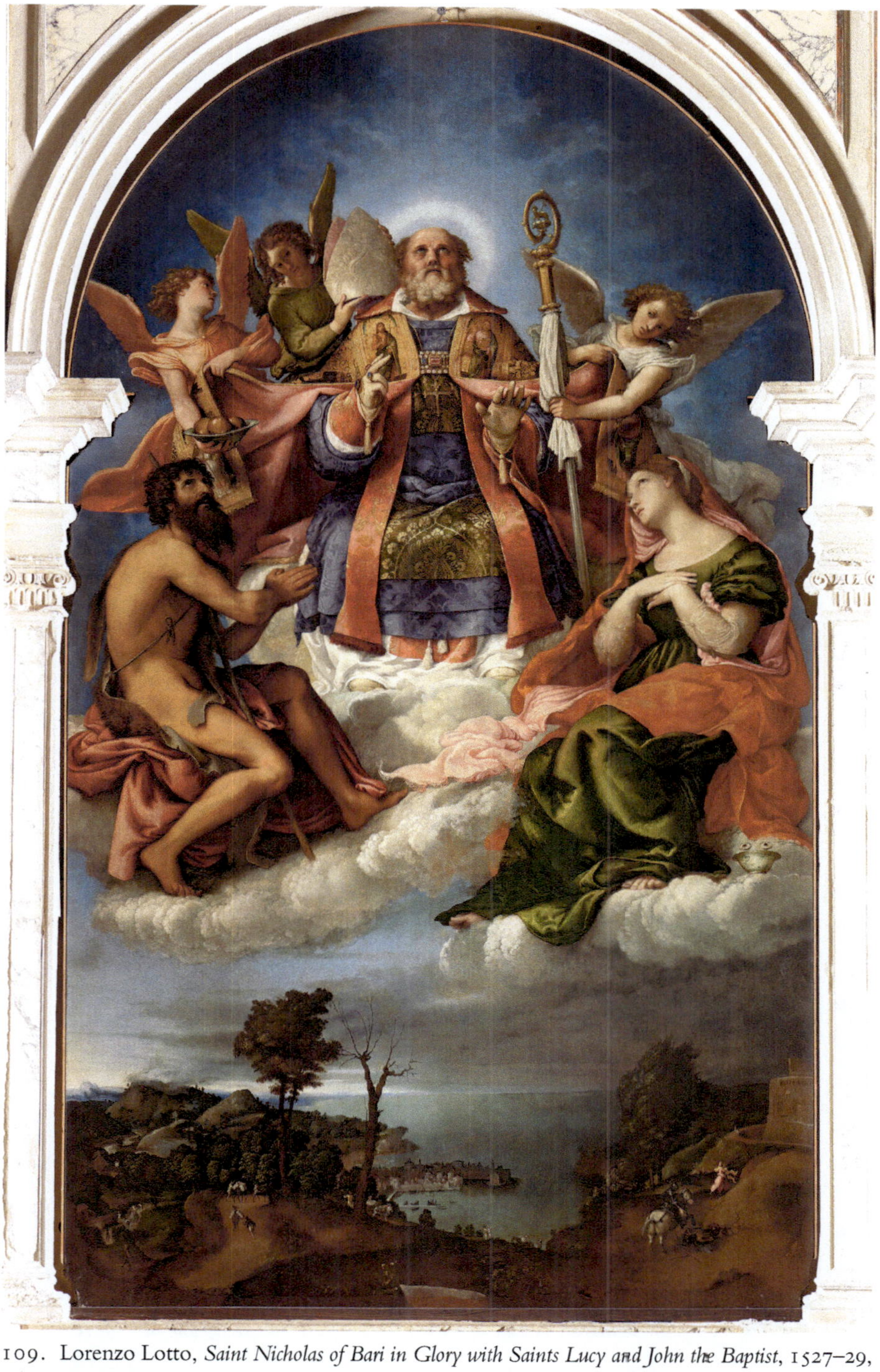

109. Lorenzo Lotto, *Saint Nicholas of Bari in Glory with Saints Lucy and John the Baptist*, 1527–29, oil on canvas, Santa Maria dei Carmine, Venice (Photo: Cameraphoto)

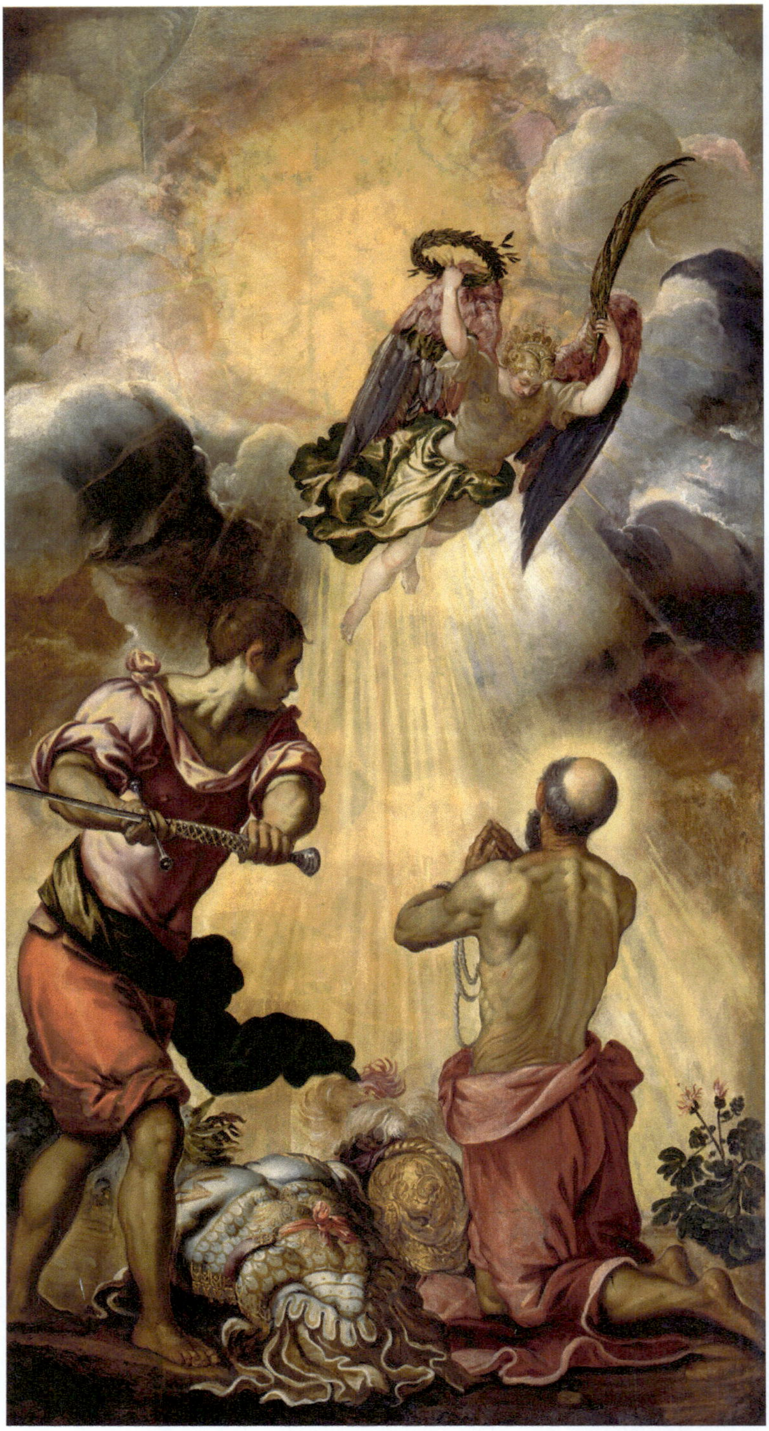

110. Jacopo Tintoretto, *The Martyrdom of Saint Paul,* c. 1556, oil on canvas, Madonna dell'Orto, Venice (Photo: Cameraphoto)

Catholic belief; and it was valued for its authorship by Titian, who was the emperor's favourite painter. The unusual iconography was even said to have been dictated to the artist by Charles himself, according to Vasari.[17] After he abdicated in 1556 the painting accompanied Charles to the Hieronymite monastery of Yuste in Extremadura, where he arrived on 3 February 1557, dying a year later in 1558. In the codicil to his will Charles requested that the painting was to reside in the same place as his body after his death.[18] Charles's son, Philip II, was left to decide his father's final resting place, but in the event that the corpse remained at Yuste then Philip had been requested to ensure that a 'retablo of alabaster or marble' was commissioned, with portraits of his family as 'as they appear in the painting by Titian called *The Last Judgment*'. This was never to be: the painting left Yuste and was moved to the Escorial in 1574, but Charles's dying wish further evinced his special affection for Titian's masterpiece.[19]

Linking the two themes of heaven and death – the heaven depicted by Titian in the *Gloria* and the closeness of the image to Charles during the last days of his life – the emperor's 'model death' was spent contemplating his impending demise in a manner that would later be emulated by Philip, who spent his final days at the Escorial with his own coffin at the bedside, his chamber abundantly covered with devotional images and crucifixes.[20] For both father and son, sacred paintings were an important element in a virtuous death, being a focus for contemplation, providing solace, and in the case of the *Gloria* perhaps even moving the King to order the extirpation of heresy with greater force, testament to its significant influence over him and in turn to the powers of its creator.[21] Referred to in contemporary documents as variously a *Last Judgment* or *Trinity* – the former title only making sense if the painting is interpreted as a specific vision of the Elect[22] and the latter inadequately reflecting only the presence of the Father, Son, and Holy Spirit in the heavens – in the painting we see God the Father and Son garbed in cornflower blue on either side of the dove of the Holy Spirit.[23] They are borne aloft by a cloud, surrounded by cherubim and suffused in the ethereal yellow radiance of paradise that cracks through the underside of the cloud in splintered rays. To the left, slightly below the central trio, the mediatrix Madonna turns to look back at the airborne Old Testament prophets and saints who strain towards the heavens, brandishing their attributes. To the right, Charles and members of his family are seen dressed in penitential white and bereft of their finery, save for the imperial crown planted at the emperor's knees. Accompanied by a host of angels, some of whom assist them in their devotions, the painting depicts the journey from earth to the heavens, or from this life to the next. In the landscape at the bottom of the painting a group of pilgrims witness the wondrous spectacle, and above them the majestic form of Moses reclines himself along the cloud. Like the putto in the *Assunta* his leg swings down into the realm of the mortals as he rides into the heavens, the saints and prophets appearing marvellously varied in terms of their dimensions, becoming smaller as they ascend into paradise and disappear from our world into the next, and larger in the immediate foreground, the monumental Old Testament figures here connecting the earthly world below with the heavenly one above.

In the *Gloria* heaven is imagined by Titian as a realm of colour and light, the powdery blues, peaches, and violets of the skies and clouds dissolving into the progressive luminescent clarity of the heavens, reaching a crescendo around the Holy Spirit, framed by the pellucid glass orbs held by God the Father and Son. We know that Charles contemplated the painting in the final stages of his life, requesting on 31 August 1558 to see three different images (the first being a portrait of the deceased Empress Isabella, the second an agony in the garden), just a few weeks prior to his eventual death at the age of fifty-eight on 21 September. The *Gloria* was the last of the trio and the one that had the most dramatic impact on the king. Whilst gazing upon it, he apparently turned to his physician to explain that he suddenly felt ill, 'with his whole body shaking'. Fray Hernando del Corral, an eyewitness to the event, interpreted Charles's impulsive request as stemming from a premonition of his imminent death. The next day the emperor then fell into a deep fever and when he had partially recovered on 9 September he had the codicil to his will executed, adding an instruction to Philip to deal with heresy firmly, summarising the instruction in the sidebar as 'Lutherans are to be punished harshly.'[24] If we link these two events of beholding the painting and writing the codicil, then rather than assuaging Charles's doubts about his salvation, the painting propelled him to ever harsher action against his religious foes. In his abdication speech of 26 October 1555 in Brussels he had described how his prerogative as holder of the imperial crown had been to bring 'peace among the Christian peoples' and to defend 'the Catholic faith against the Ottomans'. Yet of his 'great hopes', few had been fulfilled and those at 'great cost'. Thus, his decisions taken as a ruler over vast swathes of the globe weighed heavily upon his conscience and were the catalyst for his decision to live out the remainder of his days in secluded spiritual retirement where he could atone for his sins and adequately prepare for his death, 'fearing God and desirous of his own salvation', as Vasari put it.[25]

Titian's *Gloria* was thus intimately connected to the private spiritual life of its first owner. Even if Charles is shown in the company of the saints and prophets in Titian's painting, he and his family actively pray and supplicate for entry into paradise. They are close to heaven, but their salvation appears not yet assured.[26] That this was Charles's own interpretation of the scene would appear to be confirmed by his use of the term 'Last Judgment' when he asked to gaze upon the painting in the weeks before his death. Much ink has been spilled over the 'correct' title, but the truth is that none of the proposals of *Last Judgment*, *Trinity*, *Gloria*, or *Paradiso* (which is how Ridolfi named it) completely accounts for what we behold or can resolve about all the unusual elements in the iconography.[27]

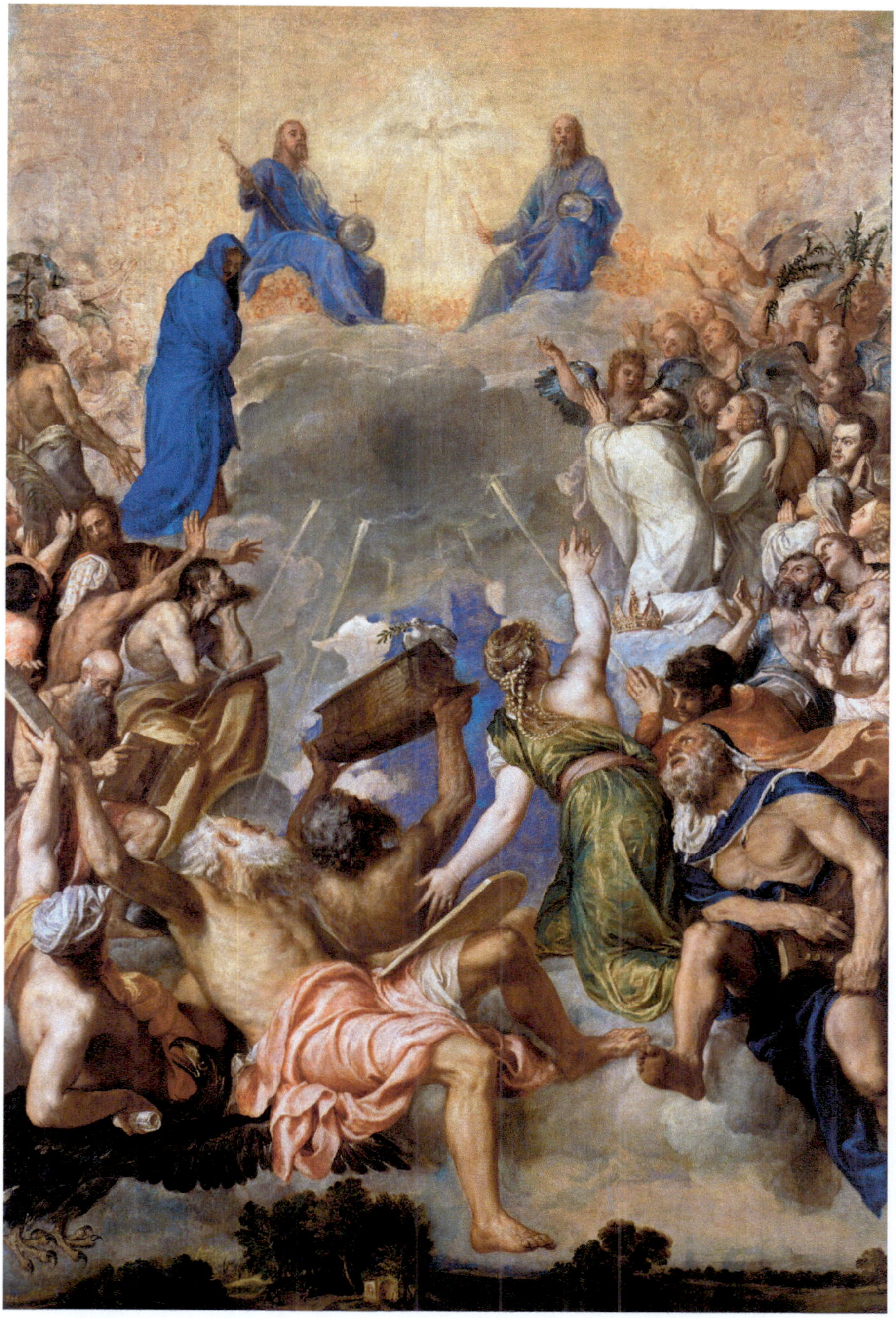

111. Titian, *The Gloria,* 1551–54, oil on canvas, Museo del Prado, Madrid (Photo: Bridgeman Images)

Indeed, Titian himself referred to the image alternately as a *Trinity* or *Paradiso*.[28] In 1556 it was transformed into an engraving by Cornelis Court (c. 1533–78), with whom the artist collaborated closely (Fig. 112).[29] In this medium both the outline of the mandorla encircling the Holy Spirit and the rays of light that it

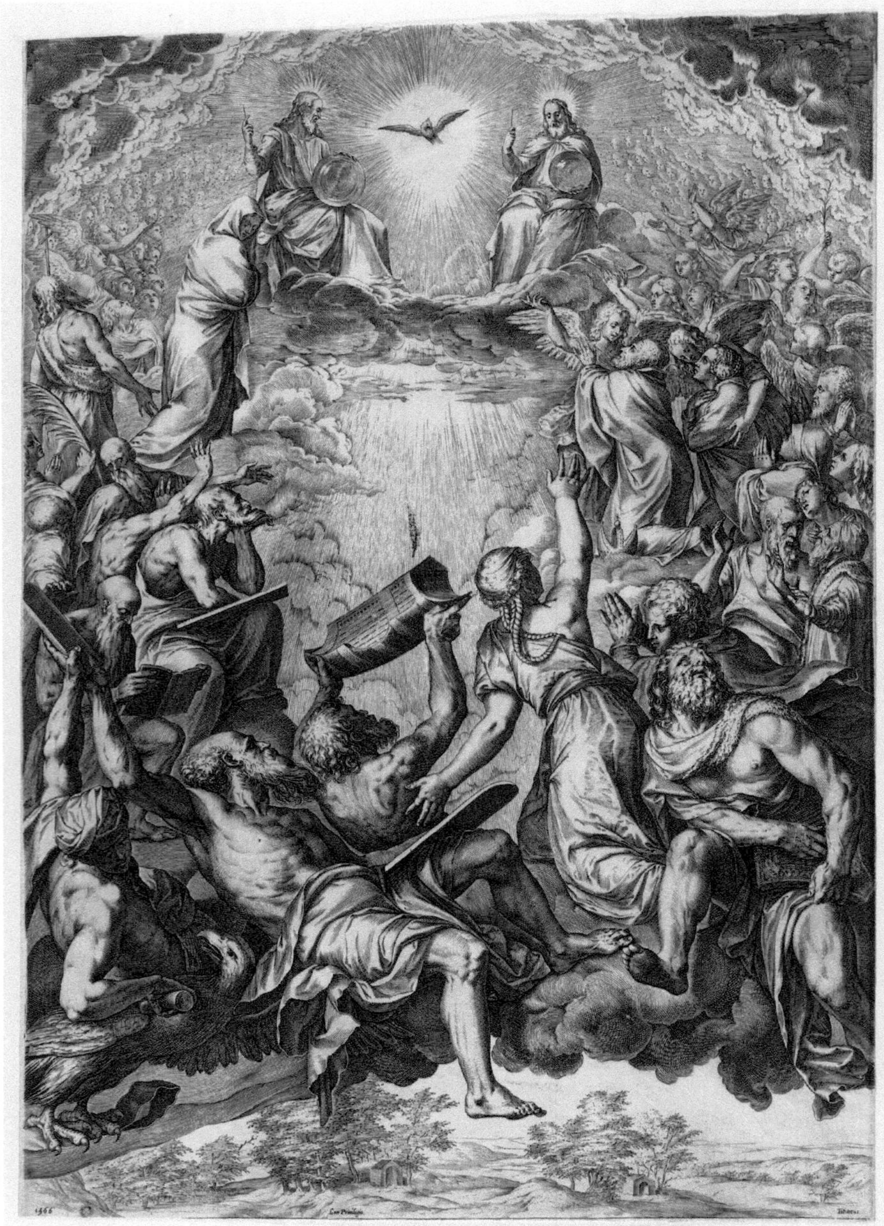

112. Cornelis Court, *The Gloria,* 1556, engraving, Metropolitan Museum of Art, New York (Photo: Open Access)

emits are understandably more defined that the melting brushwork used on the canvas. Put to brilliant effect by Raphael in the *Disputation of the Sacrament* in the early years of the century (Fig. 66) where the holy spirit appears in a perfectly defined circle of golden light above the monstrance containing the communion host, in Venice this light was shown cascading in shimmering, melting filaments upon the figures below, beautifully deployed by Titian's pupil, the Paduan painter Damiano Mazza (c. 1550–76) for the *Coronation of the Virgin* of c. 1575 for Santa Maria dei Derelitti in Venice (Fig. 113), and again at the centre of the mosaic of *Paradise* in the basilica of San Marco, completed between 1628 and 1631 (Fig. 114). The golden tesserae of mosaics are well suited to the depiction of divine light, and we can imagine that they first inspired Titian's vision of heaven for the *Assunta*. In turn, the later *Paradise* mosaic designed by Girolamo Pilotti may even have taken its cue from elements of the *Gloria* composition since it shows God the Father and Son armed with sceptres and the *globus cruciger* on either side of a mandorla from which the Holy Spirit appears, shown emitting a brilliant white light and surrounded by a host of cloud putti and embodied cherubs, whose presence recalls the *Assunta*.[30]

Writing about the *Assunta*, Charles Hope observed that it was one 'of those rare masterpieces that transcend conventional stylistic categories, having less in common with the art of Titian's own time than with that of the Baroque'.[31] Even though Hope was referring to the overall appearance of the altarpiece, rather than to the depiction of the light of the heavens specifically, his comment seems astute if we consider Gian Lorenzo Bernini's creation of one of the canonical achievements of the Baroque: his sunburst motif in the apse of Saint Peter's basilica in Rome. Redolent of the realm of the Holy Spirit reproduced both in Court's print and in the ducal basilica and closely associated with the Counter-Reformation Church, above the *cathedra Petri* gilded stucco angels are buoyed by clouds, and shards of light rendered from painted wood extend from around the amber glass with the dove at its centre in an explosion of radiance (Fig. 115).[32] If it was Bernini who initiated the motif of the Baroque glory, that Venetian artists proved of significance in this regard should not come as a surprise, since the splendour of the basilica of San Marco in Venice, sheathed in gold tesserae and marbles, was evocative of paradise itself, enveloping the visitor in its aureate, otherworldly glow (Fig. 116).[33]

PURGATORY

Images of purgatory aimed to inculcate a sense of both trepidation for the amount of time one might have to spend there and compassion for those souls trapped as its denizens. For the majority of individuals who were neither virtuous enough to enter paradise directly nor evil enough to be consigned to an eternity in hell, life everlasting could only be achieved after time spent in purgatory, where souls were purified in recompense for sins committed during their lifetime.[34] The question of how to reduce the amount of time spent in this intermediate state caused great anxiety for the living from the Middle Ages onwards. As Eamon Duffy observed, 'Purgatory, rather than Hell became the focus of Christian fear.'[35] Prayers and suffrages were

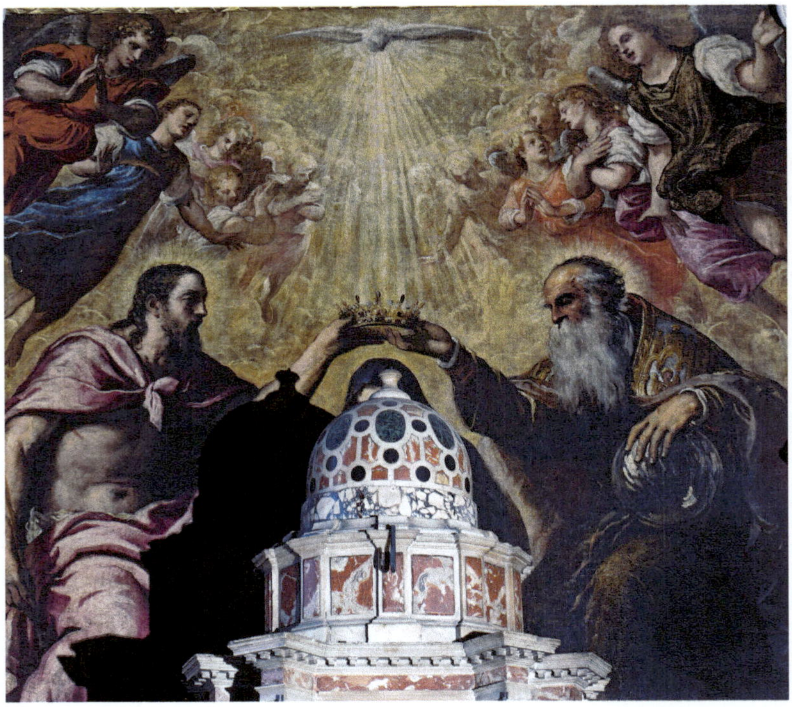

113. Damiano Mazza, *Coronation of the Virgin,* c. 1575, oil on canvas, Santa Maria dei Derelitti, Venice (Photo: by kind permission of I.P.A.V: Istituzione Pubbliche di Assistenza Veneziane)

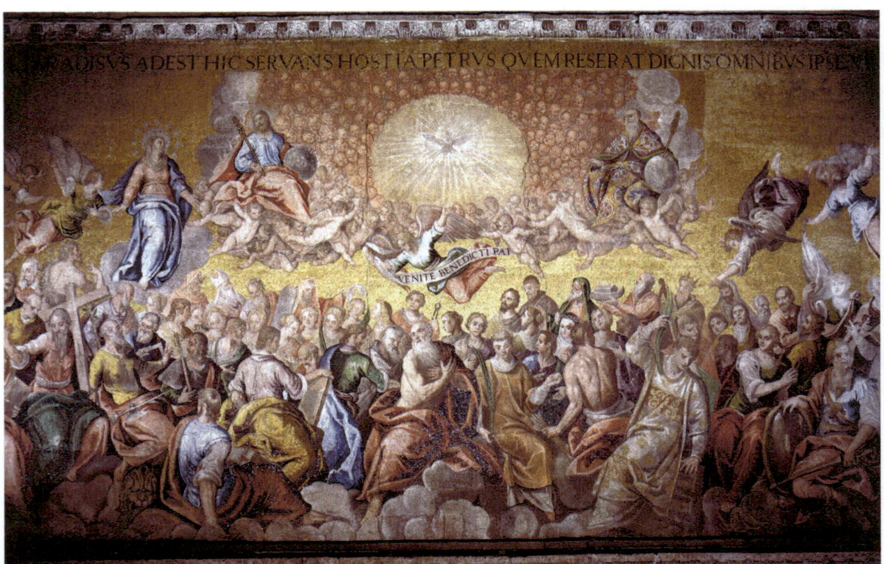

114. Cartoon by Girolamo Pilotti, execution by Luigi Gaetano and Giacomo Pasterini, *Paradise,* 1628–31, mosaic, Basilica di San Marco, Venice (Photo: Archivio Fotografico della Procuratoria di San Marco/by kind permission of the Procuratoria di San Marco)

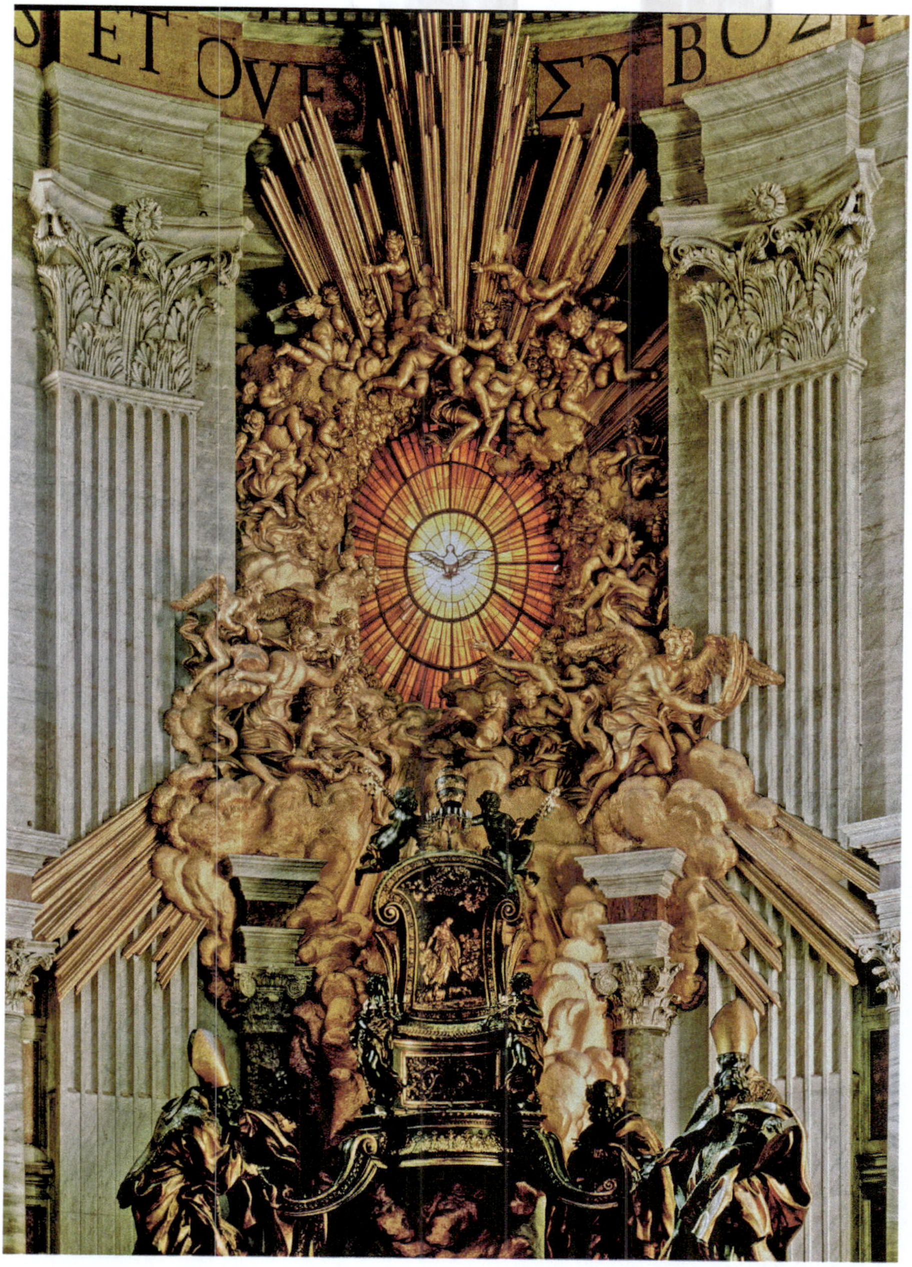

115. Gianlorenzo Bernini, *The Throne of Saint Peter,* 1657–66, Saint Peter's Basilica, Vatican City (Photo: Bridgeman Images)

of paramount importance in hastening the passage of the soul into heaven, and many resorted to the acquisition of indulgences or bequeathed considerable sums in their wills for vast quantities of requiem masses. Thus, the living were intrinsically linked to the fate of the departed. Like the destitute, the dead were dependent on charity, and it was the supplications of mortals on

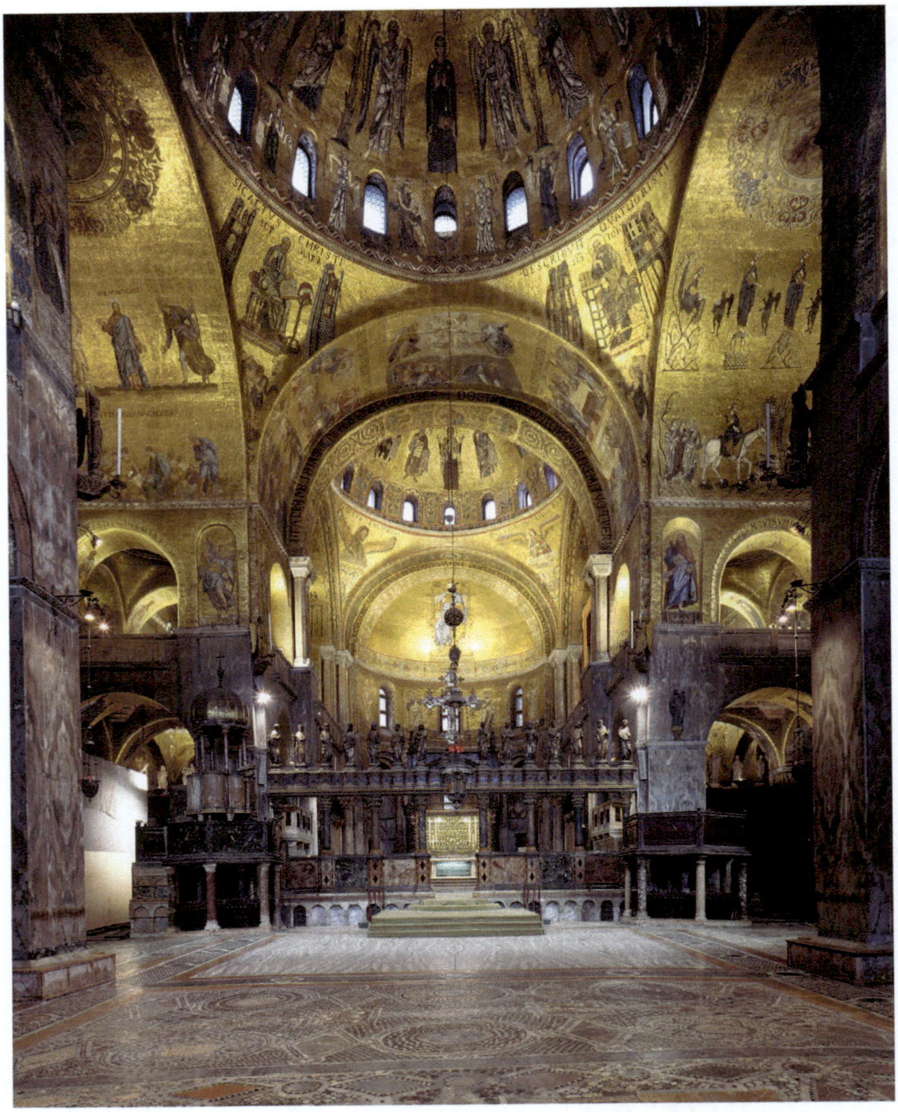

116. Interior of the Basilica of San Marco, Venice (Photo: Cameraphoto)

earth that were believed to have a tangible effect on reducing their torments in the afterlife.

Protestant Reformers rejected the dogma of purgatory and found it repellent that the sale of some indulgences detailed the precise amount of time (sometimes down to the minute) that the buyer could shave off their allotted time there. Two of the interrelated issues that sparked the Reformations, purgatory and indulgences, were consigned to short statements on their efficacy by the Catholic Church in the very final session of the Council of Trent.[36] The wills of some of the procurators of Saint Mark's basilica demonstrate an increase in requests for masses for the repose of their souls from hundreds to thousands over the course of the Seicento in the aftermath of Trent, the late sixteenth and seventeenth centuries being a golden age of purgatory, with mass requests booming and the proliferation of new confraternities dedicated to the dogma.[37] Not only were masses offered for one's own soul as well as those of one's relatives of importance, but the broader community was implicated in the fate of the dead, as concern grew for those lonely souls in purgatory without anyone on earth to pray for them. This led to the foundation of confraternities dedicated to assisting both the souls of the departed *confratelli* and those unfortunate souls who 'are without any particular help, as if forgotten by relatives, and by friends', in the words of the Scuola della Santissima Madonna del Suffragio dei Morti in Venice.[38] More broadly, the preoccupation with purgatory can be understood as developing out of a culture that believed preparing for an honourable death and providing spiritual succour to those about to die was an efficacious act of charity capable of saving countless souls. Bernini, for example, was an attendee for forty years at the confraternity of the Bona Hors at the Gesù in Rome, instigated to prepare its members for their demise, something that the artist himself assiduously planned for.[39] Indeed, Christopher Black argued that by the Ottocento the preoccupation of devotional societies with the afterlife seems to be of greater note than their traditional interest in philanthropy.[40]

PALMA IL GIOVANE AT THE SCUOLA DI SAN FANTIN

Prior to the late Cinquecento, purgatory was depicted sporadically, sometimes on tympanums over church entrances or in breviaries where the suffering were shown being pulled out of the flames by angels.[41] It was not until the late sixteenth century that it began to be widely found in Italian altarpieces, and between 1600 and 1603 Palma il Giovane completed an unusually extensive cycle of paintings on the theme for the ceiling of the ground floor of the meeting house of the Scuola di Santa Maria della Giustizia e San Girolamo, otherwise known by its sobriquet of San Fantin, now home to the Ateneo Veneto (Fig. 117).[42] In the *Divine Comedy*, Dante had imagined purgatory as a place of moral transformation, a route to the light of heaven that was distinct from hell, which was instead situated in the interior of the earth below. Artists drew upon infernal iconography to visualise the discomforts of purgatory, which meant there was often little to distinguish the purgatorial flames from those of damnation, even if for those granted access to heaven's antechamber the promise of salvation was secured.[43] Given the extent to which purgatory loomed large in lay consciousness before the Reformations, the relative dearth of representations prior to this point is significant and difficult to explain. Philippe Ariès opined that the later explosion in purgatorial images might

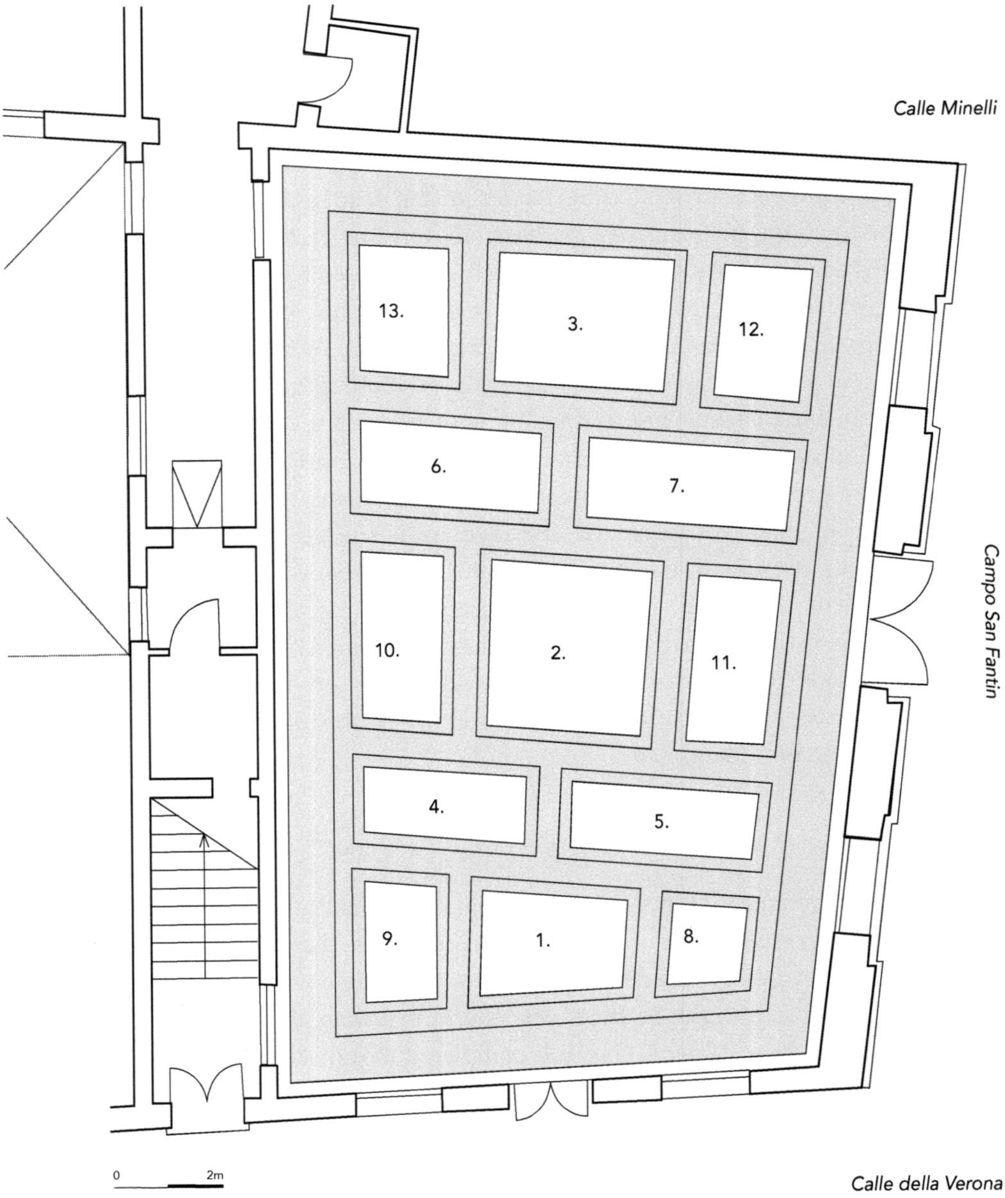

Aula Magna (Church of the Scuola)

Ceiling plan, Ground Floor

1 – Alms given to the Poor for the Souls of the Defunct, 2 – Pope Pius V distributing Indulgences,
3 – Mass in Intercession for the Souls in Purgatory, 4 – Souls Immersed in the Fires of Purgatory,
5 – Souls Immersed in the Fires of Purgatory, 6 – Souls Immersed in the Fires of Purgatory,
7 – Souls Immersed in the Fires of Purgatory, 8 – Saints Illario and Anselm,
9 – Saints Bede and Bernard, 10 – Saints Ambrose and Augustine, 11 – Saints Jerome and Gregory,
12 – Sains Athanasius and Basil,13 – Saints John Chrysostom and Gregory Nazianzus

117. Ceiling plan, Aula Magna, Ateneo Veneto, Venice (Plan: Sebastiano Giannesini)

have been the result of two phenomena: a change in outlook that saw purgatory less as an interim inferno inhabited by a few sinners saved *in extremis* than as an antechamber through which almost everyone (with the exception of canonised saints) would eventually have to pass, as well as more pronounced emphasis on a dialogue between the living and the dead through the offering of masses, ones believed to have the power to deliver contingents of souls into heaven.[44] It would also appear that the disputes of the Reformations and the Tridentine decrees played a pivotal role in stimulating the diffusion of the iconography (a motivation not considered by Ariès). Pope Leo X (r. 1513–21) defended purgatory against Luther's teachings in the 1520 bull *Exsurge domine*, and the Council of Trent was the third time in the Church's history that the dogma had been asserted, the first being at the Second Council of Lyon in 1274 and the second at the Council of Florence (1438–55). Moreover, the growth of confraternities dedicated to the dead and the papal approval given to them through the conferral of generous indulgences spurred on devotion for the purgatorial souls, as did the activities of religious orders associated with Catholic Reform. This ensured that there was an increased requirement for altarpieces and images of purgatory for the altars, oratories, and meeting houses of these associations from the end of the century onwards.

At the time of its completion, the thirteen paintings of Palma's ceiling at San Fantin constituted one of the most extensive cycles of the dogma in existence, even if the iconography of souls being liberated from the purgatorial fire by angels, the Virgin Mary, and various saints was by this point established.[45] As a whole, the embellishment of the Scuola in the Cinquecento reflected the twin dedications of the confraternity to the Virgin Mary and Saint Jerome, as well as the aims and practices of the confraternity, which was to offer comfort to the condemned, and prayers, good works, and masses for the souls in purgatory.[46] Such brotherhoods were founded from the mid-fourteenth century onwards in Italy, and they refined themselves in the fifteenth century when the oratory of San Giovanni Decollato o dei Fiorentini was founded in Rome (1488) and the two Scuole of Santa Maria della Giustizia (o della Consolazione) and San Girolamo in Venice were merged (in 1458) into one single confraternity.[47] The institutions of the two cities were eventually twinned in the year 1613, meaning that those associated with the Venetian fraternity of San Fantin could benefit from the indulgences that had been granted to the Roman institute by Pope Paul V in 1608.[48] A larger edifice for the confraternity was constructed after a fire in 1562, which was considerably expanded first in 1580 and again in 1664.[49] The confraternity's *mariegola* reports that the new expenditures on the ceiling decoration were necessary to complement 'the most miraculous Christ for which the devotions of the faithful grow daily'.[50] No written records of miracles worked by the wooden crucifix once displayed on the altar of the cross at the Scuola are recorded, but as noted by Meryl Bailey, areas of the object are overlain with an accretion of silver plaques that provide a visual record of grace received.[51] At the beginning of the seventeenth century Stringa recorded the great expense made to perfect the interior and exterior of the site and its popularity with the laity. He described how there was 'a great crowd at the oratory every Friday' (when it was opened for longer to the public) and that the site was particularly popular with women, who out of devotion had 'many masses said to obtain grace'.[52] The successive conferral of indulgences upon the confraternity would also have helped to make membership an attractive option, and in 1687 San Fantin was elevated to the status of a Scuola Grande. Unlike the hierarchical distinctions rife in the city's older Scuole Grandi, an entry of 12 March 1658 in the San Fantin *mariegola* certified that no divisions on the basis of age or sex between members were to be made. In theory, at least, the members were '*fratelli tutti*' and as such 'received that charity which will be voluntarily given'.[53]

The decoration of the Scuola di San Fantin was ranged over two floors, and the confraternity proved to be a formidable patron of the arts, being home to works by Titian, Tintoretto, and the workshop of Veronese, in addition to the later paintings of Palma.[54] The ground floor was the site of the confraternity's oratory, where Palma's purgatorial ceiling works were complemented on the walls below by Leonardo Corona's paintings of Christ's Passion.[55] There were also two altars dedicated to the Cross and Saint Jerome that were designed and decorated with bronze and marble sculptures by the hand of Alessandro Vittoria.[56] On the first floor of the Scuola was the confraternity boardroom (the *albergo grande*), home to Tintoretto's much admired altarpiece *The Apparition of the Virgin to Saint Jerome* (c. 1580).[57] Palma worked on the first floor of the confraternity building before he produced the ceiling paintings for the oratory below, embellishing the walls with eight canvases depicting episodes from Jerome's hagiography in the early 1590s, the cycle thus forming one of the most extensive dedicated to the saint in Italy.[58] Prior to this, Palma had already adorned the ceiling of the space with his spectacular *Assumption of the Virgin*. Palma was labouring on this huge painting when it was first noted by Borghini, who mentioned the 'paradise full of angels and other figures'.[59] Dated to c. 1582, the work was lost after it was removed and sold off in 1826, but we can gain some idea of its appearance from the oil sketch that survives in the collection of the Querini Stampalia (Fig. 118).[60] Although they are not possible to individuate with certainty from the *modello*, Ridolfi first detailed how the ceiling featured portraits of Titian, Vittoria, and Francesco Tedaldo, the Guardian Grande of the confraternity, who was, like Vittoria, a close friend of Palma. Painting oneself assured of a place in heaven may have been far too presumptuous for display in a church, but it seems to have been acceptable for the confines of the confraternity building. According to Ridolfi, in amongst the clouds populated by the Elect were also musician

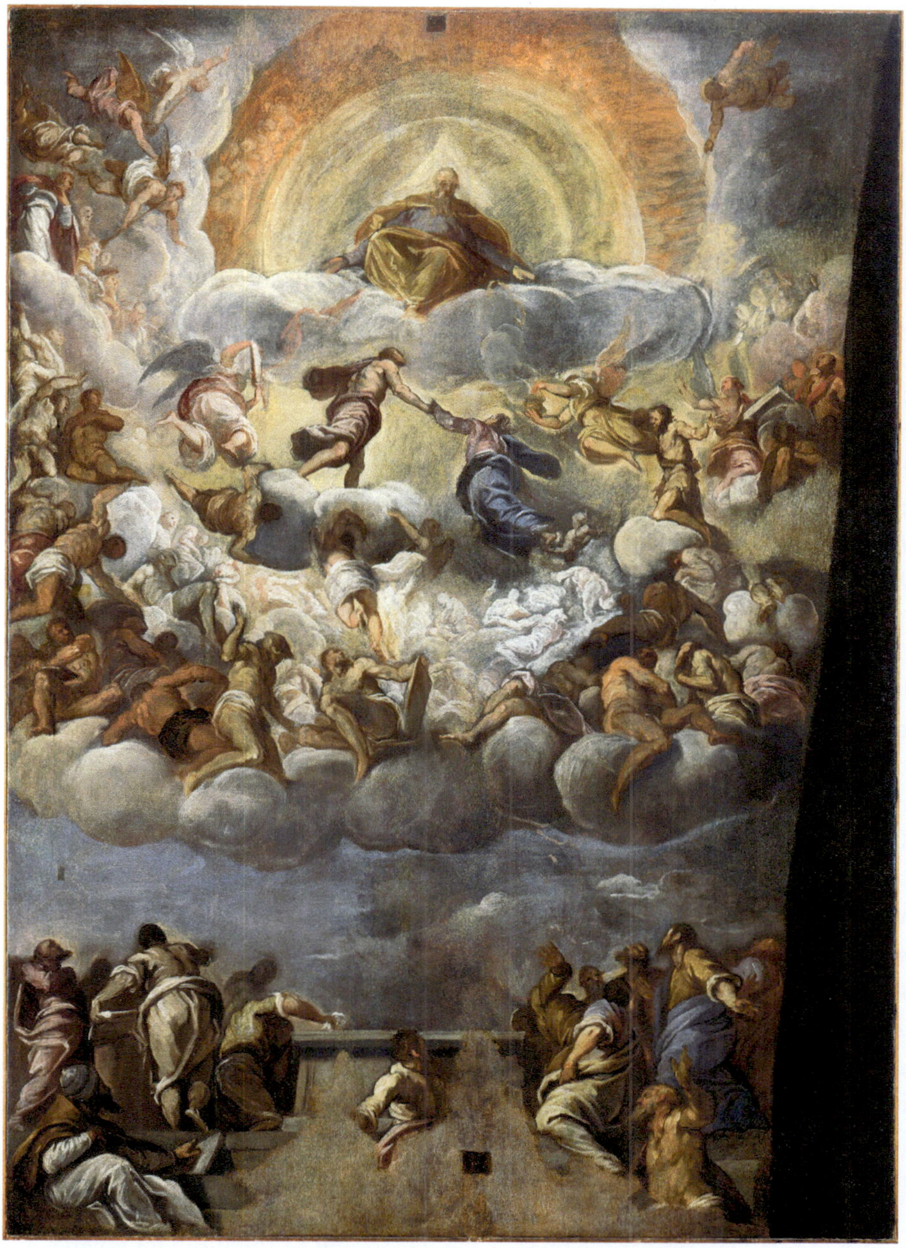

118. Palma il Giovane, *The Assumption,* c. 1582, oil sketch, Querini Stampalia Foundation Museum, Venice (Photo: Cameraphoto)

friends of the artist, as well as a portrait of Palma himself, accompanied by his consort, Andriana Palma.[61] The presence of Titian can be explained by Palma's ardent admiration for him, as well as announcing his indebtedness to the recently deceased king of Venetian painting, especially considering the subject of the ceiling and the inevitable comparison that could have been made to the Frari altarpiece.

Returning to Palma's ceiling cycle for the ground floor of San Fantin, this was the first of its kind in Venice, visualising something unseen but avidly believed in by early modern Catholics: that the world of the dead was shaped by the actions of the living.[62] It replaced an earlier ceiling decorated by Tintoretto, the subject of which is unknown.[63] The lower section of the *Baptism of Christ* by Battista Franco of c. 1552–54, mentioned in Chapter 1, has been identified as an early scene of purgatory in a Venetian altarpiece, but such an identification would inadequately account for the presence of devils in the vignette. Recently, scholars have convincingly demonstrated that it in fact depicts the resurrection of the dead, which makes the novel subject matter of Palma's purgatorial cycle all the more significant.[64] The iconography emphasised the trilogy of methods that the Catholic Church held necessary for salvation and the expiation of sin: prayer, masses, and good works. The three central paintings are the *Alms Given to the Poor for the Souls of the Defunct*, *Pope Pius V Distributing Indulgences*, and the *Mass in Intercession for the Souls in Purgatory* (Figs. 119–121). In each of these, at the same time as the charitable act is enacted on earth, angels are shown liberating suffering souls in purgatory, who then fly towards paradise. At the moment money is given to the lame man, as the pope confers rosaries and a scapular to the faithful, and as the priest raises the chalice during the mass and the altar boy rings the bell, a mystical event is shown being activated in the afterlife. They are complemented by a further six canvases depicting twelve saints and Doctors of the Church (Latin and Eastern) whose writings helped to define purgatorial dogma, all of whom were mentioned in Roberto Bellarmino's influential writings of 1588 on the theme.[65] A series of smaller canvases illustrate the souls of men and women enveloped by the purgatorial flames, reflecting an iconography that was already fixed by this point and endlessly repeated in altarpieces and devotional prints throughout the seventeenth and eighteenth centuries (Figs. 122 and 123).[66] The nude bodies writhe amongst the flames, but that this is a purging process rather than a damning one is suggested by the fact that their faces do not evidence signs of agony; in fact, they are for the most part obfuscated or expressionless.

The success of the San Fantin cycle can be gauged by the fact that Palma returned to a very similar schema for the decoration of the Grimani Chapel at the Tolentini just over a decade later, in c. 1615. The ceiling paintings of the *Sacrifice of the Mass for the Defunct*, *The Offering of Alms*, and the *Dispensing of Indulgences* are accompanied by canvases of the four Doctors of the Church, whilst the central altarpiece is *Christ in Glory between the Virgin and Saint Peter with the Souls in Purgatory* (Fig. 124).[67] These souls immersed in smoke and fire are shown being gently assisted by a fleet of liberating angels who guide their attentions to the vision above, as Saint Peter intercedes on their behalf and a mountain of putti who cushion the feet of Christ clamber over one another to

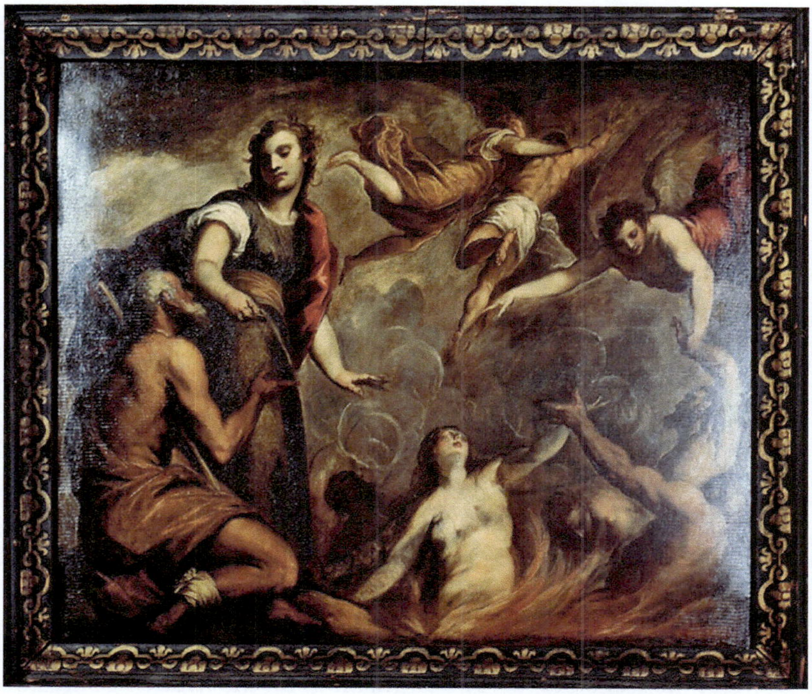

119. Palma il Giovane, *Alms Given to the Poor for the Souls of the Defunct*, c. 1603, oil on canvas, Aula Magna, Ateneo Veneto. Venice (Photo: Ateneo Veneto)

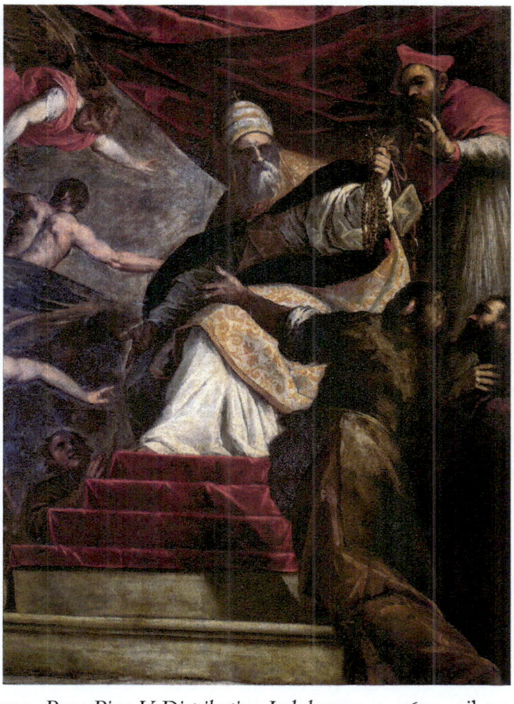

120. Palma il Giovane, *Pope Pius V Distributing Indulgences*, c. 1603, oil on canvas, Aula Magna, Ateneo Veneto, Venice (Photo: Cameraphoto)

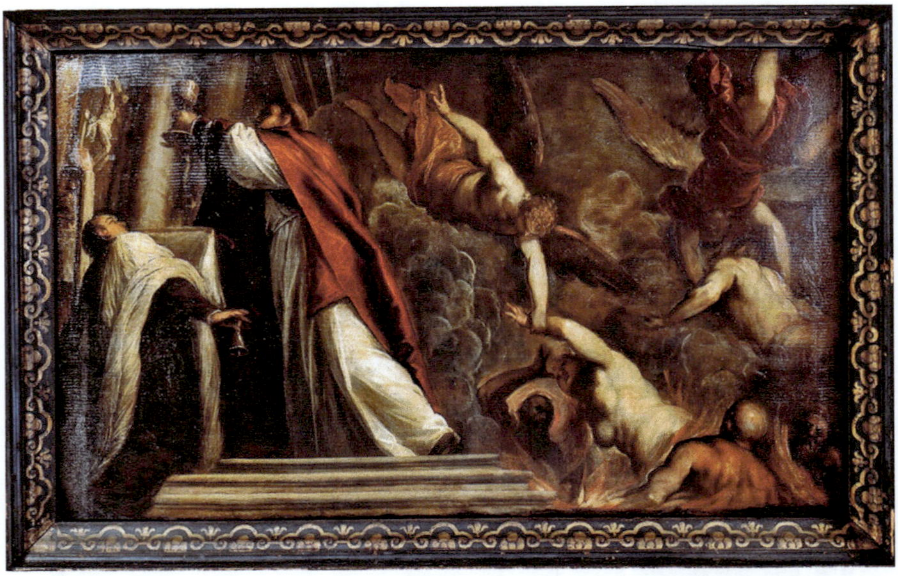

121. Palma il Giovane, *Mass in Intercession for the Souls in Purgatory*, c. 1603, oil on canvas, Aula Magna, Ateneo Veneto, Venice (Photo: Ateneo Veneto)

look down at the scene below. The affirmations on the nature of purgatory at the Tridentine Council had been brief; they never discussed the presence of flames, for example, and it was advised that 'the more difficult and subtle questions [. . .] be excluded from popular discourses before the uneducated multitude'.[68] As Mâle observed, 'it was difficult for art to express such high theology'.[69] Palma's paintings at both San Fantin and the church of the Tolentini thus offered an extensive explication of the doctrine that focused less on providing an imaginative visual excursus on what purgatory was, and more on the means promulgated by the Church in 1563 as efficacious for the salvation of the spectator's soul.

Palma's late mannerist display at San Fantin packed forms together in scenes that were densely populated with figures illuminated by an otherworldly colouring of rich coppers, reds, and ambers. This was complemented by the passion cycle of Corona, where a similar crepuscular palette dominates in his exploration of the dark night of Christ's trials. On the floor above, where Palma's ceiling of the apotheosis of the Virgin into heaven was once placed, darkness transformed itself into light. The brightness of the heavens in Palma's surviving *modello* depicted the world of ecstasy that had been promised to the virtuous, and which the comforters of the condemned were encouraged to focus their attentions upon, likening them to the penitent thief Dismas, who had been crucified at Christ's side and to whom salvation had been assured (Luke 23:43: 'today you shall be with me in paradise'). A scene of the Assumption was fitting given the context. Not only because purgatory was Mary's special realm of influence as *mediatrix*, but because on this feast day it

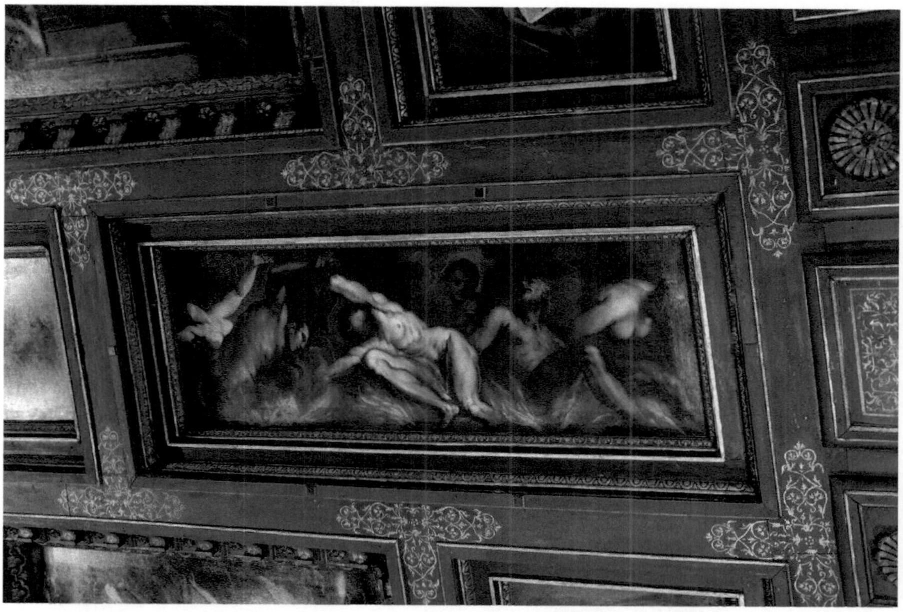

122. Palma il Giovane, *Souls Immersed in the Fires of Purgatory*, c. 1600, oil on canvas, Aula Magna, Ateneo Veneto, Venice (Photo: Ateneo Veneto)

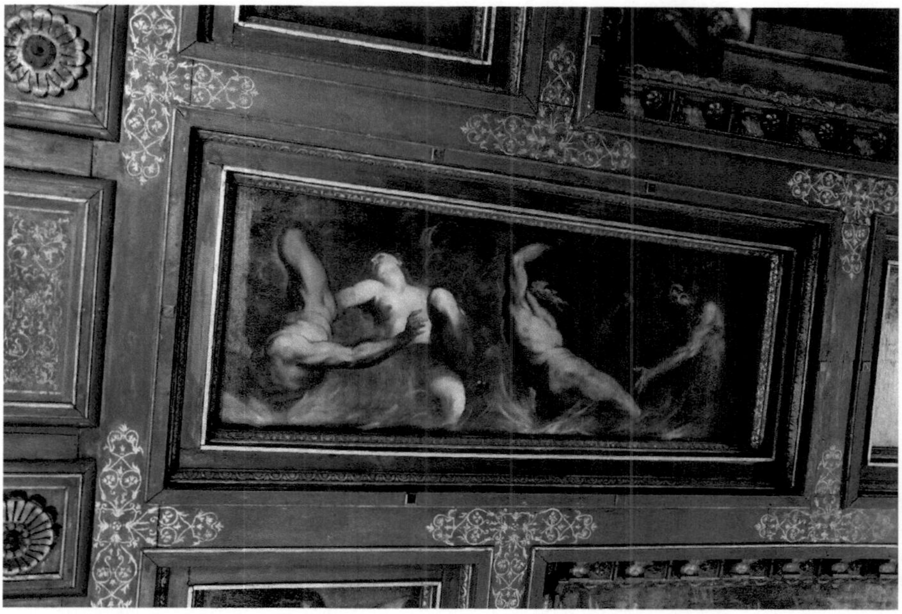

123. Palma il Giovane, *Souls Immersed in the Fires of Purgatory*, c. 1600, oil on canvas, Aula Magna, Ateneo Veneto, Venice (Photo: Ateneo Veneto)

was believed that by her grace souls were received into heaven.[70] The connection between purgatory and the assumption of the Virgin can also be seen in Federico Zuccaro's decoration of the chapel of the Angels at the Gesù in Rome, believed to have been completed in the same year that works began on

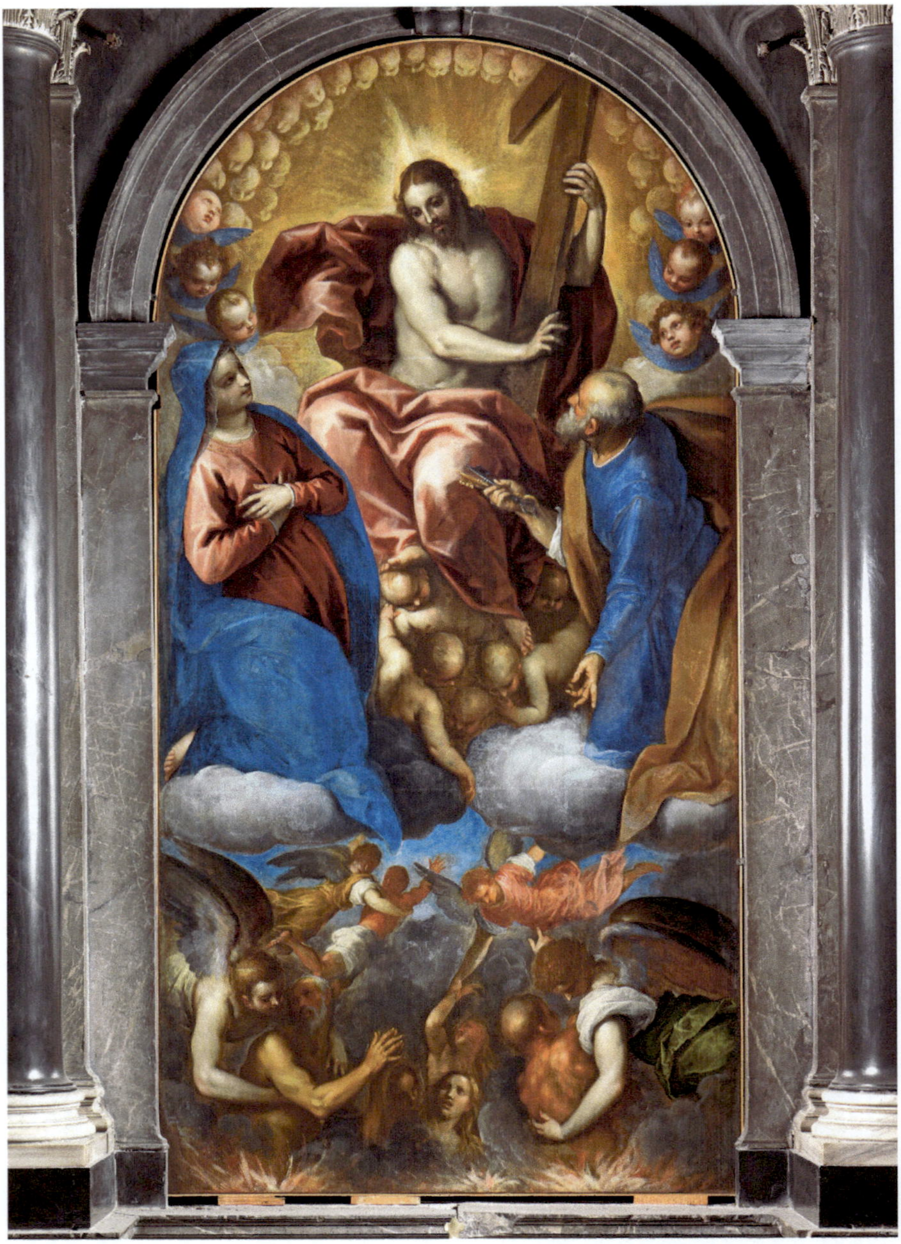

124. Palma il Giovane, *Christ in Glory between the Virgin and Saint Peter with the Souls in Purgatory*, c. 1615, oil on canvas, San Nicola da Tolentino, Venice (Photo: Cameraphoto)

Palma's ceiling at San Fantin.[71] Here the left wall fresco is *Angels Freeing Souls from Purgatory to be Presented in Heaven*, and the vault above shows the heavens opening as Mary is greeted by the Trinity above.

The decorative programme of San Fantin was intertwined with the devotional focus of its members, so the question of access and the use of the space helps us to better understand its embellishment and imagine the responses that it might have been provoked in the beholder. As comforters of criminals condemned to death, one of the duties of members of the Scuola was to accompany and console the *giustiziati* along their passage from the prisons of the Ducal Palace to the site of their execution, then bury their corpses and pray for their souls. They took over the care of the condemned individual in the days leading up to their impending demise (when they were transferred from their cells to the *chiesiola*, or chapel of the prisons) by providing a chaplain to hear their confession and help them best prepare for their miserable fate.[72] In a general way this earthy *via crucis* was reflected in San Fantin's decoration, as was the promise that the *confratelli* repeated to the contrite criminal: that on the day of their death their soul would be saved and that their brothers on earth would be praying for their swift passage from purgatory to heaven. However, there is no evidence to suggest that the condemned were ever taken to the Scuola where they would have witnessed the painting cycles, and their last mass took place in the prison chapel.[73] Nicholas Terpstra observed that hell was never depicted on the *tavolette* (hand-held painted devotional images) used to comfort those sentenced to death, and even purgatory was downplayed in the guides for comforters because the focus of the condemned was to be kept squarely on the heavens.[74] So the decoration of the space was not intended for the prisoners, but was primarily conceived with the gaze of the members (and on the ground floor, that of the wider public) in mind. On the days that an execution was to take place, the *confratelli* gathered in the Scuola and changed into the long black robes and distinctive hood of their office. In the boardroom on the first floor the rules for the accompaniment of the condemned were read aloud and a mass was celebrated at the altar adorned with Tintoretto's *Apparition of the Virgin to Saint Jerome*.[75] Having passed through the oratory below where they would have seen Palma's ceiling and the passion cycle of Corona, the members of the confraternity would have been reminded of the aims and beliefs that underpinned their imminent actions. Like Christ, the condemned was to die a violent death, an act believed to be justified as the righteous retribution for the crimes that he had committed, something that he was urged to accept. Yet in dying the condemned could become Christ-like in his suffering and was offered the possibility of redemption.[76] The execution also provided the members of the confraternity the chance to imitate the faithful followers of Christ who removed his body from the cross, as shown in Corona's *Deposition*, or who prayed and assisted him along his route to Calvary, as Veronica does in Corona's *Way of the Cross*, offering her shroud to Christ as a soldier violently attempts to terminate her compassionate act (Fig. 125).

The encounter with images did not end as the procession left the Scuola di San Fantin. Through the presence of the lay brotherhood, the whole event was powerfully steeped in Christian symbolism and its concomitant material,

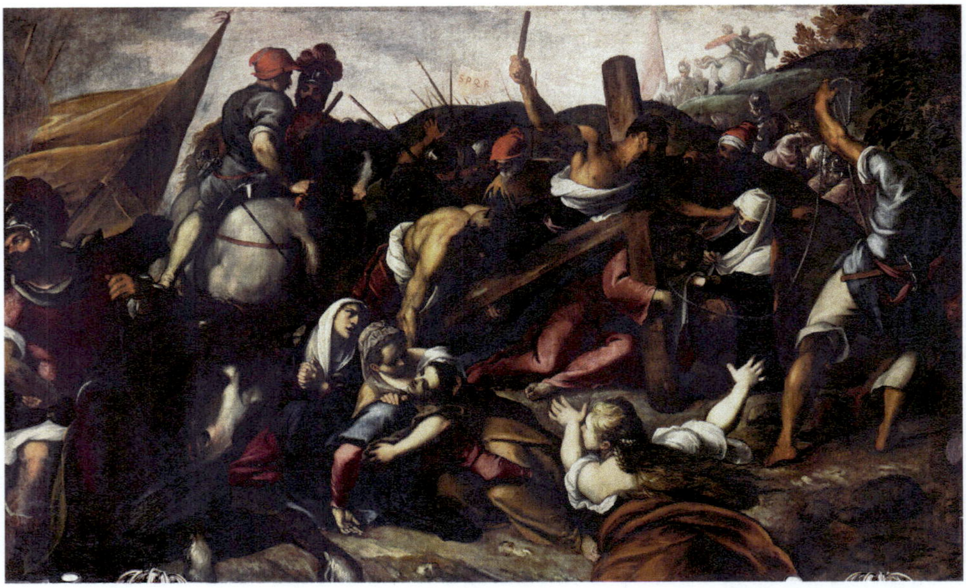

125. Leonardo Corona, *The Way of the Cross*, oil on canvas, c. 1590–96, Aula Magna, Ateneo Veneto, Venice (Photo: Cameraphoto)

sensory, and visual culture in a way that made executions in Italy distinct from those elsewhere in Europe.[77] On the day of such an event a large wooden cross was placed outside the Scuola and the *confratelli* then processed towards the prisons in pairs carrying candles, following the wooden crucifix that was detached from the altar of the cross and carried by the *vicario* (Fig. 126).[78] At the height of this object is the pelican, who rips open her breast to feed her young, symbol of the eucharist and of charity, and one of the emblems of the confraternity.[79] The brotherhood brought with them the objects necessary for the event: holy water, a second smaller crucifix of bronze, the *pazienza* or oval of fabric decorated with an image of the crucifixion to be tied to the body of the condemned, and the *tavolette*, which were to be placed before the eyes of the prisoner at all times as the procedure was enacted.[80] Having reached the prisons after stopping at the two churches of San Geminiano and San Marco, the cloak of the confraternity was placed upon the shoulders of the criminal in the chapel, a speech was made by the Guardian Grande, and the condemned man was officially a member of the Scuola, in a potent gesture of fraternal charity.[81] The procession then accompanied him to the site of his execution, attempting to distract his attention away from the sight of the executioner and the jeering crowd by enveloping his senses with prayers, songs, and images.[82] If the penalty was not of the most serious sort, then this was a short walk to between the two columns of piazza San Marco where the hanging or decapitation took place.[83] The comforter would alight to the executioner's podium and was expected to ensure that the gaze of the condemned could at all times

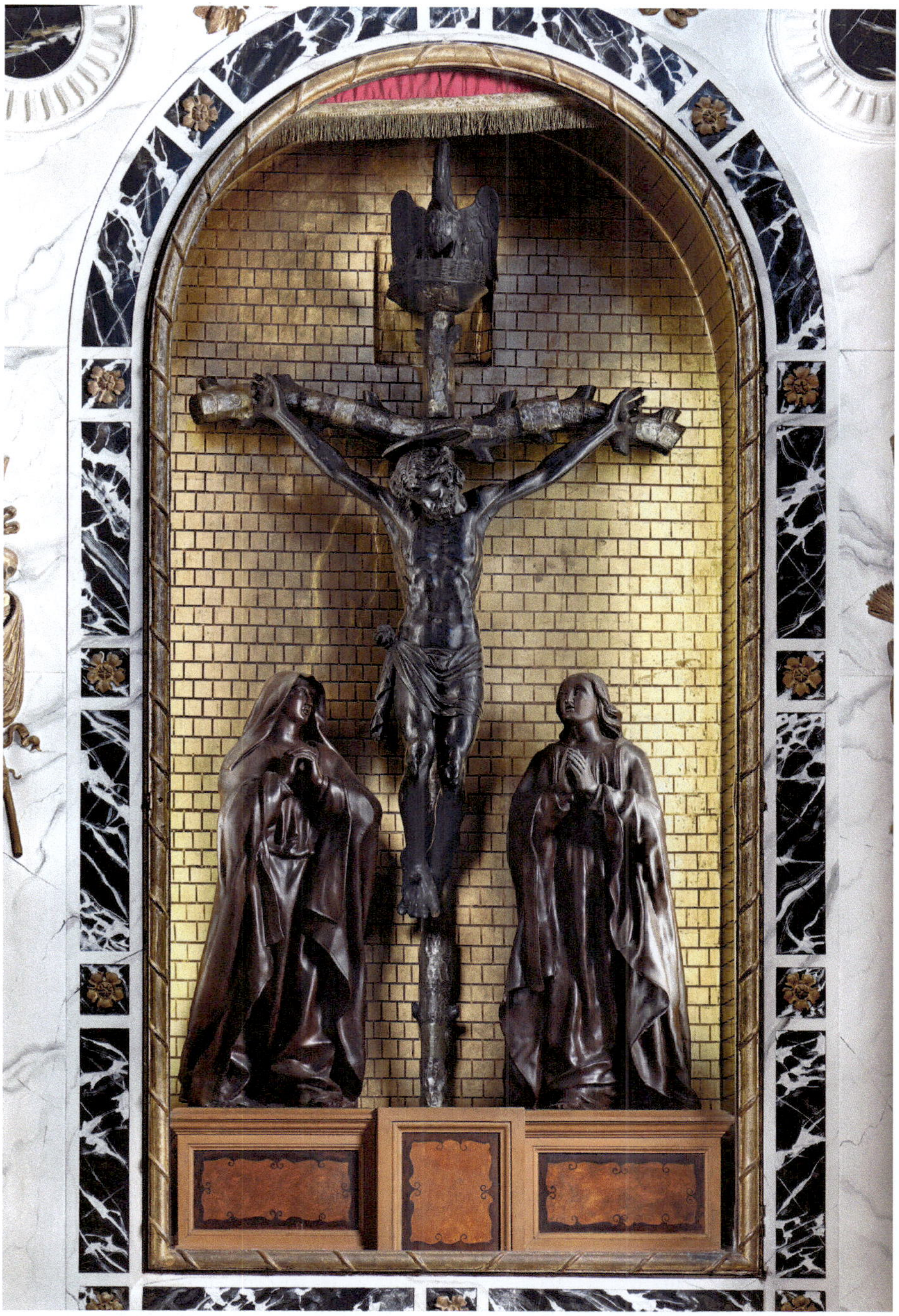

126. *Crucifixion,* painted wood, fifteenth century, Santa Maria Assunta, Codroipo (Photo: Cameraphoto)

see the wooden *tavoletta*, which he was encouraged to kiss. A surviving example from the oratory of San Giovanni Decollato depicts the suffering Christ carrying the cross, bound by a rope around his neck, and comforted by the faithful Veronica. Christ fixes his gaze upon Veronica's veil, in the same

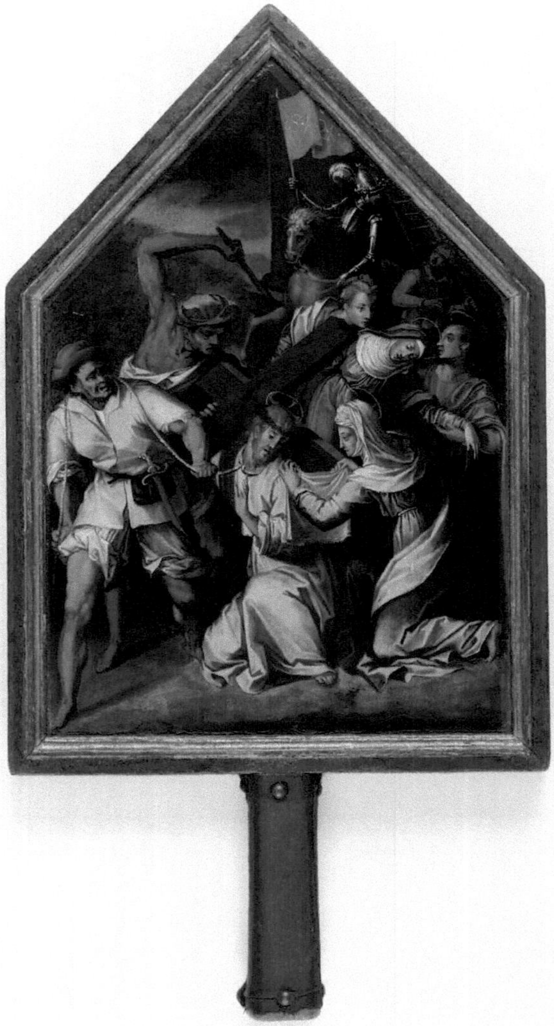

127. *Tavoletta of Christ Meeting Veronica,* painted wood, late sixteenth century, San Giovanni Decollato, Rome (Photo: Courtesy of the Arciconfraternita di San Giovanni Decollato, Rome)

way as the Christ-like criminal was to focus their gaze on the sacred painting before them (Fig. 127).[84]

This *tavoletta* was the last image seen before the condemned drew their final breaths, intended not just to distract them from the physical pain of their passing but to offer them spiritual strength at the height of their earthly trials. Some of these objects were double-sided, featuring depictions of martyrdoms on one side and paradise on the other. They could be swiftly rotated by the comforter to illustrate the belief that through mortal torments one could gain immortal paradise.[85] Samuel Edgerton described these humble *tavolette* as 'a kind of visual narcotic', arguing that they demonstrated a humanitarian bent even in their design, since in some cases they were widened at the sides to form a sort of triptych so that the prisoner's lateral vision would be blocked, ensuring that he did not lose his nerve at the sight of the executioner.[86] The practice of meditating on a devotional image at the hour of one's death was not confined to executions. Savonarola encouraged having macabre images in one's home to constantly bring to mind the imminence of death;[87] later Charles V gazed at a painting of the *Crucified Christ* in the hours before his last breaths, begging forgiveness for his sins;[88] and Bernini had a work of his own design, the *Blood of Christ the Redeemer*, painted onto a canvas in his bedchamber, which he desired to have 'always facing his bed in life and in death'.[89] This was one of the most powerful ways in which images were put to use, testifying to a confidence in the ability of the visual representation to penetrate the psyche, pacify the beholder, and help deliver their soul into the afterlife.

The black crucifix of the Scuola di San Fantin still survives in the church of Santa Maria del Codroipo, twenty kilometres from Udine. Displayed against a background of gaudy gold mosaics, for the viewer who chances upon the crucifix in its current location it gives few secrets of its past life as an object that was believed capable of working miracles, that served as the processional standard of the confraternity, and that witnessed countless individuals accompanied to the gallows over centuries of Venice's history. Both the crucifix and the *tavolette* were objects that were believed capable of influencing the fate of the soul of those whose salvation hung in the balance. Even if they were tied to the acts of a violent humanity, for their proponents they mitigated the brutality of the event for the condemned. Images were one of the primary ways through which Catholics experienced religion, and as Louise Marshall pointed out, 'images affect beholders in ways not tapped into by either text or spoken word, and in themselves actively constitute belief'.[90] The visual objects used during the Scuola di San Fantin's processions, as well as the decorative programmes at the confraternity's headquarters, expressed the community's fundamental convictions about life, death, and the worlds to come. In this sense they reflected Ernst Gombrich's grand claim that 'our attitude towards the image is inextricably bound up with our whole idea about the universe'.[91]

NOTES

1 In Giulio Romano's *Martyrdom of Saint Stephen*, Saul is the only figure, aside from the saint, who reacts to the vision above. In the biblical account the event preceded Saul's conversion, which is presumably why Domenico Tintoretto chose to depict Saul in a manner faithful to scripture in his own altarpiece of the subject.

2 For 'faith by sight', see also Cocke, *Paolo Veronese: Piety and Display*, 22–23. As Eire points out in a passage on canonisation processes and the writings of hagiographies, the process 'rested on a simple, yet immensely cheeky Catholic syllogism that offended every Protestant: humans can indeed reach a high degree of holiness, and these holy men and women (saints) can indeed work miracles; therefore, any Christian church that has no saints or miracles must be a false church'. Eire, *Reformations: The Early Modern World, 1450–1650*, 403.

3 See Ekserdjian, *The Italian Renaissance Altarpiece*, 401. Eskerdjian cites Marco Pino's *Virgin and Child between Saints Peter and Paul, with Saint Michael Freeing Souls from Purgatory* (1570s) in the church of Santi Apostoli, Naples, as one of the earliest known examples of this.

4 See Eire, *From Madrid to Purgatory*, 174.

5 For a recent study of how artists rose to the challenge faced by Dante of how to describe the extremities of divine light, see Kemp, *Visions of Heaven: Dante and the Art of Divine Light.*

6 Daniel Arasse, 'Extases et visions béatifiques à l'apogée de la Renaissance: quatre images de Raphaël', *Mélanges de l'Ecole française de Rome. Moyen-Age, Temps modernes* 84, no. 2 (1972): 404.

7 Humfrey, *The Altarpiece in Renaissance Venice*, 76.

8 For example, belief in the phenomena of levitation as a '*real* miracle flourished among Catholic Christians, especially in the early modern period'. Carlos M. N. Eire, 'The Good, the Bad, and the Airborne: Levitation and the History of the Impossible in Early Modern Europe', in *Ideas and Cultural Margins in Early Modern Germany: Essays in Honor of H. C. Erik Midelfort*, ed. Marjorie E. Plummer and Robin B. Barnes (Farnham: Ashgate, 2009), 307–23.

9 The competition was initially won by Bassano and Veronese, passing to Tintoretto after the death of the latter in 1588, with the majority of the works carried out by Domenico. Habert, *Il Paradiso di Tintoretto*, 37–38.

10 Prior to Titian, the division between the heavenly and the earthly had been clearly distinguished by artists like Botticelli in his altarpiece of the *Coronation of the Virgin with Saints John the Evangelist, Augustine, Jerome and Eligius* of 1490–92 where he used gold ground to indicate paradise (considered archaic at this time). See Charles Burroughs, 'Indicating Heaven: Botticelli's "Coronation of the Virgin" and Mediated Imagery', *Artibus et Historiae* 35, no. 69 (2014): 9–34.

11 Christian K. Kleinbub, 'At the Boundaries of Sight: The Italian Renaissance Cloud Putto', in *Renaissance Theories of Vision*, ed. Charles H. Carman and John Shannon Hendrix (Abingdon: Routledge, 2016), 122.

12 Aquinas asserted angels lacked bodies but could assume material bodies if required. Kleinbub, 'At the Boundaries of Sight: The Italian Renaissance Cloud Putto', 120–21. For Raphael's depiction of divine light, see, most recently, Kemp, *Visions of Heaven: Dante and the Art of Divine Light*, 110–23. Titian would have been familiar with the innovations of Fra Bartolomeo since his altarpiece of *God the Father with Saints Mary Magdalen and Catherine of Siena* of 1509 was intended for San Pietro Martire on Murano. Although it ended up in Lucca, it appears that Titian had knowledge of it.

13 See John Shearman, 'Raphael's Clouds, and Correggio's', *Studi su Raffaello* 1 (1987): 659; Stoichita, *Visionary Experience in the Golden Age of Spanish Art*, 86–87.

14 See Genevieve Warwick, 'Bernini (1598–1680): Sculpting Sainthood', *Studies: An Irish Quarterly Review* 104, no. 416 (2015): 450–51.

15 Kemp, *Visions of Heaven: Dante and the Art of Divine Light*, 125, 176.

16 Much has been written about this painting and so I refer readers to the following recent publications in particular: Michael Bierwirth, *Tizians Gloria* (Petersburg: Imhof, 2002); Piers Baker-Bates, 'The "Cloister Life" of the Emperor Charles V: Art and Ideology at Yuste', *Hispanic Research Journal* 14, no. 5 (2013): 427–45; Isabella Munari, *Tiziano spirituale: la 'Trinità' per Carlo V tra i venti della riforma* (Milan: Edizioni unicopli, 2019). Munari's book concentrates on dismantling the interpretation of the work as an emblem of Counter-

Reformation orthodoxy, a reading proposed above all by Craig S. Harbison, 'Counter-Reformation Iconography in Titian's Gloria', *Art Bulletin* 49, no. 3 (1967): 244–46.

17 Vasari, *Lives of the Painters, Sculptors and Architects*, vol. 2: 793.

18 Baker-Bates, 'The "Cloister Life" of the Emperor Charles V: Art and Ideology at Yuste', 431.

19 Geoffrey Parker, *Emperor: A New Life of Charles V* (New Haven, CT: Yale University Press, 2019), 485. The painting remained at the Escorial until its transferral to the Prado at the end of the 1830s. A copy by Antonio de Segura survives at the high altar of Yuste. See Munari, *Tiziano spirituale: la 'Trinità' per Carlo V tra i venti della riforma*, 47.

20 Eire, *From Madrid to Purgatory*, 7.

21 Philip displayed special reference to devotional paintings, ordering them to be covered when he used the chamber-pot, for example. Eire, *From Madrid to Purgatory*, 329–31.

22 See Kemp, *Visions of Heaven: Dante and the Art of Divine Light*, 125. The scene might refer to chapter 29 of book 22 of the *City of God* where Saint Augustine describes the Beatific Vision, a source first proposed by Erwin Panofsky in *Problems in Titian, Mostly Iconographic* (London: Phaidon, 1969), 64–65, 68.

23 The painting was referred to first as *La Gloria* by José de Sigüenza (d. 1606) when he noted the transferral of the painting to the Escorial. Charles's inventory refers to it as a Trinity, but in the codicil of Charles's will it is named *Last Judgment*.

24 Parker, *Emperor: A New Life of Charles V*, 485. For other chronicles recounting Charles's reaction to the painting, see Munari, *Tiziano spirituale: la 'Trinità' per Carlo V tra i venti della riforma*, 110–15. Reports of the existence of Lutheran conventicles in Spain had preoccupied him during his retirement. Said reports caused Charles to complain, 'I have endured and suffered so many setbacks and expenses in Germany, and sacrificed part of my health.' Parker, *Emperor: A New Life of Charles V*, 483.

25 Vasari, *Lives of the Painters, Sculptors and Architects*, vol. 2: 793. Vasari does not appear to have seen the painting. See Munari, *Tiziano spirituale: la 'Trinità' per Carlo V tra i venti della riforma*, 50.

26 Panofsky observed that 'the members of the imperial family are represented not as donors proleptically admitted to Paradise but as resurrected souls humbly praying for admissions ("Pone me cum benedictis")'. Panofsky, *Problems in Titian, Mostly Iconographic*, 69.

27 Ridolfi, *Le maraviglie dell'arte*, vol. 1: 185.

28 In both Titian's letter to Charles V of 10 September 1554 and one to Cardinal Alessandro Farnese of 16 January 1567 he referred to it as a Trinity. See Munari, *Tiziano spirituale: la 'Trinità' per Carlo V tra i venti della riforma*, 45–46. In his request for a privilege for the print he referred to it instead as a Paradise. Michael Bury, *The Print in Italy, 1550–1620* (London: British Museum, 2001), 92.

29 On 4 February 1567 Titian was granted a privilege by the Senate for the prints for fifteen years. For the Flemish engraver Court, see, in particular, Bury, *The Print in Italy, 1550–1620*, 91–92, cat. 55; Giorgio Tagliaferro et al., *Le botteghe di Tiziano* (Florence: Alinari, 2009), 390–94. See also Matthias Wivel, 'Titian and Giulio Bonasone: The Gloria That Wasn't', *Zeitschrift für Kunstgeschichte* 77 (2014): 313–32. Wivel points out that Titian had probably thought about issuing the painting as a print for some years, and may have been unsatisfied with the quality of Giulio Bonasone's work, to whom he attributes the drawing of the subject in the Louvre.

30 Andaloro et al., *San Marco*, 118.

31 Charles Hope, *Titian* (London: Chaucer Press, 2003), 48.

32 For Bernini's light effects, see Warwick, 'Bernini (1598–1680): Sculpting Sainthood', 449–51; Kemp, *Visions of Heaven: Dante and the Art of Divine Light*, 157–58. Warwick calls the motif a 'consummately Tridentine one'.

33 The Byzantine evocation of heaven at San Marco was noted also by Humfrey in *The Altarpiece in Renaissance Venice*, 24.

34 The canonical text for the history of purgatory is Jacques Le Goff, *The Birth of Purgatory*, trans. Arthur Goldhammer, first published as 'La naissance du Purgatoire', 1981 (London:

Scolar Press, 1984). Also useful is Duffy, *The Stripping of the Altars*, 338–76. For theological aspects, see Paul J. Griffiths, 'Purgatory', in *Oxford Handbook of Eschatology*, ed. Jerry L. Walls (Oxford: Oxford University Press, 2008), 427–56; Alan E. Bernstein, 'Heaven, Hell and Purgatory: 1100–1500', in *The Cambridge History of Christianity: Christianity in Western Europe c. 1100–c.1500*, ed. Miri Rubin and Walter Simons, vol. 4 (Cambridge: Cambridge University Press, 2009), 200–216.

35 Duffy, *The Stripping of the Altars*, 341.

36 Waterworth, *Canons and Decrees of the Council of Trent*, 232–33.

37 Peter Burke, 'Conspicuous Consumption in Seventeenth-Century Italy', in *The Historical Anthropology of Early Modern Italy: Essays on Perception and Communication* (Cambridge: Cambridge University Press, 1987), 149. For increases to mass requests from the late sixteenth century onwards, see also Eire, *Reformations: The Early Modern World, 1450–1650*, 398.

38 *Sommario dell'Indulgenze, Ordeni, Regole, & Oblighi, Che devono esser osservati dalli Fratelli, che vestono l'Habito della Veneranda Confraternità della Santiss. Madonna del Suffragio de'Morti* (Venice: Fratelli Pinelli, 1723), 14. The devotion existed since 1615 at the church of San Geremia according to the later *Sommario*, and was twinned with the Roman institution dedicated to the *Madonna del Suffragio dei Morti* in 1624. Martinioni points out that the Scuola was 'conceded lots of indulgences for the souls of the dead'. See Martinioni, *Venetia, città nobilissima, et singolare*, 145. For other examples in Italy, see Black, *Italian Confraternities in the Sixteenth Century*, 106. They proliferated in Venetian parishes above all in the seventeenth and eighteenth centuries, as demonstrated by the numerous entries in Vio, *Le Scuole Piccole nella Venezia dei dogi: note d'archivio per la storia delle confraternite veneziana.*

39 Irving Lavin, 'Bernini's Death', *Art Bulletin* 54, no. 2 (1972): 164.

40 Black, *Italian Confraternities in the Sixteenth Century*, 30–31. For the popularity of the suffragi in Venice in the seventeenth century, see Mackenney, *Venice as the Polity of Mercy*, 317–18.

41 Le Goff pointed out that although it has been asserted that no representation of purgatory can be traced before the end of the fourteenth century, in fact the iconography can be found in the previous century, and careful investigation may also reveal earlier examples. Jacques Le Goff, *La nascita del Purgatorio*, first published as 'La naissance du Purgatoire', 1981 (Turin: Einuadi, 1996), 367. Pilliod states that the iconography first appeared shortly after 1000 CE but does offer an example. Pilliod, *Pontormo at San Lorenzo*, 118. For the early representations of the iconography in manuscripts, see also Louise Marshall, 'Purgatory in the Medieval Imagination: The Earliest Images', in *Imagination, Books & Community in Medieval Europe*, ed. Gregory Kratzmann, Proceedings of the Conference Held at the State Library of Victoria, 29–31 May 2008 (Victoria: Macmillan Publishers Australia, 2009), 213–19.

42 The principal texts for the decoration of the Scuola are Nicola Ivanoff, *Il ciclo pittorico della Scuola di San Fantin*, fascicolo speciale per il 150 anniversario 1812–1962 (Venice: Stamperia di Venezia, 1963); Chiara Traverso, *La Scuola di San Fantin o dei 'Picai': Carità e giustizia a Venezia* (Venice: Marsilio, 2000); Pietro Zampetti, *Guida alle opere d'arte della Scuola di San Fantin Ateneo Veneto*, ed. Ileana Chiappini di Sorio, reprint of the 1973 edition (Venice: Ateneo Veneto, 2003); Meryl Bailey, 'La devozione delle confraternite, la Riforma cattolica e il ciclo del Purgatorio di San Fantin', in *Ateneo Veneto, 1812–2012: un'istituzione per la città*, ed. Marina Niero, Camillo Tonini, and Michele Gottardi (Venice: Linea d'acqua, 2012), 211–42; Meryl Bailey, 'Carrying the Cross in Early Modern Venice', in *Space, Place, and Motion: Locating Confraternities in the Late Medieval and Early Modern City*, ed. Diana Bullen Presciutti (Leiden: Brill, 2017), 244–69.

43 This follows concepts relating to flames first developed by Saint Augustine. See Le Goff, *The Birth of Purgatory*, 67–70.

44 Philippe Ariès, *Images of Man and Death*, trans. Janet Lloyd (Cambridge, MA: Harvard University Press, 1985), 167–68. Ariès includes an important image of the *Coronation of the Virgin* (1453–54) by Enguerrand Charonton showing souls being delivered by angels, which he calls 'the real ancestor of the iconography of purgatory' (162).

45 The significance of Palma's cycle has also been noted by other scholars including Black, *Italian Confraternities in the Sixteenth Century*, 261; Mason, 'Venetian Painting in the Late Sixteenth and Early Seventeenth Centuries', 535, 538. Some earlier examples of the iconography can be found in the Fondazione Zeri catalogue; see, for example, Biagio di Goro Ghezzi's 1368 fresco *Madonna Interceding for the Souls of Purgatory* in the church of San Michele, Paganico, or the predella *Saint Lawrence Liberating Souls from Purgatory* (c. 1412) by Lorenzo di Niccolò now in the Brooklyn Museum of Art.

46 A detailed history of the confraternity is provided by Traverso, *La Scuola di San Fantin o dei Picai*. See also Giuseppe Pavanello, *La Scuola di S. Fantin ora Ateneo* (Venice: Officine grafiche Vittorio Callegari, 1914).

47 The earliest example of such a confraternity was the Bolognese *Santa Maria della Morte* (1336) and then the Florentine *Santa Maria della Croce al Tempio* (1356). Around the same time similar brotherhoods sprang up in Padua, Verona, and Vicenza. See Adriano Prosperi, 'Il sangue e l'anima: richerche sulle Compagnie di Giustizia in Italia', *Quaderni Storici* 17, no. 51 (3) (1982): 964. The literature on these confraternities has flourished ever since Prosperi's important text. Of the recent publications, see, in particular, Nicholas Terpstra, ed., *The Art of Executing Well: Rituals of Execution in Renaissance Italy* (Kirksville, MO: Truman State University Press, 2008); Nicholas Terpstra, 'Body Politics: The Criminal Body between Public and Private', *Journal of Medieval and Early Modern Studies* 45, no. 1 (2015): 7–52; Nicholas Terpstra, 'Confraternities and Capital Punishment: Charity, Culture, and Civic Religion in the Communal and Confessional Age', in *A Companion to Medieval and Early Modern Confraternities*, ed. Konrad Eisenbichler (Leiden: Brill, 2019), 212–31.

48 Traverso, *La Scuola di San Fantin o dei Picai*, 75. Other indulgences followed in 1615, 1571, and 1731.

49 For the history of the building, see Traverso, *La Scuola di San Fantin o dei Picai*, 99–103, 120–21; Zampetti, *Guida alle opere d'arte della Scuola di San Fantin Ateneo Veneto*, 16–19. The Scuola first had a seat in the church of San Fantin, but in 1471 they constructed their own building close by.

50 Dated 10 October 1600. See Traverso, *La Scuola di San Fantin o dei Picai*, 106, note 22.

51 Bailey, 'Carrying the Cross in Early Modern Venice', 253.

52 Stringa, *Venetia, città nobilissima, et singolare*, 91v–92r. Pavanello assets that the oratory was open each day for three hours in the morning followed by a mass. Pavanello, *La Scuola di S. Fantin ora Ateneo*, 28. The same author documents the rich array of relics held by the confraternity.

53 Traverso, *La Scuola di San Fantin o dei Picai*, 19. Women were barred from serving on the General Chapter of the Scuola. Pavanello, *La Scuola di S. Fantin ora Ateneo*, 17. The condemned were overwhelmingly male; the few exceptions are noted by Bailey, 'Carrying the Cross in Early Modern Venice', 247, note 6. Reconstructing membership of the Scuola is complicated since rarely was the individual status or occupation described in the *sottoscrizioni dei Capitolari*, and the main registers are dispersed. Nevertheless, there were a few artisans and numerous merchants, and a number of the brothers held important governmental positions. In Rome, Michelangelo was a member of the confraternity of San Giovanni Decollato, as were the artists Baccio Bandinelli and Pietro da Cortona. See Samuel Y. Edgerton, *Pictures and Punishment: Art and Criminal Prosecution during the Florentine Renaissance* (Ithaca, NY: Cornell University Press, 1985), 172.

54 Vasari recorded a small altarpiece by Titian, *Saint Jerome in Penitence*, which was destroyed in the fire of 1562. Vasari, *Lives of the Painters, Sculptors and Architects*, vol. 2: 788. In the same year most of the confraternity's records were destroyed, so the majority of the extant documents post-date 1562. The Scuola's sacristy on the ground floor featured a cycle, *The Life of the Virgin*, by the workshop of Veronese (now in the reading room), completed in 1576. This date was recorded on four of the eight canvases, yet the cycle was only first described years later, by Boschini, in *Le minere della pittura*, 127. Boschini attributed the

paintings to Alvise dal Friso. For the vexed question of the authorship of the cycle, see Ivanoff, *Il ciclo pittorico della Scuola di San Fantin*, 14–16; Pignatti and Pedrocco, *Veronese*, vol. 2: 472–74, 521–23, cats. 372–74, A73–A77; Traverso, *La Scuola di San Fantin o dei Picai*, 140–43; Zampetti, *Guida alle opere d'arte della Scuola di San Fantin Ateneo Veneto*, 87–96.

55 For Corona's cycle, see Traverso, *La Scuola di San Fantin o dei Picai*, 124–27; Zampetti, *Guida alle opere d'arte della Scuola di San Fantin Ateneo Veneto*, 49–51; Valentina Sapienza, 'Note sulle "Storie della Passione" di Leonardo Corona all'Ateneo Veneto', in *Ateneo Veneto, 1812–2012*, ed. Michele Gottardi, Marina Niero, and Camillo Tonini (Venice: Linea d'acqua, 2012), 243–49; Enrica Folin, '"Questa breve morte, morendo ben disposto (come far devi) ti sarà un principio dell'eterna felicità e della beata vita": lettura iconologica del ciclo della Passione nella Scuola "dei Picai" ora Ateneo Veneto', *Arte Documento* 34 (2018): 176–85. Sapienza pointed out that Corona died in 1596, not 1605 as stated by Ridolfi, meaning that the cycle must have been completed around a decade earlier than previously thought.

56 These were later moved to the church of Santi Giovanni e Paolo in 1816. The altar of Saint Jerome was disassembled and its pieces dispersed, with the exception of the statue of the saint and a bas-relief, *The Virgin in Glory*. The altar of the Cross is now situated in the Chapel of the Dead. The original figure of the crucified Christ was donated to the last chaplain of the confraternity and was substituted with an example in white marble from the church of Santa Ternita by Francesco Cavrioli in the year 1817. Traverso, *La Scuola di San Fantin o dei Picai*, 108, note 25, 156–59.

57 See Ivanoff, *Il ciclo pittorico della Scuola di San Fantin*, 1–2; Pallucchini and Rossi, *Tintoretto: le opere sacre e profane*, vol. 1: 222–23, cat. 425; Peter Humfrey, 'Tintoretto and the Altarpiece', in *Tintoretto: Artist of Renaissance Venice*, ed. Robert Echols and Frederick Ilchman, Exhibition Catalogue, Palazzo Ducale, Venice, 7 September 2018–6 January 2019, National Gallery of Art, Washington, 24 March–7 July 2019 (New Haven, CT: Yale University Press, 2018), 131–33. As noted by Ivanoff, the unusual iconography of Tintoretto's altarpiece is reflected in an illustration to be found in the *mariegola* of the confraternity. This was remade in 1566 after the previous one was destroyed in the fire of 1562.

58 See Mason Rinaldi, *Palma il Giovane: l'opera completa*, 109, cats. 269–72; Traverso, *La Scuola di San Fantin o dei Picai*, 108, 150–54; Zampetti, *Guida alle opere d'arte della Scuola di San Fantin Ateneo Veneto*, 85–87. The inventory of 1786 confirmed that there were eight canvases by Palma of episodes from the hagiography of Saint Jerome, in accordance with the description of Boschini, *Le minere della pittura*, 128. Four of the works are now in the church of San Giorgio delle Pertiche in Padua, one is in the deposit of the Accademia, one is in the church of San Girolamo in Venice, and the last two have been lost. Jerome was an extremely popular saint in Venice, coming in at number two in the table of saints most frequently depicted in altarpieces for the city's churches between 1450 and 1530. See Humfrey, *The Altarpiece in Renaissance Venice*, 65.

59 Borghini, *Il Riposo*, 560–61. See also Schulz, *Venetian Painted Ceilings of the Renaissance*, 81–82, cat. 23; Mason Rinaldi, *Palma il Giovane: l'opera completa*, 144–45, cat. 558. Schulz believed that Borghini's notices on Venice dated to the summer of 1582 at the latest.

60 See Zampetti, *Guida alle opere d'arte della Scuola di San Fantin Ateneo Veneto*, 22. Two fragments of the painting have been identified, one in a Milanese private collection and the second in the Hermitage.

61 Ridolfi, *Le maraviglie dell'arte*, vol. 2: 177. This information was repeated in an inventory of 1786 and by subsequent guides. Zampetti, *Guida alle opere d'arte della Scuola di San Fantin Ateneo Veneto*, 165.

62 For this ceiling, see Schulz, *Venetian Painted Ceilings of the Renaissance*, 82–83, cat. 24; Mason Rinaldi, *Palma il Giovane: l'opera completa*, 147, cats. 574–86; Traverso, *La Scuola di San*

Fantin o dei Picai, 106, 130–35; Zampetti, *Guida alle opere d'arte della Scuola di San Fantin Ateneo Veneto*, 37.

63 See Traverso, *La Scuola di San Fantin o dei Picai*, 106. The reasons for substituting Tintoretto's work are also unknown. The ceiling may have been damaged, have gone out of fashion, or was no longer adapted to the reorganised oratory space. Some 600 ducats had been set aside by 10 August 1600 for the new work. An inscription above the door, 'MDC/MENs/DEC.s', has been suggested as the date of completion for the paintings (Mason, Zampetti, and Traverso), but Palma would have had to work very swiftly to complete everything between August and December. It is more likely that only some of the canvases had been finished by this point, as argued by Bailey in 'La devozione delle confraternite, la Riforma cattolica e il ciclo del Purgatorio di San Fantin', 217–19. The new cycle is first mentioned by Stringa, but he did not describe the three main canvases. For this reason Bailey suggests that they might not have been completed until after 1603 (the year of the dedication of Stringa's volume). Stringa, *Venetia, città nobilissima, et singolare*, 92r.

64 Firpo and Biferali, *Battista Franco 'pittore viniziano' nella cultura artistica e nella vita religiosa del Cinquecento*, 213–16.

65 Noted by Bailey, 'La devozione delle confraternite, la Riforma cattolica e il ciclo del Purgatorio di San Fantin', 221, 224. The second volume of Bellarmino's *Disputationes* contained a long section on purgatory (see book 1, chapter 10).

66 It was also popular to show the souls in purgatory being refreshed by jugs of water thrown over them. This can be seen in the title page of the *Sommario dell'Indulgenze, Ordeni, Regole, & Oblighi, che devono esser osservati dalli Fratelli, che vestono l'Habito della veneranda Confraternità della santiss. Madonna del suffragio de'Morti*. A print of the blood of Christ on the cross being directed by the Virgin Mary to relieve the souls in purgatory can be seen adjacent to the title page of the *Capitoli d'ordini, e regole da pratticarsi dalli fratelli, e sorelle della veneranda Confraternita del suffragio de' morti canonicamente eretta nella chiesa parochiale di S. Matteo di Rialto di Venetia* (Venice: Antonio Bosio, 1681).

67 Mason Rinaldi, *Palma il Giovane: l'opera completa*, 130, cats. 451–58; Manno, *La chiesa di San Nicola da Tolentino a Venezia*, 31–32. Saint Agatha and Barbara were also depicted in the chapel, as were scenes of the Annunciation and Visitation.

68 Waterworth, *Canons and Decrees of the Council of Trent*, 232.

69 Mâle, *L'art religieux de la fin du XVIe siècle, du XVIIe siècle et du XVIIIe siècle*, 60.

70 Golda Blass, 'Five Hierarchies of Intercessors for Salvation: The Decoration of the Angels' Chapel in the Gesù', *Artibus et Historiae* 24, no. 47 (2003): 182–83.

71 Mâle, *L'art religieux de la fin du XVIe siècle, du XVIIe siècle et du XVIIIe siècle*, 58–65; Blass, 'Five Hierarchies of Intercessors for Salvation: The Decoration of the Angels' Chapel in the Gesù'; Bailey, *Between Renaissance and Baroque*, 243, 245–46.

72 Traverso, *La Scuola di San Fantin o dei Picai*, 39–41.

73 Thanks to Meryl Bailey for her thoughts on the matter. Humfrey asserts that in Venice the condemned were taken to *albergo* of the Scuola where they would have witnessed Tintoretto's altarpiece. Humfrey, 'Tintoretto and the Altarpiece', 133. In other places the condemned were indeed taken to the ritual space of the confraternity providing assistance to them, where the decoration encouraged them to think of their fate in terms of a *via crucis*. The destroyed Florentine church where the archconfraternity of Santa Maria della Croce al Tempio held their devotions was site of the last rites of the condemned. It was covered with Passion scenes on the façade by Spinello Aretino and the altarpieces inside included *St James Rescuing a Pilgrim from Hanging*, perhaps by Bicci di Lorenzo, and a *Lamentation* by Fra Angelico. See Samuel Y. Edgerton, '"Maniera" and the "Mannaia": Decorum and Decapitation in the Sixteenth Century', in *The Meaning of Mannerism*, ed. Stephen G. Nichols and Franklin W. Robinson (Hanover, NH: University Press of New

England, 1972), 81–82; Edgerton, *Pictures and Punishment: Art and Criminal Prosecution during the Florentine Renaissance*, 192–201.

74 Noted by Nicholas Terpstra, 'Body Politics', 30.

75 For this reconstruction of events, see, in particular, Traverso, *La Scuola di San Fantin o dei Picai*, 46–48.

76 In the even more horrible event that the condemned was innocent, comforters were encouraged to convince them that their death was nevertheless providential, that their chances of salvation high, and that they should be grateful for the opportunity to die penitent, 'absolved of all sin', as one prison chaplain wrote in the seventeenth century. Edgerton, '"Maniera" and the "Mannaia": Decorum and Decapitation in the Sixteenth Century', 79.

77 See Nicholas Terpstra, 'Body Politics', 8; Adriano Prosperi, 'Conversion on the Scaffold: Italian Practices in European Context', in *Space and Conversion in Global Perspective*, ed. Giuseppe Marocci et al. (Leiden: Brill, 2015), 44–60. Michel de Montaigne was struck by the presence of lay comforters when he witnessed an execution in Rome during his Italian journey of 1581, since this was the preserve of the clergy in France.

78 For the account of the Scuola's procession, I am indebted to the careful reconstructions of Traverso, *La Scuola di San Fantin o dei Picai*, 45–58; Bailey, 'Carrying the Cross in Early Modern Venice', 259–62. Traverso also gives an account of the completion of the comforters' duties in accompanying the corpse to its final resting place.

79 The Scuola façade also features a relief by Vittoria of the crucifix surmounted by the pelican and the fraternity robes were also decorated with the symbol. Traverso, *La Scuola di San Fantin o dei Picai*, 157; Bailey, 'Carrying the Cross in Early Modern Venice', 248–53.

80 San Fantin had various *tavolette*, including one of *Christ Crowned with Thorns*. The first to extensively study these objects was Edgerton, '"Maniera" and the "Mannaia": Decorum and Decapitation in the Sixteenth Century', 81–86; Samuel Y. Edgerton, 'A Little-Known "Purpose of Art" in the Italian Renaissance', *Art History* 2, no. 1 (1979), 45–61; Samuel Y. Edgerton, 'Icons of Justice', *Past & Present* 89 (1980): 37–38; Edgerton, *Pictures and Punishment: Art and Criminal Prosecution during the Florentine Renaissance*, 126–221. Edgerton believed that there were no surviving examples before the sixteenth century, but earlier ones were presented in an important text by Massimo Ferretti, 'In Your Face: Paintings for the Condemned in Renaissance Italy', in *The Art of Executing Well: Rituals of Execution in Renaissance Italy*, ed. Nicholas Terpstra (Kirksville, MO: Truman State University Press, 2008), 79–97.

81 Bailey, 'Carrying the Cross in Early Modern Venice', 259.

82 Evocatively termed a 'sensory cocoon' by Nicholas Terpstra in 'Body Politics', 13.

83 If the crime was considered graver, then the tortures of the condemned were drawn out, involving a return journey down the Grand Canal to the church of the Croce (now the Papadopoli gardens). In these cases the comforters sailed alongside the raft in a gondola. Traverso, *La Scuola di San Fantin o dei Picai*, 51–56.

84 Some of these images appear to have been kissed so often that the heads of the figures had to be repainted. For an example, see Ferretti, 'In Your Face: Paintings for the Condemned in Renaissance Italy', 90. At an execution in 1514, Marin Sanudo noted that the convict kissed the crucifix held up to him by the members of the Scuola. Bailey, 'Carrying the Cross in Early Modern Venice', 262, note 42.

85 Terpstra, 'Body Politics', 24.

86 Edgerton, *Pictures and Punishment: Art and Criminal Prosecution during the Florentine Renaissance*, 172, 180. On at least one occasion these *tavolette* were used not to comfort the condemned but to prevent them from protesting their innocence. See Niccoli, *Vedere con gli occhi del cuore: alle origini del potere delle immagini*, 52–53.

87 Edgerton, *Pictures and Punishment: Art and Criminal Prosecution during the Florentine Renaissance*, 176. The *Ars moriendi* also encouraged that a crucifix or an image of the crucifixion should be in the sight of the dying person. Larry J. Feinberg, 'Imagination All

Compact: Tavolette and Confraternity Rituals for the Condemned in Renaissance Italy', *Apollo* 161, no. 519 (2005): 53.

88 Presumed to be Jan Vermeyen's 1555 *Man of Sorrows* by Parker, *Emperor: A New Life of Charles V*, 487, 688, note 89.

89 Irving Lavin, 'Bernini's Death', *Art Bulletin* 54, no. 2 (1972): 160. Filippo Baldinucci described the work as depicting blood gushing from the wounds of the crucified Christ as if to form a sea, offered by the Queen of Heaven to God the Father.

90 Marshall, 'Purgatory in the Medieval Imagination: The Earliest Images', 213.

91 Ernst Gombrich, *Symbolic Images: Studies in the Art of the Renaissance* (London: Phaidon, 1972), 125.

CONCLUSIONS

To the right of the high altar of the basilica of San Marco there is a mosaic of Christ the Saviour in the north intrados of the chapel of Saint Clement, originally dating to around 1200 (Fig. 128).[1] Above it, an inscription reads: 'Nam Deus est quod imago docet sed non deus ipsa, hanc videas sed mente colas quod noscis in ipsa.' This roughly translates as 'The image teaches what God is, but it is not God / In the image you should not adore the things you see, in your mind adore alone.'[2] A second inscription, now lost, but related to the first and cited by Stringa in 1604, once read: 'Effigiem Christi, qui transis, pronus Honora: Non tamen effigiem sed quid designat, adora. Esse Deum ratione caret, cui contulit esse, Materiale lapis, effigiale manus. Nec Deus est, nec homo, praesens quam cernis, imago; Sed Deus est, & homo, quem sacra signat imago.'[3] Travelling through Venice in the year 1594, the inscriptions caught the eye of the Scottish traveller Fynes Moryson.[4] He translated the lost distich as follows: 'As thou Christs image passest, fall the same before / Yet what this image signifies, not it adore / No reason that it should be God, whose essence stands / Materiall of stone, formall (formed) of workemens hands / This image which thou seest, is neither God nor Man / But whom it represents, he is both God and Man.'[5] The significance of the San Marco distichs have been rarely commented upon in recent times, but in sixteenth-century Europe they were sometimes inscribed upon artworks as cautionary pronouncements and were widely quoted by both Catholic theologians to defend themselves against the accusation that they worshipped holy images

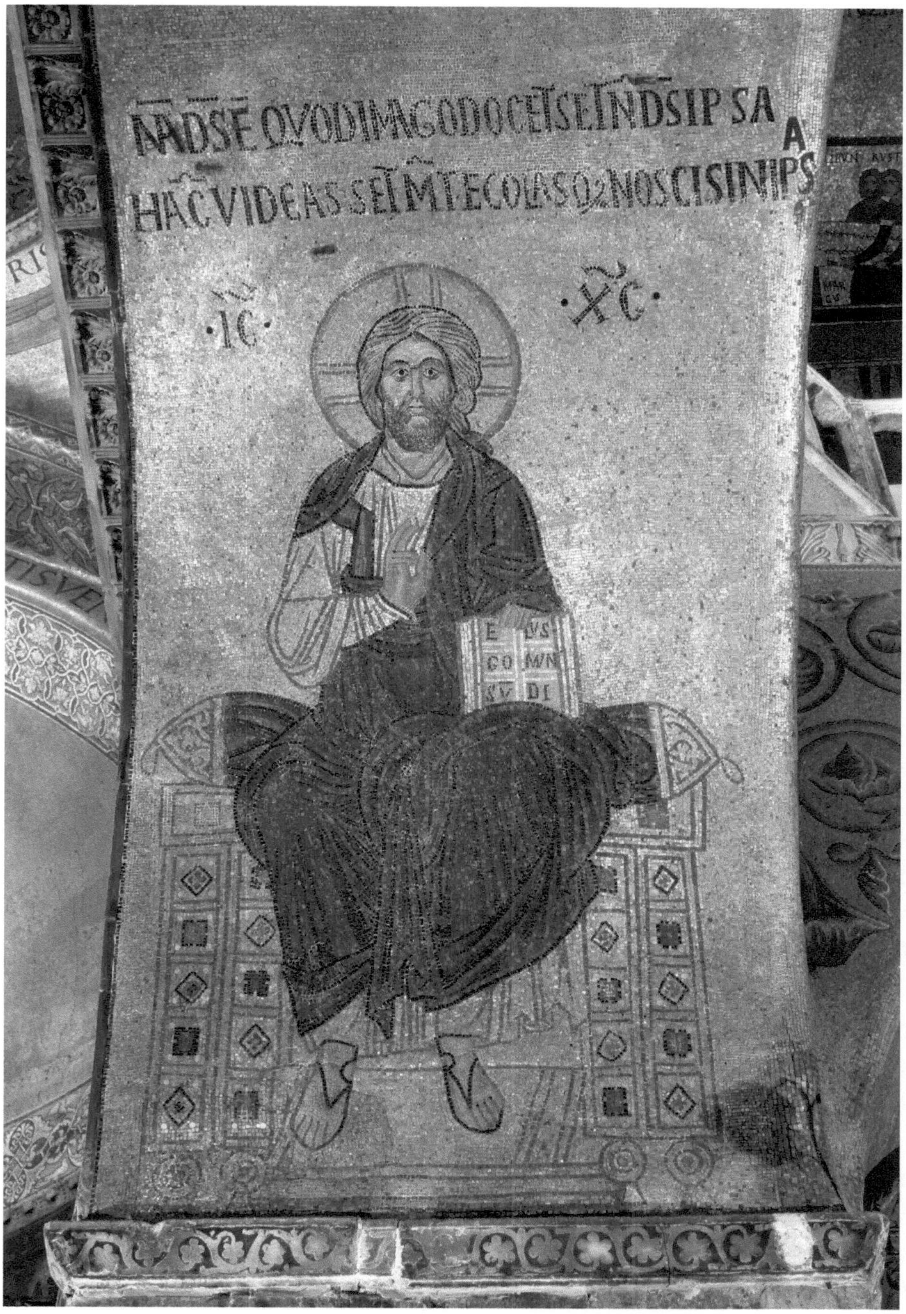

128. *Christ the Saviour,* mosaic, thirteenth century, North Intrados, Chapel of Saint Clement, Basilica di San Marco, Venice (Photo: Cameraphoto)

(since they adored not the image but that which is represented) and by Protestants as a warning against the perils of papistic idolatry.[6] Their precise origins are obscure, but in general terms they express the decrees of the Second Council of Nicaea, which condemned iconoclasm and asserted the validity of holy images after they had been suppressed by the Byzantine Emperor Leo III (c. 675–741) in 726.[7]

The words inscribed on the vault of the Saint Clement chapel hark back to the first major image controversy in the Church's almost 2,000-year history. The second of these was brought about by the Protestant Reformations. Attitudes towards the devotional image not only altered the physical appearance of early modern Europe, but played a significant role in transforming the nature of belief too. At the beginning of the Seicento, Stringa observed that the San Marco inscriptions were intended as a reminder to the viewer that should be applied to 'all the other figures, and images of saints, that one sees in painting and sculpture, not just in this church, but in all the other churches of Christendom'.[8] In the decades subsequent to the Council of Trent, when the ancient stance of the Church regarding the distinction between the worship and veneration of images was reasserted, they seem to have taken on a new resonance when they were mentioned in swift succession by both Fynes and Stringa. The words recognised the potential for image worship in Venice, a place historically linked to the Byzantine Empire, an empire in which waves of image destruction had first erupted centuries before those sparked by the Reformations, and a city home to a magnificent basilica, that in its first ninth century iteration was said to have been decorated by itinerant artists fleeing iconoclastic persecutions in Greece.[9]

An explicit warning against idolatry was also inherent in the subject matter of Tintoretto's *Making of the Golden Calf* for Madonna dell'Orto in Venice of c. 1559–60 (Fig. 129), and it was obliquely contained in some of the late sixteenth-century paintings that have been examined in the course of this book. In Veronese's two altarpieces of the martyrdoms of the Saints George and Giustina, for example, the circumstances leading to their executions were a refusal to pay homage to images of Apollo and Mars, respectively.[10] In both works the saints are exhorted by the pagan priests to turn their attention to the statues placed on the pedestals above them. But whereas these are depicted as lifeless matter, the population of the heavens above is rendered as lifelike flesh and blood. More subtly, behind Saint Lawrence in the first of Palma's paintings for the eponymous chapel at San Giacomo dall'Orio, a muscular Roman soldier with a plumed helmet can be seen, part of the emperor's entourage (Fig. 130). In the scene of Lawrence's martyrdom on the wall opposite, the figure is repeated, but this time his body has turned to stone, transformed into the statue of Mars that crowns the plinth in the background (Fig. 130). Catholics might have been accused of worshipping images by Protestants, but in these works viewers were warned about idolatry via the image itself, cleverly acknowledging and simultaneously deflecting the criticism as the preserve of a distant past.

The desire to embellish the sacred space had a venerable history in Venice long before the events of the Cinquecento, but in Chapter 4 it was shown how a love of extensive decoration prevailed in the city towards the end of the

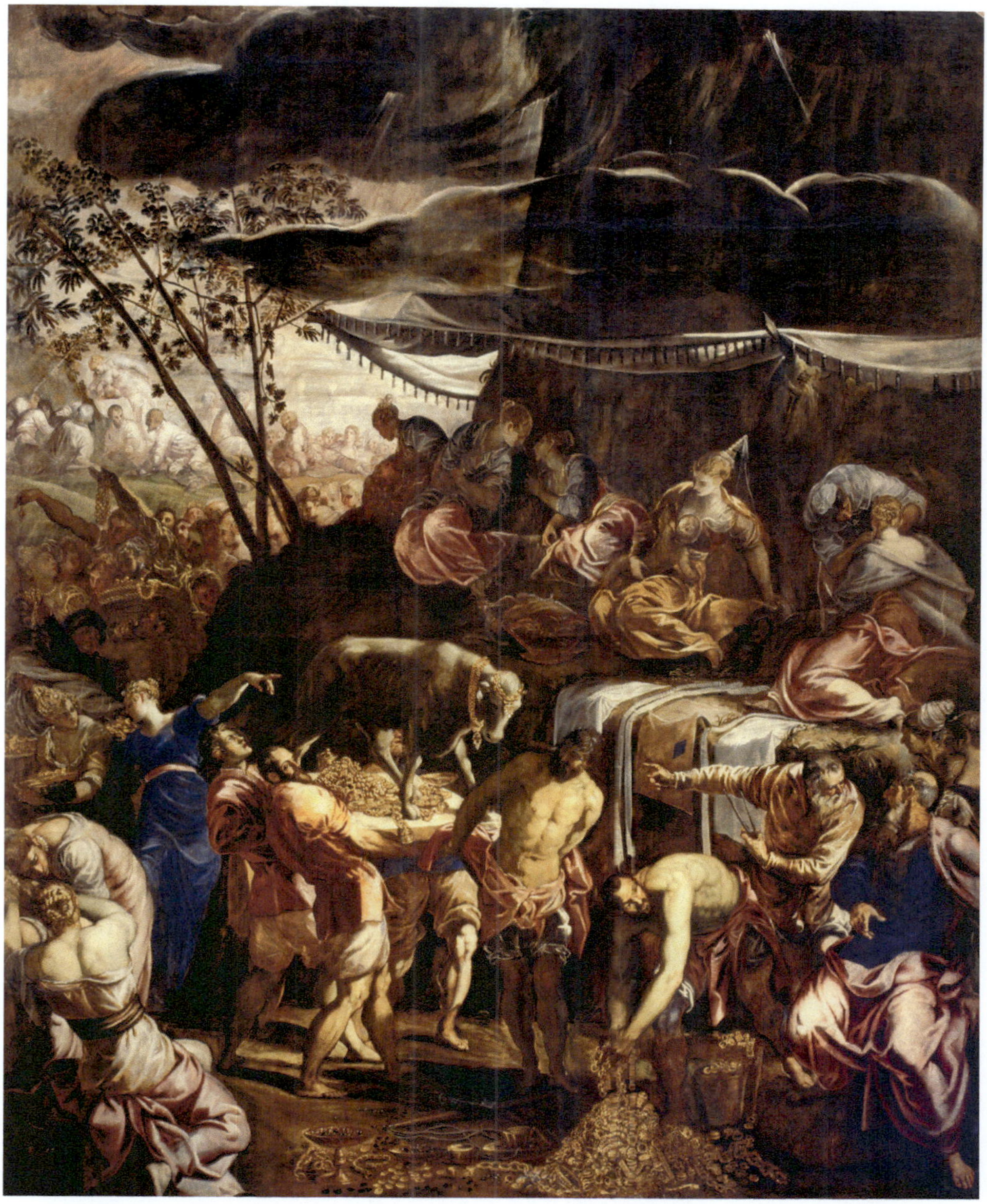

129. Detail of Jacopo Tintoretto, *The Making of the Golden Calf*, c. 1559–60, oil on canvas, Madonna dell'Orto, Venice (Photo: Cameraphoto)

century. A similar process took place in Rome and elsewhere in Italy. Church walls began to be newly enveloped with precious marbles, and costly materials like lapis lazuli, agate, and malachite were used for the reliquaries of the new saints. As Diego Angeli pointed out, these sites were thus bestowed with a sense of the eternal analogous to the precious stones themselves, and even if for some this might have been all too easily seen as evidence of the 'bad Italian taste' of the Counter-Reformation, in its time it would have been associated

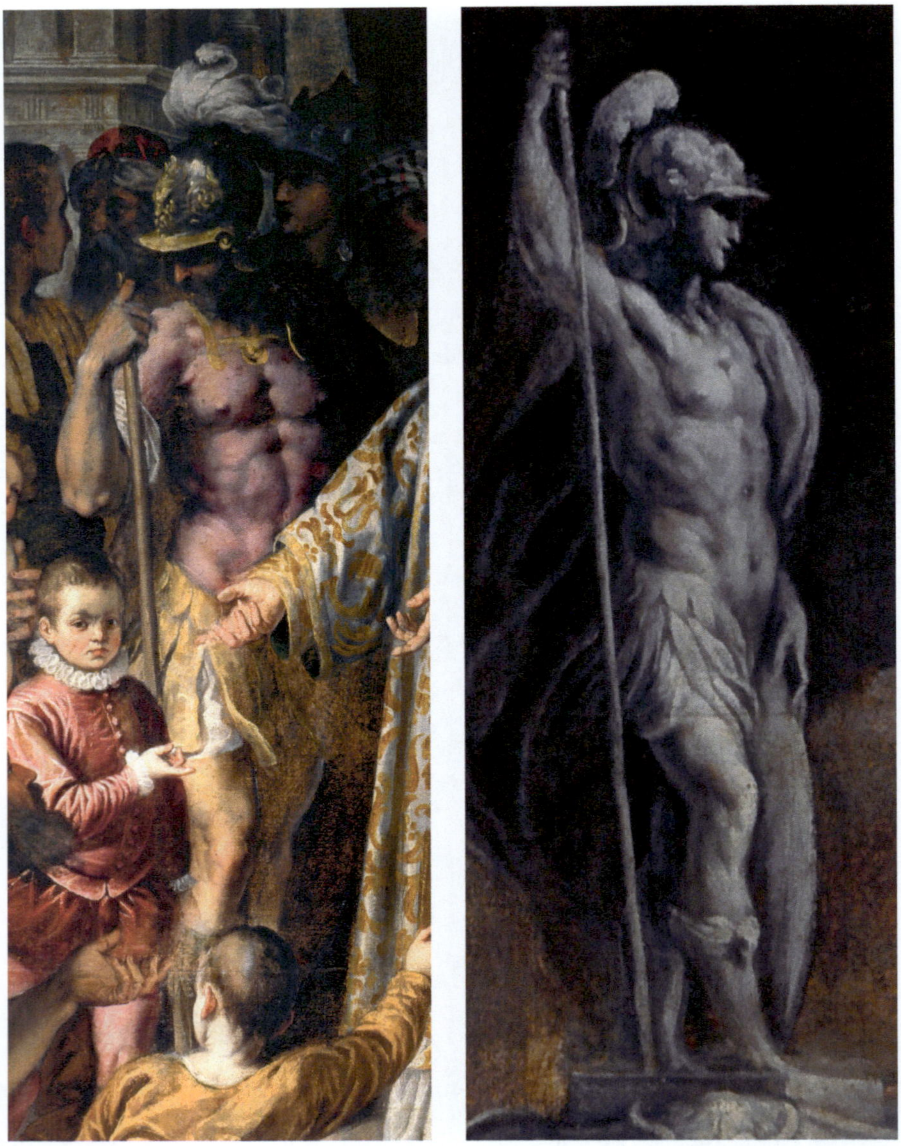

130. Detail of Palma il Giovane, *Saint Lawrence Presenting the Riches of the Church to the Emperor* and *The Martyrdom of Saint Lawrence* (Photo: Cameraphoto)

with a high intellectual theology.[11] Of all the artists examined in the course of this book, Tintoretto was probably the most wary of this materialist tendency, even if his livelihood as a painter was dependent on a steady stream of commissions. Tom Nichols expertly underlined the 'sacred poverty' of Tintoretto's devotional works at the Scuola Grande di San Rocco in light of Caravia's polemics against the exorbitant costs involved in the construction of the new meeting house, with paintings like the San Rocco *Annunciation* showing the Gospel episodes unfolding in partially dilapidated surroundings, in contrast to the more majestic settings used by Tintoretto's contemporary

Veronese.[12] In the lower section of the huge canvas of the *Making of the Golden Calf* the clay animal is shown laden down with the finery collected by Aaron (Exodus 32:2–5), as Moses receives the tablets of the law above (Exodus 24:15–17). In the left foreground two women remove their earrings to contribute to the offering that will be used to cast the cult image in gold. Piles of jewellery and coins lie scattered on the ground, abandoned to the calf. The condemnation of materialism brought about by the worship of the idol was inherent in the account of the Book of Exodus, but that a painting of this seldom-represented episode should be commissioned around the beginning of the 1560s when disputes over images had reached a fever pitch is important.[13] The idolatrous worship of the calf was used often in Protestant arguments against 'graven images'.[14] The canons of San Giorgio in Alga who were the patrons of the work, and the artist himself, would likely have been aware of this, particularly because Ridolfi tells us that it was Tintoretto who proposed the commission to the prior of Madonna dell'Orto, having offered to 'make them a gift of his labours'.[15] As Freedberg pointed out in his piercing analysis of Nicolas Poussin's (1594–1665) later *Worship of the Golden Calf* (1633–34), in the National Gallery of London, there is a deep irony in the fact that the viewer admires 'a picture that has as its subject the epitome of the negative consequences of looking, admiring and adoring'.[16] At Madonna dell'Orto, Tintoretto's painting condemned the dangers of an unfettered attraction to the image but within the boundaries of those that were deemed to be of the 'wrong' kind, in this case the idol that provoked the wrath of Moses. Whether viewers necessarily registered the 'deep irony' of warning against worshipping images via the conduit of visual representation is complicated by Moryson's reaction to the San Marco inscriptions. Rather than equate this with an ever-present risk, he understood that they showed 'how they worshipped images in a more modest though superstitious age'.[17]

As iconoclasm in Protestant countries escalated, the appropriate level of expenditure on church structures and decorations was debated by Catholic prelates. Cardinal Contarini, whom we met in Chapter 1, argued that normal expenditures on the divine cult should be reduced only if the need of the poor became so great that it was necessary to do so in order to save lives. If no such immediate necessity existed, then divine services were to be celebrated with as much splendour as possible, distributing anything left over to the needy.[18] Contarini's contemporary Giberti followed a similar line of thought. In a letter of 1533 concerning the decoration of the Holy House of Loreto by Andrea Sansovino, Giberti (as a governor of the site) stated that the central objectives of the works was that 'the honour of God and the salvation and care of souls' be conserved, pointing out that if the expenditures, even if very impressive, had a negative effect on the proper care of the laity, then 'I would deem them as nothing.'[19] Yet as we have seen, the bishop was criticised for his own profligate spending on the renovations of the cathedral of Verona. That he was cognisant of the role material splendour could play in reform efforts is demonstrated by his assertions of 1540 that this could be justified due to the fact that there is an inherent duty to honour God to the extent that this is possible, that beautiful churches encourage the laity to convene there, and because events in Germany led to no new building projects and the destruction of images.[20] These justifications provided by reformers active in the Serenissima were complemented by similar reasonings stipulated in Luigi Lippomano's popular *Confirmatione e stabilimento di tutti i dogmi catholici*, published in Venice and written whilst he was bishop of Verona. Arranged in a question and answer format where heterodox arguments were presented in italics and then vigorously refuted by the author, the treatise contained two extended sections concerning both images and the cult and ornamentation of sacred edifices.[21] In the second, Lippomano explicitly stated that building churches and decorating them sumptuously was 'something good and pleasing to God, and whoever sustains the opposite is a heretic'.[22] For Lippomano, the beauty of a majestically constructed and richly embellished church encouraged one to meditate on celestial things. The more magnificently this was done, the closer it might resemble 'the beauty of that sublime and divine heavenly Church'.[23] Lippomano cited John the Evangelist's vision on Patmos of the heavenly Jerusalem as a city made of pure gold, with walls of jasper adorned with an array of precious stones (Apocalypse 21:10–22) to argue that if the soul was to be raised to contemplating all that was 'most high, and noble, and beautiful, that surpasses all feeling and understanding', this could not be achieved with poor materials (earth, straw, tin, lead, iron), but only with those precious ones that brought to mind the kingdom of God.[24]

By the twilight of the Cinquecento, Lippomano's viewpoint came to be widely accepted amongst Catholics, spurred on by aspects of the Tridentine decrees discussed in Chapter 3. For example, although the early Jesuits decreed in 1558 that their edifices should 'visibly give testimony to poverty', they tended to distinguish between those buildings intended for practical purposes (residences and schools) that should be 'neither sumptuous nor affected in style' and the very different requirements of places of worship.[25] In 1577, Saint Peter Canisius (1521–97) argued it was right that churches should be richly decorated, and later in the seventeenth century, the Father General Gian Paolo Oliva (1600–81), a close friend of Bernini, explained in a sermon that 'For the churches therefore, both our Father Ignatius, and we, his followers, attempt to emulate the grandeur of the eternal omnipotence with ornaments of the greatest glory we can produce.'[26] This attitude was manifested already in the decoration of the Umiltà in Venice (1560–89), and above all in the embellishment of the Gesù in Rome at the end of the century. Lippomano's writings had provided a vigorous defence of such conspicuous expenditure with reference to Mary Magdalen's anointing of Christ with a costly ointment. He argued that it was Judas who had objected to her act on account of the fact that the money could have been better served by donating it to the poor (Matthew 26: 6–10), likening those who voiced this opinion to 'the voice of the traitor Judas'.[27] Nevertheless, in echoes of Contarini, Lippomano simultaneously confirmed that in times of great need (such as famines), the poor were always to take precedence, quoting the example set by saints including Lawrence.[28]

The prevailing mindset regarding expenditure on sacred art and architecture explains why it often flourished in the face of factors including economic downturns, plague, war, and famine, which could be assumed to mitigate against it. This was certainly the case in Venice, and it is a phenomenon that has also been traced in seventeenth-century Flanders and Seville.[29] But not only were elaborate public works perceived as providing a stimulus to the economy and assistance to the unemployed, but since they were considered both a charitable act and one that expressed communal devotion, it should not be so surprising that they sometimes coincided with periods of crisis.[30] As we have seen, even the poorer confraternities in Venice were keen patrons of the arts, who were content to spend considerable sums on beautifying the altars, chapels, and meeting houses of the Scuole to which they belonged. It is all too easy to condescendingly rationalise their activities as simply vainglorious or driven purely by a sense of competition. Such an attitude has a long history: when the Scottish Protestant Gilbert Burnet (1643–1715) – later Bishop of Salisbury – visited Venice in 1685, he dismissed the luxury of the city's churches as evidence of nothing more than 'a point of magnificence, or a matter of emulation among families', since he was convinced that Venetians were 'unconcerned' with religion.[31] Although these vainglorious motivations should be taken into account, most obviously when they concern monuments to a family or an individual, they should not dilute the simple truth that the overriding factor that led to much munificent patronage was religious devotion, and that images were invested with great meaning and significance for the early modern Venetians who encountered and found solace in them.[32] They were proof of belief, worship, and participation.[33] For this reason, successive patriarchs in Venice also paid a new level of attention to the organisation and decoration of the sacred space in the wake of the Council of Trent, and their endorsement of extensive decorative programmes helped pave the way for the Baroque.[34]

The principal finding of Emile Mâle's study on art after the Council of Trent was that the doctrines and traditions of the Church most despised by Protestants ironically tended to be the ones that became popular subjects in devotional art: martyrdoms, ecstasies, purgatory, and Marian subjects all abounded from the latter half of the sixteenth century onwards.[35] King Philip II's construction of the Escorial, completed in 1584, was widely understood in Spain as a heroic act, one that beautifully contrasted to the ransacking of 'ten thousand churches in England' by Henry VIII and events in France where the people 'looted and torched their temples'.[36] Yet even if the Escorial came to be promoted as a symbol of Catholic identity, it had originally been conceived first and foremost as a building complex dedicated to the cult of the dead.[37] So even if the trends that Mâle observed can indeed be confirmed, one must be hesitant about understanding this *purely* as a reactive phenomenon, where artists and patrons were instructed to deliberately exalt the beliefs and practices debated during the Reformations to refute the creeds of their spiritual foes. It seems to have been more the case that the images surveyed in the course of this book sprung from a culture that due to circumstances had emphatically confirmed the power and necessity of sacred images, and thus should be understood less as the visual outcome of specific directives from the clerical hierarchy than as part of a period of religious reform, one that had important consequences for the history of art.[38]

Be that as it may, just as the destruction of devotional images marked the dawn of the Reformations, so too did their elevation in other parts of Europe signal a deep and persistent chasm between Protestants and Catholics. Very different attitudes towards the visual and sensory world of belief deepened this rift. Luther proclaimed in his 1535 lectures on the Book of Genesis (published in 1544) that it was 'not the stones, the construction, and the gorgeous silver and gold that make a church beautiful and holy; it is the Word of God and the sound of preaching', an approach completely at odds to that of Lippomano, who believed that only the best should be reserved for honouring God, Mary, and the communion of saints.[39] In 1608, William Bedell, who was chaplain to the English ambassador in Venice, denounced the 'idolatrous' statues and images to be found throughout the city, not just in the churches, but in houses, shops, even on the boats, complaining that 'noe sooner doe their Children almost creep out of their Cradles, but they are taught to be Idolaters'.[40] Popular devotions in Catholic countries regarding pilgrimage sites like the Holy House of Loreto or masses for the souls in purgatory were often the ones that Protestant visitors found most offensive and mired in superstition. For example, the twenty-second of the thirty-nine Anglican articles of religion, to be found in all editions of the Book of Common Prayer from 1571 onward, explained that 'the Romish Doctrine concerning Purgatory, Pardons, Worshipping and Adoration, as well of Images as of Relics, and also invocation of Saints, is a fond thing, vainly invented, and grounded upon no warranty of Scripture, but rather repugnant to the Word of God'.[41] Seen in this light, Palma's work at the oratory of San Fantin was an important moment in the history of Venetian art since the decorative programme promoted every aspect that the Anglican religion warned against, including for the first time in Venice an explicit depiction of purgatory and of indulgences.

In all the areas of sixteenth-century reform for which Venice could be judged, art and architecture emerge as two of the most significant. Notwithstanding the evident importance of generous patrons, whose efforts were complemented by an ecclesiastical apparatus supportive of their aims, ultimately it was in the hands of the city's architects, sculptors, and painters to create a reformed devotional art that could adequately respond to the religious urgencies of the age. Some managed this better than others, but since it has been shown that it was unusual that the Church in Venice interfered much in their activities, the role that they played in articulating and thus moulding the spiritual world of their time should not be underestimated. This is to suggest not that the artists were themselves paragons of piety, but that the best of them were capable of inventing novel visual solutions that encouraged certain beliefs at a pregnant moment in the history of art.

NOTES

1 Demus, *The Mosaics of San Marco in Venice*, vol. 1: 56–57; Andaloro et al., *San Marco*, 47. The mosaic was restored between 1400 and 1500 and again in the 1870s. The tight hand and arm may be original, according to Demus, who notes the 'vandalism' of the nineteenth-century restorers.

2 Demus conceded that the tenor of the inscription was more Byzantine 'or more reminiscent of the original ideas of the iconoclastic controversy' compared with other parallels in twelfth-century monuments and literary works in both Italy and the north, which he thought had a more important influence than the Nicene context. Nevertheless, he also argued that 'it would certainly be tempting to see in this inscription (and in the image of Christ with which it is connected) the copy of an inscription (and image) dating back to the time of the iconoclastic controversy of the eighth and ninth centuries'. Demus, *The Mosaics of San Marco in Venice*, vol. 1: 56–57.

3 Stringa, *Venetia, città nobilissima, et singolare*, 32r–v. Neither Stringa nor Fynes Moryson (see note 4) give a precise location, with the former noting that it was by the same author 'in another place'. Demus did not comment on this inscription in his discussion of the Saint Clement chapel, and it was no longer cited by the time of Camillo Boito, *La Basilique de St. Marc à Venise étudiée au double point de vue de l'art et de l'histoire*, trans. Alfred Cruvellié (Venice: Ongania, 1889), vol. 3: 855.

4 Moryson, *An itinerary written by Fynes Moryson … containing his ten yeeres travell through the twelve dominions of Germany, Bohmerland, Sweitzerland, Netherland, Denmarke, Poland, Italy, Turky, France, England, Scotland, and Ireland*, book 2, part 1, 79–80.

5 For the Nec-Deus distich, widely used in medieval images to refer to the image as prototype as well as warning against idolatry, see Ragne Bugge, 'Effigiem Christi, qui transis, semper honora: Verses Condemning the Cult of Sacred Images in Art and Literature', *Acta ad archaeologiam et artium historiam pertinentia* 6 (1975): 127–40; Jack M. Greenstein, 'On Alberti's "Sign": Vision and Composition in Quattrocento Painting', *Art Bulletin* 79, no. 4 (1997): 674–76.

6 Bugge, 'Effigiem Christi, qui transis, semper honora', 127–29.

7 Writing in 1509, Marcantonio Sabellico noted the distich was visible in Venice 'on an edifice of gold'. He appears to have been the first to propose that its origins related to the Second Nicaean Council. Bugge, 'Effigiem Christi, qui transis, semper honora', 129.

8 Stringa, *Venetia, città nobilissima, et singolare*, 32r.

9 See Bugge, 'Effigiem Christi, qui transis, semper honora', 129.

10 Richard Cocke, 'Exemplary Lives: Veronese's Representations of Martyrdom and the Council of Trent', *Renaissance Studies* 10, no. 3 (1996): 390–91.

11 Diego Angeli, 'L'arte della Controriforma', *Nuova Antologia: Rivista di Lettere, Scienze ed Arti* 68, no. 1461 (1933): 373.

12 Nichols, *Tintoretto: Tradition and Identity*, 188. In response to Nichols's work, Cole has tentatively explored what he terms an 'anti-materialism' in aspects of both Tintoretto's pictorial practice and Renaissance artifice more broadly. See Michael W. Cole, 'Arti povere, 1300–1650', in *The Matter of Art*, ed. Christy Anderson, Anne Dunlop, and Pamela H. Smith (Manchester: Manchester University Press, 2015), 240–62.

13 Tintoretto was fond of the episode and his workshop produced at least three variations on it: two of the mid 1540s for *cassoni* (one in the Kunsthistorisches of Vienna and the other in a Turinese private collection) and a third in the National Gallery of Art, Washington, now dated either to the extremity of Tintoretto's life or later when the shop was led by Domenico. See Paola Rossi, 'Jacopo Tintoretto alla Madonna dell'Orto', in *La chiesa del Tintoretto: Madonna dell'Orto* (Venice: Parrocchia Madonna dell'Orto, 1994), 105–6. Rossi gives a much earlier date of the mid 1550s for the Washington painting.

14 Freedberg, *The Power of Images*, 384–85. For Calvin's commentary on Exodus 32, see Eire, *War against the Idols*, 210.

15 Ridolfi, *Le maraviglie dell'arte*, vol. 2: 19. Tintoretto asked only for monies to cover the materials used, but the prior agreed to pay him 100 ducats.

16 Freedberg, *The Power of Images*, 384.

17 Moryson, *An itinerary written by Fynes Moryson* . . . , book 2, part 1, 79.

18 Pullan, *Rich and Poor in Renaissance Venice*, 228.

19 Alexander Nagel, 'Experiments in Art and Reform in Italy in the Early Sixteenth Century', in *The Pontificate of Clement VII: History, Politics, Culture*, ed. Kenneth Gouwens and Sheryl E. Reiss (Aldershot: Ashgate, 2005), 403.

20 Serafini, 'Gian Matteo Giberti e il Duomo di Verona', 122.

21 Lippomano, *Confirmatione et stabilimento di tutti li dogmi catholici*, 169v–76, 178v–87.

22 Lippomano, *Confirmatione et stabilimento di tutti li dogmi catholici*, 181v.

23 Lippomano, *Confirmatione et stabilimento di tutti li dogmi catholici*, 181r.

24 Lippomano, *Confirmatione et stabilimento di tutti li dogmi catholici*, 181r. For Lippomano's defence of magnificence, see also Richard Schofield, 'Architettura, dottrina e magnificenza nell'architettura ecclesiastica dell'età di Carlo e Federico Borromeo', in *Architettura e Controriforma: i dibattiti per la facciata del duomo di Milano 1582–1682*, ed. Richard Schofield and Francesco Repishti (Milan: Electa, 2004), 137–41.

25 Contained in the *De ratione aedificiorum*. For this, see Giovanni Sale, 'Architectural Simplicity and Jesuit Architecture', in *The Jesuits and the Arts, 1540–1773*, ed. John W. O'Malley and Gauvin A. Bailey, trans. Philip J. Rosato (Philadelphia: Saint Joseph's University Press, 2005), 33. The distinction is also discussed by Richard Schofield, 'Review of Giovanni Sale, "Pauperismo architettonico e architettura gesuitica. Dalla chiesa ad aula al Gesù di Roma"', *Annali di architettura* 14 (2002): 300.

26 For Canisius, see Jeffrey Chipps Smith, *Sensuous Worship: Jesuits and the Art of the Early Catholic Reformation in Germany* (Princeton, NJ: Princeton University Press, 2002), 55. For Oliva, see Sale, 'Architectural Simplicity and Jesuit Architecture', 44; Francis Haskell, 'The Role of Patrons: Baroque Style Changes', in *Baroque Art: The Jesuit Contribution*, ed. Rudolf Wittkower and Irma B. Jaffe (New York: Fordham University Press, 1972), 60.

27 Lippomano, *Confirmatione et stabilimento di tutti li dogmi catholici*, 182r. The Gospel account does not name the woman as the Magdalen, but both Lippomano and Canisius referred to her as such in keeping with Church tradition.

28 Lippomano, *Confirmatione et stabilimento di tutti li dogmi catholici*, 182v.

29 See Peter C. Sutton, *The Age of Rubens*, Exhibition Catalogue, Museum of Fine Arts, Boston, 22 September 1993–2 January 1994, Toledo Museum of Art, 2 February–24 April 1994 (Boston: Ludion Press, 1993), 9–10; Amanda Wunder, *Baroque Seville: Sacred Art in a Century of Crisis* (University Park: Pennsylvania State University Press, 2017).

30 When Pope Alexander VII toyed with cancelling the inauguration ritual of the *possesso* to give the monies saved to the poor, he was told the sums paid craftsmen and tailors, and as such constituted an act of charity. See Burke, 'Conspicuous Consumption in Seventeenth-Century Italy', 136.

31 Burke, 'Conspicuous Consumption in Seventeenth-Century Italy', 138.

32 In his analysis of the moral purpose of confraternity membership, Rosser points out that 'moral rhetoric has tended to be underestimated by historians, in part because its repetitive character makes it seem platitudinous and in part because of a modern tendency to assume every ideal is merely a material motive in disguise'. Gervase Rosser, 'The Ethics of Confraternities', in *A Companion to Medieval and Early Modern Confraternities*, ed. Konrad Eisenbichler (Leiden: Brill, 2019), 91. Commenting on a study of death rites in Zamora that understood the rituals as revealing nothing more than material concerns with a veneer of spirituality, Eire condemned this 'perilous kind of reductionism'. Eire, *From Madrid to Purgatory*, 250.

33 See the analysis of interlocking motivations in confraternity patronage by Black, *Italian Confraternities in the Sixteenth Century*, 251–52.

34 Bailey argued that the Baroque could not have happened without the endorsement of the importance of images by the Catholic Church in the late sixteenth century. Gauvin A. Bailey, *Baroque and Rococo*, Art & Ideas (London: Phaidon, 2012), 33.

35 Mâle, *L'art religieux de la fin du XVIe siècle, du XVIIe siècle et du XVIIIe siècle*. Discussed also by Jones, *Federico Borromeo and the Ambrosiana*, 98–99.

36 Contained in the 1599 *Testimonio* of Luis Cervera de la Torre. See Eire, *From Madrid to Purgatory*, 337–38.

37 Eire, *From Madrid to Purgatory*, 338.

38 Similar conclusions with regard to the 'new spiritual intensity' of traditional devotional subjects were put forth by Humfrey et al., *The Age of Titian*, 27.

39 Jennifer Mara DeSilva, 'Introduction: "Piously Made": Sacred Space and the Transformation of Behavior', in *The Sacralization of Space and Behavior in the Early Modern World: Studies and Sources*, ed. Jennifer Mara DeSilva (Farnham: Ashgate, 2015), 15–17.

40 Chambers and Pullan, eds., *Venice: A Documentary History*, 195.

41 For the 'violently negative' opinions of Protestant reformers on purgatory, see Griffiths, 'Purgatory', 434–35. For their objections to Loreto and the exterior cult more broadly, see Schofield, 'Architettura, dottrina e magnificenza nell'architettura ecclesiastica dell'età di Carlo e Federico Borromeo', 132–37.

BIBLIOGRAPHY

ARCHIVAL AND MANUSCRIPT SOURCES

Archivio Storico del Patriarcato di Venezia (APV)
    Archivio 'segreto'

Apostolic Visit of 1581

Visite apostoliche, Visita apostolica

Nunnery Visits

Visite pastorali a monasteri femminili, Monialium visitationum sub reverendissimo domino Ioanne Trivisano patriarcha Venetiarum. 1560–1589

Visite pastorali a monasteri femminili, Visite de monache. 1592–1596 (Priuli)

Pastoral Visits

Visitationes ecclesiarum. Correr 1735–1742

Visite parochiali Zane 1601 ad 1604

Visita pastorale del patriarca Giovanni Tiepolo

Visite pastorali, Visitationes Baduarii. 1690–1698

Visite pastorali, Visitationes ecclesiarum. Liber primus (Priuli)

Visite pastorali, Visitationes ecclesiarum Venetiarum per reverendissimum dominum dominum Ioannem Trevisanum patriarca Venetiarum in anno Domini MCCCCCLXI. 1560 ad 1590

Visite Priuli, Supplemento alle visite Priuli. 1591 ad 1598

Sezione Antica

Attestazioni per le professioni di fede richieste agli insegnanti, b. 1

Archivio di Stato di Venezia (ASV)
    Notarile, Testamenti, b. 32, n. 349
    Notarile, Testamenti, b. 222, n. 960
    Notarile, Testamenti, b. 1057, n. 14
    Santa Maria dell'Umiltà, b. 2, fasc. 26b

Bodleian Libraries, Oxford (BL)
    MS. Canon It. 138, Pirro Ligorio, Libri dell'antichità

Biblioteca Nazionale Marciana, Venice (BM)
    MSS. IT. Cl. VII. 2283 (= 9121), Francesco Fapanni, Chiese claustrali di Venezia, 1884
    MSS. Lat. IV (2318–19), Acta Concilii Tridentini

Biblioteca del Museo Correr, Venice (BMC)
    MS.Cl. IV016, Mariegola della Scuola del Santissimo in San Samuele
    MS.Cl. IV025, Mariegola della Scuola del Santissimo in Sant'Agnese
    MS.Cl. IV163, Mariegola dell'Arte dei Pittori
    MS Gradenigo 228/3, J. Grevembroch, Monumenta veneta ex antiquis ruderibus, III
    MS. IV164, Mariegola della Scuola del Santissimo in San Zulian

Museo di San Marco (MSM)
    Mariegola della Scuola del Santissimo in San Giacomo dall'Orio

University of Pennsylvania Libraries
    Milledonne, Antonio. *Dell'Historia del sacro Concilio di Trento. Scritta da Antonio Milledoni segretario del Consiglio de X di Venetia in detto Concilio. Libri due.*

SECONDARY PUBLISHED SOURCES

Acheimastou-Potamianou, Myrtalē, Theopistē Liva-Xanthakē, Vyzantino Mouseio, and

Panepistēmio Athēnōn. *Byzantine and Post-Byzantine Art*. Athens: Ministry of Culture, 1986.

Aikema, Bernard. 'L'immagine devozionale nell'opera di Veronese'. In *Nuovi studi su Paolo Veronese*, edited by Massimo Gemin, 191–203. Venice: Arsenale, 1990.

Aikema, Bernard. *Jacopo Bassano and His Public: Moralizing Pictures in an Age of Reform, ca. 1535–1600*. Translated by Andrew P. McCormick. Princeton, NJ: Princeton University Press, 1996.

Aikema, Bernard. 'Les Jésuites et les arts visuels à Venise: spiritualité, propagande religieuse et raison d'État du XVIe au XVIIIe siècle'. In *Baroque vision Jésuite. Du Tintoret à Rubens*, edited by Alain Tapié, 125–39. Exhibition Catalogue, Musée des Beaux-Arts de Caen, 12 July–13 October 2003. Paris: Somogy, 2003.

Aikema, Bernard. 'Pictor religiosus'. In *Paolo Veronese: l'illusione della realtà*, edited by Bernard Aikema and Paola Marini, 241–54. Exhibition Catalogue, Palazzo della Gran Guardia, Verona, 5 July–5 October 2014. Milan: Electa, 2014.

Aikema, Bernard, and Dulcia Meijers. 'I Catecumeni: Chiesa e Ospedale di S. Giovanni Battista'. In *Nel regno dei poveri: arte e storia dei grandi ospedali veneziani in età moderna, 1474–1797*, 215–23. Venice: Arsenale Editrice, 1989.

Aikema, Bernard, and Dulcia Meijers. 'L'immagine della "Carità Veneziana"'. In *Nel regno dei poveri: arte e storia dei grandi ospedali veneziani in età moderna, 1474–1797*, 71–98. Venice: Arsenale Editrice, 1989.

Aikema, Bernard, and Dulcia Meijers. *Nel regno dei poveri: arte e storia dei grandi ospedali veneziani in età moderna, 1474–1797*. Venice: Arsenale Editrice, 1989.

Albèri, Eugenio. *Le relazioni degli ambasciatori veneti al senato durante il secolo decimosesto*. Vol. 4, Series I. Florence: Società editrice fiorentina, 1860.

Albèri, Eugenio. *Le relazioni degli ambasciatori veneti al senato durante il secolo decimosesto*. Vol. 5, series 1. Florence: Società editrice fiorentina, 1861.

Alberigo, Giuseppe. 'De Concile de Trente au tridentisme'. *Irénikon* 54 (1981): 192–210.

Alberti, Leon Battista. *On the Art of Building in Ten Books (1443–52)*. Translated by Joseph Rykwert, Neil Leach, and Robert Tavernor. Cambridge, MA: MIT Press, 1991.

Alberton Vinco da Sesso, Livia, and Franco Signori. 'Il testamento di Jacopo dal Ponte detto Bassano'. *Arte Veneta* 33 (1979): 161–64.

Alcune Interogationi delle cose della fede & del stato overo vivere de Christiani. Verona: Antonio da Portesco, 1540.

Alessandro Bonvicino, Il Moretto. Exhibition Catalogue, Monastery of S. Giulia, Brescia 18 June–20 November 1988. Bologna: Nuova Alfa, 1988.

Allen, Joanne. *Transforming the Church Interior in Renaissance Florence: Screens and Choir Spaces, from the Middle Ages to Tridentine Reform*. Cambridge: Cambridge University Press, 2022.

Ambrosi, Davide. 'La chiesa di Santa Maria dell'Umiltà a Venezia e il suo apparato decorativo: cenni storici e artistici'. *Marcianum* 10 (2014): 129–46.

Ammannati, Bartolomeo. *Lettera di messer Bartolomeo Ammannati scultore, e architetto fiorentino, scritta agli accademici del disegno l'anno 1582*. Florence: Sermartelli, 1582.

Andaloro, Maria, Maria Da Villa Urbani, Ivette Florent-Goudouneix, Renato Polacco, and Ettore Vio. *San Marco: Basilica patriarcale in Venezia: i mosaici, le iscrizioni, la Pala d'oro*. Milan: Fabbri, 1991.

Anderson, Jaynie. 'A Precedent for the Tridentine Decree on Religious Imagery: An Early Restoration of Giambattista Ponchini's "Castelfranco Altarpiece"'. *Arte Veneta* 28 (1975): 239–41.

Angeli, Diego. 'L'arte della Controriforma'. *Nuova Antologia: Rivista di Lettere, Scienze Ed Arti* 68, no. 1461 (1933): 367–78.

Antoniano, Silvio. *Tre libri dell'educazione christiana dei figliuoli*. Verona: Sebastiano dalle Donne, 1584.

Aquino, Lucia, and Simone Giordani. *Francesco Granacci e Giovanni Larciani all'Oratorio di Santa Caterina all'Antella*. Exhibition Catalogue, Oratorio di Santa Caterina all'Antella, Ponte a Ema, Bagno a Ripoli, 14 September 2013–12 January 2014. Florence: Edizioni Polistampa, 2013.

Arasse, Daniel. 'Extases et visions béatifiques à l'apogée de la Renaissance: quatre images de Raphaël'. *Mélanges de l'Ecole française de Rome. Moyen-Age, Temps modernes* 84, no. 2 (1972): 403–92.

Argan, Giulio Carlo. 'La rettorica e l'arte barocca'. *Lettere Italiane* 6, no. 3 (1954): 257–64.

Ariès, Philippe. *Images of Man and Death*. Translated by Janet Lloyd. Cambridge, MA: Harvard University Press, 1985.

Aron-Beller, Katherine. 'The Inquisition, Professing Jews, and Christian Images in Seventeenth-Century Modena'. *Church History* 81, no. 3 (2012): 575–600.

Arrigoni, Luisa. *Restituzioni 2006. Tredicesima edizione: tesori d'arte restaurati*. Edited by Carlo Bertelli. Exhibition Catalogue, Gallerie di Palazzo Leoni Montanari, Vicenza, 25 March–11 June 2006; Pincoteca di Brera, Milan and Gallerie dell'Accademia, Venice, October–November 2006. Vicenza: Banca Intesa, 2006.

Aston, Margaret. *Broken Idols of the English Reformation*. Cambridge: Cambridge University Press, 2015.

Aurenhammer, Hans. 'Venetian Painting in the Age of Titian'. In *Titian and the Renaissance in Venice*, edited by Bastian Eclercy and Hans Aurenhammer, 16–27. Exhibition Catalogue, Städel Museum, Frankfurt Am Main, 13 February–26 May 2019. Munich: Prestel, 2019.

Aurenhammer, Hans H. '"Et ne ho fatto una in Padoa ai Padri della Maddalena": una Cena perduta (e quasi dimenticata) del Veronese'. *Venezia Cinquecento* 11, no. 21 (2001): 121–40.

Aymonino, Adriano. 'La Pala di San Pantalon: immagine devozionale e manifesto politico'. *Venezia Cinquecento* 15, no. 30 (2005): 159–200.

Bagemihl, Rolf. 'Francesco Botticini's Palmieri Altar-Piece'. *The Burlington Magazine* 138, no. 1118 (1996): 308–14.

Bailey, Gauvin A. *Art on the Jesuit Missions in Asia and Latin America, 1542–1773*. Toronto: University of Toronto Press, 1999.

Bailey, Gauvin A. *Baroque and Rococo*. London: Phaidon, 2012.

Bailey, Gauvin A. *Between Renaissance and Baroque: Jesuit Art in Rome, 1565–1610*. Toronto: University of Toronto Press, 2003.

Bailey, Gauvin A. 'Review of "The Sacred Image in the Age of Art: Titian, Tintoretto, Barocci, El Greco, Caravaggio" by Marcia B. Hall'. *Renaissance Quarterly* 65, no. 3 (2012): 885–86.

Bailey, Gauvin A. '"Le style jésuite n'existe pas": Jesuit Corporate Culture and the Visual Arts'. In *The Jesuits: Cultures, Sciences, and the Arts, 1540–1773*, edited by John W. O'Malley, Gauvin A. Bailey, and Steven J. Harris, 38–89. Toronto: University of Toronto Press, 1999.

Bailey, Meryl. 'Carrying the Cross in Early Modern Venice'. In *Space, Place, and Motion: Locating Confraternities in the Late Medieval and Early Modern City*, edited by Diana Bullen Presciutti, 244–69. Leiden: Brill, 2017.

Bailey, Meryl. 'La devozione delle confraternite, la Riforma cattolica e il ciclo del Purgatorio di San Fantin'. In *Ateneo Veneto, 1812–2012: un'istituzione per la città*, edited by Marina Niero, Camillo Tonini, and Michele Gottardi, 211–42. Venice: Linea d'acqua, 2012.

Baker-Bates, Piers. 'The "Cloister Life" of the Emperor Charles V: Art and Ideology at Yuste'. *Hispanic Research Journal* 14, no. 5 (2013): 427–45.

Baldinucci, Filippo. *Notizie dei professori del disegno da Cimabue in qua*. Vol. 4. Florence: Studio per edizioni scelte, 1974.

Baldo, Vittorio. *Alunni, maestri e scuole in Venezia alla fine del xvi secolo*. Como: New Press, 1977.

Baldovin, John F. 'The Constitution on Sacred Liturgy'. In *The Oxford Handbook of Vatican II*, edited by Catherine E. Clifford and Massimo Faggioli, 148–68. Oxford: Oxford University Press, 2023.

Ballarin, Alessandro. 'Osservazioni sui dipinti veneziani del Cinquecento nella Galleria del Castello di Praga'. In *Jacopo Bassano: Scritti 1964–1995*, edited by Vittoria Romani, vol. 1: 29–36. Cittadella: Bertoncello Artigrafiche, 1995.

Barcham, William L. *Grand in Design: The Life and Career of Federico Cornaro, Prince of the Church, Patriarch of Venice and Patron of the*

Arts. Venice: Istituto Veneto di Scienze, Lettere ed Arti, 2001.

Barnes, Bernadine. *Michelangelo in Print: Reproductions as Response in the Sixteenth Century*. London: Taylor & Francis, 2010.

Barnes, Bernadine Ann. 'Aretino, the Public and the Censorship of Michelangelo's Last Judgment'. In *Suspended License: Censorship and the Visual Arts*, edited by Elizabeth C. Childs, 59–84. Seattle: University of Washington Press, 1997.

Barnes, Bernadine Ann. *Michelangelo's Last Judgment: The Renaissance Response*. Berkeley: University of California Press, 1998.

Barocchi, Paola, ed. *Trattati d'arte del Cinquecento: Fra Manierismo e Controriforma*. 3 vols. Bari: Laterza, 1960.

Barocchi, Paola, ed. *La vita di Michelangelo nelle redazioni del 1550 e del 1568*. Vol. 3. Milan: Riccardo Ricciardi, 1962.

Baschet, Armand. 'Paul Véronèse appelé au Tribunal du Saint Office a Venise (1573)'. *Gazette des Beaux-Arts* 23 (1867): 378–82.

Bassegoda i Hugas, Bonaventura, ed. *Arte de la pintura: Francisco Pacheco, 1564–1644*. Madrid: Ediciones Cátedra, 1990.

Baviera, Salvatore, and Jadranka Bentini. *Mistero e Immagine: l'Eucaristia nell'arte dal XVI al XVIII secolo*. Exhibition Catalogue, Chiesa abbaziale di San Salvatore, Bologna, 20 September–23 November 1997. Milan: Electa, 1997.

Baxandall, Michael. *Giotto and the Orators: Humanist Observers of Painting in Italy and the Discovery of Pictorial Composition, 1350–1450*. Oxford: Clarendon Press, 1971.

Bayer, Andrea. 'Bergamo and Brescia'. In *Artistic Centers of the Italian Renaissance: Venice and the Veneto*, edited by Peter Humfrey, 285–326. Cambridge: Cambridge University Press, 2007.

Bellinati, Claudio, et al. *La Basilica del Santo: storia e arte*. Padua: De Luca, Messaggero di S. Antonio, 1994.

Bellori, Giovanni Pietro. *The Lives of the Modern Painters, Sculptors and Architects; a New Translation and Critical Edition*. Edited by Alice Sedgwick Wohl, Hellmut Wohl, and Tomaso Montanari. Cambridge: Cambridge University Press, 2005.

Belting, Hans. *Likeness and Presence: A History of the Image before the Era of Art*. Translated by Edmund Jephcott. Chicago: University of Chicago Press, 1994.

Benzoni, Gino. 'Una città caricabile di valenza religiose'. In *La Chiesa di Venezia tra riforma protestante e riforma cattolica*, edited by Giuseppe Gullino, 37–62. Venice: Studium cattolico veneziano, 1990.

Benzoni, Gino. *Venezia nell'età della Controriforma*. Milan: Mursia, 1973.

Bernard Aikema, and Paola Marini, eds. *Paolo Veronese: l'illusione della realtà*. Exhibition Catalogue, Palazzo della Gran Guardia, Verona, 5 July–5 October 2014. Milan: Electa, 2014.

Bernstein, Alan E. 'Heaven, Hell and Purgatory: 1100–1500'. In *The Cambridge History of Christianity: Christianity in Western Europe c. 1100–c. 1500*, edited by Miri Rubin and Walter Simons, 4:200–16. Cambridge: Cambridge University Press, 2009.

Bertoli, Bruno, and Silvio Tramontin, eds. *La visita pastorale di Giovanni Ladislao Pyrker nella diocesi di Venezia (1821)*. Rome: Edizioni di storia e letteratura, 1971.

Bertoli, Bruno, and Silvio Tramontin, *Le visite pastorali di Jacopo Monico nella diocesi di Venezia (1829–1845)*. Rome: Edizioni di storia e letteratura, 1976.

Bianchi, Ilaria. *La politica delle immagini nell'età della Controriforma: Gabriele Paleotti teorico e committente*. Bologna: Editrice Compositori, 2008.

Bierwirth, Michael. *Tizians Gloria*. Petersburg: Imhof, 2002.

Bison, Massimo. 'Gli spazi del canto: architettura e trasformazioni dei cori abbaziali'. In *Magnificenza monastica a gloria di Dio: L'abbazia di Santa Giustina nel suo secolare cammino storico e artistico*, edited by Giovanna Baldissin Molli and Francesco G. B. Trolese, 305–18. Rome: Viella, 2020.

Black, Christopher F. 'The Development of Confraternity Studies over the Past Thirty Years'. In *The Politics of Ritual Kinship: Confraternities and Social Order in Early Modern Italy*, edited by Nicholas Terpstra, 9–29.

Cambridge: Cambridge University Press, 2000.

Black, Christopher F. *Italian Confraternities in the Sixteenth Century*. Cambridge: Cambridge University Press, 1989.

Blass, Golda. 'Five Hierarchies of Intercessors for Salvation: The Decoration of the Angels' Chapel in the Gesù'. *Artibus et Historiae* 24, no. 47 (2003): 177–208.

Blunt, Anthony. *Artistic Theory in Italy, 1450–1600*. 8th ed. Oxford: Oxford University Press, 1985.

Blunt, Anthony. *Neapolitan Baroque and Rococo Architecture*. London: Zwemmer, 1975.

Blunt, Anthony. *Sicilian Baroque*. London: Weidenfeld & Nicolson, 1968.

Bocchi, Francesco. *Le bellezze della città di Firenze* (1591). Edited by Giovanni Cinelli. Florence: Giovanni Gugliantini, 1677.

Boito, Camillo. *La Basilique de St. Marc à Venise étudiée au double point de vue de l'art et de l'histoire*. Translated by Alfred Cruvellié. 3 vols. Venice: Ongania, 1889.

Bonazza, Natalino, Isabella di Lenardo, and Gianmario Guidarelli, eds. *La chiesa di San Bartolomeo e la comunità tedesca a Venezia*. Venice: Marcianum Press, 2013.

Bordignon, Paolo. 'Antonio Vassilacchi detto l'Aliense: biografia e catalogo delle opere'. MA thesis, Università Ca' Foscari, 2015.

Borean, Linda. 'Documentation'. In *Tintoretto*, edited by Miguel Falomir, English ed., 417–50. Exhibition Catalogue, Museo Nacional del Prado, Madrid, 30 January–13 May 2007. Madrid: Museo Nacional del Prado, 2007.

Borghini, Raffaello. *Il Riposo*. Florence: Giorgio Marescotti, 1584.

Borghini, Raffaello. *Raffaello Borghini's Il Riposo*. Edited and translated by Lloyd Ellis Jr. Toronto: University of Toronto Press, 2007.

Borromeo, Carlo. *Instructionum fabricae et suppelletilis ecclesiasticis*. Milan: P. Pontium, 1577.

Borromeo, Federico. *De pictura sacra: libri due*. Milan: Mediolani, 1624.

Borromeo, Federico. *Sacred Painting; Museum*. Introduction and notes by Pamela M. Jones. Edited and translated by Kenneth S. Rothwell. Cambridge, MA: Harvard University Press, 2010.

Boschini, Marco. *La carta del navegar pitoresco: edizione critica con la 'Breve instruzione' premessa alle 'Ricche minere della pittura veneziana'*. Edited by Anna Pallucchini. Venice: Istituto per la collaborazione culturale, 1966.

Boschini, Marco. *Le minere della pittura*. Venice: Francesco Nicolini, 1664.

Boschloo, Anton. *Annibale Carracci in Bologna: Visible Reality in Art after the Council of Trent*. 2 vols. The Hague: Government Pub. Office, 1974.

Boschloo, Anton. *The Limits of Artistic Freedom: Criticism of Art in Italy from 1500 to 1800*. Leiden: Primavers Pers, 2008.

Botero, Giovanni. *Delle cause della grandezza delle citta libri 3*. Rome: Giovanni Martinelli, 1588.

Botero, Giovanni. *Relatione della Republica Venetiana*. Venice: Giorgio Varisco, 1605.

Bouwsma, William J. *Venice and the Defense of Republican Liberty: Renaissance Values in the Age of the Counter Reformation*. 2nd ed. Berkeley: University of California Press, 1984.

Bowd, Stephen D. 'Review of Marco Cavarzare, "Adhortatio ad concordiam. By Isidoro da Chiara [Temi e testi, vol. 63]"'. *Catholic Historical Review* 96, no. 1 (January 2010): 129–30.

Braun, Joseph. *Der christliche Altar in seiner geschichtlichen Entwicklung*. Vol. 2. Munich: Alte Meister Guenther Koch, 1924.

Broderick, Jarrod Michael. 'The Supremacy of Faith: Venetian Spirituality and Tridentine Doctrine in the Sala Capitolare at the Scuola Grande di San Rocco'. *Studi Veneziani* 85–86 (2022): 81–182.

Brown, Beverly Louise. 'Between the Sacred and Profane'. In *The Genius of Rome, 1592–1623*, edited by Beverly Louise Brown, 274–303. Exhibition Catalogue, Royal Academy of Arts, London, 20 January–16 May 2001. London: Royal Academy of Arts, 2001.

Brown, Jonathan. *Painting in Spain, 1500–1700*. New Haven, CT: Yale University Press, 1998.

Bugge, Ragne. 'Effigiem Christi, qui transis, semper honora: verses condemning the cult of sacred images in art and literature'. *Acta ad archaeologiam et artium historiam pertinentia* 6 (1975): 127–40.

Burckhardt, Jacob. *The Civilization of the Renaissance in Italy*. Translated by S. G. C. Middlemore. 2 vols. New York: Harper & Brothers, 1958.

Burke, Jill. 'The European Nude, 1400–1650'. In *Splendor, Myth and Vision: Nudes from the Prado*, edited by Thomas J. Loughman, Kathleen M. Morris, and Lara Yeager-Crasselt, Clark Art Institute Williamstown, Massachusetts, in association with Museo Nacional del Prado Madrid, 16–49. New Haven, CT: Yale University Press, 2016.

Burke, Jill. 'Nakedness and Other Peoples: Rethinking the Italian Renaissance Nude'. *Art History* 36, no. 4 (2013): 714–79.

Burke, Marcus B. 'Spanish Painters in the Forefront of the Tridentine Reform'. In *Art and Reform in the Late Renaissance: After Trent*, edited by Jesse Locker, 47–71. London: Routledge, 2018.

Burke, Peter. 'Conspicuous Consumption in Seventeenth-Century Italy'. In *The Historical Anthropology of Early Modern Italy: Essays on Perception and Communication*, 132–49. Cambridge: Cambridge University Press, 1987.

Burroughs, Charles. 'Indicating Heaven: Botticelli's "Coronation of the Virgin" and Mediated Imagery'. *Artibus et Historiae* 35, no. 69 (2014): 9–34.

Bury, Michael. *The Print in Italy, 1550–1620*. London: British Museum, 2001.

Caiazza, Pietro. *Un candeliere valdese nel 1540? 'La Lapidazione del Papa' di Girolamo da Treviso il Giovane*. Salerno: Scala, 2017.

Calì, Maria. 'La "religione" di Lorenzo Lotto'. In *Lorenzo Lotto: atti del convengo internazionale di studi per il V centenario della nascita, Asolo, 18–21 September, 1980*, edited by Pietro Zampetti and Vittorio Sgarbi, 243–77. Treviso: Comitato per la celebrazioni lottesche, 1981.

Camesasca, Ettore, ed. *Lettere sull'arte di Pietro Aretino*. 2 vols. Edizioni del Milione. Milan, 1957.

Camille, Michael. *The Gothic Idol: Ideology and Image-Making in Medieval Art*. Cambridge: Cambridge University Press, 1989.

Campbell, Stephen J. *The Endless Periphery: Toward a Geopolitics of Art in Lorenzo Lotto's Italy*. Chicago: University of Chicago Press, 2019.

Campbell, Stephen J., and Michael W. Cole. *A New History of Italian Renaissance Art*. 2nd ed. London: Thames & Hudson, 2017.

Cantimori, Delio. *Prospettive di storia ereticale italiana del Cinquecento*. Bari: Laterza, 1960.

Capitoli d'ordini, e regole da pratticarsi dalli fratelli, e sorelle della veneranda Confraternita del suffragio de' morti canonicamente eretta nella chiesa parochiale di S. Matteo di Rialto di Venetia. Venice: Antonio Bosio, 1681.

Caponetto, Salvatore. *La Riforma protestante nell'Italia del Cinquecento*. Turin: Claudiana, 1992.

Cappelletti, Giuseppe. *Storia della Chiesa di Venezia dalla sua fondazione sino ai nostri giorni*. Vol. 1. Venice: Tipografia Armena di S. Lazzaro, 1849.

Cappelletti, Giuseppe. *Storia della Chiesa di Venezia dalla sua fondazione sino ai nostri giorni*. Vol. 6. Venice: Tipografia Armena di S. Lazzaro, 1850.

Caputo, Vincenzo. 'Gli "abusi" dei pittori e la "norma" dei trattatisti: Giovanni Andrea Gilio e Gabriele Paleotti'. *Studi rinascimentali* 6 (2009): 99–110.

Caravale, Giorgio. *Beyond the Inquisition: Ambrogio Catarino Politi and the Origins of the Counter-Reformation*. Translated by Don Weinstein. Notre Dame, IN: University of Notre Dame Press, 2017.

Casper, Andrew R. *Art and the Religious Image in El Greco's Italy*. University Park: Penn State University Press, 2014.

Casper, Andrew R. 'Display and Devotion: Exhibiting Icons and Their Copies in Counter-Reformation Italy'. In *Religion and the Senses in Early Modern Europe*, edited by Wietse de Boer and Christine Göttler, 43–62. Leiden: Brill, 2013.

Cassese, Michele. 'I tedeschi luterani a Venezia e il loro rapporto con la parrocchia di San

Bartolomeo (dal '500 alla fine della repubblica)'. In *La chiesa di San Bartolomeo e la comunità tedesca a Venezia*, edited by Natalino Bonazza, Isabella di Lenardo, and Gianmario Guidarelli, 249–68. Venice: Marcianum Press, 2013.

Cataneo, Pietro. *I quattro primi libri di architettura*. Venice: House of Aldus, 1554.

Celio, Gaspare. *Memoria fatta dal signor Gaspare Celio dell'habito di Christo: delli nomi dell'artefici delle pitture, che sono in alcune chiese, facciate, e palazzi di Roma*. Naples: Bonino, 1638.

Chakrabortty, Aditya. 'The Billionaires' Donations Will Turn Notre Dame into a Monument to Hypocrisy'. *Guardian*, 18 April 2019.

Chambers, David, and Brian Pullan, eds. *Venice: A Documentary History, 1450–1630*. Reprint of the 1992 ed. Toronto and Buffalo: University of Toronto Press in association with the Renaissance Society of America, 2001.

Chastel, André. *Art of Italian Renaissance*. Translated by Linda Murray and Peter Murray. London: Alpine Fine Arts Collection, 1985.

Chatzēdakēs, Manolēs. *Icônes de Saint-Georges des Grecs et de la collection de l'Institut*. Venice: Neri Pozza, 1962.

Chen, Andrew. *Flagellant Confraternities and Italian Art, 1260–1610: Ritual and Experience*. Amsterdam: Amsterdam University Press, 2018.

'"La chiesa sta malissimo" Giovanni Morone e le cure di una diocesi post-Tridentina'. *Rivista di Storia della Chiesa in Italia*, no. 1 (2013): 131–64.

Cichy, Andrew. 'English Catholic Music after the Reformation to 1750'. In *Oxford Bibliographies*, 2014. www-oxfordbibliographies-com.ezproxy-prd.bodleian.ox.ac.uk/display/document/obo-9780199757824/obo-9780199757824-0009.xml.

Ciletti, Elena. 'On the Destruction of Pontormo's Frescoes at S. Lorenzo and the Possibility That Parts Remain'. *Burlington Magazine* 121, no. 921 (1979): 764–70.

Clark, T. J. *Heaven on Earth: Painting and the Life to Come*. London: Thames and Hudson, 2018.

Cocke, Richard. 'Exemplary Lives: Veronese's Representations of Martyrdom and the Council of Trent'. *Renaissance Studies* 10, no. 3 (1996): 388–404.

Cocke, Richard. *Paolo Veronese: Piety and Display in an Age of Religious Reform*. Aldershot: Ashgate, 2001.

Cocke, Richard. 'Venice, Decorum and Veronese'. In *Nuovi studi su Paolo Veronese*, edited by Massimo Gemin, 241–55. Venice: Arsenale Editrice, 1990.

Col, Andrea del. 'Problemi per la catalogazione e repertoriazione unificata degli atti processuali dell'Inquisizione romana'. *Critica Storica* 25, no. 1 (1988): 155–64.

Cole, Michael W. 'Arti povere, 1300–1650'. In *The Matter of Art*, edited by Christy Anderson, Anne Dunlop, and Pamela H. Smith, 240–62. Manchester: Manchester University Press, 2015.

Cole, Michael W. *Cellini and the Principles of Sculpture*. Cambridge: Cambridge University Press, 2002.

Coleridge, Henry James. *The Life and Letters of St. Francis Xavier*. 2 vols. London: Burns and Oates, 1872.

Concilium Tridentinum: diariorum, actorum, epistularum, tractatuum nova collectio. Vol. 9. Freiburgi Brisgoviae: Herder, 1901.

Condivi, Ascanio. *The Life of Michelangelo*. Edited by Hellmut Wohl. Translated by Alice Sedgwick Wohl. Oxford: Phaidon, 1976.

Contarini, Gasparo. *Gasparis Contareni cardinalis opera*. Farnborough: Gregg, 1968.

Conway, William Martin, ed. and trans. *The Writings of Albrecht Dürer*. New York: Philosophical Library, 1958.

Cooper, Tracy. 'The History and Decoration of the Church of San Giorgio Maggiore in Venice'. PhD thesis, Princeton University, 1990.

Cooper, Tracy. *Palladio's Venice: Architecture and Society in a Renaissance Republic*. New Haven, CT: Yale University Press, 2005.

Cope, Maurice E. *The Venetian Chapel of the Sacrament in the Sixteenth Century*. New York: Garland, 1979.

Coronelli, Marco Vincenzo. *Viaggi*. 2 vols. Venice: Gio. Battista Tramontino, 1697.

Corry, Maya, Deborah Howard, and Mary Laven, eds. *Madonnas & Miracles: The Holy

Home in Renaissance Italy. Exhibition Catalogue, Fitzwilliam Museum, Cambridge, 7 March–4 June 2017. London: Philip Wilson Publishers, 2017.

Corsato, Carlo. 'Dai Dal Ponte ai Bassano: l'eredità di Jacopo, le botteghe dei figli e l'identità artistica di Michele Pietra, 1578–1656'. *Artibus et Historiae* 37, no. 73 (2016): 195–248.

Cortesi Bosco, Francesca. *Gli affreschi dell'Oratorio Suardi: Lorenzo Lotto nella crisi della Riforma*. Bergamo: Bollis, 1980.

Cortesi Bosco, Francesca. 'Il problema della posizione religiosa di Lorenzo Lotto'. *Notizie da Palazzo Albani* 13, no. 1 (1984): 81–89.

Cortesi Bosco, Francesca. 'Riforma, religiosità, arte, alchimia negli affreschi di Lorenzo Lotto dell'Oratorio Suardi di Trescore'. *Notizie da Palazzo Albani* 9 (1980): 28–38.

Corti, Raffaella. 'Pontormo a San Lorenzo: un episodio figurativo dello "spiritualismo" italiano'. *Richerche di storia dell'arte* 6 (1977): 5–36.

Costamagna, Philippe. *Pontormo*. Milan: Electa, 1994.

Cox-Rearick, Janet. *The Drawings of Pontormo*. 2 vols. Cambridge, MA: Harvard University Press, 1964.

Cox-Rearick, Janet. 'Fra Bartolomeo's St. Mark Evangelist and St. Sebastian with an Angel'. *Mitteilungen des Kunsthistorischen Institutes in Florenz* 18 (1974): 329–54.

Cozzi, Gaetano. *Il doge Nicolò Contarini: ricerche sul patriziato veneziano agli inizi del Seicento*. Venice: Istituto per la collaborazione culturale, 1958.

Cozzi, Gaetano. 'I rapporti fra Stato e Chiesa'. In *La chiesa di Venezia tra riforma protestante e riforma cattolica*, edited by Giuseppe Gullino, 11–36. Venice: Studium cattolico veneziano, 1990.

Cozzi, Gaetano. *Paolo Sarpi tra Venezia e l'Europa*. Turin: Einuadi, 1978.

Cristellon, Cecilia, and Silvana Seidel Menchi. 'Religious Life'. In *A Companion to Venetian History, 1400–1797*, edited by Eric Dursteler, 379–419. Leiden: Brill, 2013.

Dal Pozzolo, Enrico Maria 'Anatomia di un S. Girolamo (e una postilla)'. *Il Santo* 32 (1992): 63–82.

Dal Pozzolo, Enrico Maria dal. 'Alcune precisazioni intorno al "Lignum Crucis" di Luca Antonio Busati e all'iconografia della passione in ambito francescano'. *Il Santo* 30 (1990): 107–14.

Da Mantova, Benedetto. *Il Beneficio di Cristo: con le versioni del secolo XVI. Documenti e testimonianze*. Edited by Salvatore Caponetto. Florence: Sansoni; Chicago: Newberry Library, 1972.

Daniele, Giulia. *Prospero Fontana "Pictor Bononiensis" (1509–1597): catalogo ragionato dei dipinti*. Rome: De Luca editori d'Arte, 2022.

D'Arduino, Pietro. *Vita di Antonio Milledonne secretario del Conseglio di X. Da altro Secretario Scritta*. Venice, 1618.

D'Argaville, Brian T. 'Titian's "Cenacolo" for the Refectory of SS. Giovanni e Paolo Reconsidered'. In *Tiziano e Venezia: atti del convegno internazionale di studi. Venice, 1976*, 161–67. Vicenza: Neri Pozza, 1980.

Davidson, Nicholas. 'The Clergy of Venice in the Sixteenth Century'. *Bulletin of the Society of Renaissance Studies* 2 (1984): 19–31.

Davies, Paul. 'Framing the Miraculous: The Devotional Functions of Perspective in Italian Renaissance Tabernacle Design'. *Art History* 36, no. 5 (2013): 898–921.

Davies, Paul, and David Hemsoll. *Michele Sanmicheli*. Milan: Electa, 2004.

De Ceballos, Alfonso Rodríguez G. 'La repercusión en España del decreto del Concilio de Trento acerca de las imágenes sagradas y las censuras al Greco'. *Studies in the History of Art* 13, El Greco: Italy and Spain (1984): 153–59.

De Clippel, Karolien. 'Smashing Images: The Antwerp Nude between 1563 and 1585'. In *Art after Iconoclasm: Painting in the Netherlands between 1566 and 1585*, edited by Koenraad Jonckheere and Ruben Suykerbuyk, 51–73. Turnhout: Brepols, 2012.

De Maio, Romeo. *Michelangelo e la controriforma*. Rome: Laterza, 1978.

De Maio, Romeo. *Pittura e controriforma a Napoli*. Rome: Laterza, 1983.

De Tolnay, Charles. 'Les fresques de Pontormo dans le choeur de San Lorenzo à Florence: essai de reconstitution'. *La Critica d'arte* 9 (1950): 38–52.

Dejob, Charles. *De l'influence du Concile de Trente sur la littérature et les beaux-arts chez les peuples catholiques: essai d'introduction à l'histoire littéraire du siècle de Louis XIV*. Paris: Thorin, 1884.

Delbeke, Maarten. *The Art of Religion: Sforza Pallavicino and Art Theory in Bernini's Rome*. London: Routledge, 2016.

D'Elia, Una Roman. *The Poetics of Titian's Religious Paintings*. Cambridge: Cambridge University Press, 2005.

Della Lucia, Pietro. *Giovan Battista Moroni: itinerari bergamaschi*. I quaderni del Museo Bernareggi. Milan: Silvana Editoriale, 2004.

Demus, Otto. *The Mosaics of San Marco in Venice*. 2 vols. Chicago: University of Chicago Press, 1984.

Demus, Otto. 'Probleme der Restaurierung der Mosaiken von San Marco im XV. und XVI. Jahrhundert'. In *Venezia, centro di mediazione tra Oriente e Occidente, secoli XV–XVI: aspetti e problemi*, edited by Hans-Georg Beck, Agostino Pertusi, and M. I. Manoussacas, 2:633–49. Florence: Leo Olschki, 1977.

Depasquale, Thomas. 'Epilogue Two: Michelangelo's "Last Judgment" and the Reception of the Nude in Counter-Reformation Italy'. In *The Renaissance Nude*, edited by Thomas Kren, Jill Burke, and Stephen J. Campbell, 365–73. Exhibition Catalogue, J. Paul Getty Museum, Los Angeles, 30 October 2018–27 January 2019; Royal Academy of Arts, London, 2 March–2 June 2019. Los Angeles: J. Paul Getty Museum, 2018.

DeSilva, Jennifer Mara. 'Introduction: Piously Made: Sacred Space and the Transformation of Behavior'. In *The Sacralization of Space and Behavior in the Early Modern World: Studies and Sources*, edited by Jennifer Mara DeSilva, 1–32. Farnham: Ashgate, 2015.

Ditcham, Brian G. H. Review of 'Immagini ed eresie nell'Italia del Cinquecento', by Massimo Firpo and Fabrizio Biferali. *Sixteenth Century Journal* 48, no. 3 (2017): 806–7.

Ditchfield, Simon. 'Carlo Borromeo in the Construction of Roman Catholicism as a World Religion'. *Studia Borromaica* 25 (2011): 3–23.

Ditchfield, Simon. 'In Sarpi's Shadow: Coping with Trent the Italian Way'. In *Studi in memoria di Cesare Mozzarelli*, 585–606. Milan: Vita e Pensiero, 2008.

Ditchfield, Simon. 'Of Dancing Cardinals and Mestizo Madonnas: Reconfiguring the History of Roman Catholicism in the Early Modern Period'. *Journal of Early Modern History* 8 (2004): 386–408.

Ditchfield, Simon. 'Tridentine Catholicism'. In *The Ashgate Research Companion to the Counter-Reformation*, edited by Alexandra Bamji, Geert H. Janssen, and Mary Laven, 15–31. Surrey: Ashgate, 2013.

Docampo, Javier, and José Riello Velasco. *La biblioteca del Greco*. Exhibition Catalogue, Museo Nacional del Prado, Madrid, 1 April–29 June 2014. Madrid: Museo Nacional del Prado, 2014.

Dossi, Davide. 'Tra Venezia e Roma: il "Buon Samaritano" di Marcantonio Bassetti conservato a Oxford'. *Bollettino d'Arte* 28 (Series VII) (2015): 81–86.

Douglas-Scott, Michael. 'Prohibition of Text and License of Image: Painters and the Vernacular Bible in Counter-Reformation Venice'. In *Il Rinascimento italiano di fronte alla Riforma: letteratura e arte*, edited by Chrysa Damianaki, Paolo Procaccioli, and Angelo Romano, 231–51. Proceedings of the International Conference, Warburg Institute, London, 30–31 January 2004. Rome: Vecchiarelli Editore, 2005.

Duffy, Eamon. *The Stripping of the Altars: Traditional Religion in England c. 1400–c. 1580*. 2nd ed. New Haven, CT: Yale University Press, 2005.

Duggan, Lawrence G. 'Was Art Really the "Book of the Illiterate"?' *Word & Image* 5, no. 3 (1989): 227–51.

Echinger-Maurach, Claudia. 'Models for Sculptures in Print: Michelangelo's "Samson and Two Philistines" in Lucas Kilian's Engravings'. In *Sculpture in Print, 1480–1600*, edited by Anne Bloemacher, Mandy Richter, and Marzia Faietti, 337–61. Leiden: Brill, 2021.

Echols, Robert, and Frederick Ilchman. *Tintoretto: Artist of Renaissance Venice*. Exhibition Catalogue, Palazzo Ducale, Venice, 7 September 2018–6 January 2019; National Gallery of Art, Washington, 24 March–7 July 2019. New Haven, CT: Yale University Press, 2018.

Edgerton, Samuel Y. 'Icons of Justice'. *Past & Present* 89 (1980): 23–38.

Edgerton, Samuel Y. 'A Little-Known "Purpose of Art" in the Italian Renaissance'. *Art History* 2, no. 1 (1979), 45–61.

Edgerton, Samuel Y. '"Maniera" and the "Mannaia": Decorum and Decapitation in the Sixteenth Century'. In *The Meaning of Mannerism*, edited by Stephen G. Nichols and Franklin W. Robinson, 67–103. Hanover, NH: University Press of New England, 1972.

Edgerton, Samuel Y. *Pictures and Punishment: Art and Criminal Prosecution during the Florentine Renaissance*. Ithaca, NY: Cornell University Press, 1985.

Eire, Carlos M. N. *From Madrid to Purgatory: The Art and Craft of Dying in Sixteenth-Century Spain*. Cambridge: University Press, 1995.

Eire, Carlos M. N. 'The Good, the Bad, and the Airborne: Levitation and the History of the Impossible in Early Modern Europe'. In *Ideas and Cultural Margins in Early Modern Germany: Essays in Honor of H. C. Erik Midelfort*, edited by Marjorie E. Plummer and Robin B. Barnes, 307–23. Farnham: Ashgate, 2009.

Eire, Carlos M. N. *Reformations: The Early Modern World, 1450–1650*. New Haven, CT: Yale University Press, 2016.

Eire, Carlos M. N. *War against the Idols: The Reformation of Worship from Erasmus to Calvin*. Cambridge: Cambridge University Press, 1986.

Ekserdjian, David. 'Bad Reception and the Renaissance Altarpiece'. *Mitteilungen des Kunsthistorischen Institutes in Florenz* 63 (2021): 35–45.

Ekserdjian, David. *The Italian Renaissance Altarpiece: Between Icon and Narrative*. New Haven, CT: Yale University Press, 2021.

Elliott, J. H. *Europe Divided, 1559–1598*. New York: Harper & Row, 1969.

Ervas, Paolo. *Girolamo da Treviso*. Saonara: Il Prato, 2014.

Faber, Felix. *Fratis Felicis Fabri Evagatorium in Terrae Sanctae, Arabiae et Egypti peregrinationem*. Edited by Conrad D. Hassler. Vol. 2. Stuttgart: Societatis literariae stuttgardiensis, 1843.

Falciani, Carlo. 'Il Pontormo a San Lorenzo fra echi valdesiani e riflessi conciliari'. In *Il Concilio di Trento e le arti 1563–2013: atti del convegno, Bologna, 10 dicembre 2013*, edited by Marinella Pigozzi, 53–64. Bologna: Bononia University Press, 2015.

Falciani, Carlo. *Pontormo: disegni degli Uffizi*. Florence: Leo Olschki, 1996.

Fasani, Don Antonio. *Riforma pretridentina della diocesi di Verona: visite pastorali del vescovo G. M. Giberti 1525–1542*. 3 vols. Vicenza: Istituto per le ricerche di storia sociale e di storia religiosa, 1989.

Favaro, Elena. *L'arte dei pittori in venezia e i suoi statuti*. Florence: Leo Olschki, 1975.

Feci, Simona. 'Guardare e vedere al di là del muro: immagini sacre e iconoclastia ebraica a Roma in età moderna'. In *Le Inquisizioni cristiane e gli ebrei: tavola rotonda nell'ambito della conferenza annuale della ricerca, Rome 20–21 December 2001*, edited by Giuseppe Galasso, 407–29. Rome: Accademia nazionale dei Lincei, 2003.

Fehl, Philipp. 'The Naked Christ in Santa Maria Novella in Florence: Reflections on an Exhibition and the Consequences'. *Storia dell'arte* 45 (1982): 161–64.

Fehl, Philipp, and Marilyn Perry. 'Painting and the Inquisition at Venice: Three Forgotten Files'. In *Interpretazioni veneziane: studi di storia dell'arte in honore di Michelangelo Muraro*, edited by David Rosand, 371–83. Venice: Arsenale Editrice, 1984.

Feinberg, Larry J. 'Imagination All Compact: Tavolette and Confraternity Rituals for the Condemned in Renaissance Italy'. *Apollo* 161, no. 519 (2005): 48–57.

Ferretti, Massimo. 'In Your Face: Paintings for the Condemned in Renaissance Italy'. In *The Art of Executing Well: Rituals of Execution in Renaissance Italy*, edited by Nicholas Terpstra,

79–97. Kirksville, MO: Truman State University Press, 2008.

Firpo, Luigi. 'Giovanni Botero'. In *Dizionario Biografico degli Italiani*, 13:352–62. Rome: Treccani, 1971.

Firpo, Massimo. *Artisti, gioiellieri, eretici: il mondo di Lorenzo Lotto tra Riforma e Controriforma*. Rome: Laterza, 2004.

Firpo, Massimo. *Gli affreschi di Pontormo a San Lorenzo: eresia, politica e cultura nella Firenze di Cosimo I*. Turin: Einaudi, 1997.

Firpo, Massimo. *Inquisizione romana e Controriforma: studi sul cardinal Giovanni Morone (1509-80) ed il suo processo d'eresia*. 2nd enlarged ed. Brescia: Morcelliana, 2005.

Firpo, Massimo. *Juan de Valdés and the Italian Reformation*. Translated by Richard Bates. Burlington: Ashgate, 2015.

Firpo, Massimo. 'Storia religiosa e storia dell'arte: i casi di Jacopo Pontormo e Lorenzo Lotto'. In *Storia per parole e per immagini*, edited by Ugo Rozzo and Mino Gabriele, 213–34. Udine: Forum, 2006.

Firpo, Massimo, and Fabrizio Biferali. *Battista Franco 'pittore viniziano' nella cultura artistica e nella vita religiosa del Cinquecento*. Pisa: Edizioni della Normale, 2007.

Firpo, Massimo, and Fabrizio Biferali. *Immagini ed eresie nell'Italia del Cinquecento*. Bari: GLF editori Laterza, 2016.

Firpo, Massimo, and Dario Marcatto. *Il processo inquisitoriale del Cardinal Giovanni Morone: edizione critica*. Vol. 2, part 1. Rome: Istituto storico italiano per l'età moderna e contemporanea, 1984.

Fogolari, Gino. 'Il processo dell'Inquisizione a Paolo Veronese'. *Archivio Veneto* 5, no. 7 (1935): 325–86.

Folin, Enrica. '"Questa breve morte, morendo ben disposto (come far devi) ti sarà un principio dell'eterna felicità e della beata vita." Lettura iconologica del ciclo della Passione nella Scuola "dei Picai" ora Ateneo Veneto'. *Arte Documento* 34 (2018): 176–85.

Fontana, Renzo. '"Solo, senza fidel governo et molto inquieto de la mente": testimonianze archivistiche su alcuni amici di Lotto processati per eresia'. In *Lorenzo Lotto: atti del convengo internazionale di studi per il V centenario della nascita, Asolo, 18–21 September, 1980*, edited by Pietro Zampetti and Vittorio Sgarbi, 279–97. Treviso: Comitato per la celebrazioni lottesche, 1981.

Forcellino, Antonio. *The Sistine Chapel: History of a Masterpiece*. Translated by Lucinda Byatt. Cambridge: Polity Press, 2022.

Ford, Colleen. 'Humanity Chose Notre Dame over Starving Children'. *The Easterner*, 2 May 2019.

Fracchia, Carmen. *Black but Human: Slavery and Visual Arts in Hapsburg Spain, 1480–1700*. Oxford: Oxford University Press, 2019.

Fragnito, Gigliola. 'Gli "spirituali" e la fuga di Bernardino Ochino'. *Rivista storica italiana* 84 (1972): 777–813.

Franklin, David. *Painting in Renaissance Florence, 1500–1550*. New Haven, CT: Yale University Press, 2001.

Freedberg, David. 'Art after Iconoclasm'. In *Art after Iconoclasm: Painting in the Netherlands between 1566 and 1585*, edited by Koenraad Jonckheere and Ruben Suykerbuyk, 21–49. Turnhout: Brepols, 2012.

Freedberg, David. 'Johannes Molanus on Provocative Paintings: De Historia Sanctarum Imaginum et Picturarum, Book II, Chapter 42'. *Journal of the Warburg and Courtauld Institutes* 34 (1971): 229–45.

Freedberg, David. 'Painting and the Counter Reformation in the Age of Rubens'. In *The Age of Rubens*, edited by Peter C. Sutton, 131–45. Exhibition Catalogue, Museum of Fine Arts, Boston, 22 September 1993–2 January 1994; Toledo Museum of Art, 2 February–24 April 1994. Boston: Ludion Press, 1993.

Freedberg, David. *The Power of Images: Studies in the History and Theory of Response*. 2nd ed. Chicago: University of Chicago Press, 1991.

Freedberg, David. 'The Structure of Byzantine and European Iconoclasm'. In *Iconoclasm: Papers Given at the Ninth Spring Symposium of Byzantine Studies, University of Birmingham, March 1975*, edited by Anthony Bryer and Judith Herrin, 165–77. Birmingham: Centre for Byzantine Studies, 1977.

Freedberg, Sydney J. *Painting in Italy: 1500–1600*. 3rd ed. New Haven, CT: Yale University Press, 1993.

From Quinten Metsijs to Peter Paul Rubens: Masterpieces from the Royal Museum Reunited in the Cathedral. Exhibition Catalogue, Cathedral of Our Lady, Antwerp 5 June–15 November 2009. Antwerp: De Kathedraal VZW & Bai, 2009.

Furlan, Caterina. 'La "fortuna" di Michelangelo a Venezia nella prima metà del Cinquecento'. In *Jacopo Tintoretto nel quarto centenario della morte*, edited by Paola Rossi and Lionello Puppi, 19–25. Proceedings of the International Conference, Università Ca'Foscari, Venice, 24–26 November 1994. Padua: Il poligrafo, 1996.

Gage, Frances. 'Caravaggio's Death of the Virgin, Giulio Mancini, and the Madonna Blasphemed'. In *Caravaggio: Reflections and Refractions*, edited by Lorenzo Pericolo and David M. Stone, 83–104. Farnham: Ashgate, 2014.

Gaier, Martin. 'Il mausoleo nel presbiterio: patronati laici e liturgie private nelle chiese veneziane'. In *Lo spazio e il culto: relazioni tra edificio ecclesiale e uso liturgico dal XV al XVI secolo*, edited by Jörg Stabenow, 153–80. Proceedings of the Study Day, Kunsthistorisches Institut, Florence, 2003. Venice: Marsilio, 2006.

Gaier, Martin. 'Il patriarca e il suo vicario: Lorenzo Priuli, Giovanni Mozanega e la questione dei monumenti sepolcrali nella chiesa post-tridentina'. In *La chiesa di San Pietro di Castello e la nascita del patriarcato di Venezia*, edited by Gianmario Guidarelli, Michel Hochmann, and Fabio Tonizzi, 199–217. Venice: Marcianum Press, 2018.

Galtarossa, Massimo. 'Vita d'Antonio Milledonne Secretario del Consiglio di X (1522–1588): contributo sulla concezione del "servito" burocratico a Venezia'. *Studi Veneziani* 39 (2000): 239–52.

Garnett, Jane, and Gervase Rosser. *Spectacular Miracles: Transforming Images in Italy from the Renaissance to the Present*. London: Reaktion Books, 2013.

Gaston, Robert W. 'How Words Control Images: The Rhetoric of Decorum in Counter-Reformation Italy'. In *The Sensuous in the Counter-Reformation Church*, edited by Marcia B. Hall and Tracy E. Cooper, 74–90. Cambridge: Cambridge University Press, 2013.

Gavazza, Ezia, Giovanna Nepi Scirè, and Giovanna Rotondi Terminiello, eds. *Bernardo Strozzi: Genova 1581/82–Venezia 1644*. Exhibition Catalogue, Palazzo Ducale, Genoa, 6 May–6 August 1995. Milan: Electa, 1995.

Gayford, Martin. 'How Veronese Outwitted the Inquisition'. *Telegraph*, 3 April 2014.

Gemin, Massimo. 'Riflessioni iconografiche sulla Cena in casa di Levi'. In *Nuovi studi su Paolo Veronese*, edited by Massimo Gemin, 367–70, Venice: Arsenale Editrice, 1990.

Gentili, Augusto. 'Invenzione di linguaggio, ragioni di significato'. In *Paolo Veronese: Giornate di Studio*, edited by Bernard Aikema, Paola Marini, and Thomas Dalla Costa, 91–99. Venice: Linea d'acqua, 2016.

Gentili, Augusto. 'Lorenzo Lotto, la questione della religione e l'indipendenza intellettuale'. *Bergomum* 113 (2019): 47–53.

Gentili, Augusto. 'La pittura religiosa dell'ultimo Tiziano'. *Studi Tizianeschi* 1 (2003): 9–18.

Gentili, Augusto. 'Il prudente dissenso di Tiziano: dipingere di religione negli anni del disciplinamento'. In *L'ultimo Tiziano e la sensualità della pittura*, edited by Sylvia Ferino-Pagden, 239–45. Exhibition Catalogue, Kunsthistorisches Museum, Vienna, 18 October 2007–6 January 2008; Gallerie dell'Accademia, Venice, 20 January–20 April 2008. Venice: Marsilio, 2008.

Gentili, Augusto. 'San Marco nelle immagini del Cinquecento: problemi di iconologia contestuale'. In *San Marco: aspetti storici e agiografici*, edited by Antonio Niero, 303–12. Proceedings of the International Conference, Venice, 26–29 April 1994. Venice: Marsilio, 1996.

Gentili, Augusto. 'Tintoretto in contesto tra politica e religione'. In *Jacopo Tintoretto*, edited by Miguel Falomir. Proceedings of the International Symposium, 26–27 February 2007, Museo Nacional del Prado, Madrid. Madrid: Museo Nacional del Prado, 2009, 19–24.

Gentili, Augusto. 'Tiziano e la religione'. *Studies in the History of Art* 45, no. 25 (1993): 146–65.

Gentili, Augusto, Giandomenico Romanelli, Philip Rylands, and Giovanna Nepi Sciré. *Paintings in Venice*. Boston: Bulfinch Press, 2002.

Gerola, Giuseppe. 'I testamenti di Francesco il giovane e di Gerolamo da Ponte'. *Bollettino del Museo civico di Bassano* 2 (1905): 103–14.

Giberti, Gian Matteo. *Constitutiones*. Verona: Antonio Putelleto, 1542.

Gietz, Nora. 'The Parish of San Polo and Its Patrimony after the Fall of the Venetian Republic (1797–1814)'. In *La chiesa e la parrocchia di San Polo: spazio religioso e spazio pubblico*, edited by Gabriele Matino and Dorit Raines, 325–39. Rome: Viella, 2020.

Gilbert, Creighton. 'The Archbishop on the Painters of Florence, 1450'. *Art Bulletin* 41, no. 1 (1959): 75–87.

Gilio, Giovanni Andrea. *Dialogue on the Errors and Abuses of Painters*. Edited by Michael Bury, Lucinda Byatt, and Carol M. Richardson. Translated by Michael Bury and Lucinda Byatt. Los Angeles: Getty Research Institute, 2018.

Ginzburg, Carlo. *The Night Battles: Witchcraft & Agrarian Cults in the Sixteenth & Seventeenth Centuries*. Translated by John Tedeschi and Anne Tedeschi. London: Routledge & Kegan Paul, 1983.

Ginzburg, Carlo, and Adriano Prosperi. 'Le due redazioni del "Beneficio di Cristo"'. In *Eresia e riforma nell'Italia del cinquecento*, 135–204. Florence: Sansoni; Chicago: Newberry Library, 1974.

Ginzburg, Carlo, and Adriano Prosperi. *Giochi di pazienza: un seminario sul Beneficio di Cristo*. Turin: Einuadi, 1975.

Gisolfi, Diana. *Paolo Veronese and the Practice of Painting in Late Renaissance Venice*. New Haven, CT: Yale University Press, 2017.

Gleason, Elisabeth G. *Gasparo Contarini: Venice, Rome, and Reform*. Berkeley: University of California Press, 1993.

Gleason, Elisabeth G. 'On the Nature of Sixteenth-Century Italian Evangelism: Scholarship, 1953–1978'. *Sixteenth Century Journal* 9, no. 3 (1978): 3–26.

Goffen, Rona. *Giovanni Bellini*. New Haven, CT: Yale University Press, 1989.

Goffen, Rona. 'Review of "Jacopo Bassano and His Public: Moralizing Pictures in an Age of Reform, ca. 1535–1600" by Bernard Aikema and "The Art of Giovanni Antonio Da Pordenone: Between Dialect and Language" by Charles E. Cohen'. *Art Bulletin* 80, no. 1 (March 1998): 180–88.

Gombrich, Ernst. *Symbolic Images: Studies in the Art of the Renaissance*. London: Phaidon, 1972.

Gonzalez, Xochitl. 'That's Not Censorship. Artists Are Free to Say What They Want, and Free to Face the Consequences'. *Atlantic*, 15 December 2023.

Grasman, Edward. 'On Closer Inspection: The Interrogation of Paolo Veronese'. *Artibus et Historiae* 30, no. 59 (2009): 125–34.

Greenstein, Jack M. 'On Alberti's "Sign": Vision and Composition in Quattrocento Painting'. *Art Bulletin* 79, no. 4 (1997): 669–98.

Grendler, Paul F. *The Roman Inquisition and the Venetian Press, 1540–1605*. Princeton, NJ: Princeton University Press, 1977.

Grendler, Paul F. *Schooling in Renaissance Italy: Literacy and Learning, 1300–1600*. Baltimore: Johns Hopkins University Press, 1991.

Grendler, Paul F. 'The Schools of Christian Doctrine in Sixteenth-Century Italy'. *Church History* 53, no. 3 (1984), 319–31.

Griffiths, Paul J. 'Purgatory'. In *Oxford Handbook of Eschatology*, edited by Jerry L. Walls, 427–56. Oxford: Oxford University Press, 2008.

Grubb, James S. 'When Myths Lose Power: Four Decades of Venetian Historiography'. *Journal of Modern History* 58, no. 1 (1986): 43–94.

Guazzoni, Valerio. *Moretto: il tema sacro*. Brescia: Grafo edizioni, 1981.

Guazzoni, Valerio. 'Un secolo di pittura fra Brescia e Bergamo: l'età rinascimentale'. In *Lotto, Romanino, Moretto, Ceruti: maestri della pittura a Brescia e Bergamo*, edited by Davide Dotti, 13–21. Exhibition Catalogue, Palazzo Martinengo Cesaresco, Brescia, 21 January–11 June 2023. Cinisello Balsamo: Silvana Editoriale, 2023.

Guidarelli, Gianmario. 'Gli altari nel Rinascimento prima del Concilio di Trento'. In *L'Altare: recenti acquisizioni storiografiche e prospettive di ricerca*, edited by Bert Daelemans, 119–37. Proceedings of the XVII International Liturgical Conference, Bose, 30 May–1 June 2019. Magnano: Edizioni Qiqajon, 2021.

Guidarelli, Gianmario. *I patriarchi di Venezia e l'architettura: la cattedrale di San Pietro di Castello nel Rinascimento*. Saggi IUAV. Padua: Il Poligrafo, 2015.

Guidarelli, Gianmario. 'La ricostruzione seicentesca della chiesa di San Bartolomio a Venezia'. In *Da Longhena a Selva: un'idea di Venezia a dieci anni dalla scomparsa di Elena Bassi*, edited by Martina Frank, 29–49. Università Ca' Foscari, Università Iuav di Venezia, Accademia di Belle Arti di Venezia, 9–11 December 2009. Bologna: Archetipolibri, 2011.

Guidarelli, Gianmario. 'Venice's Cathedral of San Pietro di Castello 1451–1630'. In *Architecture, Art and Identity in Venice and Its Territories, 1450–1750: Essays in Honour of Deborah Howard*, edited by Nebahat Avcioglu and Emma Jones, 185–99. Farnham: Ashgate, 2013.

Guidarelli, Gianmario, Michel Hochmann, and Fabio Tonizzi, eds. *La chiesa di San Pietro di Castello e la nascita del patriarcato di Venezia*. Venice: Marcianum Press, 2018.

Habert, Jean-Pierre, ed. *Il 'Paradiso' di Tintoretto: un concorso per Palazzo Ducale*. Exhibition Catalogue, Musée du Louvre, Paris, 9 February–8 May 2006; Museo Thyssen-Bornemisza, Madrid, 6 June–27 August 2006; Palazzo Ducale, Venice, 9 September–3 December 2006. Milan: Continents Editions, 2006.

Hall, Marcia B. *After Raphael: Painting in Central Italy in the Sixteenth Century*. Cambridge: Cambridge University Press, 1999.

Hall, Marcia B. 'Introduction'. In *The Sensuous in the Counter-Reformation Church*, edited by Marcia B. Hall and Tracy E. Cooper, 1–20. Cambridge: Cambridge University Press, 2013.

Hall, Marcia B. ed. *Michelangelo's 'Last Judgment'*. Cambridge: Cambridge University Press, 2005.

Hall, Marcia B. *Renovation and Counter-Reformation: Vasari and Duke Cosimo in Sta Maria Novella and Sta Croce, 1565–1577*. Oxford: Clarendon Press, 1979.

Hall, Marcia B. *The Sacred Image in the Age of Art: Titian, Tintoretto, Barocci, El Greco, Caravaggio*. New Haven, CT: Yale University Press, 2011.

Hall, Marcia B. 'Savonarola's Preaching and the Patronage of Art'. In *Christianity and the Renaissance: Image and Religious Imagination in the Quattrocento*, edited by Timothy Verdon and John Henderson, 494–522. Syracuse, NY: Syracuse University Press, 1990.

Hall, Marcia B., and Tracy E. Cooper, eds. *The Sensuous in the Counter-Reformation Church*. Cambridge: Cambridge University Press, 2013.

Harbison, Craig S. 'Counter-Reformation Iconography in Titian's Gloria'. *Art Bulletin* 49, no. 3 (1967): 244–46.

Harprath, Richard. *Italienische Zeichnungen des 16. Jahrhunderts aus eigenem Besitz*. Exhibition Catalogue, Staatliche Graphische Sammlung, Munich, 1 July–28 August 1977. Munich: Kastner & Callwey, 1977.

Harpster, Grace Theresa. 'Evaluating the Altarpiece: Image Decorum in Post-Tridentine Apostolic Visitations'. *Religions* 14, no. 615 (2023).

Harris, Gareth. 'Renaissance Nude Painting Row at French School Sparks Teacher Walkout'. *Art Newspaper*, 13 December 2023.

Haskell, Francis. Review of 'Painting and the Counter-Reformation', by Federico Zeri. *Burlington Magazine* 100, no. 668 (1958): 396–99.

Haskell, Francis. 'The Role of Patrons: Baroque Style Changes'. In *Baroque Art: The Jesuit*

Contribution, edited by Rudolf Wittkower and Irma B. Jaffe, 51–62. New York: Fordham University Press, 1972.

Heal, Bridget. *A Magnificent Faith: Art and Identity in Lutheran Germany*. Oxford: Oxford University Press, 2017.

Heikamp, Detlef, ed. *Scritti d'arte di Federico Zuccaro*. Florence: Leo Olschki, 1961.

Hibbard, Howard. 'Ut picturae sermones: The First Painted Decorations of the Gesù'. In *Baroque Art: The Jesuit Contribution*, edited by Rudolf Wittkower and Irma B. Jaffe, 29–49. New York: Fordham University Press, 1972.

Hiesinger, Kathryn B. 'The Fregoso Monument: A Study in Sixteenth-Century Tomb Monuments and Catholic Reform'. *Burlington Magazine* 118, no. 878 (1976): 282–93.

Hills, Helen. *The Matter of Miracles: Neapolitan Baroque Architecture and Sanctity*. Manchester: Manchester University Press, 2016.

Hills, Helen, and Melissa Caleresu, eds. *New Approaches to Naples 1500–1800: The Power of Place*. Farnham: Ashgate, 2013.

Hills, Paul. 'Decorum and Desire in Some Works by Tintoretto'. In *Decorum in Renaissance Narrative Art: Papers Delivered at the Annual Conference of the Association of Art Historians, London, April 1991*, edited by Francis Ames-Lewis and Anka Bednarek, 121–28. London: Department of the History of Art, Birckbeck College, 1992.

Hills, Paul. 'Piety and Patronage in Cinquecento Venice: Tintoretto and the Scuole del Sacramento'. *Art History* 6, no. 1, (1983): 30–43.

Hirst, Michael. *Michelangelo: The Achievement of Fame, 1475–1534*. New Haven, CT: Yale University Press, 2011.

Hochmann, Michel. *Peintres et commanditaires à Venise (1540–1628)*. Rome: Ecole française de Rome, 1992.

Hollanda, Francisco de. *Four Dialogues on Painting*. Translated by Aubrey F. G. Bell. London: Oxford University Press, Humphrey Milford, 1928.

Holmes, Megan. *The Miraculous Image in Renaissance Florence*. New Haven, CT: Yale University Press, 2013.

Holt, Elizabeth Basye Gilmore, ed. 'The Book of Suger, Abbot of St-Denis, on What Was Done under His Administration'. In *A Documentary History of Art*. New York: Doubleday Anchor Books, 1957.

Honorati, Maddalena Trionfi. 'Un tabernacolo Ligneo su disegno del Vasari e l'intagliatore Alberto Alberti'. *Antichità viva* 14 (1975): 57–61.

Honour, Hugh, and John Fleming. *The Visual Arts: A History*. 7th ed. Upper Saddle River, NJ: Pearson Education, 2010.

Hope, Charles. 'Altarpieces and the Requirements of Patrons'. In *Christianity and the Renaissance: Image and Religious Imagination in the Quattrocento*, edited by Timothy Verdon and John Henderson, 535–71. Syracuse, NY: Syracuse University Press, 1990.

Hope, Charles. *Titian*. London: Chaucer Press, 2003.

Hopkins, Andrew. *Baldassare Longhena, 1597–1682*. Milan: Electa, 2006.

Hopkins, Andrew. *Baldassare Longhena and Venetian Baroque Architecture*. Revised English ed. New Haven, CT: Yale University Press, 2012.

Hopkins, Andrew. 'Longhena, Lapislazzuli and the Pozzo Brothers: The Tabernacle of the Sacrament for San Daniele in Venice'. In *La festa delle arti: scritti in onore di Marcello Fagiolo per cinquant'anni di studi*, edited by Vincenzo Cazzato, Sebastiano Roberto, and Mario Bevilacqua, 608–11. Rome: Gangemi, 2014.

Howard, Deborah. *Jacopo Sansovino: Architecture and Patronage in Renaissance Venice*. New Haven, CT: Yale University Press, 1975.

Howard, Deborah, and Anne Varick Lauder. 'New Light on Battista Franco in Venice: Part I; The Barbaro Chapel in S. Francesco Della Vigna and the Scuola del Nome di Gesù'. *Burlington Magazine* 148, no. 1244 (2006): 747–53.

Howard, Deborah, and Laura Moretti. *Sound and Space in Renaissance Venice: Architecture, Music, Acoustics*. New Haven, CT: Yale University Press, 2009.

Hsia, R. Po-chia. *The World of Catholic Renewal 1540–1770*. Cambridge: Cambridge University Press, 1998.

Hsia, R. Po-chia. *Trent 1475: Stories of a Ritual Murder Trial.* New Haven, CT: Yale University Press, 1992.

Huber, Hans Dieter. *Paolo Veronese. Kunst als soziales System.* Munich: Wilhelm Fink Verlag, 2005.

Hudon, William V. 'Religion and Society in Early Modern Italy: Old Questions, New Insights'. *American Historical Review* 101, no. 3 (1996): 783–804.

Huffman, Kristin Love, and Iara Dundas. 'Finding San Geminiano: "A Ruby among Many Pearls"'. *Journal of the Society of Architectural Historians* 79, no. 1 (2020): 6–16.

Hughes, Anthony. 'Authority, Authenticity and Aura: Walter Benjamin and the Case of Michelangelo'. In *Sculpture and Its Reproductions*, edited by Anthony Hughes and Erich Ranfft, 29–45. London: Reaktion Books, 1997.

Humfrey, Peter. *The Altarpiece in Renaissance Venice.* New Haven, CT: Yale University Press, 1993.

Humfrey, Peter. 'Altarpieces and Altar Dedications in Counter-Reformation Venice and the Veneto'. *Renaissance Studies* 10, no. 3 (1996): 371–87.

Humfrey, Peter. 'Cima da Conegliano, Sebastiano Mariani, and Alvise Vivarini at the East End of S. Giovanni in Bragora in Venice'. *Art Bulletin* 62, no. 3 (1980): 350–63.

Humfrey, Peter. 'Competitive Devotions: The Venetian Scuole Piccole as Donors of Altarpieces in the Years around 1500'. *Art Bulletin* 70 (1988): 401–23.

Humfrey, Peter. 'Co-ordinated Altarpieces in Renaissance Venice: The Progress of an Ideal'. In *The Altarpiece in the Renaissance*, edited by Martin Kemp, 190–211. Cambridge: Cambridge University Press, 1990.

Humfrey, Peter. *Lorenzo Lotto.* New Haven, CT: Yale University Press, 1997.

Humfrey, Peter. 'Made in Venice'. *Apollo* 178, no. 612 (2013): 76–82.

Humfrey, Peter. *Painting in Renaissance Venice.* New Haven, CT: Yale University Press, 1995.

Humfrey, Peter. 'La pala d'altare veneta nell'età delle riforme'. In *La pittura nel Veneto: il Cinquecento*, edited by Mauro Lucco, 3:1119–80. Milan: Electa, 1999.

Humfrey, Peter. 'Some Thoughts on Writing a History of Venetian Altarpieces'. In *New Interpretations of Venetian Renaissance Painting*, edited by Francis Ames-Lewis, 9–16. London: Birkbeck College, 1994.

Humfrey, Peter. 'Tintoretto and the Altarpiece'. In *Tintoretto: Artist of Renaissance Venice*, edited by Robert Echols and Frederick Ilchman, 122–33. Exhibition Catalogue, Palazzo Ducale, Venice, 7 September 2018–6 January 2019; National Gallery of Art, Washington, 24 March–7 July 2019. New Haven, CT: Yale University Press, 2018.

Humfrey, Peter. 'Venezia 1540–1600'. In *La pittura nel Veneto: il Cinquecento*, Edited by Mauro Lucco, 2:455–554. Milan: Electa, 1998.

Humfrey, Peter, Timothy Clifford, Aidan Weston-Lewis, and Michael Bury, eds. *The Age of Titian: Venetian Renaissance Art from Scottish Collections.* Exhibition Catalogue, Royal Scottish Academy Building, Edinburgh, 5 August–5 December 2004. Edinburgh: National Galleries of Scotland, 2004.

Humphrey, Lyle. 'From Column to Chalice: Passion Imagery in Venetian Mariegole ca. 1320–1550'. In *New Perspectives on the Man of Sorrows*, edited by Catherine R. Puglisi and William L. Barcham, 219–56. Kalamazoo: Medieval Institute Publications, Western Michigan University, 2013.

Hurx, Merlijn. 'Bartolomeo Ammannati and the College of San Giovannino in Florence: Adapting Architecture to Jesuit Needs'. *Journal of the Society of Architectural Historians* 68, no. 3 (September 2009): 338–57.

Ilchman, Frederick. 'Tintoretto as a Painter of Religious Narrative'. In *Tintoretto*, edited by Miguel Falomir, English ed., 63–94. Exhibition Catalogue, Museo Nacional del Prado, Madrid, 30 January–13 May 2007. Madrid: Museo Nacional del Prado, 2007.

Infante, Catherine. *The Arts of Encounter: Christians, Muslims, and the Power of Images in Early Modern Spain.* Toronto: University of Toronto Press, 2022.

Ivanoff, Nicola. *Il ciclo pittorico della Scuola di San Fantin*. Fascicolo speciale per il 150 anniversario 1812–1962. Venice: Stamperia di Venezia, 1963.

Ivanoff, Nicola. 'Una ignota opera del Longhena: l'altare maggiore dei Tolentini'. *Ateneo Veneto* 132 (1945): 96–100.

Jedin, Hubert. 'Catholic Reformation or Counter Reformation?' In *The Counter Reformation: The Essential Readings*, edited by David Luebke, 21–45. Oxford: Blackwell, 1999.

Jedin, Hubert. *La conclusione del Concilio di Trento (1562–1563): uno sguardo retrospettivo a quattro secoli di distanza*. Rome: Editrice Studium, 1964.

Jedin, Hubert. 'Entstehung und Tragweite des Trienter Dekrets über die Bilderverehrung'. *Theologische Quartalschrift* 116, nos. 1–2 (1935): 143–88, 404–29.

Jedin, Hubert. 'Genesi e portata del decreto Tridentino sulla venerazione delle immagini'. In *Chiesa della fede, Chiesa della storia*, 340–90. Brescia: Morcelliana, 1972.

Jedin, Hubert. 'Venezia e il Concilio di Trento'. *Studi Veneziani* 14 (1972): 137–57.

Johnson, Geraldine A. *Renaissance Art: A Very Short Introduction*. Oxford: Oxford University Press, 2005.

Jones, Emma. 'The "cappella maggiore" of San Polo and Its Late Sixteenth-Century Reconstruction'. In *La chiesa e la parrocchia di San Polo: spazio religioso e spazio pubblico*, edited by Gabriele Matino and Dorit Raines, 231–64. Rome: Viella, 2021.

Jones, Emma. 'Priestly Patronage in Late Renaissance Venice: Antonio Gatto's cappella maggiore in San Polo'. In *Carvings, Casts & Collectors: The Art of Renaissance Sculpture*, edited by Peta Moture, Emma Jones, and Dimitrios Zikos, 218–35. London: V&A Publishing, 2013.

Jones, Jonathan. 'A Jester at the Last Supper? How Veronese Became His Era's Ai Weiwei'. *Guardian*, 19 March 2014.

Jones, Pamela M. 'Art Theory as Ideology: Gabriele Paleotti's Hierarchical Notion of Painting's Universality and Reception'. In *Reframing the Renaissance: Visual Culture in Europe and Latin America, 1450–1650*, edited by Claire Farago, 127–39. New Haven, CT: Yale University Press, 1995.

Jones, Pamela M. *Federico Borromeo and the Ambrosiana: Art Patronage and Reform in Seventeenth-Century Milan*. Cambridge: Cambridge University Press, 1993.

Jones, Pamela M. 'Federico Borromeo as a Patron of Landscapes and Still Lifes: Christian Optimism in Italy ca. 1600'. *Art Bulletin* 70, no. 2 (1988): 261–72.

Joppi, Vincenzo. 'Contributo secondo alla storia dell'arte nel Friuli ed alla vita dei pittori e intagliatori friuliani'. In *Monumenti Storici publicati dalla R. Deputazione Veneta di storia patria*. Series 4, miscellanea. Venice: Fratelli Visentini, 1890.

Jung, Eva-Maria. 'On the Nature of Evangelism in Sixteenth-Century Italy'. *Journal of the History of Ideas* 14, no. 4 (1953): 511–27.

Jurkowlaniec, Grażyna. 'Masterpieces, Altarpieces, and Devotional Prints: Close and Distant Encounters with Michelangelo's Vatican Pietà'. Edited by Salvador Ryan. *Religions* 10 (2019).

Kahr, Madlyn. 'The Meaning of Veronese's Paintings in the Church of San Sebastiano in Venice'. *Journal of the Warburg and Courtauld Institutes* 33 (1970): 235–47.

Kaplan, Paul H. D. 'Veronese and the Inquisition: The Geopolitical Context'. In *Suspended License: Censorship and the Visual Arts*, edited by Elizabeth C. Childs, 85–124. Seattle: University of Washington Press, 1997.

Kaplan, Paul H. D. 'Veronese's Last "Last Supper"'. *Arte Veneta* 41 (1987): 51–62.

Katritzky, M. A. 'Lodewyk Toeput: Some Pictures Related to the "commedia dell'arte"'. *Renaissance Studies* 1, no. 1 (1987): 71–125.

Katz, Dana E. *The Jew in the Art of the Italian Renaissance*. Philadelphia: University of Pennsylvania Press, 2008.

Kemp, Martin. *Visions of Heaven: Dante and the Art of Divine Light*. London: Lund Humphries, 2021.

Kessel, Elsje van. *The Lives of Paintings: Presence, Agency and Likeness in Venetian Art of the Sixteenth Century*. Berlin: De Gruyter, 2017.

Kiefer, Geraldine A. Wojno. 'Mid-sixteenth Century Veronese Painting in the Duomo of Mantua'. *Antichità viva* 26 (1987): 34–43.

Kleinbub, Christian K. 'At the Boundaries of Sight: The Italian Renaissance Cloud putto'. In *Renaissance Theories of Vision*, edited by Charles H. Carman and John Shannon Hendrix, 117–33. Abingdon: Routledge, 2016.

Koerner, Joseph Leo. *The Reformation of the Image*. London: Reaktion Books, 2004.

Kominēs, Athanasios D. *Patmos: Treasures of the Monastery*. Athens: Ekdotikē Athēnōn, 1988.

Koshikawa, Michiaki. 'La "Maddalena penitente" della Pinacoteca Capitolina di Domenico Tintoretto'. In *Jacopo Tintoretto nel quarto centenario della morte*, edited by Paola Rossi and Lionello Puppi, 115–18. Padua: Il Poligrafo, 1996.

Kouneni, Lenia. 'From Antiquity to Byzantium in Late Medieval Italy: Hercules on the Façade of San Marco'. In *Herakles Inside and Outside the Church: From the First Apologists to the Quattrocento*, edited by Arlene L. Allan, Eva Anagnostou-Laoutides, and Emma Stafford, 219–47. Leiden: Brill, 2020.

Kren, Thomas. 'Epilogue One: Reformation and beyond in Northern Europe'. In *The Renaissance Nude*, edited by Thomas Kren, Jill Burke, and Stephen J. Campbell, 358–64. Exhibition Catalogue, J. Paul Getty Museum, Los Angeles, 30 October 2018–27 January 2019; Royal Academy of Arts, London, 2 March–2 June 2019. Los Angeles: J. Paul Getty Museum, 2018.

Kren, Thomas, Jill Burke, and Stephen J. Campbell, eds. *The Renaissance Nude*. Exhibition Catalogue, J. Paul Getty Museum, Los Angeles, 30 October 2018–27 January 2019; Royal Academy of Arts, London, 2 March–2 June 2019. Los Angeles: J. Paul Getty Museum, 2018.

Krischel, Roland. *Tintoretto*. Reinbeck bei Hamburg: Rowohlt, 1994.

Krischel, Roland. 'Tintoretto and the Sister Arts'. In *Tintoretto*, edited by Miguel Falomir, English ed., 115–38. Exhibition Catalogue, Museo Nacional del Prado, Madrid, 30 January–13 May 2007. Madrid: Museo Nacional del Prado, 2007.

Lane, Frederic Chapin. *Venice: A Maritime Republic*. Baltimore: Johns Hopkins University Press, 1973.

Lang, Uwe Michael. *The Roman Mass: From Early Christian Origins to Tridentine Reform*. Cambridge: Cambridge University Press, 2022.

Laven, Mary. *Virgins of Venice: Broken Vows and Cloistered Lives in the Renaissance Convent*. London: Viking Penguin, 2002.

Lavin, Irving. 'Bernini's Death'. *Art Bulletin* 54, no. 2 (1972): 158–86.

Le Goff, Jacques. *The Birth of Purgatory*. Translated by Arthur Goldhammer. First published as 'La naissance du Purgatoire', 1981. London: Scolar Press, 1984.

Le Goff, Jacques. *La nascita del Purgatorio*. First published as 'La naissance du Purgatoire', 1981. Turin: Einuadi, 1996.

Leeuwen, Rudie van. 'The Portrait Historié in Religious Context and Its Condemnation'. In *Pokerfaced: Flemish and Dutch Baroque Faces Unveiled*, edited by Katlijne van der Stighelen, Hannelore Magnus, and Bert Watteeuw, 109–24. Turnhout: Brepols Publishers, 2011.

Levy, Evonne. *Propaganda and the Jesuit Baroque*. Berkeley: University of California Press, 2004.

Liberali, Giuseppe. *Documentari sulla Riforma Cattolica pre e post-tridentina a Treviso (1527–1577): La diocesi delle visite pastorali*. Vols. 7 and 8, part 1. Treviso: Seminario vescovile, 1976.

Liberali, Giuseppe. 'Lotto, Pordenone e Tiziano a Treviso: cronologie, interpretazioni ed ambientamenti inediti'. *Istituto Veneto di Scienze, Lettere ed Arti* 33 (1963): 1–121.

Libina, Marsha. *Sebastiano del Piombo and the Sacred Image: Mediating the Divine in the Age of Reform*. Turnhout: Brepols, 2022.

Lillywhite, Marie-Louise. 'Artistic Liberty and Its Limits: Tintoretto's Temptation of Saint Anthony Abbot for Antonio Milledonne'. In *Jacopo Tintoretto: Identity, Practice, Meaning*, edited by Marie-Louise Lillywhite, Tom Nichols, and Giorgio Tagliaferro, 197–232. Rome: Viella, 2022.

Lillywhite, Marie-Louise. 'The Decoration of the Church of San Giacomo dall'Orio in Venice, 1567–1606: Palma il Giovane, Giovanni Maria da Ponte and the Counter-Reformation'. *Artibus et Historiae* 40, no. 79 (2019): 117–50.

Lillywhite, Marie-Louise. 'The Decoration of the Jesuit Church of the Madonna dell'Umiltà in Venice, 1560–1606'. *Artibus et Historiae* 39, no. 77 (2018): 161–200.

Lillywhite, Marie-Louise. 'Family Values & Artistic Alliances in Seventeenth-Century Venice: The Wife and Daughters of Palma il Giovane'. *Master Drawings* 59, no. 2 (2021): 209–42.

Lillywhite, Marie-Louise. 'New Insights into the Tabernacle of the Jesuit Church of Santa Maria dell'Umiltà in Venice'. *Arte Veneta* 70 (2013): 227–33.

Lind, Levy Robert. 'The Latin Life of Peter Paul Rubens by His Nephew: A Translation'. *Art Quarterly* 9 (1946): 37–44.

Lingo, Stuart. *Federico Barocci: Allure and Devotion in Late Renaissance Painting*. New Haven, CT: Yale University Press, 2008.

Lippomano, Luigi. *Confirmatione et stabilimento di tutti li dogmi catholici*. Venice, 1553.

Locatelli, Nicola. 'Ancora sul tabernacolo della chiesa dell'Umiltà a Venezia'. *Arte Veneta* 62 (2005): 102–10.

Locker, Jesse, ed. *Art and Reform in the Late Renaissance: After Trent*. London: Routledge, 2018.

Logan, Oliver. 'Grace and Justification: Some Italian Views of the Sixteenth and Early Seventeenth Centuries'. *Journal of Ecclesiastical History* 20, no. 1 (1969): 67–78.

Loh, Maria H. '"La Custodia degli Occhi": Disciplining Desire in Post-Tridentine Italian Art'. In *The Sensuous in the Counter-Reformation Church*, edited by Marcia B. Hall and Tracy E. Cooper, 91–112. Cambridge: Cambridge University Press, 2013.

Lomazzo, Giovanni Paolo. *Trattato dell'arte della pittura, scoltura et architettura*. Milan: Paolo Gottardo Pontio, 1585.

Lowe, Kate. *Nuns' Chronicles and Convent Culture in Renaissance and Counter-Reformation Italy*. Cambridge: Cambridge University Press, 2003.

Lukehart, Peter M. 'Painting Virtuously: The Counter-Reform and the Reform of Artists' Education in Rome between Guild and Academy'. In *The Sensuous in the Counter-Reformation Church*, edited by Marcia B. Hall and Tracy E. Cooper, 161–86. Cambridge: Cambridge University Press, 2013.

MacCulloch, Diarmaid. *The Later Reformation in England, 1547–1603*. 2nd ed. Basingstoke: Palgrave Macmillan, 2001.

Mackenney, Richard. *Venice as the Polity of Mercy: Guilds, Confraternities, and the Social Order, c. 1250–c. 1650*. Toronto: University of Toronto Press, 2018.

Mâle, Emile. *L'art religieux après le Concile de Trente: étude sur l'iconographie de la fin du 16e siècle, du 17e, du 18e siècle en Italie, en France, en Espagne et en Flandre*. Paris: Armand Colin, 1932.

Mâle, Emile. *L'art religieux de la fin du XVIe siècle, du XVIIe siècle et du XVIIIe siècle: étude sur l'iconographie après le Concile de Trente, Italie-France- Espagne-Flandres*. 2nd ed., rev. and corr. Paris: Armand Colin, 1951.

Malvezzi, Virgilio. *Considerationi con occasione d'alcuni luoghi delle vite d'Alcibiade e di Coriolano*. Bologna, 1648.

Mancinelli, Fabrizio, Gianluigi Colalucci, and Nazzareno Gabrielli. 'The "Last Judgment": Notes on Its Conservation History, Technique, and Restoration'. In *The Sistine Chapel: A Glorious Restoration*, edited by Pierluigi de Vecchi and Carlo Pietrangeli, 236–55. New York: Harry N. Abrams, 1999.

Mancinelli, Fabrizio, Gianluigi Colalucci, and Nazzareno Gabrielli. *Michelangelo: il Giudizio Universale*. Florence: Giunti, 1994.

Mancini, Giulio. *Considerazioni sulla pittura*. Edited by Adriana Marucchi and Luigi Salerno. 2 vols. Rome: Accademia nazionale dei Lincei, 1956–57.

Mander, Carel van. *Dutch and Flemish Painters: Translation from the Schilderboeck*. Edited by Constant van de Wall. New York: McFarlane, 1936.

Mangrum, Bryan, and Giuseppe Scavizzi. *A Reformation Debate*. Toronto: CRRS Publications, 1991.

Manno, Antonio, ed. *La chiesa di San Nicola da Tolentino a Venezia: storia, arte e devozione*. Padua: Il Prato, 2012.

Mansi, Giovanni Domenico. *Sacrorum conciliorum nova et amplissima collectio*. Vol. 32. Paris: H. Welter, 1901.

Mansour, Opher. 'Censure and Censorship in Rome, c. 1600: The Visitation of Clement VIII and the Visual Arts'. In *The Sensuous in the Counter-Reformation Church*, edited by Marcia B. Hall and Tracy E. Cooper, 136–60. Cambridge: Cambridge University Press, 2013.

Mantas, Apostolos G. 'The Iconographic Subject "Christ the Vine" in Byzantine and Post-Byzantine Art'. Δελτίον Χριστιανικής Αρχαιολογικής Εταιρείας 24 (2003): 347–60.

Maratsos, Jessica A. *Pontormo and the Art of Devotion in Renaissance Italy*. Cambridge: Cambridge University Press, 2021.

Marciari, John. 'Girolamo Muziano, Scipione Pulzone, and the First Generation of Jesuit Art'. *Journal of Jesuit Studies* 6, no. 2 (2019): 196–212.

Marías, Fernando. 'Censuring Public Images: A Woodcut in the Inquisition Trial of Esteban Jamete'. In *The Early Modern Hispanic World: Transnational and Interdisciplinary Approaches*, edited by Kimberly Lynn and Erin Kathleen Rowe, translated by Consuelo López-Morillas, 293–318. New York: Cambridge University Press, 2017.

Marina, Areli. 'From the Myth to the Margins: The Patriarch's Piazza at San Pietro di Castello in Venice'. *Renaissance Quarterly* 64, no. 2 (2011): 353–429.

Marinelli, Sergio. 'Adesioni e resistenze al Concilio di Trento nel territorio della Repubblica di Venezia'. In *Il Concilio di Trento e le arti 1563–2013: Atti del convegno, Bologna, 10 dicembre 2013*, edited by Marinella Pigozzi, 73–80. Bologna: Bononia University Press, 2015.

Marinelli, Sergio. 'La pala per l'altar maggiore di S. Giorgio in Braida'. In *Nuovi studi su Paolo Veronese*, edited by Massimo Gemin, 323–32. Venice: Arsenale Editrice, 1990.

Marshall, Louise. 'Purgatory in the Medieval Imagination: The Earliest Images'. In *Imagination, Books & Community in Medieval Europe*, edited by Gregory Kratzmann, 213–19. Proceedings of the Conference Held at the State Library of Victoria, 29–31 May 2008. Victoria: Macmillan Publishers Australia, 2009.

Marshall, Peter. 'Angels around the Deathbed: Variations on a Theme in the English Art of Dying'. In *Angels in the Early Modern World*, edited by Alexandra Walsham and Peter Marshall, 83–103. Cambridge: Cambridge University Press, 2006.

Martin, John Jeffries. *Venice's Hidden Enemies: Italian Heretics in a Renaissance City*. Berkeley: University of California Press, 1993.

Martin, Thomas. *Alessandro Vittoria and the Portrait Bust in Renaissance Venice: Remodelling Antiquity*. Oxford: Clarendon, 1998.

Martineau, Jane, and Charles Hope, eds. *The Genius of Venice, 1500–1600*. Exhibition Catalogue, Royal Academy of Arts, London, 23 November 1983–11 March 1984. London: Royal Academy of Arts, 1983.

Martinioni, Giustiniano. *Venetia città nobilissima, et singolare, Descritta in XIIII. Libri*. Venice: Steffano Curti, 1663.

Mason, Stefania. 'Images of Christ for Venetian Piety and Devotions in the Light of the Council of Trent'. In *New Perspectives on the Man of Sorrows*, edited by Catherine R. Puglisi and William L. Barcham, 295–322. Kalamazoo: Medieval Institute Publications, Western Michigan University, 2013.

Mason, Stefania. 'La "presenza" dei committenti nei dipinti di Paolo Veronese'. In *Paolo Veronese: l'illusione della realtà*, edited by Bernard Aikema and Paola Marini, 153–63. Exhibition Catalogue, Palazzo della Gran Guardia, Verona, 5 July–5 October 2014. Electa: Milan, 2014.

Mason, Stefania. 'Tintoretto the Venetian'. In *Tintoretto: Artist of Renaissance Venice*, edited by Robert Echols and Frederick Ilchman, 36–61. Exhibition Catalogue, Palazzo Ducale, Venice, 7 September 2018–6 January 2019; National Gallery of Art, Washington, 24 March–7 July 2019. New Haven, CT: Yale University Press, 2018.

Mason, Stefania. 'Venetian Painting in the Late Sixteenth and Early Seventeenth Centuries'. In *Venice: Art & Architecture*, edited by Giandomenico Romanelli, 2:524–75. Cologne: Köneman, 1997.

Mason, Stefania, and Andrea Gallo. *Chiesa di San Nicolò dei Mendicoli: arte e devozione*. Venice: Marsilio, 1995.

Mason Rinaldi, Stefania. 'La cappella del SS. Sacramento in San Zulian'. *Atti del Istituto Veneto di Scienze, Lettere ed Arti* 134 (1976): 439–56.

Mason Rinaldi, Stefania. 'Il libro dei conti della famiglia Tiepolo per la Capella di S. Sabba in S. Antonin'. *Istituto Veneto di Scienze, Lettere ed Arti* 135 (1976–77): 193–212.

Mason Rinaldi, Stefania. 'Novità, ritrovamenti e restituzioni a Jacopo Palma il Giovane'. *Arte Veneta* 36 (1982): 145–60.

Mason Rinaldi, Stefania. *Palma il Giovane: l'opera completa*. Milan: Alfieri, 1984.

Mason Rinaldi, Stefania. 'Il tabernacolo della chiesa dei "Giesuiti" alla dogana di mare'. *Arte Veneta* 36 (1982): 211–16.

Massimi, Maria Elena. *La Cena in casa di Levi di Paolo Veronese: il processo riaperto*. Venice: Marsilio, 2011.

Massimi, Maria Elena. 'La cosiddetta "Cena in casa di Levi" di Paolo Veronese: descrizione preliminare all'identificazione del soggetto come "Cena in casa del fariseo"'. *Venezia Cinquecento* 14, no. 27 (2005): 123–68.

Massing, Jean Michel. 'Jerome Nadal's "Evangelicae Historiae Imagines" and the Birth of Global Imagery'. *Journal of the Warburg and Courtauld Institutes* 80 (2017): 161–220.

Matile, Michael. *'Quadri laterali' im sakralen Kontext: Studien und Materialen zur Historienmalerei in venezianischen Kirchen und Kapellen des Cinquecento*. Munich: Scaneg, 1997.

Matile, Michael. '"Quadri laterali" ovvero conseguenze di una collocazione ingrata: sui dipinti di storie sacre nell'opera di Jacopo Tintoretto'. *Venezia Cinquecento* 6, no. 12 (1997): 151–206.

Matthew, Louisa. 'Clergy and Confraternities'. In *Artistic Centers of the Italian Renaissance: Venice and the Veneto*, edited by Peter Humfrey, 92–150. New York: Cambridge University Press, 2007.

Mazzucco, Melania G. *Jacomo Tintoretto & i suoi figli: storia di una famiglia veneziana*. 2nd ed. Milan: Rizzoli, 2009.

McAllen, Katherine. 'Jesuit Martyrdom Imagery between Mexico and Rome'. In *The New World in Early Modern Italy, 1492–1750*, edited by Elizabeth Horodowich and Lia Markey, 143–65. Cambridge: Cambridge University Press, 2017.

McHugh, John A., and Charles J. Callan, trans. *Catechism of the Council of Trent*. Rockford, IL: TAN Books, 1982.

McNair, Philip. 'Benedetto da Mantova, Marcantonio Flaminio, and the "Beneficio di Cristo": A Developing Twentieth-Century Debate Reviewed'. *Modern Language Review* 82, no. 3 (1987): 614–24.

McNamara, Celeste. *The Bishop's Burden: Reforming the Catholic Church in Early Modern Italy*. Washington, DC: Catholic University of America Press, 2020.

McNamara, Celeste. 'What the People Want: Popular Support for Catholic Reform in the Veneto'. *Catholic Historical Review* 102, no. 3 (2016): 492–516.

Meilman, Patricia. *Titian and the Altarpiece in Renaissance Venice*. Cambridge: Cambridge University Press, 2000.

Michelson, Emily. 'Luigi Lippomano, His Vicars, and the Reform of Verona from the Pulpit'. *Church History* 78, no. 3 (2009): 584–605.

Miller, Rachel. 'Patron Saint of a World in Crisis: Early Modern Representations of

St. Francis Xavier in Europe and Asia'. PhD thesis, University of Pittsburgh, 2016.

Modesti, Paola. 'I cori nelle chiese veneziane e la visita apostolica del 1581: il "barco" di Santa Maria della Carità'. *Arte Veneta* 59 (2004): 38–65.

Molà, Luca. *The Silk Industry of Renaissance Venice*. Baltimore: Johns Hopkins University Press, 2000.

Molanus, Johannes. *De picturis et imaginibus sacris*. Louvain: Wellaeus, 1570.

Molanus, Johannes. *Traité des saintes images*. Edited by François Boespflug, Olivier Christin, and Benoit Tassel. 2 vols. Paris: Les Éditions du Cerf, 1996.

Morse, Margaret A. 'Creating Sacred Space: The Religious Visual Culture of the Renaissance Venetian "casa"'. *Renaissance Studies* 21, no. 2 (2007): 151–84.

Moryson, Fynes. *An Itinerary Written by Fynes Moryson … Containing His Ten Yeeres Travell through the Twelve Dominions of Germany, Bohmerland, Sweitzerland, Netherland, Denmarke, Poland, Italy, Turky, France, England, Scotland, and Ireland*. London: J. Beale, 1617.

Muir, Edward. *Civic Ritual in Renaissance Venice*. Princeton, NJ: Princeton University Press, 1981.

Muir, Edward. 'The Virgin on the Street Corner: The Place of the Sacred in Italian Cities'. In *Religion and Culture in the Renaissance and Reformation*, edited by Steven E. Ozment, 25–40. Kirksville, MO: Sixteenth Century Journal Publishers, 1989.

Mullett, Michael A. *The Catholic Reformation*. London: Routledge, 1999.

Munari, Isabella. *Tiziano spirituale: la 'Trinità' per Carlo V tra i venti della riforma*. Milan: Edizioni unicopli, 2019.

Murphy, Caroline P. 'The Market for Pictures in Post-Tridentine Bologna'. In *The Art Market in Italy, 15th–17th Centuries*, edited by Marcello Fantoni, Louisa C. Matthew, and Sara F. Matthews-Grieco, 41–53. Modena: F. C. Panini, 2003.

Nagel, Alexander. 'Art as Gift: Liberal Art and Religious Reform in the Renaissance'. In *Negotiating the Gift: Pre-Modern Figurations of Exchange*, edited by Gadi Algazi, Valentin Groebner, and Bernhard Jussen, 319–60. Göttingen: Vandenhoeck & Ruprecht, 2003.

Nagel, Alexander. *The Controversy of Renaissance Art*. Chicago: University of Chicago Press, 2011.

Nagel, Alexander. 'Experiments in Art and Reform in Italy in the Early Sixteenth Century'. In *The Pontificate of Clement VII: History, Politics, Culture*, edited by Kenneth Gouwens and Sheryl E. Reiss, 385–409. Aldershot: Ashgate, 2005.

Nagel, Alexander. *Michelangelo and the Reform of Art*. Cambridge: Cambridge University Press, 2000.

Nepi Scirè, Giovanna, ed. *Il restauro del Convito in casa di Levi di Paolo Veronese*. Quaderni della Soprintendenza ai Beni Artistici e Storici di Venezia, 11. Venice: Stamperia di Venezia, 1984.

Nethersole, Scott. *Art of Renaissance Florence: A City and Its Legacy*. London: Laurence King Publishing, 2019.

Newett, Margaret M., ed. *Canon Pietro Casola's Pilgrimage to Jerusalem in the Year 1494*. Manchester: Manchester University Press, 1907.

Niccoli, Ottavia. *Vedere con gli occhi del cuore: alle origini del potere delle immagini*. Rome: Laterza, 2011.

Nichols, Tom. *The Art of Poverty: Irony and Ideal in Sixteenth-Century Beggar Imagery*. Manchester: Manchester University Press, 2007.

Nichols, Tom. *Giorgione's Ambiguity*. London: Reaktion Books, 2020.

Nichols, Tom. 'Images of Almsgiving and Poverty in Venetian Art of the Sixteenth Century'. In *Armut und Armenfürsorge in der italienischen Stadtkultur zwischen 13. und 16. Jahrhundert: Bilder, Texte und soziale Praktiken*, edited by Philine Helas and Gerhard Wolf, 349–70. Frankfurt: Peter Lang, 2006.

Nichols, Tom. *Renaissance Art in Venice: From Tradition to Individualism*. London: Laurence King Publishing, 2016.

Nichols, Tom. 'Secular Charity, Sacred Poverty: Picturing the Poor in Renaissance Venice'. *Art History* 30, no. 2 (2007): 139–69.

Nichols, Tom. *Tintoretto: Tradition and Identity*. 2nd revised ed. London: Reaktion, 2015.

Nichols, Tom. *Titian and the End of the Venetian Renaissance*. London: Reaktion Books, 2013.

Nichols, Tom. 'Too Sexy for the Nude: Review of Patricia Lee Rubin, "Seen from Behind: Perspectives on the Male Body and Renaissance Art", James Grantham Turner, "Eros Visible: Art, Sexuality and Antiquity in Renaissance Italy", Jill Burke, "The Italian Renaissance Nude"'. *Oxford Art Journal* 43, no. 3 (2020): 469–76.

Niero, Antonio. 'Un episodio controriformistico di arte veneziana: l'epurazione "post-mortem" del Capp. P. Paolo Piazza'. *Arte Veneta* 28 (1975): 296–97.

Niero, Antonio. 'L'"honestas vitae clericorum" nei sinodi di Giovanni Trevisan patriarca di Venezia'. In *Il Concilio di Trento e la riforma tridentina: atti del convegno storico internazionale, Trento, 2–6 settembre 1963*, 2:745–48. Rome: Herder, 1965.

Niero, Antonio. 'Notizie di archivio sulle pale d'argento delle lagune venete'. *Studi Veneziani* 2 (1978): 257–91.

Niero, Antonio. *I patriarchi di Venezia: da Lorenzo Giustiniani ai nostri giorni*. Venice: Studium cattolico veneziano, 1961.

Niero, Antonio. 'Riforma Cattolica e Concilio di Trento a Venezia'. In *Cultura e società nel Rinascimento tra riforme e manierismi*, edited by Vittore Branca and Carlo Ossola, 77–96. Florence: Leo Olschki, 1984.

Nova, Alessandro. 'Correggio's "Lascivie"'. In *Renaissance Love: Eros, Passion, and Friendship in Italian Art around 1500*, edited by Jeanette Kohl, Marianne Koos, and Adrian W. B. Randolph, translated by Adrian W. B. Randolph, 121–30. Berlin: Deutscher Kunstverlag, 2014.

Nova, Alessandro. *Girolamo Romanino*. Turin: Allemandi, 1994.

Nova, Alessandro. 'La pittura nei territori di Bergamo e Brescia nel Cinquecento'. In *La pittura in Italia: Il Cinquecento*, edited by Giuliano Briganti, 1:105–24. Milan: Electa, 1988.

Nova, Alessandro. 'L'Ultima Cena di Giorgio Vasari per il convento delle Murate: contesto, committenza e un episodio della crisi religiosa del Cinquecento'. In *Dall'alluvione alla rinascita: il restauro dell'Ultima Cena di Giorgio Vasari. Santa Croce cinquant'anni dopo (1966–2016) (Problemi di conservazione e restauro. 47)*, edited by Roberto Bellucci, Marco Ciatti, and Cecila Frosinini, 25–32. Florence: Edifir edizioni, 2016.

Noyes, Ruth S. '"Aut numquid post annos mille quingentos docenda est Ecclesia Catholica quomodo sacrae imagines pingantur?": Post-Tridentine Image Reform and the Myth of Gabriele Paleotti'. *Catholic Historical Review* 99, no. 2 (2013): 239–61.

Nygren, Christopher T. *Titian's Icons: Tradition, Charisma and Devotion in Renaissance Italy*. University Park: Penn State University Press, 2020.

Olivieri, Achille. 'Dipingere ed immaginar: arte ed eresia nel Cinquecento veneto: Riccardo Perucolo'. *Odeo Olimpico* 22, no. 96 (1995): 99–109.

Olivieri, Achille. *Riforma ed eresia a Vicenza nel Cinquecento*. Rome: Herder, 1992.

O'Malley, John W. 'The Council of Trent (1545–63) and Michelangelo's "Last Judgment" (1541)'. *Proceedings of the American Philosophical Society* 156, no. 4 (2012): 388–97.

O'Malley, John W. 'A Historiographical Frame for the Paintings: Recent Interpretations of Early Modern Catholicism'. In *Saints & Sinners: Caravaggio & the Baroque Image*, edited by Franco Mormando, 19–27. Chicago: University of Chicago Press, 1999.

O'Malley, John W. *Trent and All That: Renaming Catholicism in the Early Modern Era*. Cambridge, MA: Harvard University Press, 2000.

O'Malley, John W. 'Trent, Sacred Images, and Catholics' Senses of the Sensuous'. In *The Sensuous in the Counter-Reformation Church*, edited by Marcia B. Hall and Tracy E. Cooper, 28–48. Cambridge: Cambridge University Press, 2013.

Ortolani, Sergio. 'Pietro Aretino e Michelangelo'. *L'arte* 25 (1922): 15–26.

Ostrow, Steven F. 'The Counter-Reformation and the End of the Century'. In *Artistic Centers of the Italian Renaissance: Rome*, edited by Marcia B. Hall, 246–320. Cambridge: Cambridge University Press, 2005.

Paleotti, Gabriele. *Discorso intorno alle imagini sacre e profane*. Bologna: Benacci, 1582.

Paleotti, Gabriele. *Discourse on Sacred and Profane Images*. Translated by William McCuaig. introduction by Paolo Prodi. Los Angeles: Getty Research Institute; Brighton: Roundhouse Distributor, 2012.

Palladio, Andrea. *The Four Books of Architecture* (1570). Introduction by Adolf K. Placzek. New York: Dover Publications, 1965.

Pallucchini, Anna. 'L'abbozzo del "Concilio di Trento" di Jacopo Tintoretto'. *Arte Veneta* 24 (1970): 93–102.

Pallucchini, Rodolfo. *Giovanni Bellini*. Milan: Aldo Martello Editore, 1959.

Pallucchini, Rodolfo. 'Una "parabola del buon samaritano" di Jacopo Bassano'. *Arte Veneta* 41 (1987): 135–38.

Pallucchini, Rodolfo. *La pittura veneziana del Seicento*. 2 vols. Venice: Alfieri, 1981.

Pallucchini, Rodolfo, and Paola Rossi. *Tintoretto: le opere sacre e profane*. 2 vols. Milan: Alfieri, 1982.

Palmieri, Matteo. *Libro del poema chiamato Citta di vita composto da Matteo Palmieri Florentino*. Edited by Margaret Rooke. Northampton, MA: Smith College, 1927.

Panofsky, Erwin. 'Erasmus and the Visual Arts'. *Journal of the Warburg and Courtauld Institutes* 32 (1969): 200–27.

Panofsky, Erwin. *Problems in Titian, Mostly Iconographic*. London: Phaidon, 1969.

Parcours: catalogue guide du Musée des Beaux-Arts de Marseille. Marseilles: Musées de Marseille, 1990.

Parker, Geoffrey. *Emperor: A New Life of Charles V*. New Haven, CT: Yale University Press, 2019.

Pascal, Vuillemin. 'Une reforme de l'interieur ... : les constitutions pastorales du patriarche de venisa Tommaso Dona (1492–1504). Presentation, examen et édition'. *Studi Veneziani* 54 (2007): 65–87.

Pastor, Ludwig von. *The History of the Popes, from the Close of the Middle Ages, Drawn from the Secret Archives of the Vatican and Other Original Sources*. Edited by Ralph Francis Kerr. Vol. 12. London: Kegan Paul, Trench, Trübner, 1914.

Paul, Benjamin. 'The Venetian Doges and Their Tombs in the Early Modern Period: Observations on Self-Representation in a Republic'. In *The Tombs of the Doges of Venice: From the Beginning of the Serenissima to 1907*, edited by Benjamin Paul, 13–28. Proceedings of the International Conference, 30 September–1 October 2010, Centro Tedesco di Studi Veneziani and the Fondazione Cini. Rome: Viella, 2016.

Pavanello, Giuseppe, ed. *La Basilica dei Santi Giovanni e Paolo: Pantheon della Serenissima*. Venice: Marcianum Press, 2013.

Pavanello, Giuseppe. *La Scuola di S. Fantin ora Ateneo*. Venice: Officine grafiche Vittorio Callegari, 1914.

Penny, Nicholas. *The Sixteenth Century Italian Paintings, Volume 2: Venice 1540–1600*. London: National Gallery Company, 2008.

Pevsner, Nikolaus. 'Gegenreformation und Manierismus'. *Repertorium für Kunstwissenschaft* 46 (1925): 243–62.

Pighi, Giovanni Battista. *G. M. Giberti, Vescovo di Verona*. Verona: Marchiori, 1900.

Pignatti, Terisio. *Veronese*. 2 vols. Milan: Alfieri, 1976.

Pignatti, Terisio, and Filippo Pedrocco. *Veronese*. 2 vols. Milan: Electa, 1995.

Pignatti, Terisio, and Giandomenico Romanelli. *Drawings from Venice: Masterworks from the Museo Correr, Venice*. London: Trefoil Books in association with the Drawing Center, New York, 1985.

Pilliod, Elizabeth. *Pontormo, Bronzino, Allori: A Genealogy of Florentine Art*. New Haven, CT: Yale University Press, 2001.

Pilliod, Elizabeth. *Pontormo at San Lorenzo: Art, History, Ritual. The Making and Meaning of a Lost Renaissance Masterpiece*. London: Harvey Miller, 2022.

Pirovano, Carlo. 'Ego vitis vos palmites'. In *Lotto: gli affreschi di Trescore*, edited by Carlo Pirovano. Milan: Electa, 1997, 31–41.

Pirri, Pietro. 'L'architetto Bartolomeo Ammannati e i Gesuiti'. *Archivum Historicum Societatis Iesu* 12 (1943): 5–57.

Pirri, Pietro. *Giuseppe Valeriano, S.I. Architetto e pittore, 1542–1596*. Edited by Raineri C. Colombo. Rome: Institutum historicum S.I., 1970.

Politi, Ambrogio Catarino. *Compendio d'errori, e inganni Luterani, contenuti in un Libretto, Senza nome de l'Autore, intitolato, Trattato utilissimo del benefitio di Christo crucifisso*. Rome, 1544.

Portogruaro, Davide. *Il tempio del Redentore e il convento dei Cappuccini di Venezia*. Venice: Libreria Emiliana Editrice, 1930.

Pouncey, Philip. 'Girolamo da Treviso in the Service of Henry VIII'. *Burlington Magazine* 95, no. 603 (1953): 208, 210–11.

Presciutti, Diana Bullen. 'Miracles in Monochrome: Grisaille in Visual Hagiography'. *Art History* 42, no. 5 (2019): 862–91.

Preston, Patrick. 'The Critical Reception of Michelangelo's "The Last Judgement": The Theological Context'. *Reformation & Renaissance Review* 7, nos. 2–3 (2005): 337–46.

Preto, Paolo. 'Un aspetto della riforma cattolica nel Veneto: l'episcopato padovano di Niccolò Ormaneto'. *Studi veneziani* 11 (1969): 325–63.

Priuli, Lorenzo. *Dottrina christiana, divisa in tre parti, da insegnarsi nella Città e Diocese di Venezia ... e per ordine di Mons. Ill. e Reverendiss. Marco Gradenigo Patriarca di Venezia*. Venice: Alvise Valvasense, 1728.

Priuli, Lorenzo. *Ordini, & auuertimenti, che si deuono osservare ne' Monasteri di Monache di Venetia. Sopra la visita e la clausura*. Venice: Giovanni Antonio Rampazetto, 1591.

Priuli, Lorenzo. *Regole della Compagnia della dottrina Cristiana per le scole delle donne. Fatte d'ordine di Monsig. Illustriss. & Reverendiss. Sig. Cardinal Priuli Patriarca di Venetia*. Treviso: Girolamo Righettini, 1634.

Prodi, Paolo. *Arte e pietà nella Chiesa tridentina*. Bologna: Il Mulino, 2014.

Prodi, Paolo. *Il cardinale Gabriele Paleotti (1522–1597)*. 2 vols. Rome: Edizioni di storia e letteratura, 1959–67.

Prodi, Paolo. *Ricerca sulla teorica delle arti figurative nella Riforma Cattolica*. Bologna: Nuova Alfa, 1984.

Prodi, Paolo. 'Ricerche sulla teorica delle arti figurative nella riforma cattolica'. *Archivio italiano per la storia della pietà* 4 (1965): 121–212.

Prodi, Paolo. 'The Structure and Organisation of the Church in Renaissance Venice: Suggestions for Research'. In *Renaissance Venice*, edited by John Hale, 409–30. London: Faber & Faber, 1973.

Prosperi, Adriano. 'Conversion on the Scaffold: Italian Practices in European Context'. In *Space and Conversion in Global Perspective*, edited by Giuseppe Marocci, Boer de Wietse, Aliocha Maldavasky, and Ilaria Pavan, 44–60. Leiden: Brill, 2015.

Prosperi, Adriano. 'Note in margine a un opuscolo di Gian Matteo Giberti'. *Critica Storica* 4 (1965): 367–402.

Prosperi, Adriano. 'Un processo per eresia a Verona verso la metà del Cinquecento'. *Quaderni Storici* 15 (1970): 773–94.

Prosperi, Adriano. ed. 'The Religious Crisis in Early Sixteenth-Century Italy'. In *Lorenzo Lotto. Rediscovered Master of the Renaissance*, 21–26. Exhibition Catalogue, National Gallery of Art, Washington, 2 November 1997–1 March 1998; Accademia Carrara di Belle Arti, Bergamo, 2 April–28 June 1998; Galeries nationales du Grand Palais, Paris, 12 October 1998–11 January 1999. Washington, DC: National Gallery of Art, 1997.

Prosperi, Adriano. 'Il sangue e l'anima: richerche sulle Compagnie di Giustizia in Italia'. *Quaderni Storici* 17, no. 51 (3) (1982): 959–99.

Prosperi, Adriano. 'Seminario sulle visite pastorali del vescovo G. M. Giberti (1525–42)'. *Richerche di storia sociale e religiosa* 39 (1991): 171–81.

Prosperi, Adriano. *Tra evangelismo e controriforma: G. M. Giberti, 1495–1543*. Rome: Edizioni di storia e letteratura, 1969.

Puglisi, Catherine R., and William L. Barcham. *Art and Faith in the Venetian World: Venerating Christ as the Man of Sorrows*. Turnhout: Harvey Miller, Brepols, 2019.

Puglisi, Catherine R., and William L. Barcham. eds. *Passion in Venice: Crivelli to Tintoretto and Veronese: The Man of Sorrows in Venetian Art*. Exhibition Catalogue, Museum of Biblical

Art, New York, 11 February–12 June 2011. London: Museum of Biblical Art, 2011.

Pullan, Brian S. 'La nuova filantropia nella Venezia cinquecentesca'. In *Nel regno dei poveri: arte e storia dei grandi ospedali veneziani in età moderna, 1474–1797*, edited by Bernard Aikema and Dulcia Meijers, 19–34. Venice: Arsenale Editrice, 1989.

Pullan, Brian S. 'The Old Catholicism, the New Catholicism and the Poor'. In *Timore e carità: i poveri nell'Italia Moderna*, edited by Franco Della Paruta, Mario Rosa, and Giorgio Politi, 13–25. Proceedings of the Conference 'Pauperismo e assistenza negli antichi stati italiani', 28–30 March 1980, Cremona. Cremona: Libreria del convegno editrice, 1982.

Pullan, Brian S. *Rich and Poor in Renaissance Venice: The Social Institutions of a Catholic State*. Oxford: Blackwell, 1971.

Puppi, Lionello. 'Il soggiorno italiano del Greco'. *Studies in the History of Art* 13, El Greco: Italy and Spain (1984): 133–51.

Puppi, Lionello. *Torment in Art: Pain, Violence, and Martyrdom*. New York: Rizzoli, 1991.

Puppi, Lionello. *Un trono di fuoco: arte e martirio di un pittore eretico del Cinquecento*. Rome: Donzelli, 1995.

Rambaldi, Susanna P. 'Ancora sull'evangelismo italiano: Categoria o invenzione storiografica?' *Società e storia*, no. 18 (1982): 935–67.

Rearick, W. R. 'Vita ed opere di Jacopo dal Ponte, detto Bassano c. 1510–1592'. In *Jacopo Bassano c. 1510–1592*, edited by Beverly Louise Brown and Paola Marini, LVII–CLXXXVIII. Exhibition Catalogue, Museo Civico, Bassano del Grappa, 5 September–6 December 1992; Kimbell Art Museum, Fort Worth, Texas, 23 January–25 April 1993. Bologna: Nuova Alfa, 1993.

Redona, Pier Virgilio Begni. 'Pitture e sculture in San Faustino'. In *La chiesa e il monastero benedettino di San Faustino Maggiore in Brescia*, edited by Gianni Mezzanotte, 99–232. Brescia: Editrice La Scuola, 1999.

Richa, Giuseppe. *Notizie istoriche delle chiese fiorentine, divise ne' suoi quartieri*. Vol. 1. Florence: Pietro Gaetano Viviani, 1754.

Richa, Giuseppe. *Notizie istoriche delle chiese fiorentine, divise ne' suoi quartieri*. Vol. 5, part 1. Florence: Pietro Gaetano Viviani, 1757.

Ridolfi, Carlo. *Le maraviglie dell'arte: ovvero le vite degli illustri pittori veneti e dello stato* (1648). Edited by Detlev von Hadeln. 2 vols. Berlin: G. Grote, 1914.

Ringbom, Sixten. *Icon to Narrative: The Rise of the Dramatic Close-Up in Fifteenth-Century Devotional Painting*. Åbo: Åbo Akademi, 1965.

Ripa, Cesare. *Iconologia overo Descrittione di diverse imagini cauate dall'antichità, & di propria inuentione*. Rome: Lepido Facii., 1603.

Ritzler, Remigio. 'Gli atti della visita apostolica del 1581 ai conventi di S. Maria Gloriosa e di S. Nicoletto dei frati minori conventuali in Venezia'. *Miscellanea Francescana* 69 (1969): 153–86.

Roberts, Joe. 'Anger at Fundraiser for Notre Dame Instead of Homeless Parisians'. *Metro*, 16 April 2019.

Rodetis, George A. 'El Greco's Statements on Michelangelo the Painter'. *Journal of Aesthetic Education* 31, no. 3 (1997): 25–37.

Romanelli, Giandomenico. *Il pittore prigioniero*. Venice: Marsilio, 2014.

Romanelli, Giandomenico. 'Tra Giovanni Battista Cima e Riccardo Perucolo: un cinquantennio speciale a Conegliano'. In *Un Cinquecento inquieto: da Cima da Conegliano al rogo di Riccardo Perucolo*, edited by Giandomenico Romanelli and Giorgio Fossaluzza, 16–39. Exhibition Catalogue, Palazzo Sarcinelli, Conegliano, 1 March–8 June 2014. Venice: Marsilio, 2014.

Romanelli, Giandomenico, and Giorgio Fossaluzza, eds. *Un Cinquecento inquieto: da Cima da Conegliano al rogo di Riccardo Perucolo*'. Exhibition Catalogue, Palazzo Sarcinelli, Conegliano, 1 March–8 June 2014. Venice: Marsilio, 2014.

Romani, Vittoria. '"Picturae opus adiecit Paulus Calliarius Veronensis celebris pictor". La pala dell'altare maggiore di Santa Giustina'. In *Magnificenza monastica a gloria di Dio: L'abbazia di Santa Giustina nel suo secolare cammino storico e artistico*, edited by Giovanna

Baldissin Molli and Francesco G. B. Trolese, 365–72. Rome: Viella, 2020.

Romano, Giovanni. 'La Bibbia di Lotto'. *Paragone* 27, nos. 317–19 (1976): 82–91.

Roncalli, Angelo Giuseppe. *Gli atti della visita apostolica di San Carlo Borromeo a Bergamo* (1575). 2 vols. Florence: Leo Olschki, 1936–57.

Rosand, David. 'The Crisis of the Venetian Renaissance Tradition'. *L'arte* 11–12 (1970): 5–53.

Rosand, David. *Painting in Cinquecento Venice: Titian, Veronese, Tintoretto*. New Haven, CT: Yale University Press, 1982.

Rosand, David. 'Palma Il Giovane and Venetian Mannerism'. PhD thesis, Columbia University, 1965.

Roskill, Mark W. *Dolce's Aretino and Venetian Art Theory of the Cinquecento*. Toronto: University of Toronto Press in association with the Renaissance Society of America, 2000.

Rosser, Gervase. 'The Ethics of Confraternities'. In *A Companion to Medieval and Early Modern Confraternities*, edited by Konrad Eisenbichler, 91–108. Leiden: Brill, 2019.

Rossi, Paola. 'Altare maggiore'. In *La Basilica dei Santi Giovanni e Paolo: Pantheon della Serenissima*, edited by Giuseppe Pavanello and Matteo De Fina, 384–87. Venice: Marcianum Press, 2013.

Rossi, Paola. 'Jacopo Tintoretto alla Madonna dell'Orto'. In *La chiesa del Tintoretto: Madonna dell'Orto*, 93–150. Venice: Parrocchia Madonna dell'Orto, 1994.

Rubin, Patricia Lee. *Seen from Behind: Perspectives on the Male Body and Renaissance Art*. New Haven, CT: Yale University Press, 2018.

Ruggiero, Guido. *The Boundaries of Eros: Sex Crime and Sexuality in Renaissance Venice*. New York: Oxford University Press, 1985.

Ruskin, John. *Guide to the Principal Pictures of the Academy of Fine Arts at Venice*. London: Hazell, Watson and Viney, 1877.

Ruskin, John. *The Relation between Michael Angelo and Tintoret: Seventh of the Course of Lectures on Sculpture Delivered at Oxford, 1870–71*. London: Smith, Elder, 1872.

Ruskin, John. *The Stones of Venice: The Fall*. Vol. 3. London: Smith, Elder, 1853.

Ruskin, John. *The Stones of Venice: The Foundations*. Vol. 1. London: J. Wiley, 1851.

Russell, Camilla. 'Religious Reforming Currents in Sixteenth-Century Italy: The Spirituali and the Tridentine Debates over Church Reform'. *Journal of Religious History* 38, no. 4 (December 2014): 457–75.

Salas, Xavier de. 'Miguel Angel y El Greco'. In *El Greco y el arte de su tiempo: las notas de El Greco a Vasari*, 33–52. Madrid: Real Fundación de Toledo, 1992.

Sale, Giovanni. 'Architectural Simplicity and Jesuit Architecture'. In *The Jesuits and the Arts, 1540–1773*, edited by John W. O'Malley and Gauvin A. Bailey, translated by Philip J. Rosato, 29–44. Philadelphia: Saint Joseph's University Press, 2005.

Salomon, Xavier F. 'Francesco degli Arbori's Chapel in Murano and Its Decoration by Paolo Veronese'. In *Veronese in Murano: Two Venetian Renaissance Masterpieces Restored*, 15–59. New York: Frick Collection, 2017.

Salomon, Xavier F. 'Review of "La Cena in casa di Levi di Paolo Veronese. Il processo riaperto" by Maria Elena Massimi'. *Burlington Magazine* 154, no. 1313 (2012): 581–83.

Salomon, Xavier F. '"A ruby among many pearls": The Lost Church of San Geminiano in Venice and Its Sixteenth-Century Decoration'. In *David Bowie's Tintoretto: Angel Foretelling the Martyrdom of Saint Catherine of Alexandria*, edited by Benjamin van Beneden and Nicola Jennings, 54–69. London: Colagni Foundation, 2017.

Salomon, Xavier F. *Veronese*. Exhibition Catalogue, National Gallery, London, 19 March–15 June 2014. London: National Gallery Company, 2014.

Salzberg, Rosa M. 'The Margins in the Centre: Working around Rialto in Sixteenth-Century Venice'. In *The Place of the Social Margins*, edited by Andrew Spicer and Jane L. Stevens Crawshaw. London: Routledge, 2016.

Sancassani, Giulio. 'Il pittore Girolamo Valenti da Vicenza in carcere a Verona per eresia nel 1559'. *Atti e memorie dell'Accademia di Agricoltura, Scienze e Lettere di Verona* 26, no. 6 (1976): 191–95.

Sansovino, Francesco. *Venetia città nobilissima et singolare, descritta in XIIII. Libri.* Venice: Giacomo Sansovino, 1581.

Sapienza, Valentina. 'L'arte dei pittori a Venezia tra Quattro e Cinquecento: Una comunità? Alla ricerca di un'identità tra pratiche di mestiere e apprendistato'. In *Comunità e società nel commonwealth Veneziano*, edited by Gherardo Ortalli, Ermanno Orlando, and Oliver Jens Schmitt, 224. Venice: Istituto Veneto di Scienze, Lettere ed Arti, 2018.

Sapienza, Valentina. *La chiesa di San Zulian a Venezia nel Cinquecento: dalla ricostruzione sansoviniana alle grandi imprese decorative di fine secolo.* Rome: École française de Rome, 2018.

Sapienza, Valentina. '(Intorno a) Leonardo Corona (1552–1596). Documenti, fonti e indagini storici-contestuali'. PhD thesis, Università Ca' Foscari, 2011.

Sapienza, Valentina. 'Note sulle "Storie della Passione" di Leonardo Corona all'Ateneo Veneto'. In *Ateneo Veneto, 1812–2012*, edited by Michele Gottardi, Marina Niero, and Camillo Tonini, 243–49. Venice: Linea d'acqua, 2012.

Savy, Barbara Maria. *Manducatio per visum: temi eucaristici nella pittura di Romanino e Moretto.* Cittadella: Bertoncello Artigrafiche, 2006.

Scavizzi, Giuseppe. *The Controversy on Images from Calvin to Baronius.* New York: Peter Lang, 1994.

Schaffran, Emerich. 'Der Inquisizionsprozess gegen Paolo Veronese'. *Archiv für Kulturgeschichte* 42, no. 2 (1960): 178–93.

Schiller, Gertrud. *Iconography of Christian Art.* 2 vols. London: Lund Humphries, 1971.

Schlitt, Melinda. 'Painting, Criticism, and Michelangelo's "Last Judgment" in the Age of the Counter-Reformation'. In *Michelangelo's 'Last Judgment'*, edited by Marcia B. Hall, 113–49. Cambridge: Cambridge University Press, 2005.

Schofield, Richard. 'Architettura, dottrina e magnificenza nell'architettura ecclesiastica dell'età di Carlo e Federico Borromeo'. In *Architettura e Controriforma: i dibattiti per la facciata del duomo di Milano 1582–1682*, edited by Richard Schofield and Francesco Repishti, 125–249. Milan: Electa, 2004.

Schofield, Richard. 'Carlo Borromeo and the Dangers of Laywomen in Church'. In *The Sensuous in the Counter-Reformation Church*, edited by Marcia B. Hall and Tracy E. Cooper, 187–205. Cambridge: Cambridge University Press, 2013.

Schofield, Richard. 'Review of Giovanni Sale, "Pauperismo architettonico e architettura gesuitica. Dalla chiesa ad aula al Gesù di Roma"'. *Annali di architettura* 14 (2002): 299–301.

Schulz, Anne Markham. *The History of Venetian Renaissance Sculpture ca. 1400–1530.* 2 vols. London: Harvey Miller, 2018.

Schulz, Anne Markham. 'The Life and Works of Jacopo Fantoni, Venetian Sculptor'. *Nuovi studi* 19 (2013): 109–21.

Schulz, Anne Markham. 'Il problema della scultura tarda di Tullio Lombardo'. *Prospettiva*, nos. 115–16 (2004): 42–65.

Schulz, Anne Markham. *The Sculpture of Tullio Lombardo.* London: Harvey Miller, 2014.

Schulz, Anne Markham. 'Two New Works by Antonio Minello'. *Burlington Magazine* 137, no. 1113 (1995): 799–808.

Schulz, Juergen. *Venetian Painted Ceilings of the Renaissance.* Berkeley: University of California Press, 1968.

Schutte, Anne Jacobson. 'Periodization of Sixteenth-Century Italian Religious History: The Post-Cantimori Paradigm Shift'. *Journal of Modern History* 61, no. 2 (1989): 269–84.

Schutte, Anne Jacobson. *Pier Paolo Vergerio: The Making of an Italian Reformer.* Geneva: Droz, 1977.

Schütze, Sebastian. 'The Politics of Counter-Reformation Iconography and a Quest for the Spanishness of Neapolitan Art'. In *Spain in Italy: Politics, Society, and Religion, 1500–1700*, edited by Thomas James Dandelet and John A. Marino, 555–68. Leiden: Brill, 2007.

Scotti, Aurora. 'Architettura e riforma cattolica nella Milano di Carlo Borromeo'. *L'arte* 5 (1972): 54–90.

Scribner, R. W. 'Incombustible Luther: The Image of the Reformer in Early Modern Germany'. *Past & Present*, no. 110 (1986): 38–68.

Scribner, Robert. W. *Popular Culture and Popular Movements in Reformation Germany*. London: Hambledon Press, 1987.

Sebregondi, Ludovica. 'Churches, Convents, Monasteries and Confraternities in Counter-Reformation Florence'. In *The Cinquecento in Florence: 'Modern Manner' and Counter-Reformation*, edited by Carlo Falciani and Antonio Natali, 107–17. Exhibition Catalogue, Palazzo Strozzi, Florence, 21 September 2017–21 January 2018. Florence: Mandragora, 2017.

Seidel, Martin. *Venezianische Malerei zur Zeit der Gegenreformation: kirchliche Programmschriften und künstlerische Bildkonzepte bei Tizian, Tintoretto, Veronese und Palma il Giovane*. Lit Verlag: Münster, 1996.

Seidel Menchi, Silvana. 'The Age of Reformation and Counter-Reformation in Italian Historiography, 1939–2009'. *Archiv für Reformationsgeschichte* 100, no. 1 (2009): 193–217.

Sénécal, Robert. 'Carlo Borromeo's Instructiones fabricae et supellectilis ecclesiasticae and Its Origins in the Rome of His Time'. *Papers of the British School at Rome* 68 (November 2000): 241–67.

Serafini, Alessandro. 'Gian Matteo Giberti e il Duomo di Verona: il programma, il contesto'. *Venezia Cinquecento* 6, no. 11 (1996): 75–161.

Serafini, Alessandro. 'Gian Matteo Giberti e il Duomo di Verona. 2: gli affreschi di Francesco Torbido'. *Venezia Cinquecento* 8, no. 15 (1998): 21–142.

Serafini, Alessandro. 'Girolamo da Treviso, il Giovane'. In *Dizionario biografico degli Italiani*, 56:591–95. Rome: Treccani, 2001.

Shearman, John. 'The "Dead Christ" by Rosso Fiorentino'. *Boston Museum Bulletin* 64, no. 338 (1966): 148–72.

Shearman, John. *Mannerism*. Harmondsworth: Penguin Books, 1967.

Shearman, John. 'Raphael's Clouds, and Correggio's'. *Studi su Raffaello* 1 (1987): 657–68.

Sherman, Allison. *The Lost Venetian Church of Santa Maria Assunta dei Crociferi: Form, Decoration, Patronage*. Edited by Carlo Corsato. London: Independent Publishing Network, 2020.

Simoncelli, Paolo. *Evangelismo italiano del Cinquecento: questione religiosa e nicodemismo politico*. Rome: Istituto storico italiano per l'età moderna e contemporanea, 1979.

Simons, Patricia. 'Artemisia Gentileschi's "Susanna and the Elders" (1610) in the Context of Counter-Reformation Rome'. In *Artemisia Gentileschi in a Changing Light*, edited by Sheila Barker, 41–57. London: Harvey Miller, 2017.

Sinding-Larsen, Staale. *Christ in the Council Hall: Studies in the Religious Iconography of the Venetian Republic*. Rome: 'L'Erma' di Bretschneider, 1974.

Sliwka, Jennifer. *Visions of Paradise: Botticini's Palmieri Altarpiece*. London: National Gallery Company, 2015.

Smith, Logan Pearsall. *The Life and Letters of Sir Henry Wotton*. 2 vols. Oxford: Clarendon Press, 1907.

Smith, Jeffrey Chipps. *Sensuous Worship: Jesuits and the Art of the Early Catholic Reformation in Germany*. Princeton, NJ: Princeton University Press, 2002.

Sohm, Philip. *Pittoresco: Marco Boschini, His Critics, and Their Critiques of Painterly Brushwork in Seventeenth- and Eighteenth-Century Italy*. London: Cambridge University Press, 1991.

Solmi, Edmondo. 'Lettere inedite di Gasparo Contarini nel carteggio del cardinale Ercole Gonzaga'. *Nuovo Archivio Veneto* 7, no. 14 (1904): 245–74.

Sommario dell'Indulgenze, Ordeni, Regole, & Oblighi, che devono esser osservati dalli Fratelli, che vestono l'Habito della veneranda Confraternità della santiss. Madonna del suffragio de'Morti. Venice: Fratelli Pinelli, 1723.

Soranzo, Giovanni. 'Rapporti di S. Carlo con la Repubblica Veneta'. *Archivio Veneto* 27, series 5, nos. 53–54 (1940): 1–40.

Sperling, Jutta Gisela. *Convents and the Body Politic in Late Renaissance Venice*. Chicago: University of Chicago Press, 1999.

Steinberg, Leo. 'A Corner of the "Last Judgment"'. *Daedalus* 109, no. 2 (1980): 207–17, 221–73.

Steinberg, Leo. *The Sexuality of Christ in Renaissance Art and in Modern Oblivion*. 2nd ed., rev. and expanded. Chicago: University of Chicago Press, 1996.

Stella, Aldo. 'La proprietà ecclesiastica nella Repubblica di Venezia dal secolo XV al XVII'. *Nuova rivista storica* 42 (1958): 50–77.

Stoichita, Victor I. *Visionary Experience in the Golden Age of Spanish Art*. London: Reaktion Books, 1997.

Stowell, Steven F. 'Purging the Eye: Images and the Cure for Lust in Catholic Reformation Italy'. In *Renaissance Religions: Modes and Meanings in History*, edited by Peter Howard, Nicholas Terpstra, and Riccardo Saccenti, 207–30. Turnhout: Brepols, 2021.

Stringa, Giovanni. *Venetia città nobilissima, et singolare; descritta già in XIIII. libri da M. Francesco Sansovino*. Venice: Altobello Salicato, 1604.

Stroik, Duncan G. 'Church Architecture since Vatican II'. *Jurist* 75 (2015): 5–34.

Strozzi, Giulio. *Venezia edificata*. Venice: Pinelli, 1624.

Strupp, Joachim. 'The Sculptured Altarpiece in Renaissance Venice, ca. 1460–1530'. PhD thesis, University of St Andrews, 1993.

Sutton, Peter C. *The Age of Rubens*. Exhibition Catalogue, Museum of Fine Arts, Boston, 22 September 1993–2 January 1994; Toledo Museum of Art, 2 February–24 April 1994. Boston: Ludion Press, 1993.

Suykerbuyk, Ruben, and Anne-Laure van Bruaene. 'Towering Piety: Sacrament Houses, Local Patronage and an Early Counter-Reformation Spirit in the Low Countries (1520–1566)'. *Nederlands kunsthistorisch jaarboek* 67 (2017): 118–59.

Tacchi Venturi, Padre Pietro. *Storia della Compagnia di Gesù in Italia*. Vol. 1, part 1. Rome: Civiltà Cattolica, 1931.

Tacke, Andreas. *Der katholische Cranach*. Mainz: Von Zabern, 1992.

Tacke, Andreas. 'With Cranach's Help: Counter-Reformation Art before the Council of Trent'. In *Cranach*, edited by Bodo Brinkmann, 81–89. Exhibition Catalogue, Städel Museum, Frankfurt Am Main, 23 November 2007–17 February 2008; Royal Academy of Arts, London, 8 March–8 June 2008. London: Thames & Hudson, 2007.

Tafuri, Manfredo. *Venezia e Il Rinascimento: religione, scienza, architettura*. Turin: Einaudi, 1985.

Tafuri, Manfredo, and Foscari Antonio. *L'armonia e i conflitti: la chiesa di San Francesco della Vigna nella Venezia del '500*. Turin: Einuadi, 1983.

Tagliaferro, Giorgio. 'Il "Mito" ripensato: trasformazioni della pittura tra Lepanto e l'Interdetto'. In *Celebrazione e autocritica: la Serenissima e la ricerca dell'identità veneziana nel tardo Cinquecento*, edited by Benjamin Paul, 193–231. Rome: Viella; Venice: Centro tedesco di studi veneziani, 2014.

Tagliaferro, Giorgio. 'Procurators on the Threshold: Sitters and Beholders in Palma Giovane's Crociferi Entombment'. *Artibus et Historiae* 37, no. 74 (2016): 153–76.

Tagliaferro, Giorgio, Bernard Aikema, with Matteo Mancini and Andrew John Martin. *Le botteghe di Tiziano*. Florence: Alinari, 2009.

Talvacchia, Bette. *Taking Positions: On the Erotic in Renaissance Culture*. Princeton, NJ: Princeton University Press, 1999.

Talvacchia, Bette. 'The Word Made Flesh: Spiritual Subjects and Carnal Depictions in Renaissance Art'. In *The Sensuous in the Counter-Reformation Church*, edited by Marcia B. Hall and Tracy E. Cooper, 49–73. Cambridge: Cambridge University Press, 2013.

Tanner, Norman P. *Decrees of the Ecumenical Councils*. 2 vols. Washington, DC: Georgetown University Press, 1990.

Tapié, Alain, ed. *Baroque vision Jésuite: du Tintoret à Rubens*. Exhibition Catalogue, Musée des Beaux-Arts de Caen, 12 July–13 October 2003. Paris: Somogy, 2003.

Tedeschi, John, and William Monter. 'Toward a Statistical Profile of the Italian Inquisitions'. In *The Inquisition in Early Modern Europe: Studies on Sources and Methods*, edited by John Tedeschi and Gustav Henningsen, 130–57. DeKalb: Northern Illinois University Press, 1986.

Tempestini, Anchise. *Giovanni Bellini*. Milan: Fabbri Editori, 1997.

Terpstra, Nicholas, ed. *The Art of Executing Well: Rituals of Execution in Renaissance Italy*. Kirksville, MO: Truman State University Press, 2008.

Terpstra, Nicholas, 'Body Politics: The Criminal Body between Public and Private'. *Journal of Medieval and Early Modern Studies* 45, no. 1 (2015): 7–52.

Terpstra, Nicholas, 'Confraternities and Capital Punishment: Charity, Culture, and Civic Religion in the Communal and Confessional Age'. In *A Companion to Medieval and Early Modern Confraternities*, edited by Konrad Eisenbichler, 212–31. Leiden: Brill, 2019.

Terpstra, Nicholas, 'Renaissance Religions – Afterwards?' In *Renaissance Religions: Modes and Meanings in History*, edited by Peter Howard, Nicholas Terpstra, and Riccardo Saccenti, 365–73. Turnhout: Brepols, 2021.

Tiepolo, Giovanni. *Discorsi et considerationi sopra il Santissimo Sacramento dell'Altare*. 2 vols. Venice: Santo Grillo, et Fratelli, 1618.

Tietze, Hans, and Erika Tietze-Conrat. *The Drawings of the Venetian Painters in the 15th and 16th Centuries*. New York: J. J. Augustin, 1944.

Timofiewitsch, Wladimir. *Girolamo Campagna: Studien zur venezianischen Plastik um das Jahr 1600*. Munich: Wilhelm Fink Verlag, 1970.

Tozzi Pedrazzi, Rosanna. 'Notizie biografiche su Domenico Tintoretto'. *Rivista di Venezia* 12 (1933): 299–316.

Tramontin, Silvio. 'La figura del vescovo secondo il concilio di Trento ed i suoi riflessi veneziani nell'interrogatorio del Patriarca Trevisan'. *Studi Veneziani* 10 (1968): 423–56.

Tramontin, Silvio. 'Gli inizi dei due seminari di Venezia'. *Studi Veneziani* 7 (1965): 363–77.

Tramontin, Silvio. 'Le nuove congregazioni religiosi'. In *La chiesa di Venezia tra riforma protestante e riforma cattolica*, edited by Giuseppe Gullino, 77–112. Venice: Studium cattolico veneziano, 1990.

Tramontin, Silvio. 'La visita apostolica del 1581 a Venezia'. *Studi Veneziani* 9 (1967): 453–534.

Traverso, Chiara. *La Scuola di San Fantin o dei 'Picai': Carità e giustizia a Venezia*. Venice: Marsilio, 2000.

Trebbi, Giuseppe. 'Lorenzo Priuli'. In *Dizionario biografico degli Italiani*, 85:435–38. Rome: Treccani, 2016.

Treves, Letizia. 'Daniele da Volterra and Michelangelo: A Collaborative Relationship'. *Apollo* 154, no. 474 (2001): 36–45.

Trexler, Richard C. *The Spiritual Power: Republican Florence under Interdict*. Leiden: Brill, 1974.

Turchini, Angelo, Giovanni Donni, and Gabriele Archetti. *Visita apostolica e decreti di Carlo Borromeo alla Diocesi di Brescia*. 6 vols. Brescia: Brixia sacra, 2003–7.

Turner, James. *Eros Visible: Art, Sexuality and Antiquity in Renaissance Italy*. New Haven, CT: Yale University Press, 2017.

Tyack, Geoffrey. *Oxford: An Architectural Guide*. Oxford: Oxford University Press, 1998.

Vasari, Giorgio. *Lives of the Painters, Sculptors and Architects*. Edited by David Ekserdjian. Translated by Gaston du C. De Vere. 2 vols. New York: Alfred A. Knopf, 1996.

Vélez, Karin. *The Miraculous Flying House of Loreto: Spreading Catholicism in the Early Modern World*. Princeton, NJ: Princeton University Press, 2018.

Viggiano, Alfredo. 'Politics and Constitution'. In *A Companion to Venetian History, 1400–1797*, edited by Eric Dursteler, 47–84. Leiden: Brill, 2013.

Villena, Guillermo Lohmann, ed. *La Basílica Catedral de Lima*. Lima: Banca de Credito del Peru, 2004.

Vio, Gastone. *Le Scuole Piccole nella Venezia dei dogi: note d'archivio per la storia delle confraternite veneziane*. Costabissara: A. Colla, 2004.

Voelker, Evelyn Carole. 'Carlo Borromeo's Instructiones fabricae et supellectilis ecclesiasticae, 1577. A translation with commentary and analysis'. PhD thesis, University of Syracuse, 1977.

Walberg, Deborah. 'Patriarch Giovanni Tiepolo and the Search for Venetian Religious Identity in the Waning of the Renaissance'. In *Celebrazione e autocritica: la Serenissima e la ricerca dell'identità veneziana nel tardo Cinquecento*, edited by Benjamin Paul, 233–52. Rome: Viella; Venice: Centro tedesco di studi veneziani, 2014.

Walberg, Deborah. 'Tradition and Propaganda in the Venetian Madonna della Pace'. *Ikon* 9 (2016): 1–14.

Walberg, Deborah. 'The Writings and Artistic Patronage of Patriarch Giovanni Tiepolo (1570–1631): A Preliminary Investigation'. *Studi Veneziani* 62–64 (2011): 193–224.

Walsham, Alexandra, and Peter Marshall, eds. *Angels in the Early Modern World*. Cambridge: Cambridge University Press, 2006.

Warwick, Genevieve. 'Bernini (1598–1680): Sculpting Sainthood'. *Studies: An Irish Quarterly Review* 104, no. 416 (2015): 444–55.

Waterworth, Rev. James, ed. *Canons and Decrees of the Council of Trent*. London: Dolman, 1848.

Whistler, Catherine. 'Life Drawing in Venice from Titian to Tiepolo'. *Master Drawings* 42, no. 4 (2004): 370–96.

Wivel, Matthias. 'Titian and Giulio Bonasone: The Gloria That Wasn't'. *Zeitschrift für Kunstgeschichte* 77 (2014): 313–32.

Wolf, Gerhard. *Salus Populi Romani: die Geschichte römischer Kultbilder im Mittelalter*. Weinheim: VCH, 1990.

Worthen, Thomas. 'The Altar and the "banco" of the Scuola del Sacramento in San Giacomo dall'Orio'. In *La chiesa di San Giacomo dall'Orio: una trama millenaria di arte e fede*, edited by Massimo Bisson, Isabella Cecchini, and Deborah Howard, 187–204. Rome: Viella, 2018.

Worthen, Thomas. 'Architecture & Sacraments in Venetian Parish Churches'. Paper presented at the Annual Conference of the Renaissance Society of America, New York City, 27–29 March 2014.

Worthen, Thomas. 'Soazoni, or the Venetian Reformation of San Nicolò dei Mendicoli'. In *Celebrazione e autocritica: la Serenissima e la ricerca dell'identità veneziana nel tardo Cinquecento*, edited by Benjamin Paul, 253–83. Rome: Viella, Venice: Centro tedesco di studi veneziani, 2014.

Worthen, Thomas. 'Tintoretto's Paintings for the Banco del Sacramento in S. Margherita'. *Art Bulletin* 78, no. 4 (1996): 707–32.

Wright, Alison. 'Tabernacle and Sacrament in Fifteenth-Century Tuscany'. In *Carvings, Casts & Collectors: The Art of Renaissance Sculpture*, edited by Peta Wright, Emma Jones, and Dimitrios Zikos, 42–57. London: V&A Publishing, 2013.

Wright, Anthony. 'Republican Tradition and the Maintenance of "National" Religious Traditions in Venice'. *Renaissance Studies* 10, no. 3 (1996): 405–16.

Wunder, Amanda. *Baroque Seville: Sacred Art in a Century of Crisis*. University Park: Penn State University Press, 2017.

Zabeo, Giovanni Prosdocimo. *Elogio a Giacomo Robusti*. Venice: Tipografia Bernardi, 1813.

Zampetti, Pietro. *Guida alle Opere d'arte della Scuola di San Fantin Ateneo Veneto*. Edited by Ileana Chiappini di Sorio. Reprint of the 1973 ed. Venice: Ateneo Veneto, 2003.

Zanardi, Mario. 'I "domicilia" o centri operativi della Compagnia di Gesù nello Stato Veneto (1543–1773)'. In *I Gesuiti e Venezia: momenti e problemi di storia veneziana della Compagnia di Gesù: atti del Convegno di studi, Venezia, 2–5 ottobre 1990*, edited by Mario Zanardi, 89–179. Padua: Gregoriana, 1994.

Zanetti, Anton Maria. *Della pittura veneziana*. Venice: Giambatista Albrizzi, 1771.

Zarillo, Taryn Marie. 'Artistic Patrimony and Cultural Politics in Early Seicento Venice'. PhD thesis, Columbia University, 2016.

Zavatta, Giulia. 'Documenti inediti per Alessandro Vittoria e il pittore Melchiorre Galluzzi da Cologna Veneta'. *Verona Illustrata* 29 (2016): 21–37.

Zeri, Federico. *Pittura e Controriforma: l'arte senza tempo di Scipione da Gaeta*. Turin: Einaudi, 1957.

Zorzi, Alvise. *Venezia scomparsa*. 2 vols, Milan: Electa, 1977.

INDEX